DATE DUE

RADIO AND TELEVISION
COMMUNICATION

RCA Building, Radio City, New York—a world center of radio and television. It is the home of the Radio Corporation of America and the National Broadcasting Company.

RADIO AND TELEVISION
COMMUNICATION

CHARLES FREDERICK LINDSLEY

Professor of Speech, Occidental College
Director of Radio, Pasadena Community Playhouse

McGRAW-HILL BOOK COMPANY, INC.

1952   New York   Toronto   London

RADIO AND TELEVISION COMMUNICATION

II

THE MAPLE PRESS COMPANY, YORK, PA.

To J. M. L.

PREFACE

"From where it happens, you hear it happen"—and see it happen. Radio and television, extending the field of auditory and visual stimuli, have reshaped the social and cultural mold. The science of electronics invests the term, "communication," with global meaning.

The subject of radiobroadcasting and telecasting has many facets. Several hundred collegiate institutions offer more than a score of differentiated radio courses. Specialized instruction is offered in announcing, production, script writing, radio music, station management, advertising, engineering, and many other phases of the general field. With the advent of television and the sharply accentuated interest in this new communications medium, college courses and workshops have begun to multiply.

These courses, depending on the way they are organized and administered, may serve three purposes: (1) They can have a professional and vocational objective. If the curriculum is sufficiently broad, it should equip the radio aspirant with basic knowledge, skill, and experience requisite to professional apprenticeship in both commercial and noncommercial broadcasting. This forthright vocational aim may be modified or restricted to the professional needs of teachers, ministers, business and professional men; for the teacher will employ audio-visual aids in the classroom, the religious director will use a public address system or the facilities of his church station, and the business leader may find opportunity to voice his opinions and views by way of the radio panel or talk. (2) Radio courses can serve the objective of general education. The electronic extension of eye and ear, and the consequent impact of the "talk box" and the picture screen, place radio within the orbit of social science. Radio is not an institution, but it affects institutions—influencing political thought, educational concepts, economic standards, and civic responsibility. The subject area of radio and television involves historical data, economic facts, political principles, social and ethical standards, and these phases of the subject should be given either a separate or associative interpretation. (3) A particular academic value of radio courses lies in the fact that they provide motivation in facilitating the speech learning process. Class members may never become professional announcers, actors, producers, or news reporters, but the quasi realism of a classroom studio provides a strong stimulus to speech improvement. In those cases where students have the privilege of using a licensed station, the motivation is increased. An effective radio talk employs the principles of attention, organization, and clarity; the radio actor, although working with a new medium, must have sensitivity and interpretative skill; the announcer, at his best, is a gentleman conversing; the dramatic narrator requires insight, imagination, and emotional control; and the director is charged with a responsibility requiring organizing ability and leadership qualities. In brief, a broadcasting class serves the objectives inherent in speech education.

The first design of this book is to familiarize the student with the influence which radio has on the thinking and behavior of society. Radio and television constitute a dynamic force. An appreciation of this force requires perspective—a knowledge of its origins and growth, the philosophy behind its operation and control, its size and potentiality. A radio or television studio is more than an aggregation of physical assets, and a radio or television program is more than words, sounds, music, and pictures flashed miraculously through the air. These are only material symbols of social and cultural standards. A microphone is not a piece of metal; it is the man who stands in front of it. The student of broadcasting and telecasting, therefore, requires more than a laboratory manual of outlined procedures and operational techniques. He should study communication not only from the standpoint of a performer, but from the standpoint of an intelligent member of society because, as a member of society, he is subject to the influence of communications media which consume his time, bite into his pocketbook, affect his standards of appreciation, and threaten him with the dual stamp of mediocrity and conformity. More students will play listening roles than acting roles, and they should learn to listen and observe objectively according to sound standards of judgment. Critical listening requires familiarity with a wide range of programs, their content, the audience for which each is designed, the motivating force behind the program, and group listening habits. With this kind of appproach to the subject and with a knowledge of basic historical and economic facts and principles, the student is better prepared to start the improvement of his own communicative skill by participating in writing and speaking exercises applicable to the radio talk, the making of announcements, acting, and panel discussion. Acquaintance with performance skills will naturally point to the field of supervision, to the direction and production of programs, and to the ultimate management of complete workshop or station operations.

Thus it is that a radio and television course, offered within the framework of general education, may strive for three objectives: (1) to familiarize the student with an influence in modern life which affects the thinking and behavior of modern society, (2) to discipline him in critical and discriminating listening, and (3) to acquaint him with the various kinds of performance and introduce him to some of the skills employed by the performer. This latter design is for two classes of people: those who may have occasional need to use radio in business, professional, or educational relations, and those who desire to adopt radio as a career.

Grateful acknowledgment is made to the many individuals who gave generous assistance in the preparation of this book. An attempt to make a complete enumeration would certainly commit the sin of omission. Specific mention of direct contributors is made in respective footnotes. The author expresses especial appreciation to the many publishing companies, radio networks, advertising agencies, industrial corporations, and authors who have allowed quotations from their publications. The Columbia Broadcasting System was particularly generous in giving advice and its consent to quote from copyrighted material. I am indebted to the Radio Corporation of America, the National Broadcasting Company, Altec Lansing Corporation, and *Time* magazine for illustrative copy, and to the Mutual Broadcasting System, the American Broadcasting Company, and the Liberty Network for important information. Finally, I wish to credit many of my graduate students, particularly Jack G. Bell, Evelyn Bell, William G. Hume, and Danny Desmond who contributed research assistance.

Charles F. Lindsley

Los Angeles, Calif.
July, 1952

CONTENTS

PART I

HISTORICAL, ECONOMIC, POLITICAL, SOCIAL, AND VOCATIONAL ASPECTS OF RADIO

CHAPTER 1

INTRODUCTION

> For I dipt into the future,
> far as human eye could see,
> Saw the Vision of the world,
> and all the wonder that would be.

The reach of imagination has ever sought to span the limits of terrestrial and temporal boundaries. Summoning mythical genii to their aid, poets and fablers traversed continents in seven-league boots and soared into the skies on magic carpets. This dream of transcending the immediate present, expressed at first in fantasy, became a practical challenge. The labyrinthine mysteries of nature invited exploration. Men heard the command, Search! Discover! and taking up the challenge began to fashion keys that would unlock the unknown. The modern scientific era emerged. Theories, principles, and methods were evolved, and necessary implements invented by which they could be tested. Great names were written in the corridors of time: van Leeuwenhoek, Newton, Watt, Priestley, Volta, Farraday. They laid foundations on which others who came after them—men like Morse, Bell, Steinmetz, and Marconi—built towering superstructures. Fantasy became fact, and dreams reality.

Comparisons and contrasts of the present and the past are considered platitudinous, and significant only to the historically curious. It is amusing to hear about the number of days it took George Washington to plod the muddy roads from New York to Mount Vernon. The item that news of an armistice, reached by England and America in the War of 1812, took more than a year to cross the Atlantic, is a museum piece, indeed, to a generation accustomed to quarter-hour reports on what is taking place concurrently in every part of the globe. The records of the fastest clipper ships have little romantic appeal to men acquainted with the stratosphere. An occasional schoolboy may declaim,

> What shall I say, brave Admiral, say,
> If we sight naught but seas at dawn?

but epic voyages of explorers are meaningless fragments to children of an atomic age. Science has produced a world inconceivable to our

3

grandfathers and great-grandfathers, but it is here, and we are a part of it. The quality of our adjustment to the modern era will tell the story of survival or destruction.

A major chapter in the relentless march of science tells the story of electricity. Within a hundred years the Leyden jar condenser (1745) and the lightning rod (1752) became the telegraph wire (1832); in something over half a century more, the click-click of the land telegraph became the crackle of the wireless transmitter (1896); and in a decade more we had the wireless telephone—the transmission of voice by electromagnetic waves (1906). A new branch of science called "electronics" had been established.

Utilization of this mystical force in industry can remove air-borne dust particles as small as 1/250,000 inch from precision machinery, "sew" aluminum plane parts together at the rate of 1,800 stitches per minute, radiograph the internal parts of a speeding motor, generate bactericidal ultraviolet radiation to sanitize working conditions, and detect minute holes smaller than $\frac{1}{64}$ inch in tin plate racing through a shearing line at 1,000 feet per second.

Radio, a means of communication, is a phase of applied electronics. It embraces a world-wide system of communication: radiotelephone circuits between the United States and foreign countries; ship and shore radiotelegraph; radiotelephone and direction-finder equipment; transoceanic radio service by which photographs, printed matter, and weather maps are exchanged between the United States and seven countries; international and short-wave broadcasts; ultra-short-wave equipment; and a multitude of special and noncommercial services. When you use the word "radio" however, you are probably referring to your home receiving set, your car radio, the broadcasting studio you have visited, the programs to which you have listened, your last repair bill, or your interest in making a professional contact with a commanding industry. The layman is content to think mostly in terms of radio's local utility. It is sufficient that he can snap a switch and establish connection with the air above the streets freighted with cargoes of words, music, and sound patterned for his enjoyment and information. We live in a push-button, gadget-laden era which we accept as commonplace and routine. We would, no doubt, miss the pop-up toasters, electric-eye doors, and telephoto news reports were we suddenly deprived of them, but in the absence of any such calamity we accept them as everyday accessories. The magic of radio is no longer magic. The thrill and wonderment first occasioned by the galena crystal and the "cat's whisker" were quickly dissipated by rapid technical improvements and the universal acceptance of a new medium. Today, radio is just another commonplace of twentieth-century living, but it is woven so intimately into the multiple strands of life that it becomes a subject of social concern.

The social impact of radiobroadcasting and telecasting is clear and impressive. By July 1, 1950, the United States government had authorized 3,144 AM, FM, and TV broadcast stations.[1] From these licensed outlets

Fig. 1. Radiophoto of Charles Evans Hughes as received in New York after being transmitted from that city to London and back on July 6, 1924. The event inaugurated the first radio transmission of pictures across the Atlantic.

Fig. 2. A radiophoto of the late Charles Evans Hughes as received in New York on July 6, 1949, after transmission over RCA's transatlantic radio facilities in commemoration of the twenty-fifth anniversary of sending pictures across the Atlantic by radio.

emanate continuous hours of music, drama, news, commentaries, public-service programs, round-table and panel discussions, voices of experts, and variety entertainment. It is estimated that over 90 per cent of American homes are radio-equipped and that there are 87 million potential television viewers in 43 states.[2]

The scope of radio's influence is practically universal. Time and space have been so contracted that the phrase, "whispering gallery," loses its

[1] AM, 2,303; FM, 732; TV, 109, Sixteenth Annual Report, Federal Communications Commission, Washington, D.C., p. 102.
[2] Ibid., p. 103.

metaphorical character. Radio has made the world a neighborhood. This universality was well demonstrated within the first decade of its official life. "In the final months of 1932 [radio listeners] became convinced that there were few spots on, above, or below the earth's surface where radio could not take them."[3] They heard a musical program from a speeding B & O train; a nightingale singing in the Pangbourne Woods near London; Auguste Piccard in Desenzano, Italy, telling how it feels to ballon 10 miles into the stratosphere; and William Beebe, off Nonsuch Island, reporting from a steel and glass bathysphere 2,200 feet below the sea level:[4]

It is absolutely black. Now there are fish two or three feet away. . . . It is the most amazing thing now: the amount of light down here. It must be the normal illuminescence of the creatures. . . . Here come loads of little— I don't know what they are—I never saw anything like them. [Then, speaking to his tugboat half a mile above.] Let's go down some more.

Pope Pius XI, "the first Pope to make use of this truly wonderful Marconi invention," spoke directly to millions of people: "give ear ye islands and hearken ye people from afar." Historic events that followed— Hitler's rise to the German Chancellory, the invasion of Ethiopia, the abdication of King Edward VIII, Neville Chamberlain's declaration of war—were heard simultaneously in every capital of the world. The catastrophic years of conflict that began in 1939 brought to mankind the real power and meaning of radio communication. The tramping boots of the German *Wehrmacht,* the strident diatribes of dictators, and the shrill flight of aerial bombs raining their "ghastly dew" were heard in almost every American home. Eyewitness reporters spoke to us from the cities of Europe. Listeners on this side of the Atlantic were linked within the space of half an hour to Paris, London, Berlin, Rome, and Prague. Foreign-language speakers and their translators were broadcast to the world at the same time. Later international events following victory days emphasized this integrating power of radio. The fourth man-made atomic explosion, climaxing the scientific experiment called Operation Crossroads, was heard through millions of radio receivers around the globe—an experiment which had its counterpart not long after when the air lanes carried the announcement that an explosion resembling the mushroom of the A-bomb had been registered in Russia. Within a few hours a billion people began to fit a new puzzle piece into the jagged framework of international relations. As a final illustration, the broadcasts from battle fronts are still vivid in our minds. Listeners, com-

[3] *The Sound of Your Life,* a record of Radio's first generation, Columbia Broadcasting System, Inc., p. 23.
[4] *Ibid.,* pp. 22–23.

fortable in their easy chairs, eavesdrop on conversations among soldiers, reporters, and interrogators stationed at such widely separated points as New York, Tokyo, Seoul, and a ship in mid-Atlantic. "The voice of radio is the swiftest and most deeply-penetrating means of reaching an entire people that the world has ever known."

The impressive story of broadcasting is only a part of radio's full importance. Radio services which are neither broadcast nor common carrier constitute a vital and dramatic document. These services are grouped in what is known as "safety and special services." They comprise a broad field of radio utilization by commerce, industry, and individuals and fall in five categories: safety services, land transportation services, industrial services, developmental services, and operator services. Authorizations in the safety and special radio services (exclusive of amateurs, citizens, and special aircraft radiotelephone) exceeded 66,000 at the close of the fiscal year, 1950. On June 15, 1949, the operation of more than 300,000 transmitters was covered in nonbroadcast radio authorizations.

The story of radio's special services constitutes a particularly dramatic chapter. The sea has been forced to relax its perilous grip on mariner and aviator. The navigator is no longer compelled to rely on sun and stars to steer his course. When elusive celestial bodies fail to set their beacons, modern radio instruments give him an accurate check on his position in relation to other vessels and to the land. Readily adapted to every type of vessel from yacht to merchant ship, radio instruments afford the skipper a powerful ally in his battle with the elements. Aerial navigation, likewise, is cloaked with protection by these same radio instruments. A plane, disabled at sea, sends out distress signals up to the time it is abandoned, and even from the life rafts, SOS signals, picked up by a ship or shore station, are relayed to the nearest Air-Sea Rescue Unit. Only the general position of the survivors is known, but the rescue plane, relying on radar, can discover the exact location of the life rafts equipped with a device on which the radar can "home." The rescue is effected and the mercy ship, as it nears its base, radios for medical aid to stand by when it lands. The safety of soldiers and sailors in a global war kept troops in contact and warned air and sea commanders against enemy forces. The ominous command, "All men man your battle stations," blaring forth from the bull horns, meant that radio devices had detected the approach of enemy planes. With radio to receive warnings and with intership communication to transmit orders, the surprise attack was apprehended. Analysts claim that one factor contributing to the defeat of Japanese fleets in the battles of the Philippine Sea was the inability of the enemy ships to maintain cooperative communications. A lack of teamwork owing to poor radio contact contributed to their rout.

The ravages of fire in the national forest and in metropolitan areas are subdued by fire fighters aided by radio apparatus. The escaping criminal knows the small chance he has of eluding the dragnet thrown out by zone and interzone police radio systems. Special emergency operations, occasioned by such events as collapse of high-tension wires or bridges, and major traffic accidents, are facilitated by radio communication. Messages can be sent from speeding automobiles. On July 16, 1946, an overseas call was made from a moving automobile from St. Louis to Honolulu. Mobile facsimile radiotelegraph services have been demonstrated. In lieu of neighborhood telegraph offices, vehicles moving about a certain area can pick up messages from the air and deliver them to local addresses. Replies can be sent by the same means.

The scientific limits of radio have not been reached. The full improvement and extension of wireless communcation will be recorded in the years ahead. Developments which now almost transcend imagination will become as commonplace as the present-day home receiver. Mechanically, it would be possible today to transmit the deliberations of the United Nations to every citizen on the planet. Tomorrow, this practicality will be a reality. Today, if you do not like a particular program coming to you over a particular channel, you "fish" for something else, hoping that another air lane will have what you want. Tomorrow, you may stay with the same channel, taking your choice from several programs beamed to you simultaneously over the same air lane. On Apr. 17, 1946, a public demonstration of a new piece of equipment, under the trade name, Faximile, produced a wave of excitement. This was a transmitter designed for the reproduction of printed or pictorial matter by radio. This machine, over FM, broadcasts printed matter, which is picked up by a receiving set, which prints it on a roll of specially treated paper at a constant speed. Today, Jones finds his morning paper under his rose bushes, in his neighbor's yard, chewed to pieces by the pup, or in his driveway where the rain has reduced the newsprint to a sodden, unintelligible blur. Tomorrow, his newspaper will be put to bed at a local radio station, broadcast by an FM transmitter, and dropped automatically from his home radio receiver. And now, of course, we have crossed the threshold of television. The nightclub, the gridiron, the political arena, and the school have been brought to the living room. "From where it happens," you not only "hear it happen," you see it happen.

This introductory statement is made to indicate the scope and interest range of our subject. It has many ramifications, all of which cannot be pursued in the present volume. It is not our purpose to treat of the technical nature of radio and television. Our ultimate aim is to make clear the performance techniques employed in these media, but a knowledge of these skills should be based on an understanding of the historical, political, economic, social, and vocational aspects of electronic communication. Therefore, before we go into the studio to learn through practice the various principles associated with the principal types of performance, we shall sketch briefly the evolution of broadcasting, trace the steps by which it reached the level of functional service, measure its economic stature, explain the relationship of government to radio communication, weigh radio's social contribution, and explore its vocational promise.

QUESTIONS

1. What are some industrial applications of electronics?
2. Name three classes of radio services.
3. What is "Faximile"?
4. Name six phases of radio communication.
5. What was the number of AM, FM, and TV stations on July 1, 1950?
6. What percentage of American homes are equipped with radio receivers?
7. Discuss: "Radio has made the world a neighborhood."
8. What technological advances in radio communication are promised for the future?

CHAPTER 2

EVOLUTION OF WIRELESS COMMUNICATION AND RADIOBROADCASTING

New ideas are challenged by conservative obstinacy and incredulity. Napoleon Bonaparte scorned a delegation which asked his patronage to promote a steamboat by saying he had no time for mere toys. When George Stephenson's locomotive, the *Rocket*, was readied for a trial run, it was opposed with the argument that a cow might get on the track. In 1875, a chugging motorist in Chicago was told to take his contraption off the street—that horseless carriages were forbidden by city ordinance. On that eventful day at Kitty Hawk, the Wright brothers' successful experiment with a heavier-than-air machine was greeted with the bewildered admission, "The dang thing flew." Every new discovery has had its doubters and scoffers, but the mental adhesions of the conservative mind are never strong enough to restrain the progress of inquiring, searching intellects challenging the unknown. Seventy-five years ago, a popular orator, given to studied alliterative effects, declaimed, "Lightning and light, wind and wave, frost and flame, and every secret subtle force of earth and air have become the tireless toilers of the human race." With what rhetorical embellishments would he characterize the twentieth century? Shakespeare's Puck claimed he could put a girdle around the earth in forty minutes. This magical power has been surpassed. Words and pictures girdle the globe with the speed of light.

Radio is the culmination of a series of inquiries, explorations, and experiments stretching over centuries and embracing many scientists of many nationalities. Dependent on the phenomenon of electricity, its origin may be traced to certain observations made by the Greek philosopher, Thales, six centuries before the Christian era. These observations had no particular significance for over 2,000 years, but when William Gilbert, an English scientist, published in 1600 his work, *On the Magnet, Magnetic Bodies and the Great Magnet the Earth,* he stimulated a series of fruitful research studies and accomplishments. In 1700, electricity was successfully demonstrated and conveyed over a distance of 866 feet; in 1744, C. F. Ludolff of Berlin ignited ether with

10

an electric spark; and a year later Sir William Watson, using a Leyden jar, conveyed an electrical discharge over metallic wires for a distance of 2 miles. By 1873 the basic laws of electrical science had been discovered and formulated. New names were fixed in the scientific firmament: Coulomb, Henry, Gauss, Faraday, Laplace, Poisson. The basic foundations were laid for the development of electrical communication.

The modern history of electrical communication as a proved and successful fact begins on May 24, 1844. It was on this day that the first telegraph message was dispatched from Washington, D.C., to Baltimore, Md.—an accomplishment which terminated 77 years of experimentation with wire transmission. Eight years earlier (1837) Samuel F. B. Morse had filed a petition with the U.S. Patent Office to protect his right to "a new method of transmitting and receiving intelligence by electromagnetism." Various similar devices had been constructed by other experimenters, but Morse's instrument was the only one to gain general approval. Every schoolboy knows the dramatic story of that day in the national capital when the first telegraph message was clicked out—"What hath God wrought."

The chain was now being forged. The 30 miles of wire that carried recordable signals in 1844 stretched to 3,000 miles 14 years later when the transatlantic cable was laid connecting England and America. After 8 years of initial transmission difficulties, two continents were joined by telegraphic communication.

The third link was completed on Mar. 10, 1876. On that date the world greeted the first successful operation of the telephone. The many inquiries and speculations of scientists concerning sound transmission found their answer in an invention by Alexander Graham Bell. The electrical transmission of sound had been expanded to make possible the transmission of speech which required a reproduction of specific tonal elements of pitch, intensity, and quality.

The situation at this point was as follows: the telegraph was a fact, and the telephone was a fact. Electrical impulses, flashed over wires, could be received and translated into meaning. The vibrations of the human voice, impressed on an electric current, could be transmitted and received over long-distance wires as normal speech. Communication by overhead wires and underseas cable was a reality. Cables, however, were expensive. Moreover, oceanic conditions made it impossible to reach many coastal areas. What was the answer? Was space telegraphy, not dependent on wires, a possibility? This was the next problem to challenge the scientist. The answer was given by Heinrich Rudolf Hertz and Guglielmo Marconi. Popularly stated, Hertz discovered (1887) ether waves, announcing the theory that electric waves travel with the speed of light in a special medium called ether; and Marconi, improving on devices developed prior to 1905, discovered a method by which feeble electrical impulses (wireless signals) could be sent and received between two points. Marconi's announcement of successful wireless communication startled the world. The response at first was incredulity, but the doubting Thomases were reduced to silence as the scientist, almost from month to month, increased the range of his signals. From 2 miles to 11, from 11 to 18, from 18 to 56. And then, on Dec. 12, 1901, the first transatlantic signals sent from Poldhu, on the coast of Cornwall on the southwest tip of England, to St. John's, Newfoundland. In the following year, Marconi

FIG. 3. Guglielmo Marconi at the receiving set at St. John's, Newfoundland, Dec. 12, 1901.

established wireless communication between Russia and England. The range and strength of the signals increased with each succeeding test. Eyewitness reporters of a naval battle between Russian and Japanese vessels off Port Arthur (1905) made direct reports to the *New York Times* by wireless; and Robert E. Peary announced his discovery of the North Pole (1909) by the same means. Wireless communication was a fact.

Science moves always with relentless logic. Bell had impressed the human voice on ordinary electric current. Why couldn't the voice also be impressed on ether waves? Of course, there was a difference between electric current and ether waves which seemed to vitiate the analogy.

The change and direction of ordinary electric current occurred 120 times a second; wireless cycles (Hertzian waves) changed their direction from 20,000 to 60,000,000 times a second. The key to this problem was supplied by Professor Richard Fessenden. It was his theory that with a sustained wave transmission and an h-f alternator he might achieve wireless telephony. He asked the General Electric Company to see what their engineers could do. The problem was assigned to a young man at Schenectady by the name of Ernst F. W. Alexanderson. The path of the inventor is never smooth. There was the usual period of trial and error, near success and failure. In the summer of 1906, however, an alternator capable of delivering a smooth and continuous flow of h-f vibrations was ready for a critical demonstration. The test was made at Brant Rock, Mass., where the experimenters were able to use the sending tower of a powerful wireless station owned by the National Electric Signaling Company.

Christmas Eve, 1906! Who can describe the emotions accompanying that first attempted broadcast? A few moments now and a supreme scientific triumph might be acclaimed. Was it actually possible to project the human voice through the caverns of space? Hundreds of miles at sea, wireless operators at their stations, headphones clamped to their ears, alert to the staccato click of their instruments, caught a repeated call—CQ, CQ, CQ. It was a strange signal. What did it mean? Then—a voice! A man was speaking. His words were understandable. A woman sang. A violin was heard. And now, words again, "If you have heard this program, write to R. A. Fessenden at Brant Rock." It was the first request for radio fan mail.

Fourteen years were to elapse, however, before the possibilities inherent in Fessenden's experiment attained the full measure of radiobroadcasting. This fact is not too easily explained, but the delay was due in large part to the difficulties that accompany all monumental scientific discoveries. Fundamentally, the Brant Rock "broadcast" was only a demonstration of what might eventually be achieved. Reception had to be improved and greater voice amplification provided. These requirements were supplied later by General H. C. Dunwoody's crystal receiver, Lee de Forest's three-electrode tube, and Alexanderson's vacuum tube—an electronic amplifier which stepped up power in kilowatts instead of watts—but there were long years of litigation and involved negotiations among rival interests trying to establish their respective claims. Moreover, strange as it may seem, the inventors seemed to be faced with an incredulous and rather apathetic public opinion. Lee de Forest, for example, when defending a patent claim to his audion in a United States court, was denounced by a Federal district attorney as a mountebank who had said the human voice could some day be transmitted across the Atlantic Ocean. Alexanderson's work was labeled by a General Electric official as a "foolish dream." More experimentation and demonstration of wireless telephony were necessary before the public was going to get excited. Therefore, step by step, the fathers of wireless telephony moved steadily ahead. Lee de Forest's experiments were in the vanguard. Tests were made in New York City between two buildings three blocks apart, between the Lackawanna and the Hoboken and Manhattan terminals, from a yacht cruising in Lake Erie, from the Eiffel Tower in Paris, and from the Metropolitan stage in New York. These broadcasts were conducted between 1907 and 1910. Meanwhile, the transmission of voice by wireless was attempted by the U.S. Signal Corps operating between Sandy Hook and Bedloe's Island, and the Navy made installations of trial equipment on two United States battleships. In 1916, de Forest enlarged his scale of operations and set up an experimental radiobroadcasting station at Highbridge in the Bronx. His demonstration at this time consisted of flashed election bulletins. Later, he transmitted recorded music from the Columbia Phonograph laboratories in New York City to the roof of the Astor Hotel. These transmissions were heard in Canada and on ships at sea. The reception was declared satisfactory. In 1918, when President Wilson went to the Peace Conference in Paris, his ship, the *George Washington,* and the Atlantic flagship, the *Pennsylvania,* were equipped with radiophones. On his return from Europe, while 900 miles from the American Coast, Wilson talked with his Secretary of the Navy, Josephus Daniels.

Another experimenter who had been vitally interested in wireless telephony during this time was a Westinghouse Company engineer, Dr. Frank Conrad. His particular concern was the development of a wireless-telephone transmitter. He conducted his experiments not only at the Westinghouse laboratories but also from the garage at his home. Following the war, when the government had reinstated amateur wireless stations, Dr. Conrad relicensed his station, 8XY (April, 1920). In the evenings he conducted a series of voice broadcasts. These were "picked up" by scores of amateur operators. Encouraged, Conrad then began to broadcast recorded music. The response of his listeners to these programs was enthusiastic. They asked for more extensive and varied programs. A regular 2-hour broadcast was arranged for Wednesday and Saturday evenings. The result was more than he had anticipated. Receiving sets multiplied and "an enterprising store in Pittsburgh inserted advertisements in the local papers announcing a supply of radio sets for those who desired to listen to the Conrad programs." The vice-president of the Westinghouse Electric and Manufacturing Company, Harry P. Davis, studying the effects produced by Conrad's 8XY, saw the possibilities in extending the scope of the programs and decided to build a broadcasting station at East Pittsburgh. He and his associates applied to the government for a commercial license. The license was granted. On election night, Nov. 2, 1920, 500 to 1,000 listeners, equipped with earphones, heard the Harding-Cox election returns. This was the first demonstration of a radiobroadcast from a licensed government station. The station was KDKA. The era of broadcasting had arrived.

Fig. 4. RCA radiophotos of President Coolidge and Austen Chamberlain, British cabinet member, sent from London to New York in November, 1924.

The chain was now complete: a piece of amber rubbed with flannel—a Leyden jar—an electric spark and a copper wire—a sustained telegraph signal—voice sounds imposed on an electric current—telegraphic communication without the medium of intervening wires—voice sounds imposed on wireless frequencies! Proceeding from an intermittent spark in the darkness, men had toiled logically and steadily forward. Radio, another miracle of the twentieth century, had joined the company of other epic achievements to further man's conquest of time and space.

At the risk of what may seem like an illogical digression and a violation of unity in this narration, it is necessary to turn back in our chronology to point the fact that radiobroadcasting, which came 14 years after the historical Brant Rock experiment, was made inevitable by the perfection of wireless telegraphy. Station KDKA was a natural outcome of wireless developments stimulated particularly by the war years, 1914 to 1918. The practical importance of Marconi's invention (the success of which up to 1906 we have recorded) was clearly realized by the United States government which played an important part in developing the new means of communication. The United States began the construction of a powerful transmitter at Arlington, Va., in 1910 and projected plans for other stations at San Diego, Calif., in the Canal Zone, and at Pearl Harbor. In 1912, the Ship Control Act was passed requiring the licensing of all radio operators and transmitting stations. When international war broke upon the world in 1914, a Federal board was appointed to reorganize the Naval Radio Service. The survey and report made by this body prompted the organization of the Naval Communications Service empowered to study carefully all the scientific developments then in progress and to channel them as much as possible in the interests of national protection. Upon the declaration of war by the United States in 1917, the President directed the Navy to take over all private wireless stations then operated principally by the Federal Telegraph Company and the American Marconi Company. Amateur wireless operators were ordered under penalty of having their equipment confiscated to disconnect all pieces of apparatus and antennae and to seal and store the same. All private companies engaged in the manufacture and operation of wireless equipment cooperated by placing all their resources at the disposal of the government under a centralized control. "The scientific resources of all electrical manufacturers were combined in one common endeavor." Radio technicians developed radio direction finders by which to locate enemy ships. The government sponsored radio training schools, particularly at Harvard University and at Mare Island, Calif., in which thousands of young men were prepared to play an important role in subsequent radio history. By 1918, the General Electric Company had so improved the Alexanderson alternator that the government was able to communicate with its military commanders on the European battlefield. President Wilson's famous address, "The Fourteen Points," was delivered to the *world* by wireless.

In view of the vast technical knowledge which man had acquired in his mastery of the ether, and the perfection of long-distance wireless telephone communication (successful calls were made from New York to Paris and from New York to Honolulu), the step to radiobroadcasting was logical and inevitable. If wireless-telephone messages were feasible, why should every home not become a listening post for voices emanating from a central sending point? Wasn't this a matter of relative simplicity? The basic principles, the basic equipment, and the technical knowledge were at hand. KDKA was the answer.

QUESTIONS

1. Summarize the evolution of the basic laws of electricity.

2. Name in historical order the principal achievements in the field of electrical communication antedating radiobroadcasting.

3. In what respect was the invention of the telephone an advancement over the telegraph?

4. What was the analogy between wireless telegraphy and wireless telephony? What facts made this analogy appear illogical?

5. What role did Fessenden play in the achievement of wireless telephony?

6. Why did so many years elapse between the Brant Rock experiment and the operation of the first licensed broadcasting station?

7. Name some of the important broadcasting experiments between 1906 and 1920.

8. What is the importance of the name, Frank Conrad?

9. Explain how the war years, 1914 to 1918, accelerated the final advent of radiobroadcasting.

CHAPTER 3

RADIO'S GROWING PAINS

Radiobroadcasting had to surmount three hurdles before it was "in the clear": a political low hurdle, an economic intermediate hurdle, and a technical high hurdle. The first obstacle presented itself 2 years prior to the construction and operation of KDKA. During the war, as we have seen, all wireless equipment had been placed under a unified control. At the end of hostilities, the private companies expected and waited for the return of their facilities to their own management. Whether this return would be made was, for a brief time, in serious doubt. Legislation (the Alexander bill) was introduced in Congress to perpetuate a government monopoly of all wireless communication. The proponents of the measure were influenced by three arguments: (1) The ether was a natural resource, the utilization of which was instinct with potential good or evil. Radio belonged to a unique category. It was a phenomenon which had no parallel in existing statutory subject matter. A telephone or telegraph company owned a right of way; it owned physical properties such as wires and cables and poles. These were concrete material things which could easily be protected by physical laws, but the radio operator owned nothing beyond his transmitter. The accepted laws protecting physical property did not apply to wireless telephony. The space over and above the earth's surface was not a tangible resource; therefore, the nature of the medium demanded public ownership and control. (2) If radio were turned over to private interests, the result would be an inevitable monopoly contravening existing laws pertaining to the concentration of industrial and financial power. (3) The war years had proved that wireless communication was vital to national security, and this security would be endangered if the government relinquished its control. This latter contention in particular was supported by the Secretary of the Navy.

The Alexander bill was, of course, stoutly contested. It was denounced as a trespass on the rights of American citizens, as a double cross of private interests which, in good faith, had "loaned" their resources to the country in a time of crisis, as a fatal check to the technical development of a new science, and a permanent fixation of unrestricted operations in the hands of government bureaucracy. Newspapers and periodicals supported the protests of the Marconi Wireless Telegraph Company of America, the National Wireless Company, and the American Radio Relay League. Congressional hearings ended on Jan. 16, 1919. The bill was tabled.

The government was handicapped in pushing its arguments because of the weight of traditional free-enterprise theory and because neither the government nor any particular industry controlled sufficient patent rights to implement a communications system at this time. Moreover, there was no legal method by which the government could commandeer the necessary patents. A merger of the various interests, it appeared, was necessary if a practical system of broadcasting in the United States were to be realized. Secretary Daniels opposed such a merger even with a quasi-governmental participation, but he found himself in a very tight situation. He was faced with the possibility of a British cable monopoly unless the patent interests concerned could be brought together. The British Marconi Company wanted to purchase the Alexanderson alternator owned by the General Electric Company, and the latter, faced with a loss of business following World War I, was tempted to make a deal with the British firm. When it was convincingly argued that the sale of the alternator to Marconi interests would "fix in British hands a substantial monopoly of world communication" it was realized that something had to be done to protect the interests of the United States in the impending race for radio supremacy. Appealed to on patriotic grounds, General Electric agreed not to put the alternator into foreign hands without some regulation and control, but made it clear that without a customer for its prized machine there were only two alternatives: government ownership on the one hand and the organization of an American company on the other. By this time the pressure for a government monopoly had relaxed, and GE was asked if it could organize such a company. The GE officials agreed to explore the possibility of consolidating rival interests in a private communications system. The detailed and elaborate negotiations which followed constitute a dramatic story. The result was the garnering of a sufficient number of rights to permit the formation of a domestic corporation; but more time was required to bring the plan to functional effectiveness. More time was required to establish cross licenses, financial backing, and cooperative agreements. At last, four major companies were brought together: the General Electric Company, the American Telephone and Telegraph Company, the Radio Corporation of America, and Westinghouse Manufacturing Company. Each party acquired rights (within limitations) to utilize patents owned by any of the four. The stage was now set. The Navy Department, which had held out for government ownership, had lost its argument in favor of private corporate agreements. Private cor-

porations had effected a consolidation which had the means to manufacture, sell, and distribute radio equipment essential to broadcasting and
radio-program reception. The initial political issue was resolved in favor
of private business.

When KDKA went on the air in 1920, the radio was open to private
interests as far as political sanction was concerned. The succeeding year
clearly revealed the unlimited possibilities of broadcasting. It was the

FIG. 5. Douglas Fairbanks and Mary Pickford in one of their first broadcasts.

dramatic period of many radio "firsts"—the first public radio address,
(Herbert Hoover), the first church broadcast, the first broadcast of a
boxing event, the first tennis matches on the air, the first National League
baseball game.

Now came radio's second hurdle which was considerably higher than
the first one cleared in 1919. The sixty-four-dollar question in 1923 was,
How can radio stations and their program operation be financed? Several
major companies, as noted above, were technically and financially endowed to manufacture and market broadcasting equipment and receiving
sets; but a radio receiver in a man's home was worthless unless there

was something to receive. Where were the radio programs coming from? Who was going to produce them? A constant playing of phonograph records would not be adequate. There was no limit to what could be put on the airways; but singers, actors, musicians, and entertainers would expect compensation for their services. Programs would become increasingly expensive. Who would pay the bill to promote a program service that would attract new millions of avid listeners and promote the sale of more and more millions of radio receivers? Could this bill be met from the profits of the equipment manufacturers? The latter said this would be highly improbable if not impossible.

The general manager and vice-president of RCA, David Sarnoff, thought the solution might be found in a system of a few superstations supported by industry itself from returns on radio sales. A prorata agreement might be reached under which each of the companies concerned would be allocated a percentage of profits derived from such sales. Herbert Hoover expressed the opinion that broadcasting could be supported by the industry if organized in a pattern of six or seven national circuits. Later, Sarnoff advanced another idea—the outright endowment of radiobroadcasting stations, putting them in the category of educational and cultural institutions deriving support from public funds. Spokesmen for GE thought the solution might be found in voluntary contributions from listening audiences. There was also the suggestion that radio sets should be licensed.

The ultimate solution was found in a system with which everyone is now familiar—commercial sponsorship. This was a system by which an advertiser purchased air time to promote his product or service and, in return, paid the station a set rate for such service. In the summer of 1922, the American Telephone and Telegraph Company, owners of WEAF, sold a short period of time to the Queensborough Corporation, a company which was promoting the development of a real-estate project. In fact, Queensborough bought time on WEAF on five consecutive days and thereby became radio's first commercial customer. In the following December, Gimbel Brothers, a New York department store, bought radio time. They were followed by R. H. Macy & Company. In the next 6 months, 34 other companies used WEAF as an advertising medium.

These pioneer commercial broadcasts had many critics and opponents. The Newspaper Publishers' Association announced that it would refuse in its columns free publicity concerning radio programs consisting of direct advertising and that it would eliminate from published program announcements the name of trade-marked merchandise or known products obviously used for advertising. The reason alleged for this decision was that radio advertising was likely to destroy the educational and entertainment value of broadcasting. The Associated Press refused to have its dispatches used over radio channels unless they could be considered of great importance. A congressman introduced a bill to abolish all advertising. Thus, commercial broadcasting, at the outset, did not have clear sailing. Furthermore, commercial anglers, the radio sponsors themselves, were loath to cast their lines into the aerial deep. Perhaps radio was a new means of sales promotion, but there was something intangible and nebulous in the process of reaching a clientele by ether waves. Therefore, as late as 1930, the sales value inherent in a radio presentation was considered problematical; but this reluctance to use the new medium was not long-lived. There was a sharp and sudden turn of sentiment. More and more pioneers brought their wares to the microphone, and the effectiveness of radio selling was so clearly demonstrated that within a year and a half advertisers had arrived in sufficient numbers to establish firmly and tenaciously the system of commercial sponsorship. Radio was over its second hurdle.

The third problem—the really high hurdle in radio's path—was a technical one. A radio message travels in every direction. "Every signal is a potential destroyer of every other one. . . . The chance for conflicts is infinite." Moreover, radio impulses (sound imposed on carrier frequencies) have no meaning or value unless they are properly received. You have had difficulty at times on your receiving set with station interference. One station overlaps another. It is not possible to tune one completely out, and the program to which you are listening is blurred or obscured. The prevention of this dual reception is what may be called an airways traffic problem. Radio traffic cops have now gained control over the aerial highways, and you seldom suffer the annoyance of program interference; but this was not the situation at the outset.

Congress had passed legislation in 1912 regulating communication, and the administration of the law had been placed with the Secretary of Commerce. The 1912 Act—a law to regulate radiotelegraphic communication—was a simple one. Its provisions required the licensing of operators, prescribed the wavelengths to be used, and stipulated penalties for malicious interference with signals and for fraudulent or false signals. The law was not designated to cope with the problems inherent in a system of national broadcasting initiated 10 years later. The technical nature of radio in particular was not understood by the lawmakers or by the administrator of the Act. This is evidenced by the fact that when private radio facilities were returned to their owners after World War I, the Department of Commerce designated one wavelength, and only one (350 meters or 750 kilocycles), for all private broadcasting. The meaning of such a limitation was this: If Jones operated a station in Center City and Smith wished to build a competing one, both owners would have to share the same wavelength. Later, if Brown, also of Center

City, entered the field, three stations would have to divide broadcasting time. In other words, no community could have more than one full-time station. In 1921, Secretary Hoover authorized the commercial use of another wavelength (400 meters or 833 kilocycles), but this improved the situation only to the extent of permitting a community two full-time stations. The broadcasting boom was setting in. Stations were multiply-

Fig. 6. Olga Petrova, noted actress, in 1921 appeared before the radio microphone in costume as actors do today before television cameras.

ing by hundreds, receiving sets by hundreds of thousands, and listeners by millions. The latter were not very happy. The air traffic snarl produced a cacophony of squeals and chatter which rendered reception almost worthless. Something had to be done.

Not only were radio-set owners very unhappy, station investors also felt that their operations were unfairly and inefficiently regulated. The Commerce Department's policy of licensing wavelengths was attacked in the courts by a licensee in New York City—the Intercity Radio Company—whose expired broadcasting grant was denied extension on the ground that there was no available wavelength. The litigation which ensued reached the Court of Appeals for the District of Columbia. This tribunal ruled that Secretary Hoover had exceeded his discretion—that the Act of 1912 was too general and too vague to permit arbitrary assignment of radio frequencies. However, in the absence of congressional readiness to deal with the total problem, the Secretary had to "carry on."

In March, 1923, he called his second radio conference. A previous conference attended by broadcasters, educators, technical experts, and industrial representatives had been held in February, 1922, but no definitive program had been consummated at that time. The second meeting produced what seemed like a practical solution. In opening the sessions of this conference, Hoover said,

When this group met a year ago, there were 60 broadcasting stations in the United States; today, there are 588. It was estimated then that there were between 600,000 and 1,000,000 receiving sets; today it is believed there are between 1,500,000 and 2,500,000 persons listening. Public broadcasting has practically been limited to two wavelengths, and I need not dilate to you on the amount of interference there is and the jeopardy in which the whole development stands.

Out of this meeting came recommendations for a new classification of stations. A different system of assigning individual wavelengths was adopted using practically the same portion of the radio spectrum as now used for long-wave broadcasting—550 to 1,550 kilocycles.

With the assignment of particular channels to particular broadcasters for their respective uses, it was hoped the system would be adequate to serve the interests of the licensees; but as applicants and permits increased in number, things did not get better. There was much jealousy and bickering occasioned by the Secretary's assignments because it was inevitable that all wavelengths were not equally advantageous. Every owner of a radio station thought he had a right in the "radio sun." Moreover, while it was expected that the new allocations would make it possible for good receiving sets to pick up and differentiate some 20 or more stations, the actual result was to render worthless many thousands of ordinary receivers not designed for selective tuning. Homemade sets, particularly, were rendered obsolete, and only improved commercial sets could make a satisfactory selection of broadcasting stations. Set owners thought they would be better off under the former system when stations used the same wavelengths and shared time with each other. When the third conference was assembled in October, 7 months later, the members were fully aware of these interference problems and realized that more operational channels would have to be assigned. Eight committees reported on the following subjects: (1) general allocation of frequency or wavelength bands, (2) allocation of frequency bands to broadcasting stations, (3) general problems of radiobroadcasting, (4) problems of marine communications, (5) amateur problems, (6) interference problems, (7) interconnection, and (8) coordination. Progress was being made. It seemed that the many technical problems which besought the new industry were being solved. Actually, however, the policies adopted at the third conference produced no tangible improvement in the situation, and when the fourth radio conference was convened in the autumn of 1925, Hoover confessed that he was at the end of his legalistic rope.

I can see no alternative to abandonment of the present system which gives the broadcasting privilege to everyone who can raise the funds necessary to erect a station, irrespective of his motive, the service he proposes to render, or the number of others already serving his community. . . . The ideal situation . . . would be traffic regulation by the Federal government . . . leaving to each community a large voice in determining who are to occupy the wavelengths assigned to that community.

For three years, certain congressmen had been pushing for a national regulatory act but they had been blocked in every session of Congress. In March, 1926, however, they got their bill to the floor. How long its passage might have been delayed at this point is pure conjecture, but certain events, no doubt, influenced the lawmakers in reaching a decision. In February, 1926, Secretary Hoover took action to restrain the Zenith Radio Corporation from "appropriating" a wavelength reserved by international agreement for Canadian broadcasters. Again, as in 1922, the Secretary received a legal spanking. The Act of 1912, said the Court, did not provide a standard of control for his discretion; and 3 months later when the acting U.S. Attorney General handed down a decision that the Secretary of Commerce had no authority to regulate the power, frequency, of hours of operation of broadcasting stations, Hoover "threw in the towel."

The period between July, 1926, and February, 1927, was a particularly confused one. Like homesteaders rushing frantically toward El Dorado, applicants besieged the Commerce Department for licenses, and the Department was virtually compelled to grant authorizations to all comers. The existing "aerial chaos" was intensified. Hoover's pious hope that the industry might achieve self-regulation proved a delusion. One hundred ninety-four new stations went on the air without regard to interference with broadcasters in both Canada and the United States.

Then came the Radio Act of 1927—a set of comprehensive regulations which discerning minds had been sponsoring for 5 years. In a sense, the clock was stopped and reset. This was necessary in the proviso requiring applicants to sign waivers "of any claim to the use of any

. . . frequency . . . because of the previous use of the same whether by license or otherwise." The lawmakers had been brought to the realization that radio could never attain its potential usefulness unless it developed according to sound engineering principles and practices and was made available equally to every section of the country—to rural and sparsely populated areas as well as to concentrated metropolitan areas. This objective, however, had to be accomplished within the philosophy of a free, competitive economic system. The conjunction of these general principles precipitated an immediate and growing series of problems.

The specific provisions of the 1927 Act were intended to implement the following principles:

1. The regulation of all forms of radio communication within the United States, its territories and possessions, is rightly inherent in the Federal government.

2. Individuals (firms and corporations) may be permitted (licensed) to use radio channels, but this permission is conditional and not granted in perpetuity.

3. Licenses should be granted only to applicants who can meet specific qualifications.

4. An applicant must guarantee that he will operate according to the standard of "public interest, convenience, or necessity."

5. Each state and community is entitled to "fair, efficient, and equitable radio service."

6. Free competition should be maintained not only among broadcasters but also among manufacturers and distributors of "radio apparatus and devices entering into or affecting interstate or foreign commerce."

7. The merits of any dissension from a commission ruling should be determined by a court of law (the District Court of Appeals for the District of Columbia).

8. Qualified candidates for public office should be given equal treatment by the radio licensee.

9. The commission should not exercise power of censorship over radio communication or interfere with the right of free speech.

The task of administering the Act was assigned to a commission of five members (Federal Radio Commission) appointed by the President with the advice and confirmation of the Senate. The country was divided into five territorial zones, and each zone had its representative in the new administrative body. No more than three commissioners could be from the same political party.

The FRC went to work immediately. The situation before them, as explained above, was extremely chaotic. An average of eight stations operated on each of 90 channels, and many of them had deserted their assigned wavelengths and were ignoring restrictions prescribing power limitations and hours of operation. Moreover, other stations were using

or overlapping Canadian channels. In areas where a 50-kilocycle separation was necessary to eliminate interference (cross talk), operators were
broadcasting with as little as 2-kilocycle spacing.

Specific and mandatory rules and regulations were needed, and the
Act gave the Commission requisite authority. It was empowered to

1. Classify radio stations in certain groups.[1]
2. Prescribe the nature of the service to be rendered by each group.
3. Assign frequencies.
4. Allot power.
5. Determine times of operation.
6. Establish locations and areas of service served by each station.
7. Regulate apparatus.
8. Prevent interference.
9. Require detailed records of operation.
10. Exercise restrictive judgements subject to judicial review.

With a critical Congress "kibitzing over its collective shoulder," the
FRC went to work. General orders were issued. Fifty-kilocycle separations were established in urban areas. A band of channels from 600 to
1,000 kilocycles was designated as exclusive clear channels on which only
one station could operate at night (from sunrise to sunset). The
Canadian exclusive channels were cleared, and the power to be used
on channels shared with Canada was limited. In general, frequencies
were reallocated in an attempt to eliminate interference and provide
equitable reception. Taking in account economic and population factors,
the FRC tried to achieve this ideal by grading stations according to a

---

[1] Standard broadcast channels are classified as clear, regional, and local. A *clear
channel* is one on which the dominant station or stations render service over wide
areas and which is cleared of objectional interference within primary service areas.
A *regional channel* is one on which several stations may operate not in excess of
5 kilowatts. A *local channel* is one on which several stations may operate with powers
not in excess of 250 watts.

Standard broadcast stations, operating on their respective channels, are classified
as Class I, Class II, Class III, Class III-A, Class III-B, and Class IV. A Class I
station is a dominant station operating on a clear channel and designed to render
primary and secondary service over an extended area and at relatively long distances.
Its primary service is free from objectionable interference from other stations on the
same and adjacent channels; its secondary service area is free from interference
except from stations on the adjacent channel. Operating power: not less than 10
nor more than 50 kilowatts. A Class II station is a secondary station which operates
on a clear channel and is designed to render service over a primary service area
which is limited by and subject to such interference as may be received from Class
I stations. Operating power: not less than 250 watts nor more than 50 kilowatts. A
Class III-A station is one which operates with power not less than 1 nor more than
5 kilowatts. A Class III-B station is a Class II station which operates with a power
not less than 0.5 nor more than 1 kilowatt at night and 5 kilowatts during the day.
A Class IV station is one operating on a local channel and designed to render
service primarily to a city or town and the suburban areas contiguous thereto.
Operating power: not less than 0.1 nor more than 2.5 kilowatts.

formula calling for low-power local, medium-power regional, and high-power clear-channel stations. According to the principle of "public interest, convenience, or necessity," some stations were reduced in power and others were placed on probation.

In 1928, Congress adopted a substitute for Section 9 of the new Radio Act. This substitution, known as the Davis Amendment, made mandatory an equitable distribution of radio facilities. It has been described as a "masterpiece of mixed motives in which misguided idealism, States' rightism, pork barrelism, and rabid monopolism joined forces to defeat the expressed aims of the Act of 1927,"[2] but the alleged intent of the Amendment was to guarantee maximum coverage, minimum interference, and uniform service. The attainment of these objectives required a comprehensive plan that could be applied on a national basis. Such a plan was advanced in 1929. It was a quota system by which each zone and state would receive equal treatment with reference to assigned radio frequencies and service according to population. This proposal encountered so much opposition that it was modified the following year. Stations were assigned numerical unit values (a full-time 1,000-watt regional channel station was given the value of one unit), each zone was to have the same number of units, and each state within the zone was likewise assigned an "equitable" share. The execution of this plan was fraught with many complications. As matters stood, some zones were already over quota. There was clear sailing for the Commission only in under-quota states and in under-quota zones. Numerous litigants assailed the quota plan as illegal, but the Commission was vindicated in a decision by the Supreme Court.

The conscientious efforts of the FRC to achieve uniform coverage through sharing devices and channel separations went on apace, but against what appeared at times to be insuperable odds. The hope that the vast areas intervening between the metropolitan centers could be served by clear channels was as yet unrealized. Fifty-five of the fifty-seven 50-kilowatt stations were located mostly on the seaboards. Their location had been determined by the availability of advertising markets and not geographical areas. The radio highway was still a complicated maze of blocks, detours, and dead ends; and unforeseen technical developments such as FM and TV were subsequently to add further complications. However, by 1930, broadcasting had been brought to the level of functional public service. The threefold problem which had existed a decade before had found its solution. The question of ownership and control, the problem of promotion and finance, and the matter of Federal responsibility for radio's ultimate development had reached the state of settled policies.

[2] Llewellyn White, *The American Radio*, p. 153.

QUESTIONS

1. What three barriers impeded the development of radiobroadcasting?

2. What were the arguments advanced in favor of government ownership and operation of radio facilities?

3. Explain the practical situation which balked the government spokesmen.

4. By what means were private control and operation achieved?

5. What proposals were made concerning radio program financing?

6. What was the origin of sponsored broadcasts?

7. What was the nature of the "technical hurdle"?

8. Why was the designation of one wavelength a source of confusion?

9. How did Secretary Hoover, in 1921, attempt to relieve this confusion?

10. What was the result of the litigation between the government and the Intercity Radio Company?

11. Summarize the accomplishments of the four radio conferences.

12. Why was the period between July, 1926, and February, 1927, a particularly confused one?

13. What was the outcome of the Commerce Department's failure to solve the broadcasting problem?

14. Enumerate the basic principles of the Radio Act of 1927.

15. What specific regulatory authority was given the FRC?

16. How did the FRC proceed to cope with the aerial chaos?

CHAPTER 4

RADIO: A BIG BUSINESS

The purpose of this chapter is to present the picture of radio's growth and development as a big business. An understanding of the data and pictograms which follow requires a brief statement about some technical aspects of broadcasting: network evolution, organization, and management; commercial operations; and audience analysis.

Recently, there was an interesting story about a government search for a radio station which was apparently functioning as a commercial carrier but about which the radio authorities in Washington had no record. Field engineers assigned to the job of tracking down the "wildcat" located it in a Middle Western city. A group of young men, erstwhile radio "hams," not satisfied with purely amateur operations, had as-

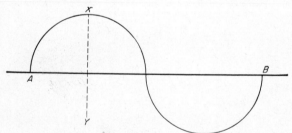

Fig. 7. Sound cycle and amplitude.

sembled the necessary equipment and were conducting regular station broadcast services. When questioned, they claimed ignorance of any law which forbade their operation. They had four requisites of an operating station—studios, control room, transmitter, and antenna—but not the fifth, a government license.

In order to establish one's self as a broadcaster, he must apply to the Federal Communications Commission (FCC) in Washington, D.C. In his application he must represent that there is an available channel in his territory, that he is financially and morally responsible, and that he will operate in the interests of the public. This license entitles him to build a station of specified power to be operated on a precise wavelength and for a stated number of hours per day.

A radiobroadcasting station, designed to transmit sound, music, and speech through the air, is a product of scientific and engineering genius. An explanation of the physical laws by which it functions belongs to technical treatises which the layman finds difficult to interpret. Satisfied with his dexterity in tuning the dial, he may simply say, "nerts to Hertz."[1] It is not easy to explain how sound waves are amplified, superimposed on carrier frequencies, picked up by receivers, and retranslated into audio sound; but let us give a few definitions that may be helpful to a better understanding of radio magic.

To understand two terms important in radio terminology—frequency and amplitude—we may recall what we know about ordinary sound waves. A vibrating body, such as a violin string, is set in motion and the vibration of the string produces condensations and rarefactions in the surrounding medium, the air. A sound wave is conventionally represented by a sine curve. The swing of the vibrating element (the violin string) from the initial point of attack to its return to the same phase condition A-B is called a cycle. The pitch of the sound depends on the number, or frequency, of these cycles. The loudness of the sound depends on the distance from the crest of one wave to the bottom of the succeeding one. This distance X-Y is called amplitude (see Fig. 7).

Sound waves picked up by a microphone are changed into electrical impulses. These are sent over wires to a transmitter which generates a powerful wave carrier—a steady signal of r-f energy. The sound impulses, originating at the microphone and changed into electrical characteristics, are carried, as it were, on the back of the radio carrier wave. The frequency of the carrier wave is expressed in degrees of kilocycles. A 1-kilocycle has 1,000 cycles per second. When you turn to the radio page in your daily paper, you find your stations listed as follows:

KECA—700
KFI—640
KWKW—1300

The numbers refer to the carrier-wave frequency, expressed in kilocycles on which the station operates, and designate the particular spot in the electromagnetic spectrum occupied by the station.

The standard aural broadcasting band uses only a portion of the spectrum, the section between 550 and 1,600. Each radio channel is separated by 10 kilocycles. This provides for 106 broadcasting channels. With more than 2,000 AM broadcasting stations in the United States, it is obvious that a great many stations use the same channel. They are so placed geographically, however, as to avoid interference.

As an applicant for a radio station license, you would be interested in the dial spot assigned you. Certain locations are considered more ad-

[1] Otis C. Ferguson, "Nerts to Hertz," *The New Republic*, Apr. 4, 1934.

vantageous than others. You frequently hear an announcer give the call letters of his station and say " . . . on the center of your radio dial." The kilocycle band placed at your disposal, however, would not be so important as the signal power allowed. Channels are classified, as previously explained, as clear, regional, and local. If you were fortunate enough to get one of the 59 clear-channel assignments, you would probably be able to operate with a maximum of 50,000 watts; as an operator privileged to use one of the 41 regional channels, you would have to be satisfied with a power of 1,000 to 5,000 watts; as a local

Fig. 9. The National Broadcasting Company Studios, Radio City, Hollywood, Calif.

station owner you would be confined to a wattage ranging from 100 to 250.

Furthermore, the conditions of your license would fix your broadcasting hours. Competitive conditions in your locale might require you to share time with another station. The policy of the FCC in specifying these conditions accords with their philosophy of providing fair, equitable service to all sections of the country.

Finally, you would be assigned identifying call letters. It is interesting to observe that, with few exceptions, all stations west of the Mississippi River are given the initial letter K; all stations east of the Mississippi, the letter W.

As of June 30, 1950, the government had issued 2,118 standard broadcast licenses. All communities over 25,000 population; 84.7 per cent of communities between 10,000 and 25,000; 52.5 per cent between 5,000 and 10,000; and 24.9 per cent between 2,500 and 5,000 had one or more radio stations. Seventy-three communities of less than 2,500 had their own radio outlets. It was thought at one time that the 500- to 1,600-kilocycle band could not accommodate the number of stations requisite for national coverage; but technological improvements in transmitter design and control, microphones, studio construction, together with a better spacing of broadcast bands, have obviated any further extension of the band.

FIG. 10. Studios of Columbia Broadcasting System, Columbia Square, Hollywood, Calif.

Broadcasting operations today flow in a smooth and established pattern. It is very much as if we had one powerful station which could reach everyone in the nation. This is due to the fact, of course, that radio transmitters are connected by telephone lines and that hundreds of stations are linked together in a gigantic chain which stretches from one seaboard to another. It is more than a matter of interest to record how chain broadcasting came about. It is true that on Mar. 7, 1924, listeners in California and England heard a radio program at the same time, but network broadcasting as we know it did not come until later.

The story of network evolution is as follows. Although scores of radio transmitters sprouted like mushrooms following the debut of KDKA, each station was an independent unit or outlet. Certain stations, however, were of particular interest because of their power and financial backing. These were the Westinghouse stations at Newark, N.J. (WJZ) and at Chicago (KYW), the GE station at Schenectady (WGY), and the A.T. & T. Co., New York station, WEAF. The most important of these from the standpoint of subsequent developments was WEAF. Under the cross-licensing agreements among the four majors, it was considered that "a monopoly of wireless telephony for profit" was invested in A.T. & T. Co. This company, acting on the belief that it had an "exclusive right to exploit radiobroadcasting for public use," built WEAF, and 12 days after going on the air sold time (leased its facilities) to a commercial sponsor. In other words, WEAF was established as a toll-broadcasting service analogous to long-distance telephone service. The possibilities of "telephone broadcasting" commanded the attention of the A.T. & T. Co. engineers and was given its first test in the fall of 1922 when a play-by-play description of the Princeton-Chicago football game was transmitted from Stagg Field in Chicago to New York. The success of this experiment established the principle of network broadcasting. Other tests were made, however, and programs were sent by radio wire from New York to Boston and from New York to Washington, D.C. The hookup was expanded and WEAF, WGY, KDKA, and KYW carried a test broadcast. On October, 1924, when President Coolidge spoke at a convention session of the U.S. Chamber of Commerce, 22 stations "from coast to coast" carried his words. By 1925, A.T. & T. Co. claimed a broadcasting chain of 26 stations.[2]

In 1926, the A.T. & T. Co., decided that it would be to their advantage to retire from the broadcasting business. A deal was made with RCA by which the latter acquired possession of WEAF, and a lease arrangement was signed by which RCA could use the A.T. & T. Co. long-distance lines. At the same time the corporation set up a broadcasting subsidiary, the National Broadcasting Company (NBC), through which advertising services could be funneled to their radio outlets. The stations to which the telephone company had been sending programs from WEAF were organized as a broadcasting network—the Red; a companion network, the Blue, was formed from those stations which had been operating under RCA's direction by use of telegraph wires. Both networks were served by NBC. It was highly advantageous for a station to become affiliated with a network because it meant better programs and more revenue. In one year, NBC member stations increased from 19 to 48.

[2] All these chain broadcasts had been promoted as experimental demonstrations. They were not permanent or commercial. Back in mid-1923, however, a station owner in Dartmouth, Mass., had asked the telephone company to connect WEAF with his station on a permanent basis so that his audience could benefit from the broadcasts emanating from the New York station. An agreement was made and confirmed. It can be recorded that this was the first commercial network.

Three more national radio networks were to follow. The first of these, the Columbia Broadcasting System (CBS), came on the heels of the NBC organization. CBS started operations in September, 1927, with an aggregation of 16 stations. A year later it had 28 affiliates. The next chain, the Mutual Broadcasting System (MBS), made its start in October, 1934. Four stations came together in a cooperative arrangement. They were strong stations serving large market areas: WOR (New York), WGN (Chicago), WXYZ (Detroit), and WLW (Cincinnati). For various reasons the owners of these stations had maintained an independent status, feeling that it was unnecessary for them to join either NBC or CBS. When several advertising agencies offered them special rate inducements to broadcast simultaneously, the owners entered a corporate agreement. This four-station network became a "cooperating" group of 107 stations by 1939. At the outset, Mutual did not support a full-time network management or an originating program organization. Member stations paid for the maintenance of network lines and "the network derived its income from a commission for selling time." Full-time management was set up in 1942, however, and today Mutual's organization and service approaches that of NBC and CBS. Owing to the fact that MBS had few 50,000-watt stations, it has had to attain its service coverage by integrating a large number of local and regional stations. In terms of member stations, Mutual is the the largest of the networks. The fourth network, the American Broadcasting Company (ABC), came into official existence in December, 1944. It was actually the Blue Network formerly owned by NBC although its station structure was radically different from the original Blue. In 1941, the FCC had promulgated certain regulations concerning chain broadcasting, and under the rules NBC was forced to divest itself of one of its networks. The Blue was put on the market and finally found a purchaser in October, 1943. On Dec. 30, 1944, radio listeners heard a new station cue: "This is ABC, the American Broadcasting Company."[3]

[3] In 1948, a fifth network was organized, and 3 years later its affiliates were outnumbered only by Mutual's member stations. This was the Liberty Network whose president, Gordon McLendon, predicted that by the summer of 1952 Liberty would be "the biggest in the business." Thirty-one-year-old McLendon, on whom publicity has fastened the appellation, "the Old Scotchman," got the idea for his network during the war when he discovered that boys from provincial mid-continent towns were avid baseball fans although the only games they ever *heard* were the World Series. On Mar. 21, 1948, from the Dallas station, KLIF, McLendon "tried out" his idea by "re-creating" from teletype a play-by-play account of an exhibition game between the New York Giants and the Saint Louis Cardinals. The response of listeners was enthusiastic. In 60 days, a 47-station network was organized, a nucleus which, by 1951, expanded to more than 300 stations in all 48 states, broadcasting to an audience of 30 million. Coast-to-coast operations were begun in October, 1951. Liberty is regarded primarily as a sports network but its 7-hours-per-day, 7-days-per-week schedule includes newcasting, special events, special Hollywood shows, mystery dramas, and a disk-jockey round table—a different disk jockey from a different city each day.

The organization of radio networks established an advertiser's paradise. The local market became a regional or national market. A sales message addressed to a microphone in New York was heard by potential customers in the Mississippi Valley and on the Pacific Coast. Not only did networks give geographical expansion to the sponsor's voice, they brought him an ever increasing number of listeners by virtue of improved programs. The "crossroads" station was now able to broadcast the best entertainment that New York, Chicago, and Hollywood could produce, and program content also constantly improved owing to the rivalry of the networks in securing preferred listener clientele.

The job of selling radio time was the primary concern of the networks. This entailed on their part elaborate administrative and technical machinery. Advertising accounts had to be secured through aggressive sales promotion, public acceptance enlarged, technical research promoted, audience surveys made, and "public-service" programs planned and executed. All of this was a burden and obligation assumed by the network. The affiliated station was the direct recipient. It made no contribution other than to lease its technical facilities through which the "net" show could be "piped."

The contractural agreement between the member station and the parent organization provides that a percentage of the station's time should be reserved for programs originating with and delivered by the network. (The time not contracted to the network is, of course, the station's own and may be sold or used as local or regional opportunities dictate.) Each station is compensated according to its location, market coverage, power, etc. The formula by which this remuneration is allowed is very complex and is of interest primarily to those involved in the business of time sales. The network, naturally, takes the larger percentage of the revenue dollar because it sells the program in the first place, pays for the use of the telephone lines, and carries an overhead expense represented by studios and administrative, technical, program, and research personnel.

An advertiser, buying radio network time, is not required to use the complete broadcasting chain. A sponsor must "take" a fixed minimum of stations called "the basic network," but beyond this prescribed limit he may add individual outlets according to his market operations. Because some manufacturers and distributors deal only in a particular area or region, such as the Pacific Coast or New England, he may wish to use only the radio facilities in his general area. Consequently, national networks are subdivided into what are called regional networks to serve sponsors within geographically defined marketing areas.[4]

---

[4] At the close of the 1950 fiscal year, the number of network affiliates were: ABC, 286; CBS, 184; MBS, 543; NBC, 176.

Radio sales promotion, synonymous with broadcasting itself, is the heart of American radio. (We shall return to this statement when we explore the social aspects of our subject because it is basic and fundamental to a philosophical appraisal of radio's influence.) How do the programs to which we are accustomed get on the air? National sponsors operate through advertising agencies which are an integral part of commercial broadcasting. The agency is presumed to know whether radio is the best means of advancing a client's name, product, and message as well as the type of program which will produce the best results. It can also give expert advice as to the best broadcast coverage, specify the time of day when the program should be presented, and serve as a liasion factor between sponsor and network.

The show or program finally agreed on may come from three sources: (1) The agency itself may conceive, build, and produce it. Many agencies employ writers and directors, buy scripts, employ acting and musical talent, and assume full charge of the broadcast. (2) The network may provide the idea, format, and personnel. The program they offer is usually one which has been tested as a sustained or nonsponsored broadcast. (3) An outside party, an independent producer, talent firm, an individual or group of individuals, may deliver a "package" which will satisfy the advertising agency and its client. By an "outside package" is meant a program which is furnished to the agency and is complete as to script, production, and cast. In this case the agency acts only in an advisory, and to some extent supervisory, capacity being fully responsible only for the commercial continuity.

All advertising is not done through the medium of "big" shows, however. One of the main sources of financial revenue is spot advertising—single-shot thrusts at a definite and localized target. This kind of promotion ranges from the short station break—Bulova watch type of thing—through 100-word and 1-minute commercials up to a full-period program. National advertisers use spot advertising technique, but it is the special medium of the local advertiser. This type of selling is handled by agencies, station commercial staffs, and by free-lance salesmen.

What is the cost of radio advertising? This question can be answered only with reference to many factors: the number of stations employed, the nature of the program, the length of the program, and the time of the day or night it is released. Every network and station has a rate card on which is listed standard costs for time and coverage. In addition to station time, the sponsor must add talent expenses. The latter are determined by the minimum scales set by the talent unions, but they will rise above this amount when particularly desired performers are paid "above scale."

There is one other question we should answer before charting radio's growth and development: How can a sponsor know about the pull of his program? Is there any way of estimating the extent of station coverage, audience size, and program appeal? At first, the problem of counting auditors must have seemed as futile as counting fish in the sea. People were asked to write their reactions and mail them to the "station to which you are listening," or they wrote in voluntarily. This fan mail was interesting but it was by no means a cross-section measurement of listener attitudes. A magazine publisher could count the names on his mailing list, and the billboard advertiser could estimate the average number of viewers who passed a given intersection each day; but the radio salesman, casting blindly into the air, could only guess. Radio field engineers could plot the coverage of a station and measure the intensity of their signal at any given point, but this had no precise relation to the actual number of people receiving the signal.

There are four techniques by which radio polls have been taken: recall, coincidental, audimeter, and mail ballot. The recall method was initiated by Archibald Crossley in 1929. Listeners were asked to report the programs to which they had recently listened. Interest in his plan attracted attention and prompted the formation of the Cooperative Analysis of Broadcasters (CAB) with Crossley as director. By 1945, the CAB was giving weekly reports to the radio industry on listening patterns in 81 cities. The coincidental method was the contribution of Clark-Hooper, Inc. This was a plan of calling telephone numbers and making such inquiries as, Are you listening to your radio? To what program are you listening? The results obtained by these two methods were considered similarly reliable. Subscribers felt that the expense of one service was all they wished to stand, and CAB went out of business at the end of 1946. The question, How's your Hooper? became the byword in professional radio circles. The third method of determining audience scope and interest, introduced in 1942, was devised by A. C. Nielsen. He used a mechanical device, the audimeter, which was attached to a receiving set and which recorded on a piece of paper the exact time when stations were tuned in and tuned out. One advantage which the audimeter held over the coincidental technique was that it could be applied to nontelephone homes and in rural as well as urban centers. With 3,000 audimeters in 20 states. Nielsen claimed that he could give reliable figures for 60 per cent of radio's over-all coverage. In 1945, the Broadcasting Measurement Bureau (BMB), endorsed by the American Association of Advertising Agencies, the radio industry, and the National Association of Broadcasters, brought forward another system. By means of a "controlled mail ballot" listeners were asked to list "the call letters of all radio stations which you or some one in your family listen to at home *at any time*," and to check "the number of *nights a week* (after dark) each station is listened to," and "the number of *days a week* (before dark) each station is listened to in the home." The Bureau undertakes to get a cross-section pattern for every county in the United States.

These four survey techniques, based on refined statistical procedure, are the principal methods of analyzing radio listening habits. There are other means of studying audience reaction, but they are reserved for more specific situations and have never been employed on a network basis. Listeners in selected homes are asked to make a detailed report on their listening, covering a period of time in units of one week. In a house-to-house canvass, radio owners are shown a list of programs recently or currently on the air and asked to check those which they have heard. People are brought into a radio studio during an actual radio-broadcast and, as the program moves along, each viewer can register his likes and dislikes by a mechanical recording device. Furthermore, a listening panel, composed of representative users of radio, is asked to report, à la Gallup-poll style, on various aspects of the program. Their answers are made to specific questions set forth in a questionnaire.

Now, with a basic understanding of how stations are assigned their respective positions on the radio dial to ensure maximum broadcasting efficiency, how they are organized in chains or networks to achieve national coverage, how they function as merchandising outlets, and how advertisers may check the effectiveness of their programs, we can chart in retrospect radio's growth and development. For standards of measurement we shall use the statistics concerning receiving sets, radio stations, radio sponsorship, associated services, employment, and compensation.

Receiving Sets. Radio growth is reflected in the steadily increasing sale of radio receivers. In 1916, David Sarnoff recommended to the Marconi Company the details of a "radio music box" supplied with amplifying tubes and a loud-speaking telephone which could be placed "on a table in the parlor or living room." Four years later he presented to Owen D. Young an estimate of a prospective radio business based on this music-box idea. It was Sarnoff's belief that 75 million dollars might be derived from the sale of this gadget within a period of 3 years. His estimate was actually exceeded by 8.5 million dollars. This phenomenon can be understood in the light of television's meteoric growth. Almost overnight, housetops by the millions have sprouted a forest of aerials. This avid, if not frenzied, buying of TV receiving sets is analogous to the enthusiasm which householders displayed toward audio receivers in the early thirties. Two years after the licensing of KDKA, there were approximately half a million radios in American homes. Today, there are over 80 million. With the exception of three war years—1943, 1944, 1945—there has been a steady annual increase in radio receiver sales. More people, year by year, have found a radio a necessary item.

One-half, or more, of the radios in the world are in the United States. Several interpretations might be given of this fact although they would probably be the same which apply to America's numerical superiority in bathtubs. Serious claims can be made, however, anent our mechanical

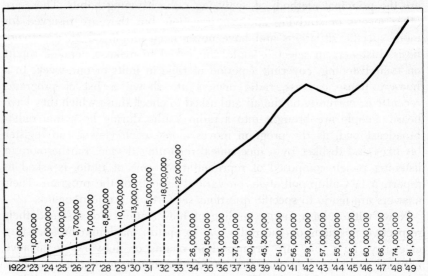

FIG. 11. Estimated total radio sets in use in the United States, 1922 to 1949.

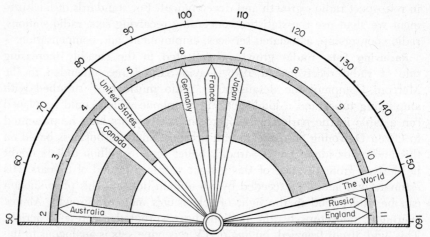

FIG. 12. Radio receivers in the world and eight leading nations.

ingenuity, production capacity, high rate of literacy, and capitalistic enterprise. A graphic account of radio-set distribution may be given by using the standard kilocycle and megacycle dials. If you know the carrier frequencies of the AM and FM stations in your region, Fig. 12 may supply a helpful frame of reference.

Using the same type of mnemonic device, we can also picturize the relation of other national radio systems in terms of radio receiving sets owned by listeners in the United States. The complete semicircle in Fig. 13 represents the total sets in the United States; the segments, or arcs, as labeled, represent the comparative number, or percentage, of radio sets owned by other countries.

Radio Stations. The annual increase of receiving sets was related to a corresponding phase of radio development—station growth. The correspondence was not exact as will be seen by comparing Figs. 11 and 14 exemplifying the respective annual expansion of receiver purchases

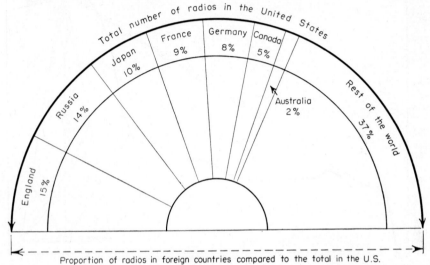

Proportion of radios in foreign countries compared to the total in the U.S.

FIG. 13. Proportion of radios in foreign countries compared to the total in the United States.

and station operation. New station construction shows slight gain between 1923 and 1934. A national depression and, later, a world war, imposed drastic restraints upon station owners, but a rush of applicants following 1944 brought the number of operating stations to a sharp peak. In 4 years, twice as many stations were constructed as in the previous 18 years.

The reason for this rapid growth was that broadcasting had proved to be a profitable venture. During the 8-year period, 1937 to 1944, broadcast revenues increased from 114 million to 275 million dollars; expenses from 92 million to 185 million dollars; and broadcast income from approximately 23 million to 90 million dollars.[5] Based on the ratio of income

[5] *Public Service Responsibility of Broadcast Licensees,* Federal Communications Commission, Washington, D.C., Mar. 7, 1946, p. 48.

to depreciated investment in tangible broadcast property, AM stations *as a whole* more than tripled their profitability between 1939 and 1945. Whereas in 1939 this ratio was 57 per cent, it had increased to 190 per cent in 1945.[5a] When comparative trends of earnings in relation to investment are reviewed for the different classes of stations, we reach the following generalizations: Local unlimited stations increased their ratio almost tenfold, regional part-time stations showed a fivefold increase, and three of the part-time stations (local part-time, 5- to 20-kilo-

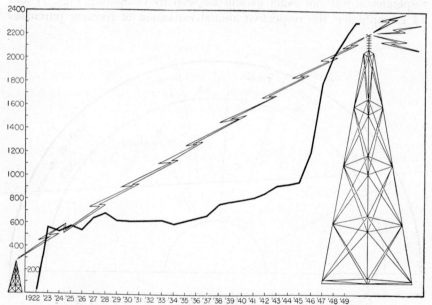

FIG. 14. Growth of standard broadcasting stations, 1922 to 1949.

watt part-time, regional part-time) increased their ratios more than fivefold.[5b]

If station profitability is measured by another yardstick—the ratio of broadcast income to broadcast revenue—every *class* of station operated with substantial plus signs. In 1939, AM stations, *as a whole*, realized an average of 19 cents of income (before Federal income tax) from every revenue dollar received. In 1944, this income was almost doubled (36 cents), and in 1945, 31 cents of every dollar was net revenue.[5c] Many individual stations lost money, particularly those which had just started operations, but every *class* of stations enjoyed marked increases. When

[5a] *An Economic Study of Standard Broadcasting*, Federal Communications Commission, Washington, D.C., Oct. 31, 1947, p. 12.
[5b] *Ibid.*, p. 16.
[5c] *Ibid.*, p. 16.

the ratio of income to revenues by class of station is considered, the degree of profitability is shown in sharper relief.

This evidence of potential prosperity influenced a flood of applications following VJ day. On July 1, 1947, there were 1,795 authorized stations and 666 applications for new stations, a total of 2,461. Many of the new applicants would be denied owing to their inability to qualify under imposed financial and technical standards, but the FCC estimated in 1947 that the following year would see 2,250 broadcasting outlets in the United States. The number of operating stations in 1945 was 909.

A further evidence of radio's profit-making potential is seen in the prices which would-be licensees were willing to pay for broadcast stations. These prices, of course, were influenced by general inflation and

Ratio of Broadcast Income (before Federal Income Taxes) to Total Broadcast Revenues, by Class of Station, 1939 and 1945, for All Commercial Stations (excluding Key Stations of the Major Networks) *

Class of station	1939 per cent	1945 per cent	Per cent increase over 1939
Local unlimited..............	5.6	23.9	326.8
Local part-time..............	5.6	20.5	266.1
Regional unlimited...........	17.6	32.5	84.7
Regional part-time...........	6.8	22.8	235.3
5- to 20-kw. unlimited........	18.5	23.2	25.4
5- to 20-kw. part-time........	14.2	28.0	97.2
50-kw. unlimited.............	32.4	37.6	16.1
50-kw. part-time.............	24.9	26.1	4.8
All stations.................	18.7	30.9	65.1

* *An Economic Study of Standard Broadcasting*, Federal Communications Commission, Washington, D.C., Oct. 31, 1947, p. 19.

by the fact that the construction freeze during 1942 to 1944 had affected station availability. Nevertheless, the fact that entrepreneurs were willing to buy at greatly inflated prices seemed proof that there was "gold in them thar hills." The total sales prices from 1938 to 1943 ranged from 139 to 260 per cent of the total original cost of fixed assets. In the 2 years following, the ante was up. The total sales price in 1944 was 327 per cent and in 1945, 343 per cent of total original cost. The 49 stations sold in 1946 brought an aggregate price of 650 per cent of the original cost of fixed assets. These stations were currently very profitable. Their net income before Federal income tax equaled 102 per cent of original cost. Even at the inflated purchase price paid, new station owners might recover their purchase price in 6.5 years if profits remained at the 1946 level. In 1938 and 1939, the stations sold earned less than 10 cents on every dollar originally invested in fixed assets; in 1944, the stations sold earned 45 cents on every dollar of original cost. This ratio climbed in the two succeeding years. Stations earned 82 cents on the dollar in 1945 and $1.02 in 1946.

Radio Sponsorship. As the number of radio receivers bears a relationship to the number of broadcasting stations, station growth and operation relate to the number of commercial sponsors employing radio as a sales medium. Station profit is in proportion to the number of clients

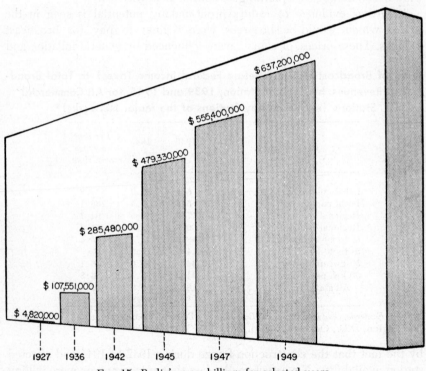

FIG. 15. Radio's gross billings for selected years.

served and the size of their radio advertising budgets. The business side of broadcasting can be measured in large part by the advertiser's use of the radio medium.

In 1927, radio's annual statement to its advertising clients approximated 5 million dollars. In 1949, this round figure had ballooned to well over 500 million dollars. With the exception of one year—1933—the advertisers of America wrote larger and larger checks each succeeding year for the privilege of proclaiming their goods and services.

The value placed on radio as a sales medium is shown in Fig. 16

by comparing the radio advertising budgets and the total advertising appropriations of 10 companies for a typical year, 1946.

The growth of radio advertising is thrown somewhat in relief when compared to newspaper advertising (see Fig. 17). The advertising revenue pie has undergone a constant resectioning. The share of national and local advertising going to newspapers dropped from 79 per cent in

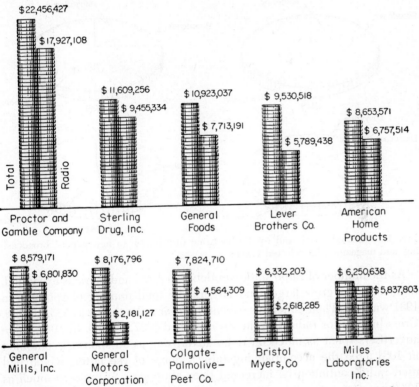

FIG. 16. Dollar comparison of radio advertising to total advertising expenditures (radio, 107 national magazines, 42 farm papers) for 10 leading advertisers, 1946. (Based on statistics copyrighted by Publishers Information Bureau and published in *Printers' Ink*, Apr. 18, 1947, p. 98.)

1929 to 53 per cent in 1946, whereas the broadcast share of total billings rose from 3 per cent in 1929 to 25 per cent in 1946.

The above statistics combine the sums spent by national *and* local advertisers. When national and local advertising are considered separately, the effectiveness of radio compared with newspapers as a national sales medium is revealed more clearly. Radio billings increased from 17 to 33 per cent (1934 to 1946) whereas newspaper revenue from national advertisers decreased from 48 to 27 per cent. This statistical relationship would seem to warrant the generalization that companies producing low-price units and depending on high frequency of purchase find radio a better sales medium. A regular radio program listened to by millions of potential customers is an effective agent in building strong mental associates and buyer consciousness.

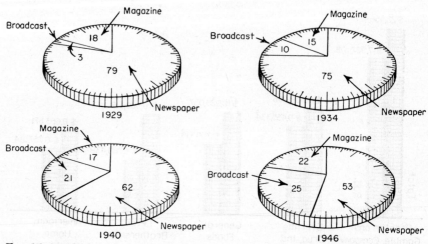

FIG. 17. National, local, and total advertising distribution to newspapers, broadcasting, and magazines, for selected years.

As the number of radio station outlets increased and markets expanded, radio budgets grew larger and larger. The total number of sponsors in 1931 was 343. Their collective expenditure for radio time was $35,536,148. Gross billings for radio time in 1949 reached $637,200,000. In 1948, three advertisers spent as much on radio advertising as all sponsors combined in 1931 (see the accompanying table). Some of the latter, which had used radio continuously, increased their allotments to radio as much as 1,300 per cent within 17 years.

	1931	1948
General Mills	$521,234	$7,200,000
General Foods	582,603	6,800,000
Colgate-Palmolive-Peet	743,465	4,300,000

Advertising is a constant day-to-day, week-by-week business. Some of the principal clients of the networks have had a long and continuous relationship with radio. Network accounts with some national advertisers span more than a decade, as may be seen by the accompanying table.

Clients	Weeks on CBS*
Proctor and Gamble.......................	688
Lever Brothers Co........................	646
William Wrigley, Jr. Co...................	810
Kolynos Co...............................	759
R. J. Reynolds Tobacco Co................	754
American Tobacco Co......................	571
Pet Milk Sales Corp......................	736
Gulf Oil Corp............................	719
Lady Esther Sales Co., Inc................	718
Liggett & Myers Tobacco Co..............	695

	Weeks on NBC†
Proctor and Gamble......................	847
Lever Brothers Co........................	450
American Tobacco Co......................	922
Liggett & Myers Tobacco Co..............	424
R. J. Reynolds Tobacco Co................	473

* *Annual Report for the Fiscal Year Ended Jan. 3*, 1948, pp. 36–37, Columbia Broadcasting System, Inc.

† *Annual Review*, 1946–1947, pp. 42–44, National Broadcasting Company.

The product groups which spend the greatest amounts in telling their story by radio are shown by the following table.

	Millions of Dollars*
Food and food products..............	47
Toiletries...	32
Drugs and remedies....................	22.5
Soap cleansers and polishes..........	20.7
Smoking materials....................	20.3
Household equipment and supplies.........	8.5

* Figures rounded for 1949. See *Broadcasting Yearbook*, 1950, p. 12, Broadcasting Magazine, Washington, D.C.

Proctor and Gamble is reputed to have spent 22 million dollars on radio advertising in 1944.

The size of radio and its great importance to the national economy are measured by the scope and character of its commercial sponsorship.

Associated Services. The size of radio business cannot be stated only in terms of radio receiving sets, stations, sponsors, sponsors' budgets, and revenue to station owners. The industry is a far-flung empire composed of many related and interlocking parts. Home radio sets must be serviced, and the annual cost to set owners for electricity, batteries, replacement tubes and parts, supplies, and shop service is over half a billion dollars.

. . . the investment in broadcasting and stations as of December 31, 1944 [compared] with an estimate of the public's investment in broadcast receivers of that date [shows] that the original cost of the public investment in broadcast receivers exceeds the original cost of the networks' and stations' investment in tangible property by the ratio of about 26 to 1.[6]

. . . a comparison of the estimated annual expenditures by advertisers for broadcast time and talent with the estimated cost to listeners [notes] that

[6] Based on an 8-year period prior to Dec. 31, 1944.

advertisers spent an estimated 2.0 cents per day per receiver to reach listeners, while listeners spent an estimated 3.1 cents per day per receiver to hear the programs provided.[7]

Somewhat as a corollary, it may be noted that the economic value added by the manufacture of radios and related products in 1947 reached a total of $773,233,000, and the value of phonographs produced in the same year totaled $75,660,000.[8]

Furthermore, broadcast stations must be built, supplied, and maintained. Two hundred or more equipment manufacturers stand by to supply towers, transmitters, tubes, transformers, amplifiers, loud-speakers, microphones, and test equipment. There are further requisites such as turntables, recorders, tone arms, equalizers, and recording stylii. The directory of AM, FM, and TV equipment manufacturers in the 1950 *Broadcasting Yearbook* lists 163 companies furnishing these kinds of materials. The brief statement of the Federal Telephone and Radio Corporation is an illustration of the technical aspect of broadcast structure and maintenance. It is the business of this corporation to supply:

AM: Complete broadcasting systems; transmitters; transmitting and rectifying tubes; consoles, microphones, and associated speech input and transmitter control equipment; field intensity meters. FM: Same plus square-loop transmitting antennae; studio transmitter links; microwave relay systems; transmitter monitors; dummy antennae. TV: Transmitter and complete broadcast equipment; high-gain triangular-loop antennae; remote pickup, studio transmitter, and intercity relay microwave link equipment; transmitter monitors and control consoles. HF coaxial cables and selenium rectifier DC power supplies.

Associated with the radio and television business are hundreds of companies which furnish a variety of functional services. These organizations manufacture sound-effects records, educational TV films, newsreels, animated TV commercials, talking-book records for the blind, industrial film, and musical spots. They provide production scripts, recording services, show packages, talent, and otherwise integrate in many ways with the needs of the industry and the requirements of the public.

Employment and Compensation. Another measurement of the scope of radio as a business is found in employment and compensation.

The first census of radiobroadcasting was taken in 1936. The Bureau of the Census included their review of radio as a separate part of the 1935 *Census of Business*. This statement was the first, complete, formal presentation of the character and extent of the radio business. The data presented represent the business of 561 stations operating on Dec. 31,

[7] *Public Service Responsibility of Broadcast Licensees, op. cit.,* p. 54.
[8] *Census of Manufactures,* U.S. Department of Commerce, Bureau of the Census, Vol. II, p. 741.

1935. On that date, networks and stations together employed an average of 14,561 persons with an annual payroll of $26,911,392.[9]

In 1948, radio engaged 34,740 full-time employees and paid them a total salary of $130,416,000. It is a significant fact, and one we refer to in our discussion of radio as a vocation, that the increase in radio personnel over the years has been relatively small compared to the annual in-

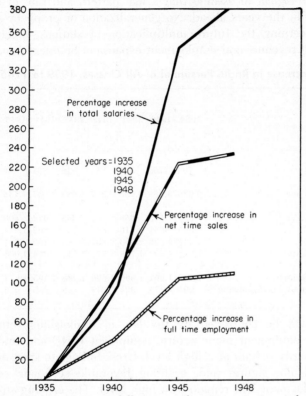

FIG. 18. Percentage increase in full-time employment, net time sales, and total salaries for selected years 1935, 1940, 1945, 1948.

crease in business volume. Stations in 1935 employing 14,000 employees did a total net sales business of 86 million dollars; stations in 1948 employing 35,000 full-time personnel did a business of more than 400 million dollars. Employees increased 1½ times; net sales increased four times.

Exact and comparable breakdown data on all classes of employment are not available except for the years 1939 to 1945 and, owing to world conditions, this is not a good sampling period. However, the data in the

[9] Radio Broadcasting, *Census of Business*, 1935, U.S. Department of Commerce, Bureau of the Census, October, 1936.

accompanying table have some bearing on the above generalization concerning employment growth in the industry.

Summary. The foregoing account of the economic growth and financial aspects of the radio industry serves the purpose, primarily, of historical interest. Its chief value lies in furnishing some perspective with reference to the development of a new type of business inaugurated in 1920.

It is not logical to assume that a like pattern and rate of expansion will occur in the years ahead. No generalization or prophecy should be made concerning the future multiplication of stations, receiving sets, advertising revenue, and employment expansion. Standard broadcasting,

Increase in Radio Personnel of All Classes, 1939 to 1945

	1939	1940	1941	1942	1943	1944	1945	Per cent increase, 1939–1945
Number of stations reporting....	705	765	817	851	846	834	866	22.8
Technical:								
Employees operating..........	3,035	3,469	3,688	3,807	3,683	3,837	4,155	36.9
Program:								
Producers....................	505	573	658	701	653	672	808	60.
Writers.....................	565	637	716	691	703	863	1,071	89.
Announcers..................	2,247	2,596	2,983	2,937	3,025	3,269	3,601	60.
Staff musicians..............	1,871	1,803	1,748	1,771	1,647	1,674	1,661	36.7
Commercial:								
Outside salesmen............	1,436	1,561	1,660	1,396	1,238	1,195	1,271	−11.5
Promotion and merchandising..	201	274	304	242	233	258	273	35.8

at least, will be controlled by the law of diminishing returns. The volume of equipment manufacture, equipment parts, and maintenance will necessarily remain at a high level. Gross billings to sponsors will be written in nine figures and, granting favorable economic conditions, radio employment will remain at a high level. The ensuing story of the communications industry, however, will emphasize quality rather than quantity and will deal with the relationship of component parts.

The radio historian of 1960 must give prominence to the advent and growth of television. Now, it is too early to treat this subject with much more than speculation. Undoubtedly, the annals of a major communications evolution (or revolution) have begun. What will be the relation of TV to AM? How will future advertising budgets be divided between these two media? Will standard broadcasting stations lose ground? We shall have to wait for the answers to such questions, but whatever the picture may be after the second 30 years of radio history, the facts of the first decades will remain as a dramatic, even sensational, epoch of American business promotion and achievement.

QUESTIONS

1. What is a carrier-wave frequency?
2. What is the standard aural broadcasting band?
3. What is the number of broadcast channels?
4. How is it possible for 2,000 broadcasting stations to operate without interference?
5. Sketch briefly the evolution of the four major networks.
6. Explain the technical, administrative, and financial relationships between networks and their affiliated stations.
7. Why is a network an advertiser's paradise?
8. How do radio programs get on the air?
9. Name and explain the four methods by which a sponsor can determine the "pull" of his radio program.
10. Sketch the growth of broadcasting in the United States in terms of the number of receiving sets, broadcasting stations, advertising budgets, and employment.

CHAPTER 5

RADIO AND GOVERNMENT: THE FEDERAL COMMUNICATIONS COMMISSION

Radio and government are necessarily related. (1) Radio is a power that exercises control over men's minds. The influence of broadcasting on mass thinking and social standards in incalculable. (2) Radio is a limited resource. The number of broadcast channels is fixed by electromagnetic laws. These two facts—radio's social importance and its technical limitations—compel supervision and control by a central agency. The type and amount of control exercised are dictated by political and economic philosophy.

The three basic control systems are best exemplified by those in Russia, in Great Britain, and in the United States. These are, respectively, state ownership and operation, quasi-governmental control by an appointed government monopoly, and private ownership and control.

The "state-owned" systems of radio vary in some administrative details, but the principle of government control, regulation, and responsibility is paramount. Government subsidies, derived in some instances from special tax levies on receiving sets, supply the financial basis of operation, and program content is dictated by appointed bureaus. The essence of state-owned radio is found in totalitarian countries. A dictator ideology is dependent on the control of mass thinking consonant with the policy of those in power. Edited facts which are constantly and persistently fed to a people will produce stereotyped thinking. Totalitarian states tell their people what they want them to believe. This means that radio in these countries is an instrument of propaganda and must be under the complete domination of the state. Radio sets may actually be built with limited tuning devices to gaurantee that only particular stations will be received.

In Great Britain, broadcasting is placed in the hands of a corporation distinct from the state but supervised by a government-appointed board. The British system is often referred to as an example of state ownership, but this is somewhat erroneous. There is vastly more freedom inherent in the British Broadcasting Corporation (BBC) than in an outright state system. In some respects, even though slight, the English

52

system is analogous to the American plan of broadcasting. In the United States, the relation of government to broadcasting is a nominal one. Originally established by private interests, the far-flung radio empire is owned and operated by individuals under a supervisory control that permits the same freedom pertaining to capitalistic enterprise in general.

Government monopoly and control are sufficiently clear as to require no particular exposition, but a review of the British system will serve as a frame of reference for the extended discussion of American broadcasting which follows. Let us look at the BBC—its origins, functions, administration, financial operation, and its program structure as it reflects government concern and direction.

RADIO AND GOVERNMENT IN GREAT BRITAIN

The BBC originated with an association of wireless-set manufacturers, organized in 1922. Certain difficulties of administration prompted the appointment of a government committee—the Broadcasting Committee of 1923—headed by Frederick Sykes. This Committee set the future tone and character of British broadcasting. After debating the issue of government vs. private ownership, it reached certain compromises. Outright state control was rejected, but it was recommended that the government exercise "watchfulness." The Committee also ruled against the selling of time to the highest bidder for his unrestrained use. A new company, the British Broadcasting Company, was organized and granted a 4-year license. Before the expiration of this period, the government appointed a second investigatory board, the Crawford Committee, to study "the whole future of the service." This group of investigators declared that the increasing power of broadcasting made inadequate the trade constitution of the established service and recommended the creation of a public corporation to remain a monopoly under a renewable license from the Postmaster General. The new authority, to be called the British Broadcasting Corporation, was to be financed by license fees imposed on receiving sets.

The functions and powers of the BBC set forth in the Royal Charter of December, 1926, are quite general. The Act prohibits agreements with other governments without consulting with the Postmaster General, proscribes broadcast advertising, and stipulates that the BBC charter and license be renewed every 10 years. In the choice of program matter, BBC is not subject to Parliamentary compulsion.

In addition to revenue from license fees, BBC's income is derived from three publications: Radio Times, The Listener, and London Calling. Radio Times, the most popular of these booklets, is a type of fan magazine that carries program schedules for the coming week; The Listener contains talks, round-table discussions, and commentary; and London

Calling is a radio information journal for overseas listeners. The BBC supplements its income by selling advertising space in these journals.

The BBC is directed by a board of seven governors directly responsible to the government, Parliament, and the people. The charter does not specifically outline their duties and responsibilities. Powers are more implied than expressed. Although the Corporation is a government-supported monopoly, the relation between the BBC and Parliament is largely anomalous. Neither the director-general nor the controllers have to answer questions to Parliament.

The work of the BBC is organized on the basis of "services" referred to as Light, Home, Third, and Regional. The Corporation operates on 13 wavelengths—one long and 12 medium—for home programs. After 6:00 P.M., nine programs are beamed throughout the British Isles. The British program most analogous to United States radio is the Light Program. Excluding commercials of any kind, this program could easily be mistaken for typical American production, affording quiz shows, popular tunes, and variety entertainment to its listeners. It commands by far the largest audience. Although all the services carry news and talks, these types of broadcast are heard particularly on the Home Service. Each political party is allotted a specific number of talks per year in proportion to its representation in Parliament, a fact which gives an advantage to the party in power. Election campaigns are never covered by the BBC. Other types of programs released on the Home Service wavelength includes operas, orchestras, sportscasts, information for women, and specially designed hours for children and young people. The Third Program, inaugurated in October, 1946, is devoted to serious music, drama, talks, and poetry. The director-general of that year, Sir William Haley, characterized the new program in this manner:

Let it demonstrate that we are not afraid to express our own culture or to give our people access to the culture of others. Let it set a standard which will not only raise the level of our own broadcasting but in the end affect the class of broadcasting in other lands.

The first week's program included G. B. Shaw's *Man and Superman*, acted in its entirety and lasting 4½ hours; Pierre Emmanual, reading his own poetry; and Lucile Watson, playing Bach compositions on the harpsichord. Under no circumstances are Third Program broadcasts to be interrupted, hurried, or cut off—important news bulletins included. Great works of literature are never altered, except the voluminous *Canterbury Tales* and similar classics. Exceptional broadcasts are sometimes repeated several times. More than one hundred of the world's greatest dramas were presented during the first 3 years of this revolutionary experiment.

The BBC has given prominence in its programing to religious worship *within the Christian tradition.* Care is taken to see that all Christian denominations are adequately and fairly represented.

The educational possibilities of broadcasting were recognized by the original BBC in 1922–1923. Some of the first evening programs consisted of talks given by the curators of, and official lectures at, the various national art galleries and museums. When the present Corporation came into being in 1926, this educational policy was expanded. A director was appointed to organize educational programs, and in 1928 the Central Council for Broadcast Adult Education was created. This interest was not confined to the adult citizenry. Great Britain was the first country in Europe—possibly the first in the world—to study systematically the possibilities of broadcasting to schools. BCC established the Advisory Committee on School Broadcasts as early as 1923, and by 1926 more than 2,000 schools were receiving regular programs. In 1929, this job was handed over to the Central Council for Schools Broadcasting. It is not a legal and functional unit within the framework of the BBC itself; it acts as an external and advisory body.

The BBC is a semi-independent, quasi-autonomous public corporation. It has functioned for more than a quarter of a century with objective concern for the public interest and is inextricably woven into the pattern of British life, thought, habit, and culture. It has never been a political instrument for shaping political opinion and social policy.

RADIO AND GOVERNMENT IN THE UNITED STATES

Wireless Ship Act. The history of Federal radio legislation in the United States begins with the Wireless Ship Act of June 24, 1910. The law was designed to protect maritime navigation. Any vessel carrying more than 50 persons was required to install radio sending and receiving apparatus that would cover a minimum distance of 100 miles.

The value of wireless communication to life and property on the seas and inland waters had been proved by a growing number of maritime incidents. The first wireless call for help was flashed by a distressed vessel in April, 1899, when the *R. F. Mathews* collided with East Goodwin Sands lightship. It was a dramatic demonstration of what Marconi's miracle could accomplish. Later, the *S.S. Republic,* colliding with the *S.S. Florida* off New York, received assistance at the scene of the accident; and 15 passengers were rescued from a Great Lakes vessel caught in an ice jam after several tugs heard their distress call and steamed to their relief. Then, on Apr. 14, 1912, occurred the greatest maritime disaster in times of peace. A White Star liner, the *Titanic,* a ship of record size and speed which men said could not sink, struck an iceberg off Newfoundland. It went down in $2\frac{1}{2}$ hours, but ships summoned by the *Titanic's* steady SOS arrived in time to save 700 persons. (Fifteen hundred lives were lost, and all would have perished had it not been for wireless communication.) This incident sped the passage of the Act of 1912.

Act of 1912. Germany and Belgium had equipped ocean-going vessels with wireless as early as 1900. Great Britain installed wireless on a merchant ship in 1901, and in 1910, as stated above, the United States had passed a mandatory law for ships of certain registry. The *Titanic* disaster made it clear that more extensive provisions should be made for the protection of life at sea. The Act of 1912, adopted in August of that year, was the first general legislation for the regulation of radio communication. At that time, however, radio communication was a matter of wireless operators, private companies engaged in shipping, and the U.S. Navy; and the primary purpose of the law was to designate the channels to be used by these three interests and to set up a licensing system under the Department of Commerce. The 1912 Act was not written as a broadcasting control law. It is true that the framers of the legislation used the phrase, "radio communication," but it was employed with the intention of providing for a day yet unborn. That day arrived more quickly than Congress previsioned. It came and there was no law pertaining thereto. The complex technical problem which developed made necessary the third major radio control law, the Radio Act of 1927. This Act, which has remained the basic radio law of the land, was explained in Chap. 3. Seven years later, however, it was rewritten as the Communications Act of 1934.

Communications Act of 1934. The title, Federal Radio Commission, was changed to Federal Communications Commission (FCC), but in all essential respects the authority of the new body remained the same as it had been under the legislation of 1927. The assignment of the exact "slice of the air" assigned to any broadcaster was still the prerogative of the Commission, and the details and conditions of station operation remained practically the same. The new Act also incorporated three fundamental principles enunciated in 1927: (1) The ether is public property, (2) the radio industry shall be privately owned and operated, (3) free speech on the air shall be preserved. The licensing practices of the new Commission have followed precedents established by the preceding authority: (1) A licensee must sign a waiver to any claim that continuous operation on a frequency gives him a property right thereto, (2) any license once granted may be revoked, (3) the Commission's basic standard of judgment shall conform to the principle of "public interest, convenience, or necessity."

The Communications Act of 1934 with Amendments and Index Thereto,[1] is an 85-page document. A detailed understanding of FCC duties,

---

[1] For sale by the Superintendent of Documents, U.S. Government Printing Office, Washington 25, D.C.

powers, and operation would require a study of this publication plus thousands of pages of transcript from numerous hearings, commission rulings, court cases, and FCC annual reports. Obviously, our statement here must be condensed. However, the relation of the FCC to radiobroadcasting and nonbroadcasting involves important issues of democratic theory and practice. After a brief exposition of the structure, organization, functions, and operation of the FCC, we shall clarify the nature of these issues.

FEDERAL COMMUNICATIONS COMMISSION

What Is the FCC? The FCC is an independent Federal establishment created by Congress and, as such, reports directly to that body. It is composed of seven men appointed by the President and confirmed by the Senate. Not more than four members may belong to the same political party. Each Commissioner is appointed for a term of 7 years.

Staff Organization. The Commission is more than a board of seven appointees, however. It embraces some 1,400 employees, 500 of whom are known as "field men." The staff of workers is distributed across the nation to district offices, suboffices, ship offices, monitoring stations, and a field engineering laboratory. The work of the Commission is administered through five bureaus all of which bear some more or less direct relationship to the ownership and operation of broadcasting stations. The accounting bureau deals with financial, economic, and rate aspects of licensing and regulation, supervises traffic, compiles and analyzes statistics. The engineering bureau checks on technical phases of operation. All legal problems arising from the exercise of license privileges, and any involved litigation, are the concern of the legal bureau. The issuance of orders or decisions affecting ownership status is released by the bureau of the secretary. The functions of the fifth bureau, the administrative, cover planning, budget, and personnel matters.

Object. The object of the Commission is to provide for orderly development and operation of radiobroadcasting services; to make available a rapid, efficient, nation-wide and world-wide wire and radio communication service with adequate services at reasonable charges; and to promote the safety of life and property through improved communication systems which will, at the same time, strengthen the national defense. The object and function of the Commission go far beyond the scope of commercial broadcasting. The Act of 1934 applied "to all interstate and foreign transmission of energy by radio, and to the licensing and regulation of all radio stations."

Licensing Procedure. A prospective station owner is required to file an application for a construction permit and an operating license. If his application is approved, he is assigned call letters, an operating or transmitting power, and a particular frequency or channel in the radio spectrum. This license may later be modified or even revoked. During the period of operation, the owner's equipment is checked and regulated according to approved methods of engineering practice, and his program service is checked by the rule of "public interest, convenience, or necessity." Any applicant who meets the physical, financial, and technical requirements may enter the field, provided there is a wavelength open in his community. The following extract from a subcommittee hearing on a Senate bill to amend the Communications Act of 1934 offers a thumbnail sketch of Commission policy with regard to the issuing of licenses. Mr. Denny, Chairman of the Commission at the time, is the witness.

CHAIRMAN: I think it would be interesting if you would indicate to us just what is your present practice and policy and rule with respect to the issuing of licenses. What do you take into account when the applicant comes in?

MR. DENNY: First, we have the regular applicant form from the applicant which shows who he is, what business he has previously been engaged in, what his citizenship is, what his financial resources are, whether he has ever been involved in any suit in connection with a violation of the antitrust laws, pursuant to the specific requirements of statute, what his plans for serving the community are, what his technical installation is going to be, where he is going to put his antenna, etc.

We then examine the applications that have been filed on the basis of file numbers, so that they come up for consideration on a first-come, first-served basis. In about half of the cases we find there is no conflicting application, and in that event the application, the man's qualifications being satisfactory in all respects, can be granted. When there is a competing application, a hearing is necessary. And there you get into the business of comparing the qualifications.

Let us assume first that the competing application comes in from a different community. Mr. A, let us say, is applying for community No. 1, and Mr. B files an application on the same frequency for community 2. The first thing that we look at is the requirement of 307(b) of the Act, which says that we must treat communities equitably; we have to treat States equitably. We decide which of those communities has the greater need for radio service, and, having decided that, and having seen that both applicants are qualified, without weighing the comparative qualifications of the applicant, we give it to the community that needs the service most.

In the second case, let us assume that Mr. A and Mr. B both want to build a station in community No. 1. Therefore, we must weigh the comparative qualifications of these applicants.

SENATOR MAGNUSON: This is all on the same frequency?

MR. DENNY: All on the same frequency, yes. Thank you, Senator. In such a case, we must weigh the comparative qualifications of the applicants. There, as are indicated by the Commission's written decisions, we look to a number of factors. One important factor is the residence of the applicant in the community. We feel that is one of the very important things that we can turn to in this business of deciding between two applicants.

And usually the case that is presented to us, Senator, is a case where we have two excellent groups of applicants, and it is a very difficult thing to choose between them. But we feel that the persons who are residents of the community should have the advantage over people who are non-residents.

We feel that people who are going to operate the station themselves on a day-to-day basis, and devote their full time and energies to the operation of the station themselves, should be preferred to a person who wants the frequency as an investment, and who is going to be simply a stockholder and who is going to hire someone to manage it for him.

We feel that the personal touch is important.

We look at the proposed program plans of the two applicants to see which program plan seems better adapted to serve the needs of the community.

We of course make sure that both of the applicants are adequately qualified financially.

That is a very brief thumbnail sketch, Senator. To carry it to its complete conclusion, you would have the whole volume of Commission decisions in cases involving choices between applicants.

This explanation of the structural organization and operational procedure of the Commission brings us to a consideration of the socio-political aspects of its supervisory responsibility. The first issue stems from the relationship of the FCC to radio programing. Although the language of the Federal statute seems explicit with regard to the Commission's jurisdiction over program material, the broadcasting industry has ever feared political encroachments which, through censorship, would make broadcasting a servant of bureaucratic caprice.

I submit with all sincerity and with all earnestness that the minute you get the government writing codes governing programs and saying who may go on the air or who may not go on the air, that regardless of the Commissioners and Congress to avoid censorship by government, that you will then destroy the present American system of broadcasting, that you will have censorship galore, that you will have dictatorship of the means of communication, and that you will shake the very foundations of our democracy.[2]

Radiobroadcasters hold that the function of the FCC is to regulate only the physical and technical aspects of radio. Broadly stated, three contentions are advanced to support their position: (1) Government regulation of programing is contrary to the principle of free speech and therefore a violation of the First Amendment, (2) such supervision

[2] From a statement of David Sarnoff before the FCC, Washington, D.C., May 17, 1939.

would be discriminatory, and (3) it would place a restraint on the capacity of radio to serve the general welfare.

The argument that the First Amendment was written at a time when no one previsioned radio waves, electronic mechanisms, and wireless communication, and therefore does not apply to radio speech, is unsound. The fact that the framers of the Constitution could not have foreseen the advent of broadcasting does not prevent the language of the First Amendment from covering anything which comes legitimately within the meaning of constitutional language. Freedom of speech as guaranteed by the First Amendment includes not only speech broadcast directly by the vocal organs and the mouth, but also speech amplified by a megaphone, a telephone, a public address system, or a radio transmitter. Radio's extension of the oral word to global distances has not changed the fundamental purpose or character of speech. Technological developments which have advanced printing from the primitive hand press and the local circulation of leaflets to the present-day high-speed multiple press, and a circulation that reaches millions, have not altered the constitutional guarantee of freedom to newspapers. Radio speech, although a new medium of presentation, is no less immune to bureaucratic control. The basic principles of free speech essential to democratic governments argued so eloquently by Andrew Hamilton in the case of Peter Zenger have been held sacrosanct throughout American history.

Governmental regulation of radio policy and broadcast subject matter would be discriminatory. This contention is somewhat of a corollary to the one just presented. The three primary media of expression and communication are the press, the cinema, and the radio. The press has enjoyed a continued immunity from government restrictions. Anyone may decide when and where he will set up a printing press, and every publisher may decide what he will print without dictation from local, state, or Federal censorship boards. His paper is not licensed by the government, and the only restraint placed upon him is the force of public opinion. Although much has been written in criticism of news editors and the manner in which they have operated under the constitutional protection of free speech, the selection, reporting, interpretation, slanting, or suppression of information has been jealously affirmed as the prerogative of an independent communications medium. Outside the boundaries of obscenity, profanity, libel, and defamation, newspaper reporting may run the gamut of lurid and sensational details. An even wider latitude, it seems, is granted the tabloids, pulp magazines, and book publishers. The motion-picture industry, too, has an autonomy under the Constitution although various censorship boards prescribe certain restrictions allegedly in the interest of public morals. If radio is a technological extension of the direct oral and printed word, it should be accorded the independence of other communication media.

Government controls, other than those purely physical and technical, would restrict the capacity of radio to serve the general welfare. A radio station should render good service to the community. Local areas, however, have different needs, standards, and tastes; different cultural, educational, and economic levels. "If seven men who sit . . . in Washington are granted the power to control program content . . . to impose their philosophies and their tastes upon all the radio listeners of the country,"[3] a radio station would not be able to adapt itself to the social needs and standards of its particular audience. It is impossible for a Federal commission to "determine the proper quality of broadcasting fare for those distant, far-flung, extremely varied communities in which broadcasters are operating."[4] The present system of unrestricted and competitive programing ensures the public the widest possible range of program selection, and broadcasters avow a sincere responsibility to serve their listeners. Standards of public taste cannot be imposed by an external authority. As one radio executive has said, "Radio is made in the image of the people." The people decide what they want and decide what is good or bad.

The three contentions summarized above find detailed elaboration in statements made by radio industry spokesmen over the years. Their fuller meaning in terms of specifics may be stated as follows:

The FCC should not:

1. Regulate the synchronization of network programs or duplication of network programs.

2. Base its regulatory activities on reported information concerning finance, labor, etc.

3. Consider applications for new licenses or modification of existing licenses on the basis of economic injury, whether there is enough business to support the new station, etc., because this is a rate regulation type of activity not applicable to radio since the latter is not a common carrier.

4. Consider a renewal application as a means of disciplinary purpose, using the renewal procedure to punish the renewal applicant for some violation of what the Commission believes to be the proper operation of a station.

5. Impose sanctions or penalties on grounds other than those *specified* in the Act. It should not be permitted to use the vague and indefinite standard of public interest, convenience, or necessity as a means of penalizing a licensee for some reason or conduct not specifically forbidden either by statute or some authorized regulation of the Commission.

6. Prohibit news analysts and commentators from talking about candidates.

[3] Harold Fair, Hearings before a subcommittee of the Committee on Interstate and Foreign Commerce, U.S. Senate, 80th Congress, 1st session, S 1333, p. 249.
[4] *Ibid.*, p. 253.

7. Prohibit discussion for or against candidates by any persons except the candidates themselves, persons designated by them, or persons designated by their political parties.

8. Place a station under hazard of discipline for rejecting a party or candidate representing a cause which is either illegal in that state or does not have the right to appear on the ballot.

9. Prohibit political broadcasts for 24 hours before and during day of election.

10. Take programs into account in applying the standard of "public interest, convenience, or necessity" because this amounts to censorship of the most effective character. No power over programs and program policies should be exercised, giving to broadcasting a status comparable to that held by the press under the First Amendment.

11. Deny the broadcaster the right of editorial selection and supervision corresponding to that exercised by the editor of a newspaper or publication.

12. Have jurisdiction over either indecent language or false charges and accusations. Such offenses should be prosecuted in the criminal courts in the district where the offender resides or does business.

The issue of government regulation of programs stems from the phrase, "public interest, convenience, or necessity." This wording in the Communications Act implies that broadcasters have a responsibility to the public which is discharged essentially through program structure and content. If this implication is sound, then there is the further one that broadcasters' operations are subject to regulation. Before giving the position of the FCC on the general issue, let us state the argument as presented by extrainterested spokesmen.

The argument begins with the premise that the ether belongs to the people and constitutes a natural resource—perhaps our last natural resource. The utilization of this resource is instinct with potential good and evil. It may be the tool of the propagandist or the voice of the educator; it can produce stereotyped opinions or stimulate critical faculties, quicken appreciation and discrimination, or deaden artisitic and cultural tastes; it can be emotionally irrational, blatantly pompous, or genuinely informative, honest, and sincere. Radio may be a garish signboard erected in the living room or a dignified statement of institutional ethics; the "continued drivel of second-rate jazz," or a "message of mercy robed in song"; a "parliament of the people," or the soapbox of the demagogue. In a brief filed with the FCC, such statements as the following appear:[5]

Gresham's law, according to which bad money drives out good, applies to the market of ideas as well, where bad ideas drive out good. Even when

[5] From a memorandum of the American Jewish Congress in reapplication of News Syndicate Co., Inc., for construction permit for an FM broadcasting station, filed Nov. 12, 1946. Quoted as footnote in *Broadcasting and the Bill of Rights*, published by the National Association of Broadcasters, p. 13.

they are presented by equal frequency and forcefulness, suggestion of suspicion and bias are much more effective than invitation to fairness and good will. . . . The United States has adopted a unique system of radio regulations unparalleled in other countries. It is a most daring experiment, substantially based on the belief that a properly selected set of private licensees prompted by the profit motive is capable of performing a delicate public duty and serving public interest, convenience, and necessity in an area as vital for the political and cultural life of a country as that of formation of public opinion and public taste through the medium of mass communications. . . . Unfortunately, instruction and information are not always entertaining, and entertainment is not always instructive and informative. It is also obvious that people, by and large, prefer to be entertained than to be instructed and informed, and that there is much more money in entertainment than there is in instruction or information. This is, in short, the whole difficulty of a public service which relies for its operation on a profit-making industry. . . . The licensee who puts "entertainment" far above "betterment" will use the sustaining time for the same purposes for which the advertiser uses the time he buys: to build up following, to increase the station's popularity, and to build an invaluable "stay-tuned-to" habit.

Radio as a communications medium is not fully analogous to the press. There are essential differences. A publisher goes into business in the same manner as a merchant or a manufacturer. He invests his money in an initial enterprise, proceeds to expand his venture in competition with any number of competitors, and succeeds or fails according to the law of supply and demand. The principle of free enterprise grants him no special protection not afforded to others. A radio station owner cannot go into business without a government license. This license permits him to operate a broadcasting station on a prescribed wavelength. This franchise is immediately worth considerable money—valuable from the time it is granted. Moreover, the license represents an exercise of power by government. The Federal government is the people. Do the people have a vested interest in the air? Should they have some rights? If so, then it may be against public interest to turn loose licenses permitting the licensees to do as they please. Moreover, radio, by its inherent nature, is a monopoly. The pathways of the air are restricted in number, and radio license grantees occupy a dominant position in the vital area of communication. Channels are usually preempted in the major cities and condensed areas of population, and owners who operate stations of superpower dominate their respective fields. Actually, one 50,000-watt clear-channel station, well located, may be worth as much as fifty 250-watt stations; and when superpower stations are owned and controlled by a network or chain which prescribes definite contractual conditions for its affiliated stations, such as the number of program hours which the affiliate must take from the network, the conditions verge on monopoly.[6]

Following somewhat this general line of reasoning, the FCC has made clear its position. In March, 1946, the Commission published a report entitled, *Public Service Responsibility of Broadcast Licensees*. It is commonly referred to as the *Blue Book*. The document may be interpreted as an expression of the Commission's philosophy and attitude. In the first section of the report, the Commission explains that it is concerned with the disparity between promises made by applicants for radio licenses and their actual performance. Knowing that the law stipulates the operational standard of "public interest, convenience, or necessity," applicants feature their prospective aims and services from this standpoint. Following is a typical representation:

1. The . . . Municipal Housing Authority would broadcast a weekly one-quarter hour program, publicizing its activities. The Council of Churches of . . . would cooperate with the applicant in presenting religious programs. The proposed religious programs consist of: a one-quarter hour morning devotional program, presented five days a week by local ministers; a one-quarter hour Jewish program on Saturday afternoon; morning church services, presented from local churches for one hour on Sundays; and vesper services for one-half hour on Sunday afternoons. Definite arrangements have been made with the city superintendent of schools for the broadcasting of school programs from one-thirty to two P.M. daily. Arrangements have been made with a State Forum Counseller, assigned by the U.S. Office of Education to the New York Council of School Superintendents, to broadcast programs in connection with this group's work in promoting adult civic education. The broadcasts to be presented would consist of: a local town meeting program (patterned after the well-known program, American Town Meeting of the Air), which would be carried on Tuesday evenings eight to nine P.M.; and three one-quarter hour programs each week. The Federation of Women's Clubs of . . . representing some 38 clubs, would broadcast a one-half hour program each week during the seasons of the year when the clubs are most active. Definite arrangements have already been made for the presentation of some 43 programs by affiliates

---

[6] In the opinion of broadcasters, an allegation that radio represents a monopoly is something of a red herring. It is pointed out that, with 2,000 stations, no more than 7 of which are in the hands of single ownership, monopolistic conditions cannot exist. Also, the FCC's rule on duplicate ownership is cited: "No one individual or corporation may own more than one station serving the same area, and in FM and in television no more than six stations in FM and five stations in television regardless of the area." Concerning the limitations of the radio field and the room for new stations, it is claimed that with AM and FM, television and facsimile, there are now more radio facilities available to any market than the market will support. Also for that same reason, hundreds of available FM facilities are still going begging despite all the pressure put upon AM broadcasters by the Commission to apply for them and despite all the encouragement the Commission has been trying to give to entrepreneurs outside the radio industry, by articles and speeches pointing to the high profits that some broadcasters have made during the recent lush years.

of the Federation. A one-quarter hour book review would be presented each week in cooperation with the city public library; and the applicant has also agreed to broadcast special announcements concerning the library.

Such representations promise much for the public interest and welfare. Should the percentage of time as specified in the above assurance be devoted to the ends named, radio would make a social impact of unquestionable value. But promises are not always kept. One's zeal for ideals is sometimes tempered by expediency. In regard to the station making the above assurances,

Commission inspectors made recordings of the programs which it broadcast on certain days. The report was that "on the first of these days the programs consisted of 143 popular records and 9 semi-classical records. There were 264 commercial announcements and three minutes of announcements concerning lost and found pets." On the second day, taken as a sample, "the programs were made up of 156 popular and 10 semi-classical records and were accompanied by 258 commercial announcements. Ten minutes were devoted to the lost and found pet column." And on the third day, "165 popular, 12 semi-classical records, 10 minutes of the lost and found pet column, and 199 commercial announcements made up the day's schedule." During these three days, which represented a total of 36 hours of broadcast time, only 23 minutes were devoted to programs other than records and commercial announcements.

The Commission does not attempt to generalize from examples similar to this one, nor does it claim that it is typical. However, the conclusion is strongly implied that, when such records are brought to the attention of the FCC, it has a right to question their application for license renewal.

The *Blue Book* also reveals the Commission's concern with over-all program structure. Does the station provide for (1) a balanced interpretation of public needs, (2) programs which by their very nature may not be sponsored with propriety, (3) significant minority tastes and interests, (4) the needs and purposes of nonprofit organizations, (5) a field of experiment for new types of programs, and (6) a forum for public discussion in which subject matter and opinions are properly balanced among various points of view? If a program service does not meet these tests, it is said to have imbalance. Imbalance results when commercial pressure precludes "programs for significant tastes and interests" and needs and purposes of nonprofit organizations. The Commission has stated that to permit advertisers to dictate either the proportion of time which stations shall devote to sustaining programs, or any other major decision, is inconsistent with the basic principles of licensee responsibility on which American broadcasting has always rested.

Thus, the case for and against Federal control of broadcasting beyond purely technical requirements resolves itself into these issues: (1) Is governmental regulation a form of censorship which violates the First Amendment? (2) Is it discriminatory? (3) Can radio be relied upon to discharge adequately its public responsibility according to the phrase, "public interest, convenience, or necessity"?

In its review of broadcasting practices and policies, the FCC has made it clear that conditions exist which require a measure of correction and restraint. The facts offered would not in themselves prove the case for government control of program policy. It would be necessary to demonstrate that the alleged abuses were so inherent in the system that they could not be remedied by self-imposed standards and disciplines. This the FCC does not attempt to do by direct argument, but they do advance their claim to jurisdictional authority on the basis of historical and legal reasoning.

It is held that the original Radio Act of 1927, in which the phrase, "public interest, convenience, or necessity," was employed, placed upon the FRC the necessity and obligation of formulating standards by which the formula could be interpreted. The philosophy of the Commission was clearly expressed in the renewal forms prepared and used in 1927, the testimony of the Commission before the House Committee on Merchant Marine and Fisheries when the 1927 law came up for renewal a year later, the 1929 formulation of a standard of program service, and in the 1934 hearings before the House Committee on Interstate Commerce. The Communications Act of 1934 was passed with full knowledge of a procedure already established by the Commission:

The Federal Communications Commission from the beginning accepted the doctrine that its public interest determinations, like those of its predecessor, must be based in part at least on grounds of program service.

Court decisions are cited to substantiate the validity of the Commission's doctrine.

The Commission licensing function cannot be discharged, therefore, merely by finding that there are no technological objections to the granting of a license. If the criterion of "public interest" were limited to such matters, how could the Commission choose between two applicants for the same facilities, each of whom is financially and technically qualified to operate a station? Since the very inception of Federal regulation by radio, comparative considerations of the service to be rendered have governed the application of the standard of "public interest convenience, or necessity."[7]

The Commission seems to have the definite conviction that there rests upon it an affirmative duty to give full consideration to program service.

[7] *National Broadcasting Company v. United States*, 319 U.S. 190, 216–217.

The logical corollaries would be somewhat as follows: broadcasting stations are licensed to serve the public; "public interest, convenience, or necessity" means service to the public; a radio station exists for the broadcasting of radio programs; the program is the yardstick by which their value is to be measured; if the programs do not serve the public, then the stations have not met the conditions of their licenses. It would seem reasonable to conclude that, in the opinion of the FCC, program regulation is legitimately within the province and legal responsibility of government.

Although the FCC has often expressed its philosophy in directives, rulings, and legal procedures, very few mandates have been issued with reference to programing or program violations. Only 10 station licenses were revoked in the first 13 years of the Commission's existence. The specific orders handed down have dealt with broad policies affecting the entire industry. At various times, the FCC has dealt with such questions as, How many stations should be controlled by a single newspaper ownership? Should a license be denied to an applicant because his operation would "cut in" on a station or stations already placed in the same area? Should any restraint be placed on a station owner who wished to sell his franchise? Do clearly defined obligations placed on a licensee require that real owners of the broadcasting stations be known at all times to the government? These inquiries have risen from the concern which the Commission has had for fair and adequate broadcasting in the public interest.

In the same mood, the FCC has diligently explored the possibilities of various new technological developments, skills, and techniques—coaxial cables, stratovision, microwave transmission, photovision, facsimile reproduction, and the possibility of transmitting several programs on the same frequency. Even the most monumental decisions of the Commission, and those which have caused the greatest outcries, have dealt with broad policies of service in the public interest rather than with specific violations of program standards inherent in the Commission's philosophy of that subject. Two of these decisions should be given a brief explanation. They are the Mayflower decision and the chain broadcasting regulations. The first dealt with the right of a station to editorialize over the air, and the second with the relation of networks to their affiliates. A station in Boston (WAAB), the Mayflower Broadcasting Corporation, was cited for using its facilities in advocating opinions and at the same time forbidding its opponents an equal amount of time for reply or rebuttal. The FCC ruled that a station owner could not "advocate." The decision concerning chain broadcasting dealt with certain business practices pertaining to network operations. The situation in 1940 was as follows:

1. A station affiliated with a network could not take programs offered by another network.

2. If an affiliate declined a particular network program, the network could not offer it to another station in the same area.

3. Affiliation contracts bound the station for 5 years; the networks for 1 year.

4. Networks held options on all the time of their affiliates, and nonnetwork programs could be canceled on 28 days' notice.

5. A station was compelled to take programs as dictated by the network. There was no basis on which they could be rejected.

6. No restraint was imposed on the number and power of network stations in a particular area.

7. A station was not free to control its time rates without offering reciprocal concessions to the network.

These conditions were changed by the Commission's Order No. 37, Docket 5060, May, 1941:

1. Network affiliation might not prevent a station from carrying the programs of another network.

2. An affiliate which rejects a program cannot prevent another station from carrying it.

3. Contractual relationships between station and network should not exceed 2 years.

4. A station was permitted to option time to a competing network; certain hours were to be reserved and not optioned to the network; and the 28-day cancellation notice to sponsors was expanded to 56.

5. A station might reject a network program if deemed unsuitable.

6. In the interests of fair competition, networks were restricted to the ownership of not more than one station in one locality.

7. Stations were permitted to fix their time rates without approval of the networks.

Our discussion of the FCC to this point has been concerned with its relation to and control over "radio broadcast service." The authority of the Commission over common carriers—domestic telephone services, domestic telegraph, international telephone and telegraph—is not a phase of the present consideration. Likewise, we waive an explanation of government control of radio operators, the details of field engineering and monitoring, and technical and laboratory activities. There is, however, a large segment of FCC authority which is vitally germane. This is the area of "nonbroadcasting services."

FCC AND NONBROADCASTING SERVICES

It is natural for you to think of radio in terms of program-sending stations. Programs are beamed to you every minute of the day and night by AM, FM, and TV. By a simple click of a switch or the push of a button, the air waves freighted by every kind of information and entertainment can be channeled through your receiving set. These programs come from stations available for hire, owned by private individuals or corporations exercising commercial privileges. The frequencies assigned to these stations, however, are only a small section of the electromagnetic spectrum. Radio, as a means of communication, is employed in a great many special areas and for a great many special services. There are nearly 150,000 radio stations in the United States grouped in some 40 categories. Authorized commercial broadcasting stations constitute only a small part of this total. The number of authorizations issued by the FCC fluctuates from month to month and from year to year, but in round numbers there are 66,000 nonbroadcast licenses, 80,000 amateur stations, and over 200,000 mobile units compared to the 4,000 authorized commercial outlets.

The complex, high-speed age of the twentieth century brought an increased necessity of close cooperation. As population centers grew more vast, the size of industrial production expanded, land and air transportation increased in scope, and new frontiers developed, it was imperative that closer and more efficient contact be maintained among the various activities in the social and economic scene. The complex metropolis provided more latitude for public enemies, magnified their field of operation, and at the same time made their apprehension more difficult. Man developed wings, but his flight through space was menaced by capricious natural and mechanical elements. Fog shut his eyes, mountains barred his way, and accident shadowed his course. The sea lanes became more crowded although the perils of ice and fog, fire and storm were not lessened. Industry probed more deeply for natural resources. Oil derricks arose 100 miles offshore; the fur trader, fisherman, and miner explored new territory, and their operations were rendered more dangerous by isolation. Speeding land craft on rails and roads found their safety more and more jeopardized by conditions incident to rapid transit. Isolated motion-picture companies in lonely locations required extra equipment as quickly as possible. Fire fighters, shrouded in choking smoke, needed direction from someone on the outside who could spot strategic areas and give prompt instructions. Flood or hurricane might tear out a section of communication lines and cut off vital messages flashing east and west. How could the break be breached and continuity of service be maintained while the lines were being repaired? Such problems as these have been solved by radio—by the creation of "safety and special radio services." These services are offered in some perspective in the table following.

Safety and Special Radio Services*

Class of Station	Authorizations, June 30, 1950
Aeronautical:	
Carrier aircraft	1,572
Private aircraft	17,856
Public-service aircraft	690
Aeronautical land and fixed	1,409
Civil air patrol	1,886
Airdrome control	53
Navigational	134
Flight test	83
Flying school	16
Mobile utility	95
Total	23,794
Marine:	
Ship	22,601
Ship radar	1,125
Coastal and marine relay	130
Alaskan coastal	340
Alaskan fixed public	524
Other	201
Total	24,921
Public safety:	
Police	5,618
Fire	276
Forestry conservation	1,307
Highway maintenance	238
Special emergency	168
Total	7,607
Industrial:	
Power	3,601
Petroleum	1,380
Forest products	246
Special industrial	724
Low-power industrial	93
Relay press	26
Motion pictures	20
Total	6,090
Land transportation:	
Railroad	450
Urban transit	100
Intercity bus	30
Taxicab	2,750
Highway truck	107
Automobile emergency	58
Total	3,495
Experimental:	
Class 1	416
Class 2	50
Total	466
Grand total	66,373

* *Sixteenth Annual Report,* Federal Communications Commission, Washington, D.C., June 30, 1950, p. 96.

The nature of radio communication in each of the categories listed in the table is as follows:

Aeronautical. *Carrier Aircraft.* These stations are placed aboard an aircraft engaged in transportation of passengers or cargo for hire.

Private Aircraft. These stations are placed on aircraft not operated as an air carrier, but rather for business and pleasure other than the carrying of passengers and cargo for hire.

Public-service Aircraft. These stations handle private communications between planes in flight and on the ground—messages pertaining to the personal business of passengers or crew. It is possible for persons in aircraft to be connected to the nation-wide land-line telephone system.

Aeronautical Land and Fixed. These stations provide service necessary for the safe, expeditious, and economical operation of aircraft. The land stations communicate between ground and aircraft; the fixed stations furnish point-to-point communication to enable the airline to carry on its business more efficiently.

Civil Air Patrol. These stations provide the necessary communication for Civil Air Control activities and emergencies pertaining to the protection of life and property—air shows, missing aircraft search missions, training missions, and communications systems at encampments, bases, and meetings.

Airdrome Control. This type of station provides communication between an airdrome control tower and arriving and departing aircraft for the purpose of regulating the separation of aircraft to avoid collisions and maintaining an efficient flow of traffic into and out of an airport. An airdrome control station also communicates with aeronautical mobile utility stations aboard essential vehicles of an airport.

Navigational. These stations involve the transmission of special radio signals to enable an aircraft to determine its position with reference to the navigational facility. Included are radio beacons, radio direction finders, radio ranges, localizers, glide paths, markers, and ground control approach stations.

Flight Test. A flight-test radio station is a station aboard an aircraft or on the ground used for the transmission of communications in connection with the test of aircraft and major components of such aircraft.

Flying School. Flying-school stations aboard aircraft and on the ground are used for communication pertaining to instructions to flight students or pilots while actually operating an aircraft.

Mobile Utility. An airfield is serviced by crash, maintenance, fire, and other vehicles. Control-tower operators maintain direct contact with these units in the case of emergencies on the field.

Marine. *Ship.* All radio stations on board ships of United States registry are required to be licensed by the FCC. Ships equipped with wireless telephony can communicate with other ships, aircraft, and coastal stations. The purpose of these maritime mobile service stations is to receive or send messages relating to the safety of life or property, to assist navigation, and to handle messages for passengers and crew.

Ship Radar. By June 30, 1950, 1,125 United States merchant ships were authorized to use radar on a regular basis as a navigational aid in assisting ships entering and leaving a harbor.

Coastal and Marine Relay. Stationed at certain fixed points on land, these stations furnish public communication service with ships at sea. Public coastal stations perform two types of service: (1) They broadcast weather reports, expedite distress, relay messages, and render such other general service to ships as may be necessary; (2) they accept messages from private telephone subscribers on land to ships at sea.

Alaskan Coastal. Stations situated on the Alaskan Coast—low-power short-range stations—transmit messages for fishing, fur trading, mining, and other similar enterprises which have dealings with areas to which there are no land-line facilities.

Alaskan Fixed Public. These Alaskan Coast stations also serve the correspondence needs of private individuals.

Public Safety. *Police.* This service embraces municipal, county, state, zone, and interzone police radio stations. Communication between police land stations and mobile units includes police aircraft and ships. Most cities over 5,000 in population are equipped with police radio. The radiotelephone provides a three-way communication for police agencies. Messages can travel from a fixed land station to a mobile unit, from the mobile unit to land station, and from one mobile unit to another.

Fire. The ravages of urban fires exact a huge toll of life and property every year. Modern radio is a vital factor in preventing and controlling fire. In the city, not only is headquarters able to keep in touch with fire apparatus, but on the scene of the fire the fire chief from his vantage point in the street or on an adjoining rooftop may talk with his firemen who carry lightweight low-powered pack sets.

Forestry Conservation. The destructive force of forest fire is an ever-present menace to one of our basic natural resources. Scattered groups of men waging their battle against fire in forest areas are linked by radio communication. In addition to the prevention, detection, and suppression of forest fires, this radio service is used in official forestry-conservation activities—in the protection of forests against insects and disease, in reforestation, in flood and erosion control. They operate from fixed land stations to mobile units mounted on trucks, and foresters and wardens receive their communications through portable pack sets.

Highway Maintenance. Radio messages are employed to speed crews to the scene of snow-laden roads, road blocks, landslides, or similar emergencies, and to keep in contact with them while on the job.

Special Emergency. Authorizations are granted to (1) establishments located at remote distances from other communication facilities, (2) emergency relief organizations such as the Red Cross which have disaster communication plans drawn up ready for instant operation, (3) physicians normally practicing in remote areas where other communication facilities are not available, (4) beach patrols engaged in lifesaving operations, (5) school bus operators of regular routes into rural areas lacking other communication facilities, and (6) communications common carriers such as telephone and telegraph companies, which use radio in emergencies involving breaks in wire lines. In these situations, trailers equipped with portable radio units are rushed to the scene, messages are relayed by wireless telephony between the ends of the break.

Industrial. *Power.* Public utilities, by the use of radio communication, can restore service interrupted by fire, storm, flood, and accident; send messages concerning routine maintenance; and coordinate construction activities. Forces in the field performing such work as cable pulling, wire stringing, and pipe laying are kept in constant and immediate contact with central headquarters.

Petroleum. The conditions which pertain to the production of oil and gas are complex and extensive. The processes of drilling, producing, collecting, refining, transporting, and storing petroleum products is a far-flung operation. Radio has served to bring these operational units of the enterprise into closer operation. Drilling activity may take place 100 miles offshore or in inaccessible and remote land areas. Fires are always an imminent possibility. Pipe lines, which span long distances, must be constantly inspected and protected. There are many field emergencies such as explosions, well blowouts, and equipment failures. Radio communication is an indispensable aid to safe and efficient production.

Forest Products. The uses of radio previously allocated to Federal and state agencies to detect, prevent, and suppress fires have been extended to privately owned timber and logging companies.

Special Industrial. This service is open to businesses engaged in production, fabrication, construction, and manufacturing, provided radio communication is used only within the confines of a plant area in connection with a construction project of a public nature, or at the site of an industrial installation or operation located in a remote and sparsely settled region. Stations assigned to these special conditions have a wider range than low-power, industrial radio. They can transmit messages up to about 10 miles.

Low-power Industrial. Radio permits are granted industrial and commercial concerns to use portable transmitter-receivers in their respective plants. Such service is suitable only for short-distance communication. The average range is approximately 1 mile.

Relay Press. Newspapers, through the operation of a central transmitter in the home office, can keep in contact with mobile radiotelephone equipment in automobiles carrying reporters and photographers. Press representatives on routine assignments can be contacted instantaneously in the event of a major news break. This service was put on a regular basis in 1949.

Motion Picture. Motion-picture companies on location can connect with the nearest wire communications to expedite the shipment of supplies, coordinate action on outdoor sets, and dovetail related activities on the "shooting" set.

Land Transportation. *Railroad.* The railroad radio service is available to all railroads providing a passenger or freight transportation service on a common carrier basis. Communications are limited to those relating directly to the protection of life or property and messages essential to the maintenance, supervision, and efficient operation of the railroad systems.

Urban Transit. This service makes radio communications facilities available for street railway systems and also for city bus lines. Its use has been of value in providing prompt aid to streetcars and transit busses in periods of emergency occasioned by power failures, collisions, or breakdown of equipment. These facilities also provide efficient dispatching of passenger-carrying vehicles during rush hours and other critical traffic periods.

Intercity Bus. The operation of radio-communication facilities by carriers regularly engaged in passenger transportation over public highways between cities is provided by this service. The use of radio for this purpose assists bus operators in providing efficient, safe, and dependable service. Communications are often necessary to expedite warnings to drivers of dangerous road conditions likely to be encountered. Mechanical trouble can often be speedily rectified by the bus driver's calling the dispatcher to facilitate the sending of repair trucks or an additional bus as needed. Schedules, too, can be more readily adjusted to fit the traffic demands. Radio is also valuable in emergencies requiring medical assistance.

Taxicab. More than 2,500 separate communication systems covering about 50,000 mobile units have greatly improved the quality of taxicab service and reduced the cost of company operation. It is no longer necessary for the driver to get his "pickup" directions by stopping periodically at a call box to phone the head office for instructions. A radio dispatcher at a central station, who is kept informed about all available cabs and their locations, communicates directly with the driver and tells him where he is wanted. As many as 14 calls a minute can be disposed of by a radio dispatcher. By means of radio, taxicabs can cooperate with police in reporting emergencies or apprehending criminals. When cabs break down and need immediate repair service, the driver does not have to trek to a telephone which may not be convenient at that place or hour. He can summon aid and receive help in the minimum time by wireless.

Highway Truck. This radio service provides communication facilities to persons engaged in trucking operations on an intercity basis or on a route basis outside metropolitan areas. Stations in this service are authorized to transmit messages relating directly to the safety of life or property and communications essential to the maintenance, supervision, and efficient operation of trucks.

Automobile Emergency. Considerable interest has been shown in this service by both automobile associations and operators of public garages. It has proved especially effective in getting emergency road-service trucks to stalled vehicles. This materially contributes toward public safety by the prompt removal of traffic hazards.

Experimental. *Class* 1. Stations used by persons engaged in fundamental or general research, experimentation and development of the radio art; or for the development, testing, and calibration of radio equipment.

Class 2. Stations authorized for the development of a new radio service or the expansion of an established service.

The above enumeration is not a complete list of nonbroadcast radio services. It indicates, however, the vast and multiform application of radio transmission and reception. We have not mentioned, for example, broadcast stations licensed to educational institutions or the type of permits granted to scientific and medical agencies. Nor does our review embrace the scope of common carrier radio. There is also a Citizen's Radio Service employed on farms and ranches facilitating communication between work parties in the field and with automobiles and other moving vehicles over limited ranges. Especially important is the Amateur Radio Service, one of the oldest and most active of radio services, which embraces over 88,000 amateur station licenses and almost 87,000 amateur operator licenses.

QUESTIONS

1. Why are government and radio necessarily related?

2. What are the three basic control systems?

3. Discuss the BBC according to its origins, functions, administration, financial operation, and program structure.

4. Trace the legislative control of radio in the United States, using the dates, 1910, 1912, 1927, and 1934.

5. What is the FCC? What is its composition, organization, object?

6. What tests are administered to an applicant requesting a license to operate a radio station?

7. Why do radiobroadcasters hold that the function of the FCC is to regulate only the physical and technical aspects of radio?

8. What arguments can you advance to support both sides of the proposition: The phrase "public interest, convenience, or necessity" bestows upon the FCC an obligation to regulate program structure and content?

9. What seems to be the position of the FCC on this proposition?

10. What are nonbroadcast services?

11. What has been the role of the FCC in promoting these services?

CHAPTER 6

SOCIAL ASPECTS OF RADIO

I

A hundred million radio and television sets in 95 per cent of a nation's homes represent a gigantic social influence. Radio is more than a huge aggregation of material assets created by science and integrated into a colossal communications structure. We are impressed by the size of radio centers, towering transmitters, and the complicated machinery which makes broadcasting possible, but these are only the foundation structure and framework of radio. One can no more judge the quality of broadcasting by its external appearance than he can judge the intrinsic qualities of a home by its ornate and glamorous facade. The social, cultural, and moral essence of radio lies in the words that are spoken and in the motivations and judgments of the broadcaster. The final estimate of radio's influence is to be found in its effect on the listening audience.

Prior to 1922, before the pattern of commercial broadcasting was established, radio was conceived as "a potent instrumentality for culture and the uplifting of America's mass intelligence." David Sarnoff envisioned it as a public service comparable to the free library. The printing press, the telegraph, the telephone, and the cinema had extended the range of literate and articulate interchange, and here was a new means of communication which could "bind the earth in a universal network of sound" and "lift cultural wastelands." A new mental, cultural, and spiritual world lay in the turning of a switch. The simultaneous dissemination of news in town and hamlet would raze the barriers of isolation and blow away the fog of provincialism; the village green would flower into a national parliament of the people; men would grow in political and civic stature; the gulfs of economic difference would be bridged; the voice of the pulpit would be expanded; and drama and music would implement precepts and ideas.[1]

For them [the middle classes and the underprivileged whose desire to share in the world of events has been most persistently thwarted] radio is a gigantic and invisible net which each listener may cast thousands of miles into

[1] Cantril and Allport, *The Psychology of Radio*, p. 259.

76

the sea of human affairs and draw in teeming with palatable delights from which he may select according to his fancy.

These were idealized hopes. The extent to which radio has attained them provides a forensic battlefield. Affirmative and negative claims meet in sharp conflict. Psychologists, sociologists, educators, politicians, reformers, businessmen, and radio executives enter the lists, jousting with an assorted artillery of invective and satire, theory and fact, prejudice and self-interest, feeble generalizations, "surveys," manifestoes and codes. It is alleged that radio's bright hopes faded when the system of broadcasting was surrendered to private-profit entrepreneurs. Established as a sales medium for commercial products, it was necessarily geared to a common denominator of mass response, inherently impotent to provide for cultural and intellectual needs. It is the purpose of this chapter to examine the merits of this allegation from both the affirmative and the negative point of view.

When radio industrialists asked, Upon what meat shall this our infant giant feed? the answer, as stated, was found in the plan of commercial sponsorship. The air lanes, leased to the soap and soup fraternity, would provide the sustenance required by the young Goliath. How the infant prodigy waxed and grew fat on this diet has been traced in Chap. 4. The laissez-faire, private-profit philosophy which undergirds American radio constitutes the platform from which the critic has loudly sung his lament. It has been a song of few verses, but with a much-repeated chorus:

A device to increase the profits of competing industrialists—the medium of special-interest propagandists—a market for goods controlled by advertisers and not beholden to the people—a monopoly for those with the most money to spend on propaganda—a one-sided advocate—a molder of mental stereotypes—an exploiter of common interests . . . (repeat—repeat).

It is an accepted fact that radio *is* a privately owned enterprise operated for personal profit. The lifeblood of a radio station is its advertising revenue. Radio is used primarily to sell goods. It is an aerial billboard on which the advertising men splash their variegated lithographs, and their purpose is to attract the greatest number of people to stop, listen—and buy. (The television formula is the same with the addition of one word: stop, listen, *look*—and buy.) A tobacco company president was quoted in the *New York Times* of Apr. 22, 1945, as saying,

We have some funny thinking here about radio, and we have been criticized for it. Taking 100% as the total value, we give 90% to commercials and we give 10% to the show. . . . We are commercial and we can't afford to be anything else. I don't have the right to spend the stockholder's money just to entertain the public.

In a New Year's statement issued in the same year by the president of the National Association of Broadcasters, the spokesman pointed to radio's record earnings and said, "One must consider balance sheets to measure the progress of radio. For balance sheets represent an index of the medium's effectiveness." A cartoonist presents the picture of a medicine man standing on the tail gate of his wagon addressing the yokels: "Before introducing to you the world-famous Kickapoo musicians, let me call your attention to the properties of this bottle of elixir in my hand." This is contrasted with a scene in a broadcasting studio. A resigned violinist sits patiently while a sleek-haired announcer breathes into the microphone: "Before we present the world-famous virtuoso, allow me to call your attention to the properties of Schmear's axle grease." The title of the cartoon is, "Who Says They Never Come Back?" Station clientele embraces the butcher, the baker, the candlestick maker—an assortment of sponsors who want to make your dentures, fix your automobile, sell you a mountain view lot, reduce your weight, put pep in your walk, serve you a corned beef and cabbage dinner, lend you money—ad infinitum.

The listener's complaint is not directed against sales promotion as such. He is willing to pay the price of enduring a certain amount of advertising chatter, but he thinks the price, in general, is too high. He is willing to have his radio fare concocted and brewed in sponsoring laboratories, but he finds that the seasoning is too heavy to make the program product palatable. He is irritated by overlong commercials, singing commercials, interruption of program continuity with selling appeals, the overuse of spot announcements, and the crowding of several announcements between two major programs. A casual glance at a bibliography of magazine articles on the subject reveals a wide expression of discontent with radio sales promotion. Some typical titles are "Medicine Men of the Air," "Old Nostrum Rides Again," "Plug-ugly Time," "Capsulating or Crooning," and "Diaper Cleanup." Opinions expressed are often more than caustic:

. . . radio, a device to sell goods by any means, fair or foul . . . vulgar and false claims of private individuals and corporations to seek money . . . the advertising business at the zenith of its arrogance and the nadir of its simplicity . . . a combination of advertising claims that offends the intelligence . . . exaggerated claims and tiresome repetition suitable to the mind of a moron . . . one long parade of headaches, coughs, aching muscles, stained teeth, unpleasant full feeling, and gastric hyperacidity.

The techniques of the advertiser attracted congressional interest as early as 1932, and the FCC was authorized and instructed to make a special study of the matter.[2]

[2] Senate Document 137, 72d Congress.

Radio commercials in themselves, however blatant, repetitive, insistent, and obnoxious, are only a clue to radio's real social import. They are surface phenomena of a sales psychology based on the principles and techniques of suggestion and propaganda. In this fact lies radio's impotence to operate as a basically sound social and cultural influence capable of "elevating the race of men." Suggestion is a technique of controlling the behavior of people, and propaganda—planned and systematic suggestion—is a large-scale suggestion phenomenon. Both the suggester and the propagandist proceed from the premise that there is a common denominator of human interest which can be manipulated. Special manipulative tools are employed to prepare attitudes in the subject which can be released at the proper moment and, when released, give increased impetus (augmentation). Preattitudinal sets—basic wants, desires, wishes, dispositions—are carefully determined and appraised. The release of these sets is effected through emotional stimuli. Words are carefully selected to set off conditioned responses; a halo is spread over the heads of celebrities who urge us to climb on the band wagon; illegitimate prestige (experts in one field posing in another) is widely employed; emotionally toned habits carefully exploited; and partial aspects of the subject are skillfully blended to block off opposed modes of conduct. This is the psychology of salesmanship, and it operates on the premise that there is a mass denominator. Radio commercials, therefore, become diagnostic clues to systemic and organic conditions fully revealed by an X-ray examination of radio's program structure.

Advertising and program structure are pieces of the same cloth. In order to sell goods, the broadcaster "attempts to provide a coarse net with which to capture the favorable attention of as many listeners as possible." The more customers, the more sales. To sell to the masses, the sponsor must reach the masses. A network executive is on record as saying that radio is made in the image of the American people—that it fits the contours of the people. These contours are the common interests of large groups.

The broadcaster . . . aims only at the average man, thus failing to reach the dullards and risking an insult to those of superior intelligence.[3]

Radio programing is dominated by an economic philosophy, not a social philosophy. The sponsor says, "I want a market—the broadest possible market. How can I capture a listening audience that will give me that market?"

"By giving them a program to which they will listen," says the advertising man.

[3] Cantril and Allport, op. cit., p. 7.

"What kind of program is that?"

"Well, let's look at the Hooper ratings. Jones is doing a bang-up job with his *Catch-'Em-Alive* drama, Smith broke all records last year with his *Ghosty-Ghoulies,* and that serial we put on for Brown is a knockout."

"Okay, give me something along that line—something a little better." Thus, concentration of program types is inherent in the business structure of radio. This is made particularly emphatic when a large percentage of radio business comes from a few major sponsors. (What would happen to the balance sheet if beer, cigarettes, and soap were suddenly declared radio contraband?) Sales philosophy is correlated with program philosophy.

A commercial broadcast supported by advertisers cannot provide a proportioned program content that will serve adequately the widest possible range of intellectual, cultural, and entertainment standards. It is a general rule of radio statistics that the more serious the content of the program, the fewer the number and the higher the level (in terms of socioeconomic and educational status) of listeners. The FCC itself has declared, as previously cited, that when programing is placed in the hands of advertisers in search of a market, each concerned with his particular half-hour, rather than in the hands of stations and networks responsible under the statutes for over-all program balance in the public interest, a well-rounded structure cannot be attained. The commercial broadcaster is not concerned with specific segments of the body politic and with minority tastes and interests. He caters to average demands—to the common interests of large groups.

Soap operas—"the most ubiquitous form of mass entertainment ever devised"—are a case in point. It has been estimated that half of the women who are at home and have radios listen to an average of 5.8 of these serials each day. In January, 1940, the four networks provided listeners with 59½ daytime hours of sponsored programs weekly. Of these, 55 hours were devoted to soap operas. Only 4½ sponsored daytime hours a week on the four networks were devoted to any other type of program.[4] In 1945, "soapers" represented about 66 per cent of the daytime revenue of two networks, about 22 per cent of their total revenue, and about 15 per cent of the gross of all network broadcasting.[5] The four major networks offered a total of 39 hours of soap-opera programs. Ten hours devoted to serials contrasted with three-fourths of an hour given, by classification, to cultural and religious programs.

Another aspect of radio programing relates to the subject of children's

---

[4] *Public Service Responsibility of Broadcast Licensees,* Federal Communications Commission, Washington, D.C., Mar. 7, 1946.

[5] *Fortune,* March, 1946, p. 120.

programs. It was the hope that radio would contribute to the proper emotional and intellectual development of young children. What was a good children's program? The question concerned parents, teachers, and organizations associated with child guidance and education. It was to receive some attention, but there has been relatively little comprehensive research on the subject. Azriel L. Eisenberg, in 1936, conducted a significant study of more than 3,000 children in the New York metropolitan area, and recommendations were made to educational organizations and the broadcasting industry; Dorothy Lewis, who has made notable contributions to radio by spearheading community councils, prepared a report in 1940–1941 on present activities in the field of children's radio programs; and an occasional graduate student has made a study in some special area. The most important study of this subject was initiated in 1938 by the Federal Radio Education Committee at Ohio State University. A staff of investigators was assigned to investigate the subject of both in-school and out-of-school radio listening. (In our present discussion we are concerned with the latter.) Studies were made of children's reactions to programs, of parents' reactions to children's listening, and of various codes and standards previously developed by broadcasters, parent groups, and child psychologists. The summarized findings and interpretations pointed by the inquiry were published by the Committee under the title, *Criteria for Children's Radio Programs.*[6] The criteria as formulated were based on previously published research findings and data derived from "close contact with broadcasters, with parental and women's organizations which have been active in criticizing children's programs . . . and with children themselves." In addition to these primary sources,

. . . the various codes which have been suggested in the course of the controversy over children's programs, have been carefully examined. Many of the constructive suggestions, contained in these codes, have been subjected to an analysis which has brought to bear upon the problem the best insights represented in the disciplines of education, psychology, and sociology.

The answer to the over-all question, By what criteria should children's radio programs be judged? was presented in three categories:

A. Considerations relating to the ethical, moral, or social ideals of American life.

B. Considerations relating to the emotional, intellectual, and social development of the child's personality.

C. Considerations relating to the showmanship or entertainment values.

[6] *Criteria for Children's Radio Programs,* Federal Radio Education Committee, U.S. Office of Education, Washington, D.C., 1942.

The specific criteria of each category are given as follows:

Category A:
1. Children's radio programs should build faith in democracy and unfaltering loyalty to the ideals of democratic living.
2. Occupational skills which are essential to American life should be honestly and sincerely portrayed.
3. The role of minority groups of races and nationalities which make up modern America should be portrayed sympathetically and realistically.
4. Children's radio programs should be authentic in broad historical or contemporary interpretation, factual detail, and artistic portrayal.
5. Children's radio programs should maintain generally recognized standards of good taste.
6. Crime is not suitable as a dominant theme in a radio program directed specifically to children.
7. The rich field of children's literature should provide the main part of the content of children's radio programs, and the main cues for handling plot and character development in the stories originating from other sources.

Category B:
1. Radio programs should arouse in children a wide range of emotional response and should avoid undue stress upon fear and aggression.
2. The child has a need for genuine characters of truly heroic proportions as imaginary playmates and models to imitate, with which to identify himself.
3. In fantasy and fairy-tale programs, the fantastic or purely imaginative elements should be clearly identifiable to child listeners as unreal.
4. Intrinsic interest, maintenance of suspense, and satisfactory resolution of suspense should be consistently observed in the development of any children's program.
5. The social problems of childhood, involving friendship, gang loyalty, and respect for one's equals, should be frequently and honestly portrayed on children's radio programs.
6. Family relationships, mutual respect and understanding between parents and children, and family problem situations should be portrayed in children's radio programs.
7. Suggestive power of radio should be utilized wherever possible in leading listeners to useful hobbies, skills, interests, activities, and knowledge.
8. Humor that is within the comprehension and appreciation of children should be used more extensively as an integral part of children's programs.

Category C:
1. The specialized technique of radio drama should contribute to the listener's visualization of the characters, situations, and the action portrayed.
2. The vocabulary and vocal inflections used in a children's radio program must be clearly comprehended by the youngest age level of intended listeners.
3. Dialogue in children's programs should not undercut, by over-narration of detail, the imaginative processes by which the listening child lives the story.

4. Sound effects, in order to be effective, should represent things or situations which can be readily visualized by the average child.

5. Music used in connection with radio drama should communicate emotions, mood, and feelings.

What have the rulers of the radio realm done to incorporate these objectives in programs designed and beamed to a juvenile audience? What place have children had in a balanced program schedule? Sponsors have produced programs to which children listen, but very few children's programs. The quarter-hours provided for child listening have been described as an unforgivable exploitation of childhood. Conditioned in part by comic books and the Saturday cinema matinee, "kiddies" are ready to respond to gun-toting cowboys, galloping rangers, shrieking sirens, and even gurgling sounds of mayhem; and they will eagerly save box tops to guarantee the continuance of their entertainment parade.

> Between the dusk and the daylight
> When the broadcasters step up their power
> Comes that large magnificent shambles
> That is known as the children's hour.
>
> The wee ones huddle together
> In time for the evening scare
> To chill their juvenile marrow
> And curl their innocent hair.
>
> Then over the waves of ether
> To fill their sweet long dreams
> Come tales of terror and torture
> And 17 kinds of screams.[7]

Assuming, as he does, the child's predilection for fantastic heroes, adventure, conflict, and unreality, it would be a most enlightened sponsor, indeed, who would substitute honest accounts of American pioneers for the Robin Hoods of the West, scientific laboratories for space ships, or even Sutter's gold for trapped bandits in a bat-infested cave. The plethora of crime, mystery, and horror drama, not particularly designed for children, but from which they can hardly escape, has accounted for more than one public outcry. In 1947, for example, 350,000 names on a petition to eliminate these types of "shows" caused a "mild case of jitters among radio men." But with the exception of minor concessions, such as the elimination of "cliff hangers" (episodes that leave the listener breathless

---

[7] By Stoddard King, courtesy of Mrs. Stoddard King.

on the brink of suspense), the program format has undergone little change.

The educative effect of radio upon the formative life of the child is only a phase of its total educative impact. By sins of omission, it has been even more devastating in its effect upon adult life. Whether radio has fulfilled its promise of adult education depends, of course, on one's definition of education. It must be conceded that literacy is more than a matter of the three R's and that ignorance is a relative term. It may be that James Jones, Tommy Dorsey, and Charlie McCarthy are elements of a cultural pattern that includes Shakespeare, Beethoven, and Mark Twain. Although the educated man travels the main highways, he is also familiar with the laterals and feeders which wind down from the hinterland. This does not mean, however, that a man who could make his living touring the quiz shows is educated. Isolated encyclopedic facts are important only as they relate to basic principles, and principles are valuable only as they fall into integrated and interpretive patterns. The purpose of education is to develop intellectual, moral, and aesthetic judgments applicable to life situations, to expand the range of stimuli, and to perfect skills of adaptation. A "full man" is one who has reached the limits of functional capacities which find satisfying completeness in social interaction.

This concept of education, as it might be implemented by radiobroadcasting, has not been the purpose of sponsored programs. The seller of goods and the seeker after markets are not guided by a philanthropic zeal to shape public opinion, guide social action, extend the scope of the classroom, promote homogeneity, or extend cosmopolitan advantages. Did you ever make a slow journey across the radio kilocycles? An experimental trip along the radio dial at 8:15 P.M. on a midweek night, moving gradually from station to station, produced the following result. The report is made without any attempt to stack the cards:

. . . stop in and see for yourself. It's the new look in cars. . . . My little Mammy, the sun shines east, the sun shines west. . . . Buy a postwar car—20 per cent down and as long as 30 months on the balance. . . . Here we go. Keep your gun handy. . . . Here we are at Cow Town. Come down to Noody's and win a new shirt. Prizes for the best dressed male and the best dressed female. . . . The most talented hillbilly band in the hillbilly business . . . (Song) "And Though You Don't Want Me Now I'll Get Along Somehow." . . . [After the closing strains of the national anthem] We are in the ring now watching the fighters get ready. Friends, if you are short of cash these days. . . . Give the kids a break when the Community Chest knocks at your door. . . . Or, if you have ulcer pains induced by hyperacidity. . . . And that's the news for tonight. . . . The price is going to scare you plumb to death, and you have 2 years to pay.

While no sound generalization can be based on such chance juxtaposition, the illustration is not altogether a logical straw man. The casual "tuner-inner," fishing for a program to suit his momentary mood, is certain to encounter a melange of sales, sex, and sentimentality. He may easily conclude that radio's function is to dispense silly sales twaddle, nostalgic ballads, and melodrama with an occasional dash of community service and news.

Robert M. Hutchins, former Chancellor of the University of Chicago, in an article prepared for the BBC *Quarterly* and reprinted in *Variety* for May 10, 1950, recalls certain criticisms he had lodged against radio 15 years previously:

The claims of the minority have been disregarded, the best hours have been given to advertising programs, the hours assigned to education have been shifted without notice, experimentation has been almost non-existent, and the financial support of educational broadcasting has been limited and erratic.

He then adds, "There has been no change." Hutchins admits there are some good plays, well presented, a few good news commentators, and "a great deal of fine music"; but from the standpoint of the overall picture he says that

. . . one of the greatest instruments for enlightenment and one of the greatest triumphs of the human mind [is] employed exclusively to debase those whom it might enlighten and ennoble.

Radio's sustaining programs, offered as evidence of the industry's contribution to public education and enlightenment, do not compensate for radio's omissions. Sustaining programs are those supported wholly by networks or stations and offered gratuitously as public service. (This phase of program scheduling is detailed in the latter portion of this chapter.) They are classified under the headings of public affairs, religion, music, agriculture, and education. It is readily admitted that these broadcasts represent the zenith of radio's genius and technical proficiency, but they fail to attain the full measure of their potential merit. The reason is that the hours assigned to "sustainers" are not so favorable for listening as those sold to sponsors and that programs originating with the networks are not carried by a sufficient proportion of the network's affiliates to guarantee more than a spotty coverage. An NBC traffic report for Mar. 5, 1950, lists all the company's sustaining shows and the number of stations which declined or accepted each show. The following table reveals how many of the better known programs fared:

NBC Report of Sustaining Shows

Program	Number of Stations	
	Accepted	Refused
America United....................	43	125
U.N. Is My Beat....................	9	158
Coffee in Washington................	19	81
Public Affairs......................	19	116
Chicago Round Table...............	69	99
American Forum of the Air...........	48	120
Living—1950......................	113	55
Kaltenborn.......................	38	75
Mrs. Roosevelt....................	66	71
Bach Aria Group..................	37	102
Boston Symphony..................	35	133
Pioneers of Music.................	102	66
NBC Symphony...................	109	58
National Radio Pulpit..............	85	83
Eternal Light.....................	81	87
Catholic Hour....................	108	59
NBC Theater.....................	111	57

Moreover, the program records of local stations charged with the responsibility of serving the public show how advertisers, in the main, dictate the schedule of operations. When aggressive sales departments produce the signature on the dotted line, it is somewhat difficult for the management to reconcile immediate financial opportunity with proclaimed public policy. The answers made to school superintendents and civic organizations may be, "We are sold across the board . . . . We won't have any time until after the elections . . . . The only spot is late Saturdy afternoon after the football games."

In 1946, the FCC stated the following conclusions after an analysis of program balance:

1. Larger stations carried a considerably smaller percentage of sustaining programs than the smaller stations.

The proportion of time devoted to sustaining programs during the best listening hours from 6:00 to 11:00 P.M., was lower than during other hours.

3. There was a tendency to crowd sustaining programs into the Saturday afternoon and Sunday morning segments, and to crowd them out of the best listening hours from 6:00 to 11:00 P.M.

4. There was a paucity of sustaining programs on particular stations.

Statistically, these conclusions may be challenged on the ground that the generalizations are derived from a sampling process. Records for a single day or week were examined, and the findings were interpreted as typical or standard practice. The conclusion that sustaining programs are disappearing from the program service of some stations, and that there is a dearth of sustaining network at convenient listening hours, probably requires a broader statistical base. However, the facts presented are significant and place a burden of proof on radio management. If we assume that the facts are typical and represent week-to-week operation, a very serious situation becomes manifest. With regard to public-service programs described above, their value is lessened when 50 per cent (and in some cases less than 25 per cent) of the network's affiliates may decline to carry them, substituting therefor local commercial programs composed of phonograph records interspersed with numerous spot announcements.

Another reason why radio has not fulfilled its educational promise is that the government refused to set aside a fixed percentage of adequate radio channels for the exclusive use of noncommercial broadcasters. In 1934, the FCC faced the question, Should a fixed percentage of radio broadcast facilities be allocated by statute to particular types or kinds of nonprofit activities? Twenty-four days of hearings produced 14,000 pages of testimony and several thousand pages of exhibits. The educators, pleading for reservation and assignment of noncommercial channels, were opposed by the broadcasting industry, the licensees of broadcasting stations, and the manufacturers of radio equipment. The outcome of the hearings was a negative recommendation by the FCC. Some of the reasons for not granting a fixed percentage of available channels for educational use were as follows:

1. There is no need for a change in the existing law to accomplish the helpful purposes of the proposal.
2. Flexibility in the provisions of the law is essential to regulation if growth and development in the art of broadcasting are to be encouraged and regulated for the best interests of the public as a whole.
3. There are insufficient broadcast facilities available in the present development of the art to provide for specialized broadcast services consistent with a fair, consistent, and equitable distribution of facilities and services throughout the country.

The result of the FCC decision was to place the "educators" in direct competition with commercial applicants.

It is true that 200 "educational licenses" were issued between 1921 and 1936 (most of them before 1927), but in the same period 154 of them either expired a natural death or were transferred to private hands. Only one-third were able to survive for 3 years or more. The principal reasons for this mortality were the financial inability of colleges and universities to maintain a broadcasting service, the lack of professional know-how or showmanship in program preparation, a general lack of faculty interest, and the failure of the FCC to fight for the educators' cause. It was evident as early as 1930 that whatever educational force radio might have lay in the hands of the radio merchants. The Commission had said, "There is no need for a change in the existing law to accomplish the helpful purpose of the proposal [fixed proportion of educational channels]." How well education has fared is a matter of record. The battle of the educator has been an uneven one. Deprived of their radio voice by reason of nonaggressive government action and their own ineptitude in using the crumbs which were allowed them, educational interests have fought an ineffectual battle. The Federal Radio Education Committee in the U.S. Office of Education, the Association for Education by Radio, the Institute for Education by Radio, the National Association of Educational Broadcasters, and the School Broadcast Conference have tried to make the best of an unequal situation, but their combined efforts have been at best a weak rear-guard action.

Another phase of radio's social influence under the philosophy of free enterprise involves its contribution to mass enlightenment through the dissemination of news and the sponsorship of discussion. It is axiomatic that an informed public opinion is basic to democratic procedures. Radio was envisioned as a means of bringing to all the people the news of the world, an interpretation of that news, and a fuller understanding of vital issues. This was thoroughly implied in the basic premise: "The ether is a public medium and its use must be for the public benefit." It may be said at this point that the most effective and significant contribution of radio to social life has been the transmission of daily news and the presentation of discussion, but inherent in this function and service have been conditions prejudicial to the full attainment of the ideal. Radio news can be selected, slanted, and colored, and the microphone can be the sounding board for the commentator's bias. Discussion can be the expression of crackpots and ism peddlers as well as the counsel of disciplined, informed, responsible, and qualified experts. Moreover, the fact that radio time is limited makes it impossible for every controversy to be aired, and someone must decide who will and who will not be heard. If controversialists are charged for the use of the airways, a premium is placed on those causes more richly financed; if time is given without charge and all comers are allotted equal assignment of air time, program balance cannot be controlled. The Communications Act is specific in forbidding FCC to apply censorship measures to radiobroadcasting, but the fact that air time is granted at the pleasure of the station licensee has invoked a long and continuing discussion of the meaning of the First Amendment as it applies to free speech over the air.

The history of radio is replete with controversy, complaints, public hearings, court actions, decisions, rules, and regulations in relation to the subject of free radio and free public discussion.

The phrase, "controversial public issues," received a great deal of consideration in the early codes of the National Association of Broadcasters (NAB). The sale of time for "broadcasts in connection with a political campaign in behalf of or against the candidacy of a legally qualified candidate for nomination or election to public office, or in behalf of or against a proposal which is subject to ballot" was approved, but it was recommended that time for other programs of controversial nature should be given gratis. It was admitted that the station had a duty to provide for the presentation of public issues, but this duty could be best discharged, it was advised, by allotting with fairness free time to all elements. The position of the Association was based on the premise: "Radio is not a common carrier, forced to sell time to all with the means to buy, first come, first served. . . . American radio is predicated upon the right to hear, not upon the right of the individual to be heard." No charge should be made for time, it was reasoned, because, first, if time were sold to all with the means to pay, controversial time could not be balanced, and a powerful public forum would inevitably gravitate almost wholly into the hands of those with the greatest means to buy it. The NAB has been charged with duplicity in framing its position, it being argued that the latter should avoid controversial programs as much as possible. The imputation may be motivated by some bias, but it is logical to assume that if a "controversialist" could not buy radio time, and that if he were given time for which the station would have to provide an equal amount of time for an adequate or satisfactory rejoinder, many requests would naturally go by default. (Specific approval was given to sponsored presentation of public-forum types of programs on the assumption that these would be constructed in such a way as to give equal weight to dissenting points of view.)

Something of a test of the NAB position came in 1942, when the Co-operative League of the United States proposed a series of broadcasts. The League was turned down by both NBC and CBS. It was deemed that the economic program of the League was in such direct opposition to standard economic practices as to make the proposed broadcast so highly controversial as to bar it under the policy tacitly in force. The action of the networks was denounced in the Senate as discriminatory and a denial of fundamental rights. Later, the League was permitted to go on the air, and the NAB attempted to cover the matter, as well as similar cases that might arise in the future, by rephrasing its code to the effect that a sponsoring organization should not incorporate in its commercial copy statements that could be construed as an attack on other business enterprise or system of distribution. This recommendation to member stations was interpreted as a restraint applicable to labor unions. The NAB thought this was an unjust apprehension, but later when the United Automobile Workers sought to buy time for a series of broadcasts, the League objected on the ground that they (the broadcasts) could not be classified as political and should not be presented on paid time.

Whether or not time should and could be sold for the discussion of public issues was dealt with in an order handed down by the FCC in the summer of 1945. Hearings had been conducted on a complaint brought by the UAW charging that a station in Columbus, Ohio, was exercising censorship over broadcasts. In effect, the FCC ruled that controversial issues were permissible broadcast material.

The foregoing account indicates how the system of private-interest control over a communications medium may work to thwart full, objective, and unbiased intellectual discussion. The radio law is clear, and the FCC, in upholding radio as a medium of free speech for the general public, has recognized the paramount right of the public in a free society to be informed and to have presented to it for acceptance or rejection different attitudes and viewpoints. The Commission has affirmed in a long list of decisions that the presentation of news and comment in the public interest requires that the licensee must operate on a basis of over-all fairness and make his facilities available for the expression of contrasting views of all responsible elements in the community. However, this is a general philosophy; the individual station owner is necessarily permitted to implement it according to his judgment. His judgment may be questioned and his license put in jeopardy, but in the final analysis it is he who guarantees the freedom of the air. It is natural, as we have seen in the case of the Co-operative League, that the economic or political philosophy of the station owner may act as a covert control at least over what is released over his station. Not only may his views be reflected in the commercial programs which he broadcasts or refuses to broadcast; he may actually engage in the direct propagation of these views by editorializing over the air. The proneness of certain station owners to use their licensed privilege in this manner produced one of the most controversial decisions ever to emanate from the FCC. This was the Mayflower decision to which we referred earlier. In this case, the Commission had before it a situation where a licensee had used the facilities of his station to promote ideas and political candidates of his own choosing. The Commission, in reviewing the licensee's operation, held that a licensee could not under any circumstances, consonant with the public interest, act as an advocate. "A truly free radio cannot be used to advocate causes of the licensee. . . . It cannot be devoted to the support of principles he happens to regard most favorably. In brief, the broadcaster cannot be an advocate." The decision, in effect, suppressed and prohibited a licensee from speaking over his microphone in behalf of any cause. The majority opinion of the Commission at that time was that overt editorialization, or advocacy by broadcast licensees, was inconsonant with the operation of their stations in the public interest and, if permitted, would result in such overemphasis on the side of any particular controversy which the licensee chose to espouse as to make impossible any reasonable balanced presentation of all sides of such issues.

In March, 1948, the Commission ordered a hearing reopening the subject of radio news and comment presentation in a democracy. The issues under consideration were (1) to determine whether the expression of editorial opinions by broadcast station licensees on matters of public interest and controversy is consistent with the obligations to operate their stations in the public interest and (2) to determine the relationship between any such editorial expression and the affirmative obligation of the licensees to ensure that a fair and equal presentation of all sides of controversial issues is made over their facilities. A new conclusion was reached, to wit: Overt editorialization, within reasonable limits and subject to the general requirements of fairness, is not contrary to the public interest.

The so-called freedom of the air as applicable to newscasters has also been a matter of discussion and concern. How should the reporting of news be handled in the public interest? Is it possible that news reporters may shape their reports in such a way as to mislead or arouse false emotions? In general, radio news reporting is patterned after the sensationalism of newspaper headlines, and the typical broadcast is a capsulated review of catastrophe, tragedy, dissensions, lawlessness, and danger. The constant impact of this emphasis can create unrest, frustration, and pessimism. Indeed, one may get the impression that the world is a realm of sharp practices, vicious cupidity, and hopelessness. A prominent newscaster begins with the question: What's going on in the world? The answer, given by the newscaster racing against the clock to telescope as much teletype as possible, does not suggest at any point that man may be "stumbling still toward the shining goal," or that the old-fashioned virtues of kindness, generosity, and neighborliness are still alive. Destructive forces are exploited; constructive forces are ignored. This is not to suggest that we should sugar-coat stern realities or ignore disintegrative forces gnawing at the heart of civilization; but it is to suggest that a one-sided emphasis may engender a defeatist, even fatalistic, personal philosophy.

The news analyst or news commentator (and there are more than 600 of them in the United States) who goes beyond the teletype facts to give his interpretation, deduction, prophecy, and personal opinion, renders a service measurable by his integrity, logical acuity, and intellectual background. The value of his commentary depends upon the accuracy of his facts, good taste, and the avoidance of sensationalism in both content and presentation. A CBS directive to news analysts in 1943 adjured them to marshal their facts with care and to present them not as pulpiteers trying to sway the people. It is not the purpose of a news commentator, said the directive, to harangue or crusade. In the opinion of some authorities, this type of imposed regulation is nothing less than "infamous." No restraint should be imposed on a broadcaster, it is said, because he is responsible under the law in matters of libel and obscenity, and beyond these bounds he should be free to edit and present his news according to his own intent and style. Regardless of which point of view is correct, the issue points the social influence which commentators may exert on the public mind.

Summary. The social promise of radio faded when broadcasting rights were assigned, under nominal government regulation, to private business. Organized primarily as a sales medium and dominated by an economic philosophy, radio was impotent to serve the intellectual and cultural needs of the people. Selling techniques compelled the shaping of program content to fit a mass denominator. The result was an unbalanced and disproportionate presentation of subject matter in which minority tastes and interests were neglected. In brief, radio developed as an entertainment and not as an educational medium. Inherent in this generalized criticism are 10 specific complaints:

1. Radio stimulates desires and wants, persuades people to reach beyond their means, and creates false economic standards.

2. The bulk of radio is geared to a low common denominator of taste, and the amount that can be labeled cultural is proportionately very small.

3. Radio news reporting, colored by the editorial style and the broadcaster's delivery, may not be objective and factual; and news commentaries, in particular, representating personal judgments may be responsible for erroneous, emotional, and distorted public opinion.

4. Radio forums and round tables are potentially an accepted form of democratic operation, but the lack of applied forensic skill to this kind of broadcasting promotes confusion and vagueness, not clarity and objective understanding.

5. Information disseminated by means of so-called quiz shows is inconsequential, if not trivial or so dressed in the garb of entertainment as to vitiate its practical value.

6. Radio has magnified the voice and influence of crackpots and isms.

7. Radio entertainment, controlled as it is by commercial interests, relies on the sensational and melodramatic.

8. The potential service which a station can render to its particular area is nullified by the economic opportunities offered by network and recorded programs.

9. Radio does not provide a forum for all controversial interests because (a) on a free sustaining basis there is not sufficient time to accommodate all parties, (b) on a commercial basis all factions are not equally able to pay for radio time, and (c) if time were made available to all who wanted to broadcast their views, the station's advertising revenue would be jeopardized.

10. Radio standardizes and stereotypes mental habits and dulls critical faculties.

II

The defenders of radio join issue with the critics and contend that their position is fallacious both in principle and in fact.

The radio critic is charged, first, with the fallacy of faulty generalization. His conclusions are not supported by a sufficient number of fair, typical, homogenous examples. The superficial generality, the endlessly repeated cliché, the snap judgment are not the marks of intelligent criticism. Complaint should be leveled at specific instances, specific programs, specific stations—actual offenders.[8] In view of the tremendous scope and variety of broadcast coverage, the institution of radio cannot be indicted on the basis of individual enumeration. It is seldom that the radio prosecutor bases his position on adequate data statistically and logically supported. It is true that he may quote the findings of surveys provided by the networks for their clients, but when he does he makes qualitative interpretations that go beyond the quantitative meaning of the findings. The Crossley, Hooper, and Nielsen techniques were designed to estimate the *amount* of radio listening. There are actually few data by which to prove that the present program pattern would change if listeners were given a choice between what they now have and a radio fare similar to BBC's *Third*. We cannot know how public preferences in the United States might be different because the people have never been given a different choice of programs accompanied by serious promotion.

The second reply to the critic's lament is that the fault is not in the vehicle (radio) itself but in the use people make of it. We might facetiously paraphrase Cassius: The fault, dear listener, is not in our radio stars, but in ourselves. If the listener were as discriminating as his radio dial is selective, there would be no problem. The real difficulty lies with the "tuner-inner." Radio can give what you want if you take the care to get it, but if you expect that a chance pushing of a radio button will miraculously deliver a program matched to your especial perference, you are pushing the magic of radio beyond its limits. A casual dial-twister, cutting across the program spectrum, is bound to catch snatches of broadcasts in which he is not interested and for which he has intellectual, aesthetic, or emotional antipathy. If listeners were as dis-

[8] William S. Paley, *Radio and Its Critics*, an address to the twenty-fourth annual convention of the National Association of Broadcasters, 1946.

criminating in regard to radio as they are toward other sources of information and entertainment, their satisfaction would be much greater. If one wishes to attend a theater or musical concert, he may choose anything from burlesque to Shakespeare, from swing band to grand opera. He can find lurid cinema fare on Main Street or Academy-award pictures uptown. He subscribes to a newspaper, but he chooses to read the financial section and not the want-ad section, the editorials and not the comics. His range of magazine choice is almost as limitless as book lists, but his predilection is for *Atlantic Monthly* or *Life* and not *Confessions* or the *Police Gazette*. For temporary escape he may pick up *Corpses for Hire*, but this will not substitute for the latest biography or historical novel which may be his customary type of reading. One does not launch a broadside attack against the cinema, theater, and press because there are individual pictures, plays, books, and newspapers which do not appeal to his tastes and interests. He can readily argue that there are aspects of these media which, in his opinion, are not socially wholesome, but he tolerantly realizes that they are due to variations in our striated sociocultural civilization. The same kind of reasoning should be applied to radio, but logic fails because radio is peculiarly different from other communications media. Whereas some effort and expense are required to find entertainment or enlightenment beyond the walls of the living room, radio is at one's elbow—a ubiquitous presence—and he does not have to drop a coin to turn on a receiving set. When we have to get out the family chariot, drive across town, and plank down good dinero to see a show or listen to a concert, we are pretty careful to select the show or the concert which we want to see, but at home it is sometimes easier to keep to the armchair than get up and "turn that darn thing off." This condition presents a challenge to the radio owner to use his set with more selective and discriminating intelligence.

A third condition which the critic disregards is that the dial-twister or button-tuner operates according to established habits and interests. A hundred million people represent a wide gamut of preferences. Listener interests vary according to factors of age, sex, education, geography, vocational and professional occupation, and socioeconomic status. The segmented partials of the over-all program structure correlate with segmented tastes and preferences. "All social groups spend approximately the same amount of time listening to the radio, but when we examine what it is that they listen to, marked group differences appear."[9] The "quantity of exposure" to a communications medium and the "quality" of listener reception are not directly related. This is evidenced by the answer to Question 14 in the Lazarsfeld-Kendall questionnaire employed in their 1947 survey.

[9] Lazarsfeld and Kendall, *Radio Listening in America.*

Ques. 14.

A. Here's a set of cards listing different kinds of radio programs. Would you mind looking through those cards, and telling me the types of programs you like to listen to in the daytime?[a]

B. Now which types of programs there do you like to listen to in the evening?[a]

	Daytime	Evening
News broadcasts	72%	74%
Comedy programs	*	59
Quiz and audience participation	27	56
Dance and popular music	33	49
Complete dramas (other than mystery)	*	46
Mystery programs	*	41
Talks or discussions about public issues	22	44
Semiclassical music .	22	33
Sports programs	23	33
Serial stories	39	*
Classical music	16	30
Homemaking programs	30	*
Religious programs	34	21
Hillbilly and western music	23	26
Talks on farming	16	*
Livestock and grain reports	14	*

$$100\% = 3.225$$

[a] More than one answer was permitted.
* Heard infrequently at the designated time.

SOURCE: Reprinted by permission of Prentice-Hall, Inc., from *Radio Listening in America*, by Paul Lazarsfeld and Patricia L. Kendall, copyright 1948 by Prentice-Hall, Inc., pp. 122–123.

Moreover, it would appear that listening preferences are consistent, as shown in the accompanying table.

The Constancy of Program Preferences

(1947 compared with 1945)

	Daytime preferences, per cent				Evening preferences, per cent	
	Men		Women		Total	
	1945	1947	1945	1947	1945	1947
News broadcasts..................	65	61	76	71	76	74
Comedy programs.................	*	*	*	*	54	59
Popular and dance music...........	15	23	35	39	42	49
Talk or discussions about public issues	22	19	21	22	40	44
Classical music...................	12	11	23	20	32	30
Religious broadcasts..............	19	22	35	41	20	21
Serial dramas....................	7	6	37	33	*	*
Talks on farming.................	13	16	12	13	*	*
Homemaking programs.............	5	5	44	48	*	*
Livestock and grain reports........	14	17	6	10	*	*

* Figures do not add to 100 per cent because more than one answer was permitted each respondent. The starred program types are not considered because of the infrequency with which they are heard at the designated times.

SOURCE: From Paul Lazarsfeld and Patricia L. Kendall, *Radio Listening in America*, p. 21, Prentice-Hall, Inc., New York, 1948.

Where do listeners derive their interests, tastes, and preferences? They are the product of environmental and institutional influences operating upon them from the time they are born. The home, school, playground, office, and church have shaped their interests and judgments. Is radio to be condemned because it has not, in 30 years, shattered the mold and recast the citizen according to an idealistic design? Even a state system of broadcasting, in which bureaucratic councils told the people what they should and should not listen to, would not "turn the trick." We have often been told that man's capacity for social adaptation has been outstripped by physical and technological progress. A machine is a static and soulless thing; its value lies in the intelligent use which men make of it. An automobile in the hands of an inebriated joy rider is an engine of lethal destruction; atomic power may be the supreme triumph of man's constructive genius, or it may blow the world to bits; medicine can cure or kill. Likewise, radio can contribute to the elevation of the race or perpetuate a static mediocrity; the *deus ex machina* is the adaptive capacity of man himself to make intelligent use of the medium.

A fourth rejoinder made to radio's critics is that, like social critics in general, they are myopic. They see too small an arc of the circle of events. They lack perspective. Their point of reference is the single one of ultimate perfection. A man-made institution grows toward perfection gradually as wisdom matures and the mistakes of experience are gradually corrected. Our standard of judgment should be a comprehensive one which embraces the Then, the Now, and the To Be. While radio's shortcomings and abuses may be many, they should be evaluated in the light of shortcomings and abuses already corrected.

Having made these general rejoinders, industry spokesmen turn to specific charges. The fact that radio is privately owned and operated as an advertising and sales medium is readily admitted; but the implication that free-enterprise broadcasting is inherently and necessarily contrary to public welfare is vigorously denied. Any credo unsupported by honest and capable intent may be innocuous as a political platform, but the broadcaster's conception of responsibility is clearly stated:[10]

We believe: That American Broadcasting is a living symbol of democracy; . . . that its influence in the arts, in science, in education, in commerce, and upon the public welfare in general, is of such magnitude that the only proper measure of its responsibility is the common good of the whole people.

The first regulatory radio code (the NAB *Code of Ethics*) was written in 1929. The principles and policies enunciated at that time were subsequently revised and amended in 1935, 1937, 1939, 1946, and 1948. The *Britannica Yearbook* in its 1939 review of major trends in the radio industry lists (1) expansion of investments, (2) upsurge of unionism, and (3) *self-imposed policies regulating programing and advertising.*

Regulations have dealt specifically with advertising. They stipulate that an advertiser should limit his statements of value and price to factual material, check his copy for false and misleading statements, adhere to a schedule of maximum time prescribed for commercials, and make all offers conform to standard requirements. The exact language of *Standards of Practice for American Broadcasters,* effective July 1, 1948, is as follows:

Diligence should be exercised to the end that advertising copy accepted for broadcasting complies with pertinent Federal, state, and local laws. Acceptance of advertising should be predicated upon such considerations as the integrity of the advertiser, the quality of the product, the value of the service, and the validity of the claims made.

In accepting advertising, the broadcaster should exercise great care that he is not conveying to his audience information that is misleading, dangerous to health or character, distasteful or contrary to the proprieties and customs characteristic of his audience, or in violation of business and professional ethics.

[10] *Standards of Practice for American Broadcasters,* National Association of Broadcasters.

NBC lists 14 types of business which are unacceptable. CBS excludes
. . . any product which describes graphically or repellently any internal bodily
functions, symptomatic results of internal disturbances, or matters which are
generally considered not acceptable topics in social groups.

It is admitted that "competition for economic survival has inflicted on
the public a percentage of irritating advertising copy," but this is denounced as unjustifiable and unnecessary. Radio codes formulated by
associations, networks, and stations are not mandatory legislative restrictions enforceable by executive and judicial authority. They are codes
of "self-regulation." The argument, however, that these statements of
practice are like political platforms which sponsoring parties use as a
"front," and which they forget once they are in power, has only partial
basis in fact. Some autonomous stations may not even subscribe to a
code, and those which do may not keep faith with the ethics of their
profession; but there is a general industry recognition of compliance
with broadcasting ethics and a consistent over-all record of managerial
attempt to follow self-imposed injunctions.

Not only are the character and content of advertising copy restricted,
but the amount of time given to the sponsor's message in relation to
program time is also prescribed by an advisory code. The maximum
time to be used for advertising, allowable to any single sponsor, regardless of type of program, should be as shown in the accompanying
table.

	Minutes	Seconds
Between 6:00 P.M. and 11:00 P.M.		
5-minute program.............	1	
10-minute program............	2	
15-minute program............	2	30
25-minute program............	2	50
30-minute program............	3	
45-minute program............	4	30
60-minute program............	6	
All other hours		
5-minute program.............	1	15
10-minute program............	2	10
15-minute program............	3	
25-minute program............	4	
30-minute program............	4	15
45-minute program............	5	45
60-minute program............	7	

Furthermore, advised standards of practice urge the avoidance of simulated spot announcements which are divorced from the program preceding the introduction of the program itself, or by following its *apparent* signoff.

The program itself should be announced and clearly identified *before* the use of what has been known as "cowcatcher" announcements and the program should be signed off *after* the use of what have been known as "hitchhike" announcements. The placement of more than one commercial announcement between two commercial programs should not be permitted.

The response of radio management to the accusation that broadcasters have been recreant to their educational responsibility is given as both constructive and rebuttal argument. Disclaiming that it is management's obligation to organize and promote educational curricula and formal extension instruction, executives point to the bulk of sustaining programs originating by networks and stations and broadcast at their expense in the "public interest." (A sustaining program is one supported wholly by the network or station and offered gratuitously in the public interest; a commercial program is sponsored and paid for by an advertiser.)

A large proportion of time is devoted to sustaining programs classified under the general headings of public affairs, religion, music, agriculture, and education. For the selected week of Mar. 5, 1950, 45.5 per cent of all broadcasting time of the NBC network was sustaining; for the week of May 7, 1950, the percentage was 46.1 per cent. For the corresponding months of May, 1949 and 1950, the proportion of total broadcast time assigned to "sustainers at KNX, the key station in Columbia's western division, was as shown in the accompanying table.

	1949	1950
Morning...............	34.7	27.7
Afternoon.............	37.6	30.9
Evening...............	44.3	29.1
Average...............	38.7	29.1

The nature of sustaining programs and of their contribution to public knowledge, morality, and appreciation is adequately evidenced by a partial listing of network offerings.[11] NBC publishes a brochure, *On the*

[11] In the following presentation no comparison or contrast of institutional offerings is intended, and the reader should draw no inference with reference to comparative merits. Enumeration is made for the purpose of illustration only. Some of the programs named are not currently offered, but have been replaced by others of similar character.

Dial, which carries a selective listing of public-service programs created, sponsored, and transmitted by the network. For 3 years, NBC was the exclusive broadcasting sponsor of *United Nations Week,* enlisting more than 100 radio and television programs to make the public more aware of the aims and progress of the United Nations. A documentary series of unusual interest and importance entitled, *Living,* deals constructively and dramatically with vital and personal social problems affecting the daily life of every American family. For example, two of the broadcasts in 1948, *Marriage in Distress* and *Mother Earth,* dramatized, respectively, the subjects of divorce and world hunger. In 1949, the *United States in World Affairs,* presented in cooperation with the Department of State, brought a discussion of national foreign policy by high-ranking government officials. Current problems affecting the national welfare are debated and clarified by representatives of industry, labor, and agriculture in the series entitled, *America United.* The efforts of the Economic and Social Council to build world-wide foundations for enduring peace, the work of the International Refugee Organization, the program of the U.S. Mercantile Commission, the medical developments made available by the U.N. World Health Organization, and the function and operation of the International Bank were some of the subjects presented in 1950. Regular Sunday network programs give voice to three principal religious faiths. The oldest religious program on the air is *National Radio Pulpit,* supervised by the Federal Council of Churches of Christ in America; the *Catholic Hour,* now in its twenty-fourth year, is presented in cooperation with the National Council of Catholic Men; and *The Eternal Light,* which demonstrates the fundamental character of democratic impulses in a good society, is produced by the Jewish Theological Seminary. (This latter series has received three first awards from the Ohio State Institute for Education by Radio as the finest religious radio program on a national network.) Two Toscanini broadcasts of *Aïda* by radio and television in 1949 representing "the most ambitious network contributions to opera in terms of personnel, time clearances, cost, and preparation in radio," were a cultural contribution to opera of the first magnitude. At other times NBC has sponsored such significant programs as the *Bach Aria Group,* the *NBC String Quartette,* the *NBC Symphony Orchestra,* and *Pioneers of Music.* Concerts broadcast under the latter title are the basis for a University of Southern California home-study course. Agricultural programs supply farmers with information that saves them millions of dollars annually. (The Department of Agriculture sends material daily to about 500 radio stations.) The *National Farm and Home Hour,* the longest established of all farm programs was originated by NBC in 1928 and was a regular sustainer until 1945 when it was adopted by a sponsor. The *NBC University of the Air* was formulated in 1948 in collaboration with several universities. Under this plan, a radio listener may register with a particular university at a nominal fee for a selected study course. The home-study courses, *World Affairs* and *Economics of the Modern World*, based on the subject matter presented in the *University of Chicago Round Table* broadcasts, are offered by the University of Chicago.

CBS has made many notable contributions to social, cultural, and educational life. The most complete, carefully planned, and executed series of programs ever introduced to the air waves was the CBS *American School of the Air*, which completed its sixteenth year in 1945–1946. Its purpose was to bring "education in an attractive form to children and young people and to their parents and friends . . . illuminate present-day problems, [and] bring enlightenment and entertainment." A national board of 21 consultants who aided in the organization of these programs was drawn from prominent universities, teachers colleges, educational associations, libraries, the National Congress of Parents and Teachers, and similar organizations. These representatives "advised on choosing subjects, on educational content, and on general policies." The programs were supplied to "hundreds of thousands" of classrooms. The full story is told in the CBS *Calendar Manual* for each season. We have space for only a brief account.

A total of 150 programs was presented in 1945–1946 covering a range of history, science, literature, music, and current events. The main subjects for each of five series, extending from Oct. 1 to Apr. 26, were as follows:

1. The Story of America
   . . . history dramatized by skilled writers and actors . . . to illuminate the gradual unfolding of that democratic experiment (creating and maintaining an independent Republic), to indicate something of its cultural characteristics, and to suggest the social principles which have been deeply cherished.
2. Gateways to Music
   The ever widening gamut of mental and emotional experience (found) in music.
3. March of Science
   . . . the reporting and interpretation of science . . . great moments in science which have shown man how to do the world's work better; science as it has brought better health to mankind; and discoveries.
4. This Living World
   An understanding and interpretation of current events
5. Tales from Far and Near
   . . . introduces books old and new and acquaints them [children] with an array of characters as varied as the Pushmi-Pullyu, Mickey the Horse, and Miss Price.

Program titles from each of these five categories will suggest the more specific nature of these School of the Air broadcasts:

1. The Story of America
   a. DeSoto's March
   b. Penn's Experiment
   c. The Genius of Franklin
   d. Frémont and California
   e. Alaskan Gold
2. Gateways to Music
   a. Music on Rails
   b. South of the Border
   c. Beethoven
   d. H.M.S. Pinafore
   e. The Martial Spirit
3. The March of Science
   a. Insect Killers
   b. Plastic Era
   c. Story of Radar
   d. Oxygen—Breath of Life
   e. Looking Ahead
4. This Living World
   a. Food for Europe
   b. The Farmer's Job
   c. Black Market
   d. Housing America
5. Tales from Far and Near
   a. The Pickwick Papers
   b. Mickey, the Horse that Volunteered
   c. Pecos Bill
   d. Dr. Doolittle's Circus
   e. Paul Bunyan

The influence of the School of the Air was officially recognized by teachers in 1940 when it became the official, nation-wide classroom radio institution of the National Educational Association of the United States. The programs commanded a wide audience beyond the schoolroom. They were released in Canada, sent by short wave to Latin America, and during the war were a part of Armed Forces Radio Service.

The American School of the Air was suspended during the year 1948–1949. The explanation given by CBS was:

A new emphasis in education has emerged in the CBS schedule during the past several years . . . evidenced in the creation of the Documentary Unit, the development of actuality broadcasts and historical recreations, the application of radio dramatic techniques to problems of human behavior, and a general increase and variety of public opinion broadcasts relating to the political, economic, and social problems. The examination of ideas distilled from human experience on *Invitation to Learning* and the discussions by informed citizens of the whole range of public policy questions on *People's Platform* and *Capitol Cloakroom* are supplemented by the newly developed daily series, *You and the World.* The programs are designed to enrich and broaden the cultural environment of both young people and adults.

News—local, special, world—is reported and interpreted for a weekly audience of 90 million. *You and the World* brings the answers of experts to vital personal questions concerning money, labor, health, and similar subjects. Opinion broadcasts clarify subjects of national and world concern. *Memo from Lake Success, The People's Platform, Capitol Cloakroom, Where the People Stand, The Church of the Air,* and *Invitation to Learning* are examples of first-rate public-service broadcasts.

The CBS documentaries (pictures of present-day cultural forces and activities) deserve particular mention. *The Eagle's Brood* (a study of juvenile delinquency), *Fear Begins at Forty* (old age and employment), *The Sunny Side of the Atom* (constructive uses of atomic energy), *Report Card* (a broad survey of education in the United States), *Shadow on the Mind* (a study of mental health), are examples of the radio industry at its best and illustrate the tremendous possibilities of radio as a social force. Five documentary unit productions planned for the first half of 1950 presented, (1) *Baseball,* radio's first full-scale study of the great American game, (2) *The American Indian,* based on an extensive investigation of the economic and social crisis now facing America's 300,000 Indians, (3) *Political Careers,* an examination of the ingredients of elective political careers in the United States, (4) *The Motion Picture Industry,* an analysis of the creative and social decisions involved in the production of motion pictures in America, and (5) *The Magazine Industry,* an examination of the *Time-Life-Fortune* publications as part of the pattern of American magazines today. CBS, like NBC, sponsors programs in the other areas of agriculture, music, religion, and education. *Country Journal, CBS Symphony Orchestra, Church of the Air,* and *Invitation to Learning* are the titles of such offerings. *Invitation to Learning* is a half-hour discussion of significant books by panels of distinguished scholars, authors, and critics. The following CBS programs for the third quarter of 1949 illustrate the potentialities of this type of "air learning":

Man and Society

July 3. Goethe, *Faust*—Special Bicentennial Program
July 10. Ruth Benedict, *Patterns of Culture*—Mold of Society
July 17. Henrik Ibsen, *Doll's House*—Woman's Place
July 24. Sinclair Lewis, *Babbitt*—Philistinism
July 31. Karel Capek, *R.U.R.*—Mechanization

August 7. Nathaniel Hawthorne, *Mosses from an Old Manse*—Puritanism
August 14. Franz Boas, *Mind of Primitive Man*—Racism
August 21. William Howells, *The Rise of Silas Lapham*—Nouveau Riche
August 28. Aldous Huxley, *Brave New World*—Standardization
September 4. John Galsworthy, *Loyalties*—Prejudice
September 11. Margaret Mead, *Coming of Age in Samoa*—Adolescence
September 18. W. Lloyd Warner, *Yankee City*—Class Distinction
September 25. James Barrie, *The Admirable Crichton*—Class Distinction

Not all public-service programs are sustaining. A commercial broadcast can have subject matter and treatment which place it in the realm of public affairs and education, and the fact that a sponsor's name may be associated with a program should not, *ipso facto*, discredit it. In fact, the expanding number of sponsored programs which can be included within the orbit of the informative, educational, and cultural attest the growth and evolution of radio from the medicine show level. Many of Mutual's (MBS) publicized public-service programs carry the names of sponsors. For example, General Foods Corporation presents *House of Mystery* ("to expose the scientific and logical foundation for happenings and stories that apparently have a supernatural basis"), and also *Juvenile Jury*[12] ("a panel of five children whose ages range from five and a half to eleven, give their views on problems that children of their own ages meet in their relationships with other youngsters and adults in their daily lives"). Special MBS educational programs for 1948 included, *To Secure These Rights, The Atom and You,* and *Children of Divorce.* Mutual received honorable mention by the Eighteenth Institute for Education by Radio, Ohio State University, "for the courage to believe in children's taste to present a varied selection of the classics in serialized form during the five-a-week block of children's programs." The Wisconsin Joint Committee for Better Radio Listening cited MBS for "contributing programs of unusual merit to the industry." Particularly mentioned programs were *Adventure Parade, Chicago Theatre of the Air, Information Please, Northwestern Reviewing Stand, William L. Shirer,* and *Symphonies for Youth.* The Committee on National Radio Awards of the City College of New York presented the network with a first prize, award of merit for the most effective all-over national radio network promotion during 1947.

The ABC, a network of 207 stations, makes the following statement concerning their program policy:

The first aim of the American Broadcasting Company and its affiliated stations is to keep you *fully* informed as to local, national and world events

[12] *Juvenile Jury* placed first among children's programs in the Second Annual Radio Awards selected by the American Schools and College Association and was chosen as an outstanding children's program in the Sixteenth Annual Poll of Radio Editors, conducted by *Billboard Magazine.*

. . . to live up to their responsibility of presenting both sides of every issue of public interest. To do this—and at the same time broadcast information that is of specific value to veterans, farmers, doctors, teachers, and the like—ABC devotes one-third of all its air time to programs exclusively dedicated to the public interest.

Examples of ABC's contribution to public interest comprise programs of discussion (*America's Town Meeting of the Air*), international relations (*To Live in Peace*), religion (*Message of Israel, The Hour of Faith, National Vespers*), juvenile delinquency (*We—The Guilty*), medicine (*The Doctors Talk It Over*), labor and management (*Labor U.S.A.*), farming (*The American Farmer*), drama (*The Theatre Guild on the Air*), and music (*Boston Symphony Orchestra* and *Metropolitan Opera*).

This review of network broadcasts is given to suggest the quality and extent of noncommercial broadcasting in the public interest. Publicized network programs designed to promote higher standards of public information, morality, and appreciation constitute an impressive picture of radio service geared to educational objectives. Collectively, they constitute a major item in refuting the charge that radio is "assorted fluff, gush, and drivel" and that the level of broadcasting is "abysmally low." The alleged lack of radio's educational influence does not lie with the broadcaster's ineptitude or lack of concern; it lies fundamentally in the auditor's failure to make a discriminating selection of program content and in his indifferent and negligent attitude toward what is available. A listener will not "tune in" a Mozart concert, a documentary social thesis drama, or a round-table discussion if his sociocultural level is not above torch songs, mystery thrillers, and the fight arena. A man is the product of his civilization. His tastes and interests are fashioned by many influences, and radio cannot compensate for their imperfections or deficiencies. It can only try to improve the over-all stimulus pattern of social influence and hope that its efforts will be matched by a personal zeal for better understanding and social effectiveness.

The impact of radio's educational potential cannot be fully realized until there is an organized and consistent program of listener education. Although the NAB has provided impetus and financial support to such a program, this is not a direct task for the broadcasting industry itself. The channeling of listening habits is a problem which radio consumers must solve for themselves under self-appointed, intelligent leadership. The National Association, in 1940, organized the Radio Council on Children's Programs which became the pattern for a number of community councils. The first organizations were established in Minneapolis, Cedar Rapids, Cleveland, and Nashville. In 5 years, under the direction of Mrs. Dorothy Lewis, there were 45 active councils.[13]

[13] Llewellyn White, *The American Radio*, pp. 114–115, University of Chicago Press, 1947.

. . . their average membership including such groups as parent-teacher associations, librarians, school boards, service clubs, women's clubs, church bodies, and an occasional labor union. Typical projects include improvement of children's programs, allocation and production of public-service programs by central committees, distribution of material, program promotion, and periodic conferences. Two outstanding councils are the Better Radio Listening Council of Wisconsin and the Greater Cleveland Listening Council. The former covers every community in the state, publishes monthly lists of "meritorious" programs, and stimulates discussion of radio problems particularly among high school students. Ready access to the University of Wisconsin's WHA (Madison) assures it a sympathetic platform which is audible throughout the state. The Cleveland group, which received its original impetus from Robert Stephan, radio editor of the *Plain Dealer,* confines its efforts to greater Cleveland; claims to speak for 155,000 women; conducts occasional door-to-door, mail, and telephone surveys; and publishes periodic "evaluative" program lists. Like the Wisconsin group, it bars anyone connected with the industry from membership or active participation.

The cliché, "What is everybody's business is nobody's business," applies to radio listening traits. Until purposive and discriminating habits are substituted for casual and haphazard ones, the cry of the critic will be abroad in the land. Placing the onus on the listener does not lessen the obligation of management and sponsor to supply better radio programs, but it emphasizes a cooperative relationship without which the people can never find the wheat in the chaff.

Another reason why American radio does not assume the task of broadcasting forthright and correlated educational programs is that this is the responsibility of educational organizations, per se, assigned channels for the particular purpose. The basic and accepted structure of broadcasting in America, established by the sanction of government, implies that a number of noncommercial channels should be assigned for the exclusive use of civic, religious, and educational institutions. True, it is only in the FM band that a portion of the band is set aside for use by educational institutions, and special rules established to provide the particular noncommercial type of operation advantageous to these institutions. (Eighty-two FM noncommercial licenses were in force as of June 30, 1950.) In the standard band no distinction is made in so far as Commission rules are concerned between licenses issued to educational institutions and those issued to the more numerous commercial operators. However, at the outset of the broadcasting era, many leading universities, realizing the possibilities of extending their facilities by means of radio, applied to the government for licenses. More than 200 such authorizations were given between 1921 and 1936. Approximately (as explained earlier in this chapter) only half of the licensees were able to maintain their position for a period of 3 years or more owing to the requisite financial burden entailed, lack of faculty interest, and the competition of commercial stations which commanded a preferred listener response; but the college stations which survived have rendered effective service. Some state universities, such as the University of Wisconsin, the University of Minnesota, Ohio State University, Cornell University, and the University of Florida, administer elaborate plans, and smaller collegiate institutions, exemplified by Oregon State College, St. Olaf, Grove City College, South Dakota State College, have made significant contributions to their areas. The work of these college and university stations demonstrates clearly and effectively the functional value of adequately furnished noncommercial stations.

The decision of government in not allocating exclusive AM noncommercial channels, did not, *ipso facto,* deprive education of radio voice. Commercial stations have given competent advice and free time to public agencies.

Broadcasters should cooperate with educators and educational groups in developing techniques of broadcasting as well as those processes of education best calculated to produce expert and skillful personnel.

While stations have reserved the better time spots for their commercial clients, and although the "educator" has been moved around, the fact remains that a definite percentage of time has been allocated to him without cost, particularly when he has been able to supply the craftsmanship requisite to effective broadcasting. Assuming that the educator can bring a needed and effective program idea to the station, he will be accommodated.

Summary. The social influence of radio is broad, comprehensive, and constructive. Admitted shortcomings cannot overbalance the effectiveness of its general influence any more than aspects of yellow journalism or "B" pictures negate the advantages of press or cinema. The critic points his finger at imperfections and cries aloud against the whole industry. Imperfections in a garment do not destroy its utility or service. Jagged holes in a raincoat may render it ineffectual, but dropped stitches in a knitted sweater do not impair its warmth. The offending cupidity of individual advertisers is not the essence of radio. A radio program may be both meat and poison, but there are more who live than die. In direct reply to those who decry radio's social influence, industry spokesmen contend that broadcasting (1) raises the economic standard of living by universalizing sales products, tying consumer and producer more closely, and making the qualities of goods and services common household knowledge, (2) expands the range of cultural influences, making available to every family the enlightenment of good literature, the inspiration of music, and higher concepts of artistic excellence, (3) brings the current, local, and international scene to the living room, (4) molds a highly informed and socially conscious public, (5) promotes a better knowledge of social issues by presenting to a national audience political, economic, and social experts—in expositions of vital issues and problems, (6) informs the electorate about municipal and civic affairs, public leaders, candidates for office, and the work of government bureaus and organizations, (7) provides entertainment and relaxation, and (8) performs a particularly vital service in times of emergency and national peril.

QUESTIONS

1. What hopes were expressed concerning radio as a social and cultural influence?

2. What basic reason is offered to support the contention that these hopes have not been realized?

3. Explain: "Radio programing is dominated by an economic and not a social philosophy." Illustrate.

4. Why has radio not fulfilled its educational promise? Discuss with reference to educational programs, per se, network sustaining programs, news commentary, and discussion.

5. Explain four alleged fallacies inherent in radio criticism.

6. What positive evidence supports the claim that radio has contributed to social, cultural, and educational welfare?

CHAPTER 7

RADIO AS A VOCATION[1]

"How can I get a job in radio?" This is a question which perplexes the vocational counselor. It cannot be answered too confidently. The number of available positions in relation to the number of applicants creates a supply-and-demand problem not easily solved. The adviser can hedge by muttering well-worn clichés: "Room at the top . . . persistence brings rewards . . . keep knocking on doors"; but concrete formulas guaranteeing bona fide interviews, auditions, and job acceptance are not easily prescribed. Is it competition that bolts the door? Is there no room for any appreciable number of newcomers? Is the radio industry so well staffed as to make unnecessary a discriminating search for new talent?

The question, How can I get a job in radio? cannot be answered until we ask and receive an answer to a second one, What kind of job do you want? In most instances the radio aspirant is thinking in terms of program performance. He wants to announce, act, play a musical instrument, sing, or direct. The first reply of the counselor should be that program performance is only one of many positions for which the applicant may qualify.

Let us begin with an outlined enumeration of the many different positions in the broadcasting industry. This will be a composite picture— a sort of radio employment spectrum derived mainly from the organization charts of the major networks. It does not follow that each network or key station provides all the employment possibilities listed, but all the jobs enumerated do exist within the over-all radio framework.

1. Administration division
    a. President or major executive
    b. Vice-president
    c. General manager
    d. Assistant general manager
    e. Department head
2. Engineering or technical division
    a. Transmitter, recording studio (audio), field (remote), maintenance,

[1] The basic material in this chapter was prepared by Jack G. Bell, Instructor in Speech and Radio, Occidental College, and was originally submitted as a graduate thesis. The author gratefully acknowledges his contribution.

109

traffic, development engineers; technical apprentices; television technicians and operators

3. Commercial division (marketing, advertising, promotion)
   a. Network sales
   b. Local and spot sales
   c. Sales service
   d. Sales traffic
   e. Institutional promotion
   f. Public-service promotion
   g. Market research
4. Program division
   a. Continuity acceptance
   b. Program schedules
   c. Producers and directors
   d. Assistant directors
   e. Continuity writers
      (1) Commercial
      (2) Dramatic
      (3) News
   f. Announcers
      (1) Commercial
      (2) Sports
      (3) Special
      (4) News
         (a) Reporters
         (b) Analysts and commentators
         (c) Special events
   g. Staff musicians
   h. Sound-effects technicians
   i. Actors
5. Traffic department (to maintain program schedules)
6. Publicity department
   a. Director of public information
   b. Press agents
   c. Photographers
7. Public-relations and public-service departments
   a. Guest relations
   b. Information
8. Purchasing and supply department
9. Office service
   a. Accounting
   b. Secretarial
   c. Stenographic
   d. Typists
   e. Mail clerks
   f. General clerical

10. Building and maintenance
    a. Carpenters
    b. Electricians
    c. Stage setup, etc.
11. Personnel division (employment)

This somewhat specific outline may be generalized as follows:

1. *Administrative Division.* Includes the top executives and division or department heads.

2. *Program Division.* Headed by the program manager, it includes the production department (production directors, assistant directors, actors, and other talent); script department (script and continuity); announcing staff; sound-effects personnel; and trancription technicians.

3. *Sales Division.* Network sales; local and spot sales.

4. *Engineering Division.* Studio and field engineers, maintenance engineers, research and development engineers or technicians.

5. *Public-affairs Division.* This division is concerned with relations between the network and its affiliated stations, radio advertisers, the listening audience, and the general public. The division includes various subdepartments: press information, education, public service, guest and audience relations, and special events.

6. *Station Relations Division.* Maintains liaison between the network and its affiliated stations. It also embraces a traffic department whose function is to maintain smooth integration of programs.

7. *Office Management Division.* Pertains to business personnel having routine office responsibilities: accountants, secretaries, stenographers, typists, mail clerks, and receptionists.

A vocational analysis of each of the many types of employment made available by the broadcasting industry would be too complex for the purpose of this chapter, but we shall discuss briefly each of the principal jobs from the standpoints of qualifications, employment policies, competition, salary, and union requirements.

Administrative. Top executive positions are reached after long and varied experience in the field of radiobroadcasting. The duties of executive officers pertain to matters of supervision, policy, and organization. Special skills and qualifications peculiar to broadcasting are essential to administrative work, but they parallel, in the main, the requirements of any large corporation.

General Manager. CBS, in its western division, delegates the duties of general manager to a vice-president of the network. This practice is not uncommon and will be found true of many networks. Qualifications for this position include all the skills necessary to the supervision of a highly complex, constantly varying, and demanding business. A network schedule of radio programs varies greatly from day to day and week to week, and every change involves some reorganization of personnel and shift in staff pattern. The general manager's job is very complex because of varying types of contracts with affiliated stations and advertisers, FCC regulations, Federal and state laws, industry codes, and government postal regulations. He is concerned with the dictates of the listening audience, audience analysis, and program planning. It is his responsibility to ensure smooth and efficient operation. Consequently, he must be familiar with all the phases of broadcasting and weld the necessary working elements of his organization into a pattern of efficient coopera- tion. Most general managers have been in the radio business from 10 to 20 years.

The general manager is usually appointed by the board of directors or president of the network. Selection is based, as in related fields, upon satisfactory service in some lesser executive position.

In one sense, competition for positions in the top brackets of the broadcasting industry is very strong; in another, it is almost nonexistent. As in any business, there are qualified individuals in radio who wish to reach the peak; but notwithstanding the tremendous volume of business handled by the networks and their affiliates, the number of administra- tive positions is relatively small. Radiobroadcasting is comparatively a new industry, and many of the men who now fill the executive chairs started with the birth of the business and climbed to their present jobs as radio gradually developed. The advent of television and frequency modulation may offer new opportunities, but present positions in the administrative area of broadcasting are quite secure.

Compensation scales for general managers vary with individual net- works. Exact minimum and maximum figures cannot be given, but it is considered that salaries paid to top executives are quite substantial.

Union affiliation is not required for administrative positions, per se.

Department Heads. The head of a department in a network must command the skills and techniques necessary to the efficient operation of his own department. In order to promote interdepartmental relations he should understand the operation of departments other than his own. Departmental isolation cannot be tolerated in radiobroadcasting. The department executive must be able to work with people in a congenial manner, even under extreme pressure. The constant necessity of meeting changing conditions requires a fine sense of adjustment and emotional balance.

The personnel assigned to departmental duties are usually selected by the general manager or other top executives who base their judgment on the experience, reputation, and proved capacity of the applicant. Promotions are usually made from "inside the ranks." Seldom is a man brought in from outside the organization. He usually moves up from a spot within the same department.

Competition in this area is analogous to the same factors discussed with reference to the position of general manager. The turnover, however, is greater. Department heads occasionally move on to accept positions with advertising agencies or to managerial positions with regional networks or local stations.

Salary scales for department administrators vary with the job, the station, and the network. Salaries are prescribed by the general manager, president, or other officials according to established policies. Again it can be assumed that the compensation in these jobs is commensurate with the responsibilities assigned and is relatively high.

There is no union requirement for department heads, but as a rule the man will be a member of the union with which most of his personnel are affiliated.

Program Division. It is the function of the program division to plan, produce, and schedule the network's programs, to supervise programs produced by outside agencies, to supervise employment and payment of talent, and to provide for the writing or purchasing of scripts. The program division personnel comprises those persons participating directly in broadcasting a radio program—producers, directors, assistant directors, script and continuity writers, announcers, actors, musicians, sound technicians, and transcription technicians.

Production director. A distinction may be made between the producer and the director. The former may be charged with the responsibility of supervising and integrating all the various elements of a program, and the latter may be assigned to a particular unit of the entire program. This distinction does not exist, however, except in special circumstances; and the title of producer, or director, or producer-director usually denominates the persons responsible for the program presentation. We shall use the term "producer." He is the man who casts the show, interprets the script, conducts rehearsals, times the show, directs the actors, musicians, and engineers, and integrates the program elements into an artistic pattern.

Requirements for this position embrace thorough knowledge of radio program skills, organizational ability, quick and sure decisions, leadership ability, and experience.

The number of producers employed by a network is regulated by the number of programs initiated by the network itself, the agencies, and free-lance production companies. The western division of CBS maintains a staff of six to eight producers, and the eastern division, four to ten. Network divisions may interchange their directors according to special needs and for particular program requirements.

Competition for production jobs is very strong. It is estimated that all programs initiated by the four major networks are handled by 170 men. In other words, there are 170 professional network radio producers. In addition to these, there are some 400 men employed by the advertising agencies. There are some 125 advertising companies which engage in the sale and production of radio programs, and these agencies employ their own producers. In the light of the vast amount of radio programs carried by more than 2,000 stations, the over-all employment picture in this vocational phase of broadcasting is not too bright for the large number of people interested in program directing.

The basic salary prescribed by the union for producers is $100 a week, but this varies with individual contracts and types of shows. In their 1945 study of employee compensation data, covering 9 networks and 876 stations, the FCC reported the average pay to production personnel to be $62.50 per week. The basic pay for network production today is considerably higher, and individual salaries may reach a figure between $6,000 and $10,000 a year.

Producers are required to join the Radio Directors' Guild, a union limited to production-directors and assistant producers.

Assistant Producers. Networks employ assistant producers in connection with programs produced by outside agencies. The primary function of the assistant is to interpret to the agency matters of network policy. The position requires a man who has a knowledge of policies, organization procedure, industry controls, and network rules and codes. He must be familiar with the regulations of the FCC, the NAB code, Federal and state laws, and individual station policy.

Assistant producers are hired by the head of the program department. They are usually young men who have come up through the ranks.

Again, competition for these positions is very strong. The number of assistantships is not large. A key station in New York, Chicago, or Los Angeles will probably hire not more than seven or eight staff assistants. It is true that there is a greater turnover in this area because every assistant wishes to climb the ladder and quickly avail himself of a new location which may promote his advancement.

The union minimum salary is $72.50 and, unlike the figure for producers, does not vary a great deal.

Assistant producers are also members of the Radio Directors' Guild.

Announcers. Announcers are classified as free-lance announcers and staff announcers. The free-lance man is hired by individual sponsors, advertising agencies, or stations for specific jobs. The staff announcer is retained on a weekly or monthly basis and works regularly scheduled hours. He may be expected to handle a wide variety of assignments, and usually does; but his main task is to handle routine announcements, station breaks, spot announcements, time signals, program signatures, and possible recordings.

The qualifications of the announcer are described in Chap. 12 on radio announcing where it is pointed out that the announcer is a salesman who captures attention, holds it, and persuades his listeners in accordance with the sponsor's objective. A "melodious voice" is not the ultimate requirement for an announcer. He must have a pleasant voice, of course, but it is all-important that he speak clearly and distinctly without affectation, unnaturalness, theatrical styling, or provincial mannerism. The personality behind the words is very important because the radio listener is quick to associate with the stimulus word the quality and character of the speaker behind it. A staff announcer should have great flexibility and be able to adapt himself to a wide variety of commercial copy and programs. He must think quickly and confidently, meet emergencies easily, be punctual, cooperate with his associates, and have a knowledge of codes and procedures that relate to his phase of radio work.

Announcers may become specialists according to their individual talents and interests. The various areas of sports, news, dramatic narration, musical programs, special events, and commercial advertising offer particular fields of specialization.

The supply of announcers in proportion to the available jobs is very large. Some 500 announcers are affiliated with the Los Angeles branch of the American Federation of Radio Artists (AFRA), and their field experience ranges from 2 to 20 years. The southern California area is saturated with radio stations, but they cannot begin to employ any appreciable percentage of the available personnel. KNX, the major originating network station for CBS, maintains a staff of 10 or 12 announcers, and the turnover is almost negligible. KNX receives three or four applications per week, and when a free-lance audition is announced, 50 to 70 competitors will make their appearance. There has been no appreciable change in the announcing personnel of the networks in the past 5 years.

Salaries for network announcers vary greatly according to program, sponsor, station, and demand for a particular announcer. A free-lance man may earn from $50 to $300 for a single program, but the starting base salary for the staff announcer as fixed by union negotiation, is $100 for a 40-hour week. This pay may be increased if the announcer is engaged by a sponsor or sponsor's agent to handle commercial programs. The range of compensation in this area is indicated by the following table reported by the Los Angeles AFRA local in its 1949 September-October issue of *Afra Dial-Log*. The figures pertain to announcers' incomes for 1948.

Approximate Gross Income for 1948
for 426 Announcers Reporting

	Full-time employment	Part-time employment
To $2,000...................	190	7
$ 2,000 to $ 5,000...........	108	2
$ 5,000 to $10,000...........	66	2
$10,000 to $20,000...........	29	1
$20,000 to $50,000...........	15	0
Over $50,000.................	6	0

Union dues are assessed on a sliding scale according to gross income—income derived from radio employment. Some of the income listed above may have come from types of employment other than announcing, per se; and no analysis of the figures is possible with regard to free-lance jobs only, free-lance and staff jobs combined, station or network affiliation, additional income derived from acting or other program responsibilities.

Union Requirements. All announcers, staff or free-lance, appearing on network broadcasts must be members of the AFRA.

Actors. Qualifications for radio acting comprise the skills and abilities requisite to acting in general, but the microphone imposes restrictions, adjustments, and demands upon the radio actor. These are explained in detail in Chap. 14. Summarized very briefly at this point, it suffices to say that audio broadcasting places primary and almost complete emphasis on vocal interpretation, that the actor must convey mood, character, and pictures of movement by voice alone, that he must learn to perform within a more intimate frame of reference, be flexible and versatile, be familiar with the limitations of the medium with which he is working, and be able to give what is very close to a sight reading of the printed page. Small-station experience is not so essential in this area of employment. An actor is hired on the basis of his ability to fill the role. No specific stipulation is made concerning the length or nature of apprenticeship. He is employed according to his reputation, proved ability, or audition rating.

There is more competition for acting jobs than in any other branch of the industry. The reason is found in the well-known supply-and-demand formula. Thousands of people trained in colleges, private radio and dramatic schools, little theater and stock companies, vie for the glamorous radio spotlight, but their ambitions are restricted by several conditions. Stage and screen stars are being used in an increasing number of dramatic shows because stage and movie idols guarantee a large listening audience. The number of programs requiring actors is only a portion of radio's daily program schedule, and many of these programs and serials are unit shows using the same principals. Furthermore, casting directors, working under the demands of a tight time schedule, will select proved and experienced actors on whom they know they can rely. There is no time to coach actors in any detail, and it is hazardous to take chances with an unknown quantity. Another reason why the profession of radio acting is an uncertain one and why it does not offer sustained continuity of employment is that too many broadcasts are "one-shot" affairs. The great majority of program assignments are for a single performance. The characters in the script, except for principals and the established characters in strip or serial shows, are changed from week to week. This general situation gives an advantage to a minority group of actors, but it operates against the majority, especially those who are trying to break into the business.

The rate of pay for radio actors is fixed by agreement between their bargaining agency, the AFRA, and the employing agencies, stations, or networks. Individual compensation may run higher than AFRA rates, but no contracting party may pay less. The minimum fees for actors who appear on transcontinental (TC) and Pacific Coast regional broadcasting are given in the accompanying tables.

National Network Commercial Rates for Actors

Length of program	Fee	Re-broadcast fee
15 minutes or less.............	$21.75	$14.50
16 to 30 minutes..............	36.25	18.25
31 to 60 minutes..............	50.75	25.50

REHEARSAL: $8.75 per hour, first hour required; after first hour, rehearsal may be computed and paid in half-hour periods at the rate of $4.38 per half-hour or part thereof.

THIRTEEN WEEKS' NONCANCELABLE CONTRACTS
(Single broadcast per day)

Times a week	Discount per cent	Guaranteed minimum
5	15	$203.25
4	10	145.25
3	5	116.25

REHEARSAL: $8.75 per hour. Total compensation shall be the applicable fees plus rehearsal pay, less the discount, or the guaranteed minimum, whichever is higher.

Regional Network Commercial Rates for Actors

Length of Program	Fee
15 minutes or less.............	$15.50
16 to 30 minutes..............	19.25
31 to 60 minutes..............	27.00

REHEARSAL: $4.75 per hour, first hour required; after first hour, rehearsal may be computed and paid in half-hour periods at the rate of $2.38 per half-hour.

THIRTEEN WEEKS' NONCANCELABLE CONTRACTS

Times a week	Discount, per cent	Guaranteed minimum
3	5	$ 60.25
4	10	80.25
5	15	100.25

REHEARSAL: $4.25 per hour. Total compensation shall be the applicable fees plus rehearsal pay, less the discount, or the guaranteed minimum, whichever is higher.

The portions of all the above schedules of rates that are designated as 13 weeks' noncancelable contracts apply only to 15-minute programs. On all similar types of contracts for half-hour and hour programs, a discount from scale of 10 per cent is allowed.

While AFRA regulations govern the actors' minimum rates of pay, higher compensation can be paid by the station, network, or agency. Top-flight actors, or "stars," are usually paid in accordance with contract between themselves and the organization producing the program. These rates of pay, of course, vary a great deal. An indication of the average yearly income of the radio actors is offered by the *Afra Dial-Log*, September, 1949.[2]

Los Angeles Local of AFRA

(Sept. 14, 1949)
Total number of actors—1,638

Approximate gross income for 1948	Full-time employment	Part-time employment
To $2,000...................	710	429
$ 2,000 to $ 5,000...........	153	31
$ 5,000 to $10,000...........	99	12
$10,000 to $20,000...........	96	8
$20,000 to $50,000...........	49	0
Over $50,000................	51	0
Total...................	1,158	480

[2] *Afra Dial-Log*, September-October, 1949, Hollywood, Calif., p. 12. Hollywood AFRA official monthly publication for its membership.

There is never any assurance that you will have continuous employment unless you have a leading role on a serial. In other words, one works from show to show depending upon a call from the director or sponsor's agent. Irregularity of employment is a condition inherent in the structure of radio acting. Moreover, even among proved and seasoned actors, there is a considerable turnover, because new programs want new characters, not the same voices. This statement would seem to contradict the above assertion that directors are loath to try new talent. There is no actual contradiction, however, because the availability of proved and seasoned actors is sufficient to permit a good deal of shifting.

Is there no opportunity at all for the newcomer to radio? Yes, there is. The above facts are stated to make clear that the problem is a difficult one. There are some stations which will give you an honest audition. Some agency departments will do likewise. It is unfortunate, however, that where such auditions are given, the results are disappointing. About the most you can expect is a courteous statement that your name will be placed on file and that you will be notified if "something turns up." It is probably true that your name will be placed in a casting file together with a record of the producer's impressions of your abilities and potential usefulness. Talent is made available to producers through talent registries or talent agencies, talent agents, talent scouts, and through AFRA, although the latter organization does not engage in the business of selling or contracting the services of its members. There are in the United States some 160 agencies which handle radio talent, supply users of talent, and make artist contact. Acting talent is employed for the most part by the advertising agencies and not by the station or networks. Contacts for acting jobs are best made by interviewing agency producers. It may not be easy to see the producer in each case, but one thing the job hunter will soon learn is that he must be eternally persistent. Many doors will be closed, at least temporarily, but constant application and patient renewal of potential job opportunities will probably pay dividends. Information about jobs may also be gained from the trade magazines—*Billboard, Radio Daily,* and *Broadcasting.*

Compensation received by actors today signifies a major improvement in the actor's financial position and personal bargaining power. The current schedules are a far cry from the days when actors were not organized and worked for as little as $2.50 or $5 per program, partook in free auditions, and often worked on "spec"—the speculation that a job might eventuate. Again, the figures cited above might easily give the impression that radio acting is a lucrative profession. This is true for some and would be so for many more were it not for the conditions already explained. Employment survey figures put the matter in a less favorable light than one might anticipate.

On Mar. 9, 1949, the U.S. Department of Labor, Bureau of Labor Statistics, released its first report on the employment and earnings of radio announcers, actors, singers, and sound-effects artists for use in vocational guidance of young people planning radio careers. The investigation was conducted in cooperation with the AFRA. Questionnaires sent to AFRA members in 16 cities were returned by 3,742 artists. Information was requested concerning employment for a particular week ("a survey week") and from this data the Bureau made a statement under the heading, "Employment status in the spring of 1948." The percentage is estimated for announcers, singers, actors, and sound-effects men. At the present point we are concerned with the figures revealed for actors. The report stated:

The rate of unemployment among radio actors was 8 or 9 times as high as among all working people in the country in the spring of 1948 . . . in Los Angeles, one-third of the actors had no work during the survey week . . . . Nearly one of every five actors in the study was entirely without work and looking for work during at least one-half of the weeks of 1947. . . . The largest percentage of unemployment was in Los Angeles. [New York and Chicago rated second and third, respectively.]

The report gives some indication of average earnings of radio actors. For 1947, 1 out of 10 had gross earnings under $2,000 from all sources. For all actors (fully employed and partly employed) one-third earned under $2,000. On the other hand, one out of two actors reported earnings over $3,400 in 1947, and one out of four made over $10,000.

Perhaps the first criterion of a vocational position is economic security. Judged by this standard, radio actors, compelled to follow the free-lance market for the most part, do not find radio offering much stability. Work is infrequent except for a relatively few. There are good months and there are bad months. Bit parts or supporting parts do not carry through an entire series of programs. The program season, or period of employment, may terminate after any 13-week interval. Competition seems to increase, not decrease. One's income may vary radically from year to year. One case reported in the above survey shows an income fluctuating from a $10,000 top to a low of $1,600 within a space of 3 years. As one experienced actor put it, "getting a job and keeping it means a relentless drive year in and year out to keep your name and personality before the directors."

Union Requirements. Acting personnel are members of the AFRA.

Musicians. The place of musicians in the field of radiobroadcasting is an extremely broad and varied one. Probably half of all radio time is filled by music—music of all kinds involving musicians of all types. Singers, choirs, organists, string quartets, concert orchestras, symphony orchestras, bands, and opera companies all make their appearance before the microphone within an average weekly program schedule. A discussion of each type of radio musician is not feasible at this point, but certain observations can be made concerning "staff" musicians hired by the network stations as steady employees. The training, experience, skills, and talents necessary for the majority of musicians do not differ greatly from the qualifications of good musicians in general although radio emphasizes certain aspects of musical skill. The radio musician must be highly adaptable, able to read music quickly and accurately and to execute a musical score with precision. If he is versatile enough to play two or more instruments, he is more useful than a musician who is a specialist on one instrument only. He should be able to interpret a wide variety of musical compositions and relate himself to the general emotional and artistic framework of programs of which he is a coordinate part. Extensive musical training, consummate technical skill and versatility may not in their respective selves be sufficient qualifications for radio work. These elements must be blended with many coordinating, cooperative factors, radically changing program demands and work conditions, and showmanship requisites inherent in various types of programs. Personal and personality factors are also important. Egocentric vagaries are never conducive to organizational cohesion, and radio programing and production require the utmost in team play, mutual respect, and cooperation.

There are additional qualifications for the job of music director. The first of these is a familiarity with the requirements and operational practices of program production. He is called upon to supply music of an extremely wide variety and for a number of specific purposes. Music in a dramatic program, for example, may have to fulfill one, or all, of the following: (1) open and close the program, (2) set the mood and scene, (3) indicate transition of time and/or locale, (4) imitate special sound effects, (5) punctuate divisions of the programs, and (6) furnish background for dialogue. Each bit of music must be carefully timed and made to supply the particular effect called for by the script. Unless the music director knows something of the techniques and demands of program production, it would be nearly impossible to integrate his contribution with the other elements of the broadcast.

The music director is also concerned with purely musical programs. His duties in producing such a program are numerous and call for many talents. First, he is required to pass judgment on all types of talent—conductors, composers, and arrangers as well as performers. Next, he must select music which will fit the talent available as well as appeal to the listening audience. Since he deals with the whole field of music literature, his musical knowledge needs to be almost encyclopedic in scope. As popularity of music follows constantly changing patterns, he must couple an awareness of listeners' current demands with an insight into the potential popularity of any piece of music. The musical program should have a structure as well planned as that of a dramatic show. The music director is often responsible for framing his program around a format which meets artistic demands of variety and interest.

Finally, while the duties of program pickup are allocated to the program engineer, the music director must also take an important part in achieving correct balance of all elements of the musical broadcast. He is more apt to detect improper balance than the engineer and should be able to correct the flaws he hears. He must, therefore, know something about the placement of the instruments and artists with relation to each other and the sound properties of the studio; the number, placement, angling, height, and kind of microphones to be used; and the kind and amount of distortion suited for best results.

Employment policies concerning the radio musician are bewilderingly complicated in their detailed analysis. Union regulation and restrictions, multiplicity of contractual agreements between talent and station or agencies, and variations in numbers and use of employed music personnel—all serve to prevent a generalization of employment policies which would apply to all networks or stations. It can be safely stated, however that staff musicians for the most part are employed by either the music director of the network station or by the orchestra manager of the staff orchestra. The production director, in a few instances, will hire music personnel for a specific program.

Large stations and networks are almost 100 per cent union-organized under the American Federation of Musicians (AFM), a closed shop union for instrumentalists. Union regulations demand certain jurisdiction over the hiring of music personnel. For example, the Musicians Mutual Protective Association of Los Angeles, Calif., states:[3]

A local Orchestral Manager, in addition to leader, shall be required for each Radio Staff Orchestra. On class B Local Station, leader is also permitted to serve as Orchestra Manager.

A local Orchestra Manager, in addition to leader, shall be required for each orchestra playing any Chain Broadcast.

The local Orchestra Manager shall engage all musicians in a given orchestra; he shall be the official representative of this Association and shall be held responsible to the Association for conditions in his respective orchestra. . . .

Orchestra Manager in charge of any engagement shall have complete supervision over the work of Arrangers, Orchestrators, Copyists, Librarians, Proofreaders, and Instrumentalists employed thereon.

[3] *Price List and Regulations of the Musicians Mutual Protective Association of Los Angeles, California, Governing Radio, Phonograph Recordings, Electrical Transcription,* Local 47, American Federation of Musicians, 1949, p. 9.

Union agreements with the network also specify how many union musicians the station must employ on its regular staff. This number may or may not coincide with the number of staff musicians actually employed by the station. Large stations frequently maintain more than the minimum number required by union contract.

Another of the clauses in standard union agreements specifies the working hours for staff musicians. Local 47, AFM agreement with NBC, CBS, ABC, and NBS, calls for a 4-hour day, 5-day week. Work must be performed between 8:00 A. M. and 12:00 P. M. Rehearsal or performance in excess of 4 hours per day or outside of the specified hour span is considered overtime.

Music directors are usually employed by the general manager of the network on the basis of reputation and experience.

Competition for radio musicians' jobs is extremely keen. Staff orchestra positions are comparatively few in number and, because of the salaries paid, are highly desirable. Turnover of staff musicians is very slight.

Salary Scales. Minimum free-lance fees and salary scales for staff musicians (instrumentalists) are determined by the AFM. In the following tables, are the AFM minimum pay rates for staff and free-lance musicians on transcontinental, Pacific Coast, and local broadcasts.[4]

National Network Rates for Musicians

Staff orchestras
(Sustaining and/or regional and local commercials)
STEADY-ENGAGEMENT PRICE PER FIVE-DAY WEEK*

	Per Man
Four hours per day, per week	$115.00
Overtime, per half-hour or fraction thereof	2.88

Leader and/or orchestra manager, 50% extra
Doubling: First double, 15% extra; additional doubles, 10% extra
Playing alone, any instrument, 25% extra

* All national-network commercial broadcasts must be paid for at single-engagement prices.

SINGLE ENGAGEMENTS (COMMERCIAL)

	Per Man
Half-hour program (including 3½ consecutive hr. same day as broadcast)	$37.50
One-hour program (including 5 hr. rehearsal)	62.50
Rehearsal overtime, per half-hour or fraction	3.75
Broadcast overtime, per 15 min. or fraction	3.75

SINGLE ENGAGEMENTS (SUSTAINING)

	Per Man
Half-hour program (including 1½ hr. rehearsal in one session same day as broadcast)	$23.00
One-hour program (including 2 consecutive hr. rehearsal)	33.93
Rehearsal overtime, per half-hour or fraction	2.88
Broadcast overtime, per 15 min. or fraction	2.88

Leader and/or orchestra manager, 50% extra
Doubling: First double, 25% extra; additional doubles, 10% extra
Playing alone, any instrument, 50% extra

[4] *Ibid.,* pp. 11ff.

Regional Network Rates for Musicians

SINGLE ENGAGEMENTS (COMMERCIAL)

	Per Man
Half-hour program (including 2½ consecutive hr. rehearsal same day as broadcast)	$23.00
One-hour program (including 4 hr. rehearsal)	32.78
Rehearsal overtime, per half-hour or fraction	3.45
Broadcast overtime, per 15 min. or fraction	3.45

SINGLE ENGAGEMENTS (SUSTAINING)

	Per Man
Half-hour program (including 1½ hr. rehearsal in session same day as broadcast)	$15.53
One-hour program (including 2 consecutive hr. rehearsal)	20.70
Rehearsal overtime, per half-hour or fraction	2.30
Broadcast overtime, per 15 min. or fraction	2.30

Leader and/or orchestra manager, 50% extra
Doubling: First double, 25% extra; additional doubles, 10% extra
Playing alone, any instrument, 50% extra

Local Rates for Musicians

SINGLE ENGAGEMENTS

	Per Man
Half-hour program (including ½ hr. rehearsal in one session same day as broadcast)	$ 9.20
One-hour program (including 1 hr. rehearsal)	16.10
Rehearsal overtime, per half-hour or fraction	2.30
Broadcast overtime, per 15 min. or fraction	2.88

Compensation for network musicians is generally in excess of required pay, owing to the high caliber of personnel demanded for network broadcasting. Minimum salary fees and working conditions for radio singers are governed by the AFRA. A membership tabulation for September, 1949, in *Afra Dial-Log* gives the 1948 gross income for singers in the Los Angeles local of AFRA as shown in the following table.[5]

Los Angeles Local of AFRA

(Sept. 14, 1949)
Total number of singers—442

Approximate gross income for 1948	Full-time employment	Part-time employment
To $2,000	142	128
$ 2,000 to $ 5,000	52	27
$ 5,000 to $10,000	33	13
$10,000 to $20,000	19	4
$20,000 to $50,000	9	0
Over $50,000	15	0
Total	270	172

[5] *Afra Dial-Log, loc. cit.*

Union Requirements. All radio musicians must be members of the AFM.

Sound Technicians. The job of producing or creating and executing with artistic accuracy the sound effects called for by the radio script requires a number of qualifications. Most sound effects today are available on recorded disks, but many script exigencies depend upon manual or live effects created by the ingenuity of the technician. Furthermore, the sound man must be more than an intelligent robot who plays records on cue, walks in a gravel box, or closes doors. He must have a showmanship ability to integrate his work with the over-all artistic pattern sought by the director. This requires a sense of proportion, timing, imagery, and dramatic appreciation. He must picture the dramatic scene to be registered upon the mind of the listener and execute the program elements assigned to him with a clear realization of their ultimate effect. He must know how to operate recording equipment because recorded sounds are usually played from turntables in the studio. To some slight extent his knowledge and skill parallel the work of the studio engineer.

Sound technicians are employed by the head of the sound-effects department and are in many instances recruited from personnel within the organization. Young men are frequently promoted from less responsible positions such as messenger, mail clerk, and transcription assistant according to their general interest in their work, background, proved initiative, and responsibility. Likewise, the sound department is a springboard to higher positions in the radio employment structure. Some engineers, producers, and even announcers have advanced from the ranks of the sound department although the majority of men in these positions, because of the highly specialized value of their work, remain in this particular field.

The number of sound-effects personnel is very small. The CBS station, KNX, employs about 6 technicians. The Los Angeles AFRA local lists only 33 sound men in their membership tabulation for 1949. The number of employees in this category is limited by the simple fact that a few men can easily handle the work assigned even in a major key network station. One technician can usually take care of the sound problems incident to one broadcast, and he may work several programs a week. Because of the limited job availability in this area, competition is acute. The jobs are few in number, they offer possible training ground for other types of responsibility, the work has a fascination and is an outlet for persons who want to work in radio but who realize they do not possess acting or musical skill. The majority of sound technicians are staff employees, but transcription agencies hire a few men on a 13-week contract basis.

Salary Scales. Salary scales for sound technicians are governed by contracts between the network or stations and the AFRA. AFRA does not list minimum fees for staff or free-lance sound men, scales being determined by individual contract with each network, station, or independent contractor. National network rates for transcription programs are as follows:[6]

National Transcription Program Rates for Sound-effects Artists
MINIMUM FEES

. . . must be paid not less than a minimum fee of $9.00 per hour, first hour required, and thereafter time to be computed and paid at the rate of $2.25 per quarter-hour or part thereof. This hourly rate begins at the time of call and runs continuously thereafter.

At this minimum fee, the sound-effects artist is not required to furnish any equipment. If equipment is furnished, the technician and the producer shall mutually agree on satisfactory compensation which must be in excess of $9 per hour for performance and equipment.

WEEKLY STAFF CONTRACTS

Minimum compensation:
  For first 6 months of employment: $360 per month
  For second 6 months of employment: $420 per month
  Thereafter, $480 per month
Work week:
  Forty hours in 5 days
Overtime:
  At the rate of time and a half
Employment:
  Employment shall be on the basis of a 13-weeks' continuous, noncancelable guarantee with the right of either party to give 2 weeks' notice of termination prior to the end of any 13-week period.
Work day:
  The work day begins with the time reporting and ends at the conclusion of the last assignment. All intervening time excepting 1 hour for lunch constitutes part of the work day.
Applicability:
  This permission to have staff sound-effects artists applies only to transcription companies and only to transcription work. Sponsors, agencies, independent contractors, stations, and networks may not engage staff sound-effects artists under this schedule.

It can be speculated that salary scales for live commercial and sustaining programs and experienced staff employees are somewhat parallel to

[6] *AFRA Handbook,* 3d ed., pp. 74–75, American Federation of Radio Artists, Los Angeles, 1947.

these fees listed for transcription work. Junior sound men, however, probably make below the minimum fee for transcription staff contracts.

Afra Dial-Log, September, 1949, lists the approximate gross income of sound-effects artists who belong to the Los Angeles local of AFRA (see following table).[7]

Los Angeles Local of AFRA

(Sept. 14, 1949)

Total number of sound-effects artists—33

Approximate gross income for 1948	Full-time employment	Part-time employment
To $2,000	25	0
$2,000 to $ 5,000	6	1
$5,000 to $10,000	1	0
Total	32	1

Writers. There are many distinctly different types of writing for radio. Broadcast prose runs the gamut from commercials (advertising copy in its many forms—straight; dramatized, singing), continuity (the connective material of a musical or variety program), news programs, talks, and local-interest programs, through the various classifications of dramatic presentations (unit and episodical series, serials and soap operas, adaptations, documentaries, variety sketches, public-service drama, and children's programs), to stylized comedy and "gags" for professional comedians.

It is an amazing fact that[8]

. . . twenty million words are broadcast daily to the American air. Take all the words in all the full-length pictures produced in Hollywood in a year, and you do not have enough words to keep radio in the United States going for twenty-four hours. Twenty million words, 17,000 different programs—every day.

The bulk of this written material is not produced by the staff writers employed by the networks. Almost all commercials come from the advertising agencies, public-service organizations, public-relations firms, publicity organizations, and advertising departments of business establishments. All "gag" writers work directly for the professional comedians or the agencies that produce the comedy programs. Much of the dramatic material is written by the staff writers of advertising agencies,

[7] Afra Dial-Log, loc. cit.
[8] Erik Barnouw, Handbook of Radio Writing, p. 3, Little, Brown & Company, Boston, 1947.

radio production firms, and transcription producers, or bought from free-lance writers either by contract or as unsolicited scripts.

Therefore, while the network staff writer makes a contribution to daily broadcasting, it is also important to include other writers who are responsible for material heard in network broadcasting.

Job Qualifications. The duties of a radio writer vary greatly. In a network, staff writers fall into two classifications: continuity and news. The continuity writer may be called upon to write almost any type of material, with the exception of news, as the situation demands. The network staff newswriter devotes his time exclusively to writing copy for radio newscasting.

Advertising agencies maintain staffs of writers. In the larger agencies some of the personnel write exclusively for radio, turning out commercials and sometimes connective material for music and variety programs. In the smaller agencies, writing for radio is only part of the copy writer's job. Staff writers for public-service organizations generally work on talks, documentaries, miscellaneous announcements, interviews, and special programs. Often they do not write for radio alone but work on other fields of writing as well.

The written material heard over a network is provided in two other ways: (1) by writers under contract to professional comedians, advertising agencies, radio production firms, or transcription producers for specific programs and (2) by free-lance writers who submit scripts to open-market dramatic series. Contract writers are obligated only to produce the prescribed number and quality of scripts on time. How, when, or where they work is usually of no concern to an employer. Free-lance writers work at their own discretion, the only demand being the production of salable scripts.

No matter what arrangement a writer works under or what type of material he produces, certain basic skills are essential. A radio writer must know the limitations and requirements of the medium thoroughly. As radio is entirely auditory, he can use only three tools: dialogue, music, and sound effects. He must know how to set a scene, describe action, bridge time, establish spatial relationships, portray emotion, and create convincing characterizations without any visual aids. Also, radio has developed distinct script forms and a directive vocabulary peculiar to the medium. A writer must know the proper mechanical details of making up a script in the standard stylized manner acceptable throughout the industry.

Apart from technical and mechanical skills, a radio writer must be as imaginative and creative as a writer in any other field of literature, and most of the time he must be more prolific in producing new material. The transitory nature of radiobroadcasting makes great demands on writers. Any single piece of drama, continuity, or comedy is seldom heard more than once over the air, yet the daily broadcasting schedule goes on as usual. To make a living, a radio writer must be prepared to turn out a constant volume of fresh and original material for there are no long-run engagements and few royalty returns on even the best writing.

News writers must have the general skills necessary to all news reporters. In addition they must have the ability to write news to conform with the special requirements of radiobroadcasting. This means that radio news writers need a special talent for brevity and clarity. Much news is packed into the 5 to 15 minutes usually allotted to a newscast, and each item must be written with exceptional clarity because listeners do not have a chance to reread details that are not immediately understood. Also, a news writer is required to adapt material to the special abilities and style of individual announcers.

The best training and experience for radio writing is writing. It is helpful to have a background in all forms of narrative literature. If a writer has the ability to write good short stories and plays, it is comparatively easy to learn the special techniques of radio writing. These techniques can be learned in radio-writing schools, courses offered by colleges and universities, participation in community workshops, or from a number of excellent books available on the subject. However, contact with some form of instruction group gives the new writer the opportunity of hearing his work produced by casts of live actors under real or simulated studio conditions. It is extremely helpful to get the "feel" of aural writing by some kind of production experience.

It is almost impossible to obtain a staff position, either with a network or agency, without some evidence of radio experience such as the free-lance sale of scripts, or at least part-time writing at a small station. Occasionally people enter radio writing from acting, directing, advertising, or newspaper work.

Before a news writer can obtain a place in a network newsroom he should have had at least 5 years of experience in writing news. People who have had the most experience in writing for radio have the advantage. Work on college newspapers, participation in educational groups, and the study of journalism may be counted as experience in some cases.

In the specialized field of writing advertising commercials, the emphasis lies more in merchandising ability, selling experience, advertising background, and the knack of turning out the type of prose currently popular for selling products over the air.

Employment Policies. At a network station, staff continuity writers are hired by the head of the program department, and news writers are usually under the jurisdiction of the head of public affairs. In an advertising agency the person in charge of hiring new employees varies with the size and organization of the agency, but an interview with the copy chief is usually correct for an initial step.

The opportunity for advancement in a staff job is very limited. There are only two rungs on the ladder in the continuity department: junior and senior positions. The more lucrative and spectacular carreers are in the free-lance and contract fields.

Competitive Factor. There is some turnover of writing personnel because the contract and free-lance fields offer higher remuneration, but it is quite moderate. Staff writers are assured reasonable continuity of employment; free-lance and contract writers are relatively insecure. The business of a network or large agency is a continuing business, and a writer is given successive assignments; but in the free-lance field the employment contract is for a particular job and may terminate with the conclusion of the program.

Salary Scales. Contracts with the Radio Writers Guild (RWG) govern salary scales for staff writers in most network stations. The average compensation for continuity writers ranges from $75 a week for junior writers to $110 for senior writers. News writers receive approximately the same scale of wages. A few continuity writers draw additional compensation from commercial programs.

Contract writing is regarded as the "big money" field. Fees paid for unit plays, series, and "gag" continuity range up to four figures per week.

The position of the free-lance writer has become more profitable in recent years since the RWG negotiated a minimum basic agreement with most of the networks. This agreement establishes fees ranging from the low of $45 for a single 15-minute script on a regional sustaining broadcast to the highest minimum of $250 for a single half-hour script. A similar agreement with the agencies and other independent program producers is presently pending. Competition is keen in this field, and it is not easy to place scripts.

The competitive factor is clearly shown by the annual earnings of the membership of the western region of the RWG for 1947. The figures in the following table are based on the quarterly report made in connection with the payment of Guild dues.

Los Angeles Local of the Radio Writers Guild

(January, 1948)

Number of Writers	Receiving an Income of
172	Less than $ 2,000
172	$ 2,000 to $ 5,000
25	$ 5,000 to $ 6,000
25	$ 6,000 to $ 7,000
20	$ 7,500 to $10,000
50	$10,000 to $20,000
50	$20,000 to $30,000
5	Over $30,000

Union Requirements. Most professional radio writers belong to the RWG. Almost all networks and stations have a union shop of continuity writers and news writers. The only requirement for active membership in the Guild is the authorship of two paid-for broadcast scripts, regardless of length.

Radio Sales. An important field of radio employment is prescribed by the functions and responsibilities of the sales department. The sales division of a network comprises the network sales department and the local and spot sales department. The first is responsible for time sales to national advertisers, and the second handles local business carried by the network stations. In addition, some networks include a sales traffic, a sales service, and a sales promotion department. Sales service, however, is akin to sales, and all sales personnel have some responsibility for the servicing of accounts.

The qualifications for radio selling are those which pertain to effective salesmanship in general, but the seller of broadcast time handles a particularized and highly competitive commodity which must be geared to the specific needs of his clientele. A radio program is an advertising device to sell goods. In order to sell goods, the sponsor must reach prospective customers. Where are these customers? When can they be reached? How can their interest be established and maintained? What will the program cost? These are some questions the salesman must be prepared to answer. He must know markets, radio listening habits, the relative strength of program ideas, and promotion techniques. If the program is bought by the sponsor, the salesman then becomes a liaison agent between sponsor and network or station. He may have to confer with as many as nine different departments to see that the account is properly serviced. Program and production details, promotion methods, press relation, traffic arrangements, and accounting credits are all a part of his concern. He has sold the sponsor; he must now keep him sold and at the end of the contract persuade him to renew it. Thus, the radio salesman must be familiar with many phases of radio business and operational procedure. His training may be secured in connection with newspapers, general sales work, and more specifically in the operation of the small radio station.

Considering the dollar volume of business carried by the radio networks, the number of salesmen employees is very small. Approximately 100 representatives handle all the network time sales for the four major chains. The limited number of local and spot salesmen is indicated by the fact that KNX, the CBS key station in Los Angeles, employs only four station salesmen and one spot salesman. Competition for these sales jobs is sharp, and employment turnover in this area is very small. The future development of FM, world-wide short wave, and television broadcasting may provide larger opportunities for radio salesmen.

Salaries for sales personnel are among the highest in the broadcasting industry. Network representatives are seldom paid on a commission basis owing to intricate accounting difficulties, but local and spot salesmen are paid a commission plus salary. Naturally, compensation scales vary according to the size, locale, and importance of the station.

Salaries for network salesmen are among the best in the radiobroadcasting industry. Table 15 of the FCC publication, *Statistics of the Communication Industry in the United States*, 1945, lists the average weekly compensation for 165 outside salesmen of four nation-wide networks and their 10 key stations as $139.22 per week. Five regional networks averaged $109.73 per week. It may be assumed that these average figures are greatly increased in the instances of particular individuals servicing key stations in particular locales.

Union Requirements. Salesmen are not unionized, but their duties call for a familiarity with the union requirements of other types of radiobroadcasting jobs.

Engineering Division. The engineering division of a network is headed by a chief engineer who is in charge of all purchases, installation, operation, research, maintenance, and repair of the technical equipment of the network station. Under him are a large number of skilled technicians who are directly responsible for getting the program from the microphone to the loud-speaker in the individual radio set. In network broadcasting, the process of technical transmission of a program breaks up into many different phases, with personnel typically specializing in one or more types of engineering work. Commonly the division of duties is as follows: (1) studio engineers, (2) field engineers, (3) master control engineers, (4) transmitter engineers, (5) maintenance engineers, (6) research engineers, (7) transmission engineers, and (8) recording and transcription engineers. While the duties and specific qualifications for each of these types of engineers differ, employment policies, competitive factors, and salary scales are similar.

1. *Studio Engineers.* In the operating schedule of a network station every program broadcast is assigned a radio engineer to carry out certain technical duties in connection with that program. Those engineers assigned to handle programs originating in the studios of the station are called "studio engineers." They perform their duties for the most part in control rooms of the studios and are the only engineers who have an actual physical association with the programs in the studios.

The demands placed on the studio engineer vary depending upon the complexity of the program, but whether it is a 1-minute news announcement or a full hour of drama, the studio engineer, in the final analysis, is primarily responsible for the same things. His duties include the checking and placement of all microphonic equipment used on the broadcast, and the making of suggestions for correcting any acoustical defects or obtaining any desired acoustical effects. During rehearsals and while the program is on the air, he opens the microphones as they are needed, mixes the output currents of each, and closes them when they are no longer required. He also, when necessary, blends the microphones, balancing the orchestra, sound effects, and voices. The studio engineer is responsible for controlling the over-all volume from his studio, watching a volume-indicator meter, and adjusting the volume to keep it within required limits. This process is commonly called "riding gain" and may be defined as " . . . the maintenance of a program's proper volume: loud enough to be heard plainly on the air and yet not so loud as to destroy the fidelity of its reproduction."[9]

The studio engineer must follow every move of a program, being thoroughly cognizant of its technical requirements from its initial rehearsal to its completed presentation. The requirements for his job are more general and inclusive than some other types of engineering positions. First, he must possess an adequate technical knowledge of radio, including radio engineering and acoustics. The essentials of program production and radio showmanship should be familiar to him. He must be able to make fast judgments because problems periodically crop up in rehearsals and during broadcasts which require instantaneous decisions. The constant mental pressure of the job demands a calm temperament. Close association with artists, salesmen, announcers, producers, sponsors, and executives requires a pleasing personality with consummate forbearance and tact. As he handles all types of programs from symphony or jazz musicals to large cast plays and single speakers, he is helped in his job by a knowledge of music, drama, and voice. J. L. Hornung lists the qualifications for the studio engineer as follows:[10]

(a) Knowledge of drama
(b) Knowledge of music and musical instruments
(c) Voice and dynamics of speech
(d) Audio engineering and its applications
(e) Acoustics and acoustic principles
(f) Recording principles
(g) Radio engineering and its principles
(h) Experience
(i) A pleasant personality

In addition to the above general qualifications, network stations usually require that all studio engineers possess either a first- or second-

---

[9] J. S. Hayes and J. J. Gardner, *Both Sides of the Microphone*, p. 84, J. B. Lippincott Company, Philadelphia, 1938.
[10] J. L. Hornung, *Radio as a Career*, pp. 90–91, Funk & Wagnalls Company, New York, 1940.

class radiotelephone operator's license. The majority of men hired have a first-class license.

2. *Field Engineers.* All radio broadcasts do not originate in station studios. Football announcers have a 50-yard-line seat at football contests. Special-events programs originate where the action is taking place. Programs of dance music originate with orchestras playing in hotel restaurants, night clubs, or dance halls. Whenever a broadcast originates outside the main studios, a field engineer is needed to install, operate, and dismantle the broadcasting equipment used. His duties are similar to those of a studio engineer. He needs practically the same background and training as the studio engineer plus the ability to listen to a program and judge its quality through earphones instead of the loud-speakers found in studios. The nature of the job also demands more training in telephone engineering, Morse code, and radio engineering. This is particularly true if he handles a large number of special or single broadcast pickups.

In some large stations, studio engineers and field engineers are segregated. More commonly no distinction is made, engineering personnel being drafted for either type of job as the situation demands.

3. *Master Control Engineers.* "The master control room of a broadcasting station is a clearing house for all programs which are broadcast, produced, recorded, auditioned, received or conveyed through and by the station."[11] Here the sequence of programs from different studios, remote pickups, and other stations is switched along proper line channels. The process is somewhat as follows:[12]

When one program ends—say, in one of the local studios—it will be followed by another program from a different location which may be another local studio, a temporary "nemo" pick-up point, or a network studio hundreds of miles distant.

To execute these changes rapidly and smoothly, so that listeners are not annoyed by abrupt changes from one program to the next or by long awkward pauses between, semi-automatic switching equipment is used. The control-room engineer has in front of him a switchboard with several score push-button keys and signal lights. This board is called the master control desk and looks somewhat like an oversized organ console. It is frequently called the "nerve center of broadcasting" (although some people who try to operate it prefer the name "nervous center").

By pressing certain keys, the control engineer starts a chain of automatic magnetic-switch operations which disconnect and reconnect until all circuits are properly set up for the next program. The signal lights "report" back to him the progress of events, and one final light indicates completion of the switch.

[11] Hayes and Gardner, *op. cit.,* p. 86.
[12] Judith C. Waller, *Radio: The Fifth Estate,* p. 374, Houghton Mifflin Company, Boston. Courtesy of the publisher.

The entire operation has required about one second, and everything is in readiness for the next program to start.

The work of a master control engineer reaches its peak immediately before and after every program. The majority of programs are of 15 minutes duration; as longer shows have frequent station breaks, this peak comes practically every quarter-hour.

The master control engineer must be absolutely familiar with his own station and its facilities, as well as with all network member stations and the complete technical setup which connects them on the master control board. Since the master control engineer works under tremendous pressure, he must have a stable personality. He often listens to three or four programs simultaneously and is expected instantly to pick out flaws which may occur in any one of them.

4. *Transmitter Engineers.* The basic duties of a transmitter engineer are the maintenance and operation of the technical equipment used to transmit the station's programs. He usually:[13]

1. Places transmitter in operation
2. Adjusts volume and tone of programs during broadcast
3. Maintains transmitter and associated equipment
4. Shuts down transmitter at close of broadcast

FCC regulations require that a licensed radio operator must be in charge of the transmitter at all times while it is in operation. Licenses for operators are granted by the FCC and are issued upon the successful completion of a written and performance examination which must be taken at any one of several Commission offices located throughout the country. This examination is highly technical and is designed to test the applicant's knowledge of the care and operation of the transmitter and broadcasting transmission laws and codes. The qualifications for such positions have been set up by Radio Corporation of America Communications as follows:[14]

1. Foresight, judgment, resourcefulness, industry, and cooperation
2. Knowledge of radio engineering and associated branches of electrical engineering and detailed knowledge of plant he supervises
3. Knowledge of radio laws and regulations and possession of a radio telegraph and/or a radio telephone operator's license.

The job of transmitter operator is a responsible, yet routine one. It demands little of the imagination and diplomacy required of a studio or master control engineer. Though great care is taken for the safety

[13] *The Job of the Radio Operator,* Occupational Briefs, Brief No. 77, p. 1, Industrial Service Division, Government Printing Office, Washington, D.C.
[14] Waldo Abbot, *Handbook of Broadcasting,* 2d ed., p. 326, McGraw-Hill Book Company, Inc., New York, 1941.

of personnel because of the high voltages employed, it is more dangerous than other types of radio engineering jobs.

5. *Maintenance Engineers.* Maintenance engineers have been called the "trouble shooters" of the radio station. Radiobroadcasting equipment is extremely delicate and ever subject to wear and breakdown. Playing a vital role in the technical performance of any network station are the men who service its equipment. On a moment's notice they must be prepared to hunt out and correct any mechanical failure which may occur in the complex maze of amplifiers, volume indicators, electric switches, batteries, clocks, and all the other pieces of intricate radio equipment. Furthermore, " . . . good maintenance, like good doctoring, requires the ability not only to locate and fix troubles after they occur, but to anticipate them and make repairs before the failure happens."[15] A large part of the maintenance engineer's job is to make numerous routine tests on all apparatus at regular intervals, and replace any weak or defective pieces of equipment.[16]

. . . the radio maintenance engineer is the man who fixes the machine which does not run when the button is pushed. In radio studios the "machine" consists of many electronic and other devices, from amplifiers to storage batteries. To be able to handle any situation, the maintenance engineer must be a combination general repairman, radio operator, chemist, mechanical engineer, electrical engineer, radio trouble-shooter, telephone man, electrician, and mechanic. In addition, he must be a sort of "technical detective," anticipating when the machine threatens to stop and fixing it before it does.

The essential requirements for this type of engineering job are sound technical knowledge plus training in radio and telephone repair. The maintenance engineer must also be deft with tools and know the various instruments and intricate little mechanisms used in broadcasting.

6. *Research and Development Engineers.* Research constantly goes on in the radio station's laboratories to develop newer and more efficient methods of transmitting its programs to the listener. The group of men most directly concerned with this phase of radio engineering are commonly called "research and development engineers." This highly specialized phase of radio engineering calls for excellent qualifications in technical knowledge and background.

7. *Transmission Engineers.* Large networks such as NBC, CBS, and ABC usually include the job of transmission engineer.[17]

The transmission engineer's job is to keep the studio and control-room equipment in adjustment, so that the program currents from microphones to amplifiers are maintained at their proper values and so that no distortion

[15] Waller, *op. cit.*, p. 391.
[16] *Ibid.*, p. 392.
[17] *Ibid.*, p. 384.

occurs. He also tests the wire lines which carry the programs from point to point in the studios and control room, from the field or nemo pick-ups to the control room and from the control room to the transmitter. In other words, he is constantly measuring and testing to keep the quality of transmission through all the lines and equipment up to the high standards required.

This job is closely akin to that of maintenance engineer with similar qualifications and skills.

8. *Recording and Transcription Engineers.* Another classification of engineering personnel frequently listed in large networks is the "recording and transcription" engineer. Transcriptions of programs are manufactured on special recording equipment. The person who operates this equipment is called the recording engineer.[18]

Recording and transcription engineers (the first man makes the recording, and the second plays it) require the background and training of studio engineers. Whether they record the program or play the transcription matters little. If the engineer is a capable studio operator, he is a capable recording or transcription engineer.

These eight classifications comprise the major engineering jobs found in the radio network station. While it has been evidenced that qualifications for the radiobroadcasting engineer are determined in part by the specific type of engineering job he performs, it should be recognized that certain qualifications apply to all radio engineers. Engineering divisions do not operate as mutually exclusive units. Personnel is frequently interchanged. Each division interlocks and dovetails with the others, working rather as one cog in a considerably larger wheel. The broader and more flexible a person's abilities, the more apt he is to find a starting position in this "wheel," and the more likely he is to advance to higher positions.

Employment Policies. Network engineering personnel are hired by the head of the engineering department directly from the radio engineer's union hall. If the union does not have a qualified man available, the head of the engineering department can select an individual not affiliated with the union. However, the person chosen for the job must become a member within 90 days after employment. All newly employed technicians are considered to be on a probationary basis for that time. If retained after 90 days, the technicians enjoy all the rights and privileges of a regular technician.

Competitive Factor. Radio engineering is one of the most stable positions in the entire employment scale. The number of replacements is very small. This has been a matter of disappointment to many veterans

---

[18] Hayes and Gardner, *op. cit.*, p. 94.

who were trained in the broad field of electronics and who hoped to find in the radio field a demand for their services.

Salary Scales. Minimum salaries for network radio engineers are set by the International Brotherhood of Electrical Workers. The following table shows the weekly pay scale as listed by the union's Los Angeles Local, No. 45.[19]

Pay Scales for Radiobroadcasting Technicians

Length of Employment	Weekly Wage Rate
3 months	$ 62.50
3 months to 1 year	67.50
1 to 2 years	77.50
2 to 3 years	87.50
3 to 4 years	97.50
4 to 5 years	110.00
5 years or more	125.00
Assistant supervisors	143.50
Supervisors	150.50

NOTES: Work for all technicians shall be 40 hours within 5 work days. Work in excess of work week shall be paid for at overtime rates of time and one-half.

Work day is 8 consecutive hours, exclusive of assigned meal period. Each technician shall be granted 2 consecutive days off each week.

Technicians shall be allowed 12 hours rest between completion of any one day's tour of duty and beginning of next day's tour of duty. Technicians will be paid $1.50 for each hour worked prior to the completion of a given rest period.

Part-time work is in proportion to above scale.

Radio-engineering personnel sometimes receive compensation in addition to the above union scale in the form of bonuses from individual sponsors or advertising agencies.

Union Requirements. There are four unions covering radio technicians: National Association of Broadcast Technicians, American Communications Association, International Alliance of Theatrical Stage Employees, and International Brotherhood of Electrical Workers, Radio Division. The last represents the majority of network radio technicians.

Public-affairs Division. The public-affairs division is a grouping of several departments: promotion, press information or publicity, education, public service, guest relations, news, special events. Each has specific duties, but they function collectively to publicize the network—its services, programs, and performers—create good will on the part of its listening clients, promote effective station relations, and provide for studio and program visitors. Personnel in the departments are under the supervision of the director of public relations.

The job promotion is to make the public conscious of services and values, to win acceptance, and to expand public clientele. A radio station or network sells a service. Its life blood is sales. The volume of sales

[19] *Union Agreement,* CBS International Brotherhood of Electrical Workers, Radio Division, Local No. 45.

is in proportion to audiences range and size. Why do people listen to one station rather than to another? It is because they believe that that outlet will furnish them most consistently with the best information, entertainment, and talent. A broadcasting station is concerned with "winning friends," and this is the job of promotion. Witness the various slogans adopted by radio stations which tend to create the impression that they are the most powerful, the first in public service, and the most blessed with good will. But prestige cannot be attained, and certainly not sustained, by this type of suggestion. "Influencing behavior" is a day-to-day business requiring the most adroit application of selling principles. Moreover, the station is not only concerned with the consumer or listener but derives its sustenance from the sponsors who buy time. These advertisers, too, must be persuaded that X station offers the best facilities for promoting the distribution and sale of the client's product; advertising agencies must be convinced; and civic organizations, clubs, and associations duly impressed. All this is a major part of promotion.

There are many specific kinds of work required to achieve promotion objectives. Direct mail advertising, the preparation and dissemination of bulletins, pamphlets, brochures, program schedules, special announcements; advertising in newspapers, magazines, and trade publications; direct air advertising—telling the station's story by means of its own primary medium, broadcasting itself; the formulation of special campaigns; contacts with selected groups, such as schools and civic organizations. The promotion department aids the sales staff by preparing maps showing network coverage, checking audience listening response, preparing program reports, and even by suggesting sales ideas.

Specific skills requisite to public-affairs employment depend, of course, on the particular type of service required of the employee. Research workers should be grounded in investigatory techniques, methodological formula, statistical procedures. The majority of promotion jobs call for writing ability and an understanding of advertising techniques and principles. To these skills must be added a knowledge of network or station objectives as they apply particularly to sales and programing. Previous training that may serve as a preparation for this field of employment is often found in general advertising, journalism, and art design. Small-station experience may also be a valuable prerequisite. There is no union for promotion of personnel although some employees belong to the International Office Worker's Union. It is therefore difficult to state minimum salary scales for this type of work, and this difficulty is increased by the fact that the jobs available in the public-affairs division of a network range from simple types of clerical or office work to skilled promotion executives.

This general statement in regard to the public-affairs division as a whole may be amplified by a brief exposition concerning some of its subdivisions.

Press Information (Press Agents). The press information department provides material for newspapers, magazines, and other publications which issue news and program bulletins. Its aim is to publicize radio as an entertainment medium by supplying data about the station, its activities, and its artists. The leading trade publications are *Broadcasting and Broadcasting Advertising, Radio Daily, Advertising Age, Tide, The Advertiser, Billboard, Variety,* and *Motion Picture Daily.* Such fan magazines as *Radio Mirror, Tune-In,* and *Radio-Television Life* are not neglected. This department prepares the network's daily information bulletin which is distributed to all affiliated stations as well as to newspapers and magazines. It deals especially with personal data about performers and new programs. These articles often feature picture material produced by the staff photographers.

Qualifications for press information personnel center around the ability to write interesting news copy and feature material. The press agent's previous experience has usually been in journalism. A college education is preferred as an additional prerequisite, particularly if the applicant has had college training in journalism. A background derived from other broadcasting industry jobs is not essential although familiarity with network operations, particularly programing, is necessary.

Press information personnel are hired by the head of the press information department.

Positions in this area are more open to the radiobroadcasting initiate than most of the jobs previously discussed. It is quite a general policy to select young people who can be trained for the work.

Compensation for press-agent jobs is very high. Turnover is small and the number of job openings is small. CBS maintains only 12 employees in their western division office to handle written publicity. Ten of these are press agents, one a secretary, and one a general clerk. Ten persons are employed in the photographic section of the publicity department: one head cameraman, two photographers using Speed Graphic cameras, three

Guild Salary Scales for CBS

Position	Time employed	Compensation per week
Junior press agent	To 6 mo.	$42.50
Intermediate press agent	6 mo. to 1 yr.	57.50
Senior press agent	1 to 1½ yr.	70.00

retouchers, and four clerks. These numbers are significant when it is realized that the bulk of CBS publicity is handled on the West Coast.

Minimum salary scales for press information employees are set by the Screen Publicist Guild, Radio Division. Press agents are under the jurisdiction of the same.

Education and Public-service Personnel. NBC in using the phrase, "public service," has attempted to coin a term that will be more acceptable to the public generally than the word, "education," which seems a little austere and does not connote the type of program that should be amusing, entertaining, or easy to listen to.[20] As suggested by this statement, it is not easy or perhaps logical and desirable to distinguish between public-service programs and educational programs. It is for this reason that the same personnel may be concerned with both so-called public-service and educational broadcasting.

The responsibility for public-service operations rests specifically with the director of education and public service. His duties relate to the selection, evaluation, and acceptance of program ideas and program content which merit consideration under the heading, Public Service. Civic, educational, and religious organizations wishing to speak to the public through the medium of sustaining programs will work through him. The position requires a person of broad education, endowed with personal qualities of tact and a friendly ease with a wide clientele. Although he may have efficient and trained assistants, he should be familiar himself with program techniques and be able to forecast the probable favorable reception of the broadcasts sponsored under his direction. In other words, he should be able to apply the criteria of effective, radio showmanship to the script and its production, and know how to blend entertainment of interest value with information, to stimulate to desired action without being stodgy or drab. In brief, he will be well acquainted with broadcasting techniques, radio writing, network organization, station function and policy.

The director of education and public service is engaged by the general manager of the network division. The position is one of the few administrative posts open to women. Competition is very high, and turnover is exceptional. There are no union requirements for the job.

Special-events Personnel. The job of director of special events is closely allied with that of the position just discussed and some networks include it under the public-affairs division. Special events comprise particular occasions which have significant social, dramatic, or educational value. Dedications, conventions, anniversary commemorations, catastrophes and emergencies, political debates, and important "openings" may be listed under this heading.

[20] Waller, *op. cit.*, p. 171.

The director of special events must have a wide knowledge of the techniques of radiobroadcasting, possess imagination and showmanship, be able to write and produce continuity when necessary, and in some instances participate in a broadcast as announcer, narrator, or actor. These abilities are developed during apprenticeship years in which the elements of his craftsmanship are acquired through experience. Special-events operations often utilize regular staff announcers and engineers, but the overall responsibility falls on the shoulders of one man. He will probably be affiliated with the AFRA, the RWG, and the Radio Directors Guild.

Guest and Audience Relations. Practically every employee is a "front man" and is directly or indirectly responsible for selling good will, but the guest and audience relations division or department is set up specifically to achieve this objective. The department includes receptionists, ushers, pages, stage setup men, ticket and information-desk attendants. Receptionists receive and route callers to the proper offices; ushers guide visitors to studios or conduct building tours; pages deliver important messages or direct artists to specific and assigned locations; stage setup men prepare commercial exhibits for studio lobbies and stage backgrounds and provide required stage props; ticket and information clerks distribute tickets and answer inquiries.

Guest and audience relations employees are selected by the director of personnel on the basis of personal qualities which evidence an ability to meet and deal successfully with the public. Such elements as physical appearance, courteous demeanor, and pleasing voice are important characteristics. A college education is not a requisite but is usually preferred. No previous broadcasting experience is required, but it is usually understood that the person employed in one of these positions has an ambition to progress in the industry. In fact many people now employed in the positions of broadcast responsibility found public-relations work a good steppingstone. There is a good deal of competition in this area and at the same time a considerable turnover. This is due to the fact that unless the employee can soon climb from his steppingstone to a higher one he becomes discouraged and seeks new employment.

Salaries on the whole are quite low, especially when viewed in relation to the education and personal qualities of the personnel employed. CBS pays receptionists, ticket and information clerks $35 to $45 a week. Ushers receive $1 per show (limited to a maximum of 20 shows per week). Stage setup men are paid an average base wage of $35.

Guest and audience relations employees are unionized only in certain geographical areas. Where they are unionized, the jurisdictional union is the AFL, Office Employees International Union.

Station Relations Division (Traffic). If you will look at a United States map on which are drawn lines indicating the possible interradio station connections of a national network, and then consider the smoothness with which continuous broadcasting takes place 24 hours a day, it will be obvious that there is a traffic problem more complicated than an automobile jam at Fifth and Broadway on New Year's Eve. Confusion, delay, and conflict would be inevitable unless stop-and-go signals were properly posted and precise instructions given and obeyed. An almost infinite number of program parcels must be fitted in a close time sequence to make the daily broadcast pattern. The picture is not unlike a huge jigsaw puzzle, but it is a puzzle constantly changing its basic design. The work of the traffic department is to effect smooth station and program integration. A complete network may involve hundreds of stations, but seldom does every member station release the same program or at the same period of time. Commercial programs go to those stations best qualified to serve a sales campaign. Sustaining programs are not, in most instances, obligatory upon affiliates and may be replaced by local sustaining or commercial broadcasts.

The routing and release of programs to specified stations and the pickup of programs from various points of origin are jobs for "traffic." The work performed by this department calls for meticulous and constant attention, and the amount of logs, records, and memoranda is voluminous. Orders for temporary telephone circuits must be placed, operational information sent to telephone companies, affiliated stations advised of network programs, the beginning and termination of commercial contracts noted, detailed records kept of commercial and sustaining programs handled by the affiliates, and "certifications of performance" sent to advertising agencies handling the sponsors' accounts specifying that the required stations have or have not fulfilled the exact terms of their contracts. The volume of communications effected largely by teletype and amplified by mail and telegraph reaches astounding proportions. "Approximately 125,000 thirty-word messages pass through the communications office of NBC each month, which is comparable to the telegraph traffic of a good-sized city."[21]

Much of the traffic department's work depends on skilled clerical help, but traffic employees are usually well versed in network policies, association, network and station codes, and Federal regulations.

Prerequisite experience for "traffic" varies a good deal, and employees may receive most or all of their training after arriving on the job, but previous experience in radio programing and salesmanship may be very helpful. The majority of employees are women chosen on the basis of

[21] *Ibid.,* p. 360.

general qualifications and experience in network operations. Frequently, personnel are appointed to jobs in traffic from other divisions in the network, usually from a less skilled clerical or secretarial position. The top jobs, of course, are highly complicated and require years of experience in broadcast operations including sales and promotion. The association of the traffic and the engineering departments is very close. Sometimes personnel from engineering will perform traffic duties, but the progression is more often from traffic to engineering than vice versa.

The number of responsible and well-paid positions in traffic is small, and the competition for top placement is high. Inconsistent, though it may seem, the turnover in this area is relatively more than in some other divisions inasmuch as traffic operation is good training and background for other network positions, particularly nonperformance jobs such as sales and programing.

Salaries for traffic personnel vary with the importance of the job performed. The manager's salary is comparable to that of other department heads, and the majority of traffic employees are paid on a scale similar to that of clerical (office management) personnel. There are no union requirements for traffic employees.

Office Management Division. The volume of network business requires a large force to handle the routine matters common to any large commercial organization. The work, performed, of course, is peculiar to radiobroadcasting management. The division includes secretaries, stenographers, script typists, mail clerks, and general clerical help. Private secretaries perform ordinary secretarial work and in some cases fulfill functions which require knowledge of broadcasting operations. (Some secretaries act as junior executives or subdepartment heads. Network training and experience are required in these instances.) Script typists prepare the many copies of program scripts needed by professional personnel. Mail clerks handle the volume of incoming, outgoing, and interoffice mail.

Qualifications for these jobs are standard. Private secretaries and stenographers must be able to take shorthand and type proficiently. Script typists should be able to type accurately at a speed of approximately 65 words per minute, and mail clerks and general clerical help are expected to be intelligent enough to handle more or less routine jobs.

Office employees are hired by the director of personnel, and the general hiring procedure parallels the employment considerations applied to guest and audience relations employees except that more stress is necessarily laid on secretarial skills. Some office jobs offer opportunities to learn network operations and the skills incident to other positions in the organization. It is for this reason that the director of personnel receives applications from young men and women who hope that the office management lane will lead them to the royal road. Competition for office staff positions is not so great as in other areas owing to the fact that there are more positions to be maintained.

Except for the small number of private secretaries who act as sub-department heads, the salary scale for office workers ranges between $30 and $45 per week.

Office management personnel, in general, are not unionized although they may be affiliated with the AFL, Office Employees International Union.

For convenient reference, the foregoing discussion is tabulated in parallel summary in the following. The information in column 4, how-ever, must necessarily be interpreted with some latitude because com-pensation standards vary considerably from year to year, particularly during the history of an inflated economy.

Our analysis of network organization and the vocational aspects of net-work employment does not answer certain questions which the reader is asking. What about the opportunities in the small station? Isn't it true that small-station experience is necessary before one can break in with a key network station?

A differentiation of the so-called small station and the network station should be made clear. According to a "FCC Box Score," published in *Radiobroadcasting*, Apr. 10, 1950, there were 2,118 AM licensed standard broadcasting stations in the United States. Approximately half of these are affiliated with the four major networks. Only a few of them, however, are owned by the networks. The CBS chain includes 173 stations, but Columbia owns only 7; NBC broadcasts over 164 member units, but National owns only 6; Mutual owns no stations but operates entirely through contractual relations with independents. This means that about 50 per cent of AM stations in the United States are not related to network broadcasting. They build their programs to meet local com-munity interests, relying on an inexpensive formula of recorded "popular music, news, and sports." A definition of the small station cannot be based on the difference between its affiliation or nonaffiliation, although the popular concept and definition of the small station would probably apply to nonaffiliates only. In so far as the affiliated station and its operation can be considered in terms of autonomous and purely local functions, we would classify it as a small station.

The organization of small stations varies greatly. Some of them maintain departmental structures, and some are practically solo oper-ations. In general, however, the organization of the independent station embraces five departments: executive and administrative, program, sales, technical, and news. There will be various degrees of overlapping among these five divisions, and one department may be charged with dual

Summary of Job Opportunities and Requirements in the Network

Qualifications	Employment policies	Competitive factor	Salary scales	Union requirements
1. General manager				
Executive leadership. Thorough knowledge of nature of broadcasting and broadcasting policies, government regulations, codes. Years of experience.	Appointed by the board of directors or president of network.	Almost nonexistent. Jobs fixed with few changes.	Exact figures not obtainable but salaries presumed to be very high.	None.
2. Department heads				
Thorough knowledge of skills and techniques of jobs in his department. General knowledge of station organization. Executive ability.	Selected by general manager or other top executives of network. Usually advanced from job in department he heads.	Similar to that of general manager. Turnover greater—men going to advertising agencies, and general managers of small radio stations.	Known only to officials of network and employee. Presumed to be high.	Usually belongs to union covering his personnel.
3. Production directors				
Artistic judgment and interpretation. Knowledge of music, acting, and understanding of technical problems and limitations of medium. Background in drama and literature. Leadership, assurance, imagination, and creative ability.	Hired by advertising agencies and networks on basis of reputation and experience.	Highly coveted position. Limited number of jobs available. Assignments vary but actual turnover of personnel small.	Minimum scale $85 a week for staff personnel. Top men receive $125 to $150 a week. Free-lance men range from $200 to $500 a week or more.	Radio Directors Guild, union shop limited to production directors and assistant production directors.

4. Assistant directors

Knowledge of policies of station, FCC regulations, NAB codes, and Federal and state laws applicable to radio. Needs diplomacy and common sense. Duty to see that network programs comply with above regulations.	Hired by program manager in conjunction with general manager. Job frequently used to test relatively inexperienced personnel for advancement to higher positions.	Affords good opportunity for training and experience and contacts so finds much competition. Turnover to higher jobs fairly rapid.	Minimum scale $72.50 a week. Bonuses sometimes received from sponsors.	Radio Directors Guild.

5. Announcers

Pleasing voice and personality, salesmanship. Adaptability of speaking manner. Familiarity with all elements of programming. Some technical knowledge of microphones. Knowledge of musical and foreign terms and names. Small-station experience usually demanded. College liberal arts education desirable.	Staff announcers hired by chief announcer or program director. Free-lance announcers hired by production directors of individual programs. Selection based on reputation and/or voice audition.	Highly competitive. Large number of small-station announcers seek network positions, but turnover of personnel small.	Minimum scale set by union contract. Staff minimum $85 a week; average approximately $100 a week. Free-lance scale varies from $50 to $300 for single half-hour show.	Must be members of AFRA.

6. Actors

Ability to read lines interpretatively. Versatility of characterization. Ability to project action by means of voice. Ability to double and do dialects. Knowledge of microphone techniques and radio sign language.	Normally hired by production director of specific program or series. No network staff actors. Selection based on auditions and reputation. Directors have tendency to rely on a few known personnel.	Popularity of job makes competition extremely great. Allied fields furnish many actors for top roles.	Salary scales based on minimum rates established by union. Earnings of some high. Average annual pay of majority low.	Actors performing on network shows must be members of AFRA.

Summary of Job Opportunities and Requirements in the Network. (Continued)

Qualifications	Employment policies	Competitive factor	Salary scales	Union requirements
7. Musicians				
Technical musical skill and training. Versatility. Uniqueness of style an aid to soloists. Radiobroadcasting background also advantageous.	Complicated by numerous union regulations, but generally employed by musical director of station or orchestra manager.	Extremely keen because of high pay and large number of applicants for few positions.	Minimum union scale for staff musicians $115 a week for 4-hr. day. Commercial shows vary in rate according to coverage.	Must be members of AFM
8. Sound technicians				
Creative imagination, dramatic understanding, and auditory imagery. Manual dexterity. Knowledge of program production in general desired.	Hired by the head of the sound-effects department. Personnel frequently selected from other positions in network.	Number of men employed limited so competition is high.	Minimum wage scales determined by contract between network and union. Pay varies according to seniority. Not highly paid field.	Sound technicians are members of AFRA.
9. Writers				
Creative writing ability. Skill in specific type of writing—dramatic, continuity, news, commercials. Must know limitations and requirements of medium. Must know mechanical details of making up a script. Previous writing experience demanded.	Staff continuity writer personnel employed by head of program department. News writers hired by head of public affairs or head of news department. Free-lance writers sell to advertising agencies, network stations, or individual production directors.	Applications for staff positions greatly exceed demand. Free-lance field also highly competitive.	Ranges from $75 a week for junior writers to $110 a week for senior writers. Free-lance payments vary from $42 to $1,500 depending on type, length, and coverage.	Represented by RWG.

10. Salesmen

Familiarity with nearly every phase of radiobroadcasting. Training in sales, sales promotion, and advertising best preparation for job. Networks typically require previous experience in radio selling.	Hired by sales manager. A few chosen from within network on ability in other jobs and suitability for work. Majority come from selling jobs in small stations.	Number employed extremely small for volume of business handled. Turnover limited.	Salaries vary, but typically among highest in industry for nonexecutive positions.	No union requirements although duties call for familiarity with union requirements of other jobs.

11. Engineers

Vary with specific type of engineer but all must possess thorough technical training. Studio engineers must be familiar with production techniques. 1st- or 2d-class radiotelephone operator's license needed. Foresight and resourcefulness called for.	Hired by head of engineering department directly from union hall. New employees serve 90-day probationary period.	Relatively large number of men needed but turnover of personnel extremely limited. Competition, therefore, high.	Minimum wages set by union. Varies with length of employment from $62.50 a week at 3 months to $125 a week at 5 or more years. Supervisors paid additionally. Bonuses from sponsors sometimes received.	Four unions covering radio technicians but majority of contracts with International Brotherhood of Electrical Workers, Radio Division.

12. Promotion personnel

Understanding of advertising principles and techniques. Writing ability. Creative advertising imagination. Familiarity with network operations. Part of work clerical and does not call for special training.	Hired by head of promotion department and/or director of personnel. Offers good opportunities for learning business aspects of radiobroadcasting.	Number of employee turnover higher in some jobs, for it is popular training for novice radio workers.	More skilled promotion men may earn $100 to $250 or more a week. Many in job paid comparably to office management workers.	None.

Summary of Job Opportunities and Requirements in the Network. (Continued)

Qualifications	Employment policies	Competitive factor	Salary scales	Union requirements
13. Press information personnel				
Ability to write news copy and feature material. Experience in journalism demanded. College graduates preferred.	Hired by head of press information department. Majority have done professional writing of some type prior to employment by network. Policy to train some young people in work.	Number of applications received very high. CBS's western division receives 12 per week. Turnover small.	Minimum wages set by union: Junior press agents, $42.50 a week. Intermediate, $57.50 a week. Senior, $70 a week. Photographers, $100 to $150 a week.	Employees are members of Screen Publicist's Guild, Radio Division.
14. Education and public-service personnel				
Familiarity with educational and service organizations and civic bodies. Pleasant personality, tact, even temperament. Knowledge of programing and station organization.	Hired by general manager. Position carries high prestige and often filled by a woman.	Determined by turnover, usually rare so competition keen. One of few administrative jobs open to women.	Prestige of individual governs salary level.	None.
15. Special-events personnel				
Combination of abilities of production director, writer, and announcer. Must be able to ad-lib proficiently. Knowledge of techniques and operations of broadcasting.	Hired by general manager. Position carries high prestige and usually filled by man of high reputation.	Job often utilizes staff announcers but responsibility rests with one man, so competition almost nonexistent.	Set by general manager and varies with network and man.	Usually a member of AFRA.

16. Guest and audience relations personnel

No previous broadcasting experience required. Pleasant personality and appearance. Strong interest in field and desire to progress. College education desirable.	Hired by director of personnel on basis of application and personal interview.	High when considering low salaries paid, but serves as steppingstone to higher jobs. Turnover heavy.	Low for caliber of people employed. Wages range from $20 to $45 a week.	Not unionized at most networks. CBS employees affiliated with AFL, Office Employees International Union.

17. Traffic personnel

Largely clerical. Calls for knowledge of network policies, NAB codes, and government regulations. A few jobs highly skilled, requiring knowledge of sales and programing.	Selected by head of traffic department with director of personnel. Frequently chosen from other network jobs.	High competition for top jobs. Less exciting work than most radio jobs so competition not so keen for lower positions.	Vary with importance of job. Traffic manager's pay comparable to department heads. Most wages similar to that of clerical personnel.	None.

18. Office management personnel

Largely secretarial. Must be able to type 60 to 70 words a minute. No previous radio experience demanded. Private secretaries must be able to take shorthand.	Hired by director of personnel on basis of application and interview. Stress placed on secretarial skill.	Along with guest and audience relations personnel the major inlets to network, so relatively competitive.	Range between $30 and $45 a week. Starting salaries may be lower. Private secretaries may be paid more than above.	Not unionized in most stations. CBS employees affiliated with the AFL, Office Employees International Union.

responsibility. Paralleling in part the more extended analysis of network operations, let us take a look at a small station as a vocational medium.

The office of general manager combines several duties. He is responsible to the station owner and board of directors for the profitable conduct of the business. He may make decisions on program schedules and direct or supervise sales. This position normally calls for considerable experience in various aspects of practical broadcast operations. On the basis of his experience and reputation in the radio field, the manager is employed by the station owner. Because the position of general manager is the highest to be found in small-station operation, it is widely sought by qualified people, and competition is acute. Managerships change hands rather frequently, however, because the area of employment, nationally speaking, is wide and because almost any small-station manager would consider a network assignment a favorable promotion.

Salary scales for general managers vary according to station size and location and according to personal ability. An NAB report in 1946, *Eight Management Surveys of Small Market Stations throughout the United States,* listed the average compensation for the eight stations named as $8,400 a year. An FCC report in 1945, covering 852 stations, listed the average compensation paid general managers as $160.01 a week.

The independent's program structure is very simple. With a few exceptions there are no elaborate musical, dramatic, or studio audience shows. Commercial ends can be satisfied in the main by recorded program material and run-of-the-mill teletype news reporting. Sustaining programs, produced allegedly in the public interest, may be limited to interviews, talks by "distinguished" citizens, remotes, and some dramatic and children's programs arranged and produced by outside agencies. There is no need for a large staff of producers, directors, announcers, actors, musicians, sound technicians, and writers. There must be sufficient announcing personnel to keep the program schedule running, to play records, to make spot announcements and necessary introductions. There must be an engineering crew to operate the transmitter, to maintain and operate studio equipment, and to function as needed at the mixing panels. Salesmen must be relied on to bring in new accounts and keep old ones. These three essential groups are expanded as the over-all business of the station dictates.

The work of the announcer in the small station is more varied than in the network or fully organized independent outlet. Announcing may be combined with such tasks as continuity preparation, the playing of records, control panel operation, and he may even help with publicity and sales. This is to his advantage and leads to a versatility and knowledge that will aid his advancement. General qualifications are substantially the same as those specified above for the network announcer. The applicant to the small station may be expected to have had some training and experience in a college or private radio school. A liberal arts college education, with an emphasis on speech and dramatics, may be valuable. Announcers in the independent stations are employed by the general manager on the basis of interview, audition, on the applicant's personality and background. While audition tests vary a great deal, the employer will consider factors of appearance, personality, and education. He will also wish to satisfy himself concerning the aspirant's voice and speech, reading ability, and general interpretative skill. Competition for announcing positions is very high when compared with other types of radio jobs. A single example is illustrative. When station KWIK in Burbank, Calif., was established in 1947, over 200 announcers were auditioned. The majority of them had had some previous experience. Only 50 were judged as "acceptable," 25 were "more than acceptable," 10 were "excellent." Six men were hired, and five of these had worked previously as announcers for major networks. In 1948, KWIK received approximately six applications a week for announcing positions. Burbank is in a large metropolitan area, one of the broadcasting centers of the United States, and these figures are not typical of the small station, but they are probably relative. The dark side of the competitive picture is lightened somewhat by the fact that the small stations hire more announcers than any other single type of personnel. The Industrial Service Division of the U.S. Employment Service stated in 1947 that in their opinion the number of positions available in small stations would be increased by the growth of television and FM broadcasting.

Compensation for the small-station announcer varies with the station. The average man can expect a salary ranging from $35 to $60 per week. If station personnel are members of the AFRA, the weekly earnings are slightly higher than the average small-station scale. AFRA minimum pay rates for local staff announcers vary according to the class of the station, upon its coverage or power, and are established by individual station contract. Salary scales range from $85 per week in small local stations. Small-station announcers may or may not be members of AFRA, depending on the station policy.

The sales department of a typical small station comprises a sales manager, head or executive, and three salesmen. In some cases the number of salesmen is greater, and in others the sales manager may operate without assistance. Sales revenue is derived from services rendered to the network, national spot advertising, and local or direct sales to community sponsors. The skills requisite to radio selling are fundamentally the same in all locations although the problem varies in complexity according to the nature of contracts, the character of the program, the relationship to agencies, and the production problems. Salesmen in the small stations are usually hired by the general manager, sometimes by the sales manager. The choice of applicants is based on experience and suitability for the work. The number of salesmen engaged is small, and the turnover is not very large. However, the qualified person with ideas and new approaches to selling the station's product has a good chance of finding a job. Salesmen are paid for the most part on a commission basis, but some may receive a straight salary only, or a salary plus a commission. Average earnings are among the highest in the small-station organization. There are no union requirements for radio salesmen.

The duties of the engineering department consist of studio operation and transmitter operation. The chief engineer may be responsible for the building and maintenance of equipment. If the station is a 24-hour station and if it handles a large number of remote pickups and perhaps operates a mobile transmitter, the size of the engineering staff is correspondingly enlarged. The duty of the studio engineer is to maintain and operate studio equipment. The transmitter engineer cares for the transmitter. Engineering personnel must be familiar with the rules and regulations issued by the FCC and see that the station is operated to comply with these regulations. A licensed radiotelephone operator (first class) must be on duty at all times when the station is on the air. Most engineers possess this license which has become one of the primary qualifications of the technician.

The engineer in the small station may do more than perform technical work. He may, indeed, serve as announcer, spin platters, and assume public-relations responsibility by meeting visitors and helping to put them at ease during their broadcasts. Since capacity for radio engineering requires a long period of technical training, the competition for technical jobs is not so high as in other departments. The turnover, though, is relatively small because the training, skill, and know-how which the engineer possesses can be utilized in many allied or accessory branches of the radio field. Radio-engineering salaries are not so high as the required job preparation would indicate. The NAB survey of eight small stations indicated an average salary of $42 per week for technicians and $57 for chief engineers. These figures are larger for stations in metropolitan areas. The union which covers this employment branch is the International Brotherhood of Electrical Workers, Radio Division.

The radio news editor in the small station is not primarily a reporter. It is his duty to take the information that comes in from the wire services such as Press Association, Associated Press, United Press, and

Summary of Job Opportunities and Requirements in the Small Radio Station

Qualifications	Employment policies	Competitive factor	Salary scales	Union requirements
1. General managers				
Executive ability. Thorough knowledge of broadcasting operations and regulations. Familiarity with all jobs in station. Years of experience.	Hired by ownership of station on basis of reputation and training. May or may not be stockholder or owner.	While not comparable to network, competition high. Sought by both small-station employees and network employees.	Vary with the station size and prestige of man. Average can be estimated around $8,500 a year.	None.
2. Announcers				
In degree same as for network. Must be versatile. Previous professional experience not demanded if sufficiently qualified to meet standards of station.	Hired by general manager on basis of audition and background. Policy of some stations to hire combination announcers and engineers.	Small-station field large but popularity of job and training opportunities make job much sought.	Vary with station. Average individual can expect $35 to $60 a week.	Some small stations have contracts with AFRA.
3. Salesmen				
Same as for network; more frequently called on to write client's advertising copy.	Hired by general manager, sometimes in conjunction with sales manager. Based on individual's background and suitability.	Qualified man has good chance for employment though numbers demanded not high. Turnover low.	May be paid on commission or salary, or both. Earnings typically vary between $300 and $400 a month or more.	None.
4. Engineers				
Technical knowledge. 1st- or 2d-class radio operator's license. Knowledge of FCC technical rules and regulations. Frequently need announcing ability.	Hired by general manager in conjunction with chief engineer. Based on background and training.	Not so high as some other types of jobs. Turnover relatively high. Men leave for networks or allied field.	Low considering training demanded. Average approximately $40 a week.	Some stations are covered by the International Brotherhood of Electrical Workers.
5. News editors				
News editing and general news writing skill. Occasionally announcing.	Hired by general manager on basis of background and experience.	Rural areas offer good chances for employment.	Averages between $50 and $60 a week.	None.

Station Personnel Survey

Location: South
Power: 250 watts
Network: Yes

Total number employees—14
Full-time—11
Part-time—3

Department and personnel	Duties	Sex M	Sex F	Age	Length of employment	Total years radio experience	Education H.S.	Education Coll.	Pay
Executive Dept.:									
General manager	Executive responsibility	X		33	6 yr.	18			$10,000 yr.
Bookkeeper	Keeps accounts		X	41	3 yr.	3	X		$25 wk.
Program Dept.:									
Prod. manager	Programs, copy, auditions, announcers, music, library, traffic recordings	X		28	4 yr.	4		X (degree)	$45 wk.
Continuity writer A	Routine writing, steno work		X	20	6 mo.	½			$33 wk.
Continuity writer B	Writing and traffic		X	20	6 mo.	½			$33 wk.
Announcer A	Also music librarian	X		25	8 mo.	1½		Part	$35 wk.
Announcer B	Also special-events director	X		26	7 mo.	1		Part	$37.50 wk.
Announcer C	Sports announcing	X		24	9 mo.	1¼		Part	$40 wk.
News Dept.:									
News editor	Handles all news	X		20	3 mo.	1			$47.50 wk.
Sales Dept.:									
Sales manager	Also asst. gen. mgr.	X		32	4 yr.	4			$7,042 yr.
Technical Dept.:									
Chief engineer	Participates in public service	X		30	6 mo.	15		2 yr.	$60 wk.
2d-class oper.	Routine technical duties	X		25	6 mo.	1	X		$40 wk.
Operator A	Runs board	X		17	1 yr.	1	Std.		$15 wk.
Operator B	Runs board	X		18	1 yr.	1	Std.		$15 wk.

Source: *Eight Management Surveys of Small Market Stations throughout the United States*, a report made at the direction of Small Stations Committee of the NAB, National Association of Broadcasters, Washington, D.C., 1946.

Station Personnel Survey

Location: Middle West
Power: 250 watts
Network: NBC Supplementary

Total number employees—14
Full-time—12
Part-time—0

Department and personnel	Duties	Sex M	Sex F	Age	Length of employ-ment	Total years radio experi-ence	Education H.S.	Education Coll.	Pay
Executive Dept.:									
General manager	Absolute responsibility for station operation	X		30	2½ yr.	12	..	3 yr.	$5,200 yr.
Office manager	Sec. to gen. mgr., purchasing agent; writes continuity		X	25	2½ yr.	2½	..	2 yr.	$40 wk.
Program Dept.:									
Program manager	Responsible for all programing. Director special events; writes local news copy; holds school for announcers	X		31	3 mo.	6	..	X	$50 wk.
Announcer A	Announces; handles electrical transcriptions; keeps program chart; writes continuity	X		28	3 yr.	5	::	X	$42.50 wk.
Announcer B	Announces, special-events continuity	X		23	2 yr.	3	X	..	$37.50 wk.
Announcer C	Announces; staff pianist; continuity	X		24	6 mo.	3½	..	2 yr.	$35 wk.
Sales Dept.:									
Sales manager	Handles local sales; continuity chief, play-by-play sports; football, baseball, etc.	X		35	2½ yr.	8	..	X	$57.50 wk.
Technical Dept.:									
Chief engineer	1st-class ticket	X		37	2½ yr.	16	X	..	$57.50 wk.
Operator A	1st-class ticket	X		37	2 yr.	3	X	..	$40 wk.
Operator B	1st-class ticket	X		47	1 yr.	17	..	X	$40 wk.
Operator C	2d-class ticket	X		26	1½ yr.	1½	X	..	$42.50 wk.
Traffic Dept.:									
Traffic clerk	Responsible for all traffic continuity types		X	20	1 yr.	1	X	..	$32.50 wk.

Source: *Eight Management Surveys of Small Market Stations throughout the United States*, a report made at the direction of Small Stations Committee of the NAB, National Association of Broadcasters, Washington, D.C., 1946.

Station Personnel Survey

Total number employees—18
Full-time—17
Part-time—1

Location: Southeast
Power: 250 watts
Network: Yes

Department and personnel	Duties	Sex M	Sex F	Age	Length of employment	Total years radio experience	Education H.S.	Education Coll.	Pay
Executive Dept.:									
General manager	Responsible for station operation	X		37	6 yr.	20		3 yr.	$7,500 yr.
Sales Dept.:									
Sales manager	Sales and bookkeeping	X		33	5 yr.	5	X		$3,000 yr.
Salesman	Sales service	X		31	3 yr.	3	X		$1,920 yr.
Program Dept.:									
Production manager	Program supervision, part-time announcing	X		27	5 yr.	8	X		$2,160 yr.
Continuity chief	In charge of all copy. Asst. to prod. mgr.	X		26	3 yr.	3		X	$1,920 yr.
Traffic manager	Full-time devoted to traffic; bills accounts		X	24	4 yr.	4	X		$1,420 yr.
Continuity writer A			X	27	2 yr.	2	X		$1,320 yr.
Continuity writer B			X	22	1 yr.	1	X		$1,320 yr.
Announcer A		X		24	5 yr.	5			$1,920 yr.
Announcer B		X		27	4 yr.	4			$1,800 yr.
Announcer C		X		20	6 mo.	½		In coll.	$1,420 yr.
Announcer D	Also types affidavits schedules		X	23	5 yr.	5	X		$1,680 yr.
Receptionist			X	22	3 yr.	3	X		$1,320 yr.
Music director	Music librarian; sings; piano		X	26	2 yr.	2	X		$1,320 yr.
Technical Dept.:									
Chief engineer		X		42	15½ yr.	15½			$2,160 yr.
1st-class oper. A		X		31	6 yr.	6			$1,920 yr.
1st-class oper. B		X		27	4 yr.	4			$1,800 yr.
3d-class oper. C		X		27	1 yr.	1			$520 yr.

SOURCE: *Eight Management Surveys of Small Market Stations throughout the United States*, a report made at the direction of Small Stations Committee of the NAB, National Association of Broadcasters, Washington, D.C., 1946.

Station Personnel Survey

Location: Middle West
Power: 250 watts
Network: Yes

Total number employees—19
Full-time—17
Part-time—2

Department and personnel	Duties	Sex M	Sex F	Age	Length of employment	Total radio experience	Education H.S.	Education Coll.	Pay
Executive Dept.:									
Owner-manager	Head of all departments	X		45	5 yr.	5 yr.		X	$9,724 yr.
Assistant manager	In charge of all operations except sales promotion and finance; former chief engineer	X		27	5 yr.	5 yr.	X		$3,840 yr.
Sec. to owner	Also handles traffic		X	18	1 yr.	1 yr.	X		$1,425 yr.
Bookkeeper	Bookkeeping only duty		X	32	7 mo.	7 mo.	X		$1,855 yr.
Clerk	Typing, filing		X	18	5 mo.	5 mo.			$725 yr.
Program Dept.:									
Program manager	Does not perform actual duties of title, owner does. Assigned to develop public interest programs	X		35	5 yr.	5½ yr.		1 yr.	$2,385 yr.
Asst. program mgr.	Also women's editor; prepares and broadcasts all women's shows; handles accounts		X	37	5 yr.	5 yr.		X	$2,700 yr.
News editor	Edits, reports, writes, broadcasts. 60-hr. work week	X		25	1½ yr.	1½ yr.		X	$2,700 yr.
Music director	Selects music, electrical transcriptions, live talent, announces	X		28	10 mo.	10 mo.		X	$1,825 yr.
Continuity editor	Assigns accounts, checks copy, 30 hr. per wk. Announces 18 hr.	X		32	4 mo.	4 mo.		X	$2,385 yr.
Announcer	Announces 18 hr. per wk., 30 hr. on sales promotion; sells evenings on 15% commission	X		30	13 mo.	13 mo.	X		
Director of education	Now vacant. Formerly handled all school and university contacts; coached station dramatic club		X	26	2 yr.	2 yr.		X	$2,130 yr.

Station Personnel Survey

Total number employees—19
Full-time—17
Part-time—2

Location: Middle West. (Continued)
Power: 250 watts
Network: Yes

Department and personnel	Duties	Sex M	Sex F	Age	Length of employment	Total radio experience	Education H.S.	Education Coll.	Pay
Sales Dept.:									
Salesman A	Sales and service	X		47	5 yr.	5 yr.	...	X	$4,600 yr.
Salesman B	Sales and service	X		36	1 yr.	1 yr.	X	...	$3,480 yr.
Technical Dept.:									
Chief engineer	Supervises bldg. and ground; helps asst. mgr.	X		33	2 yr.	3 yr.	X	...	$3,010 yr.
1st-class oper.	48-hr. week	X		26	1 yr.	1 yr.	X	...	$2,080 yr.
3d-class oper.	48-hr. week	X		30	13 mo.	13 mo.	X	...	$2,086 yr.
3d-class oper.	Replaced by 1st-class man	X		24	7 mo.	7 mo.	X	...	$2,068 yr.
3d-class oper.	High-school senior who operates 8 hr. Sat. and Sun.	X		17	2 yr.	2 yr.	Sr.	...	60¢ hr.
Buildings & grounds	5 days work as janitor; Janitor, works Sat.	X		16	6 mo.	6 mo.	Jr.	...	40¢ hr.

SOURCE: *Eight Management Surveys of Small Market Stations throughout the United States*, a report made at the direction of Small Stations Committee of the NAB, National Association of Broadcasters, Washington, D.C., 1946.

Station Personnel Survey

Location: Southwest
Power: 1,000 watts
Network: Member of regional network fed by ABC and MBS

Total number employees—7
Full-time—7
Part-time—0

Department and personnel	Duties	Sex M	Sex F	Age	Length of employment	Total radio experience	Educ. H.S.	Educ. Coll.	Pay
Executive Dept.:									
Owner-manager	Operating head of all departments	X	..	40	10 yr.	10 yr.	..	X	$1,000 mo.
Secretary	Announces part of 1 day weekly	..	X	25	2 yr.	2 yr.	..	3 yr.	44¢ hr.
Program Dept.:									
Program manager	Owner-manager								
Announcer A	Sells by telephone; writes copy; announces 60 hr. per wk.	X	..	45	3 yr.	6½ yr.	X	....	55¢ hr.
Announcer B	Announces 60 hr. per wk.	X	..	33	5½ mo.	17½ mo.	..	2 yr.	50¢ hr.
Sales Dept.:									
Sales manager	Sales; writes copy; announces 1 newscast a day and commercials on football games	X	..	38	9 mo.	18 mo.	..	Some	$65 wk.
Technical Dept.:									
Chief engineer	Owner-manager, has 1st-class ticket								
Operator A	3d-class ticket, 60–70 hr. per wk.	X	..	22	1 yr.	1 yr.	X	....	40¢ hr.
Operator B	3d-class ticket, 36–40 hr. per wk.	X	..	18	1½ yr.	1½ yr.	..	....	40¢ hr.

SOURCE: *Eight Management Surveys of Small Market Stations throughout the United States*, a report made at the direction of Small Stations Committee of the NAB, National Association of Broadcasters, Washington, D.C., 1946.

Station Personnel Survey

Location: Northeast
Power: 250 watts
Network: ABC basic, supplementary

Total number employees—21
Full-time—19
Part-time—2

Department and personnel	Duties	Sex M	Sex F	Age	Length of employment	Total radio experience	Education H.S.	Education Coll.	Pay
Executive Dept.:									
General manager	Entire responsibility for station's operations	X	..	35	7 yr.	7 yr.	..	X	$8,500 yr.
Secretary	Liaison between gen. mgr. and whole operation; handles payroll	..	X	38	7 yr.	7 yr.	X	.....	$55 wk.
Business manager	Assists gen. mgr.; handles some sales	X	..	33	4 yr.	8 yr.	.	X	$75 wk.
Program Dept.:									
Program manager	Real manager; responsible for traffic	X	..	31	12 yr.	12 yr.	X	.....	$65 wk.
Asst. program manager	General promotion and publicity; ½ hr. daily woman's program	..	X	34	2½ yr.	2½ yr.	X	.....	$32.50 wk.
Announcer A	Special-events announcer	X	..	34	1½ yr.	1½ yr.	..	X	$40 wk.
Announcer B	Announces only	X	..	24	1 yr.	3 yr.	..	X	$35 wk.
Announcer C	Announces only	X	..	30	6 mo.	3 yr.	X	.....	$35 wk.
Announcer D	Announces only	X	..	28	9 mo.	9 mo.	X	.....	$35 wk.
Continuity writer A	Also calls on accounts	..	X	23	2 yr.	2 yr.	X	.....	$32.50 wk.
Continuity writer B	Also calls on accounts	X	..	22	8 mo.	8 mo.	.	Coll std.	90¢ hr.
Sales Dept.:									
Sales manager	Sales	X	..	34	4 yr.	4 yr.	X	.....	$70 wk.
Saleswoman A	Sales	..	X	34	1 yr.	1 yr.	X	.....	$40 wk.
Salesman B	Services Italian accounts; writes program; announces in Italian	X	..	31	8 mo.	8 mo.	.	X	$50 wk.

Station Personnel Survey

Location: Northeast. (Continued)
Power: 250 watts
Network: ABC basic, supplementary

Total number employees—21
Full-time—19
Part-time—2

Department and personnel	Duties	Sex M	Sex F	Age	Length of employment	Total radio experience	Education H.S.	Education Coll.	Pay
Technical Dept.:									
Chief engineer........	....	X		34	4 yr.	12 yr.	X		$75 wk.
Operator A..........	1st-class ticket	X		28	2 yr.	2 yr.	X		$35 wk.
Operator B..........	1st-class ticket	X		23	6 mo.	1½ yr.	X		$35 wk.
Operator C..........	1st-class ticket	X		22	4 mo.	2 yr.	X		$35 wk.
Operator D..........	1st-class ticket	X		20	8 mo.	8 mo.	X		76¢ hr.
General Dept.:									
Bookkeeper.......	Sole duty		X	29	3 yr.	3 yr.	X		$35 wk.
Receptionist.......	Also sec. to sales and programing		X	23	2 yr.	2 yr.	X		$27.50 wk.
News editor A......	....	X		41	3 mo.	6 mo.	X		$75 wk.
News editor B......	....	X		31	3 mo.	....		X	$40 wk.

Source: *Eight Management Surveys of Small Market Stations throughout the United States,* a report made at the direction of Small Stations Committee of the NAB, National Association of Broadcasters, Washington, D.C., 1946.

Station Personnel Survey

Location: Mountain Time Zone
Power: 1,000 watts
Network: MBX Supplementary

Total number employees—11
Full-time—11
Part-time—0

Department and personnel	Duties	Sex M	Sex F	Age	Length of employment	Total radio experience	Education H.S.	Education Coll.	Pay
Executive Dept.:									
Owner-manager	General supervision of entire station; handles public relations, news departments, broadcasts 3–4 news shows daily, 1 commentary show Sun., 2 musicals. Has 1st-class ticket	X	..	38	20 yr.	25	..	..	$90 wk.
Co-owner	Treasurer and office manager	X	..	65	15 yr.	15	..	..	$90 wk.
Program Dept.:									
Program manager	Supervises all programs; handles women's programs; services accounts; does recording	..	X	32	6 yr.	6	X	..	$67.80 wk
Traffic manager	Office secretary; writes some copy and handles traffic	..	X	25	3 yr.	3	X	..	$62.40 wk.
Musical director	Staff organist and music librarian; writes some copy; holds 1st-class ticket	X	..	33	3 mo.	10	..	X	$62.40 wk.
Senior announcer	Announces; holds 1st-class ticket	X	..	40	5 yr.	20	X	..	$62.40 wk.
Announcer A	Announcer; E.T. librarian	X	..	22	6 wk.	3	..	X	$57.20 wk.
Announcer B	Announcer; E.T. librarian	X	..	..	2 mo.	6	..	X	$57.20 wk.
Sales Dept.:									
Sales manager	Sales	X	..	46	2 mo.	5	..	X	$57.20 wk.
Technical Dept.:									
Chief engineer	Does all maintenance; operator part-time	X	..	27	1½ yr.	4	..	X	$75 wk.
Operator	Holds 1st-class ticket	X	..	27	1 mo.	8	X	..	$57.20 wk.

SOURCE: *Eight Management Surveys of Small Market Stations throughout the United States,* a report made at the direction of Small Stations Committee of the NAB, National Association of Broadcasters, Washington, D.C., 1946.

Station Personnel Survey

Total number employees—14
Full-time—13
Part-time—1

Location: Pacific Northeast
Power: 250 watts
Network: MBS Don Lee Supplementary

Department and personnel	Duties	Sex		Age	Length of employment	Total radio experience	Education		Pay
		M	F				H.S.	Coll.	
Executive Dept.:									
President	Over-all responsibility	X		46	19 yr.	20 yr.	X	1 yr.	$875 mo.
President's sec.	Handles correspondence and bookkeeping		X	27	5 yr.	5 yr.	X		$215 mo.
Station manager	Also sales manager	X		41	15 yr.	16 yr.	X		$700 mo.
Secretary-treasurer	Handles payroll	X		43	18 yr.	18 yr.	X		
Program Dept.:									
Program manager	Also chief announcer and continuity chief responsible for traffic	X		43	12 yr.	20 yr.	X		$450 mo.
Announcer A	Announces; writes continuity	X		24	4 yr.	4 yr.	X		$225 mo.
Announcer B	Announces; writes continuity	X		25	4 yr.	4 yr.	X		$187.50 mo.
Announcer C	Chief engineer; some announcing	X		23	3 yr.	6 yr.	X		$275 mo.
Announcer D	Operator A; some announcing	X		34	4 yr.	4 yr.	X		$250 mo.
Announcer E	Operator B; some announcing	X		25	1 mo.	1 mo.			$225 mo.
Traffic manager	Handles all traffic	X		28	6 mo.	6 mo.	X		$200 mo.
Sales Dept.:									
Manager	Sells; services accounts	X							
Salesman A	Sells; services accounts	X		43	2 yr.	2 yr.	X		$275 mo.
Salesman B	Sells; services accounts		X	40	5 yr.	5 yr.	X		$275 mo.
News Dept.:									
News editor	Writes local news; announces 2 daily news programs	X		27	1 yr.	1 yr.	X		$250 mo.
Technical Dept.:									
Chief engineer	Maintenance and operation	X		23	3 yr.	6 yr.	X		$275 mo.
Operator A	40 hr. per wk. on board; announcing	X		34	4 yr.	4 yr.	X		$250 mo.
Operator B	40 hr. per wk. on board; announcing	X		25	1 mo.	1 mo.	X		$225 mo.

SOURCE: *Eight Management Surveys of Small Market Stations throughout the United States*, a report made at the direction of Small Stations Committee of the NAB, National Association of Broadcasters, Washington, D.C., 1946.

International News Service and set it down in an accurate, condensed, vivid, and swiftly moving continuity. He will attempt to acquire an informal and colloquial style. He will be a good judge of news values and be able to write with facility and ease in the medium of auditory journalism. News editors are hired by the general manager of the station. Not many news editors are employed by small stations; therefore, competition is high. The average income of news editors is between $50 and $60 per week. These employees are not obliged to join a union but they are eligible for membership in the RWG.

Traffic operations in most small stations are handled by an office secretary or an individual employed in some other station job. Usually, traffic is assigned to the program or sales office. Although the traffic department is important in small-station operation, it is largely clerical in nature.

The tables, "Summary of Job Opportunities and Requirements in the Small Radio Station" and "Station Personnel Survey" outline the positions and conditions of small-station employment in detail. The former is similar to the tabulations made for network employment. The latter is from a study conducted by the NAB in 1946 and includes data from eight locations in the United States. The salary figures are subject to change today owing to changes within the industry since the survey was made.

QUESTIONS

1. Enumerate the employment classifications inherent in network broadcasting operations.

2. Name seven types of employment embraced by the network program division.

3. Discuss the vocations of radio announcing and radio acting from the standpoint of competition.

4. How are radio engineers classified? Explain their respective duties.

5. What departments are embraced by the public-affairs division?

6. Discuss radio employment from the standpoint of compensation.

7. Compare network and local station employment according to opportunity, types of work, compensation, and continuity of employment.

8. On the basis of the information in this chapter, how would you answer the following questions: How can I get a job in radio? Will a radio job guarantee me continuity of employment? What compensation can I expect?

CHAPTER 8[1]

RADIO TALENT UNIONS

Radio employment is subject to conditions and regulations negotiated by the industry and the various craft organizations. Musicians, actors, announcers, writers, and technical personnel are covered by these agreements. Rates of pay, hours, and working conditions have undergone periodic adjustment and revision since the late thirties. Radio employers have also had to deal with union control over music and literary rights. As early as 1938, the American Society of Composers, Authors, and Publishers (ASCAP) was paid $3,845,206.34 for permission to use copyrighted music, a condition which prompted the NAB to find a new source of program material in a specially created association, Broadcast Music, Inc. On Feb. 12, 1939, the AFRA was awarded a code of minimum terms for actors, singers, and announcers. The minimum quarter-hour pay scale agreed on for actors and announcers was $15; for singers, $40. A new contract was signed a year later granting a 10 per cent increase to artists working on sustaining programs. In 1945, a general increase of 20 per cent was given to actors, singers, and announcers working on commercial programs and to actors and singers employed on sustaining shows. The salaries of sound-effects technicians were boosted from 20 to 30 per cent. Further substantial increases were gained in 1947 and 1950. These contractual changes have been effected through peaceful bargaining and without serious interruption of broadcasting continuity. The periodic demands of ASCAP and AFM, however, have provoked industry resistance involving boycotts, strikes, and court injunctions. In 1940 when AFM wanted a 5 per cent increase in their guarantee, the request was denounced as exorbitant, and under political pressure the demand was dropped. In the same year, ASCAP's insistence on the payment to them of 7½ per cent of network revenue, a battle ensued in which the Association was beaten and forced to settle for rates lower than those in force at the time of their new demands. The order of James C. Petrillo, president of AFM, in 1942, banning the making of transcriptions and phonograph records on the grounds of unfair competition with live musicians, produced a congressional inquiry

[1] For assistance in gathering much of the information in this chapter, the author expresses his appreciation to Evelyn Bell.

(January, 1943), an antitrust action in a Federal court, and a final hearing before the U.S. Supreme Court. The result was a victory for Petrillo and netted his Association members 4 million dollars from royalties assessed against the production and use of phonograph records and transcriptions. A large proportion of this cost was carried by the radio industry. Shortly thereafter, however, Petrillo lost his fight when he sought to enforce another demand that members of his union be hired exclusively to play records ("spin platters") in the radio stations, a job being performed by members of the National Association of Broadcasting Engineers and Technicians. But the aggressive activity of the AFM continued and led to congressional legislation, the Lea Act (Apr. 16, 1946), making certain practices of the union unlawful. Almost immediately Petrillo called a strike against a Chicago station because it refused to employ three additional music librarians. He was upheld by a local tribunal, but the Supreme Court reversed the decision and remanded the case for retrial. At midnight on Dec. 31, 1947, the AFM again threw its full weight. A Petrillo order forbade 195,000 musicians to play for any recording or transcription company and for recorded and transcribed radio shows. (This was the period when the American public became very familiar with "Jeannie with the Light Brown Hair.") The dispute terminated in a compromise settlement, transcription and recording companies agreeing on royalties to be paid into an unemployment fund for musicians.

The above items are sufficient to illustrate the relationship between radio management and the organizations representing its employees. Every field or branch of the entertainment industry has its particular protective agency, and radio employees—performers, technicians, writers, and others—have their guilds, unions, and associations. The two organizations most likely to concern you are the AFRA and the RWG. The radio student should have a knowledge of both organizations. Their structure, aims, and procedures typify the various bargaining agencies designed to protect the radio artist.

AMERICAN FEDERATION OF RADIO ARTISTS (AFRA)

What Is AFRA? AFRA is a collective bargaining agent for wages and working conditions representing actors, singers, announcers, and sound artists.

The unionization of radio actors began in 1937, and in the following year codes were drawn up and submitted to the networks and agencies for ratification. The initial reluctance of the employers to accede to these new employment terms and conditions was successfully overcome, and the codes were signed late in 1938. Eddie Cantor was the first AFRA president. Working conditions as originally established have undergone slight change although pay rates have been substantially increased.

Organization. AFRA was organized to meet adverse employment conditions. Fees paid performers were very small. Not only did actors receive as little as $5 or $7.50 for a single performance, but rehearsal time was unlimited and calls could be canceled without obligation to those engaged. Actors were not paid for audition programs or programs produced as a speculation. Rehearsal days or times could be changed without notice. Breaks during rehearsals were of indefinite length, but the actors were told to "stand by."

Structure. The national organization comprises three major locals—New York, Chicago, and Los Angeles—and about 30 smaller locals. Its work is directed by a president, five vice-presidents, an executive secretary, and a board of directors to which each local elects members according to the size of the local chapter. The national membership is approximately 30,000.

The local organization as exemplified by the Los Angeles chapter is headed by a president, four vice-presidents, and a board of directors composed of six actors, four announcers, and one singer. The office staff includes an executive secretary, three field supervisors, and several office secretaries. The present membership of the Los Angeles local is about 2,700 members: 1,700 actors, 400 announcers, 550 singers, 50 commentators, writers, and emcees.

AFRA is not an employment agency and does not secure jobs for its members.

Qualifications and Conditions Pertaining to Membership

1. Membership is open to any qualified person—anyone who speaks, acts, or sings professionally over the air.

2. One is qualified when he has had one paid performance on the air.

3. A nonmember, if engaged for a performance, may secure a clearance for that one performance, but subsequent employment is forbidden until union membership is effected.

4. The nonmember may be engaged to work as many as four sustaining programs, provided he applies for and receives work permits. The fees for these permits range from $5 to $7.50, but the total amount may be applied to the initiation fee when the performer becomes a member of AFRA.

5. Persons appearing on round-table discussions or public-service programs, or persons "outstanding in another field appearing as themselves on any type of show," may make one appearance in a year without having to join the union.

6. As long as he keeps his dues paid and adheres to codes and regulations, one retains his membership. A member may be granted an honorable withdrawal from the union if he leaves the profession by giving notice to AFRA in writing of his intention. He is eligible to become active again without a second initiation fee. However, if he returns at the end of 6 months, he must pay dues for two quarters. After an absence of 18 months, he may be reinstated upon the payment of the current quarter dues.

Cost. The initiation fee in most locals is $50. Dues are based on the income derived solely from radio employement during the previous year.

Up to $ 2,000	....	$ 24
5,000	....	36
10,000	....	48
20,000	....	60
50,000	....	72
Over 50,000	....	100

Disciplines or Penalties. Infraction of AFRA codes or regulations is subject to disciplinary action ranging from fines and penalties to expulsion. Infraction by members include lateness, absence, insubordination, misconduct, failure to report infractions by producers, to sign claim sheets, or to report auditions. For such infractions the member may be brought before the board for a hearing which may result in fines, suspension, expulsion, or other disciplinary measures if the charges are sustained.

Objectives. The union's objectives are to procure reasonable and fair working conditions and adequate compensations for performance in the radiobroadcasting industry. With personnel supply much greater than job availability, all kinds of exploitation would result without the protection of a strong bargaining agent. AFRA ensures standard practices in auditions, engagements, rehearsals, broadcasts, and transcription work. It enforces air practice codes and prevents producers from deviating from equitable employment procedures. These objectives are stated as follows in the AFRA constitution:

We . . . hereby constitute ourselves a voluntary association to advance, foster, promote and benefit all those connected with performances in radio as actors, singers, announcers . . . all . . . persons who sing, speak, act . . . or create sound effects . . . : to protect their professional activities; to secure proper legislation upon matters affecting their professions; . . . to prevent and abolish abuses . . . ; to assist such persons in securing just and equitable contracts, agreements, working conditions, and minimum compensation in their dealings with their employers, agents, managers, impressarios, and others connected directly or indirectly with the radio business; . . . and to take united action to abolish any unfair dealings or abuses or other conditions which are detrimental to persons engaged in the said profession; . . .

Gains for Its Members. AFRA has succeeded in obtaining standard contracts which run for 2 years and are then renegotiated, minimum wages, and fair working conditions. Comprehensive contracts cover every phase of broadcasting: commercial network, regional and local; sustaining network, regional and local; rebroadcasts; transcriptions; auditions; dramatized commercials; dramatized news broadcasts; rehearsal fees for various classifications of shows. Each type of performer—actor, announcer, singer, sound-effects man—has an individual schedule of minimum wages.

Minimum Fees. Performers' fees range from $10 to $100 according to air coverage and the commercial aspects of the program. Payment is also made for rehearsal time. The complete schedule of fees is complex and comprehensive.

Audition Programs. Program auditions are paid for at half the basic fee with full rehearsal fee.

Doubling. Doubling may be permitted on commercial, sustaining, and transcribed programs if the actor plays only one additional part. If he is required to play more than one part in addition to his principal role, he is entitled to another full fee at the standard commercial rate. Under no circumstances, however, may a performer double in another category without an additional fee; that is, he cannot double as an announcer and as an actor, or as an actor and singer.

Air Credit. On programs longer than 15 minutes, identifiable billing must be given leads not in excess of two. On 15-minute programs, identifiable billings must be given leads not in excess of two at least once weekly. Billing may be deleted in the event of contingencies occurring during the broadcast, at the producer's discretion, but subject to arbitration if AFRA does not consider the contingency justifiable.

Special Services. 1. An important service rendered by the union to its members may be called, *grievance investigation.* AFRA is the place of appeal for all grievances claimed by its members. There are about six levels of appeal in the organization. A member would first place his complaint with his local head supervisor. If the supervisor's efforts are unsuccessful, the local executive secretary attempts a conciliation, and in the event of another failure the matter is brought before the local board of directors; if it reaches a deadlock in negotiations there, it may be turned over to the American Arbitration Association. In cases of jurisdictional disputes, the final level of authority is the International Board of Associated Actors and Artists of America. When an actor's claim is justified, the union makes every attempt to attain redress quickly and peaceably by direct contact with the producer. If this fails, the union is prepared to file claims with the American Arbitration Association or fight cases through the courts. AFRA members are notified and instructed not to accept work from him until further notice. Failure to observe the non-work ruling results in disciplinary action against the offending member. Although a national strike has never been carried out, there have been instances of strike action against local stations.

2. *Contract Supervision.* All members are urged to submit all contracts to the AFRA office before signing. This is primarily to protect the actor in two ways: (1) there may be unfair options or services, or a

number of other unfair provisions that the AFRA staff is trained to detect. (2) Records may be kept of approved or disapproved contracts if deemed necessary.

3. *Claim Sheets.* The AFRA office makes files and claim sheets on every broadcast program, audition, or transcription. These claim sheets record the name of the show or transcription, all the details of the call, any overtime that occurs, and a list of all performers engaged on the program with the amount of the fee due each individual being paid scale, or a notation—over scale. Claim sheets are kept on file in the AFRA office for a number of years and are considered authoritative in any disputes over payments. These claim sheets have proved their worth many times and are invaluable in substantiating claims that are brought against an employer some time after the actual broadcast of a program. Fair settlements of contract terms are generally reached quickly in individual performer cases because of the complete and accurate system of AFRA records.

4. *News Publications.* AFRA clientele is served with a monthly publication of trade news and information of interest to radio performers, union activities, a list of programs combined with pertinent information concerning producers, directors, networks, and agencies. It gives information about new shows coming on the air, those being canceled, changes in program policies, activities of members, television news, and special information such as lists of unfair producers.

AFRA exerts a constant vigil with reference to employment practices in order to protect its membership. The union stands firmly on the premise that producers shall not consider actors as pieces of property, and members who may not possess sufficient individual bargaining power are protected from signing inequitable contracts.

AFRA and Television. With the sudden mushrooming of television, the problem of union jurisdiction and control became a very complex one. The AFRA, the Screen Actors Guild (SAG) and the Screen Extra Guild (SEG) were involved in serious dispute. SAG and SEG took the stand that their unions, respectively, should represent television performers. They based their claim on the fact that TV was making general use of films and was apparently dependent thereon. AFRA, on the other hand, contended that TV shows involved many radio elements, that in many instances entire radio shows with practically no change in format or cast were televised, and that working and employment situations in TV were, in general, more comparable to radio practices than to those in the movie industry. In most cases, AFRA pointed out, employers were the same advertising agencies and radio networks that its union had been negotiating with since its inception. However, AFRA conceded that TV was a new and individual industry in which jurisdiction cut across pre-

Financial Agreements With Major Networks

Number of lines	Length of show, minutes	Pay	Rehearsal hours	Pay for each extra hour
		Actors with lines		
Five or more.......	15	$ 70	5	$5
	30	125	12	5
	60	170	22	5
Less than 5........	15	50	4	5
	30	62.50	6	5
	60	75	9	5
		Walk-ons and extras		
	15	$ 20	3	$3
	30	35	6	3
	60	45	9	3

SPECIALITY ACTS

	Pay	Acts
Single performer.........................	$200	6 in 2 days, one day being broadcast day
Two performers...........................	275	
Three performers.........................	375	
Four performers..........................	475	
Each additional person over four...........	100	

SPORTSCASTERS

	Pay per event	Weekly pay (seven events)
Class A contests:		
Play-by-play announcing.....................	$200	$550
Assistant play-by-play reports.................	125	350
Minor sports:		
Play by play...............................	100	225

rogatives claimed by various agencies, and expressed willingness to join Actors Equity, Chorus Equity, American Guild of Variety Artists, and the American Guild of Musical Artists in establishing an individual and separate agency in television called Television Authority. This proposal, at first, was unacceptable to SAG and SEG, and they refused to cooperate and insisted on retaining complete jurisdiction over their members, film components of television, and programs consisting entirely of films. Accordingly, they forbade their members to work with other union members and attempted to force all performers desiring work in television to become members of SAG and SEG. AFRA persisted in working for an amicable and acceptable agreement. The continuing discussion resulted in the formation of the Television Authority (TA) in December of 1949, representing the American Guild of Variety Artists, the American Guild of Musical Artists, Actors and Chorus Equity Associations, and AFRA. Eleven months later, TA was successful in effecting agreements with the four major networks. Some of the financial terms agreed on are shown in the table on page 173.

Live signature numbers and company announcements, termed in the trade as "cutters," "hitchhikers," and "cowcatchers," receive $40 including dress rehearsal and $50 for brief sponsor announcements.

Summary. AFRA has done much to unify and standardize employment conditions in the radio industry. Show business, at its best, has always been competitive and insecure. Radio with its transitory quality, a grist mill of dramatic material, its one-shot shows, and consequent turnover, was at one time a perfect stage for exploitation. Not only was competition keen, but jobs were short-lived. There were no long-term contracts for the average actor. With the organization of AFRA and the negotiations of standard minimum-wage rates, with the establishment of favorable rehearsal conditions and call regulations, and with the protection of actors' rights concerning cancelations and auditions, considerable stability was given to the radio industry. The sale of talent was raised to a more dignified and professional basis, and better talent was attracted to radiobroadcasting. Because of well-defined responsibilities on the part of both producers and performers, the artistic and creative levels of radio are higher than they would be without such regulation. AFRA has been a stabilizing and beneficial influence in the radiobroadcasting industry.

RADIO WRITERS GUILD (RWG)

What Is RWG? It is a collective bargaining agency representing staff and free-lance professional writers in the field of radio. It is a member guild of the Authors' League of America, Inc., as are the Authors' Guild, the Dramatists Guild, and the Screen Writers Guild. RWG was established in 1939.

Structural Organization. There are three regional groups—eastern, middle-western, and western—with headquarters, respectively, in New York, Chicago, and Los Angeles. The national officers comprise a president and three vice-presidents, one from each regional group. There is a national council composed of 30 active members, 10 from each of the regionals.

A writer is eligible when he has had two scripts purchased and broadcast within 12 months prior to his application. No minimum length is prescribed for these scripts. Any broadcast dialogue which is paid for, no matter how short, will qualify the member for acceptance. A writer who has had one script broadcast within 12 months prior to his application is eligible for associate membership. This script need not be paid for. Community or college programs broadcast over local or campus facilities are acceptable.

Membership is designated as executive and regular. An executive member is one who consistently employs other writers or acts as purchasing agent to buy the work of other writers. All others are classed as regular members.

Associate members do not have voting privileges but receive all other services of the Guild. They must apply for active membership upon the sale of qualifying scripts.

Members in good standing of other Authors' League Guilds may request transfer to RWG with no initiation fee.

Cost. The initiation fee for active members is $10; for associate members, $8. Minimum dues are $5 quarterly. Associate members pay only the flat rate of $8, but active members are assessed on a sliding scale according to their income derived from the sale of scripts. This scale ranges from $7 for those making from $500 to $750, to $56 for those whose income is over $12,500.

Membership Tenure. Members retain permanent tenure and good standing by the regular payment of dues. They may request honorable withdrawal in writing. Dues do not accumulate. The reinstatement fee is $5.

Objectives. RWG has several objectives. According to its constitution it strives to "promote fair dealing and to cultivate and maintain cordial relations, unity of action, and understanding among the members of the Guild, and between them and their employers." The union tries to improve conditions of employment and correct abuses to which members may be subjected. It attempts equitable adjustment of all work disputes and protects the rights and property of its members. Finally, RWG establishes and enforces minimum contracts covering wages, hours, and working conditions. In addition to employee-employer relationships, the Guild has consistently upheld the position that radio exists to serve the public interest—a position that correlates with the basic philosophy of the FCC as set forth in the Commission's *Blue Book*.

How Does the Guild Work to Secure Its Ends? In attempting to effect just compromises between writers, the agency depends on peaceful negotiations with networks, agencies, and packagers. However, there is a provision in the RWG constitution that obligates all members, upon a two-thirds vote of active members and consent from the Authors' League Council, to refrain from working for, or disposing of radio or television material to, any specified employer in the radio industry. Negotiations have almost led to extreme measures in two instances, but there has never been a nation-wide strike. RWG has been supported in its negotiations by the other three league guilds. There have been instances of alleged unfairness to writers by individual producers—various tricks of pirating scripts or program ideas, violation of contracts, nonpayment of fees, and other injustices. In these cases, the Guild, if it deems necessary prints the names of such producers on an unfair list in its monthly bulletin sent to members, and this is usually sufficient to correct the alleged abuse or practice.

Does RWG Represent Both Staff and Free-lance Writers? RWG has negotiated contracts for staff continuity and news writers since 1941, and represents them in collective bargaining with networks, stations, and any other type of employer. On Oct. 31, 1947, a contract was signed with the four major networks establishing minimum script fees and ownership rights for free-lance writers. This agreement, subject to periodic renegotiation, extends to May 15, 1954. Ninety per cent of the free-lance writers were covered by this minimum basic agreement. The details of writers' contract agreements are comprehensive, but the general principle involved is important. This principle establishes the writer's ownership and control over his material. There was a time when the author was forced to abandon all claims to ownership after receiving a flat purchase price. His material could then be reused without further payment or payments, sold for use in the movies, television, anthologies, on the stage, or in any other way without further financial benefit to the author.

Special Services. *Publications.* Members of RWG receive the *Authors' League Bulletin* (published by the Authors' League) which contains articles of interest to writers, market digests, lists of managers in good standing, and other important information. Each regional office edits a monthly bulletin of Guild activity news, market information, local and regional events. The eastern region publishes the *Script Writer;* in the west, the bulletin is called the *Radio Writer.*

Contract Supervision. The Guild requests all members to submit every new contract to the local Guild office before signing it in order that the executive secretary may check the contract terms in detail and advise the writer whether they are in line with current agreements and standards.

Grievance Investigation. There are grievance committees consisting of representatives from RWG and networks or producers as specifically provided for by the two national agreements. These committees hear claims, complaints, or grievances and try to arrive at a satisfactory settlement. If not settled in this way, cases may be taken before the American Arbitration Association. These committees hear cases of action sought against the employer only.

Market Surveys. The Guild issues free-lance market lists to members. These contain pertinent details as to format, air time, producer or network, mailing address, customary fee, etc.

Craft Seminars. From time to time, the Guild sponsors craft seminars for its members. These instruction sessions deal with such topics as writing for television and studies in specific types of continuity.

Credit Bulletin. The Guild compiles periodically an index of radio writers and their work which it sends to all networks, agencies, producers, and packagers, as well as to each Guild member.

Manuscript Registration. Members of RWG are entitled to use the Screen Writers Guild registration service at a reduced rate. This service is designed to protect rights on new literary material. The writer files his script and receives a dated, numbered receipt and may have additional show copies stamped "registered" to indicate that he has copyrighted his work. The registration fee is $1 to Guild members and $1.50 to nonmembers.

Are Writers for Television Protected by the Guild? At a national conference in New York on July 17, 1948, representatives from all the guilds of the Authors' League of America met and organized the National Television Committee. There are at present no particularized contract terms for writers of televised programs, but RWG is concerned with this problem and is making an effort to achieve television writing standards.

Summary. RWG operates to give the writing profession protection, reasonable security, adequate compensation, and professional dignity. These objectives are associated with the belief that an adequately protected and compensated writing profession will improve the literary, entertainment, and cultural quality of radio programs.

QUESTIONS

1. What is the relation of ASCAP to radiobroadcasting?
2. What are the three radio talent unions most closely associated with radio performance?
3. What is AFRA?
4. Why was it organized?
5. Who can belong to AFRA?

6. What are its principal objectives?
7. What has AFRA gained for its members?
8. What special services does the union give to its members?
9. What is the position of AFRA in the field of television?
10. What is RWG?
11. Who can belong to RWG?
12. What are its principal objectives?
13. What special services does RWG extend to its members?
14. What is its position in the field of television?

PART II

BASIC PRINCIPLES AND
TYPES OF PERFORMANCE

CHAPTER 9

BASIC PRINCIPLES

A radiobroadcast is governed by four factors: (1) the nature of the medium, (2) the program purpose, (3) the audience, (4) the studio equipment and working conditions. They apply in varying degree to the writer, the performer, and the producer and may be considered the basic principles of performance.

NATURE OF THE MEDIUM

Social communication is achieved through the use of written and oral language symbols. Writing is a process of transmitting thoughts to paper; speaking is a process of transmitting thoughts by vocalized sounds and physical action. Television involves both audio and visual elements of communication, but radio is a projection of sound patterns only. Radio is an aural medium. Comprehension of the radio message is in proportion to how we listen and how auditory stimuli produce meanings, excite the imagination, and stir the emotions. In order to achieve maximum auditor response, these auditory stimuli must be planned, arranged, and presented according to the limitations of ear listening alone.

The aural nature of radio imposes restrictions on the writer. Communication, minus the interpretative symbols of seen movement and gesture, and minus the opportunity for reflective analysis and review, requires a style that is instantly intelligible. The commercial announcer must get attention, make clear his subject, arouse interest, and secure action; and he must do it in a fixed period of time and in a limited number of words. The writer of the radio talk, addressing the ear of his listener, must likewise strive for "easy listening" and maximum comprehension of ideas. The dramatist who produces his play upon the stage of imagination and is concerned with its emotional impact upon the hearer, integrates selected elements of sound, music, and speech in conformity with aural demands. Divested of conventional stage trappings and accessories, he must compensate for their lack by giving proper attention to the selection of details, dialogue style, connecting narration, and other aspects inherent in the over-all quality of dramatic vividness. The composer of narration understands that such matters as word choice, sentence structure, grammatical devices, rhythm, and concreteness are related to expositional clarity and dramatic mood and movement.

The radio speaker is affected and controlled by the aural character of his medium even more than the author. This is because the speaker projects a personality picture. He makes an impression on his listener that is either agreeable or disagreeable, favorable or unfavorable. Psychology has established the concept of personality as the total organization of one's reaction tendencies, the cross section of his behavior patterns, or his characteristic behavior in typical situations. "Speech style is an index of productivity or sterility of one's social life."[1] Attitudes toward life are revealed through speech. Pronounced personality traits are encountered every day. There is the person who is suffering, or who makes others suffer, because of "I strain," the dogmatist whose arrogance is arrayed against the spirit of compromise; the man who goes busily about unconcerned with the opinions of others; the fair-minded man who meets you in the spirit of, "Come, let us reason together." We are familiar with the exuberant exponent of ideas, causes, and institutions—the enthusiast and the eccentric who seem to delight in making radical departures from social norms. Our attitudes toward life are revealed in part through speech.

The relation of speech and personality has been studied objectively. Cantril and Allport give an account of controlled laboratory experiments in which "twenty-four male speakers and over six hundred judges participated. The method consisted chiefly in matching objective information obtained for twelve features of personality . . . with the corresponding voices."[2] The resulting data pointed the generalization that many features of personalities can be estimated from the voice. An English investigator, working in collaboration with the BBC, conducted a series of experiments which went beyond the point of correlating voice and personality features.[3] Listeners at large described in great detail a series of selected subjects reading assigned material over the air. They recorded their impressions concerning the speaker's age, profession, appearance, professional qualities, personality components, and other characteristics. Judgments were expressed in such phrases as "a most bullying, unpleasant person," "diffident disposition," "fearless, reliable, capable of leadership," "kindly and thoughtful," "determined and persevering," "independent disposition," "inclined to be sullen," "diligent and persevering," "vivacious," "good opinion of himself," "unassuming with refined tastes," "probably would never like responsibility." The

[1] Elwood Murray, The Speech Personality, p. 112, J. B. Lippincott Company, Philadelphia, 1937.

[2] Cantril and Allport, The Psychology of Radio, Chap. VI, p. 109, Harper & Brothers, New York, 1935.

[3] T. H. Pear, Voice and Personality, Chapman & Hall, Ltd., London, 1931.

experiments which produced these results were not controlled, and the accuracy of the opinions or reactions expressed may be questioned. However, whether such judgments are accurate is largely beside the point. The fact of the judgment is important. The audience does associate the vocalization of language sounds with the speaker's personality.

In our discussion of radio acting, the problem of projecting a characterization is explained as the process of counterfeiting a stereotype. This means that we tend to associate a particular kind of voice with a particular kind of character. It is true, of course, that all members of a class do not speak alike, but there are elements common to the group—elements which become significant and interpretive when employed by the actor. Our appraisal of people is conditioned by experience. We meet someone whose voice attracts or repels us, someone who impresses us favorably or unfavorably by his manner of speech; and when we encounter the same quality in another, the original agreeable or disagreeable impression is transferred to him. People carry about with them a host of preconceptions and predispositions, and a voice will touch off these mental sets in proportion to the stereotyped elements in the presentation. If you talk with dogmatic positiveness, you will be classed as a dogmatist; if you speak with nervous, clipped utterance, you will register another impression; you cannot rant and appear conservative or emotionally balanced; and affectation will place you in still another light. Your speech will stamp you as boastful or considerate, egotistical or friendly, dictatorial or respectful, superficial or earnest, pessimistic or cheerful. It is important, therefore, that the radio speaker be concerned with the impression he makes upon his audience.

What are the qualities, or aspects, of speech which contribute most to the impression we make on others? What is agreeable, favorable, or pleasing speech? It is difficult to describe acceptable speech standards by "terminology officially blessed by science," because there is no fixed physical or psychological scale by which to classify vocal types. Speech patterns do comprise particular tonal elements—timbre, intensity, pitch, and duration—but they are so closely integrated that it is difficult to deal with them practically as separate entities. Speech is a series of configurations, and any analytical treatment of it is a pedagogical device. Social experience superimposes upon the primary voice structure psychological components which affect the response and functioning of the vocal mechanism, and expression should always be considered in the light of basic mental and emotional processes. However, let us consider five specific aspects of speech which affect listener reactions. The first of these is vocal quality.

1. *A Good Radio Voice Has Pleasing Quality.* To understand voice quality, we should understand the meaning of resonance. Perhaps you

have heard a demonstration of sound filters in which various frequencies in the lower, higher, and middle portions of the vocal range (tonal scale) have been suppressed or attenuated. Rather weird effects were produced. There is still a great deal of theorizing about the exact nature of voice production, but we are quite certain that in addition to laryngeal structure and functioning, vocal resonance structures are very important. Voices vary because no two amplifiers are identical. The individual voice is imperfect because the human loud-speaker filters out some of the sound frequencies. This is the explanation of voices described as muffled, nasal, throaty, high, or harsh. The cause may be functional as well as organic, and in so far as quality deficiency is due to improper use of the voice—voice production, or the use of the vocal mechanism—it may be overcome through the application of standard speech therapy. A good radio voice should possess pleasing voice quality.

2. *Good Radio Speech Is Clearly Enunciated.* The aural character of radio communication places a premium on distinctness. The electrical transmission and reception of sound have been perfected to such a point that imperfect diction is probably no worse than it would be in the face-to-face situation. That is to say, we hear the speaker very much as we would were we talking to him directly. Granting the best of high-fidelity transmitters and receivers, speech distortion has been practically overcome. Nevertheless, because we are unable to interpret the physical gestures, movements, and expression of the speaker in action, the clarity and distinctness of his utterance become more important.

Speech is a series of related sounds interpreted by the hearer as meaning. In a primitive culture it is possible that isolated, phonated elements conveyed meaning and guided social reaction, but speech as we know it today consists of 40 or more phonetic elements woven into complicated language patterns. These phonetic elements are classified as vowels and consonants.

A vowel is a sound that comes directly from the vocal cords through the tone passage (glottis to lips) without interference or modification by the intervening structures. A vowel is a stream of tone. When it is acted upon by the articulators—tongue, teeth, lips, jaw, and the hard and soft palates—the tone is changed, stopped, or modified. The sounds resulting from this action of the articulators are called consonants.

Vowel sounds are of fundamental importance. The quality of the tone is related to vowelization, the word attack or loudness of tone is associated with the projection of the vowel, and the length or duration of the word depends on the "stretch" of the vowel. It is also the vowel which carries the frequencies that blend in the pitch patterns of speech.

Consonants give intelligibility to speech. Distinctness depends on the accuracy of vowel modifications. Speech that is described as mouthy, chewed, cluttered, and mumbled is due to faulty muscular coordinations. Too many speakers are guilty of smashing consonants, spoiling vowels, and crushing phrases into a grunt. Americans, especially, are allegedly guilty of this lingual mayhem, the statement being made that we "write English but speak American." The aural character of radio speech requires clarity and distinctness of utterance.

3. *Pronunciation.* The radio audience is particularly censorious with regard to the speaker's pronunciation. This attitude stems from the fact that the listener finds an opportunity to arrogate to himself a bit of superiority. It is natural to take delight in the fact that you are enlightened and that the other fellow is ignorant. Whatever the reason, the prestige of the speaker suffers when he commits grievous errors. How can a congressman be wise when he violates pronunciation standards? How much faith can we place in a public leader when he cannot manipulate properly the ordinary words of his mother tongue? We can expect "hillbillies" and the run-of-the-mill quiz contestant to amuse us with language atrocities, but we expect perfection from our straight men. Radio announcers, particularly, are regarded as paragons, and when they slip from grace, as they often do, we are inclined to relegate them to the "sticks." Perhaps too much value is placed on this phase of speech, but in view of the low esteem in which the listener may hold the violator, the radio performer should be mindful of the rules of popular acceptance.

It is not always easy to distinguish between the mispronunciation of a word and its faulty enunciation or articulation. In some instances, these processes overlap in such a way as to render them identical. The contraction, or slurred articulation, of *government* produces a wrong pronunciation; a vowel substitution in either of the words, *get, dog,* and *for* is faulty enunciation and also incorrect pronunciation. However, pronunciation is usually regarded as a process of stress, vowel and consonant accuracy, and syllabication. The words *abdomen, address,* and *detail* may be articulated and enunciated correctly but mispronounced by placing wrongly the syllable accent. The pronunciation of *bade, comely, gape,* and *blackguard, cupboard,* and *flaccid* would be correct, respectively, according to vowel and consonant enunciation; whereas the words *glacial, extraordinary,* and *folio* are examples of terms requiring particular syllabification. The favorable or unfavorable impression of the radio speaker upon his audience may be due in part to the accuracy of his pronunciation.

4. *Vocal Evidence of Emotional Poise and Balance.* The radio speaker should give evidence of emotional poise and self-control. This, of course, is an attribute of effective speaking at all times, but there are inherent in the radio speech situation conditions which produce self-consciousness and nervousness. The sound-deadened studio, a directional microphone,

the red light that says, "You are on the air," a clock ticking off the minutes, a producer and technicians hovering in the background, and the consciousness that somewhere, perhaps, there is a listening audience may be devastating factors. Anyone who has worked his first network show, appeared in competitive auditions, or worked under other critical conditions has experienced the tensions that have clutched his midriff, dried his throat, tightened the articulators, and shortened his breathing. The author recalls a young actor who had such a bad case of mike fright that he could speak only in gasps. Fortunately, he was playing the role of a man who had just carried a buddy across the frozen stretches of Arctic waste land and was supposed to be in the final stages of collapse.

Summarizing in brief, radio speech is oral communication. The speaker projects a personality picture. The auditor draws conclusions concerning the emotional and mental make-up of the speaker and is impressed favorably or unfavorably. These impressions are influenced by the speaker's voice quality, the character of his diction, and his emotional poise. The fact that radio is an aural medium places a particular premium on oral proficiency.

PROGRAM CHARACTER AND PURPOSE

Radio performance is governed by program purpose. Versatility is the real hallmark of the skilled and effective performer. He must know how to adapt himself to the type of continuity dictated by the program and the program objective. This applies with particular directness to the announcer. His primary function is to sell, but the commercial copy put before him varies with the product to be presented and according to the requirements specified by the sponsor. He must run the gamut from the hot-shot-barker type of commercial to the dignified institutional advertisement. He introduces a variety of guests, handles special news bulletins, guides his listeners on miscellaneous musical journeys, makes courtesy and discrepancy announcements, and may even come forth with, "We regret to inform you that owing to circumstances beyond our control, the program to which you have been listening will be resumed in just a moment." The staff announcer is a hard-working, sometimes confused, but versatile spokesman. He sells, makes simple explanations, reports, and creates listening attitudes. He is all things to all men. The narrator, too, is a versatile artist who ranges through a variety of dramatic moods, creating vivid pictures in the mind of the listening audience, but he does more than arouse images of galloping hoofs, heroic rescues, and sinister prowlers. Radio narration may be simple exposition, biographical portraiture, satirical commentary, or objective description. The narration in a "cops and robbers" or murder mystery script is different, indeed, from that in a documentary dealing with atomic energy or the United Nations. The narrator must adapt himself to many types of programs, and his performance is effective in proportion to the quality of his adaptation.

The person who makes a radio talk should be guided by the purpose of the program. If his object is to make a detached explanation, his manner of address will be different from his attacking a political opponent or pleading a humanitarian need.

The discussion participant (the round-table or panel member) represents a point of view or cause, but his radio delivery is restrained by the program's purpose to offer enlightenment and a rational presentation of a controversial issue. The panel member may be an advocate, but he is confined by the bounds of honest inquiry; he argues, but with strict deference to opposing views. He is tolerant and judicial. The debater has more latitude and may properly be more aggressive and more contentious.

The actor is not constrained by the program purpose in quite the same manner as the announcer, narrator, speaker, and discussion participant. He belongs to a somewhat unique category. However, the dramatic script calls for specific acting abilities, and his skill is measured by the effectiveness of his interpretation.

RADIO AUDIENCE

Radio programing and performance are governed in part by the audience addressed. The radio audience is a classified one; that is, people listen according to personal interests and tastes. Intellectual, economic, occupational, age, and sex strata are clearly indicated by various audience surveys and analyses. Some programs, of course, reach a much less interested listening group than others, and the ideal program, perhaps, would be one that had a uniform appeal; but actually every broadcast is typed and reaches only a fractionated part of the general public. Who listens, for example, to soap operas, western music, symphony orchestras, mystery melodramas, the various grades of quiz shows, giveaway programs, financial counselors, and individual news commentators? Each type of program has a well-defined clientele. Thus, listening tastes, preferences, and habits—audience character—should be considered by the radio performer. It is dangerous to assume that radio's listening millions are cast from the same mold. Some people resent the hard, driving insistence of commercial advertising. Others are annoyed by the rattling, machine-gun type of news reporting and are disgusted by the lugubrious tones of a sad-voiced prophet of doom. Some listeners may be entertained by an emotional, combative, chip-on-shoulder attitude, but others prefer a calm, deliberative presentation.

Fɪɢ. 19. CBS (Hollywood) News Bureau. Note teletypes. The clocks show Greenwich mean time, Moscow time, and Chungking time.

Potential audience response should guide the techniques of writer and speaker. The implications of this statement will be developed in the discussion of program types and program performance.

STUDIO EQUIPMENT AND WORKING CONDITIONS

A third set of principles related to program broadcasting pertains to studio construction, equipment, working conditions, and regulations. The physical and electronic phase of broadcasting belongs to the realm of engineering science. It is not essential that one who addresses a microphone should be able to trace his voice vibrations as they are converted into electrical energy, amplified, controlled, sent to a transmitter by telephone lines, imposed on a carrier frequency, picked up by an intercepting aerial, reamplified in a receiving set, and changed back to sound energy. The function of vacuum tubes, oscillator tubes, conductors, resistors, amplifiers, and transmitters concerns, primarily, the radio engineer. *But some knowledge of studio arrangement, basic equipment, and operation is essential to performance.*

Studios. "Studio" is the term applied to a room constructed for the special purpose of radiobroadcasting. It is designed to meet three basic requirements: purpose, the elimination of extraneous sound, and the control of reverberation.

From the standpoint of purpose, studios vary in size from the very small room, equipped with a table and chair and used by an individual speaker, to the auditorium which accommodates hundreds of auditors, and a stage large enough to seat a symphony orchestra. A "small" station may crowd all its programs into one general-purpose studio; a key network station may use 15 or more studios.

The studio should be isolated from extraneous sounds and noises. It is frustrating to have your dramatization of a James Fenimore Cooper

Fig. 20. A CBS theater studio. Note the control booth located to the left of the stage; above it is the client's booth.

Indian raid punctuated by sirens or the roar of a Douglas bomber. A glee-club rehearsal adjacent to the college radio workshop will not harmonize with *The Fall of the House of Usher*. Professionally, studios are planned with great care in order to "seal away any possible seeping-in of outside noises." Sound engineers have designed rooms that are literally and actually suspended on cushioning devices within the framework of the building. Usually, a studio is not entered directly, but through a "sound lock" or entry chamber. In other words, two doors shut off the broadcast area from possible outside interference.

It is even more important that the reverberations of sound originating within the studio be reduced or controlled. You are familiar with the phenomenon of reverberation. You have experienced it many times when speaking or listening in a classroom or auditorium. The room, you have said, is "boomy," hollow, acoustically imperfect. The voice seemed distorted and harder to understand. That was because the speech sound waves were reflected at intervals too short for the ear to detect, and the sound, therefore, seemed to be continuous. The impression was a blending or overlapping of sound. Maximum intelligibility requires the full perception of exact sound characteristics. How can this reverberation and consequent distortion of vibrational elements be corrected? How

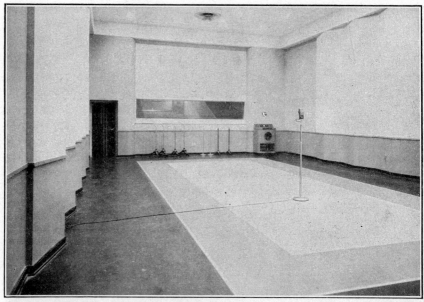

Fig. 21. Studio H in NBC's new Hollywood Radio City. One of four "blind studios" where programs are broadcast which depend on illusion created by the voice alone to make situations and characters real to the audience. The rectangular slit in back of the wall is the engineer's and director's control room. The V formation of side walls splays sound to prevent it from bouncing back into the microphones.

can we eliminate the persistence of a tone after it has been sounded? By cutting down the period of reverberation. What should that period be for broadcast speech? Scientifically, opinions vary slightly, but the estimate is 0.6 to 1.2 seconds.

To achieve this reverberation period, many experiments have been made with sound-absorbent materials and studio architecture. Curtained walls, hanging drapes, movable panels, and permanent walls treated with rock-wool insulation and various materials have been used to achieve studio conditions requisite to the accurate broadcast of voice, sound, and music. The problem of acoustical design is always a difficult one, and the answers derived by the experts are still somewhat varied.

It is possible for a studio to be too "dead" or too "live." The amount of permissible studio reverberation differs slightly with the type of broadcast. Consequently, a studio may be constructed which has varying resonance characteristics; that is, one section may be treated to suppress almost completely the reflection of sound waves, and another arranged to permit a very definite "bounce." The third section of the same studio may have resonance characteristics between these extremes. Moreover, broadcast rooms differ in design. They vary in dimensional proportions, contour, and the use of aids such as revolving panels and irregular, saw-tooth wall design.

There are other considerations to be observed in placing your broadcasting working space such as lighting, ventilation, microphone connections, and its relation to the control room and adjacent studios, but these are relative to individual requirements and situations. It is especially important, however, that the problems of general utility and sound shielding be carefully considered.

Microphones. A microphone is a device used in radio by which sound waves are changed to electrical impulses that permit them to be amplified and transmitted.

The quality of a microphone is judged by its capacity to reproduce both tonal and volume ranges of sound over the entire limits of human hearing. Its technical performance is described by the engineer in terms of frequency response, dynamic range, directional uniformity, transient properties, power output level, and sensitivity. These physical specifications, meaningful and important to him, are jargon to the layman and are of little, if any, practical value to the performer. The studio engineer and radio technician know that particular types of microphones should be used according to the nature and condition of the broadcasting situation. Does the acoustical nature of the studio require a reduction of echo? Is the program accompanied by an excess of audience noise? Do conditions require the artist to work at some distance from the microphone? Is there a problem of acoustical feedback? Is the program a remote broadcast from an outdoor point of pickup and subject to wind noises, air currents, and moisture? Is the program one of audience participation, round-table discussion, direct personal address, or a play? Is it a broadcast of a string quartet, orchestra, soloist, or choral group? Microphones are used according to the nature and conditions attending the broadcast situation, but their selection and installation are the responsibility of the engineer. The problem does not concern the performer or program participant.

Nor is it altogether necessary for the latter to know the various kinds of microphones. The speaker is not aided by the knowledge that one microphone employs a free-moving ribbon; another, a fixed diaphragm;

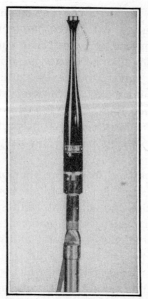

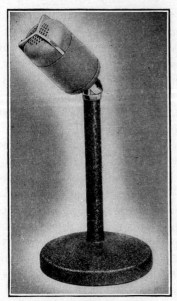

Fig. 22. The Altec 21B microphone. Miniature in size, light, inconspicuous, uniform in response. Free from bass build up.

Fig. 23. Western Electric 633A microphone. A rugged, dependable microphone, either directional or nondirectional.

Fig. 24. Western Electric 639B cardioid microphone, on desk-type base. Combines a dynamic moving-coil pressure element with an improved ribbon-type velocity element.

Fig. 25. RCA, type 44BX. Intended primarily for studio use where the highest quality reproduction is required. Bidirectional.

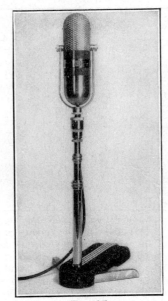

Fig. 26   Fig. 27

Fig. 26. The RCA Starmaker. The company's first streamlined microphone designed to afford a better view of television entertainers and programs.

Fig. 27. RCA type 77-D, MI-4045, and banquet stand MI-4095. Has best features of velocity and pressure microphones.

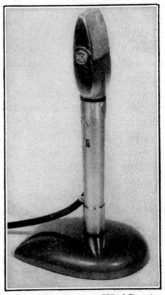

Fig. 28. RCA type KB-2C. A new miniature velocity microphone. Ideal for remotes, clubs, conventions.

Fig. 29. RCA microphone (Varacoustic) MI-6203. Ideally suited for public-address use.

Fig. 30. RCA pressure microphone, type 88-A (MI-4048C). This microphone is ideal for general remote pickup use. It has good frequency response and is relatively free from effects of wind and moisture. Its rugged construction withstands the hard usage of remote work.

and a third, the principles of the other two. However, as a matter of interest, we offer illustrations and brief descriptions of velocity (ribbon), pressure (dynamic), and cardioid types of microphones.

While it is not necessary for the speaker to understand the technical construction, function, and characteristics of a microphone, there are certain facts which do affect his use of the instrument. These can be gathered in a set of instructions under the heading, "microphone technique," a phrase that has been given more prominence than it deserves. A list of 13 points stated as injunctions will cover the subject rather adequately. They apply to performance in general but especially to the radio actor.

1. *Do not handle the microphone.*
   a. Do not tap or blow into it to test if it be alive.
   b. Do not lower or raise an adjustable-stand microphone.
   c. Do not move it from one floor position to another.
These tests and adjustments are made by the engineer or technical assistant on duty. A microphone is a very sensitive instrument. Careless handling may damage both it and related control-room equipment.

2. *Know the directional characteristics of microphones.* They are classified as unidirectional, bidirectional, and nondirectional. This means, respectively, that the microphone may pick up sound vibrations from one direction only, from two opposing directions, or from any point within a circumference of 360 degrees. The angle which subtends these vibrations is called the "beam." When you are "on-beam," you are speaking directly to the ribbon, diaphragm, or receptive element in the mike.
   a. Study the effect of moving to the right or left upon audience audibility and volume unit (V.U.) registration. Just what is the width of the angle of pickup?
   b. The beam of the bidirectional mike will be approximately the same as above, but repeat the same test, moving over to the dead side. How far can you move without changing the voice level or quality of the tone?
   c. In the case of the nondirectional mike, the voice level should remain constant for the same distance—for any equally distant point within the circumference of 360 degrees.

3. *Determine the various distances required for different voice levels dictated by the speaking situation.*
   a. Normal conversational speech.
   b. Intimate and suppressed speech.
   c. Calling to someone at a distance.
   d. Shouting, as a member of an excited crowd.
   e. Varying degrees of emotion.

Voices vary in natural intensity. Two speakers working opposite each other will probably take positions of varying distance.

4. *Understand the difference between off-beam and off-mike.* Off-beam and off-mike are different terms. One can stand in the beam but off, or away from, the mike. Experiment with the effects produced as you move away from the microphone keeping within the beam and as you move away from the mike but outside the beam. An on-beam voice decreases very rapidly, somewhat according to the formula, "intensity of sound varies inversely with the square of the distance."

5. *Radio, or microphone, speech is not projected speech.* This means that speech is not projected in the sense that the stage speaker must project. The latter must use more than normal emphasis and intensity. His vowels have more force, and most of the consonants are energized. (This is said with primary reference to the radio talk, the discussion, the announcement, the news commentary, and panel participation. The actor's role calls for wide variation of intensity, but even acting lines require a suppression of certain articulative processes.) Radio transmission of sound is achieved at the speed of light. Thus, the distance between the radio speaker and the hearer is practically nonexistent. There is no back row or balcony which one must try to reach. If consonantal energy is not suppressed, the result produces an effect called "popping," "blasting," or "peaking."

6. *Control audible breathing.* Avoid audible inhalation or exhalation except when these are requisite to emotional interpretation. Conditions or feelings such as fatigue, excitement, physical effort, resignation, and fear are accompanied by the audible intake and release of breath; in normal speaking, one's breathing should not be heard. It is distracting. To achieve the ideal is not easy because of the sensitivity of the microphone. The radio speaker should have perfect breath control, being able to breathe in "without making a sound as of the tide coming in," and be able to control the exhalations so that the sentence is not followed by the release of unused breath.

7. *Know how to make fades.* The term "fade" means that the sound (voice, sound effects, music) is gradually diminished in volume. It comes in (increases) from a partially audible level to full broadcast level, or goes out (decreases) from normal level to less audible level. Fades are described by the adjectives, "live" and "board." A live fade is made by the speaker; a board fade is achieved at the monitor panel by reducing the level as regulated by the potentiometer. A live fade occurs in proportion to the decrease or increase of vocal sound vibrations upon the microphone ribbon or diaphragm There is no fixed mathematical or mechanical rule to regulate the degree or quickness of the fade. The speaker will learn through trial and error the method that is best

for him. In fact, this is something that might be called "mike sense" or "mike feel." There is one aspect of the problem which is overlooked by the average performer. You should not depend entirely on radio mechanics to achieve your purpose. You should supplement these by fading your own voice—by decreasing the intensity level of the line. If you were reading a radio play from an auditorium stage and you wished to indicate the integration or separation of scenes by the fade technique, how would you do it? By naturally lowering your voice, letting it trail off to an indefinite or inaudible level. You can do something of the same thing when making a mike fade.

Any method which produces the proper effect of diminished intensity may be used by the radio performer, but four methods may be specified:

a. Back out of the beam into the dead area.

b. Turn gradually from the normal microphone position and keep turning as you walk into the dead area.

c. Back away from the microphone, remaining in the beam.

d. Turn slowly and face away from the mike.

A "fade-in" may be called an entrance fade, and a "fade-out" may be called an exit fade.

8. *Understand perspective.* The term "perspective" refers to special relationship of voice, sound, and music. A mother is telling her daughter who is upstairs where she may find a mislaid purse; a workman is giving directions to another workman at the bottom of a shaft; enemy planes are flying at a faintly audible distance; the mob is outside the jail; music playing in the ballroom is heard by the lovers on the balcony outside. These situations involve elements of perspective achieved by the proper balance of sounds. The balance may be the product of skillful mixing when two or more microphones, or sound input channels, are used, but in situations like the first one listed above, the speakers will create the pictures by their positions and mike techniques.

9. *Don't be a "mike creeper."* Maintain your position at the microphone, moving only in accordance with level, perspective, or balance requirements. Some people want to keep moving until they are literally caressing the microphone.

10. *Don't be a "mike hog."* In acting and some other types of performance, you will not always have a microphone to yourself. You will frequently have to share it with others. This means a sharing of the beam. You may have to adjust your position, moving slightly on word cues so that the person performing with you is not shut off from free access to the microphone.

11. *Handle the script so that the rattle of the pages is not picked up and broadcast.* The care with which you manipulate the pages of your script is very important. Paper rattle, like breathing, can be very annoying. Very slight paper noises are greatly magnified. Don't slide your pages. It is better to hold the page from which you are reading at the lower right-hand corner, keeping it in such a position that when you have finished the last speech you can *lift* the completed page and place it under the script. There is some authority for dropping pages on the floor, but this practice has disadvantages. It is possible that pages dropped by the speaker may be heard as they fall or that

they may be walked on and thereby produce a crackling sound. Moreover, the habit of strewing pages over the studio floor is an untidy one, and should you want to save the scripts, the job of reassembling them is no small chore.

12. *Watch the director for cues and signals.* It is of utmost importance that the actor coordinate his performance with direction. There are many things your director may want to tell you during the program. He may wish to stretch a bridge, delay a sound cue, increase or decrease tempo, change your mike position, and many other things. If he cannot catch your eye, it is difficult for him to communicate with you. Although it is not easy, or perhaps possible, to keep following your script and watch for directions at the same time, you can contact him between speeches.

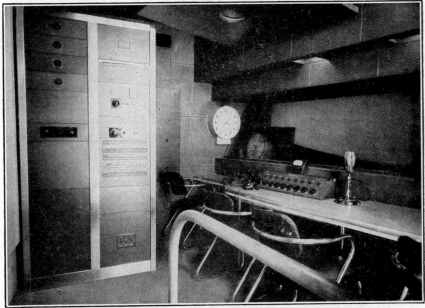

Fig. 31. Studio control booth. Note the "talk-back" mike which is used by the producer to talk to his cast in the studio.

13. *Keep your eye on the script.* The script is the audience to which you are playing and the actor, or actors, with whom you are playing. It is also the dramatic stage itself. Although this is something of an exaggeration, it is fundamentally true. When you begin to play with the actors around you, two things may happen: (1) you are apt to lose your place on the page and (2) you will bob from side to side, changing vocal direction with relation to the beam. This may produce a kind of in-and-out picture, a fuzziness, or variation of level. In general, keep your eye on the script, but when you do look away from it, the place at which you stopped should be marked by the free index finger.

Control Room. The control room is a small area about 6 by 8 feet, visible to the studio but sealed off from it by sound-insulated walls and a specially constructed double glass window. Why is it called a control room? What is controlled? A microphone converts sound into electrical energy, but the energy is a weak signal which must be boosted or amplified to controllable volume. This is accomplished in the control room where the microphone cable terminates in an amplifier. The increase of energy is fed to a monitoring panel, board, or console equipped with variable attenuators called "gain controls" or "pots." Each microphone has its individual control on the console, and energy originating thereat

Fig. 32. Radio control panel.

is registered on a meter or volume indicator called a V.U. meter. This original sound (*e.g.* the speaker's voice) may be too weak for what the engineer calls "requisite broadcast level" and must be "cranked up" or given additional amplification; it may be too intense and have to be reduced. The gain control is advanced (turned up) or retarded (turned down) to a point directed by the V.U. meter. Monitoring would be a simple job if only one microphone were used and if the sound input were fairly uniform. Some programs, though, require several microphone channels. In a dramatics show, sound effects, voices, and music may be fed to the console over three channels. The problem now is to control relationships of sound. Voices must be balanced, background music should not override dialogue, and effects of general confusion should be kept in perspective. A clear picturization of the dramatic scene requires a sense of proportional relationships. This is achieved by the engineer at the mixing panel. An experienced technician can mix a program and maintain the sound level necessary to program transmission by watching the V.U. meter. In fact, this is what he does, but the control room is also a listening post and is therefore equipped with a monitor speaker over which the program is heard as it will be received by the radio audience. Thus, a director, working from the con-

Fig. 33. A view of the master control, the nerve center of a network operation. The CBS station, Hollywood, Calif.

trol booth, is able to detect in rehearsal the possible flaws in the production and work for their elimination. The purpose of the control room, then, is to receive and mix the various sounds emanating from the studio, to control the output of sound going to the transmitter, and provide an intermediate listening, or monitoring, station.

While control function and operation are vitally related to broadcasting, they are not of direct concern to the performer. He should, however, understand the general relationship of microphones and studio to the control board, and also how his performance is regulated at that point. It is much more important for the program producer-director to

Fig. 34. Stand by. Be quiet. We are ready to begin.

Fig. 35. Begin. It is your cue.

Fig. 36. You are too close to the microphone. Move back.

Fig. 37. You are too far from the microphone; move in.

Fig. 38. You are using too much voice level; hold it down.

Fig. 39. You are not using enough voice. Speak louder.

Fig. 40. How is the balance?

FIG. 41. Watch me for cue.

FIG. 42. Are we on time?

FIG. 43. We are behind time; speed it up.

FIG. 44. We are coming out ahead of time; slow down.

FIG. 45. We are on time; maintain established pace.

FIG. 46. Everything is OK.

FIG. 47. Cut; stop operations.

know control-room operations because he is dependent upon them for many of the effects he wishes to attain.

Working Conditions. A radio studio is not a place to play. The professional, of course, understands the conditions which attach to his employment, but not all amateurs are mindful of the proper conduct and use of time required of them. We are speaking particularly of students in the college radio workshop and amateur groups who are privileged to produce sustaining programs on a local station. Studio conduct is always a matter to be stressed. As actors, you will find that it requires a lot of patience to sit through hours of rehearsal time. As we have previously said, there is always much trial and error, backing and filling, stopping and starting. Those who have "bit" parts will become especially restive. The attitude of every performer should be that the preparation of every broadcast is an opportunity to learn, to grow, to achieve—to reach the maximum. This attitude, if genuine, will be manifested in attentiveness, cooperativeness, courtesy, observance of ordinary social amenities, and concentration. These traits are essential to a closely organized unit engaged in a common pursuit. They are essential to group morale.

It is under the topic, Studio Working Conditions, that we would place a knowledge of radio sign language. Pantomimic communication is necessary during the actual broadcast, and pertinent physical signals must be understood by all "hands." The 14 instructions most commonly used, together with their corresponding expression through signs, are as follows:

1. *Instruction:* Stand by. Be quiet. We are ready to begin.
   Sign: The palm raised in warning signal.
2. *Instruction:* Begin. "It is your cue." Hand cues are given to actors and technicians as required by the program or production situation.
   Sign: Point the index finger directly and sharply at the performer.
3. *Instruction:* You are too close to the microphone. Move back.
   Sign: Gesture with the palm of the hand as if pushing the speaker away from the microphone.
4. *Instruction:* You are too far away from the microphone; move in.
   Sign: Gesture with the palm of the hand as if pushing the speaker toward the microphone.
5. *Instruction:* You are using too much voice level; hold it down.
   Sign: Gesture with the palm or palms downward.
6. *Instruction:* You are not using enough voice. Speak louder; bring it up.
   Sign: Gesture with the palm or palms upward.
7. *Question:* How is the balance?
   Sign: Hands moved alternately up and down, palms downward.
8. *Instruction:* Watch me for a cue to begin or proceed.
   Sign: Point to your eye.

9. *Question:* Are we on time?
   Sign: Bend the forefinger over the nose.
10. *Instruction:* We are behind time; talk faster; speed it up.
    Sign: Move the hand or forefinger in a circular motion.
11. *Instruction:* We are coming out ahead of time; slow down; stretch.
    Sign: Place the fingertips together and pull them apart as if stretching an elastic band.
12. *Instruction:* We are on time; maintain the established pace.
    Sign: Place the forefinger on the tip of the nose.
13. *Instruction:* Everything is OK.
    Sign: The thumb and forefinger, or middle finger, form a circle.
14. *Instruction:* Cut; stop operations.
    Sign: The index finger is drawn across the throat.

Summary. Radio program broadcasting is governed by basic principles which apply to speakers, directors, and technicians. Each performance is restricted by conditions inside and outside the studio. These principles apply with some uniformity, however, to all basic types of production, and we shall now consider in turn the major kinds of radio performance, pointing up the utilization of the four major factors explained in this chapter.

QUESTIONS

1. Name the four basic factors which govern radiobroadcasting.
2. Explain how the aural nature of radio imposes restrictions on the writer, speaker, and actor.
3. Name five aspects of speech which stimulate listener reaction.
4. How do program and audience factors affect radio performance?
5. Explain: Radio studios are designed to meet special acoustical requirements.
6 What is a microphone? Name five types of microphones.
7. Why is a particular type of microphone chosen for a given broadcast?
8. Enumerate and explain briefly 12 points of microphone technique.
9. What does the control room control?
10. Give to the class an oral and physical explanation of radio sign language.

CHAPTER 10

THE RADIO TALK AND THE RADIO SPEAKER

You may never be employed as a professional broadcaster, but other business or professional connections may require that you address a radio audience. The effectiveness of a radio talk depends on what is said and how it is said. Composition and delivery are organically related. A speaker's command of his subject, the judicial quality of his mind, his sincerity of purpose, and adaptation to the response nature of his audience are revealed in the clarity of thought, cogent organization, and the choice of language symbols as well as by vocal presentation. Let us consider the radio talk from the standpoints of preparation and presentation.

Preparing the Talk. In preparing a radio talk, we should recognize that there are differences between what we may call the essay style and the speech style. A composition prepared for oral delivery will differ in some respects from the paper prepared for publication. Lord Macaulay said of Sir James Mackintosh, "He tries to speak essays." On one occasion, when a speaker was praised in the presence of an English statesman, he inquired, "Does it read well?" "Yes, grandly." "Then it was not a good speech." A vigorous defense of this difference between the styles of speaker and writer is found in William Hazlitt's essay, *On the Difference between Writing and Speaking.* Himself a master of English prose, Hazlitt affirms: "Few persons can be found who write and speak equally well. Not only is it obvious that the faculties do not always go together in the same proportion, but they are usually in direct opposition to each other." Herbert Spencer, in his essay, *The Philosophy of Style,* discusses composition from the standpoint of economizing the mental energies of the reader or listener. "Language is an apparatus of symbols, and the more simple and better arranged these symbols, the greater the effect produced. Force in language depends upon the economy of mental energies."[1] The general principle may be stated as follows: "Other things equal, the force of all verbal forms and arrangements is great in proportion as the time and mental effort they demand from the recipient is small."

[1] Herbert Spencer, *The Philosophy of Style,* Allyn & Bacon, Boston, 1917.

The basic difference between the speech and the essay lies in the fact that one deals with author-reader relationship, and the other with speaker-auditor relationship. A reader may proceed at his leisure and reread the page he does not understand, whereas the auditor must assimilate the speaker's ideas during a limited period of time with no chance to rehear points that are not clear. This places a special burden upon the speaker and demands that he use techniques to make his material instantly intelligible. The comprehension of language symbols requires some mental effort. Therefore, "the effectiveness of language as a bearer of thought is measured by the ease with which it gives up its contained idea—the cheaper the transportation, the larger the freight."[2]

The mental energies of a listening audience are "economized" by the use of particular techniques. Basically, it is necessary to command the listener's attention. Beginning with the opening sentences or paragraph, the speech should command a continuing interest through the use of the unusual or novel, the concrete or specific, and items related to the personal and vital interests of the listener. Listening ease is also aided by clear speech structure. The conventional rhetorical principles of unity, coherence, and sequence should be adhered to. Unity is violated when the speaker departs from a pronounced assertion, theme, or proposition and makes excursions into nonrelated and extraneous fields—when he does not "stick" to the point. Coherence results when thoughts are properly integrated and are related to each other by clear transitional devices. Sequence pertains to the order of the several speech parts. Facts and ideas may be arranged chronologically, logically, or psychologically, depending upon the nature of the subject matter and the purpose of the address. The speaker's choice of words—his vocabulary—is related to the economizing principle.

When articulating your superficial sentimentalities, beware of platitudinous ponderosity. Let even your conversational communications possess a clarified conciseness, a compound comprehensibleness, coalescent consistency, and a concatenated cogency. Eschew conglomerations as asinine affectations. Let your extemporaneous descantings have intelligibility without rhodomontade. Sedulously avoid polysyllabic profundity, pompous prolixity, and vain vapidity. In other words, say what you mean, mean what you say, and don't use big words.[3]

Words should be clear and purposive. Colorful, connotative, short, Anglo-Saxon, and easily recognized words compose the clearest picture. Sentence structure cannot be too involved. In general, sentences should be short, simple, loose, declarative, and interrogative rather than long, complex, periodic, and compounded. The use of the second person,

[2] *Ibid.*
[3] Anonymous.

direct quotation, and the rhetorical question helps to effect rapport with the listener. Illustration, expository analogy, specific instances, comparison, simile, and metaphor add to vividness and clarity. These are some of the principal tools which the speaker uses in fashioning his thoughts for oral presentation.

Easy comprehension is aided further by relating the subject to the understanding level of his audience. It is a pedagogical law that we understand a new thing, principle, or idea only as it is interpreted in the light of the known and the familiar. The abstract or abstruse proposition must be brought into the realm of the listener's experience and related to something he has seen, felt, thought, already accepted, or believed. A new size, shape, or dimension has no meaning unless it can be focused within some frame of reference. An illustrative analogy is effective because the speaker says implicitly. "This is like something you understand or which you have already accepted." Abstractions and generalities awaken small response in the listener's mind unless some concrete correlative is furnished by the speaker.

Statistics are rather meaningless unless a comparable standard is supplied. When the speaker says that the amount cited is equivalent to the cost of 10 state universities, or represents $11 for every minute of time from the birth of Christ to the first day of 1950, he conveys the impression that the amount involved is of immense proportions. The function of graphical representations or pictograms is to make the statistical story clear and easily understood. Such subjects as "How Pay-roll Taxes Rise to Meet Increased Welfare Costs," "Sources of Government Revenue for the Year Ending June 30, 1950," "Where Our Defense Dollars Go," would be dull, indeed, if offered without the benefit of reference levels. It was said of a speech to be delivered by Henry Woodfin Grady, "Mr. Grady will have statistics, but they will not smell of the census." The illustrations used by the speaker will be selected according to the acting nature and interests of his listeners. The choice of subject matter and its organization should be governed by the speaker's purpose and the receptive faculties of the audience addressed.

Listen to a radio talk and appraise its effectiveness according to the following tests:

1. Does the first paragraph secure attention?
2. Is the speech clearly organized?
3. Is there a clear sequence of ideas?
4. Does the speaker use concurrent and recurrent restatements for clarity and emphasis?
5. Does sentence structure aid intelligibility?
6. Does the speaker use words that are familiar to the audience?
7. Is the subject developed within the experience of the audience?

8. Do various metaphors, illustrations, and specific instances serve as "windows that let in the light"?

Reading the Speech. Practically all radio addresses are read. The elements of time and station protection require speakers to write their talks and deliver them as recorded on paper. However, the phrase, "reading the speech," is misleading. One should talk his speech—not read it. He should converse, not recite; communicate, not bombard his hearers with words. Social behavior is activity which seeks the satisfaction of a basic need. Speech is one means by which this satisfaction is attained. The need may be that others understand us, agree and cooperate with us, or share in the ordinary pleasure of gregarious association. There cannot be speech without an auditor any more than we can have sound (in a psychological sense) without an auditory receptor. The process of circular stimulation which goes on during conversation guarantees communicative directness. The inner play of ideas and emotions dictates the rate, emphasis, inflection, pause, and other elements of the speech pattern; when one is conversing "solo," as it were—talking to an invisible auditor without interruption—it is difficult to capture the normal and circular character of the speech process. Nevertheless, you are talking to another. Presumably, your words are provoking a movement of wheels in his consciousness. It is a one-sided conversation in that one party thereto is a silent partner, but in essence the mutuality of social intercourse is nonetheless present. It is important, therefore, that you read the speech as if you were talking it or addressing it, idea by idea, to a visible auditor.

The artificiality and unnaturalness inherent in the average reading performance are due, chiefly, to the fact that people seldom write as they talk. This is to repeat what we have said above: essay style is not the style of oral discourse. It is not meant that, when writing for publication, we should write as we talk. We are emphasizing only that words set down on paper to be addressed to the radio listener should approximate a more personal, colloquial, and communicative style. Let us try to make this clear by three examples. The following paragraph might be acceptable in a magazine article, but would it be equally acceptable if read over the air?

The growing complexity of modern life and the tremendous increase of student enrollment have produced a searching examination and evaluation of educational curricula. Various attempts have been made to adapt the college curriculum to a more pragmatic philosophy of education, and not a few departures from traditional theory and practice appear on the educational horizon. Greater initiative and self-reliance of the student by lessening his dependence on the instructor; stimulation of independent thinking through honor courses; the grouping of subjects into divisions rather than departments; an emphasis on the importance of social feeling and an understanding of human nature appear as clearly defined aims in the curriculum changes adopted at the University of North Carolina, Reed College, Rollins, the University of Oregon, and the University of Wisconsin.

The above sentences are involved, and the vocabulary is not in the range of the general radio audience. The following revision attempts a simplified expression of the proposition that curricula are being revised to meet changing educational philosophy. There are more words in the rewriting of the paragraph, but radio speech in general will have less compactness than composition written for publication.

More young men and women are going to college. This fall college classrooms will be crowded by applicants who want more academic training. What is the explanation of this increased enrollment? The high-school graduate is told that education is the key to a better understanding of our complex modern life. Education is the means by which he may meet the problems of life. It will prepare him for a vocation, for a profession, for citizenship, for parenthood. But will a college course do this? College administrators are asking themselves this question. The result is that the college curriculum is being examined. How practical are the courses now required? Does a college course really prepare a student for useful pursuits? Or, are the courses theoretical and impractical? If a man is to get on in his chosen field, he should have initiative and self-reliance and know how to apply what he has learned. College administrators agree with this, and that is why they are giving the old courses and requirements a thorough going over. The result is that some very important changes are popping up on the educational horizon. There is the Reed College plan, the Rollins plan, the Experimental College, the Great Books idea, and the University of Chicago experiment. All of them have something of a common objective. Help the student to think on his own. Don't let him become a copycat, a parrot, or a reflection of the professor's notebook. Let him see that education is a pattern, not a lot of puzzle pieces or unrelated parts. Prepare him to function as a citizen as well as a business or professional man. Teach him about the forces of his own nature—where they come from, how they function, and how they can be controlled. This is the new trend in education. This is the reason why curricula are undergoing change.

A second example of the difference between conversational speech patterns and formal written expression is drawn from a congressional hearing on a bill proposing amendments to the Communications Act of 1934. The published account of this hearing gives us prepared statements filed by various witnesses, and also the stenographic report of what they said on the same points when interrogated by the committee. In the following paragraphs we have, then, the statements of the same spokesman. The first is from his prepared manuscript as filed for the printed record, and the second is from the transcribed record of his speech conversation with the examiners. Both quotations relate to the same subject.

Study them carefully. What are the differences in sentence structure? What evidences of thought (mental activity) do you find in the second statement that are not so clearly indicated in the first one? Is one more colloquial than the other? What phrases seem to qualify, amend, or give a different direction to the argument?

(a)

Evidence to support this request for specific language in the act to prohibit the Commission from regulating the business of the licensee is available in the Commission's prevailing practice of requiring the licensee to devote a stated percentage of his time to various types of programs, including such categories as education, religion, agriculture, news, entertainment, fraternal, and so forth. Yet the nature and the needs of the community may change completely over the years. The character of the population may change. Local customs and institutions may change. What was once a definite need in the community, to be served by the broadcaster, may have become a surfeit, and the licensee may be powerless to supply a new need of the community because of the arbitrary limitations and antiquated obligations imposed upon him. Again, he can petition the Commission for relief or for permission to change his arbitrary table of percentages, but this takes time, may involve some extensive hearings, and forces the Commission to investigate the economic factors which are, and should be, outside their jurisdiction.

(b)

I would like to point out that an applicant might come in, either an applicant for a new station or a renewal applicant, and in perfectly good faith state that he intends to operate, say, 60% commercial and 40% sustaining. He only says that, Sir, because the Commission requires that he say it. So in perfectly good faith he states whatever his per cent would be in his opinion, 60–40, 70–30, or whatever it is. Then he is committed to that firmly. He cannot change that without going through all sorts of expense and time and trouble and delay; he cannot change it without in some instances, the way he thinks anyway, and the way things have been, jeopardizing his license. Yet he is powerless to control the conditions under which he will operate. Because during this three-year period of his license, conditions in his community change radically, as we in the business end of radio certainly know.

A third example illustrating the characteristics of conversational discourse is found in the record of the same hearings. In reading the following dialogue, note what we have referred to as the circular character of conversation—the interplay of minds, the clash of divergent opinions, the give-and-take of spirited colloquy. Notice the sentence structure. The units of thought are brief and terse. Check colloquial phrases, such as "Oh, yes"; "And, as I say"; "Oh, well"; "Just let me say a word, please"; "Oh, sure."

CHAIRMAN: I cannot help barging in for a moment. You speak about freedom.

MR. PELLEGRIN: Yes, sir.

CHAIRMAN: You do not accord a person who wants to advertise over your stations full freedom. You tell him what time he can have, and when he can have it. And you take the script, if that is what you call it, the advertisement to be put out over the radio, and you do not give to the advertiser complete liberty with respect to the terms of the subject of that broadcast, do you?

MR. PELLEGRIN: Senator, you have asked two questions, and I would like to answer them both, sir. On that time question, I think it would be a more accurate statement from our point of view to say that we give to the advertiser complete freedom of time in so far as time is available. We submit to him our availabilities, and he takes his choice.

CHAIRMAN: Oh, yes. I understand that.

MR. PELLEGRIN: But of course we could not take you off the spot you have to give the time to him.

CHAIRMAN: But that is simply admitting there is not complete freedom.

MR. PELLEGRIN: The freedom we are talking about is not the same kind of freedom.

CHAIRMAN: The situation is one in which you control the time that the advertiser may have.

MR. PELLEGRIN: Yes; that is our obligation. As licensees of the station we must do that.

CHAIRMAN: But that is not freedom. It is not freedom to the advertiser who would like to utilize your services. And as I say, as I understand the situation, you exercise the right to edit the material which the advertiser puts out. You do not agree to take it just as he prepares it.

MR. PELLEGRIN: Senator, we must do that, to make sure that his copy does not violate the laws.

CHAIRMAN: I say again that it is not freedom that you are talking about.

MR. PELLEGRIN: It is freedom, and not license. There is a great difference in the kinds of freedoms we are talking about. One thing we are talking about is free speech and free press, the freedom guaranteed to us under the first amendment. The other freedom, the freedom of the advertiser to say what he wishes, is another matter. We are not restricting his rights, under the first amendment. We are not restricting his rights of freedom of speech.

CHAIRMAN: You are denying him, though, the absolute right to determine what the terms of his advertising shall be.

MR. PELLEGRIN: No, sir, we do not limit him, within those limitations that are imposed upon us by the FTC and the other rules and regulations, and the standards of good taste that we must maintain in order to serve our listeners. That is a point that I want to come to in a moment, if I may.

CHAIRMAN: I understand that but I am suggesting that all this talk about freedom is a lot of talk about something that does not exist. You do not accord the advertiser complete freedom. He takes what you tell him he can have.

MR. PELLEGRIN: Oh, well, you will not find any advertisers coming in and complaining to this committee that they do not have freedom to advertise over the radio, any more than that would be the case as to the press.

SENATOR JOHNSON: Do not be too sure about that statement.

MR. PELLEGRIN: Let me give you a parallel as to the situation in advertising, as between radio and the press. The same companies use both media. We do not question the freedom of the press. There is no question about it.

CHAIRMAN: Just let me say a word, please. I realize that there is not time to give to everybody everything that he wants. I realize also that you cannot give to everybody the complete and absolute freedom to write his own script.

MR. PELLEGRIN: Oh, no; we cannot do that.

CHAIRMAN: And to require you to put it out as he prepares it.

MR. PELLEGRIN: No, Sir.

CHAIRMAN: Now, those things, I think are difficulties from which you cannot get away, it seems to me. But they negate, to me, at least, all this talk that is being indulged in about complete freedom. You do not grant it yourselves.

MR. PELLEGRIN: Senator, I must insist that we do grant it, within the limitations imposed upon us, you see.

CHAIRMAN: Oh, sure, within the limitations.

MR. PELLEGRIN: We cannot go beyond our limitations.

CHAIRMAN: And subject to those conditions.

MR. PELLEGRIN: Subject to our limitations, of course.

CHAIRMAN: I just do not call that complete freedom.

MR. PELLEGRIN: Well, Senator, that is true of everything in American life. And yet when people do not exceed the limitations imposed upon them, we do not say that their freedom is infringed upon. I am sure that is a reasonable statement.

The reading of a speech may be artificial and unnatural even though the composition conforms to the above principles and characteristics of effective oral discourse. The reason is to be found in the mental attitudes of the speaker. Reading is a psychological process. The student of speech learns such terms as phrasing, emphasis, stress, quantity, rate, inflection, modulation, and key; but these words have no significant value other than to define the mental and/or emotional process underlying speech motivation. Reading faults may be traced always to faulty reactions. If one thinks clearly, he will phrase, emphasize, and vary his reading rate accordingly; if he does not think clearly, he will read poorly. Qualifying, explanatory, or parenthetical phrases are read more rapidly because they are usually subaddenda—echoes of main ideas; correct phrasing depends on the perceptions of thought centers; and the allocation of stress or force to words or phrases signifies thought or emotional differentials.

You can quickly satisfy yourself concerning the psychological aspect of interpretive expression. Analyze a sentence. What are the parts of speech and what function does each serve in implementing the idea? What is the subject or noun, the predicate or verb, the adjective, the adverb, the object of the verb? Name the parts of speech in the following sentence:

We condemn any affectation or show, believing in the encouragement of sincere, vivid, and direct communication of ideas.

Which words are nouns? verbs? adjectives? What is the subject of this statement? What is the speaker's attitude concerning the subject? What is the reason for this attitude? How sincere or strong is the belief expressed? Are the qualities enumerated really important? These questions are answered by the reader in terms of accent or stress, the rate of the expression, and the particularization of the thought components.

What differences in time pattern do you find in this example?

One day last month, we were coming out from town—Saturday afternoon as I recall—and ran into George Biggs. You know, the man who built our garage. I asked him about his boys. He said that Joe—Joe was the one who helped him here—had moved to Oakely—gone into the real-estate business, I think he said. And Timmy was planning on college this fall.

What is your oral punctuation (phrasing) of the following quotation?[4] (Readers may differ in their word grouping because they will interpret differently.)

Before the reader can render ideas as well as images, he must get the thought of the poem clear in his own mind. This grasp of content can be conveyed only by correct pronunciation and clear enunciation of the words, by proper breathing so that the pauses aid the phrasing, by the inflections of vocal pitch to show questioning or exclamation, by changes in tempo, and by emphasis of volume upon the important ideas. To point a climax, gestures may sometimes be added, though they should not be overused. The most important fact is this: if the reader does not have the meaning of the poem clearly in mind and the desire to communicate that meaning to another, all training . . . will be of little avail; if the ideas are firmly grasped, the other aids should come as a matter of course and taste . . . .

How are the ideas and zeal of the speaker reflected by word, phrase, and sentence stress in the following quotation from a speech made by Lloyd George in defense of a new tax law?

This is the first conscious attempt on the part of the state to build up a scientific organization of society. Heretofore, the only question the tax gatherer has asked was—"How much have you got?" We ask that still, but we add another—"How did you get it?"

[4] Untermeyer and Davidson, *Poetry: Its Appreciation and Enjoyment*, Harcourt, Brace and Company, Inc., New York, 1934, p. 489.

It is a tremendous question never before asked so plainly, a new idea, formidable, full of life—I do not wonder that it has raised a great stir. I do not wonder that there are heart searchings and angry words, because this simple question—this modest proposal which you see embodied in the new tax provisions—means and can only mean the refusal of the modern state to bow down before the authority of wealth.

Patterns of vocalization are the result of mental and emotional activity. "Read-y-ness" is overcome in proportion to the reader's purpose, clear understanding, and personal identification with the thought behind the words. Psychological completeness of speaker-subject and speaker-audience relationships is requisite to effective oral presentation of ideas. It is not easy to achieve these relationships, and the radio speech situation involves elements which make the speaker-audience adjustment particularly difficult. In the first place, the audience is unseen. The speaker finds himself in an acoustically treated studio, and his voice does not sound natural. There is a clock on the wall and he must begin and close on the half-minute. The microphone is not a very sympathetic companion. There are the mechanics of sitting or standing, turning pages, watching the time, maintaining a microphone position. All these things produce an unreal or artificial speaking situation that adds to the normal amount of self-consciousness, and the emotions engendered militate against the directness, simplicity, and ease requisite to good radio delivery. What can be done? Has any one ever written a prescription which will dissipate stage fright? "If to do were easy as to know what were good to do, chapels had been churches and poor men's cottages princes' palaces." However, it will help to remember that we should talk *with* and not *to*—that we should hold the object of our communication before our eyes and speak personally, directly, even intimately with him. This is what we mean by saying we should not read the speech, we should talk it.

QUESTIONS

1. What are some of the recognizable and defined differences between essay style and speech style?

2. What particular elements of style are dictated by the speaker-auditor relationship?

3. Describe several techniques by which the writer of a radio talk economizes the mental energies of his audience. How does the writer facilitate comprehension?

4. Enumerate the criteria by which to judge the effectiveness of a radio talk.

5. Why is it difficult to attain a personal and communicative style when presenting a talk from manuscript?

6. What do we mean by saying we should not read the speech, we should talk it?

7. How can "read-y-ness" be overcome?

CHAPTER 11

DRAMATIC NARRATION AND
THE DRAMATIC NARRATOR

NARRATION

"Your narrator has been . . . ." What is narration? How does a narrator differ from an announcer or an actor? What are the purpose and the nature of radio script material classified as dramatic narration? These questions apply to an important phase of radio performance.

Excluding argumentation, there are three forms of composition: exposition, description, and narration. Exposition is interpretation or explanation. It is detached and objective. The hearer is informed and enlightened. His response is, I understand, I see, it is clear. Description involves an emotional element. It is the expression of how the stimulus-object affects you empathically. The geologist's explanation of a rock formation would not be the same as the artist's description of the phenomenon. As one philosopher has said, "The scientifically trained mind is not the artistically trained mind." The statement does not mean that the scientist is unable to see with the artist's eyes or vice versa; but only that the scientific process of relating objective facts is not the same thing as expressing in imaginative and emotional words the effect of these facts. Narration is the telling of an event or a series of related happenings. It may be a simple incident or a concatenation of factors involving complications. These three types of recorded experience are not discrete forms of composition. It is not always easy to classify a given paragraph rigidly. Narration may be simple, unemotional, and expository in nature; description may be objective and detached; and exposition may involve interest elements which place it beyond the line of factual objectivity. For these reasons, the phrase, "dramatic narration," as applied to radio writing and performance must be defined somewhat arbitrarily. Although script material labeled "narration" or "narrator" may serve the needs of clarification only, program narration is used far more often as an element of entertainment. We would therefore define dramatic narration as a combination of expository, descriptive, and narrative elements designed to effect an imaginative and

214

emotional response in the listener. In composition it is different from the straight commercial and the radio talk: in delivery, it blends the skills of announcing and acting.

The function of the narrator is clearly expressed by Stephen Vincent Benét in the opening lines of his radio play *A Child Is Born*.[1]

NARRATOR: I'm your narrator. It's my task to say
    Just where and how things happen in our play,
    Set the bare stage with words instead of props
    And keep on talking until the curtain drops.
    So you shall know, as well as our poor skill
    Can show you, whether it is warm or chill,
    Indoors or out, a battle or a fair,
    In this, our viewless theatre of the air.

This brief definition of the narrator's role in a radio play suggests the wide range of narrative composition and treatment. Narration serves several dramatic purposes:

1. *The play is given a setting, characters are introduced, the dominant mood of the drama is indicated.*

(a)

ANNOUNCER: This is the home of Dr. Jim Northrup's family in one of those quiet small American towns. Perhaps the nicest thing about the Northrup place is the cool, grassy yard, shaded by a gnarled old apple tree. Opposite the tree is a screen door leading to the comfortable living room, where Granny Northrup usually does her knitting; while Gramps Northrup, on a summer afternoon like this, is apt to be tinkering at his basement workbench on some gadget for his five-year-old grandson, Pud. Before long Granny will call . . . [2]

(b)

(*Music: A few introductory chords and then it segues into "Bedelia." The melody seeps in, and then, as the strings take over, the music fades underneath until cue*)

NARRATOR: Tonight we turn back the pages of time for a nostalgic hour. It is the year 1906 in the United States of America. Teddy Roosevelt is in the White House, there's a blacksmith on every Main Street, and the automobile is a luxury item. The women are wearing Merry Widow hats, chatelaine bags, and black lisle stockings with lace open-work. And the men? Ah, the men have discovered peg-top trousers, those strange indispensables you can climb into only by removing your shoes. There is a

---

[1] From *We Stand United and Other Radio Scripts*, published by Rinehart & Company, Inc. Copyright, 1942, by Stephen Vincent Benét.
[2] Opening narration, Act I, from Paul Peters' radio adaptation of *On Borrowed Time*. *Theatre Guild on the Air*, p. 139, Rinehart & Company, Inc., New York. Quoted with the kind permission of the author.

pug dog and a zither in every home. And the title on the sheet music on every piano is . . . "Bedelia" . . . .

(*Music: Up* . . . *Two young, fresh voices, a boy's and a girl's, are heard singing the words*)

NARRATOR: And now that we've established the color and the period, I'd like you to meet the Miller family. They live in a large small town in Connecticut, where Nat Miller is the owner and publisher of the local newspaper . . . . First, there's Tommy, the youngest . . . .

(*Running footsteps approach.*)[3]

(c)

EARL: The long war was over. And the tall man with the sad eyes and the stooping shoulders was tired. And so one night he did what everybody likes to do sometimes when they are tired. He went to a show. He went down to Ford's Theatre in Washington town and he sat in a box and it was the Number I box because he was a pretty big man.

Well, the play went on, and along about the middle of the evening something happened that wasn't on the program. I guess you all know what that was. The news spread pretty fast . . . .[4]

(d)

(*Sound: Footsteps on pavement. Slow. Deliberate*)

NARRATOR: Manhattan! City of hope. City of despair. Its towering steel gods control men's lives by day and brood like sleeping monsters by night. It is midnight. Jeff Ramsay, successful playwright and critic, walks the silent streets. In one hour he has an appointment with death. Just five hours before, Fate had laid its iron grip on Ramsay. (*Fading*) It was shortly after the rush of the lunch hour on 41st Street . . . .

(*Sound: Fade in street traffic*)

(e)

(*Sound: Low wind*)

NARRATOR: Ajax McPherson died tonight. Within the grim stone mansion, things are more dismal and foreboding than usual. Peering through the black, wrought iron gates, one sees only the bulky outline of an ugly building, and the dull glow of a single light. That light is in the bedroom of Ajax McPherson. Within that room a will has just been read. The lawyer has left. Still present is the McPherson clan—and the corpse of Ajax McPherson.

(*Effect: Organ chord breaks narration. Crescendo. Cross fade to background of low voices*)

---

[3] Opening narration, Act I, from Arthur Arent's radio adaptation of *Ah, Wilderness. Theatre Guild on the Air*, p. 175, Rinehart & Company, Inc., New York. Quoted with the kind permission of the author.

[4] From, *The Lonesome Train*, by Millard Lampell. Copyright, 1943 and 1945, by Pickwick Music Corporation, New York, N.Y. Used by permission of the copyright owner.

2. *Narration is used to bridge dramatic scenes.* In general, a radio play should not be cemented with narrative passages because the movement and impact of the story are retarded by this device. The historical evolution of an institution or business may be told dramatically. Such subjects as medicine, oil, and aviation lend themselves to the professional script writer as excellent themes, but the sweep of the story requires an episodical treatment, and the episodes must be bridged. Historical and biographical subjects may also necessitate a similar dialogue-narration format. A news dramatization patterned after the justly famous *March of Time* program requires the services of a narrator to tie together the series of events.

(a)

(*In a surgical ward in Washington, D.C., Clara Barton meets one of her former pupils who has been badly wounded.*)

BARTON: Dr. Coolidge, that boy is going to die.

COOLIDGE: No—I—I think . . .

BARTON: I know it. And he'll die because he had no one to nurse him—to care for him at the battle line. You say I can't go to the front. I tell you I will go. I'll go in spite of conventions, army regulation—and you. I want a pass to Surgeon General Hammond. I want it at once.

(*Music: Transition*)

NARRATOR: Clara Barton—a nurse on the battlefields of the American Civil War. Amidst the leaden hail of Bull Run and Chantilly, at Harper's Ferry and South Mountain; Antietam and Fredericksburg; before the belching walls of Fort Wagner; mired in the muddy swamps of the wilderness— on through every major engagement up to the climax of the great Amen before Richmond, the noble heart of this noble woman beat in tempo to the suffering of her fellow countrymen. (*Pause*) The war was over. Destiny had written a tragic finis to a fratricidal strife. President Lincoln asks her to assume the gigantic task of locating over 80,000 men. Largely at her own expense, Miss Barton set to work and against almost insuperable odds gradually brought order out of chaos. Then early one winter evening in 1868, she stood on a lecture platform in the east. A great throng was listening to the woman whom John B. Gough regarded as one of the greatest orators in America.

(*Sound: Mixed chatter and applause on cue*)

CHAIRMAN: Ladies and gentlemen.

(*Sound: Applause up*)

CHAIRMAN: Ladies and gentlemen ! ! !

(*Sound: Gradually fades and tacets under first words of chairman*)

(b)

From the story of the Donner party. The emigrants had taken a wrong route and encountered grave obstacles. The "cutoff" proves to be a trap.

(*Organ: Transition*)

REED: Hastings, it's your duty to go back and lead us out.

HASTINGS: My duty is with this caravan here. They're paying me.

REED: It isn't a matter of pay; it's a matter of life and death. There are 87 people in Webber Canyon—women and children.

HASTINGS: The trail across the mountain is perfectly safe.

REED: We are afraid to try it without a guide. We'd rather risk the canyon.

HASTINGS: Well, I've warned you. We had to lower every wagon over a hundred foot precipice. . . . It took days.

REED: We took this cutoff because of you and Bridger. You've no right to go back on us now.

HASTINGS: I'm sorry, Mr. Reed, but I won't leave my party. I will go with you tomorrow to the top of the Wasatch Mountains and point out the route you can travel; and if you make some notes of the country and occasionally blaze some trees, you can do as much as I could. That's all I can promise you.

(*Organ: Transition*)

NARRATOR: On Reed's return the Donner party decides to travel across the mountains in a direct line to Salt Lake. Their passage was blocked by narrow canyons filled with huge rocks fallen from precipitous cliffs on either side. Thirty days of grueling labor—and with every hour King Winter was gathering his icy hosts in the mountain fortresses of the Sierras. The teams were well-nigh exhausted and the emigrants' stock of provisions nearly consumed.

DONNER: I have asked you to meet me out here, men, out of ear-shot of the women. I have taken an inventory of the provisions. There is not enough to carry us through. We must get food or starve to death.

3. *The dramatist may tell his story through the medium of first-person narration.* Here, the actor is both actor and narrator. The lines he reads as an actor are dialogue and those which he interprets as story teller are narration. The two are not identical. This dual role—actor-narrator— has become very familiar to radio listeners. It is used occasionally on the screen.

(*Sound: Rain and thunder: car motor in high, then under*)

GODFREY: It was a night that was never meant for driving. I didn't know where I was going. I didn't care. I had left the city a couple of hours before and decided to drive up state. I'd made good time . . . I was in a hurry. Strange, I didn't have anybody to meet. I just wanted to get away from the city. . . .

(*Sound: Loud thunder clap*)

GODFREY: I was getting into the high mountain region. The road was steep and narrow. I didn't see any lights or houses anywhere. I was cold and tired. The white line in the road started to weave in front of me. I was getting sleepy . . . . Suddenly a sharp turn loomed up. I swerved too fast. . . . The road was slippery. . . .

(*Sound: Screeching brakes: motor off*)

GODFREY: Somehow the car stopped and I was sweating all over. Why was I in such a hurry? Why was I risking my life out here on a slippery mountain road? And then for the first time I saw the lights. They came from a small café by the side of the road. Maybe, I could get a hamburger and a cup of coffee and rest for a while . . . .

4. *A music program frequently uses a narrator.* The continuity may give us the story behind the song, an account of the composer's life, the circumstances accompanying the writing of the composition, or an interpretation of meaning and mood. It may offer a mental frame or emotional setting.

(a)

(Orchestra: Russian background music)
NARRATOR: The *Musical Mirror* turns and reflects vast, imperial Russia in the year 1876. Russia is engaged in a bitter war with the Turks and the Serbs, the Grand Duke Nicholeavich plans a group of September concerts for the benefit of the wounded. The country is experiencing a renascence in music. . . . The borders of the Empire are not wide enough to confine the fame of Rubenstein . . . Rimsky-Korsakov. Yet, when the Grand Duke wishes a composition especially written for his war benefit, he turns to one Peter Tschaikowsky, to fill the commission. Tschaikowsky is a sensitive, tortured soul, burdened with a restless, deep-rooted unhappiness. He is both awed and honored by the Grand Duke's request. As he begins to work, he envisions a composition that will translate into music the vastness, the majesty, the many-faceted glory of Holy Russia . . . a composition that will sing in the heart of the world for all the varied peoples who live under the double eagle. Into his work he puts not only notes and measures, but the hopeless resignation of a caravan of exiles, plodding doggedly toward the barren wastes of Siberia. . . . He includes the smothering loneliness of the endless steppes, and the wild exultation of a Cossack song . . . the glittering pomp of the Court, and the touching faith of the simple peasants . . . a vision of long, dark shadows on icy snow, and of fertile fields basking in the sun. When he is finished, he has before him the composition which will live forever as a musical symbol of Imperial Russia; the Russia of Peter and Catherine and Ivan . . . the old Russia that is no more. Tschaikowsky has written "The Marche Slav."[5]
(Orchestra: Marche Slav)

(b)

(Orchestra)
NARRATOR: Next Thursday is Memorial Day . . . and it is only fitting that the *Musical Mirror* should turn to honor the one figure that symbolizes the sacrifice of "those who gave their last full measure of devotion," that this country might live.
[5] Jack Van Nostrand.

(*Orchestra: Taps*)

NARRATOR: Tonight we look deep into this image in the *Musical Mirror,* but somehow it fades before our eyes . . . and vision-blurred we close our eyes . . . content to hear . . . (*Pause*) . . . "You wonder who I am. . . . You will never know. Unknown Soldier, they call me . . . and unknown I shall remain. I rest here in my lovely tomb at Arlington— content . . . and happy that it is so. Here I can almost forget the horror of that night at Bar-le-Duc. The raid we had to make there in the dark that never stayed dark enough. I can forget how brave we were, and how we laughed half to ourselves, and said: "They will never see us out there in the wires . . . even if they do shoot up their cursed flares."—And how we couldn't hear each other for the din and fury of the bursting shells . . . but just went on where we were sent. And how there was a sudden blaze of awful light! And Hell broke loose in a thousand different ways! . . . And then . . . grew black. But a blackness I came to learn to love. . . . And with beauties you will have to die as well—to know. And so, I am happy here to still be called, "Unknown." I'd rather have it so . . . for every year a little host of mothers come and stop beside my tomb . . . and more than one has whispered down, "My boy . . . I know it's you," and gone away believing it is so. And so you see that even if I knew a way to let you know the man I was before that night at Bar-le-Duc . . . I would not tell. Still, let me be unknown to all the rest, and bring heart's peace to just a few. Dear God, let me forever be "unknown."[6]

(*Orchestra: The Unknown Soldier*)

5. *Dramatic narration may occur outside the play itself.* That is, a complete program unit may be taken by a narrator whose purpose is to entertain by relating in dramatic or semidramatic style deeds of heroism, historical incidents, personal achievements, dramatic life stories, and strange facts and oddities.

NARRATOR: The great dream of your life is coming true. The floating palace that has carried you across the blue waters of the Pacific is slipping silently into Honolulu Harbor. You have heard about this Paradise of eternal summer and you are to live under its rainbowed skies for two whole weeks. Haunting strains of Hawaiian music, flower leis, surf-board thrills, long hikes on hibiscus bordered trails! You stand breathless at the rail of the boat. Suddenly you hear some one at your side: "Here come the diving boys." Oh, yes, you have heard of them, too—sleek, brown lads who swim out into the bay to display their agile skill in diving for coins. Pieces of money flash in the bright sunlight and strike the water, zigzagging toward the bottom. But before they have traveled far, the tawny swimmers catch them in their mouths and rising to the surface gesture for a new shower of gifts. *Diving boys catch coins in their mouths.* Bunk! It is possible for a skillful swimmer to catch a coin in his mouth but this feat is rarely performed. The picture of diving boys catching pennies in their mouths is fiction.

[6] True Boardman.

6. *A sixth type of narration is found in the play which employs primarily an extended amount of free-verse commentary interspersed by short dialogue passages, verse speaking groups, and montage effects.* The difference between this construction and any third-person narration lies principally in the semipoetic character of the composition.

(*Music: Establish and down to BG*)

NARRATOR:

There was a day last summer, a year ago,
When a world came back to life
To live a while in jubilation,
For peace had come in place of sudden death,—
The dove of peace that fleetingly appears
To wing across the calm horizon and replace
The scavengers, the vultures in the gutted streets,—
Peace had come to heal the wounds of war.

(*Sound: Music segues to motif of exploding bombs and changes to lyrical theme*)

It hardly seems a year has passed
Since August days brought soothing winds of peace
To silence with their sweeping motion all the noise of war,
From the blast of flame throwers on Pacific isles,
To endless patterns of exploding bombs on continents,—
Winds that sway the grasses and flowers,
That mark the graves of white and black and yellow races,
Winds of peace touching every land.
A war binds nations in unity and singleness of aim,
But peace again destroys the unity that danger brings,
And, striving for self interest, the harmony of the whole machine is lost
In frictions of many little groups of many little people.

THE NARRATOR

The narrator is an interpreter. The copy assigned him will be expository, descriptive, and narrative. Generally, however, the purpose of the script is to effect an emotionally toned response. It will help the narrator achieve this result if he understands some of the principles emphasized by the writer. We can parallel in outline the thesis advanced in our explanation of the radio talk: Effectiveness lies in what is said and how it is said.

Writing the Narration. The writer of narration employs specific principles and devices. Word choice is particularly important.

There are colorful words that are as beautiful as red roses; and there are drab words that are as unlovely as an anemic-looking woman. There are concrete words that keep people awake; and abstract words that put them to sleep. There are strong words that can punch like a prize fighter; and weak words that are as insipid as a mama's boy. There are warm and sympathetic words that grip men's hearts; and cold detached words that leave an audience unmoved. There are noble words that lift every listener, at least for a moment, to the sunlit heights of God; and base words that leave an audience in the atmosphere of the cabaret.[7]

Radio narration, as a rule, paints a picture, describes action, stirs the imagination, and arouses emotion. In depicts a scene, establishes a mood, gives climactic impetus to the story. Words are stimuli. When properly selected, grouped, and patterned, they will produce the desired listener response. Tense, exciting, narrative passages and descriptive paragraphs are loaded more heavily with words of Saxon origin; the more intellectual appeals of exposition and argumentation utilize a more Latinized diction. Saxon derivatives which are directly imitative (splash, bang, whiz, roar) and analogically imitative (rough, blunt, keen, smooth) have a greater or less likeness to the things symbolized; and "by making on the senses impressions allied to the ideas called up, they save part of the effort needed to call up such ideas, and leave more attention to the ideas themselves." Saxon and other primitive words possess a quality of concreteness. A concrete word is one that is suggestive—clearly and sharply definitive of feeling or object. It is a word that does not compel the hearer to choose from his stock of images one or more by which he may figure to himself the genus mentioned. Radio narration employs a high degree of concreteness. The writer prefers and chooses specific words in contrast to generic words. "This superiority of specific expression is clearly due to a saving of the effort required to translate words into thought. . . . If by employing a specific term an appropriate image can at once be suggested, an economy is achieved and a new impression produced."[8] In the following illustration, the Saxon derivatives are italicized. It is these words which give sharpness and vividness to the picture:[9]

The British column *marched steadily* on, while from *trees, rocks,* and fences, from *houses, barns,* and *sheds, blazed* the *withering* American *fire.* The *hills* echoed and *flashed.* The *woods rang.* The *road became* an *endless* ambuscade of *flame.* The Americans *seemed* to the appalled British troops to *drop* from the clouds, to *spring* from the *earth.* With *every step* the attack was *deadlier,* the *danger more* imminent. For *some time* discipline and the plain extremity of peril sustained the order of the British *line.* But the *stifling* clouds of *dust,* the consuming *thirst,* the exhaustion of *utter* fatigue, the *wagons* full of *wounded men moaning* and *dying, madly* pressing *through* the *ranks* to the front, the constantly *falling* of their comrades, officers captured and *killed,* and

[7] From an address, "Learning to Speak," by Earnest F. Tittle. Courtesy of Mrs. Tittle.
[8] Herbert Spencer, *The Philosophy of Style,* Allyn & Bacon, Boston, 1917.
[9] George William Curtis, *Orations and Addresses of George William Curtis,* Harper & Brothers, New York, 1894, Vol. III, p. 107.

through all, the fatal and incessant *shot* of an unseen *foe, smote* with terror that *haughty* column which, *shrinking, bleeding, wavering,* reeled through Lexington, panic-*stricken* and broken.

Sentence structure and the sequence of sentence parts are associated with the problems of mental economy and emotional response. Details should be arranged in an order that will promote quick comprehension. A rhetorical principle of expository writing applicable to dramatic narration for the air is: "A growing thought requires the inductive exposition; the applied thought, the deductive." Sentence structure in radio narration is direct, rather short, sometimes elliptical, and not involved.

Another quality of effective dramatic narration is rhythm. This applies to certain types of narration as dictated by subject, program subject, and the desired emotional impact. Some dramatic purposes require a terse, staccato accent—a jarring and irregular beat; in other instances a mood is best expressed in smoothly flowing and rhythmical lines. Gifted writers like Benét, MacLeish, Corwin, Wishengrad, and Rosten infuse their work with poetic sensitivity and moral earnestness. Inspired by a stirring theme, they transform the irregularity of ordinary prose into poetic rhythm.

The Tender Grass[10]

(*Music: Tinkling and frail*)

NARRATOR: There are so many questions that no one ever asks. Like how is April and when does the night-time sleep? I like such questions. They are rounder than gladness and very important. No one thinks of that. I will ask you a question. Suppose once upon a time there was a boy who never was and who lived in a story that never happened. And perhaps he cried a long time because he wanted you to hear the story that never happened. Wouldn't it be terrible to let him cry? Isn't that important? I think so. I will tell you his story.

(*Music: Up and down*)

NARRATOR: Shalom means peace and Shalom was his name. But there were bad things in his heart. (*Music fading*) Once upon a never time when the forest ferns were lit by the moon and the rain was hiding from April, this boy Shalom found a bird's nest which had fallen from a tree. And in the nest were seven little birds who did not know how to fly . . . . He took each of the seven little birds and he tore out each of the seven little tongues. There was no sound left, nothing except the sound of nothing. And the boy went home to grow a day older.

(*Music: Narrative theme and down*)

The mother bird flew back and a neighbor bird told her what had happened. Then all the crickets beat their breasts, and the wind whimpered and the animals of the forest began to cry because seven little birds would never sing again.

[10] Morton Wishengrad, *The Tender Grass, The Eternal Light,* Crown Publishers, New York, pp. 3–4. Used by special permission of the author.

This brief characterization of radio narration is made to point the purpose and skill of the narrator. It is his job to translate and vivify the writer's message by vocal interpretation. He should understand the purpose of the narration and appreciate the basic elements of the writer's craftsmanship.

Reading the Narration. The narrator is an interpreter. He brings to life the structure and style of narrative composition. To discuss in detail the training and performance of the narrator, we would have to include here the subject matter presented in speech texts which deal with the art of interpretive reading. We must assume, however, that the radio student has been introduced to this aspect of speech training and that the present subject can be presented without a preface of elementary principles pertaining to reading in general. Naturally, the radio narrator must know how to read easily, fluently, and expressively, but the radio medium makes his job more exacting than this. Reading skills must be refined to an advanced degree.

Reading is a process of infusing words with a meaning which gives them empathic force.[11] The printed word is given increased semantic intensity by the way it is spoken. The tonal elements of quality, force, time, and pitch fuse in sound patterns of interpretative significance according to the sensitivity, imagination, and emotional responsiveness of the reader.

The narrator should identify himself, first of all, with the total dramatic picture and program purpose. He is an integral part of a whole—not a perfunctory performer who steps in occasionally to read a few casual lines or paragraphs. If the narration occurs in a radio play, the narrator will ask himself, What is this play about? What type of play is it (comedy, tragedy, farce, fantasy, melodrama)? What mood or moods are introduced and sustained? How does the narration aid the dramatic movement? How can the narration be coordinated effectively with the dialogue? Is the narration a part of the suspense and conflict structure, or is it primarily exposition and explanation? Similar questions should be asked when analyzing and preparing any kind of narrative material whether it occurs in a fictional play, the factual documentary drama, a musical program, dramatized news, or other type of continuity.

Having made a basic psychological adjustment to the radio script, the narrator then turns to the particular problem—the interpretation of written words. (A reader, of course, is not a mere manipulator of words, per se, because words make sense only when arranged functionally and in conventional designs or socially recognized patterns. The narrator should at all times be genuinely motivated by a continuity of thought

---

[11] The concept of empathy as related to interpretation is presented in the chapter on Radio Acting (Chap. 14).

and feeling. We may speak of word interpretation, however, without committing an elocutionary fallacy.) A word is a symbol, but meaning does not reside in the symbol. The real meaning is in the referent or that for which the word stands. But the same word to different people may have many different meanings. Words have force in proportion to the emotional associations discharged in the recipient. Individual social experience determines the meaning of a word read or heard, and since these experiences vary in considerable detail, the meanings of words also vary. As explained above, the writer is familiar with this fact and uses words according to a basic design of dramatic purpose and audience appeal. Particularly in the forthright propaganda play which makes a frank appeal to predispositions and fixed attitudes, words are chosen which touch off highly charged emotional associations. A day is not hot, it is "close and unbearable"; it is not a hot night, it is a "sticky, sleepless night." The gold star mother opens not a box, but a "little box." The body floating on a raft must be a "lifeless body." Somehow, a sea burial from a "small American naval vessel" is more poignant than it would be from a dreadnought. The ruined stone wall is a "shattered" stone wall, tanks "embattle," and the snow on the battlefield is "red." Artillery "rocks and thunders." Young priests trade "the quiet flame of a sanctuary lamp for the ravaging flames of war." We see in these examples the use of the connotative word as distinguished from the denotative word. The latter signifies a literal meaning; the former suggests related qualities and attributes. Such word pairs as "house-home," "woman-mother," "woods-wilderness," "dark-gloomy" involve this difference in word force.

The parallel problem of the narrator is to accentuate the force of these descriptive, connotative, emotionally toned words. It is not an easy problem. The reader may easily err by exaggerating or forcing the interpretation to the point where he appears insincere, artificial, and sentimental. On the other hand, if he is too restrained, the reading will be ineffective. The difference between these extremes is a qualitative and not a quantitative one; that is, there is no way to prescribe the precise degree of stress, intonation, or "word color" to be employed. The only prescription lies in the judgment and artisitic sensitivity of the interpreter.

There are many "color" words in the above examples of dramatic narration. For example,

towering	wistfully
steel gods	exhausted
sleeping monsters	vultures
iron grip	smothering loneliness
swerved	endless steppes

Make a list of similar words and phrases. What is the complete and potential force of the word? Can its full meaning be vocally interpreted by the reader? Read each one in its proper context and study the nuances and tonal gestalt which interpret the height of skyscrapers, menace, relentlessness, sudden decision and movement, loneliness, weariness, repulsiveness, deafening noise, and inexorable fate. The interpreter's appreciation and understanding will be evidenced by a fusion of resonance, timing, attack, register, and intonation.

The reading of narration, of course, is not the single matter of coloring words. If that were so, performance would be artificial and sterile. Words have meaning only if placed within a comprehensive frame of psychological understanding. The reader's identification with his material and his grasp of the communicative problem are manifested in many ways. Sympathy, insight, and understanding—the keys of the interpretative artist—dictate registration, time patterns, inflectional changes, and timbre differences with regard to the complete composition. The good reader does not rely on penciled notations or symbols to guide his work. Mechanical markings would only confuse him and interfere with a free release of honest experience.

The radio narrator is an interpreter. His script material is a combination of expository, descriptive, and narrative elements of composition, but in general it is imbued with an emotional quality. It will help him to study the nature of the narration from the standpoint of writing principles, the author's purpose, and the program function. He will read well in proportion to this understanding and in proportion to his intellectual and emotional identification with the spirit of the author's words.

QUESTIONS

1. What is dramatic narration?
2. What is the function of narration?
3. Explain several specific purposes of narration.
4. Name some of the specific principles and devices employed by the writer of narration.
5. What is the function of the narrator?
6. What are the narrator's qualifications?
7. Discuss: Reading is a process of infusing words with a meaning which gives them empathic force.
8. Explain how the narrator should study his material to achieve maximum effectiveness of presentation.

CHAPTER 12

THE RADIO ANNOUNCER

The subject of radio announcing can be considered from three points of view: (1) vocational opportunities, (2) job routine, and (3) skills or abilities. The vocational aspects of radio announcing are reviewed in Chap. 7, Radio As a Vocation. Job routine pertains to such matters as station organization and policy, staff relationships, working conditions, and station and network protocol. The announcer's duties vary with the size and organization of the station. In some situations he may need to know and have knowledge about such things as copyright restrictions, union regulations, the operation log, transcriptions, turntables, and even control-board operation; but training in these responsibilities, which are adjuncts to his primary function, is best secured on the job itself. We shall deal with announcing as one of the performance skills.

Who Is the Radio Announcer? The radio announcer is the link between the seller and the customer, the station and its public, the performer and the audience. He is the salesman who rings your doorbell, the club chairman who presents the speaker of the day, the messenger who brings good news, and the gracious host who introduces you to his guest. He is an ambassador of good will. But what kind of door-to-door salesman are you willing to tolerate? When does the chairman's introduction of a speaker win a receptive hearing? What do you mean by a gracious host? The announcer-auditor relationship is a problem in human relations.

General Criticism of Announcers and an Explanation. The radio announcer has become a stereotype, the victim of a system whose watchword is, "Buy now." Place a typical commercial announcement in the hands of 20 announcers selected from 20 different stations and geographical areas. Have each announcement recorded. Listen to them. The platters will match like so many paving blocks. This statement, no doubt, will offend the announcing fraternity. Their reply will be that there are patterned announcers and flexible announcers and that our generalization does not take into consideration the variety of material handled by the announcer. To both of these rejoinders, we would agree, but still insist that radio announcing, broadly considered, is patterned speech. The examples of individualisitic style, communicative directness, "the gentleman conversing," are the exceptions, not the rule.

There are three reasons which explain the stereotyped character of announcing: (1) The typical commercial announcement (also stereotyped) is a sales pellet compacted of common ingredients. Injunctions to buy vary only slightly in their basic formats. People are urged to buy because they will safeguard or lengthen their lives, save dollars, enhance their social prestige, prove their humanitarianism or civic virtue, or be able to ride higher than their neighbors. With a limited number of compelling motives and a legion of commercial products, it is inevitable that we get the same notes in a slightly different key. (2) The work conditions enforced on a station announcer, particularly in the smaller stations, produce an automaton who intersperses recordings with "spots" according to the work sheet and sales chart for the day. Reading becomes an automatic performance, made all the more so by the first factor just explained. (3) Another factor which explains the uniformity of announcing style is imitation. A pattern was established. Newcomers picked up the style that was current and therefore evidently acceptable, and a vogue ensued.

Criteria. We suggest seven criteria by which to judge the announcer's skill and effectiveness.

1. *Personal Qualities.* Our previous discussion of speech and personality pertains directly to the radio announcer. His real influence lies in individual qualities which elude particularized description. It is not easy to say in clear, definitive terms why you like one person and not another. We use certain adjectives such as friendly, natural, sincere, and vital, but what does each one mean? In spite of the complex batteries of personality tests, diagnostic procedures, and analytical formulas available to psychological laboratories, personality factors have not been refined to the clarity of mathematical concepts. Much progress has been made in this direction, of course, and the trained investigator can produce quantitative and qualitative data about a subject's intelligence, temperament, motility, expressional and social traits; but as layman meets layman, personality remains an intangible and indefinable "something." And this intangible, indefinable, and elusive something is a composite of hereditary and socially conditioned elements peculiar to a particular individual. "He's got it or he hasn't got it." This vulgarian summary of the point contradicts by no means the effect of education or the possibility of reconditioning, but it does argue that there are basic and fundamental limitations which differentiate people socially and that disparate qualities cannot be equalized by training.

This, perhaps, is to raise the moot question, Is a performer made or born? Or, asked in another way, Will competent instruction and patient, persistent application produce an announcer? Our answer to these questions is both negative and affirmative. Certain levels of ability can be attained through disciplined drill; but one may achieve mechanical competency and yet fail to "make the grade." On the other hand, an announcer may fail to meet the conventional textbook formulations of proficiency and yet "come out on top." To begin with, then, the qualities of the effective announcer lie deep within the personality structure of the man. The following requisites are additive refinements.

2. *Reading Proficiency.* The announcer is primarily a reader, and a mastery of reading techniques should precede the study of announcing problems, per se. The principles we have explained in connection with the delivery of the radio talk apply to him. The announcer's problem begins with the analysis of his copy. What are the subject, the product, the sponsor, the chief sales arguments, and the audience for whom they are designed? Then, the text is studied as to its rhetorical and grammatical style. Different sentence structures require variations in delivery. Communicative and interpretive completeness depends on oral punctuation, allocation of stress, time variations, and inflectional patterns. These climaxes, or high points, are achieved through pacing, transitions, and emphasis. They are reading techniques and are developed by continued practice with all kinds of subject matter. The gamut of prose, poetry, and drama which the college student encounters in interpretation courses contributes to his flexibility and ready adaptation to the printed page.

3. *Voice.* This criterion is often misunderstood. Many people believe that a "rich, deep, resonant" voice is the *sine qua non.* This is far from the truth. An announcer who has a middle register, and even higher than middle register, may be very effective. The "pleasing" voice is not altogether a matter of fundamentals and overtones. Voice timbre, or resonance, is only one tonal element and means little unless it is associated with pitch, time, and stress variations. Don't feel assured of radio success because you sing bass in the village choir. This is another place where we meet that indefinable "something." A harmonic analysis of your tone production will offer no guarantee of success or failure.

4. *Standard Speech.* The announcer's speech is free from regional and local peculiarities. This has been a condition imposed on announcers since the early years of broadcasting, and radio has contributed to a standardized speech.

The announcer must also be familiar with musical terminology, geographical and biographical names, and place names.

5. *Extempore Ability*. There are frequent instances when an announcer must meet broadcasting emergencies. Circumstances arise for which no provision is made in the script. Moreover, his work may extend to remote broadcasts requiring ad-lib descriptions and accounts of public events, accidents, parades, etc.

6. *Versatility*. This criterion covers the meaning of flexibility and adaptability. The announcer who has a patterned style of reading and makes little differentiation between the peace of Shady Rest Cemetery and the get-rich-quick opportunities in the new Sunshine Subdivision is guilty of a reflex vocal activity that cuts off just above his Adam's apple. He must have the skill to handle the particular public-relations equation set for him by the copy, the program type, and the class of sponsor. He should be able to officiate as the sponsor's or station's representative in many different situations. He may be called on to introduce a variety of musical programs—popular, light, classical, symphony, religious, folk, ballad; dramatic programs that begin with farce and range through comedy, serious drama, mystery, biographical, historical, and crime drama. He will have occasion to present to the public a variety of prominent personalities, newscasters, and commentators. And not only will the program content and program personnel be varied, but the aims and purposes of the sponsors will vary as will the audience groups for which the program is designed. To meet this range of demand, flexibility and versatility are paramount. The announcer shoud guard against becoming typed or grooved and should not read everything put into his hands as if it were a typical spot commercial requiring the usual blatant soap-box driving harangue to buy XYZ now, today, at once.

7. *Persuasiveness*. Persuasion is the process of evoking a desired listener response. To attain a given response, it is necessary first to select adequate stimuli. This adequacy is found in the acting nature of the auditor. The writer relates his copy to the action grooves of his audience, trying through the use of words to set off "highly charged tendencies" within the hearer. This material is given its ultimate force by the voice of the announcer who is at all times selling something—an idea, an impression, a box of soap. To define the quality of persuasiveness brings us back to our first criterion—personal qualities. We know that the favorable or unfavorable impression of the announcer's delivery is due to such matters as vocal quality, distinctness, pronunciation, variety, and emphasis; but these are only the bright jacket on the book. The true causal factors underlie external elements of vocalization. The meaning of this assertion can be clarified by explaining the difference between the mechanical and the *live* announcer—the physical and the psychological.

	Mechanical	*Psychological*
1. Reading proficiency:	eye movements, fixation, optical perception, and perception span are perfected through consciously controlled exercise and drill, and function in	the grasp of associated meanings and quickened comprehension of words and ideas.
2. Voice:	may be improved by learning how to compensate for physical inadequacies, and also by developing through practice a better control over phonation; but this will not overcome the effect of	tensions which accompany emotion.
3. Speech standard:	objectionable speech variants can be eliminated through practice, provided the problem is clearly objectified and sound drill disciplines are maintained, but	this phase of the speech problem is psychological in that pronunciation is a product of environmental associations.
4. Extempore ability:	can be developed through practice, but it reflects	command of vocabulary, logical facility, subject knowledge, and concentration.
5. Versatility (vocal flexibility and variety):	conscious study of speech patterns may develop an insight with reference to the monotonous voice, but such terms as range, inflection, modulation, syllable quantity, pace, and stress are only words describing	the mental and emotional processes underlying speech. Variety results from understanding and feeling; it is not the product of conscious voice manipulation.
6. Persuasiveness:	mechanical drills can do little if anything to supply the	sincerity, naturalness, earnestness, friendliness, and similar qualities which constitute the character of persuasiveness.

An announcer whose performance incorporates the above principles and skills may approach his job with confidence.

The Announcer's Continuity. What types of continuity does the announcer handle? A detailed breakdown of script material may serve the purpose of interest and information, but from the standpoint of performance, purpose-classification is more important than name-classification. Referring to our discussion of basic principles, the announcer is controlled by program nature, the audience addressed, the sponsor's objective, and station operation. Broadly stated, his functions are to sell and to give information. The kinds of material he reads over the air may be listed under these headings.

1. *Selling*. The sales message takes various forms:

a. The *service announcement*. "The correct time as verified by ——————— watch company."

b. The *spot announcement*. A commercial plug usually given between station breaks or program intervals.

c. The *full-length commercial*. The sales presentation which may be a minute or more in length and which precedes, interrupts, and closes the program.

d. *"Cowcatchers and hitchhikes."* Commercial plugs somewhat shorter than the regular or main program announcements but at the beginning (cowcatcher) or end (hitchhike) of the program, and within the time frame of the program.

e. *Institutional*. A more formal and dignified presentation emphasizing abstract qualities of the sponsor's service—ethical ideals rather than commercial details.

f. *Promotional*. To call attention to new programs and station or network services.

g. *Public service*. Similar to the promotional statement but aimed particularly to serve community events, drives, and civic needs.

2. *Information*. In addition to the important job of selling, the announcer is the voice of information.

a. *Station sign-on and sign-off*. The Federal law requires that the day's operation begin and end with the announcement of the station's call letters, authorized wavelength, and power.

b. *Station identification and program breaks*. It is also required that a station identify itself at periodic times during its operational hours.

c. *Discrepancy*. Explanations of sudden program change—irregularities and interruptions of program service.

d. *Introductions*. Presentation of guest speakers, program panels, emcees, or other program personnel.

e. *Commentary*. Expository statements regarding musical numbers, ranging from the introduction of popular music to the formal presentation of a symphony program.

f. *News*. The reporting of news as gathered from the leading news services. This may be a regular assignment. The reporting of news, however, is not news commentary. The commentator belongs in a particular classification.

g. *On-the-scene reporting*. The announcer may be assigned to cover parades, civic events, and special operations.

This listing does not cover every type of continuity or service associated with announcing, and it does not fully indicate the range of programs to which the announcer must adjust himself. However, it is sufficient to indicate the scope of his work. Your vocational aptitude and skill can be tested by the following examples compiled from active broadcast files:[1]

(1)

There is only *one* hospital in Southern California that offers complete Sister Kenny treatment to polio-crippled children. Yet, lack of funds keeps two of its three hospital wings unopened. By giving a few hours, you can help open those empty wings . . . that more may walk! Call DUnkirk 8-2271. . . . Volunteer your services.

(2)

This is Public Schools Week! You are cordially invited to visit your community's schools. Your interest and support of public education are the best guarantee of a sound public-school system. This is the finest way to protect your family's investment in democracy and secure the future for your children.

(3)

The Red Cross Campaign must go over the top. Here is why: when a dying soldier needs four pints of blood, one pint is not enough. Should a million people need food, clothing, and shelter . . . facilities for 250,000 are not enough. So . . . "on the double." Let's give *double* to the Red Cross 1952 campaign.

(4)

Good government is the job of every citizen. In order to let your municipal, county, state, and Federal government officials know where you stand on the vital issues of the day . . . write to them. For the names and addresses of your elected representatives . . . send a postcard with your name, address, and postal zone number to this station.

(5)

Young men . . . want a job where you can go swimming all summer and get paid for it? Then this is for you! The city is hiring life guards and swimming pool managers for summer jobs. For further information inquire now. Call at Room 5, City Hall, Los Angeles, or dial MIchigan 5211, Extension 734.

(6)

For a comprehensive picture of sporting events around the nation and the news headlines of the world . . . listen to CBS Newsroom, Sunday Desk . . . a half-hour with Tom Harmon and Dick Joy. Yes . . . it's Tom Harmon with a 15-minute summary of sports activities . . . and Dick Joy with late week-end dispatches from around the world . . . on CBS Newsroom Sunday Desk . . . five-thirty today over this station.

[1] The first eleven examples of public-service and promotional advertisements are supplied by the courtesy of the CBS station, KNX, Columbia Square, Hollywood, Calif.

(7)

You'll hear great radio entertainment tonight on KNX. Hopalong Cassidy starts at six . . . followed by Broadway's My Beat . . . Sing It Again . . . Vaughan Monroe . . . Gene Autrey . . . Gang Busters . . . and O'Hara. Four hours of great listening. Stay tuned tonight to KNX . . . the stars' address.

(8)

Sunday is *star-time*—on KNX. The great stars lining up to provide you with the best in radio entertainment—include the old fiddler Jack Benny himself—Amos 'n' Andy—Edgar Bergen and Charlie McCarthy—Janet Waldo—as Corliss Archer—Horace Heidt and his original *Youth Opportunity Program*—these and many more great stars ready to entertain you every Sunday—KNX—the stars' address!

(9)

Great Drama . . . brilliant performances! That's the *Hallmark Playhouse!* Where Hollywood's most glamorous stars visit your host, James Hilton, to bring you exciting radio adaptations of your favorite novels. They're the stories you love to hear . . . thrillingly brought to life. Listen to the *Hallmark Playhouse* —tonight—at six-thirty over this station.

(10)

Listen to Ed Morgan today for a 15-minute summary of late world news developments. Make this experienced reporter's roundup of world headlines a regular part of your Sunday listening schedule. Hear Ed Morgan and the News at two-forty-five today and every Sunday afternoon.

(11)

Listen to one of radio's most instructive and constructive programs! *The Housewives Protective League*—with Philip Norman as your host. Mr. Norman comes to you every day—with informal chatter and suggestions—concerning your health, happiness, and prosperity. Listen to the *Housewives Protective League Program*—with Philip Norman today, at one-thirty.

(12)

If your vacation trip means you're going to be motoring through a lot of western territory, take a tip from independent Chevron Gas Stations, and Standard Stations. Use *Chevron Supreme* Gasoline! It's climate-tailored to give your car peak performance wherever you drive . . . in cool mountain country, in hot deserts, and along the coast. When you get premium-quality Chevron Supreme, you can be sure of ping-free power. That's because it's specially blended to give faster starts, quicker pickup, and extra power on hills, with never an engine knock. A pinging engine is a strained and laboring engine that's wasting both power and fuel, you know. So rely on Chevron Supreme for thrift—and for more pleasant motoring, whether you are on vacation or just driving around town. Remember: You can't buy a better gasoline for today's high-compression engines. Get Chevron Supreme at *Standard* stations, and independent *Chevron* Gas Stations . . . where they say, and mean, "We take better care of your car."[2]

(13)

ANNOUNCER: Not all highway robbery is committed at the point of a gun . . . some of it is perpetrated by the unseen bandits of Grit and Dust who take command of defenseless bulk oils and "bore from within" to undermine the efficiency of your motor, shatter its morale, and ultimately send it to "condemned row." For that reason, tens of thousands of western motorists are entrusting the lives of their motor to Rio, the great lubricant that wears the impenetrable armor of sealed, tamper-proof cans, making Rio the perfect bodyguard of every vital moving part. This pure, 100 per cent paraffin-base motor oil is so completely de-waxed and de-jellied that the most severe cold weather cannot change its quick, smooth flow to every part of your motor. If 1,000 miles have rolled by since your last oil change, do this: When you turn in at your nearest Rio station in the morning for that tankful of *Cracked* gasoline, have the crankcase drained and take aboard Rio Pennsylvania. There is no finer motor oil sold in the west.

(14)

ANNOUNCER: The forthcoming World Series prompts me to remind you that all-purpose Rio already has won the gasoline championship by a score of six to three. Yes, this great public-serving gasoline holds the title because it is made up of *six* vital, power-developing ingredients . . . *six*, as compared with the *three* usually found in "run-of-the-mill" gasolines. This means . . . and the drivers of such emergency equipment as police cars, ambulances, and fire engines were quick to recognize the fact . . . this means that with each ingredient accounting for a different quality of performance, Rio's balanced combination of all *six* provides *your* car with the maximum performance of which it is capable. And, by "maximum performance" I mean more power, swifter pickup, smoother acceleration, and more miles per gallon than you ever experienced before. It is this *all-purpose* quality of the radically different Rio which has convinced tens of thousands of western drivers to make their neighborhood Rio station their motoring headquarters. Get that tankful in the morning and find out for yourself just why *all-purpose Rio is* the most highly recommended, public-serving gasoline sold in the west.

(15)

ANNOUNCER: Most of us want to economize these days and put off 'till tomorrow what we can't afford today. But—we can't afford to neglect our homes! Du Pont, as part of its program of *Better Things for Better Living* . . . *through Chemistry*, offers an economical wall paint in "Speed-easy." With du Pont Speed-easy it costs less than $3 to paint an average-sized room in one color. Not only is this oil-type paint economical, but it's so easy to use. Thin it with water and apply over stained or drab walls or

[2] Courtesy of Standard Oil Company of California.

wall paper with a large brush or roller. It dries in an hour, leaving your walls with a smooth, beautiful finish in a white or any one of eleven lovely colors. It's economical—it's easy—it's Speed-easy, one of the du Pont Company's *Better Things for Better Living . . . through Chemistry.*[3]

(16)

ANNOUNCER: Did you ever watch a kitten roll in a bed of catnip? Well; dogs like chocolate as much as cats like catnip—most dogs anyhow. My dog does. If your pup likes chocolate, and you want to keep him from climbing up on a chair and getting his nose into that box of Christmas candy, you can now buy him a toy shaped like a bone that has the flavor of chocolate. It's made of du Pont neoprene rubber with the chocolate added—and that means it is tough enough to stand the teeth of a great Dane and at the same time soft enough to be chucked around the living room without marring the furniture.

Just so you won't think chemistry is going entirely to the dogs this week, you can buy toys for the children, too, that are made of neoprene. Mothers will appreciate these new neoprene toys because they can be sterilized in boiling water. Neoprene stands boiling water and after-the-bath oils better than natural rubber.

A doll called the "Magic Skin" doll has neoprene skin in natural color that you can hardly tell from the skin of a real baby. A little girl can give the doll a bath without it suffering any harm from soap and water. There is a lamb with a nubby coat like wool, there's a duck, there's a dog named "Poochy"; there are baby chicks and a whale that spouts water like a real whale. The colors are mixed right into the du Pont neoprene, going all the way through. Manufacturers say they are harmless and will not come off if a baby chews them—as he will! For older youngsters there is a submarine—and a ship with three smokestacks. There are balls of all sizes. There are balloons, too, that hold air longer than balloons of natural rubber. These bright little toys represent only one of the many developments in which rubber made by chemical science is proving better than natural rubber from trees. They illustrate the way in which ingenious American manufacturers, quick to use a promising development, pass the achievements of science along to you almost as soon as they leave the laboratory. Neoprene chemical rubber is one of du Pont Company's—*Better Things for Better Living—through Chemistry.*[4]

QUESTIONS

1. What are the various functions of the announcer?

2. To what extent do you agree with the general criticism of announcers as expressed in this chapter?

3. How do you explain the stereotyped announcer?

4. Name the criteria by which to judge an announcer's skill and effectiveness.

[3] Courtesy du Pont Company (E. I. du Pont de Nemours & Company).
[4] Courtesy of du Pont Company (E. I. du Pont de Nemours & Company).

CHAPTER 13

RADIO DISCUSSION

* **The Role of Discussion in a Democracy.** It is an axiom of democratic theory that education is essential to popular goverment. A free people must have access to facts, be able to interpret them, and have the opportunity to direct their actions according to convictions derived from independent analysis. Untrammeled expression of ideas and freedom of action are basic to the Anglo-Saxon heritage. Iron manacles are less symbolic of slavery than ignorance and indolence. The story of religion is the evolution of the freedom of conscience and the right to liberty in religious development; the story of law details the means by which man has sought to control violent antisocial impulses in the interests of the community; and the growth of political stature is proportionate to successfully directed and controlled social activity.

Free public discussion and the interchange of opinions and ideas have been a process of democratic procedure since the early period of town meetings. The rise of popular education and its sharp acceleration following the war between the states evidenced faith in universal education as the means of solving problems incident to growing social complexities. The pious hope of an early colonial governor that we would never have free public schools in America, "because education has brought heresies and sects into the world and libeled the best governments," was not to be a part of the philosophy of a people striving for political independence. Recognition of the importance of mass enlightenment motivated the Chautauqua and Lyceum movements of the late nineteenth century. An informed citizenry, it was held, was best able to select representatives to decide in legislative halls the issues of state; and the American political forum became a "parliament of the people." Political and economic history is filled with critical issues and vital differences of public opinion; but no matter how violent the dissenting points of view, the solutions have been sought in orderly processes of oral and written expression, discussion, and debate and in the final arbitrament of the ballot box.

The democratic process of free discussion is an instrument to promote the ideals of social solidarity. Society is divided into a large number of partial and discordant selves. These selves or social variants, have different interests, motivations, ideals, and needs. Group and sectional interests spring from separate standards of education, economic thought, and racial and religious backgrounds. Each social segment has a particular something for which it is striving; each is motivated by a special self-interest. The task of democratic leadership is to reconcile divergent opinions and interests and reduce their number according to a concept of unitary good. A growing spirit of divisiveness impairs democratic achievement; an increase in the number of cooperating groups facilitates democratic aims. It is the faith of men who would be independent that this ideal of national unity is advanced by free discussion.

Can discussion clarify misunderstandings, reconcile differences, and effect wider agreements in the spheres of thought and action? We may properly question whether much change of opinion is achieved by discussion. One purpose of education is to teach respect for facts, detached thinking, analysis, and the logical bases of judgment. The college graduate, however, faced with the realistic problems of competition and survival, is prone to ally himself with agencies calculated to promote his special interests. It is generally conceded that men think with their emotions. It can be doubted that conclusions are ever entirely objective and logical. Political managers spend large sums to "sway the vote," committees argue long hours, and the public is harangued by all the agencies of communication; but how many votes represent a change or reversal of opinion due to the force of logical persuasion? One easily believes that which conforms to, or corroborates, his established views; and he likewise resists tenaciously all arguments opposed to his mental set. Predispositions are fixed according to environmental control and the laws of conditioned behavior. "Mental adhesions" are characteristic not only of octogenarians.

Instead of discounting the value of discussion, however, this situation presents a challenge. If we hold to the democratic way of life, we must believe that the conclusions of public issues should be hammered out on the anvil of debate; and we must have faith that larger areas of social cooperation can thereby be achieved.

In the attainment of this ideal, radio, which has produced a twentieth-century village green, has a dynamic function. Every radio home is a listening post and a unit of response which, when aggregated, spells a gigantic potential. Ideas can be presented more effectively to individuals, or small groups of individuals, than to mass audiences. The reason is found in the characteristics of the "crowd mind." The theory of a crowd mind, implying a collective consciousness that is different from individual mental activity, is not tenable in the light of current psychological doctrine. However, crowds are composed of individuals who may be, and usually are, influenced by the behavior of those around them.

Crowds are highly suggestible, emotional, and predisposed by organic pressures. The totality of crowd behavior is influenced by the principles of facilitation, social projection, and universality. The reserve, inhibition, and reflective delay which accompany individual response in relative isolation are surrendered in the urgency of a crowd situation. Orators, propagandists, and sales promoters understand how to use these principles in influencing mass judgment. They employ a set of psychological factors which would not be effective if their audience numbered 10 and not 10,000. The radio speaker addresses his tens of thousands but not en masse. He is actually speaking to you at your family "fireside." This fact gives discussion by radio a particular value. The individual radio listener (or small group of listeners) will be freer to make evaluations which conform less to a central tendency of judgment than a man who listens to an address in a crowded auditorium.

It is the purpose of this chapter to review the preparation of a discussion subject for radio presentation and to explain the mechanics of pointing and controlling the discussion on the air. There are several discussion formats, variously termed panel, round table, dialogue, symposium, conversation, debate, and forum. They differ in some respects. For example, in the symposium, each speaker is assigned a stated time for an uninterrupted presentation of his ideas; in a debate, spokesmen are also allowed a fixed time to present formal constructive and rebuttal speeches; and the forum program implies audience participation. However the plans or procedures may vary, each is governed by basic discussion principles. We shall explain these principles as they apply to a particular type of presentation—the radio panel or round table.

A Subject Is Chosen. *Why a Subject Is Selected.* The radio discussion will reach thousands and millions of listeners according to the time of the broadcast and the coverage of the station or network. The purpose of the program is to inform, stimulate, and persuade. Its value should be judged by its effectiveness in clarifying the subject and the extent to which listener thought is affected. The program is not planned to exhibit erudition, feature names, or entertain by means of verbal pyrotechnics. The subject selected should have direct and immediate appeal to the audience addressed. This audience may be local, regional, or national. It is a natural error to think of a radio program in national terms because it is the "coast-to-coast" broadcasts which have the spotlight, are most ably supported and executed, and command the largest ratings; but we must not overlook the potential community services of hundreds and thousands of independent stations. Indeed, as we have seen, one of the criticisms of chain broadcasting is that the contractural relationships involved preclude the fullest measure of local broadcasting in the public interest. Every regional and local area has many problems of vital interest, and the local radio station provides an expressional outlet for a great number of business, civic, religious, and social agencies. Subjects selected for air presentation should be geared to the prevailing interests and needs of the area concerned.

Wording the Subject. Careful thought should be given to the wording of the discussion topic derived from the general subject. The distinction between topic and subject implies the importance of limiting the area of discussion in such a way as to promote a direct clash of viewpoints— avoiding cross purposes, vagueness, and circumlocution. For example, the question, Is radio an agency of free speech? would lead to a more discursive treatment than, Should radio management have the right to censor the radio speaker's manuscript? Likewise, an attempt to answer the query, Is radio commercialism opposed to the public interest? would probably lead to more generality than, Should the FCC increase the proportion of time devoted to noncommercial programs? The topic should be stated simply, involve only one main thesis, and avoid ambiguity. Furthermore, the subject should be debatable. It must be neither obviously true nor false, and one side of the controversy should not be outweighed by a preponderance of contrary evidence. There would be small point in talking about, Is radio a social force? or, Is there a future for television? On the other hand, we might properly inquire about the effect of crime programs on children, or whether standard broadcasting will be rendered obsolete by television. Moreover, the subject topic should not be a double-barreled one, containing two ideas or aspects of the field under examination. If it were proposed to present the question, Should Mr. X. be recalled and Mr. Y. elected in his place? we would be confronted with two sets of arguments not necessarily related. The topic formulation, Do chain broadcasting and commercially sponsored radio programs operate in the public interest? may appear to present a unified and single phase of broadcasting, but upon examination it is seen that we have two nonrelated phases of a general subject.

The wording of the subject for the radio panel usually takes the form of the interrogation. This is different from the form employed in formal debate where we have a proposition beginning with the word, "Resolved." For example, "Resolved, that 30 per cent of available standard broadcast channels should be allocated to educational institutions." The panel discussion and the formal debate differ in many respects. The debate is conducted according to formal rules applying to the order and length of speeches, admissibility of evidence, and refutation. The panel discussion is informal and not circumscribed by fixed regulations. Speeches are in the nature of conversational rejoinder, and no distinction is made between constructive and rebuttal arguments. There are rules, as we shall see, but they are not of the debate manual variety.

One is probably a better panel participant if he is versed in the techniques and methodology of reasoned discourse as used in formal, logical debate, but his adaptation to the round-table situation calls for an entirely different attitude of mind and quality of approach.

A Panel Is Organized. *Size of the Panel.* It is presumed that men and women who have professional relationship to the subject and are qualified spokesmen, will be invited to form the panel. The number of participants should be limited because it is difficult for the radio listener to maintain a clear image of the round-table picture if too many speakers are involved. Moreover, the discussion itself is likely to become confused. Four speakers (exclusive of the chairman) are probably the maximum number permitting a unified and coherent impression. Two speakers, as a rule, will not produce enough variety or differentiation. An even number comprises the usual panel in order that opposing views and different subject facets may be equally represented. When several interests are involved, each with a different philosophy or plan of attack, all parties should be represented, if possible, in order that the subject may be fully covered.

Qualifications of Panel Members. What are the qualifications of the panel member? It is obvious that he should be well informed, able to reason cogently, and express himself with ease and clarity. However, a man may have these qualifications and not be able to contribute effectively to the project. His real strength lies in a full appreciation of the purpose of round-table discussion and in the mental and emotional attitudes required by the situation. We have defined discussion as a means of democratic government. This implies an association of free men, tolerance of ideas, and protection of minorities. Democracy is a market place of ideas. There are buyers and sellers, but goods should be marked plainly, and the rule of *caveat emptor* cannot apply. No man should suffer duress or coercion. Exchange and substitution should be allowed. Should the metaphor be too involved, let us say that discussion is a meeting of free minds—a process of arriving at conclusions by persuasion and logic—and that results are accepted by loser and winner in a spirit of cooperation. Round-table members are engaged in a search for a feasible and practicable solution, but whatever decision is derived the result will be a compromise. One cannot expect the conclusion to be satisfactory to all concerned. Disappointments and frustrations are inevitable, and the loser must yield gracefully and wait until a change of conditions swings the pendulum in his direction. Nor, does the victor gloat in his triumph. He realizes that the search for truth is never ending and that "new occasions teach new duties." Our feet are guided by the "lamp of experience," and our constant hope is that tomorrow will be better than today. Led by these considerations and believing that codes of present action are relative to changing conditions, the panel member should not carry to the microphone a fixed, dogmatic, and unyielding attitude. He will state his convictions and defend them tenaciously in so far as experience, evidence, and logic will stand by him; but he will be flexible enough to realize that he may not comprehend the full circle of events, that no position is impregnable, and that good and bad are sometimes inextricable. His demeanor, then, is one of restrained courtesy and tolerance for other men's views. He will be firm but not dogmatic, positive but not always unyielding, strong in his convictions but not blind to new evidence. Panel discussion should not provide the opportunity for self-exploitation or aggrandizement. In a sense, the speaker is a trustee. He is engaged in helping to decide what is "best interest," "public good," or "social expediency." He speaks not for himself, but in behalf of a group, clientele, section, association, or society at large. Hence, he assumes at the outset a judicial attitude, cognizant of all the interests involved.

When a panel is organized, it is wise to exclude extremists unless they can qualify under the above criteria. It is not the suggestion that "rightists" or "leftists" should be denied, nor is it our thought that all people representing liberal or radical points of view are bigoted, clamorous, and narrowly insistent. In fact, extreme conservatists may be most obnoxious. All points of view must be heard in a democracy, but our half-hour radio program is designed to give a fair, balanced, and judicial consideration of a public question, and whatever position is held by the discussion participant, it should be expressed with dignity, self-control, and respect for opposed opinions. If one delights in a verbal fracas and seeks entertainment in a forensic arena where temperament, emotion, and prejudice clash, such a spectacle might be arranged for him; but this is not the type of discussion we wish to promote. The panel should not be a sounding board for special issues nor a public-square miniature of soapboxers at work. Panel deliberations are a careful and rational weighing of social problems.

Differences between Panel Discussion and Formal Speech and Debate. Another requisite of effective panel participation is that the panel member understand the differences between round-table discussion and formal public address and debate. The main differences between the panel situation and the usual speaker-audience situation is that the panel spokesman is not "flying solo." He is now a member of a team. He cannot make a straight-line development of his ideas. There is the give-and-take of conversation. Thought processes will be interrupted, challenged, and blocked. Yet, the speaker must maintain a continuum of purpose and thought. There is a dynamic quality in motivated conversation seldom attained in formal discourse. The faults present in the average classroom speech—such as monotony due to even stress, time, and intonation pattern—are absent from animated conversation. The circular stimulus character of face-to-face speech produces a quickening of thought processes and a consequent expressional variety.

Panel discussion is not formal debating. Formal college debating has fallen into disrepute in some quarters. The reason is that debating is too often mere contentiousness. Each speaker feels that he is appointed from on High to defend his assigned position to the bitter end. Sharp practices result. The debate becomes a game, and the rules are manipulated to outsmart the opposition. There is no honest attempt to search and evaluate. The all-or-none principle is invoked; one side is completely right and the other completely wrong. Certainly, not all college debating is so prostituted to the fetish of winning a judge's decision, but the above characterization is true in many instances. It was this condition that gave rise to decisionless debates, open-forum debating, the audience decision, split teams, and various other innovations. The radio panel begins with the invitation, "Come, let us reason together," and then proceeds to determine, if possible, the wisest course of action. The discussion proceeds in the spirit of mutual faith, good will, and common good.

The Panel Member Prepares. The discussion participant should be thoroughly conversant with the subject. He must command a wide knowledge of related facts and comprehend their organic relationship, because a partially informed and illogical mind cannot contribute effectively to a panel discussion. The common weaknesses to be found in round-table presentations are the unsupported assertion, loose generalization, and faulty logic. By logic is meant the processes by which conclusions are drawn from facts, isolated facts associated with pre-established conclusions, and the proper interpretation of causal agencies. It must be assumed here that the college student of broadcasting techniques has had a basic training in discussion methodology, but a brief review of some of the preparation steps and dialectic skills involved in group discussion is offered to assist in preparing the assignments connected with this unit of work.

The Reading Program. The panel member begins his preparation by compiling a bibliography from the various indexes in order to establish an acquaintance with the main sources of material. The use of indexes to periodical and standard literature, reference books, encyclopedias, special bulletins and publications, and government documents is basic to the research problem. The reading program begins with the more general books, articles, surveys, and reports. This reading for orientation is governed by a particular set of questions which should be answered before continuing with a more detailed scrutiny of the topic. These questions are as follows:

1. *What are the particular facts or circumstances which give immediacy to the subject?* That is, why is there any point of holding our discussion at this time? Any worth-while discussion is motivated by special social, economic, and political conditions now present. A subject chosen arbitrarily, or selected only because it has forensic possibility, may lead to nothing but an academic exercise. Forces are taking shape today. Needs cry for solution, causal forces are leading to "boom or bust," ideologies clash, proposed legislation is fraught with serious import, and the whole problem of day-to-day living is a conflict of insurgent forces which must be directed and controlled now. The nature of discussion, as we have defined the term, implies the effort of reconciling opposed interests and points of view, each of which is seeking ascendency. First, then, we ask, Why are we discussing the subject? What is its present-hour importance? What are the facts and conditions which precipitate it at this time? A discussion of the college honor system in an institution where the system is operating smoothly, without criticism or doubt as to its effectiveness, would be an example of what we have called a manufactured academic exercise. On the other hand, if this same system, which has been operating successfully, were suddenly brought into question by an outbreak of violations and a consequent dissatisfaction, the question of its continuance would be a proper subject for investigation and debate. The *status quo* is not a field of debate if everyone is satisfied, but the presence of liberal or radical dissent will precipitate controversy. A critical inquiry into the social value of radiobroadcasting would be unnecessary if everyone were satisfied with the content and quality of radio programs, but a barrage of protests from responsible sources may force radio executives and program makers to defend their policies. Hereby, an issue is formed and must be tested in the give-and-take process of argument. Such questions as, Can we win the next war by air power alone? Should the United States develop a national system of state-supported medicine? Will television eclipse and render obsolete AM broadcasting? are examples of topics that find their cause for discussion in suddenly generated conditions which one must understand and appraise before leaping into a forensic battle.

2. *What are the principal facts in the historical background of the subject?* The answer to our first question leads logically to this second point of inquiry. The historical approach to the discussion will not only cast in relief the importance of the subject, but also will contribute to a discovery of the issues or essential points of difference. The issue of

government versus private control of the air is derived from the circumstances attending a new scientific discovery, the original positions taken by government and private industry spokesmen, and the policies adopted by various governments on the same subject. Present debates in the United States on the subject of foreign policy stem from an entirely different set of premises than ever existed at any other time in our national history: We are living in an atomic age. Measures applicable to a new situation are derived in large part from preceding experience. Man moves through a series of cycles. An understanding of the new cycle is made possible by our knowledge of the preceding one. The basic causes of recurring depressions are not completely analogous, but they do have common elements, and a knowledge of past causes and conditions may help us formulate practical remedies dealing with such phenomena as available bank credit, bank balances, speculative excesses, balance of trade, and production levels. To find the issues in a discussion of TV channel allocation to educational institutions would carry us back more than 25 years when it was proposed that radio channels should be reserved for institutional use.

3. *What is the meaning of the terms in the subject?* The third point of information requisite to a direct clash of argument is a clear-cut definition of the terms used in the subject statement. These terms must be defined sharply and discretely because, otherwise, opposed participants may be speaking in different concepts. The symbols used may be the same, but their referents will be poles apart. If we are discussing a plan, law, method, or process, it should be analyzed and broken down into objective elements which everyone can accept. If definition by authority is employed, a basis for interchange of opinions cannot be reached unless the authorities cited are mutually accepted. A dictionary definition may be different from the meaning employed by specialists or experts who speak from a particular frame of reference. If panel members do not get together on their definition of terms, they will be running on separate and parallel tracks. Definitions are especially important when the subject under consideration is stated loosely or employs vague and general terms. Such words and phrases as communism, education, democracy, labor unions, social security, state rights, in the best interest, and practicable are too inclusive. The more precise and definitive the subject statement, the better chance we have for a direct meeting of minds.

4. *Can the subject area be limited by common agreement?* Sometimes broad and inclusive terms cannot be avoided. In these instances particularly, the pointedness of the round-table presentation can be aided by an accepted narrowing of the subject. This is achieved either by waiving certain aspects of the general field or by agreeing on as

much of the subject area as possible. Fair-minded people will seldom find themselves totally at variance. They may agree on a principle but disagree on a proposed implementation of that principle. The advocates of simplified spelling have not insisted that all words be spelled phonetically, or as they sound. Spokesmen in labor-management disputes are, in general, not opposed to collective bargaining. The issue is always a detailed one concerning such matters as speed-up practices, rates of pay in reference to prevailing living costs, and jurisdictional rights. Foreign aid may be recognized as a necessary program, but honest differences of opinion may exist concerning the extent of the aid required, the over-all period of payment, and the allocation of funds to particular nations. Again, the need for a civic improvement may be admitted, and the issue be entirely one of expediency. Shall it be delayed in view of present construction costs? Shall the project be financed by a bond issue, and over what period of time? Disputants may agree that the system of privately owned and operated radio is the only one for the United States, but clash in their views concerning the social effectiveness of the system. In other words, what is the exact area we wish to scrutinize? The more the subject can be limited and the more we can focus the discussion upon points commonly agreed upon, the more profitable will be the debate.

So far in our preparation, then, we have tried to ascertain four things:

1. What is the immediate cause for discussion? What are the prevailing conditions which press for solution? The discussion is prompted by what state of affairs?

2. What are the historical facts which throw light upon the present problem? What are the antecedent factors which better enable us to interpret the current problem?

3. What is the meaning of the terms or phrases in the question or subject for discussion?

4. What are the areas of admitted matter? Are there certain partials which may be agreed upon? How far can both sides of the case be reconciled at the outset? How can we narrow the ground in an attempt to get the most direct clash of opinion?

5. *Continue the reading program to discover the issues.* The next step in preparing for our panel participation is to continue our reading to discover the pro and contra contentions. The investigator is now faced with the problem of discriminating note taking. One of Napoleon's biographers explains the Little Corporal's military success by saying that he always perceived where the matter hinged. The number of *main* contentions will not be great. Different writers will state their positions differently, but in essence the discussion will move about a few salient points. Each of these main positions will be supported by subassertions,

but the final outline will embrace a limited number of main headings. In the process of reading on both sides of the question (and one should cover the affirmative and negative cases with equal thoroughness) the opposing points of view should be set down on opposite pages of a notebook. Each list will grow and take shape as the reading continues. Another way of putting the matter is to say that you are seeking the principal guideposts by which you may orient your continuing journey through the field of source material. Or, to change the figure, we follow a jigsaw puzzle technique of locating the most obvious elements in the picture and then fitting together the detailed and smaller pieces of the puzzle. This latter process is more or less a constant one because it can never reach true completeness so long as source material is still available, and one can hardly expect to encompass all the available data relating to his subject. The lists of contentions, when completed, should be matched. The aggregate number of contentions on each side of your central line will not correspond in each instance. There will be more negative than affirmative contentions, or vice versa; but this does not alter the final determination of what is to be treated as issues.

An issue in an argument is a vital point of difference. A vital contention is one that is essential to the affirmative case. Technically, at least, affirmative proponents must establish all the main contentions. Conversely, negative advocates can vitiate or greatly weaken the affirmative position by disproving successfully *one* of the affirmative's *main* positions. A proposed plan may find adequate basis in need and meet every logical challenge from the standpoint of theory or principle, but prove weak or untenable against facts and arguments which prove indisputably the impracticability of the plan. In the same manner, feasibility alone would not be adequate ground for the adoption of a proposal completely at variance with established and accepted policy. A state-owned and controlled system of radio could, no doubt, be made to function in the United States, but to discuss its substitution for the system which has evolved in accordance with our philosophy of private enterprise would be highly perfunctory and academic. Likewise, when there is no alarming need, no crying abuse, no condition demanding correction, a proposed change or alteration of the *status quo* has little room in court.

6. *Arrange evidence to support the main contentions.* When the main issues are discovered, the next process is to arrange selected evidence in their support. (We have consistently used the word "discover" in connection with the term "issues." This word is used advisedly because issues are inherent in the subject. They cannot be arbitrarily determined. They emerge in the process of research and analysis. They are to be found.) Arranging evidence, or supporting material, in defense of the main theses, is the process of brief making. A brief is a series of logically re-

lated assertions defending the validity of the main propositions. Properly drawn, the brief is an assurance of unity, sequence, and coherence. It begins with a series of foundation stones, main uprights, and crossbeams and grows into a finished structure as the connecting and finishing materials are added and put into place. At first, briefing may seem a laborious process. It does, indeed, make rigorous exactions and involves some mental discipline. Later, however, briefing, which is really an orderly and connected process of thinking, becomes quite easy, saves time, and ensures accuracy. A complete brief of your subject is a kind of ready reference file to which you add the new information supplied by further reading and investigation.

Let us now assume that we have read widely in the more important reference sources, that we understand the main theses upon which there is a difference of opinion, and that we have prepared a detailed outline of factual evidence supporting the position we wish to maintain. If this assumption is correct, we are ready to join a round-table group, or discussion panel, and make our contribution to the honest effort of ascertaining the rightness or soundness of a proposed policy, principle, or plan.

The Panel Members Hold a Conference. The panel members should hold a prebroadcast conference, plan the scope of their discussion, agree on the main subject divisions, and establish a major blueprint for program guidance. Anyone who has listened to a variety of radio panels will testify that the impression often received is that of jumbled speeches, chaotic thinking, and general lack of cohesiveness—an awkward and confused performance. Highly trained and experienced speakers may achieve a closely knit and coherent performance, but even they cannot always be relied on to achieve this result. Some radio sponsors seem to feel that the phrase, "totally unrehearsed," constitutes a claim of merit. This may be true in those cases where quiz contestants are awarded huge prizes for brilliant feats approaching clairvoyance. The radio audience would feel betrayed should they learn that supposed bona fide contestants were tipped off in advance of the program and that what appeared as a display of brillance or acumen was, in reality, a hoax. This does not apply to the radio forum. In our opinion, the panel discussion should be "rehearsed." We do not mean that the exact pattern, organization, content, and sequence of the program should be established beforetime. While it is conceivable that a discussion might take place prior to the broadcast—even be recorded and analyzed—this would probably rob the final program of spontaneity. How far, then, should we go in settting up a panel discussion? The following suggestions are made subject to variation according to the make-up of the panel, the discussion subject, the time available, and other related circumstances.

Great variation will be found with regard to the preliminary conferences recommended by panel sponsors. The methods employed may
range from a plan of no previous discussion to one of detailed layout.
The first may be satisfactory when expert panel personnel, experienced in
and accustomed to panel *modus operandi,* are involved; and the latter
process, may promote too much formality and eventuate in a wooden
and uninspired performance. The best plan lies between these two extremes, each of which will be approached according to the composition
of the panel. In the case of the student panel, or when inexperienced
professional people are invited to make up the group, it is obvious that
more time may be devoted to a preliminary survey of the program objective and to the organization of program content.

This takes us back to what has been said about subject analysis and
outlining. Try to agree upon the issues to be discussed. State these issues
as interrogatives. Determine the order in which they are to be considered. Much time will be saved if the panel chairman, or an associate,
draws up a tentative brief of the main and subordinate propositions to
be presented at the preliminary conference. From this outline, the
principal points to be covered in the final discussion can be selected.
They may be modified, limited, or expanded by mutual agreement. No
attempt is made to select or control the choice of supporting material
or prescribe rules pertaining to the admissibility of evidence. Our purpose is to guarantee that too much ground will not be covered, that
propositions are clearly presented, and that the discussion will proceed
toward an intelligent summary.

With this preprogram conference we are now ready to present our
views to the radio audience. The effectiveness of the presentation will
be in proportion to the speakers' background preparation, their success
in maintaining a closely defined discussion outline, and the adequacy of
logical method. Logical process in discussion consists of (1) the clear
formulation of the contention thesis—making a simple and direct assertion of that which is to be proved, (2) supporting the assertion by
relevant evidence, and (3) pointing the validity of the conclusions derived according to the principles of reasoning. Logical disputants will
necessarily apply certain tests to opposing arguments in an attempt to
prove them weak, incomplete, or inadequate. In practical argumentation
these logical tests are relatively limited in number compared with the
possible number of rules prescribed by formal logic.

In general, an advocate attempts to establish the soundness of a
principle, rule, or thesis by proving the homogeneity and sufficiency of
related data; showing that a particular phenomenon, condition, or incident comes within the circle of an accepted principle or that causal
forces are correctly associated. These argumentative processes are

scrutinized for inherent fallacies. A fallacy is an error in the reasoning process. It may be one of several different kinds—ignoring the question, begging the question, statistical fallacy, imperfect analogy, wrong interpretation of cause and effect—but each is related to the basic processes of induction and deduction. A discussion participant should be conversant with these processes and adept in their use. The two particular weaknesses common to discussion are hasty generalization and the unsupported assertion. These two pitfalls in particular should be avoided.

The Panel Chairman. A successful panel discussion depends very largely on the skill of the chairman or moderator. He is at no time a participant in the exchange of views and opinions. He never argues or contends with the panel personnel or offers a personal evaluation of the merits of the arguments presented. But, although he remains detached and objective, he is the guiding force who gives point, direction, and summation to what is said. These responsibilities demand special qualifications: a comprehensive knowledge of the subject in outline, clear and logical thinking, fluency in extempore and impromptu speech, a sense of balance and proportion, tact, poise and self-control, and a sense of humor.

It may be argued that the chairman's function is an incidental and perfunctory one—that his job is to introduce a number of qualified experts, interject a few words from time to time, attempt a summary, perhaps, at the end of the program, and that he has no need for more than a superficial acquaintance with the subject under discussion. This is to take too light a view of the round-table moderator. While we cannot expect him to be a fully qualified expert in many areas, he should be conversant with major issues in several related fields. This is not too much to expect of a man who stands in the position of directing public thought and action. The emcee is not just a glib, facile, artificial poseur. His attitude should be serious, and he should be qualified for the intellectual nature of his responsibility. This requires that he have a perspective view of the question area, understand some of the inherent and basic implications, and be acquainted with the major divisions of thought that are involved.

Since discussion is the art of reasoned discourse, the chairman should know the tools which qualified speakers are presumed to use. This knowledge may help him direct the course of the discussion and keep it within bounds. When digressions and question-begging tactics develop, he is in a better position tactfully to rechannel the talk. He will know how to distinguish between relevancy and irrelevancy and make a more discriminating summary.

A forum leader must be able to speak easily, fluently, and clearly. Speech, of course, is an expression of thought. Words are symbols, and the areas of one's expression grow with the expansion of vocabulary. One cannot think clearly in a particular field unless he commands the verbal symbols pertaining thereto. Vocabulary alone, however, is not a guarantee of lucid expression. Words can be multiplied without wisdom, and Shakespeare has something to say about "sound and fury signifying nothing." Words serve their purpose in oral discourse only when combined in simple sentence patterns matched to the comprehension of the auditor. A graduate thesis on the evolution of Abraham Lincoln's literary style traces the lucid character of Lincoln's writing and speaking to the influence of *Pilgrim's Progress, Aesop's Fables,* and the *King James Bible.* When Lincoln's adversary, Stephen Douglas, completed an address, the people said, "It is a great speech." When Lincoln stepped from the rostrum, they said, "Old Abe is right." Lincoln at one time compared Douglas with a cuttlefish, a sea animal which, when attacked, secretes a dark substance in the water to hide its exact location. The masterpieces of English literature are written in simple language. The adjective, "simple," however, does not mean that clear and accurate speech is easy. There is less effort in stringing together "polysyllabic profundities" than in using accurate terms which refine the idea. Consult a standard work on synonyms and observe the nuances of meaning among words which are associated with the same basic concept. It is not the size of one's vocabulary which guarantees his ability to sculpture an idea.

Fluency in the use of definitive symbols is gained through practice. Too much of our conversation is confined to bare essentials. We are too easily satisfied with the perfunctory response. We reply in compressed phrases. Class recitations are usually made from a semirecumbent position and in semicoherent sentences which must be interpreted by the instructor if the student is to receive full credit for the answer. Ability to sustain orally a continuum of thought is rather rare owing to insufficient thought range and command of words. The radio chairman's ability to extemporize easily depends on his relation to the subject, language command, and practice in the acquisition of fluency. Can fluency be gained through practice? Assuming at the outset that one has an inquiring and aggressive interest in a realm larger than his immediate bread-and-butter existence, he will achieve conversational and extempore stature with the habit of engaging in social interchange on a variety of topics. His reading will become more purposive. Instead of scanning a magazine article to while away a tedious hour in a railway terminal, or instead of trying to comprehend chapter headings only, hoping these will suffice for the forthcoming quiz, he will read more slowly and comprehendingly, trying to relate the subject matter to established interests. Furthermore, he will try to retain what seems to be important.

Retention is aided by reflecting upon what is read, fitting it to some established frame of reference, repeating silently (or aloud) the essence of the article, and trying later to bring it into conversation. The proportion of material which we read and forget is appalling. The mind, like fallow ground, receives seed but does not yield at harvesttime. The investment return on the time and energy spent in reading would be considered low by any market standard. The wide disparities of reading comprehension are indicated clearly by college-entrance tests, and the subsequent correlation between these scores and college grades are fairly predictable. If one aspires to fluent, extempore speech, he will subject himself to mental disciplines. He will read more selectively and inquiringly, and he will achieve retention of important details through reflection and by using them in conversation. It is in this latter way, particularly, that motor speech skills, essential to extemporaneous speech, can be developed. The effectiveness of the radio panel chairman depends on his ability to extemporize fluently and clearly.

A moderator may have a comprehensive knowledge of the subject, reason clearly, express himself confidently and fluently, and yet fail to meet the tests imposed by the radio panel situation. He must add to informational backgrounds, logical acuity, and expressional ability personal qualities of poise, tact, and sense of humor. It is the chairman who makes the initial impression upon the audience and who represents throughout the program its general tone, quality, and demeanor. He is the symbol of fairness, emotional control, good will, balance, and proportion to which a public discussion should aspire. He is a leader and director—a mediator. His personal convictions are not under fire. His own beliefs and prejudices are subjugated to the interest of a balanced presentation of the discussion subject. To prevent the clash of personalities and verbal excesses incident to vigorous controversy, he must employ nice discretion and know how to change tactfully the course of the argument.

Conversely, panel members may need prompting if not prodding. Owing to embarrassment, lack of motivation, inexperience, or lack of pertinent information, they may not give to the discussion the momentum and animation required, and the moderator must keep the discussion moving and help it attain cumulative force. His ability to follow the course of the discussion, sense the anticlimactic lulls, ask pertinent questions, and keep the interchange of opinions sharply pointed, may spell the difference between a dull and a lively program.

Duties of the Chairman. The chairman has particular duties in directing the discussion. His opening remarks are the conventional kind. He will address his radio audience, state or restate the subject for discussion, and present the members of the panel. The normal purpose of any chairman's introduction is to attain good will for his program personnel. Restricted by time limitations, the radio panel chairman must be brief, state the name of each speaker, and identify him sufficiently to suggest his competency or prestige.

Next, he presents the first topic for discussion and calls upon a particular panel member to respond. This is better than to start with a general invitation such as, Would one of you gentlemen care to open the discussion? The reason for addressing an individual is to get an affirmative or positive position established as the main reference level for the program. This, furthermore, is good deliberative technique because divergent views are brought into clash by starting with a burden of proof. If any one is allowed to "pop off," we may begin with a subordinate proposition and a series of tangential responses. Someone has said that a text is a point of departure to which the speaker never returns. We should start with a text (a basic issue) in our panel discussion and remain with it until it can be resolved.

The speaker addressed, either because of previous instruction or because of personal knowledge of panel procedure, will reply succinctly. Another speaker then signifies that he wishes to make a rejoinder (this technique will be explained later), is recognized by the chairman in order that the speaker may be identified for the listening audience, and proceeds with his remarks. The issue is now the property of the panel, and the discussion will proceed as normal conversation might ensue. Statements should be brief. Given the problem of a half-hour program, embracing a panel composed of four members, a chairman, and an opening and closing sponsor's message, what will be the maximum time available to each speaker? If each one consumes an equal amount of time, he will not have more than 5 or 6 minutes. This is one reason why the participant should be concise and why irrelevancies and discursiveness must be avoided. Speeches should be short and terse and follow in tight sequence. These attributes of discussion, however, are achieved only by highly experienced and skillful performers. We state them as ideal objectives to be attained.

The moderator can assist to some extent by recognizing speakers and suggesting, mostly by sign language, the alternations in the dialogue. His chief problems are to keep the comments directed toward the issue or subject under discussion, judge when it has had adequate treatment, and after a brief restatement or summary of what has been said up to that point, make a transition to the second division of the general topic. For example, to use a generalized and abstract illustration, the chairman may say,

So far in our discussion, gentlemen, it would seem that there is a great deal of dissatisfaction with this new ordinance, but there is no agreement as to who is responsible. Mr. X assesses the blame against the city council, and Mr. Y feels that the real trouble lies in the Mayor's office. It is established that these two groups are opposed to each other and operate according to fundamentally different policies. What we want to know now is whether it is possible for the Mayor and the City Council to reconcile these differences and get together on this city improvement. Is the difference really a fundamental one, or can it be compromised so the project can go ahead? What practicable program can you offer which might be accepted by both parties? What is really practicable? How can the deadlock be broken?

By this summary and transition, the ensuing discussion is directed into a new channel. Expediency becomes the issue, and the speakers proceed to offer, from their respective points of view, compromise proposals which might break the political impasse. These proposals clash, are attacked and criticized, and substitute measures are advanced. When these have been sufficiently "kicked around," the moderator makes another summary and leads the talk to the final phase of the outline: What will be the effect upon the city if this conflict is not adjudicated? What will be the effect of a continuing stalemate? Then, at the conclusion, the chairman makes a brief review of the three main issues discussed and points out that an urgent city problem exists, that the solution is blocked by what appears to be an irreconcilable political conflict, that several compromises are possible, and that if one of these is not reached, the city may suffer serious economic loss. He may then rename the members of his panel, thank them for their participation, and give the program back to the announcer.

Ordinarily, a discussion program will have sufficient momentum, but if it should stall, the chairman, sensing the fact, will seek to accelerate the talk by shifting attention to another focal point, or by directing a specific question to a panel member. In this case the chairman may be fortified if he knows the members of his panel—their professional, business, and social backgrounds. He may say, for example, "Mr. Y, you were a member of the City Planning Commission between 1942 and 1946. You were, in fact, largely responsible for this zoning ordinance. Do you think this proposed industrial site is a violation of agreements reached at that time?" Or, "Mrs. B, you are a member of the PTA Council. What do your members think about half-day school sessions for the primary grades?"

The chairman's problem is not so much that of keeping the program moving, but rather one of controlling enthusiasms and confining the interchange of opinions to the radio time assigned. In the first place, no subject of any consequence can be covered in half an hour. We have recognized that in our injunctions concerning the importance of limiting the discussion area. The real problem for the chairman is to keep the discussion within these pretermined bounds, but even when these bounds are set, the chairman must keep a close eye on the studio clock. The inexorable minute hand is sweeping him relentlessly toward a dead line. If it is planned to discuss three major points, each should be proportioned according to its importance. It is very embarrassing to realize suddenly that you are about to go off the air and have not reached the climactic point in the discussion outline. Timing, therefore, is very important, and the problem belongs to the moderator even though a producer may be standing over him with a stopwatch. The moderator confronts a dilemma, however, because he faces the obligation of giving to each division of opinion an equal hearing. If an enthusiastic advocate has run overtime in his defense of an idea, it does not seem fair to penalize the opposition by reducing the length of their reply. To allocate time equally, and at the same time give adequate consideration to all essential points, sometimes becomes a nice problem in diplomacy as well as program balance.

Another function of the moderator—a more mechanical one—is to prevent overlapping dialogue and the confusion of two or three people talking at once. The problem is a very difficult one for the chairman to solve. In the last analysis, evenly joined speeches—smooth continuity of dialogue—stem from the self-control and cooperativeness of the panel members themselves. Normally, one is considered rude if he breaks constantly into another's speech or refuses to pause long enough to give the other man a chance to complete his reply. Some overlapping does occur, but the social convention calls for the offender to apologize and desist until his companion is finished. Under the stress of emotion associated with argumentative discourse, these interferences are more marked, and special restraint must be exercised. If the panel members work together according to accepted social amenities, interferences may be reduced to a minimum.

A panel member, while his colleague is speaking, will indicate his desire to take up the discussion by means of a predetermined signal such as simply raising the hand, although any schoolroom display of waving hands will only confuse and distract. A better plan is for the speaker to move his hand to the top of the table, calling to the moderator's attention (as well as the panel members') that he wishes to speak. Members of the panel should give the right of way to the person who first declares his intent, or it may be agreed that the moderator, by a nod or other gesture, will designate the next speaker. It may be better, in some instances, for the chairman to call the plays, figuratively speaking, although this has some disadvantages. Let us conclude by repeating that the program is a cooperative endeavor to present clearly and logically an analysis of an important subject, and that the ladies and gentlemen of the panel will conduct themselves with consideration for their associates. The mechanics essential to a smooth production are more a matter of common sense and courteous demeanor than textbook rules.

Studio Setup. The seating of the panel will be different for an audience "show" and a nonaudience, studio presentation. In the first case, the speakers face the audience, and in the second they may be grouped at a circular table, vis-à-vis. The exact arrangements—such as spacing, number of microphones used, the relationship of the chairman to the group— will vary according to personal choice. They are guided by convenience and the requirements for the best microphone pickup and monitoring conditions. It is possible that a separate directional microphone be set for each speaker although two people can use one between them without interference. In the strict round-table arrangement, one nondirectional mike may be sufficient if the panel is not too large. The announcer, who puts the program on the air and signs it off, will have a separate position somewhat removed from the chairman and participants. The principle governing microphone arrangement is that speakers are not made conscious of studio paraphernalia—that they are free to speak and converse with one another, or to the studio audience, without feeling that they have to "talk into something." Crowding should be avoided, but a feeling of intimacy, solidarity, and close relationship should be preserved.

Audience Participation. The round-table program may provide time to entertain questions from members of the studio audience. This is a complicating feature of the discussion program and must be handled with some care. Several difficulties may be encountered. To rise in a public meeting and direct a question to the program chairman involves some degree of self-consciousness or embarrassment. One may have a very important question concerning the subject under discussion but be considerably inhibited by stage fright or nervousness. On the other hand, there are highly extroverted people, usually motivated by a special bias, who have no inhibitions and no hesitancy in placing themselves and their ideas before the meeting. Moreover, it is not easy to state a question simply and concisely, and questions may become very involved. The extroversion of which we speak, and which may be associated with egocentricity, sometimes prompts the questioner to deliver his own opinions, and he prefaces his question with, "Before I state my question, I would like to say . . . ." Usually it is the "antis" in the house who are most vocal. This means that the questions will center toward one side of the controversy, and the balance which the main discussion has tried to promote will be partially destroyed.

These problems can be solved for the most part by applying certain rules. Questions can be stimulated by explaining the audience participation part of the program before the broadcast begins and by presenting carefully the requirements of an effective question period. Auditors are not to make speeches, questions are to be short and to the point, addressed to particular members of the panel, and so far as possible, cover all the main issues involved. A person wishing to ask a question will stand and raise his hand. He will wait until he is recognized by the chairman and speak only when he is recognized. He will not attempt a reply to the panel member's answer to his question, even if he feels it to be unsatisfactory, unless recognized again by the chairman. Questions will be entertained from different sections of the audience and not from particular areas only. The moderator may not be assisted by a number of associates carrying traveling microphones, and he cannot use the "I have a lady in the balcony" technique, but he will try to make the audience feel that all have been included and given a chance.

The larger the audience, of course, the more difficulty there will be in getting the questions on the air. Audience mikes may be sufficient to pick up voices from different areas of the room, or it is possible to use a system of portable microphones, but in either instance, however, the pickup may not be too clear owing to the questioner's voice level and lack of microphone technique. Or, if the question is understood by the radio listener, it may not be fully audible to the panel member addressed.

In some round-table programs, it has been the practice to require that audience questions be written, with the understanding that they may be selected at the discretion of the chairman or assisting committee, and that they may be reworded. Distributing and collecting question slips and selecting the most pertinent ones are time-consuming and mitigate against a somewhat dramatic element arising from direct questioner versus panel member relationship.

Conclusion. Discussion participation requires greater competence than any of the performance types we have discussed. It imposes upon the speaker the demands of subject knowledge, semantic skill, logical techniques, and speech fluency. These are exacting disciplines and are attained only with practice and maturity. Radio and television are media of communication which can expand the circle of social understanding. They offer a distinct challenge to the leader in public affairs, and anyone who aspires to influence in the councils of democracy should master the art of group discussion.

QUESTIONS

1. Why is discussion by radio psychologically more effective than mass-audience participation?

2. Outline the procedure to be followed in preparing a radio discussion.

3. Why should the size of the panel be limited?
4. Who should be selected as panel members?
5. What is the purpose of the preprogram conference?
6. What are the qualifications of the chairman or moderator?
7. What are the chairman's functions?
8. What criticisms would you make of radio discussion programs to which you have listened?

CHAPTER 14

RADIO ACTING

Acting is the process, technique, or skill by which one lives for a moment a vicarious experience, adapting himself to the motives, moods, and environment which actuate the dramatic character. Acting is essentially a process of re-acting. You are acting every day. You are meeting people in various social situations, and your life is checkered by a range of emotional experiences—happiness, despair, hope, anger, resentment, suspicion, fear. The untrained or uninitiated individual will behave dramatically in normal life if the stimulus is sufficient really to motivate his prepotent habits of response. Watch children at play, adults suddenly forced to meet a crisis, or the reactions of team mates in victory or defeat.

There are two differences, however, between everyday acting and "stage acting." The primary element of drama is conflict, and conflict arouses emotion, because of the thwarting which produces disequilibriums, tensions, and neural blocks. While normal living has its share of frustrations, most of these are rather trivial, personalized, and quickly dissipated. The conflicts represented in dramatic literature, on the other hand, are selected by the playwright with respect to their inherent force and impact, and the actor is thrown into a situation that transcends his normal experience. Furthermore, the chain of circumstances in the play are so telescoped as to require a substantial degree of intense feeling.

Why can't we act on the stage? The stimulus is not sufficiently present. We are inhibited, and our self-consciousness reveals itself in awkward and unconvincing behavior. If the stimulus were sufficiently present, would our arms and legs and voice go in the right direction? It is quite probable that even if one "lived the part" he still would be inept and poorly coordinated in his emotive response. There are such matters as entrances and exits, dialogue pacing, pause, sitting, walking, and standing, and we should know what is acceptable. These are associative elements which must be learned. Nevertheless, the fundamental basis of acting is stimulus awareness (subjective and objective) and an awareness of the reaction.

Radio acting and stage acting are essentially more alike than different. In radio we are not concerned with, as has been said by Selden,

. . . the medium of the body and the agents of physical expression (torso, legs, arms, body as a whole); the cultivation of the physical instrument (pantomime, bodily control, grace, presence); or posture and movement (characterized posture and movement, gestures, significant action).[1]

Bodily movements are involved in the reading of dramatic lines, but they serve only the purpose of facilitating the actor's emotional release; they are not communicative cues for a visible audience. The radio actor is dependent entirely on his voice to project the scene, the characterization, the emotional conflict. A radio play takes place upon "the stage of the audience's imagination." The listener's imaginative creation of the action is effected through aural stimuli. The voice in both types of acting is an agent of paramount importance. Furthermore, neither stage nor radio actor can possibly succeed unless his words are the expression of centrality. We avoid a categorical statement regarding technique versus "complete feeling," but at least the artist's words must convey the convincingness of genuine and sincere feeling.

RADIO ACTING SKILLS

There are eight particular skills, techniques, or abilities which the student of radio acting should master.

1. Discriminating sensitivity
2. Sight reading
3. Ability to read naturally without giving the impression of reading
4. Characterization
5. Emotional interpretation
6. Dialectal skill
7. The creation of pictures in the mind of the hearer
8. Doubling

Discriminating Sensitivity. The actor is an interpreter, an instrument of the dramatic message, the translator of dramatic situations, the medium linking the message of the play and the dramatist's objective with audience response. In the sense that the actor himself becomes the playwright and the personification of the character portrayed, he is the direct communicant of dramatic forces; but the equation of vehicle, actor, and auditor completes the actual cycle. The lines which the player speaks at the outset are not his own. They are words written by an author and put into the mouth of a character. As the actor "grows into the part," he may effect such a close identification with the script that he gains an independence which pronounces him a free agent. He *is* the character in the play, these are *his* words, this *is* his experience. But

---

[1] Selden, A *Player's Handbook*, p. viii, Appleton-Century-Crofts, Inc., New York, 1937.

this nascence of spirit, or attained synthesis, requires intense study and long practice.

An explanation of the nature of reading requires a brief excursion into the field of psychology, and we shall approach the subject from the standpoint of empathy, a principle of aesthetics. "Empathy" is Professor Titchener's translation of Theodore Lipps' word, *Einfühlung*. It means self-activity in an object of sense. Wherein does beauty reside? in the painting? in the sunset? in the marble frieze? Or, in the quality of one's perceptive response to the stimulus object? Beauty is not in the thing; it lies in the nature of the response to the thing itself. Likewise, such judgments as, the stone is heavy, the marble is smooth, or the mountain is high, are expressions of the biophysical sets or attitudes induced by the stone, marble, or mountain. What is the great difference between the perception-response characteristics of two people at the rim of the Grand Canyon, one of whom says, "What hath God wrought," and the other, "Gee, I can spit a mile"? The handwork of nature is a constant. It is there for all to see, but its effect on tourists varies with the potential of their conditioned responsiveness. Laboratory experiments show that vertical, horizontal, and angular lines engender different emotional effects, a fact that finds practical demonstration in Doric, Ionian, and Corinthian architecture, in painting, and in sculpture.

The principle of empathy is inherent in poetry, particularly of the sensuous sort. There is a reason why a verse is written in a particular meter. Iambic, trochaic, anapaestic, and dactylic meter have their respective justifications just as stanzaic form varies with subject and mood. The art of poetics is based on scientific principles. Moreover, the poet selects words with great care because "words are colors rightly laid" and invoke response in proportion to the receiving nature of the reader or hearer.

The principle of empathy operates reciprocally. First, the proper stimulus is provided by the artist—a stimulus calculated to set off the physical reaction identifiable as the emotional response—but the artist fails unless his public can see with the seeing eye and hear with the hearing ear. He depends on the capacity of the perceiving subject to respond to the stimuli submitted, but the subject cannot respond unless his sense organs have been tuned by previous experience and training. Many people profess a distaste for poetry. This is because they do not have the "openness to experience," the sympathy, or imagination that prompts a response to the condensation of poetic imagery. Professor George Edward Woodbury's statement is to the point: "To love the poets is a certificate of manhood."

You may be asking, What has this to do with the reading of the radio script? The radio drama is certainly not poetry. It is usually not literature.

But the principle of empathy is applicable because we must ask in turn, What do words in the script mean to you? What reactions, sets, or attitudes are touched off by the black marks on the page? Words are symbols attached to referents. The latter remain constant, but the symbol takes on colorings and shadings according to our personal association with the referent. The same symbol has different meanings to different people. Combinations of words expressing ideas, emotions, and situations have different meanings conditioned by social and cultural experience. By discriminating sensitivity, therefore, we mean a quality of experience which can express the connotative coloring inherent in words and phrases. But it is more than this. It pertains also to the flow of sensory awareness and emotional discrimination. Each speech has its particular motivation, and the divisions of the speech may have varying motivation. Generally speaking, one does not proceed from one word cue to the subsequent word cue without pause, change of pace, modulation, or varying stress. The current of response is checked, redirected, modified, and may even take a tangential direction from the original point of response. Let us use a dialogue sequence to make this clear.

Read through the following scene until you are familiar with it. Then ask yourself certain questions. What do I know about Byron? Why are the Byrons referred to as "mad"? How old is Byron at this time? Who is Mary Chaworth? How old is she? Are the boy and girl neighbors? How long has this infatuation being going on? How strong are the sentiments expressed? What degree of sophistication do you wish to give these youngsters?

When you are familiar with the scene and think you understand the characters involved, enumerate or explain the motivation which prompts each speech. Furthermore, indicate where and how the motivation takes a new tack. Since the speeches are short, there will not be many changes within them, but there are several instances of pronounced nuance of attitude, purpose, or mood.

Lord Byron[2]

ANNOUNCER: Our story concerns Byron's first romance when the poet was yet a boy. The year is 1803. Byron is strolling through Sherwood Forest with Mary Chaworth.

1. (*Sound: Steps on gravel path*)
2. MARY: Release my hand. I didn't tell you you could hold it.
3. BYRON: I love you, Mary. I . . . .
4. MARY: Don't. Don't ever use that word to me again.
5. BYRON: Why won't you listen to me?
6. MARY: The Byrons are mad—all of them.
7. BYRON: I'm not mad.

[2] From a radio play by Laurence C. Cook.

8. MARY: You are branded with the mark of Cain. I've heard you say so yourself.

9. (*Sound: Twittering of birds*)

10. BYRON: All right. Then marry me and remove the brand.

11. MARY: George, you must not say such things.

12. BYRON: Why?

13. MARY: To a family like mine—Oh, look, there's a robin—there in that oak tree.

14. BYRON: Spring.

15. MARY: Yes.

16. (*Sound: Steps tacet*)

17. BYRON: Sit beside me on this bench.

18. MARY: For just a moment.

19. BYRON: Mary, why—why don't you—like me? Why haven't you invited me to your dance?

20. MARY: Oh!

21. BYRON: Tomorrow night.

22. MARY: I—I can't, George.

23. BYRON: But why?

24. MARY: Well, you don't dance.

25. BYRON: You have invited Mr. Musters.

26. MARY: Yes.

27. BYRON: I suppose you are afraid I will make a scene.

28. MARY: John Musters can take care of himself, thank you. I must get home for my music lesson.

29. BYRON: Mary, give me something to remember you by—something I can keep.

30. MARY: What?

31. BYRON: That ring.

32. MARY: I prefer to wear it myself, my lord.

33. BYRON: Oh, why do you make fun of me? Let me have it.

34. MARY: But wouldn't you rather be invited to my dance?

35. BYRON: So you can laugh at me before John Musters?

36. MARY: I have made up my mind. You are to come, sir.

37. BYRON: It's too late now.

38. MARY: Please, George—you must come.

39. BYRON: No.

40. MARY: If you will, I'll—

41. BYRON: Give me the ring?

42. MARY: Yes.

43. BYRON: I'll come. . . . (*Pause*) Thank you, Mary. I'll wear it always.

44. MARY: You are satisfied now, I hope.

45. BYRON: I shall never be satisfied until you are Lady Byron.

46. (*Transition*)

There is no *one* way to read a line. Interpretations will vary with individual understanding, insight, and identification, and it should not be the function of the director to *pattern* a reading according to *his* analysis. He may seek legitimately to get the kind of reading he thinks best, but his method should not be that of establishing an interpretation to be imitated. He will, by adroit questions and suggestions, bring about an understanding of the role and the dramatic picture he desires, but he must, in the last analysis, allow for the reader's individuality and personal grasp of the idea. He will not prescribe a stress, but he may change a stress by asking, What is the point? Why do you stress this word? What would be the meaning if you changed the accent? A case in point is found in line 7. A defense could be made of placing the accent on any one of the three words: *I'm* not mad; I'm *not* mad; I'm not *mad*. These choices may be argued, but the actor must read the speech in the way he understands it and feels it, and not according to a dogmatic injunction.

It is for these reasons that we will not attempt to analyze the discriminations and transitions of thought and feeling in the above scene. We attempt only to enumerate some of the motivations as we understand them. Our language is not sufficiently refined to designate the finer distinctions of mood, but you will find in the interactions of the two people whose conversation is recorded, some of the following aspects of feeling. Expressed in the lines are resentment, petulance, pleading, irritation, self-assurance, querulousness, positiveness, naïveté, pride, gayety, reluctance, personal hurt and injury, coyness, taunting, regret, jealousy, decisiveness, belligerency, selfishness, imperiousness, hope, satisfaction, boastfulness. How many of these elements can you find there? Are there others not here named? Would you eliminate some of the above terms or replace them with more discriminating appellations?

Regardless of any exact "count," agreement, or disagreement, the point is that there is an emotional fluidity in the scene to be interpreted by vocal shadings—variations in voice timbre, intensity, pitch, and time. As so often stated, these shadings are not affected by the conscious employment of the voice. Their presence in the reading is the manifestation of so-called "inner processes." The effectiveness of the interpretation will be related to these experiential processes and not to artificial voice mechanics.

Go over the scene again and check those points at which the initial motivation arising with the line changes its direction. What takes place in speeches 2, 4, 6, 8, 13, 19, 28, 33, 38, 43?

This single example of a dialogue is probably sufficient to make clear the criterion, *sensitive discrimination*. The evidences of this attribute are the vocal responses of the reader. The voice apparatus is an instrument played upon by sentiments, feelings, perceptions, and imagination. It is an effector mechanism responding to neurological and cortical activities. "The nervous system receives impressions from the sense organs and initiates the movements that are made by the speech organs in making the sounds."[3] The plasticity of the nervous system, the hierarchy of neural pathways, and the refinement of associative connections in the cortex are all tested in the reading performance of a radio actor. The timing of syllable, word, phrase, and sentence, the resonance response of the various amplifiers, the intonation patterns, the varying degrees of stress, and the entire configuration of the tonal elements are the products of psychological activity.

Sight Reading. A radio program is presented with relatively little rehearsal compared to the time normally consumed by a cast preparing a stage play for which the parts are memorized. The air drama is put together in a few hours. You are called to a rehearsal, a script is put into your hands, you are assigned a particular role, and you are expected to read your lines at once intelligently and interpretatively. There is no time to overcome basic imperfections or to drill on interpretation. Therefore, if you cannot read fluently and expressively at sight, if you require time for study and practice to make your reading smooth and confident, you cannot qualify as a radio actor.

Some people do not read well at sight. The reasons are mainly psychological and belong to the field of remedial reading. Such problems as eye span, eye movements, dark spots, and inversion require special treatment. Lesser degrees of abnormality may be overcome by conscious practice if guided by proper counseling. The most usual difficulty arises from the fact that the "eye is not ahead of the mouth." If the word stimulus and the vocal response are synchronous—if the eye is not ahead of the word being spoken—it is certain that you are relying on a purely automatic response rather than a thought process. You are reading words, not phrases. Sentences are composed of phrases. A phrase, in the speech sense, is a word or group of words containing a "center of attention." In writing, rhetorical phrases are set off by punctuation marks; in speech they are usually demarcated by pauses. Phrasing may be defined as oral punctuation, although rhetorical and oral phrases do not always correspond. One device by which to improve sight-reading ability is to practice the trick of comprehending the subsequent phrase while voicing the antecedent one, or during the split second of intervening pause. Test this operation with the following quotation from *Les Miserables*. The phrases are obvious, each designated by punctuation. Do not read the phrase until it is visually recorded. But this anticipatory

---

[3] Pillsbury and Meader, *The Psychology of Language*, p. 91, Appleton-Century-Crofts, Inc., New York, 1928. The authors of this book make an excellent presentation of the nervous mechanisms of speech, the speech organs, and the mental motor processes of speech.

visual perception should take place while you are reading the previous phrase or during the phrase pause.

He had fallen again upon these fearful things; they were before him; they moved, they had being; it was no longer an effort of his memory, a mirage of his fancy; he saw reappearing and living around him, with all the frightfulness of reality, the monstrous visions of the past.

This technique is called "reading ahead." Can you read ahead as you speak? This is not the panacea for the sight-reading problem, but it will go far toward speeding reading rate and will guard against minor "fluffs."

Ability to Read Naturally. We would like to use a coined word at this point. Don't be read-y. The line or speech you read should sound as if you were talking and not as if you were reading it. The ability to translate the printed form into the pattern of colloquial address is probably the most difficult problem one encounters. We can rationalize somewhat by saying that writing style is different from oral style. Ideas put down on paper seldom have the structural form of ideas expressed extemporaneously or impromptu in the normal give-and-take of social intercourse. Only the most skilled scriptors can write as characters speak in daily life. Even if this were not true, the problem of infusing the printed copy with realism and life-likeness is the most challenging one we encounter. Why?

The answer is found in a differentiation of speaking sense and nonsense. In his book, *Public Speaking,* Professor Winans quotes a statement made by Professor Titchener to the effect that in speaking sense we are aware of the discharge of an aggregate idea, but in speaking nonsense we are primarily conscious of the sound and feel of the words. Reading can be a purely autonomic process. The central portion of the recognition process seems to be short-circuited, and the sensory motor response takes place without thought. You have found yourself at the bottom of a page and suddenly realized that you have comprehended nothing of the contents you have just scanned. Your mind was miles away. It is actually possible for the oral reader to have the same experience, actually to visualize words while thinking about the hands on the studio clock, confusion in the booth, or something else that demands momentary attention. Although such complete lapses of concentration are rather rare, reading is accompanied by some degree of inattention and to that extent the expression is only partially complete and accurate. Speech is circular stimulation. One speech provokes a response from the person addressed. His reply elicits a reciprocal response, and the ensuing dialogue is a back-and-forth give-and-take. Almost any casual bit of dialogue illustrates the point.

Example 1

(1) What time is it?
(2) Five-thirty.
(1) Too late.
(2) Why?
(1) They'll be closed.
(2) But this is Saturday. They're open till nine.
(1) Oh, fine. I've just got to get—. Oh, I forgot.
(2) What?
(1) Helen's bringing over that dress I promised to help her with.
(2) When?
(1) About six, she said.
(2) Leave a note for her. We won't be gone long.

The same relationship exisits between speeches that are longer, but there is a longer sustension of thought processes before the overt expression.

Example 2

(1) Mary Jones was here this afternoon.
(2) Yeah?
(1) I feel awfully sorry for her.
(2) What is it now? Seems to me she has a hard luck story every time she turns around. I sometimes wonder if she doesn't enjoy having something to cry about.
(1) Tom, that's not fair. She's really had bad luck. First one thing and then another.
(2) People make their own bad luck. Negligence—lack of foresight.
(1) As a rule, maybe; but when someone runs into your car parked at the curb in front of your house—
(2) She ought to have a garage.

The words put together in the above dialogue are conventional remarks designating aspects of feeling, intuition, and attitude. The individual speeches may be characterized as expressing concern, casualness, disappointment, curiosity, irritation, assurance, eagerness, regret, sympathy, indifference, impatience, reproof, dogmatism. If the speeches arise from the force of attitudes, feelings, or purposes, the interpretation will "ring true." If not, the reading will be wooden, stilted, "read-y."

Let us try another experiment to make this point clear. Read the following speech silently three or four times until you are familiar with it, and then present it orally giving the best interpretation you can. Now, put the script down and give the speech from memory, trying to make the ideas as pointed and personal as possible. You will not be able to quote the lines verbatim, and you should not try to do so. We want the purpose and intent of the speech, and if you make some minor substitutions and alterations, they will only serve the purpose of the demonstration.

Example 3

Listen, John, I am not going to have any interference from a lot of immature, theorizing college boys. I've worked this business for twenty years, and I know when we are on the down-grade. This is no time for a lot of fancy advertising spreads. The market's shot. The people are broke. I say, trim sail and sit it out, hold on to what we've got, and wait for the tide to turn.

Example 4

Really, my dear, she was the dowdiest old frump you ever saw. You never saw such a get-up. And when she started telling Mrs. Spendover about the new styles she saw at Vogue's, I couldn't keep my face straight. 'Cause if anybody knows about good taste in everything, it's Caroline Spendover.

Do you observe differences between the speech patterns when the paragraph is read and when it is spoken? Normally, these will be quite different. There will be rate, pause, stress, and inflectional variations from the reading style. Why? Because you are thinking more vigorously, trying to reach into the consciousness of the auditor. The printed page is not a brake upon the stream of free associations and natural impulses. You are talking and not reading.

Another way of giving the impression of reading, rather than one of live communication, is to organize the word elements into their respective ideational patterns and then connect them in a synthetic whole. Words should not be particularized except in special cases where the definitive meanings are essential to emphasis. Normally we should read by phrases, or ideas, and not in the long-ago, schoolroom fashion, "I—see—a—cat."

Sentences are unitary, meaningful wholes. This unity, articulation, and meaning are the *gestalt*, pattern, or configuration. But the whole is made of parts or units, and the unit has meaning only as we understand the larger system in which we find it. The small uniform part, medium, or process is called a "differential," and many dependent differentials may exist in an "equilibrium distribution of a large area." A complex and abstruse sentence becomes clear and centrally organized as the "dynamic influences" of the parts become clear. Another way of stating this is to say that the sentence, other than a very simple one, is composed of "relatively independent optical units," all of them together constituting an "optical constellation." But the constellation, the meaning of the whole, becomes clear only with the realization of the relationship of internal parts. The visual field is composed of parts. These parts have functional interdependence according to the subjective evaluation of the reader.[4]

[4] See Wolfgang Kohler, *An Aspect of Gestalt Psychology*, Psychologies of 1925, Clark University Press.

This explanation of sight perception, applied to reading, means that neither the reader nor the hearer is dependent upon the sensory recognition of *each* word. Sense perceptions are organized into patterns, and a complete thought as recognized by the reader or hearer is a series of units having various degrees of value and importance. Our interpretation of the complete "mosaic" depends upon our recognition of the "differentials"—the key, or cue, elements. By a process of what the gestaltists call insight, these cue factors fuse and produce the meaning of the whole. It is not necessary to objectify each particular word in order to express meaning. There is a subjective element which carries us from point to point and fills in the gaps.

The meaning of this configuration figure theory applied to reading is to be found in the nature of syllable stress and quantity. The stressed and expanded syllable is the unitary element which is the key to the structural whole. The comprehension of the polysyllabic word lies primarily in the stressed syllable, which also carries an expansion of time. For example: miscon*cep*tion, in*tel*ligent, super*sti*tious, fal*la*cious psy*chol*ogist. The phrase is clarified in proportion to the prominence given the key word:

This is the *man.*

I *think* he was *right.*

No *one* of them ever *equaled* . . . .

The *pris*oner took the *stand* to make his *state*ment.

Now, using a larger whole, a sentence made up of phrases (interior forces), we can see that syllable point, word stress, and the phrase time are the cues to the meaning of the whole.

These and a thousand other misbeliefs, misconceptions, and superstitions, enchain us moderns as firmly as the Mumbo-Jumbo of the witch doctor enchains the souls of jungle savages. These and a thousand other fallacies will be unmasked and revealed to the clear light of truth as we explore the interesting and often amazing realm of *bunk* with Dr. Richard Graham, noted educator and psychologist. But first,

Any gasoline can make claims for highest anti-knock—more power—more mileage, but the intelligent motorist bases his purchase on facts, not advertising claims.

The meaning of the above paragraph would be clear if we practically suppressed all the unstressed words and syllables:

These and a *thou*sand *oth*er *mis*beliefs, miscon*cep*tions and super*sti*tions en*chain* us *mod*erns as *firm*ly, etc.

In other words, our mental organization of meaning depends upon the perception and organization of certain parts inherent in the expressional phrase or sentence.

We do not imply that the unstressed elements are so rushed or crowded that the sound elements are poorly enunciated. Each syllable and each sound in the syllable must be formed and connected, articulated with all the associated sounds. It is a matter of organic relationship. Speech is a rapid alternation of long and short, accented and unaccented syllables, and these proportional relations must be accurate. If these proportional relations are achieved and a nicety of balance is effected, two results will ensue: (1) The reading pattern will approximate more closely the syllable-word sequence of conversational speech wherein the fixations are dictated psychologically and (2) the reading will possess rhythm and legato.

If your own sense patterns are governed by clear perception of organic parts, and the same key elements are focused for your auditor, your reading will be more intelligible and more similar to impromptu conversational address. You will achieve smoothness and flow in your reading and not go clopping along like a lame horse.

Characterization. The radio actor is called on to create and project a characterization. His only method, or tool, by which to make his characters convincing is the voice. Unless the personality in the dramatic story corresponds with his own age and status, he has the problem of using voice patterns which will identify for the audience the role he is portraying. The problem is a difficult one because there is no benefit of grease paint, costume, scenery, characterized posture, movement, and action. The radio play presented by student actors fails primarily because of the inability of the cast to embrace the range of the ages, professions, and personalities of the dramatis personae. Student actors are of the same average age, and their voices lack certain qualities identified with maturity. This fact, rather than inherent acting skill and understanding of the parts, is the greater obstacle in radio acting. An average radio play cast comprises characters of varying age levels, social and professional strata, and cultural streams. They are young and old, sophisticated and naïve, ignorant and learned, regional and national, and as wide apart as the poles in their emotional make-up. Perhaps it is too much to expect a twenty-year-old woman vocally to portray a grandmother, or a young man to represent a hard-bitten old sourdough; and the professional casting director will no doubt type-cast for the most part using voices which naturally suit the roles assigned. Although it may seem to be as difficult to turn the clock forward in the span of years as it is to set it back, it is easier to add age to voice than to subtract it. Some students possess unusual vocal variety, and everyone can develop a measurable versatility by the correct application of vocal technique.

Let us consider first what is meant by characterization by listing the variety of character types you may be called on to play. First, we should make clear that most of these are stereotypes; that is, all cops, telephone operators, westerners, gangsters, grandmothers, society matrons, butlers, and cab drivers do not speak alike. But there seems to be a generic sort of picture of each of these classifications, certain main characteristics abstracted from the whole, and generalized as the character. By analogy, a vocal portrayal is something akin to cartooning. The cartoonist selects the most prominent features of his subject and by exaggerating these to the exclusion of less significant details achieves an effect that is recognized as the intended subject. The long cigarette holder, the big teeth, the bushy eyebrows, the eyeglasses, the facial contour, or any one of many factors is used as the identifying symbol. Likewise, in effecting a vocal portrait of any type there are key elements which, if accurately revealed and held in constant focus, will serve as recognitive symbols. The telephone operator speaks with an impersonal, detached, and characteristic inflectional pattern; age is indicated by less brilliance and resonance of tone; the insincere pretender has an authoritative manner; and the D.A. is pointed, crisp, and emphatic.

The following list of character types is by no means an exhaustive one. It is offered to illustrate the range of acting parts which you will meet in a series of average plays. You may extend the list according to your own knowledge of people.

Character Types

1. "A small man in a small way." Retiring, humble, inferior, respectful, slightly effeminate
2. Aggressive, dogmatic, "sure-shot," conceited
3. Blustering authority
4. Dignified authority
5. Slow, drawling, tobacco-chewing, lazy, farmerish, ranch hand
6. Pompous, self-satisfied, benevolent padrone
7. Hard-fisted, bigoted, unrelenting tycoon
8. Judge: sympathetic but firm
9. Father: dominant, narrow-minded, harsh, inflexible
10. Cop (the stereotype)
11. Cabby
12. Newsboy
13. Lazy, stupid, half-witted, bemused loafer
14. A rustic: old gentleman, a bit absent-minded, good-natured, slightly troubled by his dentures
15. A forty-niner type: the old scout, the old-timer
16. Gangster: tough, clipped, uninhibited
17. Old man:
    a. Mellow, patient, understanding
    b. Straight
    c. Impatient, short-tempered, egotistic

18. Sanctimonious parson
19. High-pressure, fast-talking, uninhibited promoter
20. Butler
21. Young woman: spoiled, petulant, whining, unreasonable
22. Grandmother
23. Daughter
24. Old woman:
    a. Genial, kind, tolerant
    b. Embittered, suspicious, crotchety
    c. Eccentric, suggesting mental aberrations associated with delusions of
       paranoia (not a Macbeth witch characterization)
25. Head nurse: official, brusque, nervous temperament, rigid mental set
26. Schoolteacher: rigid, sour, strait-laced disciplinarian
27. Mother:
    a. Easy-going, changeable, sentimental, long-suffering
    b. Scolding, shrewish, nagging
28. Club woman: artificial, pedantic, condescending
29. Telephone operator

In the material offered for microphone practice you will find individual speeches or dialogue passages in which these types might presumably speak. How many of these speeches can you read and differentiate?

Your ability to adapt yourself to a wide range of speaking parts may be acquired through observation, imitative practice, and conscious control of your vocal processes. To know how a character should speak, it is best first of all to have a personal contact with a prototype. We can comprehend the new and unfamiliar only in the light of the old and familiar. An abstraction remains obscure until it is translated or expressed in some concrete correlative. A character whom you meet for the first time in a radio script will be difficult to create because there is no frame of reference, no comparable standard. But the character is neither a totally mythical creation nor a complete caricature. The character exists. There are people like him. However, we do not quite "see" him because we have never met him. There are many opportunities to build up a mental repertoire of personality graduations. Everyone you meet possesses some qualifying differential, and the more pronounced variations are to be found on the streetcars, in public parks, at travel centers, in public libraries, or on the screen and radio. These character types should be observed carefully and analytically and filed away, so to speak, for future reference.

Observation, though, is not enough. What you observe that is imitable should be made the basis for practice, and although radio is an aural appeal, this practice should embrace not only the speech of the person observed but his general manner of walking, gesturing, and movement. Some people, of course, seem to have a greater mimetic sense than others, but this is due largely to differences of personal interest, attention, and response. Learning is associated with interest, and if you become interested in developing facility in imitation, you will find your life models really stimulating.

In the final analysis, characterization skill depends on vocal flexibility and control. The subject of voice and voice sound, and the physical conditions attending voice production have been presented above. The elements of vocal tone, we said, are quality or timbre, intensity, pitch, and duration. One impression that might have been gained from the foregoing discussion should be corrected at this point. Vocal tone is analyzable into four parts or elements, but each one is so closely related to, if not dependent upon the other three, that we cannot consider the elements of tone as discrete entities. Quality, force, time, and pitch are fused in the process of speech and the composite effect depends on the kind of blending that occurs. It is true, of course, that we may be more conscious of any one of the four elements at a time, and that is why we often speak as we do. We disregard physical fact for immediate psychophysical clarity. With this explanation, then, we say that vocal quality differences are of primary importance to the differentiation of radio characters. How would you describe the voice quality (the impression the voice makes on the ear) of the following six character types?

1. Old man: mellow, patient, understanding
2. Pompous, self-satisfied, benevolent padrone
3. Lazy, stupid, half-wit
4. Schoolteacher: rigid, humorless, straitlaced disciplinarian
5. Telephone operator
6. Old woman: genial, kind, tolerant

Your answer to the question should be based on your knowledge of how age, emotion, occupation, and other factors affect the functioning of the vocal mechanism, particularly, the vocal resonators. The characterized voice is not a matter of saying, "Well, on this one I'll use voice X-2-y. So I'll push these stops, press these pedals, and choose this registration." While the various vocal sets may be considered somewhat objectively in the trial-and-error learning period, characterization, like your own expressions, stems from a psychological identification with the motivating forces of the dramatic personality. The voice of old age is less brilliant, less resonant, and less resilient than the voice of youth. Time affects the speech musculature and the resonating cavities as it does all metabolic functions. The tonal vibrations are less strong, and the frequencies are damped by particular conditions in the resonators. The difference between Mortimer Snerd and Charlie McCarthy is explainable in terms of resonance. The first is a low pharyngeal amplication and the second employs the upper resonators. Emotions involve muscular behavior and cause varying degrees of tension and relaxation throughout the tone passage. Unpleasantness constricts; pleasantness relaxes. The harsh throaty voice quality of anger is a result of psychological changes. The voice of the patient, tolerant, and sympathetic individual differs from the tonal complex of the acid type of crotchety and spiteful person because the emotions produce distinct physical differences. Occupational habits may be responsible for vocal elements associated with character stereotypes. All schoolteachers do not sound alike, to be sure, but there is something about the job of handling 40 restless youngsters and the unimaginative facts of the three R's that seems to produce a pinched and unsympathetic voice if the task is adhered to for several years. You do not expect a funeral-parlor director to talk like a truck driver, or a librarian like a militant, equal-rights crusader. This thesis is elaborated further in Chap. 12 on the Radio Announcer where we discuss the relationship of voice and personality.

Characterization is marked not only by voice quality. There are also differences of pitch, time, and intensity. Again, we are particularizing these elements of tone, but not forgetting that they fuse in the synthesis of tonality. Resonance changes take place with pitch changes. Different resonators are brought into play as the frequency of the tone varies. Other conditions being equal, the resonance is a function of amplitude or force. Referring again to our list of character types, however, we note that a tonal element is prominent in each case. A faster rate and more staccato attack would differentiate blustering authority and dignified authority. An old gentleman, "slightly troubled by his dentures," would be characterized not only by tonal quality, but by rate of speech. The old-timer speaks slowly. The aggressive and dogmatic man speaks more rapidly and with more force than "a small man in a small way." Inflectional patterns vary with characters variously described as energetic, lazy, pious, scolding, condescending.

Experiment with your ability to use different voices. What is your range of pitch, resonance changes, inflectional patterns, stress variation, time control? Begin with the widest possible variations, going even to the points of caricature. Then gradually refine the interpretations until you reach the limits of plausibility and acceptance. Your value and excellence as a radio actor are measured by your flexible and versatile interpretation of a variety of dramatic roles.

Emotional Interpretation. The primary element of drama is conflict, and conflict arouses emotion because of the thwarting which produces disequilibriums, tensions, and neural blocks. A need exists in the organism. A certain objective must be attained to satisfy that need, but there is an obstacle interposed between that need and the satisfaction. The organism must struggle to overcome the obstacle, and the tensions and disequilibriums are not dissolved until the difficulty is conquered. The solution may be worked out in a detached, rational, intellectual manner, but seldom is this the case. In fact, there is probably no purely intellectual behavior in a crisis. If this were true and if people in radio plays solved their problems by a detached and unfeeling analysis of the pros and cons, there would be no radio drama. Drama is conflict, and conflict involves emotion, and the radio actor must interpret emotions. A mother pleads for her boy in court, a father deals with a recalcitrant son, an innocent man protests his arrest, an employee resigns his job because of an alleged injustice, a jealous wife threatens divorce proceedings, a temperamental actress flouts her director, a wife is faithful in spite of rumor and gossip, another is enraged by a practical joke, despair drives to suicide, a woman kills her feeble-minded son to keep him from the penalty of the law. Every dramatic story has its protagonist and antagonist, actual or implied. Forces meet in shock and countershock. There is the situation, complication, and solution. The struggle is between man and man, man and nature, man and the forces of his own nature. There are obstacles which test character, atmosphere which influences behavior, a maze of frustrating complications, or the testing of social and moral theses. Thrust into any of these situations, the actor is involved in the struggle which eventuates in release or defeat. Unless you can live vicariously the emotional upsurgings of people caught in the web of circumstance and adequately manifest the emotional struggle involved, you cannot give an acting performance.

Your next acting problem, then, is emotional responsiveness and release. Responsiveness is one's reaction to the stimulus. What does a particular situation expressed in words arouse in you? Is the excitation so great as to inhibit the expression? Is the final expression a clear and convincing interpretation?

The criticism of your reading is more likely to be that you do not express enough feeling. This arises from two causes: (1) You are afraid of overemoting. You have been warned against insincerity and sentimentality. You fear you may be melodramatic, and the term applied to the exaggeration connoted by this word is "hamy" or "corny." No one wants to be a "ham," and therefore he fails to let himself go. Consequently, he doesn't quite reach the peak of emotional force. (2) The response is inadequate owing to your inability to identify yourself with the dramatic character and situation. You live on the periphery of the scene and not in it. The process by which we effect an amalgamation with the total personality of the character portrayed is essentially the same as the process of effecting rapport with what the character says from moment to moment. If a sound psychological process is engendered in you by the lines, you should not fear that abandonment will lead to distortions and fulsomeness. The haminess of which we speak is due to a sort of blind, guesswork type of expression guided by imitative concepts.

We are again faced with the controversy concerning the relationship of technical performance and control, on the one hand, and complete emotional experience, on the other. *Masks or Faces*, is the title of a book in which is recorded a celebrated controversy between William Archer and M. Diderot. The authors represent the extreme points of view. One claims that the actor must actually live the dramatic forces, and the other that the lack of emotion is the essential of great acting. The argument will probably never be resolved. The safest position to take would seem to be a middle one. The actor must experience emotional activity, but he should also have a mastery of vocal techniques. These vocal devices, if used correctly, are accepted by the audience and interpreted as the manifestation of what the actor is supposed to be experiencing. This middle-ground position, however, does not mitigate our position that the experiential processes are a part of the actor's performance. An emotion is a fused complex of sensory awareness, and the true emotion is identified with the psychological changes accompanying the changes. In normal life, why does the pattern vary with the emotions of the moment? It is because the physical changes produced by sensory stimuli create effector and motor changes affecting respiration and muscle and glandular activity. The natural expression of pain, rage, disgust, sorrow, anger, and love is due to the inherent bodily activity. One needs no lessons in acting to express fear, happiness, or grief; to congratulate a friend on some signal achievement, or to console him for the loss of a loved one. Why, then, do we need acting lessons when similar expressions are required by the line in the script? The answer has been given. The line is not the equivalent of the actual life situation. The circumstances of the life situation are not actually present, and we cannot bring them into the present. We are dealing with artifacts. We cannot clothe them in complete reality. All we can do is try to focus them in the light of imagination and achieve approximate reality. It is for this reason that we recognize the importance of technique.

Technique is the use of stereotyped vocal patterns accepted as emotional equivalents. The bases of emotions as expressed in normal life are essentially similar. People express pain and anger, joy and sorrow, in a language that is universally understood. S. S. Curry uses the phrase, "unprinted elements of expression." The phrase means that many of our expressions cannot be reduced to printed symbols. We cannot write the sounds of sobbing, chuckling, disgust, laughing, temporary confusion, or embarrassment, but there are sounds that symbolize these reactions, and they are generally understood and accepted. The actor makes use of these unprinted symbols, but his utilization of them must conform to the social norm.

The acquisition of vocal technique is complicated by self-consciousness. As said above, we seem to have a certain reticence about showing our emotions. Spontaneity of expression is impeded by a subconscious fear. Will somebody laugh at me? Will I appear ridiculous? This apprehension or dread of embarrassment inhibits our release. But the attempt must be made, and a successful execution of the problem will go far to establish confidence.

A series of reading problems will exemplify our discussion of emotion and interpretation. One of the most difficult, and at the same time, most frequently encountered emotional demands is found in the line requiring laughter; the opposite emotion expressed by crying is a frequent script demand. It is not easy to do either of these convincingly. Laughter is probably the more difficult. The usual performance, when the line specifies laughter, is a decidedly half-hearted, "he-he" or "ho-ho," almost completely isolated from the words and expression of the line itself. Read (that is, interpret) the following speeches:

(1)

(*Laughing.*) Say, where did you get that hat? . . . It must have come out of the attic . . . . (The speech begins with laughter. The sight of the hat greatly amuses. The laughter continues through the question, rises between the sentences—the hat is funnier the more you look at it—and builds to hearty merriment.)

(2)

(*Laughter that rises to almost inhibitory paroxysm.*) And there we were in the middle of this old row boat . . . and Jim . . . and Jim was trying to bail it out . . . he was trying to bail it out . . . with . . . an old shoe . . . he looked over to me and said . . . really, when I tell what he said . . . you'll . . . die . . . laughing.

(3)

(*Satisfaction and amusement at another's discomfiture.*) I really told him off. And you should have seen his face. (*Amused*) And boy, was he burned up?

(4)

(*An old woman is recounting a memory. She is recalling the day she heard her son had been killed.*) He had been away for months. Every day I thought we'd hear. Every time I heard our mail box I was sure it was a letter. But one never came. Then, one morning last June—the day before his birthday—we got the news. Jim Tolliver brought it up from the valley depot. He seemed awfully old as he shuffled down our lane, and in his hand was a yellow envelope. I knew then—that Tom was never coming home.

(5)

(*Angry, indignant, belligerent.*) Of course I'm sore. I'm not going to be a sucker for any heel. What? Yeah. Sure, you can tell him. And get this, Harrigain! If those birds down there think they can run this deal better than I can, you can give them the Hollywood pass sign for me right now.

(6)

(*Fear.*) There's someone in there—I can hear them. I'm sure it's the man who followed us. Oh, please, let's go.

(7)

(*Pain.*) You're hurting my arm. Oh, please, don't—please don't.

(8)

(*Sarcasm, taunting.*) So, I'm your buddy now, eh? What changed your mind, pal? Yesterday you thought I was giving you the double cross. Come on, talk. You're not going anywhere—come on, give.

(9)

(*Enthusiasm.*) We had a marvelous time, Frances. Tom and Virginia and Harold—the whole gang came down. And is Harold's yacht a dream! We went over to Beaver Island for a picnic on Friday, and on Saturday the Hills gave a beach party for the gang. Oh, it was heavenly. Something every minute. You ought to have been there, May.

(10)

(*Despair, resignation.*) I just don't understand him. We've given him every chance—every opportunity in the world, and he just makes a mess of everything. Fifteen years of plans and hopes gone to ruin. We're licked. There's nothing more to do.

Dialectal Skill. Facile dialect skill is an advantage to the radio actor. His value is enhanced by an ability to interpret a range of racial and national types. Audition record forms, as a rule, provide for a detailed notation concerning the applicant's dialectal talent.

The mastery of dialects requires both extensive and intensive study. The authentic dialectician should have a knowledge of comparative languages and of speech variants within the same language. A Southern accent (United States) varies greatly as one moves from Texas to Virginia to Alabama, and one who has traveled in the British Isles knows that the English speech pattern is not uniform. Few students, or even professional radio actors, however, possess a knowledge of comparative languages, and although their approximation may produce reasonably satisfactory stereotypes, most accents you hear are phony.

There are only two points we wish to make in this very brief discussion of the subject. In the first place, a mastery of phonetic peculiarities is not the ultimate guarantee of dialectal proficiency, although the phonetic approach is basic. There was a radio program on which a speech authority could place the geographical location of an individual by hearing him pronounce certain words or phrases. To many listeners, this ability appeared almost magical. The authority, however, was quite honest and sincere. He had a knowledge of speech provincialisms as compiled, classified, and recorded by research men who had made a phonetic transcription of speech patterns in selected towns, cities, and regions. If one had available and could master a dialect dictionary, one would possess a basis on which to develop an imitative speech; but even this phonetic accuracy would not insure an accurate reproduction of alien accents. A knowledge of regional and/or national accents, pronunciations, articulation, and enunciation is only the beginning, fundamental as it is, because each dialect has other distinctive characteristics such as rhythm, pace or tempo, voice quality, inflectional pattern, and linguistic identities. For example, Oriental speech and Negro speech are distinguished by characteristic voice qualities; the Scandinavian talks with a particular inflectional pattern; the Mexican pattern is rather slow and monotonous; and the clipped and somewhat staccato English accent contrasts with the slurred and legato pattern of American speech. Phonetic accuracy alone will not result in a convincing dialect.

In the second place, facility for imitation is a primary requisite to the acquisition of dialectal proficiency. One who does not have what is called a good ear for language differences is handicapped in his study and attainment. There are many opportunities to hear dialectal speech. It is constantly before us on the radio, stage, and motion picture and television screens; and in real life we are frequently associated with people who are making their adjustments to English speech. How good an imitator are you? This is the first key to the problem. The learning process can be further implemented by the use of tape recorders, constant practice, and by consulting a standard manual of dialect exercises.

Pictures in the Mind. The entire drama takes place, as we have quoted, on the stage of the imagination. There is a type of imagination for each of the sensations. We construct the past, or the unseen, in visual, auditory, olfactory, gustatory, kinesthetic, and tactile images. The problem of radio acting is to stimulate vocally as much imaginative response as possible. The situations, of course, are in the written script, and the "imaginary stage" is of primary concern to the writer; but granting that the author has provided the correct stimuli, the actor must implement what is present. The phrase, pictures in the mind, refers chiefly to movement, motor, and kinesthetic activity. A few examples only will be sufficient for illustration. You will constantly encounter pictorial demands such as the following:

1. Walking with effort
2. Riding horseback
3. Lifting a heavy weight, or other similar exertion
4. Striking a blow or receiving a blow
5. Shivering in the cold
6. Swimming
7. Struggling
8. Scrutinizing a puzzle picture
9. Creeping cautiously

A line or speech expressing activity, movement, or effort may be accompanied by sound. If so, the line read by the actor and the effect produced by the sound engineer should be complementary. They should blend into a unified impression. The following lines illustrate further the nature of the problem:

Walking

1. I don't think I can walk much further. I'm terribly tired . . . .
2. We'd better step up, or we'll miss the curtain. I hate to be late . . . .

Riding

3. (*Trotting*) That valley down there is where we camped last summer. Bass Lake is over to the right. You'll have some fine fishing while you are up here.

4. (*Galloping*) If we don't head them off at the pass, we haven't a chance unless Barlow can block 'em at the junction.

Exertion

5. Let's set this trunk over here. Ready? O.K. . . . Hey, what's in here, gold bricks? Steady . . . all right . . . let her down in the corner. Good.

6. This door's stuck tight. I guess the rain caused it to swell. . . . Ahhh! there she is.

Struggle

7. Come on, give me that book. All right, I'll have to take it from you. I hate to be a little rough with you, but—Thank you.

Striking a Blow

8. That's what you said before, Jackson; but this time you're on the receiving end (*blow*) twice (*blow*).

Shivering with Cold

9. We can't wait for them any longer. I'm freezing to death. They never could keep an appointment on time.

Swimming

10. All right, take it easy, I'm coming. I told you to stop moving around in the boat. Keep your head up. I'll get you.

The clarity of dramatic action can be sharpened if the picture is first created in the mind of the actor and if he can give an adequate vocal description of the activity involved. It is suggested you make your own list of "pictures" and practice reproducing them.

Doubling. A radio actor is frequently called upon to read two or more parts. Indeed, his ability to do so increases his value to a director. Versatility is an asset to be prized. Your skill in handling several parts in the same script depends on the range of your characterization and dialectal facility. Doubling means, simply, the ability to play a variety of parts. Characterization techniques and dialectal proficiency have been treated elsewhere. The point we make here is that doubling is an important phase of radio acting ability.

Summary. In the preceding pages we have explained the nature of acting from the standpoint of radio demands and have examined the basic skills involved in this aural medium. In order to bring into perspective the scope of acting knowledge and technique, we offer an outlined recapitulation of the implicit and explicit elements in the foregoing analysis.

1. Drama defined:
    a. Drama is the blending, by an individual or a group of individuals, of locale, character, situation, and theme according to principles of unified emotional effect.
    b. Drama is the representation of human forces in conflict.
    c. Drama is a narrative story which produces a particular emotional effect.
2. Kinds of drama:
    a. Conventionally, drama is divided into two broad categories: tragedy and comedy.
    (1) Tragedy calls for a serious theme, dignified treatment, and, usually, a disastrous ending.
    (2) Comedy calls for a lighter theme which is developed in a manner that produces amusement.
    b. Melodrama is the name given to drama that is sentimental, sensational, and extravagant.
    c. Farce is a dramatic composition which incites to laughter by an exaggerated distortion of situation and character.
    d. Basic drama types may be characterized by descriptive terms: historical, romantic, social, educational, thematic, mystery, detective, etc.
3. Radio drama defined:
    a. Radio drama, played upon the stage of the listener's imagination, is the projection of a dramatic story by means of voice, sound, and music.

    b. Although radio dramatic types fall within the conventional classification of drama, radio plays are catalogued according to theme and theme treatment.

        (1) Public-service drama, documentary, the woman's serial, the children's serial, detective, crime drama, mystery, family life drama, adaptations, biographical, historical, educational.

4. Acting defined:

    a. Acting is the process, technique, and skill by which one lives a vicarious experience, adapting himself to the motives, moods, and environment which actuate the dramatic character.

    b. Acting is creative communication.

    c. "Acting is real life reorganized and put in a frame by an artist."

5. Radio acting defined:

    a. Radio acting is the portrayal or revelation of the thoughts, emotions, struggles, conflicts, and experiences of dramatis personae by means of *voice.*

6. Differences between stage acting and radio acting:

    a. Stage acting is performed within the sight and hearing of an audience.

    b. Stage acting employs the medium of the body and the agencies of physical expression.

    c. Radio acting is performed for a hearing audience only.

7. Relation of the radio actor to the writer:

    a. Acting proficiency is aided by an understanding of the writer's art, for

        (1) The writer constructs a dramatic situation using elements of sound, music, and voice, and the actor should understand how his reading of lines is enhanced by the addition of sound and music, how the dramatic action is augmented thereby, and how the dramatic mood is likewise facilitated, for

            (*a*) The writer gets his play started quickly—has little time for a first-act exposition.

            (*b*) The writer gets attention, arouses interest with his first lines.

            (*c*) The play is compact and condensed—compressed without suppression.

            (*d*) Emotion, essence of dramatic conflict, is intense and concentrated.

            (*e*) For effective endings, scenes often depend on decisive, clipped, staccato, stablike or "stinger" lines intensified perhaps by music or sound transitions.

            (*f*) Confined by an aural medium, the writer uses clearly differentiated characters.

            (*g*) The writer at all times creates pictures in the mind of his audience both by dialogue and by the use of spatial effects.

8. Relation of the actor to the director:

    a. Acting proficiency is aided by an understanding of some of the director's problems; for the director who, with the aid of actors and technical assistants, brings to life the writer's art, is concerned with such problems as,

(1) Completing the show within an exact time limit.
(2) Perspective and spatial relationships.
(3) Tempo.
(4) Climactic movement.
(5) Tightness.
(6) Balance of program elements.
9. Radio acting principles:
   a. The actor creates the part and identifies himself with it through an understanding of human psychology.
   b. The radio actor reacts fully and accurately to imaginary stimuli. He cannot interpret what he does not see or feel. He must have the power to visualize—to make mental pictures. His reading is the result of sensitivity, not imitation.
   c. The actor takes his line motivation from his fellow actor and returns a motivation to him.
   d. The actor produces illusions of intimacy. He talks humanly.
   e. Characters should not be exaggerated. They should be kept normal and simple.
   f. The voice is an expression of personality and portrays the gamut of characters represented in the play.
10. Radio acting skills (as correlated in part with the principles):
   a. Ability to read at sight.
   b. Ability to read without giving the impression of reading.
   c. Vocal picturization of varied characters.
   d. Emotional range.
   e. Picture painting.
   f. Dialectal skill.
   g. Doubling—to play more than one part in the same script.
   h. Microphone adaptation.

QUESTIONS

1. What is acting?
2. What is the difference between everyday acting and stage acting?
3. What is the main difference between stage and radio acting?
4. Enumerate and explain each of the radio acting skills discussed in this chapter. Explain how they are essentially related.

CHAPTER 15

PRODUCTION-DIRECTION

The purpose of this chapter is to discuss the subject of radio production. We shall not review all the conditions and procedures which attend commercial employment. Production details incident to professional operations will be learned on the job. We are concerned here with the application of basic principles to the college class program.

Every broadcast involves the associated activity of several people working in different capacities. This fact makes it necessary that one individual assume over-all executive responsibility. This person is called the producer.[1] His problems and duties vary with the scope and character of the program, but his main purpose at all times is to deliver to the airways a properly timed and executed broadcast. The nature of production is best exemplified by the radio drama. Let us use this program type as a basic example because it incorporates the *duties, knowledge, techniques,* and *qualifications* that apply to program supervision and direction. We assume that a dramatic script is delivered to a director, to be presented on a scheduled date, and trace step by step its preparation and final presentation.

Duties

1. *Study the Script.* Read the script and evaluate it as a dramatic vehicle. How does it affect you? Do you see clearly the dramatic picture the author has drawn? Is your imagination stimulated? Are your emotions aroused? Does the script have a purpose other than direct entertainment? That is, do you find a thematic purpose, an educational aim, or a documentary objective? Is the main interest to be found in an idea, a character unfoldment, the dominance of atmosphere, or the complication of events and their inherent suspense? What is the picture, or pictures, you wish to create in the minds of your listeners? The final

---

[1] The titles, "radio producer" and "radio director," are basically synonymous. The first suggests a wider scope of responsibility. A complicated show involving the synthesis of many program parts may require the services of a trained executive who can supervise the integration of the program sections, and this person may be called a producer; whereas the individual appointed to perfect one of the units of the broadcast may be termed a director. The distinction is without too much basis in fact, however, and the titles of producer, director, and producer-director are used interchangeably.

quality of your production will be infused with the quality of your own imagination. If the lines, characters, and situations are only so many sticks and stones, you will not build a strong and artisitic production.

After reading the script and formulating your evaluations, go through it again and begin to plot the dramatic action in terms of rising and falling interest. A good radio play is a highly compressed dramatic narrative with a single emotional effect. It gets off to a quick start, swings through a series of sharply integrated scenes, reaches a climax, and ends with a rapid solution. Not all plays follow the some format, but in general this is the pattern. Very seldom will you find a continuous, straight-line development. Rather, your interest line will be a jagged one, although the over-all development will show an ascending scale of interest. How can these various points of climactic growth be emphasized? It is a matter of dialogue pace and the effective use of sound and music.

2. *Edit the Script.* You are not bound to follow precisely the exact text of the script. Unless you are handling the material of a top-flight professional writer, you may have to edit the play to achieve your dramatic ends.

Are locales clearly established: ballroom, street corner, department store, water front?

Are perspectives always indicated: entrances, fades, space relationships?

Do you find any dead spots: business without lines?

Is the dialogue always in character: wrong colloquialisms, stilted?

Is sound overused or underused at particular points?

Are there items which violate rules of plausibility; (*e.g.*, the length of time it takes to get from one point to another, talking on telephone before placing a call)?

Are there too many choppy scenes that should be telescoped?

Are all the minor characters—bit parts—necessary, and can some of them be eliminated?

These are some of the elements of construction and content which should be checked by the producer.

3. *Analyze the Characters.* Having edited the play to your satisfaction, you should next make an analysis of the characters and fix each one in your mind. It will be helpful if you insist on writing a brief description of each of your dramatis personae. This will aid in giving to your players an idea of the characterization desired in their performance; but you cannot discuss the thoughts, attitudes, and motivations of your play characters unless you first identify yourself with their behavior patterns.

4. *Cast the Show.* When you have studied and analyzed the script and projected it upon the stage of your own imagination, you are ready to move toward the achievement of your mental pictures. A cast of characters is selected, and the play is put into rehearsal. Casting is the process

of fitting real personalities to fictional personalities. How accurately can the actor selected project the character to which he is assigned? In casting a college program, the director is torn between the ideals of educational casting and the rules of professional casting. By the latter, a director tries to achieve a natural correspondence, whereas educational ideals demand that students be developed to play roles for which they are not especially endowed. It is natural for the student director to select "heavy" voices to play "heavies," and light voices to play ingénues; but this practice should be modified in the interests of personal development.

5. *Rehearse the Program.* Rehearsals proceed in stages.

a. At the first meeting with the director, the cast is instructed about the nature of the play and its acting demands. The story is sketched in brief and the individual roles described. Scripts are distributed, and a sight reading is conducted to acquaint everyone with the play. Brief comments may be interjected by the director during this reading, but a detailed critique of the interpretations is not made until the reading is finished. This run-through, and perhaps a second one, take place around a table. It is informal and designed for orientation.

b. If the director feels that his actors now understand their individual assignment, he will conduct his second reading "on-mike" to check voice levels, balance, scene perspective, and characterizations. In stage parlance, this might be called a rough blocking of the show. The final selection and assignment of players should not be made until after the first mike rehearsal. The voice you listen to over the monitor speaker will not be quite the same as the one you listened to in the first reading. The characterization, balance, and contrast of voices may be missed unless you rely on auditory impressions coming from the microphone.

c. The third cast rehearsal is coordinated with the work of the technical staff. Dramatic pictures involve the blending of voice, sound, and music. This is the longest and most painstaking of the rehearsal periods. Sound-effects personnel, the music director, and the monitoring engineer join with the actors to complete preparations for the broadcast. At times progress will be very slow. Effects must be checked and rechecked; music bridges, backgrounds, and curtains (introductory and final music) cued and recued; balance and perspective reset; interpretations changed or corrected. The final judgment in each instance is made by the director, and he will call for many retakes before he is satisfied. When this process of trial and error, backing and filling, stopping and starting is completed, we are ready for a "dress."

d. This fifth rehearsal is an attempt to achieve the perfection which you hope will distinguish the broadcast. It proceeds exactly as if you were on the air. There are no stops or corrections. The director follows carefully every minute detail of the production and makes notes about the things he finds unsatisfactory. He also makes accurate time notations on the margin of his script to guarantee that the program will exactly fit the time period allotted to the show.

e. The sixth session is not a rehearsal in the exact sense of the term, but following the "dress" a conference is conducted with all the participants at which the director reviews the performance and makes necessary last-minute adjustments. At various points, he has noticed that the sound effects were too late or too early, the music too loud or wrongly timed, that an actor didn't wait for the sound man to pick up the telephone receiver before starting his conversation, off-mike newsboys were too heavy, the balance between party sounds and dialogue was incorrect, the level of the filter mike was too low, etc. If the production was particularly faulty at certain points, these spots, if there is time, may be rerehearsed. Then, there should be a break—an interim—in which the performers may lose their emotional tensions and prepare for a fresh start.

f. And now the red light says you are on the air. The director throws his first cue and the program is under way. No stopping or turning back now. It's the broadcast! This does not mean that the director may now settle nonchalantly in a chair and watch results. The production itself is his real trial. More or less, he holds the program literally in the hollow of his hand. All the details which have been pieced together during the rehearsals must be executed promptly, efficiently, and with stop-watch precision. He directs the coordination of the many program parts, anticipates each action of cast and technical staff, and carries in mind the auditory pictures being transmitted to the radio audience.

During the broadcast the director is the focal point in the operations. He is situated either in the control room or in the studio. The latter location is probably the better one because he will be closer to the performers, and this proximity enables him to secure better cooperation among the associated program personnel—actors, sound men, musicians, and monitor engineer. In the studio he should wear earphones attached to a cord long enough to permit a limited area of movement. The program starts on a cue from the director, and throughout the broadcast the players and technical assistants will receive from him many hand signals. Music is brought in, held, cut, or faded out; sound effects introduced and coordinated with the dialogue; actors told when to begin a scene and directed as to their mike positions, level, and distance; the monitor given warning about board fades, the cut-in of a special mike, and consulted about the audio qualities of the program.

Knowledge. The above outline of a program rehearsal and performance makes clear that the director's work is based on a defined body of knowledge.

1. *Drama.* The thoroughly skilled radio director should have a technical understanding of dramaturgy, the art of dramatic composition and execution. The nature of conflict and suspense ever present in effective drama should be evaluated and implemented with the resources at the director's command. He should be familiar with the various patterns of dramatic format. Character, complication, atmosphere, and thematic stories require different accentuation. Moreover, dramatic ends and forms are modified when adapted to radio. Radio drama becomes a special medium quite different in many respects from a stage play. Some of these differences are suggested by the following questions:

Does the program have a fast getaway? Does it capture attention? Does the action unfold swiftly?
Is the plot simple and compact?
Is the writing designed for listening? Is the story clear at all times? Are the scenes differentiated and do they tie together and build toward a major climax?
Do the characters remain in sharp focus? Are there too many characters?
Is the action furthered by properly paced dialogue, or does it become stalled in long speeches?
Does the writer, in expressing himself through the radio medium, demand too much by his use of sound and music? Can the dramatic pictures be made vivid by eliminating some of the suggested effects, or has he failed to employ audio aids which should be written in?

A director who can evaluate a radio drama and make requisite editorial changes should know dramatic rules and the principles of script writing. In some radio departments a study of radio writing is made the intermediate course between radio acting and radio production.

2. *Studio Equipment.* Knowledge requisite to program direction is reviewed in Chap. 9. The director must learn about studios, microphones, turntables, control-room operations, and studio working conditions. These constitute the platform on which he conducts his operations.

3. *Music.* Music is a functional tool in radio production. It may establish a mood, intensify an entire scene, punctuate action sequences, emphasize the emotional climax, create impressions of unreality, bridge time, substitute for sound, paint mental pictures, suggest movement and action, and otherwise perform many dramatic and narrative functions.

The service of music to radio drama can be illustrated in part by the phraseology employed by writers when indicating in their scripts the effects desired. Script directions vary from simple, conventional terminology to detailed and explicit expositions. Furthermore, writers use different phrases according to their individuality and, presumably, their desire to be somewhat original; but music cues as variously written have

the same general meaning. A casual reading of a radio play anthology
will afford a wide range of illustrations. For example,

(*Music: Bridge*)
(*Sneak*)
(*Up and fade under*)
(*Out*)
(*Up and into*)
(*Middle curtain*)
(*Tag*)
(*Sneak under last line . . . up into love theme . . . minor in mood . . .
     to B.G.*)
(*In . . . sock and to B.G.*)
(*Sting and out under*)
(*Heavy and regal*)
(*Music hits . . . down and continuing behind*)
(*Dramatic swipe and under*)
(*Accent*)
(*Out with dissonant chord*)
(*Sneak in above . . . whirl around and out*)
(*Dramatic bridge into fogged effect*)
(*Sharp dramatic climax . . . but short. This is a punctuation*)
(*Steals under and thunders up*)
(*Brief upsweep of chords*)
(*Stream of consciousness music begins through above . . . fade . . . this is
     quiet eerie strain*)
(*Slow questioning note into a short bridge*)
(*Sweep up into short bridge . . . out sharply for a discordant chord on the
     piano*)
(*Orchestra carrying theme of nocturne dies out until only piano remains.
     It finishes playing and there is a long pause. Then a single haunting
     chord is struck by full orchestra and is held under for. . . .*)

The emotional quality of music complements the emotional ends of
drama. Just why this is so constitutes a problem in psychology. The
reason probably lies in the nature of conditioned behavior, but it is true
that music can accentuate, sharpen, and intensify the audio interpretation of the dramatic scene, point, or climax. Music can do more than
this, of course. Instruments can simulate the roar of dive bombers, the
rattle of machine guns, marching men, moving trains, and be substituted
for many other sound effects, supply comedy emphasis, transport the
listener from one locale to another, bridge and clarify dramatic structure.
We cannot expect the radio producer to have the knowledge of a trained
music director or arranger, but he should have an appreciation of what
is musically appropriate to his dramatic purpose. Instrumentation, registration, key, tempo, melody, harmony, dissonance, incomplete phrasing,

intensity, and attack are elements of composition variously employed to produce specific ends. How do the elements of musical composition relate to the interpretation of fear, frustration, anger, resignation, grief, excitement, struggle, apprehension, sudden relief? This is a question the director should be able to answer. He does answer it, rightly or wrongly, when he selects the music for his show or passes judgment upon the selections made for him by his musical director. The wisdom of his judgment contributes to the success of his program.

The student director, like the producer of the low-cost commercial show, is dependent on recorded ("canned") music. These records are expensive. The funds at his disposal will be limited. It is necessary, therefore, that he carefully select his purchases. This will entail many hours of listening, but assuming a knowledge of music as used in radio, he should be able to equip his workshop station at a cost of $100 or $150. Each recording should be played several times until the producer is thoroughly familiar with the composition, and then analyzed section by section in terms of descriptive, pictorial, and mood pictures. Resulting notations may be somewhat as follows:

1. Tempestuous. Action packed, heavy drama. Excitement. Clash of arms. Good for scene climax

2. Ominous, foreboding, tragic. Sadness, loneliness. Tempo slow. Use for dramatic setting, foreshadowing

3. Brightness, hope, spirited energy. Quick tempo

4. Fear, awe; ghostly, supernatural

5. Pastoral. Early morning. Dawn breaking, morning on the plains, quiet, peace

6. Romantic, sentimental, melodious

7. A tremendous build reaching a climax and falling to a stealthy, plodding effect

8. Suspense build, climax to catastrophe

9. Slow movement, going through a dark cave; background mood of suspense or waiting

10. Stately, *religioso*, regal

11. Comedy effect (horse laugh)

12. Passing of time

13. Stinger

14. Plaintive

15. Festive, holiday mood

The fallacy in this procedure is that a given passage of music presented to several people will be classified differently. The director can only hope that his judgment will be confirmed by the conditioned response of his listeners.

In order to help the producer arrive at a sound decision in selecting music, let us review some of the principal elements of music and the relation of musical composition to functional ends.

The first and most obvious component of music is *pitch.* Higher frequencies, in general, are more exciting and attention-getting than low frequencies. The latter, on the other hand, are slower and more pompous. Consequently, if a fast passage is desired, it most likely would be placed in the higher registers. To write for a bass instrument as you would for a flute would be ridiculous unless the aim were to produce a ridiculous or comedy effect.

The next characteristic is *tempo.* The concepts derived from relative tempi are fairly common and generally universal because of the close association with relative speeds of everyday living. Slowness conveys ideas of relaxation, thoughtfulness, sleep, open country, nature, death, morbidness, tragedy, and love. Speed creates thoughts of cities, crowds, gaiety, restlessness, business, liveliness, frivolity, and childhood.

Another basic element is *rhythm.* Here, perhaps, is where music is most closely linked with the world of reality and the mechanics of living. Rhythm may be loosely defined as a series of pulsations or sounds that form or fit into some sort of accent pattern. Through rhythmic devices, and often through the rhythm of sound effects alone, we can create the mood and often the locale of a particular scene. A steady, monotonous beating of drums would suggest an African or tropical location; the familiar "dotted-quarter" dance rhythms are associated with the Spanish cultures. In selecting music for a script, a working knowledge of rhythms of different cultures can be a useful tool and, at the same time, make the musical background more effective.

Another useful device which has been exploited by contemporary, serious composers is that of *polyrhythm*—the superimposition or rhythmic patterns. This device is effective in montages and transitions involving a sustained train of thought.

Rhythm can be used effectively as a linking device. A show can be unified musically by having one established rhythmic pattern which fits the rhythm of a dialogue and situation, and by superimposing on that rhythm the other musical elements desired. Caution must be exercised, however, to ensure that the rhythm is not monotonous, overused, or generally distracting. Besides being a good linking device, rhythm can be a handy instrument for establishing moods and mood contrast. A steady, martial rhythm creates a military air; a steady, unemphasized beat can offer serenity and calm. On the other hand, syncopated or uneven rhythm can convey impending disaster, great joy, or great tragedy. In other words, an uneven rhythm can implement dramatic climax and contrast.

Another basic element of music is *melody.* Melody is that essential part of a musical composition which is composed of a series of notes arranged in a recognizable and appealing order. It is that component of music which you can take home with you from the concert hall and enjoy months after you first heard it. The function of melody in the radio drama does not assume the same role of importance as it does in absolute music. Since melody is the most attention-getting element of music (excepting some rhythmic patterns), it is not well suited to situations where the music should be unobtrusive. Music with a strong, easily identifiable melodic line should not be used as background or for bridging scenes requiring smooth and flowing continuity. A short melodic motif may be used where there is a radical change in situations, because a brief melodic motif or fragment can arrest the listener's attention and make him conscious of the change. Moreover, music with a dominant melody can be used to advantage where the music serves as punctuation for a scene or story. In this instance, the attention is directed to the music since it serves as a climax and often as a recapitulation of the scene or the entire show.

Long, legato, melodic lines with few dissonant intervals convey moods of calmness, serenity, romance, and even spirituality; a comparative lack of dissonance creates a feeling of relaxation. A gradual rise in pitch and dynamics conveys impressions of climax and, possibly, exultation, whereas a fall in pitch and dynamics creates feelings of approaching finality and conclusion. A line characterized by large leaps, dissonant intervals, and irregular rhythm causes a great deal of tension even when it is not harmonized.

Let us now apply the foregoing explanations to a number of specific situations and see how they relate to functional problems.

Example 1 (Scene Ending)

MAN 1: We're going in there. Get your flashlight.
MAN 2: It's not my plan, Pal—but it's your show.
MAN 1: Come along.
MAN 2: I didn't like it, but we started to inch our way farther into that cavern of blackness.

Dramatic effect desired: suspense, eeriness, gloom, haunting.

Musical effects desired and methodology: Since the scene obviously contains more than a small degree of tension, the first problem is how much and what types of tension are to be used. The scene does not end on an unresolved note; there is no feeling of indecision; and melodic content would be out of place. Consequently, the best means of obtaining tension in this instance would be through the use of dissonant harmonies, perhaps over a pedal point.

The second step is to examine the list of characteristic elements and decide how each element should be used.

Pitch—probably in lower registers, not too extreme.

Tempo—the script indicates hesitancy of movement, therefore tempo should be moderate to slow.

Rhythm—fairly steady with some syncopation perhaps, to indicate hesitancy and nervousness.

Melody—not called for; transition should be one of mood.

Harmony—fairly full and dissonant, block harmonies, consistent tension.

Instrumentation—use low winds and strings for dark coloring.

Example 2 (Scene Ending)

MAN: I promised to take you to the stars, but it was an empty dream. I dragged you down instead—into the dust of failure and hopelessness. Oh, my dear, can we ever regain the promise and the dream?

Dramatic effect desired: despair, yet with a sense of power, futility, and questioning.

Musical effects desired and methodology: The music for this scene ending should be more of a punctuation than a transition. The music must convey the despair of the man and at the same time give a feeling of universality, spirituality, and frustration. The despair can be indicated best by low register. To get the spiritual effect, the music should rise and finish in a big climax at the end of the bridge.

Pitch—should begin in low register and rise to high point at end.

Tempo—slow at the beginning, picking up to moderately fast at the end.

Rhythm—the script seems to need no particular effect, probably steady rhythm in duple time.

Melody—can rise out of low register, become the dominant element, climb, and follow in "exultant" manner.

Harmony—should be dominant element at first, somewhat dissonant, giving away to more consonance and melody at end.

Instrumentation—begin with low winds, join later by strings, with all instruments joined in tutti at the end.

Example 3 (Scene Ending)

MAN: This is the end, my friends. I sell my soul to the devil. And for you, may ghouls and afreets rise from their caverns to haunt you forever.

Dramatic effect desired: eeriness, mystery, despair, threat, and revenge.

Musical effects and methodology: The effect should be one of tenseness and extremes. Tensions could be created by use of the tremolo, dissonance, and prolonged resolution. Ending the bridge with an altered tonic chord containing sharp dissonances.

Pitch—either very low or very high, emphasizing mystery, despair.

Tempo—probably slow and heavy, but it could also be fast and "tight."

Rhythm—even and marked, or dotted, rhythm with heavy chords.

Melody—unnecessary, but fragments could be used in sequence.

Harmony—thick, heavy, and dissonant.

Instrumentation—plenty of noise, use of brass, especially trombones with strings playing tremolo.

Example 4 (Scene Ending)

MAN: Wait, they're turning back . . . . Yeah, it's our planes—they've seen us. Feast your eyes, lads, they've found us—we're going home—home—home . . . .

Dramatic effect desired: exultation, freedom, escape, promise.

Musical effects and methodology: This music must echo and punctuate the feeling of exultation. It must be full and sonorous, building to a climax.

Pitch—should begin high and loud and progress even higher and louder at the end.

Tempo—fairly fast, could have a swirl at the end.

Rhythm—free choice, wide range of possibilities.

Melody—could be dominant, climbing scalewise in strings to final high chord.

Harmony—full with block chords, fairly consonant.

Instrumentation—full and rich with brass joining in at the end.

Example 5 (Scene Ending)

BOY: Gee, I didn't realize when you said—

GIRL: That I wasn't coming to the dance?

BOY: Yeah. But now, it's wonderful . . . . Gee . . . it's wonderful.

Dramatic effect desired: happiness, freshness, sweetness, youthfulness, hopefulness.

Musical effects and methodology: The whole effect here should be one of simplicity and gaiety. Dramatic effects and tension are not needed.

Pitch—middle registers.

Tempo—frisky, light, gay.

Rhythm—skipping, full of life.

Melody—light dance-type motif, should be a short motif in sequences.

Harmony—thin, bare block outline for accompaniment of the melody.

Instrumentation—thin, sparing use of instruments, no brass. Dominance of violins and flute.

The above analyses are not offered with any dogmatic claim. Individual taste and judgment will dictate dissenting opinions so far as such specific instances are concerned; but the exposition is offered to point the fact that the director's choice of functional music in the production of radio drama is governed by definite principles and a knowledge of music composition.

4. Sound Effects. The execution of sound effects belongs to the province of the sound technician or engineer, but the subject is discussed at this point because the dramatic program director should also be competent in this field.

Sound effects are classified as *live* and *recorded.* Most of the sound used to vivify dramatic action will probably be recorded. This is a generalization, however, to which there are many exceptions, and even when an effect record is available, it may be better, even necessary, to substitute manual sound to achieve sharp timing, more flexibility, and greater realism. Thunderclaps, wind, and crashing glass are three examples of "canned" sound which, as recorded, may not fit the exigencies of the dialogue. A thunder sheet, a wind machine, and a crash box may be employed to better advantage. The sound-effects technician should exercise discretion in choosing between the two means of effecting the desired auditory impressions. Many people working in radio today can remember the period of radio programing when sound records were unavailable—when all sound was performed manually. The men who went into this phase of the business were clever and ingenious and seldom failed to come up with the prescribed effect. The author recalls an instance when a script called for *marching steps* and the *flapping of fish on boat deck.* The two results were achieved by a single gadget. When the handle of this contraption was turned to the right, soldiers marched; when operated to the left, fish flopped. Anyone who has visited the sound department of one of the major motion-picture companies (*e.g.,* the department at Walt Disney's) can understand the inventiveness employed in this realm of make-believe. One of the satisfactions derived from a radio production course comes from your success in devising credible, realistic sound effects. Your sense of achievement stems from the fact that the device actually employed will usually be entirely different from what it purports to be. Coal cars are roller skates pushed over an iron plate sprinkled with sand; steps on snow are simulated by the manipulation of a box of cornstarch; the whir of the elevator is an electric vibrator; the squeaking door is a swivel chair that needs an oil-can; and thudding hoofs may be produced by thumping a manly chest with coconut shells or teacups. The full range of sound possibilities is limited only by the imagination. Following is a partial list of live or manual sounds and an explanation of how they may be produced.[2]

---

[2] The effects described here are definitely of the "home-made" variety and are, in some instances, relatively crude compared to devices created by professional studio men. However, they illustrate what may be achieved when material and financial resources are limited.

The most comprehensive presentation of sound effects will be found in Robert B. Turnbull's book, *Radio and Television Sound Effects,* published by Rinehart & Company, 1951.

Bird Wings (Flapping). Flap pieces of canvas near the microphone.

Bones Rattling. Suspended wooden sticks with strings from a board. Manipulate the board so that the sticks clack together.

Breeze. Fold two sections of newspaper in half, then cut each section into parallel strips. When swayed, these strips produce a rustling sound.

Brook Babbling. Blow air through a straw into a glass of water. Experiment by using varying amounts of water and by blowing at various speeds.

Bushes Crackling. Manipulate a small bundle of broomcorn close to the microphone. Actual tree branches may be used.

Coal Cars. The sound of small loaded coal cars approaching can be made by rolling a pair of roller skates over a piece of iron. Experiment by sprinkling gravel on the iron plate.

Door (Hollow Clang of Iron Doors Opening). Draw a roller skate over an iron plate, rattle a heavy chain, and operate a key in a lock.

Echo Effects. (1) Suspend a solid wastepaper basket, open and facing the diaphragm of the microphone. Actor stands behind the mike so that his voice goes into the container and is reflected back into the microphone. (2) The actor cups his hands and talks into a length of pipe. (3) A person in front of the microphone talks directly into a large glass jar. (Try this for telephone or talk-back effect.)

Falling Body. A gunny sack half filled with sand is dropped to the floor or ground; or the sound man does a "live body fall."

Fighting Sounds. Whack a rubber sponge with the fist.

Fire. Twist cellophane, break stems of broom straws, crush tissue or wrapping paper.

Hail. Drop rice on glass, tin, or wood.

Hinges Squeak. Turn wooden pegs in holes drilled in a block of wood to make a snug fit.

Hoofbeats. Coconut shells clapped together ("clappety clap"); two plumber's suction cups pounded against the chest (turf); half shells in a box containing sand, gravel, or other material.

Ice Crackling. Crumple an electric-light carton near the microphone.

Ice Jam Creaking. Twist a child's balloon which is inflated.

Marching Feet. Construct a wooden frame about 2 feet square. Across the frame string wires or cords laterally about 2 inches apart. From the wires suspend wooden pegs about 5 inches long and 1 inch in diameter. Space the pegs so that they are about 2 inches apart along the wires or cords. By dropping and raising the edges of the frame so that the pegs drop upon different surfaces in the proper rhythm, the sound of marching men can be produced.

Oars in Oarlocks. Twist or turn one block of wood on another. Turn simultaneously an ordinary doorknob in rhythm with the intended action of the oars. This is for oars working in metal oarlocks.

Screech of Automobile Brakes. Slide a drinking glass with the top placed against a pane of glass . . . try driving two or three nails through a piece of wood and rubbing the points of the nails on a pane of glass.

Ship Pulling at the Mooring Lines. Draw the bow of a bass viol across the edges of a strawberry box.

Shots. (1) A tambourinelike frame and an attached pliable metal spatula. (2) Strike a padded cushion with a thin, flat stick (shot pad). (3) Prick a balloon with a pin. (4) Sound-effects pistol.

Surf. (1) Rub a stiff scrubbing brush with a rotary motion over the head of a drum or tympani. (2) Roll beans on a window or drum head. (3) Use a splash cradle, a watertight box mounted on rockers and containing 2 or 3 inches of water.

Thunder. An inflated basketball bladder containing about 50 small buckshot will give a convincing rumble when agitated close to the microphone.

Wind. A drum of screening material set up so that it can be rotated against a fixed piece of canvas stretched across the revolving surface of the drum is most effective. The intensity of the wind may be governed by the speed of the rotary drum.

Wood Splintering. Crush matchboxes, strawberry boxes, or fruit crates according to the sound required.

Inventiveness and imagination are not the only requisites of a competent sound technician. He must be able to execute his assignment with skill and with a sense of artistic appropriateness. He is not an automaton who steps, closes doors, snaps on lights, or falls to the floor "with a lifeless thump" whenever a director points a finger at him. He does these things, of course, and on cue, but his performance is an integral part of the show and, like the actor's performance, has shading, sensitivity, timing, balance, and proportion. A routine, mechanical performance of sound directions may ruin a performance. Does a door slam on or off mike? Do footsteps express weariness or elation? Is the struggle a light scuffle or angry brawl? Is the liquid being poured water, tea, or a liquor? Is the coin thrown on the counter a lead nickel or a silver dollar? Is the counter glass or wood? Does the effect come with the word or phrase, before, or after it? Is the sound man concerned with dramatic timing? Every effect has its particular genre and focus. In the final analysis the director is responsible for the selection, execution, and integration of sound effects. Therefore, a knowledge of sound production is a vital and integral part of his craftsmanship.

5. *Turntables.* The execution of recorded sound effects requires a knowledge of turntables and their use. Ultimate skill in this technical field will be attained through practice, but the following explanation will serve as a guide to the beginner

a. Conventional turntables have two speeds—revolving at either 78 or 33⅓ times per minute (rpm).

b. Records may play from either the inside out or the outside in. Those you will normally use track from outside in, but this item should be checked.

c. Volume is controlled by a related rheostat, sometimes called "pot."

d. The pot should be turned off before the tone or pickup arm is placed on the record, and turned off before it is picked up.

e. *Dry grooves* (grooves which carry no recorded sound) will produce an audible sound. Start the record on a live revolution.

f. Record starts should be marked. The mark can be made with a wax pencil (red or yellow preferably), soft blackboard crayon, or a piece of colored tape. The starting of a record on a particular groove or section of a groove is a delicate operation. Play the record and stop it at the point where you want to pick up the phrase. Place a marker at this spot. Then back up the record 1 or 1½ turns and stop the turntable if you have an automatic starting switch. Otherwise, hold the record in position until you get the cue to release it. In the latter method be careful not to stop the table itself because you will burn out the bearing in the turntable motor. You can keep the recording in position by holding it lightly at the edge or by holding the felt padding which covers the revolving surface of the table.

g. In starting your record be careful to avoid a "wow." A wow results when the table is not up to full speed. Do not open the pot until the record has attained the full 78 or 33⅓ rpm. You will probably not have a table rigged for instantaneous starts, and it will take about 3 seconds before you can safely turn in the gain.

h. A sound truck usually has at least two turntables. The tone arm for each is so placed that the two can be used on the same record. This permits the playing of a record indefinitely. As the first arm reaches the end of the platter, the second arm is put down at the beginning. This is useful when it is necessary to sustain a sound such as rain through a long dialogue sequence. The technique is called "double-tone" arming.

i. The pickup or playback arms should be handled very carefully. Do not drop the arm on the record or let it fall on the surface of the turntable. The needle is easily dulled or broken, and a good pickup unit is expensive.

j. Before the broadcast be sure to arrange your records in the exact order of their use. If the sound table is equipped with a rack, the records can be spread out for ready use, or a portable wire rack is very convenient. Records should be handled with care to avoid scratching and finger smudging. They should not be transported without protective jackets.

6. *Control Board.* The operation of a control board is an engineering job. Under professional conditions the director is not directly responsible for program monitoring, but he should be able to understand the technique, and in the college workshop, take his turn as engineer. His knowledge need not extend to the technical construction, maintenance, and repair of equipment, but only to the function of the control board itself and to its manipulation during a rehearsal and broadcast. Control-board function is to mix, blend, and balance the program and sound elements and to deliver a requisite level to the transmitter. This is accomplished by managing various potentiometers or gain controls and by maintaining a level of sound as indicated by a V U. meter. The job becomes

complicated when three or four mike channels are in use and several sound sources have to be played against each other. Again, experience and a good deal of trial and error will ensue before one learns to operate a board efficiently. It requires concentration, quick perception, and most of all an artistic sense. Control engineering is very important to the director. Programs can be ruined by a careless and indifferent handling of monitor dials. Elements of balance and perspective, scene introductions and endings, and special effects depend on how the gain controls are handled. The director should maintain close liaison with his monitoring engineer.

Qualifications

1. *Executive Ability*. A director is an executive. He plans, organizes, and carries projects to completion. He weaves a great number of details into a finished pattern. This executive ability is measured by his efficiency —his capacity to complete the job in minimum time and with the maximum conservation of energy. He works according to a precise schedule, driving toward a fixed goal. A director cannot be confused, lackadaisical, indecisive. He knows what he wants and knows how to get it.

2. *Leadership*. Executive ability is related to traits of leadership. A leader can command followers only if he has their confidence and respect. He will have their confidence if he is efficient and evidences mastery of his job; he will secure respect if he can establish a spirit of mutuality, tolerance, and understanding. The primary requisite of personal success is to be well liked, and one is not liked if he is arrogant, hypercritical, unyielding, and not willing, up to a point, to share with others. There are times when the director must be firm and positive. He can go only so far in reconciling divergent opinions, and he should never give the impression that he is confused or in doubt. Program personnel should recognize that the director is the "boss." This is understood clearly enough by professionals, but in student and amateur groups divided counsels and gratuitous suggestions about this and that often threaten efficient teamwork. Let the director make the decisions. Should his judgments be in error, he is the one who should, and does, get the blame.

3. *Emotional Stability*. A director must be able to work under pressure. This calls for emotional stability. You will never have as much time as you need for program rehearsal. The minute hand on the clock moves inexorably and relentlessly toward that dead line. Only an hour or half an hour remains before broadcast time and every thing seems "snafu." There are technical failures, some of the production spots are still rough, the dialogue interpretations are unsatisfactory, another cut in the script seems necessary, your script timing data are confused, a

cast change may be necessary owing to some emergency, and so it goes. The situation may not be quite so bad, but you can be certain that problems similar to these will always be present, and the pressure of the moment requires calm deliberateness and a placid exterior. Actually you may be a mass of jangling nerves, but this excitement and insecurity must not be conveyed to your performers.

4. *Good Taste*. The work of a program producer calls for the exercise of good taste and a sense of appropriateness. Intellectual and artistic standards apply to every performance. This is especially true with reference to program content and organization. Keeping in mind the college workshop or college station as the level of our activity, what types of continuity would you approve for particularly significant dates in the broadcast schedule? Assume, for example, you are assigned to build the following programs:

> *a.* The opening program for the season
> *b.* A radio play for Religious and Spiritual Emphasis Week
> *c.* A program to advertise the annual Shakespeare Drama Festival
> *d.* A program combining music, a discussion of the New England poets, campus news, and current events
> *e.* The closing program for the season

It is apparent that the objective in each instance challenges inventiveness and, at the same time, one's sense of appropriateness. Standards of good taste could easily be offended. The opening program should be entertaining and calculated to arouse interest in subsequent programs; a sophisticated play would not fulfill the second objective; a Navy band tooting an arrangement of Casey Jones, plus news commentary about spring house parties, will not match a discussion of New England poetry; and the closing program should bring a satisfying retrospect and promise of another profitable and enjoyable season. Perhaps no director would commit such atrocities as illustrated above, but the author recalls a college broadcast over a commercial station which presented the college president speaking on the aims of liberal education, a one-act play about cancer, and a dramatic reader reciting Kipling's "Boots." The director exercises good tastes when he adapts himself to the audience and the occasion.

Summary. The knowledge, procedures, techniques, and personal qualifications which pertain to radio production have been explained by using a basic example—the radio play. While the director will be commissioned to plan, supervise, and execute other types of programs (the radio talk, the interview, the round table, a musical program, the variety show, news and special-events broadcasts), he will find that the knowledge and techniques employed in dramatic production will apply in general to all of them. Let us make this general statement somewhat more specific:

1. Assume that a faculty member comes to your college station to make a talk. He should be properly greeted and made welcome. When the program is over, he should be thanked for his participation and interest. This is a matter of public relations. The producer will have provided the necessary studio setup for him (table, chair, microphone) and will explain to his guest, depending on the speaker's previous radio experience, about microphone technique (angle of pickup, distance, voice level, paper rattle, etc.), time limitations, starting cues, time warnings, and the meaning of sign language that may be used. Before the broadcast, the producer asks the speaker to read a few lines over the mike in order to check his voice level. If it is the policy of the station to ask for copies of broadcast material in advance, an additional function of the producer would be to read the speech for the purpose of making suggestions about style, treatment, and content.

2. In the case of a panel or round-table discussion, the procedure would be essentially the same: seating arrangement planned, appropriate microphone setup, the speakers briefed, a short rehearsal conducted to check on voice balances, and production signals explained. During this broadcast the producer may assist the chairman or moderator in timing the progress of the discussion, suggesting by signals the major transition points and the time to close the discussion for recapitulation and summary. The program announcer works on cue from the producer.

3. A live music program is only another variation. Here you have a continuity, an announcer, and musicians performing as individuals and as an ensemble. You may also employ a special narrator or narrators. Physical arrangements for the best microphone pickup must be planned and tested, the program rehearsed and timed. During the broadcast the producer follows his continuity and cues the program personnel as in the radio play. His objective is to produce a coordinated and smoothly flowing performance.

A recorded music program is much easier to control. Again, the producer follows a prepared continuity, but he deals only with the turntable technician and the announcer who makes the accompanying introductions, explanations, or commentary. Program timing, however, is very important. It may be the producer's job to build a music program; that is, he may have to select the music and construct the program format. This, of course, calls for a special knowledge of program material, a flair for showmanship, and a sense of good taste.

4. All these procedures are involved in producing a variety program. The conventional air show labeled "variety" embraces music (instru-

mental and vocal), gag routines, featured artists, and special comedy acts; we use the term to describe any segmented program employing diverse but related parts. The college workshop producer could probably find sufficient local talent to emulate a Bob Hope or Fibber Mc-Gee and Molly show, but it is more likely that for him a variety program will consist of such items as campus news, interviews, talks, panel discussions, dramatic spots, recorded music, high lights from recorded sports events, soloists, quiz features, and public-service items. The production of any one of these units will follow the pattern already explained. All that is added in the case of a variety show is the task of integrating the several units in a coherent program continuity. The scope of rehearsal is expanded, the performing personnel is enlarged, and technical problems are complicated.

The foregoing account is a summary presentation of radio production and the problems of the radio producer. The latter will gain proficiency only as he engages these problems in practical laboratory performance. To that end we have provided in Part IV an extensive series of problems covering basic production techniques arranged with some regard to progressive difficulty. Careful and repeated rehearsals of these exercises will implement the four aspects reviewed in this chapter: duties, knowledge, techniques, and qualifications. Production and performance skills should be developed prior to full-scale workshop operation, a subject to which we give detailed consideration in the following chapter.

QUESTIONS

1. What is the distinction between the titles, producer and director?
2. How does the director attack the problem of preparing a dramatic script for broadcast? What are the steps in this preparation?
3. Outline the rehearsal procedure to be followed in preparing a show for the air.
4. What are the duties of the director during a broadcast?
5. What body of specialized information is requisite to effective radio direction and production?
6. Explain in some detail the principles which govern the selection of music to be used as a functional tool.
7. What are the requisites of competent sound execution?
8. How is control-board operation related to program quality? How can the control-board operator "make or break" a show?
9. Enumerate and explain briefly the qualifications of a good radio director.

CHAPTER 16

THE COLLEGE RADIO WORKSHOP

In addition to general education objectives, college radio courses have a functional design. Learning is implemented by practice. This practice, however, should be directed toward practical goals whenever possible. When efforts are channeled toward meaningful objectives, the learning stimulus is greatly accentuated. In this chapter we shall discuss the plan, organization, and operation of a college radio workshop, bringing to focus in coordinated activity basic principles, basic types of performance, and production techniques discussed in foregoing chapters. Even when a station—campus network, FM, or local AM—is not available, it is suggested that the radio or speech department studio and class should plan "closed-circuit" broadcasts, organized and executed as if a station were in operation.

Workshop Defined. The term "radio workshop" cannot be defined in a single sentence. It is generic rather than specific and does not embrace common purposes, institutional aims, and organizational patterns because these vary with educational philosophy and available equipment. The workshop may embrace a summer term of 6 weeks, a semester, or a year. It may be wholly professional in aim and character, quasi-professional, or entirely academic and educational. It may be a production group, an experimental laboratory, or an integration of several related courses. The workshop curriculum may combine lectures, collateral reading, program observation, reports, and criticism with studio production problems, or it may be restricted wholly to the preparation and broadcast of programs. Each of the following groups of courses announced by two different universities indicates the scope that may be given to a summer radio workshop:

1. The American System of Broadcasting, Principles of Radio Direction, Radio Script Writing, Script Seminars, Guest Lecture Series, Radio Station News and Publicity, Radio Acting, Radio Utilization (radio programs for classroom education and adult education in community problems), Music in Radio, and Rehearsals and Broadcasts.

2. Introduction to Radio, Radio Sales, Radio Announcing, Radio Continuity Writing, Control Room Techniques, News Broadcasting, Radio Dramatic Writing, Program Planning and Building.

Space does not permit a detailed explanation of the various types of workshops. We offer the outline of one particular plan which may be expanded or modified according to local conditions. In this sense, the college radio workshop is a production laboratory in which educational programs are planned, written, and produced. This may seem to be an arbitrary limitation, but it is made with the assumption that there will be other courses in the department—a curriculum dealing with historical, social, and economic phases of the subject, basic principles of performance, and types of performance. We present the following workshop plan as a *part* of a comprehensive radio-training program.

Purpose of the Workshop. The college radio workshop is an educational broadcasting unit. It has two main objectives: (1) to produce programs which contribute information, promote public-service needs, and stimulate interest in vital subject fields and (2) to offer practical student training in broadcasting skills and methods.

This statement of aims does not employ the word "entertainment." It is omitted intentionally, but this does not mean that a workshop program should lack interest appeal or entertainment value. "Radio is more than entertaining, though it need never be less."[1] No presentation can be successful unless it holds the listener's attention. However, the workshop is not a commercial station. It is not tied to a sponsor or advertising agency and does not compete for a rating; it is free to use subject matter normally considered not salable, albeit meritorious. This very freedom from commercial demands places on the workshop an onerous obligation to make its presentation as attractive as possible.

The number of licensed "educational stations" is less today than shortly after the rise of broadcasting to national proportions. While the reason for the decline is partly financial, the chief one is the lack of program know-how which places them at a disadvantage with the professional stations. Radio programing, in the final analysis, is a highly specialized technical and artistic accomplishment, as evidenced by the superlative productions of the networks and major stations which command the finest talent in the writing, acting, and production fields. No amateur group or weakly endowed commercial station can compete with these standards of perfection. But this realization should be a stimulus and not a deterrent; the handling of educational materials, so-called, should challenge every resource.

Organizational Personnel. The workshop personnel will include a manager, production director, program director, script department, sound and music department, technical or engineering staff, a public-relations committee, and a librarian.

[1] Niles Trammel, president of NBC.

Workshop Manager. Some one person should serve in a chief executive capacity. He corresponds to the commercial station manager.

Production Director. A production director, coordinator, or supervisor should be appointed.

Planning Board. The office of the production director can be helped a great deal if supported by a policy or planning committee.

Script Department. The general program format and the specific ideas pertaining thereto are passed on to the continuity department which prepares the scripts and submits them to the production office for approval.

Program Director. The program, finally approved and accepted, is turned over to the program director who coordinates the actors, speakers, and other program participants with the technical facilities required.

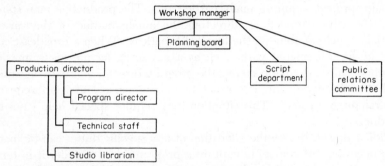

FIG. 48. Organization chart for radio workshop.

Technical Staff. The technical department is comprised of sound and music personnel and the studio engineer.

Public-relations Department or Committee. The ultimate success of the program is measured in terms of audience response. The building of the audience is the work of a public-relations director and committee.

Librarian. Station records and supplies should be accurately catalogued.

The relationship of these various offices and departments is shown in Fig. 48.

Personnel Duties. Each member of the workshop staff has specific duties.

The *manager* is a coordinator of activities who maintains a smoothly running and efficiently integrated station. (The term, station, is used synonymously with workshop. A college broadcasting group may function through a licensed FM or AM station, a campus network, or within its own studios; but management and operation are essentially the same.) He will be concerned with all the departments of his organization but will permit autonomy within the areas of delegated responsibility. The job of publicizing the workshop and promoting public relations is most specifically his concern. The duties of the station manager are essentially the same as those normally assumed by the instructor. However, in order to afford training in executive management, it is well to appoint a student to the position. The instructor is then free to devote his time to teaching problems.

Production Director. A distinction is here made between the production director and the program director. The difference becomes more significant as the scope of workshop activity is broadened. The production director is an executive who has certain coordinating duties. The type of program to be produced, the casting and direction of the program, the knitting together of various production elements constitute a major project requiring many participants. The production man stands over the whole procedure, directing the amalgamation of the various partials which combine in the finished broadcast. When a broadcast consists of several related parts such as a newscast, an interview, musical numbers, and a dramatic sketch, the program director is usually occupied with the dramatic unit. He is not free to rehearse and coordinate the several program parts. This situation may require special help from the producer.

Policy Board. Before the allocation of any specific duties can be made, it is necessary, of course, to capture a program idea, consider it in terms of audience value, and reduce it to some practical format. This is the work of the production executive in consultation with his policy board. These consultants will be guided in their deliberations by such questions as, What is the audience we wish to reach? Will this program hold their interest? Is the program schedule sufficiently varied? What is the educational value of the program? Can the idea be adequately executed within the limits of our resources? Guided by principles of feasibility, audience interest, educational and entertainment value, public service, and student training, the producer and his committee will make decisions on submitted program suggestions. Those accepted will be assigned to the continuity department for scripting.

Script Department. A college radio workshop should include a class in continuity writing. Radio writing is a specialized field which offers vocational opportunities to original and talented craftsmen. Practically all radio programs require scripts. The various types of musical programs, talks and interviews, variety and feature programs, commercials, news broadcasts and dramatic shows, must first be set down on paper. There are many royalty-free scripts available to the amateur broadcaster, but the workshop that can develop and produce its own copy offers a wider educational scope than one which is dependent on borrowed material. Assuming, then, that our organization has a sufficient number of capable writers, we should assign to them the script writing job. When the continuity is completed, it is returned to the production manager who, after further conference with his advisory group, may accept it and send the material to a program director to prepare for broadcast.

Program Director. The program director studies the requirements of the script and proceeds with preparations requisite to its broadcast release. He must choose a cast, conduct rehearsals, integrate dialogue with sound, music, and technical elements of production as required by the program. He has complete charge of the entire process, and his decisions control the final outcome. The director of a dramatic program requires the assistance of three departments: sound, music, and engineering. The responsibility for these aspects of production will rotate, as well as all other responsibilities, because one purpose of the workshop is to give everyone as much and varied experience as possible.

Sound Department. The individual assigned to handle sound effects on a show should know the method of producing the various live sounds, the sources of recorded sound, how to operate a sound table or sound truck, and how to achieve an artistic blend of sound with dialogue and dramatic action.

Music. Since recorded music will be used in the workshop programs, the musical director should have a familiarity with a wide range of musical composition in order to select passages required for backgrounds, bridges, introductions, and finales. The ease and accuracy with which he uses these recordings require practice in marking, scoring, starting, and fading them.

Engineering. The studio engineer has charge of the physical equipment utilized in broadcast operations—the microphones, sound tables, monitor panel, recorder. His chief function is to operate the control board, mixing the program elements and "riding gain" on all the levels.

Publicity and Public Relations. The chairman of the public-relations committee outlines and implements procedures by which listening interest is secured. Follow-up techniques are employed to check on program reception and acceptance.

Workshop Librarian. The efficient operation of a workshop depends on an efficient organization of records (cast lists, authors, royalties, evaluation reports, production records, log sheets), scripts, music records, sound-effects records, live sound effects, and publicity material. Confusion easily results unless the station maintains a practical filing system. The manager and his program executives should have quick access to whatever is required. This is all the more important because of frequently changing personnel. The maintenance of a workshop filing system is the duty of the librarian.

Studio Plan. Your studio plan and equipment will depend on available space, the money you have to spend, and the over-all objectives you have in setting up the workshop schedule. Again, these elements vary with different situations. The approach should be made by asking, What do we want to accomplish? What are the needs? How flexible should the equipment be? The answers may fall into a pattern somewhat similar to the following:

1. I want a room in which I can conduct a radio rehearsal (Studio A).

2. I need a second and associated studio which I can use for a simultaneous rehearsal, or as an audience room (Studio B).

3. These rooms should be connected by a monitor booth, and occupants in either A or B should be able to audition what is going on.

4. I want microphone outlets in both studios.

5. Five studio microphones will give me required flexibility: one filter, one nondirectional, one cardioid, and two bidirectional.

6. The radio console should have five mixing input channels permitting, if required, an adequate pickup of dialogue, sound, music, and filtered voices.

7. The booths should be connected with the studios by a talk-back microphone.

8. I shall require at least one sound truck equipped with not less than two two-speed turntables. (According to the suggestions made below for keeping the class fully occupied, you will probably require two of these portable sound units.)

9. I shall find one 16-inch turntable located in the monitor booth adjacent to the console very useful as an auxiliary playback.

10. Earphone connections should be installed in both studios.

11. Recording equipment in the sound booth will make it possible to play back workshop performances, objectifying the quality of the student's work.

12. A radio tuner in the booth will permit the reception and recording of radio programs.

13. I should have adequate storage space for records, sound effects, and scripts.

14. It is important that the studios be adequately soundproofed and all rooms be provided with sound-locked doors.

Workshop Operation. The most difficult problems normally encountered by the instructor in charge of the radio workshop are twofold: (1) the difficulty of keeping all the members of the group equally busy and (2) the rotation of the various jobs enumerated above so that each student will have experience in the different positions.

If you have a class of 25 and your project for the day requires the participation of only 11, what will you do with the other 14? Let them observe? Perhaps, but this is not a too engrossing activity in itself, especially when each student is anxious to "get into the act" and does not always appreciate the value of observational learning. The solving of this problem in particular requires some ingenuity and organizational skill. The following plan of operation is suggested as a means of keeping everyone busy:

1. It is well to have two or more programs in rehearsal at the same time.
2. While one group is working on the microphone, a second can be reading another script to familiarize themselves with the story, the required interpretation, sound and music needs.
3. This reading may be conducted by a student director, or by the instructor during the time he is not required to supervise the microphone rehearsal.
4. If you have portable turntables and sufficient studio space, appointed workshop members may be working simultaneously on sound-table operation, musical analysis, sound and music coordination.
5. When the main studio program is ready to be auditioned, all members not involved in that performance may form a listening group for purposes of analysis and criticism. In general, this plan of operation will keep everyone busy.

The second problem of rotating key assignments is not so difficult although you may not be able to give everyone an opportunity to serve in all the positions on your organization chart. It is obvious that in a class of 25 you cannot have 25 different managers, production and program directors. A partial solution is found in the fact that all the class personnel may not wish to have these responsibilities. They may be more interested in acting or technical assignments. It will be natural to assign the more experienced and capable students to the executive jobs, and if the assignment schedule is changed each month it is possible that all interests may be cared for. Program assignments should be made in advance. For example,

Assignment Sheet

Program Number:
Date:

Director:
Live Sound:
Recorded Sound and Music:
Monitor Engineer:

Difficult or complicated programs may require two people on sound and music. Even when the program is relatively simple, it may be advantageous to assign technical assistants, each of whom will take over on the subsequent broadcast and, in turn, be helped by an assistant. This procedure should enable every member of the group to have a proportionate share in the over-all workshop activity.

Workshop Programs. The ultimate objective of the college workshop as explained is to devise, write, and produce programs which utilize subject matter that has social, cultural, and educational significance, but with a showmanship quality sufficient to command audience interest. This final purpose, however, can be realized only after we attain certain techniques, abilities, and craftsmanship. In the training process it is advisable to use the conventionalized type of commercially acceptable continuity. Students have been conditioned by their radio listening, and they will have more interest at the outset in producing a romantic comedy, the typical mystery complication, or a dramatic spot. This approach seems a better conjoining of interest and learning. When the various acting skills and production procedures are established, we may then turn to the documentary, historical, biographical, and thesis formats.

The character of public-service programs has been discussed in Chap. 6, the Social Aspects of Radio. The scope of these network offerings is too large for the workshop group to encompass, but the subjects listed indicate the general nature of our program attempts in the workshop. The college radio production group should limit itself to lesser areas and more local needs. Two procedures are recommended.

In one sense, a series of college broadcasts is an extension of classroom and curricular subject matter restated in a new pattern and with particular direction. Look over the departmental offerings as stated in your college catalogue. You will find several subject areas which might be presented with interest and dramatic effectiveness to the average radio listener. For example,

1. An understanding of the major arts of architecture, sculpture, and painting:
   a. Ancient art: architecture, sculpture, and painting in Egypt, Mesopotamia, Greece, and Rome
   b. Christian art from the catacombs of Rome to the end of the Gothic period
   c. The fine arts in Italy
   d. Sculpture and painting in the United States
   e. Trends, ideals, and events depicted by contemporary artists
2. Biology:
   a. Structure and life history of the animal parasites of man; methods of infection and prevention
   b. The fundamental facts concerning dietary factors including the vitamins, the physiological effects of these dietary factors on the health at all age levels
3. Chemistry:
   a. Industrial chemistry
   b. Chemistry of medical compounds

4. Economics:
   a. A study of the location of raw materials and their significance to trade and industry
   b. Principles of money, credit, and banking
   c. The relationship between business and government
   d. Techniques of collective bargaining
   e. A critical review of state and Federal labor legislation
5. Education:
   a. Child growth and development
   b. Current trends in American education
6. English:
   a. Prose and poetry
   b. The modern novel
   c. The background of literary movements and the major poets and prose writers of the eighteenth century
7. History:
   a. The Westward movement and California
   b. The history of Mexico
   c. The rise of the American Republic
8. Music:
   a. Influence affecting the growth of American characteristics in music
   b. Music appreciation
9. Philosophy:
   a. Ethics: definition of the good and right; evaluation of individual and group motives and goals
   b. American philosophical thought in the twentieth century
10. Physical education:
   a. Basic hygienic materials and their adaptation for health instruction
   b. Safety and health instruction
11. Physics:
   a. Sound
   b. Optics
   c. Electronics
12. Political science:
   a. Political institutions and processes in the United States
   b. American political parties: principles and problems, history, structure, and methods
   c. Commercial law
   d. State and local government
   e. Problems of creating public opinion and organizing public action through propaganda and pressure groups
13. Psychology:
   a. Personal and social problems of everyday life
   b. Investigation of the lives and mental processes of some eminent figures of the recent past (psychobiography)
14. Sociology:
   a. Social processes in personality development
   b Family problems

15. Speech:
    a. A study of words and their ways in English speech
    b. Literary interpretation

These subjects are quite general and comprehensive, but each is capable of analysis and refinement, and each is amenable to radio script treatment and broadcast. The striving of an artist—his initial rejection by society and his final acceptance—man's triumphs over the perils of contagion and disease, the revolutionary discoveries of industrial chemistry, the conflicts between labor and management, parental problems, the social message of great literature, the operation of ethical concepts in social reactions, preventive medicine, the contribution of electronics, the conduct and influence of pressure groups, domestic conflict, and the functioning of political machinery, civic institutions, and the appreciation of poetry are vital aspects of purposive, effective, and intelligent living. The writer, of course, must know the subject and must have originality, dramatic sense, and a command of attention-control methods in presenting it. The script is the *sine qua non.*

The range of potential workshop subjects is also indicated by the programs presented by the various "schools of the air," the audio-visual departments of city schools and educational stations. A bulletin of the University of Minnesota lists the programs of the Minnesota School of the Air, beginning its second decade (September, 1940 to May, 1949), and operating "in the belief that facts are important only in their relationship to ideas, and that radio is a particularly able medium for the development of ideas and attitudes." Some of the subjects listed in KUOM's schedule follow:

1. *Old Tales and New* (kindergarten through grade 3): Dramatization of social problems through stories within the young listener's frame of reference, in addition to continuing emphasis on broadening horizons and general enrichment.

2. *Look What We Found* (grades 4 through 8): " . . . this series will consider through interviews, drama, music, narration areas of interest to children in the cultural, social, educational, and entertainment aspects of our upper midwest life."

3. *Penny and Paul* (grades 4 through 8): " . . . history and development of Minnesota . . . a picture of the growth of the state, its current problems, and future possibilities."

4. *Following Conservation Trails* (grades 4 through 8): " . . . emphasizes man's careful use of our God-given natural resources."

5. *Current Events* (grades 4 through 9): " . . . based on the belief that the imperative need to develop critical thinking in tomorrow's citizens is a responsibility that must be met by every branch of our educational system."

6. *Let Science Tell Us* (grades 4 through 8): " . . . the application of scientific achievements, familiarity with scientific thinking, knowledge of out-

standing scientists and their contribution, interest in the problems of simple science."

7. *Your Health and You* (grades 5 through 9): " . . . the vital importance of health and health practices."

8. *Journeys in Art* (grades 4 through 6): " . . . deeper cultural appreciation through the enumeration of the oustanding work of famous artists and craftsmen."

The Federal Radio Education Committee's (FREC) catalogue of radio recordings—a transcription service for schools—is a listing of recorded programs available to schools.

Research and experimentation in the field of education by radio have shown that radio programs and transcriptions can be used to convey useful knowledge to listeners, to sharpen their discernment of social significance, to fortify socially desirable attitudes with rational concepts, to embrace aesthetic appreciations, to stimulate systematic inquiry, and to implement convictions with an impelling urge to action.

The following is a partial listing of these programs:[2]

1. *Life for Wildlife*
   a. *Watch Out.* This program outlines the general theme of the series and emphasizes the history of wild-life destruction in the United States, together with the menace to wild life.
   b. *Wildfire G-Men.* Titled to capture the interest of students of the intermediate and junior-high-school grade levels, this program explains the system of enforcing our wild-life conservation laws.
2. *This Land We Defend*
   a. This program emphasizes the seriousness of floods by dramatizing the story of the Ohio flood of 1937—the flood that swept away life and property, destroyed homes and hopes, and left in its wake a sterile mass of muck and debris. This program also explains the relation between soil conservation and floods and tells what American farmers are doing to help reduce the danger of floods.
   b. *The Mormons.* This program uses the story of the Mormons to illustrate how carefully planned irrigation and soil conservation can transform a desert into a land of trees and flowers, and fields of vegetables and grains.
3. *Health, Welfare, and Safety*
   a. *A Story for Tough Guys.* This is the story of an interstate truck driver who takes dangerous chances, and a wife who worries about him. Told

[2] Students of radio education should be familiar with the work, services, aids, and publications of the Federal Radio Education Committee, U.S. Office of Education, Washington, D.C. The assistance offered by this committee is outlined in a bulletin, *What the FREC Offers You.* Two publications in particular should be in the hands of every workshop director: *Radio Script Catalogue* (Educational Radio Script and Transcription Exchange), and *Catalogue of Radio Recordings, A Transcription Service for Schools.*

with action and suspense, the story drives home the "safety-first" message in a forceful way. Much of the program content is based on actual findings of fatigue studies conducted by the Division of Industrial Hygiene, National Institute of Health.

b. A Day at the Dentist. With a dry sense of humor and some ironic comment, a dentist discusses failure of people to take proper care of their teeth. The program emphasizes the importance of dental health and the means of obtaining it.

4. *Literature and Speech*

   a. Statue of Liberty. This is the story of a Frenchman's talk with the Statue of Liberty.

   b. Citizen Tom Paine. This historical program portrays the philosophy of Tom Paine and Thomas Jefferson.

5. *Music and Art*

   a. The Ballad Hunter. This is a series of 10 programs of authentic American folk music—spirituals, blues, "fiddle tunes," old country ballads, railroad songs, sea chanteys, and cowboy tunes. . . . The series was prepared as a part of the Radio Research Project of the Library of Congress.

   (1) *The Boll Weevil.* This is a program of songs about "the little black bug" that challenged King Cotton.

   (2) *Chisholm Trail.* This program is a collection of cowboy songs of the old Chisholm cattle trail.

6. *Science*

   a. Laboratory Detectives. This program describes four of the analytical tools of the research scientist, the X ray, the spectroscope, the microscope, and microchemistry.

   b. Virus—Enemy of Life. This program tells of the long search for the viruses which cause such diseases as influenza, the common cold, and infantile paralysis, and explains what scientists are doing to combat them.

7. *Social Studies*

   a. Americans All—Immigrants All. This is a series of 24 recorded programs presenting the story of the contributions which those who have immigrated to the United States have made to the social, economic, and political development of this country.

   (1) *Our English Heritage.* This program is a dramatization showing how the English impressed upon our country their culture, their language, their laws, and their burning desire for personal and political freedom.

   (a) *Winning Freedom.* This program dramatizes an exciting chapter of our national history, showing how peoples of various national backgrounds—Scots, French, Poles, Irish, and others—fought side by side to make America free.

8. *This Is History.* This series consists of six programs which were produced under the direction of the Recordings Project of the Library of Congress, in an experimental attempt at using recording to provide documentary samples of public opinion within local regions that represent distinct cultural patterns.

Radioways to Learning is the title of a bulletin published monthly by the audio-visual aids section of the curriculum division, Los Angeles City Schools. It carries a recommended list of Los Angeles radio programs for the current period. These programs are listed under five headings:

News
    Public Affairs
    International Relations
Social Studies
    Current Events
    Geography
    History
Drama
    English-Speech
    Biography
    Story Telling

Music
    Art
    Variety
Miscellaneous
    Science
    Health
    Sports

There are over 300 listings (counting duplications) of programs broadcast more than once a week.

The breakdown treatment of any classroom subject, governed by audience levels, is extremely broad. The subject of science, admittedly a wide general field, is almost limitless. To mention only a few aspects of the applied-science field, we may refer further to such areas as weather forecasting, foods, conservation, use of waste materials, plastics, and safety; and each of these has many possible subdivisions. Each one can be presented from many concrete points of view. Children's lives are saved by vitamins, quarantine laws are essential, water and milk supply must be protected, free health clinics render vital service to those who may qualify, canning inspection and food-preservation methods are essential to health, effects of poisoning may be combatted by proper antidotes, many accidents around the home are the result of simple negligence and need first-aid treatment.

The field of biography is an almost inexhaustible source of good radio material. Great personalities leave their "footprints on the sands of time." The social forces of our time are released by the incentive, daring, and genius of men, and the record of human progress is the story of their accomplishments. The victories of medicine, engineering, social reform, statesmanship, and education were achieved by men and women who led the vanguard. One's choice of biographical subject matter may be influenced by specific broadcasting objectives as determined by factors of geographical location, the audience, and educational aims, but biography is an excellent source of vital, dramatic, and purposive material.

The second general category of programs planned by the college workshop is insitutional in character. They are devised to serve the purposes of specific organizations which have special messages for the public. Again, the list can be only illustrative. The American Red Cross, the Parent-Teachers Association, Chambers of Commerce, Better Business Bureaus, departments of city government, safety councils, various civic and professional organizations, and child-guidance clinics can use radio in presenting their purposes, work, and needs to the public. A workshop that is equipped with writers, directors, actors, and speakers may implement these institutional aims and appeals. In our proposed station organization, one function of the manager may be to contact the agencies in his community, suggest program ideas, and offer the cooperation of his workshop group.

A third source of program materials is to be found in the resources of the college faculty and student body. In general, radio "lectures" are pretty dull. It is the rare individual who can take his classroom podium before a microphone and hold the attention of an unseen audience. And yet the great fund of information represented by the scholarship and research of a college faculty has profound and vital significance, provided it can be interpreted within the interest frame of the lay radio listener. Faculty members, then, may cooperate with you in projecting a series of programs by supplying references, data, suggested treatments of subjects, and by actually taking part in the broadcasts. The form of the broadcast will probably not be that of a straight lecture. You will experiment with interviews, round tables, quiz formulas, debates, simulated classroom situations, etc. Within the student body and the college organizations there is much program material and talent that can be adapted to workshop broadcasts. Glee clubs, choral groups, band and orchestra, the dramatic organizations, the Cosmopolitan Club, professional organizations sponsored by the various academic departments, the campus church or religious groups, and the athletic interests may all make contributions to your general program pattern.

Summary. As stated at the outset, the workshop best adapted to your situation will vary from any one prescribed pattern. You will find it necessary to make departures from the details of the plan here offered, but there are fundamental principles which should apply to a successful workshop format. These may be summarized as follows:

1. To offer practical training in radio speech, acting, direction, production, technical skills, program construction, and the preparation of simple continuity types.

2. Workshop activity should be administered through an organized staff, the responsibilities of each position being rotated during the term, semester, or year.

3. Programs are designed for educational and public-service needs, but

the elements of showmanship and interest value should always be fully emphasized.

4. A regular schedule of programs should be formulated by a program committee, planning committee, or policy board. This schedule should be prepared well in advance of actual broadcast dates and with reference to an over-all program pattern.

5. All accessory workshop materials should be filed and kept in order.

6. The workshop schedule should be so organized as to maintain the constant interest and activity of every member of the group.

7. A publicity and public-relations committee should be appointed to bring the workshop and its programs to the intended clientele.

QUESTIONS

1. What is a college radio workshop?

2. What is the purpose of such a workshop?

3. Draw a schematic design representing the organizational pattern of such a workshop.

4. What equipment is needed for adequate workshop production?

5. What type of program should the college radio workshop emphasize? Why?

6. Name several sources of program ideas for such a workshop.

PART III

TELEVISION

CHAPTER 17

TELEVISION: THE NEW CHALLENGE

Now we add sight to sound. It is with a feeling of humbleness that I come to this moment of announcing the birth in this country of a new art so important in its implications that it is bound to affect all society. It is an art which shines like a torch in a troubled world. It is a creative force which we must learn to utilize for the benefit of all mankind.

"Now we add sight to sound." These words were more prophecy than concrete realization when spoken by David Sarnoff at the New York World's Fair in the spring of 1939. Today, television is a fact. It is here. It has come with dramatic swiftness and suddenness. Another major phase of communication is firmly established.

What Is Television? Technically, it is a highly specialized field and, pictured in scientific terms, is unintelligible to the layman. It is not easy to give a simple explanation of how pictures are transmitted from their point of origin to the home receiver. The transmission and reception of pictures depend on the conversion of light into electrical impulses, their propagation through space, and their conversion to original optical forms. The process involves such elements as electron lenses, deflection coils, electric scanning beams, multiconductor cables, dipole antenna, blanking pulses, link transmitters, and photoelectric globules. A condensed translation of these terms in popular language is no more necessary to the appreciation of television's evolution and social significance than similar explanations of vacuum tubes, grids, condensers, carrier waves, directional antenna, master control rooms, and console construction would be to the study of radio from a social and performance point of view. However, the following statement by a pioneer television engineer and authority offers a certain frame of reference:[1]

Television is a process by which successive images are taken of a scene, sliced into many horizontal strips, and the lights and shadows of each slicing conveyed one after another from the scene of transmission to the scene of reception. There they are reassembled so rapidly that the many images give the

[1] Harry R. Lubcke, "Radioways to Learning," Los Angeles City Schools Bulletin, May, 1949.

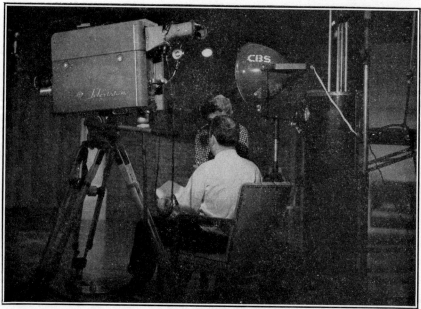

FIG. 49. Lights, camera, and mike boom on a typical TV set.

illusion of motion. This is the same as occurs in the motion picture. Actually only one very small dot of the scene being televised is transmitted at any instant of time, and there is only a single spot on the television receiver screen which reproduced the image.

Thirty Pictures per Second

In order that the eye will see continuous pictures instead of a succession of stills, television transmits 60 half pictures of alternate lines, each second. Thus, 30 whole pictures are formed each second. The little spots referred to must go over the whole field of view within this time. A little mental arithmetic will show that if there are 525 lines in the picture it must travel at frightful speeds. Actually, it moves through its own width in about 1/4,000,000 second, and in order to paint a beautiful lady's eyebrows, should they be in the scene, the spot must turn on and off with this rapidity.

Such speed as this can only be accomplished by all electronic television means and so today's cameras utilize photoelectric plates and electron streams while television receivers use cathode-ray tubes.

Camera to Receiver

The television camera, utilizing the usual photographic lens and its special electronic camera tube, forms and dissects the television image into impulses. These are amplified and in the usual case of television broadcasting are transmitted to the public on high frequencies from the top of a mountain or building.

In the home, a television antenna, either outdoor or indoor, picks up the transmitted waves. They are amplified and in the usual case of television impulses, which are fed to the control electrode of the cathode-ray tube, form all the lights and shadows of the reproduced picture.

The process of methodically slicing the image in strips is known as scanning. At the transmitter, impulses are formed which trigger-off the scanning lines, and these are transmitted along with the picture signals to the receiver. Here they trigger-off the receiver scanning circuits which position the little spot of cathode-ray tube in the same relative position in the field of view which was occupied by the sensitive area in the television camera. This process is known as "synchronization."

Should the picture on your home receiver roll vertically or tear horizontally, your reciver is not in synchronism with the transmitter, and adjustment of either the vertical or the horizontal hold controls will bring forth a perfect stationary picture.

Behind each of the instrumentalities mentioned above lie innumerable tubes, resistors, and other components. Television transmitters and receivers have as many mystical parts as the latest hydromatic transmission for automobiles. In this age of electronics, however, there is no reason why equipment cannot operate satisfactorily and dependably over long periods of time despite much complication of structure.

Brief History. Television, like radio, has a historical heritage which spans hundreds of years—reaching back almost to antiquity. The Assyrian knowledge of optics, reflecting mirrors, and refracting lenses; Thales' observation on the properties of amber; and William Gilbert's important publication, *De Magnete*, which stimulated investigations concerning the importance of the magnet, laid an initial foundation on which subsequent scientists built an ever growing superstructure eventuating in video broadcasting. The present-day fact of color television, for example, is related to Sir Isaac Newton's work with the spectrum and his discovery that all the colors of the rainbow are present in pure light.

It is the opinion of some authorities that television, as a distinct field of development, began in 1817 with the isolation of selenium by a Swedish chemist, Jöns Jakob Berzelius. This scientist did not understand the nature of photoelectricity, but selenium proved to be a substance which made possible the conversion of light energy into electrical energy. The discovery that selenium would react to light was accidental. A young telegrapher, working at Valentia in Ireland, was worried by an unfamiliar hum which developed in his code receiver. He noted that a shaft of sunlight was playing on an electrical resistor. He passed his hand through the beam, cutting off the receiver. The hum stopped. Why? The resistor was coated with selenium, and the young telegraph operator deduced that it must have what we now know as photoelectric properties. In other words, selenium was a substance that could convert light values into electrical values. This discovery was a key piece in the jigsaw puzzle soon to be completed.

We have sketched elsewhere a series of discoveries which related to the ultimate perfection of radio—the audio phase of television: a steel needle magnetized by an electrical discharge from a Leyden jar, the electric telegraph, the production of h-f electric oscillations, Maxwell's theory of electromagnetism and electric waves, and the demonstration of these phenomena. Paralleling these advances, concurrent investigations were pointing toward the achievement of television—the video phase of radio. George Stokes wrote his famous paper describing the phenomenon of fluorescence as exhibited by fluorite and uranium glass. Stokes believed these materials had the power to convert invisible ultraviolet rays into rays of visible length. An English scientist, Sir William Crookes, was working on his cathode-ray tube, an investigation which found fulfillment in the discoveries of Van Ardenne in Germany in 1930. The discovery that selenium had photoelectric properties stimulated research and pointed it toward a more definite objective. A selenium cell, it was known, would release electrical energy in proportion to the amount of light thrown upon it. Well, suppose a picture of varying brightness were thrown on a group of closely assembled selenium cells, and each cell were connected by wires to a corresponding lamp. What is a picture? It is a composite of light and shade. Thus, the energy released by the cell would vary in intensity according to the light details of the picture. Would it be possible to send a picture by such an arrangement? The theory seemed feasible, but it was discarded owing to the fact that thousands of wires would be necessary to reproduce the original picture. The experiment, however, and the reason behind it, were significant.

The next attempt to achieve this transmission of pictures was by the so-called "scanning" method. Scanning was a process of breaking the picture into small segments and then sending each segment in succession to a receiving point where the total number of elements would be reassembled. It was believed at first that this scanning method could be implemented by a system of revolving mirrors, but this proved to be impractical. The scanning disk offered more promise. The first scanning-disk patent was taken out in Germany by Paul Nikow in 1884. This device was a circular plate or disk with punched holes arranged in the pattern of a spiral. When the disk was rotated, the eye could see only the top line of the picture through the first hole in the disk, the second hole scanning the second line, the third hole the third line, etc., until the whole picture became visible line by line. The system was designed to deliver each line of a picture to a selenium cell behind the disk, and since the cell would react to the amount of light thrown upon it, the strength of each signal sent would vary with the shades of black and white in the original picture. The process was reversed at the point of reception. A light source was to distribute the varying degrees of light and shade to another disk spinning in exact synchronization with the one at the point of pickup. However, the problem of a practicable system by which the light components of a picture could be transmitted successfully remained unsolved. Further technical advances were necessary before Nikow's principle could be proved practicable.

The final answer was found in an electronic system of pickup, and in 1923 television evolved as an electronic science. On Dec. 29 of that year, Dr. V. K. Zworykin, an assistant director of RCA laboratories, filed a patent application for his basic invention, the iconoscope. The iconoscope is described as the eye of the camera. Television pictures were demonstrated on Nov. 18, 1929, at a meeting of the Institute of Radio Engineers at Rochester, N.Y. By 1933, television technology had produced equipment and methods by which electronic transmission was possible, and 3 years later RCA demonstrated outdoor telecasting, broadcasting pictures over a distance of a mile. Two months later this feat was surpassed when pictures transmitted from the Empire State Building were received 50 miles away. Mobile television vans appeared on the streets of New York and proved their usefulness by relaying outdoor track meets, baseball and football contests, prize fights, and parades to the main NBC transmitter.

With NBC's field tests in 1938 and the successfully televised opening of the New York World's Fair in April, 1939, it seemed that television in the United States had leaped the major hurdles. TV milestones began to whiz by with bewildering rapidity. A Cambridge-Princeton baseball game, King George and Queen Elizabeth at the Fair, a Brooklyn Dodgers contest on Ebbet's Field, and a football game between Fordham and Waynesburg were brought to incredible eyes. Observers on a plane 18,000 feet over the capital saw a program taking place in New York 200 miles away, and a bird's-eye view of Gotham was telecast from an airliner to shipboard passengers 250 miles at sea. A coaxial cable linking the camera in the political arena at Philadelphia with the transmitter at the Empire State Building brought to New Yorkers pictures of the 1940 Republican Convention. Television cameras, scanning press teletype machines, telecast the election returns. Television, said the promoters, was here.

The public, however, was not too certain about this new communications miracle. Perhaps it would be just as well to sit on the side lines and let the engineers experiment a while longer. Not more than 1,000 receiving sets were sold in 1939. This delay of public acceptance is interesting in view of the fact that television in Great Britain was rather well under way. England had been supplying public programs as a public service since 1936, 2 years before American interests announced plans for a 2-hour per week program schedule. By 1939, 20,000 English viewers were provided a varied TV schedule of plays, ballet, illustrated talks, variety, and music. It is estimated that the coronation of George VI and Queen Elizabeth was seen by 50,000 televiewers. In the United States, however, television was not quite ready "to go." It is true that the FCC thought well enough of its progress to issue an order on Feb. 2, 1940, permitting partial commercialization of existing facilities, but its directive was rescinded almost immediately on the ground that more time was required to effect an industry agreement concerning the way TV should be presented to the public. There were questions about technical standards, line definition, and channel limitations. Picture synchronization was not perfect, and pictures were not altogether satisfactory in terms of color and contrast.

The delay occasioned by the FCC order of February was not of long duration. A special study of the involved problems was made by the National Television Systems Committee and the Radio Manufacturers' Association. When the findings of their investigation were reported, the effect was to expand the existing 441-line definition to 525 which produced a picture that approached the clarity of a 35-millimeter film and provided the maximum detail possible within the limitations of channels 6 megacycles wide. The FCC now flashed the green light again, and in May, 1941, set the date on which TV stations could begin commercial broadcasting, July 1, 1941. On that day NBC's WNBT began commercial operations with five sponsored programs. Six other television pioneers were ready with their stations: CBS (WCBW-NY), Dumont (W2XWV-NY), General Electric (WRGB-Schenectady), Philco (WPTC-Philadelphia), Zenith (QTZR-Chicago), and Don Lee (KTSL-Los Angeles). Then came a series of world-shattering events virtually to stifle the new industry. World War II made further commercial expansion for the time impossible. The scientists and technicians were confined to their laboratories to wait until peace was restored to a chaotic world. Not until then could this new prodigy, television, be properly nurtured.

TV Development Following World War II. Immediately following the cessation of armed conflict in Europe and Asia, the national economy began to adjust itself to normal peacetime schedules. The television industry sprang into new life. By the end of 1946 there were 50 licensed, or authorized, commercial TV stations, 6 of them in operation, and 67 experimental stations were operating or authorized to operate. The A.T. & T. Co. completed a coaxial cable between New York, Philadelphia, and

Washington making possible a TV network. Commercial sponsors became interested, and 22 companies were telecasting programs by the end of 1946. Confidence in this new medium was mounting so rapidly that the FCC took under advisement a CBS petition asking that the ultrahigh-frequency (UHF) band (480 to 920 megacycles), which had been set aside for experimental work, be assigned for commercial color operations.

The period of 1947 to 1949 was a time of perfection and expansion. Television growth was so rapid and the economic picture changed so quickly, that statistics have little meaning other than to indicate how this new medium took form with startling and dramatic suddenness. One million receiving sets had been sold by Christmas of 1948, and in the following year, 850,000 joined the ranks of set owners. The amount spent for receivers in 1948 totaled $353 million dollars, and this was in 23 states only. The number of set owners in the City of New York doubled between December, 1947, and February, 1949. When film recordings for TV transmission became possible in the early months of 1949, making cable connections no longer necessary, 31 new stations went on the air. This brought the number of television stations to 55, broadcasting to more than 50 million people in 31 different market areas. TV sponsors increased 500 per cent in 16 months, and the 10 million dollars billing of 1948 soared to over 30 million dollars in 1949. The 35 stations mushroomed to 92. (There were 7 stations in 1946.) The FCC expressed the opinion that by using UHF channels, 2,181 stations could be made available to more than 1,400 communities. This is approximately the present number of AM radio stations.

By the early spring of 1950, the television industry was riding the crest of public acceptance and establishing its claim to the fastest growing industry in the history of American business. Television stocks on the New York Stock Exchange soared to new highs with each passing day. In 2½ months the closing averages jumped as much as 50 to 75 per cent in some instances. High industry earnings and rosy predictions were luring thousands of avid investors. The public had good reason to be excited over the swiftly expanding television business. By early summer in 1950, 104 stations were operating in 61 cities, broadcasting to an estimated audience of 19 million, and 6 new stations were under construction. There was evidence that television at last could be made to pay. Station and network operators began to see red ink turn to pale pink. The 8.7 million dollars spent by advertisers in 1948 had amounted to 27.5 million in 1949, and billings going to 2,300 concerns in March, 1950, would no doubt top this figure. More than 100,000 TV units were flowing from the factories each week. This meant an annual retail counter trade of 1 billion dollars—a peak of gross business that had been reached in 3 years. Television manufacturers had achieved in this time a gross volume of business which an infant automobile industry had attained only after 10 years. It appeared that the total investment of TV manufacturers and broadcasters would exceed the total investment of the entire motion-picture industry, including its studios and public theaters.

This acromegalic phenomenon was only beginning to take form. Subsequent developments were no less astounding. TV set production for the first 6 months of 1950 equaled the total output for 1949. By October, manufacturers were producing 200,000 receivers per week. The total production for 1950 was 5,661,000, and by Dec. 1, 1951, the total number of sets in use passed the 13 million mark. Owners of these sets were receiving programs from 108 stations in 63 market areas. The four networks (ABC, CBS, Dumont, NBC) saw their 1950 gross billings shoot up from the 8 million dollar level of 1948 to approximately 45 million, a figure exceeded by 28.5 million dollars in the first 8 months of 1951. In other words, 1950 revenues almost tripled those of 1949, and 1951's income for January to August showed a growth of 400 per cent. This phenomenal expansion is particularly significant considering that the FCC "freeze" order was still in effect and that the number of TV stations was relatively fixed. Nevertheless, expanding facilities were bringing video closer and closer to the status of national coverage. Coaxial cables and microwave relays, which would link Omaha and San Francisco, were under construction. A Southern cable, when completed, would connect Atlanta, Dallas, Phoenix, and Los Angeles.

Coast-to-coast television was dramatically demonstrated on Oct. 4, 1951 when a national hookup over the A.T. & T. Co.'s new microwave radio relay system enabled TV to span the continent for the first time. Ninety-five per cent of the television sets in use throughout the United States, linked by radio relay and underground coaxial cable, enabled 85 million of the nation's population "to be present" at the opening of the Japanese Peace Treaty Conference in San Francisco. This milestone in communication history was an achievement of Western Electric and Bell System engineers who, in 3 years, had built the transcontinental system comprised of relay stations about 30 miles apart permitting the transmission of superhigh-frequency radio waves in the 4,000-megacycle range compared to the ordinary radiobroadcasting range of 500 to 1,600 kilocycles.

The advent of national TV lent credence to some of the prophecies regarding television's future. In April, 1950, David Sarnoff had declared that television would be a 3- to 5-billion-dollar per year industry within 5 years, and that by the end of 1952 there would be 20 million sets and 80 million viewers. The chairman of the FCC, speaking to the Rocky

Mountain Council at Denver the following month, predicted a total
of 25 million sets within 3 years. A General Electric spokesman, looking
into the seeds of time, projected his estimate to the year, 1961. Within
this decade (basing the estimate on the cost of equipment, station
operating costs, advertising revenue, and population, and the assumption
that the freeze would be lifted before the end of 1950) 666 TV stations
would go on the air and 75 per cent of the families in the United States
would be within range of at least one TV station.[2] Other prophets, less
realistic perhaps, said that newsreels would be replaced by news tele-
service, special events would appear simultaneously on theater screens
from coast to coast, video phones would replace telephones, and black-
and-white television, subsidized by the government, would make the new
medium available to every corner of the United States.

How Will Television Affect Radio? With these enthusiastic prophets
came other seers, who declared the doom of AM broadcasting. One
survey in a metropolitan area revealed that at the start of 1949, radio's
nighttime broadcast audience was 81 per cent compared to television's
19 per cent; but at the year end radio listening had dropped to 59 per
cent and television viewers had risen to 41 per cent. Audio sets, it was
said, would be obsolete by 1955. Was it natural that people would be
satisfied with a hear box when they could have a hear-see box and
watch their favorite programs and program artists in action? On the
other hand, others were just as certain that radio would not be eclipsed.
It was admitted that television was practicable and effective, that it was
here to stay, and that it would become increasingly important in shaping
social and cultural patterns; but it was not agreed that television would
usurp completely the standard broadcast field.

Four arguments were advanced to support this position:

1. New developments cause adjustments of competitive services, but
they do not extinguish competition unless they are totally and completely inconsistent with the established order. There have been new
media of advertising and communication from time to time, and each
has made its impact on the *status quo*. The economic pie has undergone constant resectioning. The size of the pieces passed around at the

[2] The long anticipated thaw of the FCC "freeze" came in April, 1952, bringing
the goal of "television in every American community" much nearer realization. An
allocation table announced by the Federal Communications Commission ended the
ban of new station grants, and new assignments provided for 30 channels in the
very high frequencies (VHF), now in general use, and 57 channels in ultra high
frequencies (UHF). Eight outlets were specifically reserved for noncommercial,
educational broadcasting. The ruling opened the door to 2,053 stations in 1,291
communities scattered over the country. A scramble for places in the television
sun is under way, and it will be interesting to check later a prophecy made by the
chairman of the FCC near the end of 1951 when he expressed the view that only
a handful of new stations would be on the air in 1952 and not many more in
1953.

economic board have shrunk or expanded—slices have grown smaller or larger—but they have always made the equivalent of one pie. Movies did not doom the stage; radio did not kill newspaper advertising; trucks, pipe lines, and airplanes did not bankrupt the railroads; and FM broadcasting threw a very slight shadow over AM broadcasting.

2. Audio broadcasting will not be extinguished by television because the two media serve different needs. Let us assume for the moment that we had nothing but televised programs and that they were accessible in every place where there is now a radio receiver. What percentage of present radio listening time would be cut off? The businessman driving to work would miss the financial news beamed through his car radio. The housewife, preparing the evening meal, would find it a bit hazardous to keep one eye on the kitchen television set and the other on her meat thermometer or pressure cooker gauge. The cross-word-puzzle fan would find his hobby severely hampered when substituting baseball, vaudeville, jazz orchestra, and live dramas for familiar music. A TV program is something to be seen, and it is not easy to work and look, to play bridge and look, to sew a fine seam and look, or even converse and look. Indeed, it may be argued that some programs of strictly informational character may be more effective when listened to than when viewed. Depending on the time of day, the location of the TV set, the occupation of the listener, the particular nature or purpose of the program, an audio program may be more acceptable than the video one.

3. Another reason why we may not expect television to blank out AM broadcasting is that the look-hear boxes will not be universally accessible. This statement, however, should be modified because it is impossible to predict with safety the things to come in this technological era. One can say with moderation, though, that universal television will not prevail for some years. There are many obstacles to full national TV coverage, and these will delay the prophesied demise of radio. Television, at present, is very costly. A TV station costs five times as much as an AM station and a TV program several times as much as a comparable radio show. These costs are changing so rapidly and are subject to so many elements, that detailed and specific data at present would be misleading. However, a television program *is* expensive.

It is true, indeed, that the advertiser's cost per 100 sets has dropped, but nevertheless the budget in round dollars is very large. A single spot announcement may cost $1,000, and a single program may draw a sponsor's check for $50,000. The program on which Bob Hope made his TV debut cost Frigidaire $135,000. Proctor and Gamble paid $640,000 for the TV rights to 60 Broadway musicals to be produced at an average cost of $32,000. The operating budgets of video theaters range from $2,000 to $30,000 per week.

The following makes possible a comparison of television dollar, personnel, and hour production costs with radio costs.

(a) *Simulcast Programs.* Programs which are broadcast simultaneously to radio and television audiences—result in additional production costs of from $1,200 to $2,200.

(b) *Remote Pickups.* The controlling factor in sports is the cost of the rights to televise ranging from $100 per game for small high school and college football games to $18,000 for the Army-Navy type game. Boxing matches range from $3,000 per event for the weekly Friday night fight to $4,000 to $6,000 for outstanding contender fights and up to $100,000 for championship matches like the Louis-Walcott bout. The rights for the World Series cost about $140,000, while the 1948 rights to broadcast and televise all the home baseball games of the New York Giants was about $400,000. Production costs on these events range from $1,100 to $2,000 per event.

(c) *Live Shows.* A very popular dramatic presentation now heard in radio requires a crew of 10, over and above the cast and orchestra; its television counterpart requires a crew of 40 people. A widely heard "winner quiz show" in radio requires a crew of 10 people; in television it requires 34 people.

(d) *Films.* (1) Films made especially for television are priced on an individual station or network showing. The half-hour mysteries on a five-station eastern network hook-up cost $2,500 for a single release. (2) Theatrical films not originally made for television, such as westerns, have a wide cost range, being priced on a "per market" basis. Cost of theatrical films per hour range from $75 for the older films for use in smaller television cities to several hundred dollars per hour in larger markets for newer features.

(e) *Kinescope Records.* These cost $500 for a 1-hour program and $168 for the original "master" and $10 for each set of pressings.[3]

The production of a TV show is analogous to the production of a motion picture. It requires studio space, lights, sets, directors, producers, and a wide miscellany of "props." A very mediocre B picture will cost, on the average, about $2,500 per minute for the completed film, allowing for the film cutting, retakes, and the elimination of imperfections. Studio costs are only the initial expense. The process of sending the program into your home is no small item. In addition to station or network compensation, the owners of the coaxial cable exact a rental fee of at least $35 per mile per month. The rental of cables and relays to

[3] *Television As an Advertising Medium,* U.S. Department of Commerce, pp. 5–6. The cost figures cited in this report pertain to 1949. They are offered primarily as a reference level and should be revised upward in view of subsequent current operation budgets and increased market areas. By the latter part of 1951, a 1-hour dramatic show on the 125-station network cost 3.4 million dollars and a quarter-hour news strip (five times per week for 1 year) cost 4.6 million dollars. It is estimated that these costs will jump to 5 and 6 million dollars, respectively, in 1955. A network vice-president in charge of TV sales and operations makes bolder predictions. The 1951 half-hour show for 50 weeks will jump from the current $19,000 to $50,000 in 1955, and the 15-minute period will cost almost three times the current rate.

provide a television hookup would cost 10 or 11 million dollars a year. It is not surprising that television broadcasting lost 15 million dollars in 1948 and 25 million in 1949, and that the deficit was extended to 1950.[4]

Assuming that all technical barriers could be removed to make possible TV reception in every town, hamlet, and village, would the sponsor find it profitable to finance such an extension? Ultimately, it is the commercial sponsor who pays the bill. Will he be able to meet the cost of a national TV network? Millard C. Faught has estimated that a 70-hour program service on 1,000 stations would cost (including reasonable profit) 1,740 million dollars.[5] The commercial development of television will parallel the history of radio. Profit—not public philanthropy—will, in the last analysis, be the motivating force behind its growth. Television must bring revenue to the business organizations which finance the building and maintenance of TV service. This revenue will not be forthcoming, however, unless the advertiser can reach adequate markets. These markets are to found, first, in the teeming centers of population, but in order to package more and more soap, sell more automobiles, and supply more medicine cabinets with gargle compounds, city markets alone are insufficient. Remote and less populated areas must be embraced. Television's problem at present is to build a communications structure which will duplicate the universality of radio's appeal. How quickly can TV, now confined chiefly to the metropolitan areas of the East, Middle West, and the Pacific seaboard, be spread evenly over the entire United States? Until the customer market can be united and consolidated by cables and relays, and covered at a cost that is not prohibitive, many sponsors will be forced to rely on radio as a supplementary medium of appeal. The FCC has a huge backlog of applications for TV permits, and it may not be too long before all restrictions on new entrepreneurs will be removed. One is impressed by the Commission's belief that it will be possible to operate ultimately 2,200 telecast stations, but the date on which we may reach this goal is not stated and the estimate is affected by the practical

[4] An analysis of FCC figures, as of Dec. 31, 1949, reveals that the four networks with their 13 stations had an aggregate loss of 11.7 million dollars, 61.3 per cent of their aggregate capital investment of 19.1 million at cost; the 84 independent stations had a combined loss of 13.6 million dollars, 36.9 per cent of their combined capital investment of 36.8 million dollars; and all 97 stations had a combined loss of 25.1 million dollars, 42.2 per cent of their aggregate investment of 55.9 million dollars.

These loss figures, of course, are understandable in view of the fact that they represent pioneer years of promotion. The risk capital expended in developing television is beginning to pay dividends as increased revenue from an ever-growing number of sponsors pours into station and network coffers. While the industry as a whole ended 1950 in the red, the over-all loss compared to that in 1949 was reduced by 66 per cent. Out of 79 interconnected stations, 47 showed a profit during 1950.

[5] Millard C. Faught, "TV: An Interim Summing Up," *Saturday Review of Literature*, Aug. 26, 1950.

factor of cost operation. New applicants will want to locate in profitable areas. Will there be enough population centers to absorb the possible television output? These are some of the economic considerations advanced by those who do not see the early demise of radio.

The argument that economic road blocks prevent, or delay indefinitely, radio's eclipse might be refuted if every TV home were to become a television box office. This could be achieved by a government tax, but such a plan probably would be unacceptable to a people who have long enjoyed free radio entertainment. The Zenith Radio Corporation has advanced a method of television reception (coded television) that might be an answer to the financial riddle. The name of this system is Phonovision. A regular television receiver, tuned to a Phonovision station, will get only a blurred and wriggly picture on the screen. This distortion is caused by the absence of a key part of the signal. When this key is restored, the picture clears and then one can settle down to enjoy the program.[6] An owner requests that he be supplied a given program, agrees to pay a fee for this service, and the "missing link" necessary to clear reception is supplied.

In February, 1950, the Zenith Corporation was granted permission (with certain restrictions) to experiment with their "pay-as-you-see" brand on TV. The tests were to be made during a 90-day period with 300 Chicago families. For each program released—a full-length motion picture—the company was to charge the TV owner $1. Immediate opposition was voiced by local theaters and motion picture distributors who saw in Phonovision a competition that might prove disastrous. Neither were commercial television interests too enthusiastic although Zenith contended that Phonovision would supplement TV's income, produce an additional source of revenue, speed TV's costly growth, and pay for the uses of television that are not profitably sponsorable by advertising.

After several delays and postponements, Zenith began its tests of Phonovision on Jan. 1, 1951. The results were described by the company spokesmen as "terrific." Calls flooded the switchboard at such a pace that two operators were rushed throughout the day and evening. In September, 1951, FCC was asked to commercialize the Phonovision system of subscription television.

The economic potentiality of Phonovision is impressive. Mr. Faught's summary of the point is succinct:[7]

[6] In mid-1950, the FCC was asked to consider a rival "pay-as-you-see" plan, Subscriber-Vision, produced by Skiatron Corporation, New York. It does not require intervening telephone connections. A special key inserted in the receiver supplies the code to unscramble the picture. (Zenith's Phonovision requires a telephone line to supply a signal which unscrambles the telecast picture.) The Skiatron plan entails a simple, inexpensive receiving tube; Zenith's system requires the installation of special decoder outlets.
[7] Faught, *op. cit.*

Assuming that there is a rapidly achievable market for 25,000,000 Phono-vision sets (which will cost approximately $10 more than an ordinary tele-vision set) and that the families owning these sets would buy $2.50 worth of box-office programs per week over and above the free sponsored programs they will continue to see, the resulting $3,250,000,000 is more than was spent last year to produce all the stage plays, movies, and radio programs, write all the novels, and play all the big league baseball games put together. There should be some reasonable expectation, therefore, that Phonovision stands a chance of delivering television from the economic shackles of costly pro-graming that now binds the feet of this infant giant.

4. The immediate and universal availability of television is affected not only by the inherent cost problem but also by technical barriers. The FCC has been hard pressed to find a sufficient number of television channels. The Commission's original allocation plan provided for 410 stations. This number was later increased to 955, but operational dif-ficulties arose. Stations were interfering with one another. A television signal requires a roadway 6 megacycles wide which is 600 times the width of the electronic band used by an AM signal. Television stations operating on the channel had to be widely separated. The exact distance is still a matter of investigation, but it approximates 150 miles. The FCC estimated that the number of low-band stations that could be accom-modated would be about 600; but this number of outlets would be in-sufficient to serve the country. What to do? On July 11, 1941, the Commission proposed that the 12 very high-frequency (VHF) channels be supplmented by 42 UHF channels to be numbered 14 to 55. The ultimate division of stations between the so-called l-f and h-f bands would be as follows: 499 on the VHF band serving 205 cities and 1,682 on the UHF band serving 1,330 cities. When new UHF assignments are made, however, present receiving sets will not be operative without the use of attachments called "converters," and the future buyer of a TV unit will require a set specially designed to bring in both VHF and UHF. When the problem of color television is added to this complication, we have a real difficulty. You, the owner of a television receiver, will want to receive both black-and-white and color pictures beamed to you by both the VHF and the UHF stations. These "technical road blocks" in TV's path will no doubt be solved, but they are of sufficient magnitude to delay the fear of audio's complete extinction.

Television: Pro and Con. The sudden descent of television made its impact on social consciousness. A new phenomenon emerged: the gather-ing of families in semidarkness to gaze sans conversation, to commercially sponsored entertainment. Millions of people were suddenly transported to a new world of vicarious adventure. An Elysian field of inquiry in-vited a host of survey-conscious investigators. What was this new medium doing to reading habits, stay-at-home habits, and study habits?

Were new patterns of social adjustment taking shape? A flood of reports deluged the news press, magazines, and trade papers. The conclusions of reporters were too often suspect, owing to poor sampling or personal bias, but their cumulative weight gave impetus to a rising public concern. A poll of TV sets in Washington, D.C., produced the conclusion that adults were going to movies about one-fourth as often and spending almost one-third less time on books and magazines. Audience Research, Inc., made a study of reading habits in TV homes and non-TV homes in New York, Philadelphia, and Los Angeles and reported that people in TV homes compared with those in non-TV homes were listening much less to radio and reading fewer newspapers, magazines, and books. These facts were corroborated in another area study conducted by Advertest Test Research, New Brunswick. Los Angeles set owners reported that they were going to fewer movies and sports events and were doing less pleasure driving.

The effect of TV on children became a subject of particular concern. A Middle Western high-school principal decided to lengthen school hours because television was interfering with home study habits. Pupils were spending 2.8 hours every day watching television scenes and only 1.6 hours in study. An investigator in Evanston, Ill., disclosed that in video homes the average student was spending 4 hours a day watching television—almost as much time as he spent in the classroom.[8] Among Roselle, N.J., high-school students who watched TV regularly, grades dropped more than 15 per cent.[9] A teacher of fourteen-year-olds in New York declared, "Students' grades are 25 to 50 per cent lower than last year. The cause is television."[10] Many similar reports from school officials were offered to support the generalization that TV was having a harmful effect on scholastic standing.

According to other observers, TV was having an even more adverse effect on young children. A United Parents Association survey in New York City discovered that the heaviest group of child viewers were in the five-and six-year-old bracket, and that the children spent 4 hours a day at their TV sets. The alleged over-all effect was less outdoor play, less arts and crafts, interruption of eating habits, and harmful emotional stimulation.[11] The nature and effect of TV viewing were given point by certain statistics afforded by a program and audience analysis made in Los Angeles by Coffin, Cooper, and Clay:[12]

On the night of Tuesday, August 1, 1950, at 7:15 P.M., a total of 176,800 children were watching a program . . . called *Cowboys 'n Injins*, an hour and a half show combining live action with an old western film. At 8:00 P.M. this

[8] *Survey*, 86, 482–486, November, 1950. Illustrated.
[9] *Scholastic*, 57, 20–21, Sept. 20, 1950.
[10] *Nation*, 171, 87, July 22, 1950.
[11] *Saturday Review of Literature*, 33, 9–11, Nov. 25, 1950.
[12] *Survey, op. cit.*

number dropped slightly to 142,000 but at the same time another Los Angeles station started a double feature film that pulled an audience of 132,800 children. The *Cowboy 'n Injins* program ended at 8:30 P.M. and by 8:45 P.M. the total children's audience for the double feature . . . had jumped to 174,330. When the double feature ended at 10:00 P.M. there were still 110,800 . . . red-eyed children in the audience.

The above reports at this time do little more than indicate an attitude and a possible temporary effect. The data do not warrant extended generalizations approved by sociological norms. The sampling is small, the conclusions are likely to be slanted, and the novelty of television should wear off before reliable dicta are pronounced. In fact, later studies of TV's effect on children indicate that earlier complaints and fears were exaggerated. A report of more than 100 *New York Times* correspondents in cities and towns throughout the United States was summarized by the *Times* radio-TV editor in a series of seven articles published Jan. 24–31, 1951. The articles, acclaimed as "one of the most comprehensive appraisals yet attempted," report that state superintendents of school systems, principals, and teachers agree that, although children at first may look at the video screen excessively or neglect other activities, they soon return to their old habits and maintain their scholastic standing. "The use of television to introduce children to many personalities, events and topics to which they might not otherwise be exposed [is] contributing to the education of the younger generation." TV is credited with improving vocabularies, providing a new tool of learning and an outlet for children's hostility and aggressiveness. A dissenter from this consensus, however, is quoted as charging TV with leading children to "confuse violence with strength, low necklines with feminine ideals, sadism with sex, and criminals with police."

Although it is too early to make sound judgments about the results of juvenile viewing of TV programs, there is one particular aspect of this new communication medium that causes considerable alarm. There is a strong suspicion, if not actual fear, that TV will follow the main pathway already carved by standard broadcasting. A Washington columnist puts the matter rather pointedly:[13]

No discussion of life in this town would be complete without mentioning the acid comment of a local critic who asked rhetorically, "Who says we aren't making progress? Why, television has almost overnight reached a level of mediocrity that it took radio a quarter of a century to achieve!"

Television, as already emphasized, is a sales medium. The substructure of TV and radio are the same: sponsorship, sales, commercialism. Will television give us the same commonplace standards, the same passion for quick monetary returns, and promoters primarily in-

[13] Bill Henry, *Los Angeles Times*, Oct. 20, 1951.

terested in advertising commodities? Will television become chiefly the expanded and glorified voice of salesmanship? Can we expect this new communications medium to do more than extend the commonplace, the sensational, and the vulgar? The point is well stated by Val Gielgud:[14]

At the moment when the unseen drama was beginning to stand on its own legs, television came along to give the audience back its eyes. . . . It is for the listener-viewer to determine that this money [cost of television] shall not be spent unwisely or in vain; to remember that such money—even though it be siphoned through the medium of sponsors' advertising accounts—comes out of their own pockets; that *video* even more than sound-radio, affects them in their homes, and to a degree which is likely to condition to some extent the future of the civilized world. The control of radio is synonymous with Power. It is of the essence of Democracy that Power shall not be exercised without responsibility.

The topic for discussion on The Town Hall Meeting of the Air program, Jan. 3, 1950, was *Television: 1950. Is It Good or Bad?* (See Appendix I). The speakers were Al Capp, creator of "Lil Abner," and Norman Cousins, editor of the *Saturday Review of Literature*. Mr. Cousins stated that television, like its predecessor radio, was talking down to a twelve-year-old mentality. He deplored this as a "billion dollar blunder." Paraphrasing his wording, millions for mechanics and pennies for programs is not a formula to guarantee TV's boast that it is the supreme triumph of invention. Television must give us more than "an endless procession of murders, gang wars, terror and horror acts, substandard shows and wrestling matches."

Other critics have spoken even more caustically, complaining chiefly about the "grisly gamut" of killers, corpses, and private eyes, the "shrieks, groans, and the ominous dripping of blood, and horror enough to send the lily-livered skittering."

Television program merits were discussed at the 1950 Institute for Education by Radio. The usual differences of opinion were expressed. Both critics and defenders stated their positions. Certain arguments, long heard in connection with radio programs, were pointed toward TV which was charged with giving us "too much blood and alcoholic humor," "a plethora of killing and thievery." On the other hand, speakers thought any adverse effect which radio and television programs might have was due to wrong parental guidance, improper program selection, and "adult projection." The controversy is a perennial one and will never be satisfactorily resolved although it is agreed that radio and television programming is vitally related to sociocultural standards.

Substantial outpourings of public criticism have made the television

[14] Val Gielgud, "Ideas to Watch in Television and Radio," Reprinted from *Vogue*, January, 1949, p. 171. Copyright 1948, The Condé Nast Publications, Inc.

industry fully aware that it has a public-relations problem. "The mail at the FCC grows and the protests get louder and louder. . . . The obscenity on the screen is getting worse."[15] The text of a House Resolution (HR 3482) introduced Apr. 3, 1951, reads:

Congress should set up a censorship board within the FCC to pass on every telecast in advance . . . to cut all words and actions that arouse the passions, or that hold up any individual, race, creed, or group to mockery and derision.

The father of this resolution explained that his object was to clean up "lewd and repulsive" television programs. Another congressman sponsored a proposal for the establishment of a National Citizens Advisory Board to oversee radio and television programing.

Faced with public censure and the imminence of legal restrictions of censorship nature, the television industry deemed it expedient to formulate a code of practice covering programing and advertising techniques similar to the Code of Practices for Broadcasters. Such a code was adopted by the National Association of Radio and Television Broadcasters (NARTB) in October, 1951.[16] It proclaimed television's responsibility to the American public for respect for the special needs of children, for community welfare, for the advancement of education and culture, for the acceptability of program material, for decency and decorum in production, and for propriety in advertising. This code, which also set up a review board and stipulated certain penalties and rewards concerning station compliance, met violent opposition in some quarters, but regardless of possible subsequent revision, the industry had expressed its intent to impose a self-regulation which might alleviate public and individual criticism.

Criticism of televised broadcasts are offset by TV's many obvious advantages. "From where it happens, you hear it happen," is the caption of a radio network news broadcast, and in the space of half an hour you hear on-the-spot voices coming from every corner of the United States and foreign countries. From the committee rooms of Congress, the flood-periled Mississippi Valley, the council chambers of Lake Success, and the strike-bound front of industry, the words of officials, participants, and observers come to your living room. Change the caption as it now reads: "From where it happens, you see it happen." The President makes an inaugural address, the fleet parades in solemn might through the Golden Gate, the Supreme Court makes a historic decision, a ticker-tape welcome is given to military heroes, and a Rose Bowl deadlock is broken by

[15] Wayne Coy, Chairman of the FCC, in an address to the NARTB, District 5, meeting in St. Petersburg, Fla., Nov. 1, 1951.

[16] The text of the Code originally approved in Chicago in October, 1951, is printed in *Broadcasting-Telecasting*, Oct. 22, 1951, p. 23.

a desperation pass in the last seconds of play. These are events to see. Milady may now shop by television, watching merchandise displays and fashion styles on a television screen. Audio instruction is vivified by pictures. The Nelsons, Hogans, and Sneads may still write golf treatises for the Sunday morning dub, but the latter can learn about grips, stances, follow-through, slices, and hooks by watching the expert demonstrate on the video screen. The range of educational instruction by TV is unlimited. The school youngster is finding a substitute for field trips, a factory can be brought to the schoolroom, and what possibility there is to teach safety in the home, on the playground, and on the highway.

Television and Education. The educator heralds the new communications medium as education's greatest boon—the strongest possible means of inculcating ideas and ideals, and the most effective instrument of social progress. Such claims have a nostalgic echo, and only future experience can unveil an answer to the question, Will the history of educational radio be repeated? The reports of public-service and adult education programs already in operation, or definitely planned for the future, give hope that educational institutions will not this time be lost in the shuffle. By June, 1950, 45 colleges and universities, 21 school systems, and 5 medical schools were engaged in the preparation of television programs. One hundred seventy-nine other institutions reported to the Federal Office of Education that they were definitely interested in TV or were preparing to produce programs in the next few months.

Important educational contributions by way of television have been made by colleges and universities in the East, Middle West, South, and on the Pacific Coast. In 1950, Johns Hopkins University was continuing for the third year a science series over WAAM-TV, Baltimore. The Television University of the Air, a joint enterprise of 20 colleges and universities, in cooperation with WFIL-TV, Philadelphia, began its first week of regular adult education telecasting on Dec. 29, 1950. On Nov. 5, 1950, the University of Michigan made its official television entrance into adult education with a "home study by video" plan embracing a 14-week science course, *Man in His World—Human Biology*, a 7-week course, *Living in the Later Years*, and a series of teletours which took reviewers to the campus to see the use researchers make of rare, original, historical documents. Syracuse University received a special gift of $150,-000 to construct and fully equip studios for the transmission of programs over WSYR-TV, Syracuse. Iowa State College was the first university to own and operate its own TV station. The University of Texas found an outlet for its educational program through the TV stations in Fort Worth, Dallas, and San Antonio. WSB-TV, Atlanta, releases a daily adult education series in cooperation with eight Georgia institutions of higher learning. On the Pacific Coast, TV programs are presented by the

University of Southern California, the University of California at Los Angeles, Loyola University, Oregon State College, and the University of Washington. KRON-TV, San Francisco, has presented *Operation Education*, a thrice weekly 30-minute series in cooperation with Stanford University, the University of California at Berkeley, and the public-school systems of Alameda and San Francisco counties. City school systems engaged in pioneer TV testing include New York, Buffalo, Cleveland, Detroit, and Chicago. In Cincinnati, the Crossley Company has equipped 14 schools for test programing, and a full complement of programs in science and social studies has been demonstrated in a Philadelphia high school. The most ambitious and comprehensive plan of noncommercial educational telecasting was proposed by the Board of Regents of the University of the State of New York. In May, 1951, the Board advanced a plan which called for the construction of such stations in each of the population centers of the state. Under its supervision, programing would be apportioned among 120 institutions of higher education, 7,000 secondary and elementary schools, 640 libraries, 60 museums, and 140 historical societies. The objective could be attained, it was claimed, for 3.5 million dollars.

It is evident that TV is regarded as an important educational vehicle. Just how it can best function as an educational agency, however, poses a debatable question: Can educational objectives be attained if educators are made dependent on channels leased to private commercial ownership? In other words, should the government allocate a percentage of available frequencies for the exclusive use of noncommercial telecasting?

The issue has been a matter of legislative concern. A congressional resolution proposed that the FCC "study" the subject of TV educational channels. A second one, more specific, called for the FCC to set aside in each metropolitan area and major educational center one VHF channel. The Cellar Resolution (HR 3543), concerned with the same general objective, specified that 25 per cent of the operating schedule of each commercial television station should be devoted to noncommercial educational programs. The specific request that finally reached the Commission was that one VHF channel be set aside in each metropolitan area and major educational center; that where all VHFs are already assigned in such areas, existing stations be required to share an unspecified amount of time with educators; and that 20 per cent of UHF channels be reserved for education. The proponents of this proposal were the educators who organized the Joint Emergency Commission on Educational Broadcasting (JCEB). Their position and objective were stated in a memorandum accompanying a letter soliciting funds to fight the cause "to protect one of our greatest cultural resources from almost total debasement."

It is regrettable that the heads of our universities must now go hat in hand to a government agency to plead to have our cultural values recognized in the utilization of perhaps the most potent educational medium of our day. Over a period of nearly three decades, the FCC has shown extreme reluctance to make any decision contrary to the immediate interests of the large commercial networks.

We have allowed radio to be despoiled. A large part of the present television service is used to show grade B, C, and Z moving pictures, with occasional interludes for commercials. We do not suggest any unfair restriction of free competition for product merchandising. We merely insist that universities and public-service agencies devoted to the physical, mental, and moral well-being of the population have a right to operate their own television facilities.

Singly, even the greatest universities are powerless before the legal onslaught of several billion dollars represented by NBC, CBS, MBS, ABC—the major manufacturers and merchandisers of our business economy. There need be no such conflict if all concerned will come to a temperate agreement. There is considerable danger that the commercial interests will demand and get the whole hog.

The tedious hours of testimony and cross-examination which began on Nov. 27, 1950, paralleled a similar set of hearings from Oct. 1 to 20 and Nov. 7 to 12 in 1934. These sessions produced 14,000 pages of testimony and several thousand pages of exhibitors. The educators at that time were pleading a cause and were opposed by the broadcasting industry, the licensees of broadcast stations, and the manufacturers of radio equipment. The issue in 1934 was, Should the FCC recommend to Congress that a fixed percentage of radiobroadcast facilities be allocated by statute to particular types or kinds of nonprofit activities? The outcome of those hearings was a negative recommendation by the FCC. Some of the reasons for not granting special educational channels were stated as follows:

1 There is no need for a change in the existing law to accomplish the helpful purposes of the proposal.

2. Flexibility in the provisions of the law is essential to regulation if growth and development in the art of broadcasting are to be encouraged and regulated for the best interests of the public as a whole.

3. There are insufficient broadcast facilities available in the present development of the art to provide for specialized broadcast services consistent with a fair and equitable distribution of facilities and services throughout the country.

In 1950, the basic problem was again before the FCC. The arguments of the JCEB were opposed by industry representatives who challenged the capacity of noncommercial agencies to provide adequate and effective telecasting and who argued that cooperative agreements rather than specific allocations were the more realistic solution.

The issues which developed in these hearings were brought to focus in a Town Hall Meeting of the Air program on Nov. 28, 1950 (see Appendix II). The subject for consideration was, *Who Should Be Responsible for Education on Television?* The question was debated by Dr. Ernest Dichter, business and advertising consultant for radio and TV sponsors, and Miss Frieda B. Hennock, a member of the FCC. The latter took issue with Dr. Dichter's proposal that advertisers and educators form an "over-all organization to exert moral control [to] improve those programs already reaching the public." She stated as her opinion that

. . . educators . . . are qualified to determine whether we will be a better informed, better educated society in an expanding democracy, or whether we will be a nation of household gadgets, $50,000 jackpots, and home libraries stacked with comic books. . . . Television can be put to better use as an electronic blackboard rather than as an electronic billboard.

Dr. Dichter, in reply, challenged the "right of educators to usurp this title exclusively," and their ability to bring their subject to the people "in a format . . . psychologically accessible and comprehensive." If TV becomes "commercially profitable and culturally beneficial," it will be necessary for professional TV producers and educators to work together and not separately.

The problem before the FCC was a very real one. Would the social force of television be impeded by having one-tenth or more of TV channels handed over to nonprofessional hands? Would these hands prove to be inept and incapable? On the other hand, would a commercial monopoly guarantee that TV would go the way of radio and a "magnificent and cultural medium be lost to the people irrevocably"? However, the Commission was apparently impressed by the inpouring of the educators' representations, and the result of the hearings was a consensus that a definite perecentage of TV channels should be held open for educational institutions. The latter were advised, though, that unless they could prove their financial and engineering capacity to operate stations assigned them, the reservations would not be held open indefinitely. Thus, the decision was somewhat of a tentative one, and the debate over the question of who should be responsible for education on television will continue throughout the years.

Color Television. While the television industry was murmuring over its first growing pains, it was afflicted with a technological complication. The laboratory doctors injected into the blood stream of the infant a color compound. The FCC was asked to approve the transmission of pictures in color. Three companies claimed they had achieved this possibility. They were CBS, RCA, and Color Television, Inc. The first two claimed they were ready to demonstrate color transmission.

On Tuesday, Jan. 10, 1950, the *Washington Post* carried the following advertisement:

THE COLUMBIA
BROADCASTING SYSTEM
ANNOUNCES
THE FIRST PUBLIC EXHIBITION OF
COLOR TELEVISION
Beginning Thursday, January 12, at the Walker Building
734 Fifteenth Street, N.W., Washington, D.C.
Twice daily at 11 A.M. and 1 P.M.

The advertisement was significant in that it announced "for the first time in history a series of television broadcasts." Both CBS and RCA, of course, had conducted many hours of test operations prior to this date. RCA had telecast 718 hours of experimental programs between Sept. 18 and Dec. 30, 1949.

The FCC faced a new problem that called for Solomonic wisdom. Was color actually practicable? Was it still in an experimental stage, and was further improvement necessary to bring it within the framework of established standards? Could television standards, once adopted, be changed without rendering obsolete all transmitting equipment? Was color television compatible with black-and-white service? If a satisfactory color system is demonstrable now, would not any delay in adopting it be a financial injustice to millions of future TV set owners! The Commission began hearings on the issue in September, 1949. The "color sweepstakes" was one descriptive epitome of the ensuing storm of claims and counterclaims, involving as it did millions of dollars for the victor. Many interests were involved. The decision, if forthcoming would be an important one.

The FCC heard testimony and arguments for 9 months, and on July 11, 1950, went behind closed doors to wrestle with the problem and reach, if possible, a solution. A Senate advisory committee on color television had asserted that color TV was practicable in the channels already assigned to black-and-white operations, but recommended that the Commission select only one of the competing companies for commercial licensing. Three months later, Oct. 11, 1950, the Commission announced its decision. It was in favor of CBS color standards. The ruling was effective as of Nov. 20, but it stipulated that RCA have a specified time to prove that they could outperform their competitor. The decision of the Commission was five to two and evoked violent dissention from the press, set manufacturers, and rival interests. It was denounced as a usurpation of authority, a premature commitment, an abuse of authority, and a block to further research in television. The inevitable result was a legal challenge before a Federal court in Chicago. RCA charged that the Commission's order approving CBS color was illegal, void, and beyond the power, authority, and jurisdiction of that body. Almost immediately the court issued a temporary restraining order pending further consideration. On Dec. 21, 1950, a three-man tribunal rendered a decision upholding FCC's approval of the CBS system, but at the same time prohibited Columbia from engaging in commercial operations until Apr. 1, 1951, or until such time as the Supreme Court might resolve the restraint. In the language of the court (one opinion), the action of the FCC was "precipitant [and] an abuse of discretion . . . arbitrary and capricious."

The majority ruling of a special three-judge Federal court in Chicago was supplanted on May 28, 1951, by an eight-to-one opinion of the U.S. Supreme Court. The high tribunal held that the lower court had erred in overruling an administrative decision because they disagreed with its wisdom and that the discretion of the FCC had not been abused. The decision was an important one. It affected the interests of nearly 13 million owners of black-and-white television sets who would be unable to get CBS color programs without installing converters that would cost about $100. It affected manufacturers, now faced with the problem of making sets that could receive color. The latter argued, however, that it would be a long time before color television would reach any substantial proportion of the general public and that color broadcasts would be special programs outside regular black-and-white schedules. Whether this argument was primarily a rationalization would be shown by subsequent developments. The CBS seemed to feel that the period of experimentation had passed and announced that they would begin commercial color television on June 25. This inaugural program, an hour in length, would be commercial, marking a 7-day-a-week schedule that would be expanded to 20 hours per week by the fall of 1951. The promise made for June 25 was fulfilled. On that day, 16 advertisers joined in sponsoring a 60-minute telecast on a five-station CBS hookup. This color telecast came (within 6 days) on the tenth anniversary of sponsored black-and-white telecasts.

What Is Color Television and How Does It Work?[17]

Stripped of technical embroidery, the basic theory of color television is fairly simple. Even a black-and-white television picture is an optical illusion. All there is on the screen at any instant is a fast-moving bright spot that "scans" back and forth, covering the whole screen with 525 lines of light which the slow-reacting human eye (if not brought too close) sees as a picture. The pictures follow one another so fast (30 a second) that they are blended by the eye to give the illusion of motion—just as the eye blends the frames on a strip of movie film. Pictures or elements of pictures in the primary colors will blend too, giving a scene in reasonably natural colors.

[17] Courtesy of *Time*, Nov. 28, 1949, p. 49, copyright Time, Inc., 1949.

The last step, adding color, is easy in theory but exceedingly difficult in practice. The systems proposed by CBS and RCA approach the problem in fundamentally different ways.

Color with Fields. In the CBS color system (called "field sequential"), the transmitting camera, like the ordinary black and white camera, has a single Image Orthicon "seeing" tube. In front of it is a spinning disc with segments of blue, green, and red transparent plastic. When a blue segment is in front of the tube, the camera sees only the blue light coming from the scene being televised. When the disc has turned a little, putting a red segment in front of the tube, the camera sees only the scene's red light. Next, it sees green through a green segment of the disc.

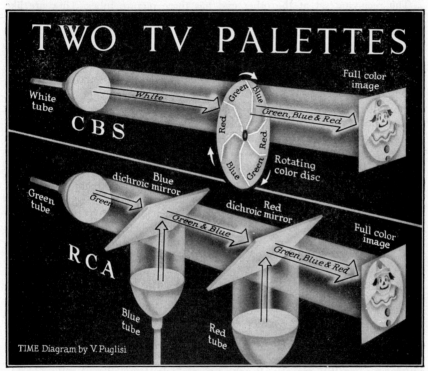

Fig. 50. Diagram of CBS and RCA color television methods.

If the disc is properly synchronized with the scanning speed of the tube, one-color "fields" go out over the airwaves and appear one after the other on the face of the receiving "picture" tube. All of them are white, since the "phospor" (the luminescent substance) on the tube's face glows only in white light. But in front of the receiving set's picture tube is a second spinning "color disc" (see Fig. 50). This disc is synchronized so that a blue segment is between the tube and the eye of the viewer whenever a "blue" field is flashing on the tube. So the eye sees the field in blue. When a "red" field is on the tube, a red segment of the disc makes that frame look red. In the same way, "green" fields are made to look green. The three one-color fields, following one another quickly, are blended by the eye to form a full color picture.

Color with Dots. RCA's system, called "dot interlacing," is entirely electronic, needs no spinning disc. In the transmitting camera are three tubes. In front of them is a system of "dichroic mirrors" which allow each tube to "see" in one color only. All three tubes scan the scene continuously, but an electronic switching device, turning their signals on and off 11.4 million times a second, allows each tube to transmit over the telecasting station only one-third of the time. In this way the "video signals" from all three tubes are strung together like trains made up of red, blue and green freight cars, and sent over the air on one wave band.

The receiving set at the other end has three picture tubes. They are like black and white tubes except that each has on its face a phosphor that glows in a different basic color. Each little impulse (the colored freight cars) arriving over the beam is electronically switched to the properly colored tube. They arrive so fast that each tube-face is covered 15 times a second with a pattern of tiny dots corresponding to the blues, reds and green in the screen being televised. The more red there is in a part of the screen (*e.g.*, a red dress), the brighter the red dots on the corresponding part of the red tube.

Next step is to combine the three colored images in the eye of the viewer. The combining is done with two "dichroic mirrors": plates of glass with one surface covered with a thin layer of a colorless, transparent substance. Because of the special way in which this combination affects light of different wave lengths, each mirror reflects only one color. The other two colors pass right through it.

The mirrors are arranged so that red light from the red tube is reflected to the eye of the viewer from the red-reflecting mirror (see Fig. 50). Blue light from the blue tube is reflected by the blue-reflecting mirror to the eye. Green light from the green tube is not reflected at all. It reaches the eye direct. The viewer sees the three pictures superimposed so that they blend to form a full-color picture.

How Will Color Television Affect Black-and-White Reception? The FCC, when ruling in favor of color television sets, had no intention of substituting them for existing black-and-white receivers. Color will come gradually and will supplement rather than suppress the programs now appearing on TV screens. By the use of "adapters" placed either inside or outside the set, present owners can receive color programs in black and white; and by the use of "converters," a unit placed in front of the present black-and-white picture tube after the set has been adapted, black-and-white sets can receive color. Once a set has been converted for color it can still get regular black-and-white programs simply by switching off the converter. As early as October, 1950, manufacturers were producing these conversion media, and retail outlets were guaranteeing the public color conversion for any black-and-white set sold before commercial color sets were available.

Advantages of Color Television. The superiority of color for all television pictures is a matter of debate although it is admitted that some programs would gain in sensory appeal. Telecasts of the Pasadena Tournament of Roses Parade and similar spectacles, for example, would be vivified if presented in color, but it is doubted that the run-of-the-mill TV show would be greatly enhanced. Technological progress is slow. Although the analogies are not completely sound, primarily owing to differences in cost factors, technicolor has not supplanted black-and-white films, and color slides have not replaced pictures in half tone.

The most dramatic demonstrations of color television so far have been in connection with hospital surgery. In fact, medical television is heralded as the most important teaching aid ever devised. It makes possible accurate, close-up pictures which can be viewed by a large group of observers. The superiority of color to black and white is explained by Dr. I. S. Ravdin, head of the department of surgical research at the University of Pennsylvania, as follows:

Color television provides a sense of depth which is necessary for the adequate teaching of surgery. The deeper recesses of body cavities which ordinarily are difficult to discern can now be readily observed because of the various color gradations. Moreover, color permits recognition of changes in human tissue during the course of an operation; and this is all-important to the surgeon. Then, too, color television permits the student to gain immediate anatomical orientation which otherwise could not be achieved.

The University of Pennsylvania made their first demonstration of televised surgical operations on the first Sunday of May, 1949. The accuracy and detail of the surgical field reproduced on the viewing screens were highly satisfactory, and 2 months later, 400 people in a hall half a mile from the operating room in an Atlantic City hospital, watched the minute details of the surgeon's performance. These pictures were so clear and effective that similar telecasts of surgical operations and clinical procedures were provided members of the American Medical Association in Atlantic City a month later. The pictures were viewed by more than 30,000 people. It is prophesied that color TV installations will ultimately be standard equipment in each of the 70 accredited medical schools in the United States.

Television as a Sales Medium

As an advertising medium, television has inherent qualities that enable it to reach the masses of consumers in an effective and interesting manner. It can employ the visual impact of newspapers and magazines, the oral persuasion and personal immediacy of radio, and, in addition, by combining sight and sound with motion make product demonstration possible.[18]

[18] Philip A. Bennett, *Television As an Advertising Medium*, p. 1, U.S. Department of Commerce.

You are a manufacturer. You produce an article or commodity which you wish to sell. You want to sell as much of this item as possible. How do you achieve the objective? (1) It is necessary to locate prospective customers, as many as you can find, (2) you persuade them that your "mousetrap" is the best of all mousetraps, barricade yourself behind an attractive counter, and await results. Stated more formally, the production, distribution, and sale of manufactured goods in a free-enterprise economy is achieved by stimulating human wants and by the competitive demonstration of product superiority. The story of advertising is a fascinating account of man's ingenuity, skill, and artistry. With the evolution of technology and the multiplication of commodities adapted to human needs and desires, the seller has constantly improved his methods of promotion. From barn to billboard, from the medicine man's harangues to the radio announcer's demands, from crude drawings to vivid color pictures, and from static white lights to whirling constellations of variegated brilliance, the science and art of advertising have assumed the proportions of complex psychological warfare.

When an advertiser enters your home through the magic portals of radio, he says to you in substance, "I bring you half an hour of entertainment. It costs me thousands of dollars, but the price you pay is practically nothing. In exchange for my generosity I ask only three things—that you remember my name, what I sell, and that my service or commodity is better than any other." The return on radio advertising investment is measured in terms of sponsor identification and recall and the hearer's response to the sales message. Judged by these criteria, radio has been a successful sales medium; but television provides a more vivid and intense customer appeal. Whatever may be the criticisms of TV's program content, video's ingenious commercials command respect. A radio announcer may intone the virtues of that "g-o-o-o-d" bread, but on the television screen a piece of toast made from that same bread becomes a gourmet's delight. Television is more than an advertising medium; it is a sales medium.

The vast sums spent for television advertising support by inference, at least, TV's claims to superiority as a sales medium. Following the "freeze" of the FCC (Sept. 30, 1948) withholding further channel allocations and station construction, the number of stations remained relatively fixed. However, while the market areas served by TV increased from 57 (Dec. 31, 1949) to 63 (Dec. 31, 1950) the number of receiving sets in the same areas grew from 3,395,000 to 10,190,000. Markets, in terms of possible consumer contacts, were expanding with incredible swiftness. Sponsors look to markets. Consequently, the number of companies willing to buy television time likewise skyrocketed. In July 4 to 10, 1948, TV was selling time to 280 customers; 10 months later, May 1 to 7, this clientele had mounted to 1,343.[19] The volume of time sold to advertisers continued to shoot up.

The U.S. Chamber of Commerce addressed a 10-point questionnaire on TV dimensions to operators of TV stations.[20] Asked what type of goods or services TV is better adapted to sell, broadcasters replied: "Any product that can be demonstrated in use and all goods that lend themselves to counter and show room display, especially brand name products. . . . TV is nearly as effective in moving merchandise as personal selling and much less expensive." Typical results ascribed to television's ability to move goods were as follows:

One TV announcement sold one carload of electric fans in twelve business hours. . . . A De Soto dealer ran one sixty-second film spot, cost $30, and sold four automobiles as a direct result. . . . Eight thousand and two hundred dollars worth of Vitamix machines were sold at $29.95 each on a single half-hour film program which cost the sponsor only $270. . . . An expenditure of $100 moved goods valued at $30,000. . . .

Total TV broadcast revenue almost quadrupled between 1948 and 1949. Revenues for the networks and their owned and operated stations, and revenues for all other operating stations, also increased by the same amount. The total time expenditure in 1948 was approximately 9 million dollars; in 1949, it was 27.5 million.[21] Total gross TV network time sales in the 10 months of 1950 was 27.2 million. (The comparable network figure for 1949 was 8.3 million.)[22]

There are few statistical data at present on which to base adequate conclusions concerning TV's sales effectiveness, but further studies similar to the Hofstra investigation sponsored by NBC may warrant sound generalizations. Interviews were conducted with TV set owners and non-set owners "matched for neighborhood, age, education, family size, standard of living, and buying power." The tabulations derived from the investigation indicated that TV "not only increased sales of television advertised brands [but that] it cuts down sales of nontelevision brands in the same homes." There is a 40.1 per cent gain in television advertised brands after TV enters the home. An over-all interpretation, as made by NBC, is that the TV advertiser may find 193 extra customers for every 1,000 sets receiving his sales presentation.

The table on page 350 presents comparative data for the TV broadcast industry, for 1948 and 1949.

Although all stations and networks showed a loss from operations in 1948 and only three stations showed an operational profit in 1949, ad-

[19] *Ibid.*, p. 7.
[20] *Advertising News Letter*, U.S. Chamber of Commerce, June–July issue, 1950.
[21] *Sixteenth Annual Report*, p. 121, Federal Communications Commission.
[22] *Broadcasting-Telecasting*, Jan. 8, 1951, p. 57.

TV Broadcast Data for 1948 and 1949

Item	Networks and their owned and operated stations*			All other stations†			Industry total		
	1948, millions	1949, millions	Per cent change	1948, millions	1949, millions	Per cent change	1948, millions	1949, millions	Per cent change
Total broadcast revenues	$ 4.8	$18.9	293.8	$ 3.9	$15.4	294.9	$ 8.7	$34.3	294.3
Total broadcast expenses	11.8	30.6	173.2	12.4	29.0	133.9	23.6	59.6	152.5
Total broadcast loss	6.4	11.7	.....	8.5	13.6	.....	14.9	25.3	.....

* In 1948 the four networks (NBC, CBS, ABC, and Dumont) owned and operated a total of 10 stations; in 1949 they owned and operated a total of 13 stations.

† Refers to 40 stations in 1948 and 85 stations in 1949.

SOURCE: *Sixteenth Annual Report*, p. 122, Federal Communications Commission.

vertisers were diverting larger and larger amounts to television budgets. The proportion of television broadcast revenues to total (AM and FM) and video broadcast revenues in 1949 was 2⅓ times greater than in 1948. The following table presents the proportion of TV broadcast revenues to total aural and TV revenues in specified metropolitan districts for 1948 and 1949.

District	TV per cent of total 1948 broadcast revenues	TV per cent of total 1949 broadcast revenues
Baltimore	7.5	20.8
Los Angeles	7.7	17.3
New York	8.2	16.9
Chicago	4.2	12.2
Cleveland	1.7	7.4

SOURCE: *Sixteenth Annual Report*, p. 123, Federal Communications Commission.

The power of television as an advertising and sales medium was evident almost with the advent of the new communications medium. TV receiving sets were bought with almost fanatical enthusiasm. Prospective markets expanded with each rising sun. Commercial sponsors, skeptical at first, like the first radio advertisers of the 1920's, lost their temporary timidity and rushed to buy time. A new era of sales promotion was born and well under way by the end of 1950.

Television Production. Television is a blending of radio, the stage, and the motion picture. Story material, actors, producers and directors, stage sets, electronic equipment, cameras, lights, visual aids, music, and other elements are integrated to produce pictures on your TV set. The following is a condensed explanation of television production and a comparison of audio and video techniques.

Studios. The studio setup for a radiobroadcast is relatively very simple and fundamentally of the same pattern. Studio space and equipment for a radio program vary with the size of the program. A radio talk requires only a small room, a table and chair, and a unidirectional microphone. A dramatic program will employ one or more microphones of different type, turntables, and live sound effects. When live music is added, the floor space is enlarged to accommodate the musicians, and in the case of a large orchestra, additional mikes may be placed to facilitate the blending of orchestral sections. In a variety show involving many performers and musical units, studio organization becomes increasingly complex. In each instance, of course, the program is related to a control room where an engineer at a mixing panel regulates the sound output and balances the various sound levels. In brief, the physical equipment requisite to a radiobroadcasting studio consists of microphones, turntables, and live sound effects.

The studio setup for a television broadcast involves a much more elaborate and complicated organization of equipment. A TV set rigged for action resembles a motion-picture stage. Program action takes place against scenic backgrounds or within prescribed settings. These may range from a simple forestage and curtain backdrop to a realistically furnished scene or room. The scene is lighted, the action photographed, the sound and dialogue picked up by microphones, and the result is monitored in a control room.

Control Rooms. Again, by comparison, a radio control booth is a very simple installation compared to the space and equipment required for monitoring a televised program. The audio control room is furnished with a monitor console which, in outward appearance, is a panel equipped with several volume controls, switching levers, and a volume indicator. The engineer has available a vertical rack and panel for the reception and switching of programs, an interdepartmental telephone, signal light switches for communication with the studio during a broadcast, a talk-back microphone, and one or more turntables. The room is also equipped with a clock and a monitor speaker. Adjacent to the console there is usually a table or counter which can be used by directors, assistant producers, and other personnel. The monitoring of a radio program is a process of riding gain on various sound levels—dialogue, sound effects, and music—and blending them in proportions requisite to over-all artistic demands. The job is achieved by the proper manipulation of gain controls on the monitor panel. When the performance requires the use of several microphones (microphone channels), monitoring is a skillful and exacting activity. Communication between the booth and the action in the studio is effected by light signals or sign language. The director of a program may work from the control room, but usually he is in the studio in direct contact with the performers.

There are some similarities between functions of the radio and the television control rooms, but in the main they are radically different. There are sound output levels to be regulated, but at this point the analogy ends. Engineers who monitor a TV program are concerned primarily with the transmission of pictures. These pictures, emanating from each camera (camera channels), are registered on viewing screens in the monitor booth (the monitor panel) and are regulated as to wave form, brightness, contrast, size, horizontal and vertical setting, and shading. Oral instructions must be given to cameramen, floor managers, and other personnel on the set; and recorded music, film slides, or film sequences must be cued as required by the continuity. The TV control room, like the one for audio broadcasting, is the nerve center of the entire system, but there are more nerves, both efferent and afferent, converging on the focal area. One engineer can monitor a radio show, but a TV production requires three or more technicians. These are seated at two consoles: a monitor console and a program console. The latter is usually situated directly behind and above the monitor panel. A TV monitor panel is a series of frames (monitor units) on each of which appears a picture coming through a particular camera channel. The program console is constructed to accommodate the producer, the video operator (technical director), and the sound engineer. During the re-

Fig. 51. A TV control room (NBC).

hearsal, the program director or producer communicates with the actors via a studio loud-speaker; during the broadcast he talks with the stage manager, camera, and dolly men via earphones. He is also connected by telephone with the film projectionist. The video operator employs a series of switches by which to control camera channels and, like the performer, has P.A. and telephonic communication with the technical staff working in the studio. The sound operator is also connected with the studio, the film projection room, and in some types of installations, the dressing rooms. His console is equipped with the necessary means of controlling film and studio sound levels, and he supplies through his turntables the recorded material incident to the broadcast.

To the layman, the television control room, in comparison with the standard radio booth, is a mass of complicated and bewildering scientific apparatus.

Fig. 52. A TV control room (CBS).

The function of the control room and the duties of the personnel associated with it are clearly epitomized in *Close-Up* published by CBS:[23]

Nerve center for the whole complex of television production is the control room. Here behind a battery of buttons and knobs sit the ones who make the decisions guiding the quality of the picture the audience will see, the sounds it will hear. It is an atmosphere of quiet madness, of many voices, quiet but urgent. Each key figure concentrates on his own area of operation . . . calling directions out to the floor, to galleries above and rooms below, through an intricate interlocking communication system. Director, assistant director, switcher, shaders, audio man, announcer . . . these are the control room people, guiding our show through its final phases, onto the air. The director tensely watches his three monitors—one for each camera—and calls out the number of the camera whose picture he wants to use at each moment: "Take ONE! . . . Take TWO!" He's hooked up directly by 'phone with cameras and technicians, but makes his wants known to the cast and stage crew through his field general on the set, the floor manager. Floor man receives instructions by one-way walkie-talkie and can move freely about to give entrance, exit, and time cues to actors, directions to crew. Assistant

[23] *Close-up*, Columbia Broadcasting System, Inc., 1949. Pages unnumbered.

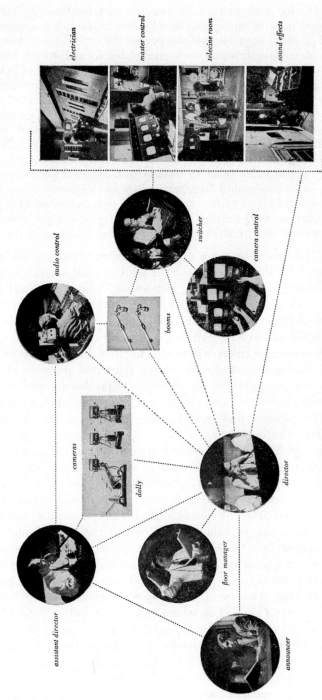

electrician

master control

telecine room

sound effects

audio control

switcher

camera control

booms

cameras

dolly

director

assistant director

floor manager

announcer

FIG. 53. Picture diagram of a television production staff.

director—"A.D." for short—precues the cameras, readying them for each shot
. . . also keeps track of timing, and directly cues music and announcer, who
has a sound-proof booth of his own just beyond the control room. Audio man
controls sound volume, bringing each microphone in and out of play. The
control room's technical supervisor is the switcher, with a battery of lights and
buttons before him. He's the one who actually puts the show into action . . .
punching up each camera's picture as the director calls the shots . . . switching in film sequences or slides as they are called for. Switcher maintains
alert and watchful contact with everybody in and out of the control room, on
and off the floor. He is also liaison man with the master control room, dispatch-
point for the show. Master control puts the show on the air locally, on the
cables going to other cities, or on TV recordings. Below directors and switchers
are shaders, or camera-control men, who watch camera monitors and control
the quality and brightness of the picture. Above their individual camera controls is the line monitor, carrying the picture being used right now. Above
that, the system monitor, with the show that is being broadcast to the public.

Director. Television program production extends the knowledge and
skill employed by the radio director. It adds to audio broadcasting the
various elements based on "stage and screen," plus specialized factors
inherent in this new type of communication. The radio director is a
craftsman who integrates the audio elements of voice, sound, and music
into meaningful and artistic patterns. Television extends the canvas and
gives the director new colors with which to paint. In radio, the producer
exercises supervisory control over all the associated program elements.
He directs the interpretation of dialogue, expresses judgment on the
selected music, instructs sound-effects men, is responsible for the projection of audio pictures that have balance, proportion, and perspective,
and to a limited extent, utilizes a knowledge of engineering practices to
achieve his end. The radio director is a coordinator. He cues dialogue,
sound, music, and incidental acoustical effects. Actors watch for his
signals, the orchestra conducts on cue, live and recorded effects are
executed on direction, and certain control-board operations may be
performed on cue. The TV director is also a coordinator, but he has
many more elements to bring into a unified pattern. Paralleling the
routine of preparing a theater production, he must assemble a suitable
script, a cast of characters, a stage set, conduct rehearsals to set the
action, select costumes and properties, and arrange a lighting plot. Associated with him, of course, is a staff of technicians who are specialists
in their respective areas and on whom he can rely, but he should be able
at all times to express intelligent opinions about every phase of the
production. Added to basic procedures, similar to theater staging, are
cinematic skills. The production is not for a theater audience, it is for the
eye of the camera. The director must be able to evaluate the effectiveness of particular camera shots—up-shots, tilt-shots, split focus, fades,

cuts, dissolves—and in this field his decisions may be very important. The problem of television lighting is different from that of stage lighting and, because of the color sensitivity of the television camera tube, particular care must be exercised with regard to colors in relation to the pickup and their relation to mood. The ultimate synthesis of picture components projected to the television screen is the responsibility of the director.

Actor. As television, in general, is a synthesis of the theater stage, the radio studio, and the motion-picture set, the performance of the television actor embraces skills and techniques common to these three media. A stage is a room from which one wall has been removed. The people in the room (on the stage) are presumed to behave (act) as people in a room normally behave. Actually, of course, there is an audience watching all that goes on. This audience is composed of customers. They pay money to be entertained, and the actor on stage cannot be mindless of their presence. The actor-audience relationship is never completely lost. This relationship, however, does not exist for the radio or television actor. The former plays to a microphone and to associated actors who maintain relatively fixed positions; the latter plays to a camera and associates who move in a comparatively restricted area. Neither of them experiences an audience identification like the one felt by the stage Thespian. The footlight performer projects. Every meaning, attitude, and emotion must reach the last row—under the balcony and in the balcony. This requires vocal intensity, broad pantomime, and exaggerated movement. On the other hand, the TV and radio actors play to a very immediate audience—to small congregated groups in a living room. The dramatic story presented may be just as intense, or more so, but this dramatic projection is not due to the kind of vocal intensity and physical communication used by the stage actor. The effective microphone performer knows how to achieve the impression of intensity through suppression. Intensity is not loudness. Physical movements are likewise restrained and limited when acting before a microphone and camera. Because of the close proximity of the television screen and the viewer, exaggerated movements are unnecessary and would, in fact, be ludicrous —a throwback to the melodramatic manners of the early "flickers." The TV actor, like the stage actor, must give an even and sustained characterization, but the television medium makes this somewhat more difficult because of peculiar distractions occasioned by the presence of light, cameras, moving microphones, a smaller playing area, and usually a more artificial stage set. Stage scenes are viewed from a fixed position, and each scene is sustained from curtain to curtain. Television is seen from many points of view as cameras move from spot to spot or scene to scene. TV "juggles time, place, and action," and more rapidly than is possible on a theater stage. The technique of television action is basically the same as stage technique, and stage training, particularly the type involved in central staging, is an important preparation for one interested in television. There are differences, of course, but these are largely matters of modification and adaptability.

Writing for Television.[24] Television has provided a new medium for writers. The aspiring television scriptor asks two questions, What are the comparisons and contrasts inherent in television and radio dramatic script writing? How can I sell my services to the industry?

The basic answer to the first question is that all good dramatic writing, whether it is for stage, screen, radio, or television, springs from the ability of the writer to originate an interesting story, tell it in terms of characters who are themselves interesting and believable within the premise of the story, and who are endowed with the rare gift of talking like people. Each writing medium, however, has its limitations, its advantages, its disadvantages.

There are five respects in which the problem of the television writer differs from that of the radio author:

1. The TV writer is free from the necessity of writing dialogue which is purely expository. In television it is no longer necessary to write, "Look out, he's got a gun." The audience can see he has a gun—if the actor remembers to come to the right marking at the right time and remembers which camera is supposed to be on him, if the camera is where it is supposed to be at that point in action, if the camera director calls the right shot, and if the dialogue director pushes the right button. When one of these things goes wrong—which doesn't happen often—the audience may be treated to a masterpiece of unself-conscious performance by a stagehand walking across the field of action totally unaware of his little moment.

2. Unlike the radio author, the TV writer is helped by the use of sets. A typical home set, for example, tells the audience what sort of home this is, something of the income bracket of the occupants, and implies whether the people who live there are neat or sloppy, old-fashioned or modern, literate or illiterate, all of which would require more expository dialogue in radio. On the other hand, sets place a limitation on television. If a bit of action involves a really grandiose setting, the radio audience can visualize it better than a television presentation can afford to do it or have the physical space in which to do it. This applies particularly to exteriors. You have noticed, perhaps, that practically all live television drama is confined to indoor settings. Exteriors, unless quite small and extremely well executed, are not too satisfactory. A program

[24] Special information on the subject of writing for television was supplied the author by Jack Van Nostrand, vice-president, Sullivan, Stauffer, Colwell & Bayless, Inc., Advertising, New York.

may employ some filmed exterior shots, but they seldom involve dialogue, being backed by the narrator working live and unseen from the studio. This is an expensive procedure and is not used by many current programs. In fact, some experimenting has been done in solving set problems by eliminating sets altogether. Actors work in either close-ups or medium shots against an absolutely black background, and only the slightest props are used such as a telephone, the corner of a counter, or a mailbox. The experiments may prove that certain types of stories can be done better through symbolism and suggestion than complete realism.

3. The TV writer is helped by the writer's pantomime. Audio drama, which takes place wholly on the stage of imagination, now becomes both aural and visual. A good actor can, with facial expression or some slight physical movement, give a poignancy or touch of humor which vocalization alone cannot achieve. It will be argued for some time, though, whether the purely imaginative drama does not require a more delicate and deft handling of spoken language.

4. The fourth respect in which the radio and television authors find themselves dealing with contrasting problems relates to technical problems incident to the job of moving live characters in continuous sequence before the eye of the camera. In going from one scene to another, the actor must be allowed time to get there; either he must have a logical exit from the first one before its conclusion or there must be a bit of business on stage in the seconds before he makes a logical entrance. If a costume change is required, the problem is more than doubled, although sometimes a change can be made by hastily donning or changing a jacket. Unless considerable lapses in time or changes of locale are involved, audiences will allow, or not even notice, the same costumes throughout a story if they are not too conspicuous. Another problem is how to get gracefully from scene to scene. If no particular need exists for definitely establishing locale or time change, this can usually be done by a simple dissolve. The easiest, and probably the least artistic, way to do it is to go from one scene to a completely black screen, then up to the new scene. However, many people in the business do not like this technique and try to avoid it whenever possible. When a narrator is used as a regular part of the show's format, the problem is easier, but he must not be allowed to become merely a writer's convenience. There are many devices to set locale changes, such as superimposing a Rome baggage sticker upon a New York sticker, cross-fading from a New York phone book to a Paris book, and fading up to see the same character handling each. Such devices can be clever but can easily be overworked. If an audience becomes too conscious of them, they defeat their own purpose. The same thing applies to time lapses when established by shots of a watch, a calendar, etc. *These things are the basic responsibility of the*

writer. The editor, producer, or director will help him, but none of them feels well disposed toward the writer who ignores these factors.

5. The physical nature of television drama makes necessary a script format quite different from that used in radio. The TV author must set down not only dialogue but stage directions as well, involving cameras, moving microphones, lights, and production personnel. Script formats may differ somewhat according to preferences of directors. One director prefers his format with the narration to the right of the description of the film action; another prefers to have the entire right side of the page blank to allow him, the camera director, technical director, audio and video directors to mark cameras and camera shots in advance. This latter form is a little difficult to read at first until one learns that narration and visual action written in sequence will occur simultaneously. It is vitally important to the various directors, however, to have the shots at their fingertips because they have no time for "second thoughts" when they are on the air. The convenience of the actors is not considered in deciding script format since they work from memory and not from the written page. (CBS uses still another format similar to the second one explained above, but with the blank space to the left of the page.)

The two shows, *The Big Story*[25] and *The Door with No Name*,[26] are both sponsored by Pall Mall cigarettes and although handled by the same agency and broadcast over the same network, the scripts contain marked differences in format as shown by the excerpts on pages 361 to 374.

6. A sixth comparison of the radio and television author is that the latter functions much more as a team member. It is still possible for a radio man to "do" a show in the sense that he originates the idea, writes the script, casts the show, directs the performance, and even supervises the selection of music. This cannot be true in television. The author is an integral part of a large team each member of which has specific and coordinate responsibilities. He is definitely allied with the technical and production staff. The number of players on a television team is incredibly large compared to the staff required for an audio broadcast. This point is emphasized by a personal experience related by an advertising agency executive in a personal letter to the author:

I've been doing the agency supervision on a show for ――――――. It's an average show—average size, average budget, not big, not small. The client wanted to give a party back-stage when we went off the air for the summer,

(*continued on page 375*)

[25] Excerpt from *The Big Story*, written by Arnold Perl, is used by courtesy of American Cigarette and Cigar Company and Bernard J. Procktor Productions, Inc.
[26] Excerpt from *The Door with No Name* used by courtesy of American Cigarette and Cigar Company.

THE DOOR WITH NO NAME

(FILM)

FADE IN ZOOM SHOT OF PELL MELL PACK	CHAPPELL: PELL MELL Famous
TO CU. HOLD FOR:	Cigarettes present: -
	"THE DOOR WITH NO NAME"

(THE MUSICAL THEME WILL, OF COURSE,

ESTABLISH AND BACK THIS ZOOM AND

FOLLOWING NARRATION.)

DISSOLVE TO:

THE DOOR WITH NO NAME

FADE IN: (LIVE)

INTERIOR - HALLWAY

LONG SHOT - "THE DOOR"

(THIS IS A VERY SOLID LOOKING DOOR,
DRAMATIC IN ITS PLAIN, BARE SURFACE.
THE ONLY ADORNMENT IS A HEAVY, METAL
DOORKNOB. IN SEQUENCE TO THE
NARRATION, THE CAMARA MOVES IN UNTIL
THE DOORKNOB FILLS THE SCREEN.)

NARRATOR:

The Door With No Name -- quiet passage

into an arsenal of espionage and

counter-espionage -- port of doom to

smugglers and subversives -- point

of no return to enemy agents and

international racketeers. Behind

this mute panel is housed the Star

Chamber in Government Intelligence.

Here, hand-picked Operatives receive

instructions to solve the unsolved

crime, meet the unknown and call it

by its proper name, accomplish that

which to all others has proven

impossible. The man who crosses this

threshold carries life or death in

his hands -- the life or death of

one - of many - or of entire nations.

It's more often just one -- his own!

361

(DISSOLVE TO:)

(INTERIOR - OFFICE BEHIND DOOR)

(CLOSE SHOT - ASHTRAY ON DESK)

(IF POSSIBLE, THE ASHTRAY SHOULD
CORRESPOND TO THE DOORKNOB AND THE
DESK TOP TO THE SURFACE OF THE DOOR.
DOUG CARTER'S HAND COMES INTO SCENE
AND FLICKS ASHES FROM HIS CIGARETTE
INTO TRAY.)

CARTER'S VOICE:

(O.S.) Before we go on, Mr. Randolph,

I have a question.

RANDOLPH'S VOICE:

(O.S.) By all means.

(THE CAMERA MOVES UP TO A CLOSE SHOT
OF DOUG CARTER. CARTER IS AN
AGREEABLE BLEND OF INTELLIGNCE,
ASSURANCE AND PHYSICAL CHARM. WE
LIKE HIM.)

CARTER:

(EARNESTLY) Why did you call me in

for this assignment?

(THE CAMERA PULLS BACK TO A MEDIUM
SHOT TO INCLUDE JOHN RANDOLPH. MR.
RANDOLPH IS. BEYOND MIDDLE AGE,
EXTREMELY BUSINESS-LIKE, BUT NOT
WITHOUT WARMTH AND, FROM TIME TO
TIME, A CERTAIN HUMOUR. THE OFFICE
IS TYPICALLY GOVERNMENT, WITH A FEW
EXTRAS. POSSIBLY A LARGE MAP COVERS
ONE WALL. SEAL ON WALL.

RANDOLPH:

We've had our eyes on you ever since

the war, Mr. Carter. (INDICATING A

LARGE DOSSIER ON HIS DESK) If you're

interested in the life history of

Douglas Carter, you'll find it all

right here.

Your background is excellent. Your

war record with Army Intelligence is

remarkable. We need you.

CARTER:

(PLEASED) Well, naturally, I'm

grateful for the honor —

RANDOLPH:

(FLATLY)   When I outline your
assignment, you may not be so
grateful.

CARTER:

(CHALLENGE WITH A SMILE)   I'm ready
to listen.

(RANDOLPH MEETS THE CHALLENGE IN
CARTER'S EYES, THEN, CONVINCED THAT
HE HAS CHOSEN THE RIGHT MAN, HE
BECOMES VERY MATTER OF FACT.)

RANDOLPH:

(TERSELY)   You will leave for Paris -
tonight.   There you will make contact
with an Operative who calls himself
Poska.

(CLOSE SHOT - CARTER AS HE LISTENS
INTENTLY)

RANDOLPH'S VOICE:

(O. S.) (Cont'd) ˙ We don't know this
man, personally - few people in the
world know what he looks like.   This
fact, alone, makes him very useful.

(ANOTHER ANGLE - TO INCLUDE RANDOLPH)

RANDOLPH:

(CONT'D)   However, the important
thing is the information he carries -
top secret.   It's in document form.
But -- (WITH EMPHASIS)   the documents
are worth absolutely nothing unless
they're combined with certain
information in our possession.   Do
you understand?

CARTER:

(HE DOES)   A jigsaw.

RANDOLPH:

Exactly.

                    CARTER:

Is this man, Poska, an American?

                    RANDOLPH:

No - but his work in the Underground

proved his loyalties beyond a doubt.

He's worked assignments through New

York for many years, but he's never

been in this country - we've never

been able to get him across. Now,

it's your try.

(HE TAKES UP AN ENVELOPE FROM HIS
DESK AND GOES TO CARTER.)

                    RANDOLPH:

Your specific job is to. bring the

man - and the information - back to

this office. It may not be easy.

(OMINOUSLY) You may have interference--

deadly interference.

(ANOTHER ANGLE - CARTER AS HE REACTS
TO THIS WARNING.)

                    CARTER:

How do I make contact?

                    RANDOLPH:

A book shop on the Rue de Charlot.

(HANDING HIM THE ENVELOPE) These

are plane tickets and passports --

yours and Poska's. (HANDING HIM A

PAPER) Your verbal codes. Naturally,

you will memorize them before you

leave this room.

(TWO SHOT - CARTER AND RANDOLPH AS
RANDOLPH'S LOOK AND TONE OF VOICE
SOFTEN FOR AN INSTANT.)

                    RANDOLPH:

I think you know how important -

and how dangerous this is.

(CARTER NODS, KNOWINGLY)

364

(WIDER ANGLE - AS RANDOLPH SHEDS
THE WARMTH AND TIGHTENS UP AGAIN.)

        RANDOLPH:

Once you leave, you're on your own.

And understand this - it's vitally

important. Under no circumstances

are you to contact this office --

any change of plan - any message from

you will mean just one thing to us -

complete failure.

(CLOSE SHOT - CARTER -- HE STARES,
LEVELLY, AT RANDOLPH INHALES
CIGARETTE WITH CHARACTERISTIC
GESTURE.)

        CARTER:

(A PROMISE) If I'm able to send a

message, it will never be sent.

(STILL LOOKING AT RANDOLPH, HE
REACHES FOR THE ASHTRAY. THE CAMERA
MOVES DOWN TO A CLOSE SHOT OF THE
TRAY AS CARTER CRUSHES OUT CIGARETTE.
THE CAMERA MOVES IN UNTIL THE TRAY
AGAIN COVERS THE SCREEN AS WE--

FADE OUT:)

(MUSIC: BRIDGE)

(DISSOLVE TO: (FILM)

CLOSE-UP OF CREST ON PELL MELL

PACK, DOLLIES BACK TO FULL CLOSE-

UP OF PACK. FADES INTO FIRST

COMMERCIAL.

AMERICAN CIGARETTE & CIGAR CO. PELL MALL FAMOUS CIGARETTES	DOOR WITH NO NAME TELEVISION OPENING COMMERCIAL - FILM #15
SIGHT	SOUND
(LITTLE MAN TAKES PALL MALL FROM PACK.)	CHAPPELL:

(LITTLE PEOPLE MARCH, IN RHYTHM, Smokers ... listen!
CARRYING CIGARETTE ON THEIR SHOULDERS.)

   GROUP: (SINGING)

Guard against throat-scratch!

Guard against throat-scratch!

(CU OF MAN #1) Guard against throat-scratch!

Enjoy the smooth, smooth

smoking of fine tobaccos.

Smoke a PELL MELL!

   CHAPPELL:

Yes, smoke PELL MELL - the

cigarette whose mildness you

can measure.

(INSERT APPROVED PUFF CHART) Puff by puff you are always

ahead when you smoke PELL MELL.

The further the smoke is

filtered through fine tobaccos,

the milder it becomes.

(AT THE WORD "5" CIGARETTES ARE At the first puff PELL MELL
CUT OFF. BETWEEN THE WORDS "5"
AND "17" CIGARETTES SHRINK GRADUALLY) smoke is filtered further than

that of any other leading

cigarette.

Moreover, after 5 puffs of each

cigarette, or 10, or 17, by actual

measure, PELL MELL's greater

length of traditionally fine

tobaccos still travels the smoke

further - filters the smoke and

makes it mild.

CU OF MAN #1 Thus, PELL MELL's fine mellow

tobaccos give you a smoothness,

mildness, and satisfaction no other

cigarette offers you.

DISSOLVE TO PACK IN MAN'S HAND. Smoke PELL MELL FAMOUS CIGARETTES
PACK ZOOMS THROUGH SCREEN. "Outstanding!" And - they are

mild!.

366

DISSOLVE TO: SUITCASE

CLOSE SHOT - SUITCASE

THE SUITCASE IS OPEN. CARTER'S
HANDS COME INTO SCENE, DEPOSIT A
LAST PAIR OF SOCKS IN THE SUITCASE,
THEN SNAP IT SHUT.
SUPERIMPOSED ON THE SUITCASE. WE
SEE A VISA BEING STAMPED, THEN
DISSOLVE OUT. AGAIN, CARTER'S HANDS
COME INTO SCENE, OPEN THE SUITCASE
AND START TO UNPACK THE CONTENTS.

(MUSIC: BG)

            NARRATOR

Three hours after receiving his

assignment, Doug Carter is on his

own - and on his way -- betting his

life for his country. A quick mind

and a strong heart are his only

weapons of defense against the

known quantity - the enemy agent -

the deadly interference.

(MUSIC: OUT)
THE CAMERA PULLS BACK TO A MEDIUM
CLOSE SHOT. WE SEE CARTER IN A
PARIS HOTEL ROOM, THE SUITCASE
ON A TABLE BESIDE HIM. HE GLANCES
AT HIS WATCH, GRABS HIS HAT UP OFF
THE TABLE AND PUTS IT ON. HE REACHES
IN A COAT POCKET AND BRINGS OUT A
SLIP OF PAPER.

INSERT: PAPER IN CARTER'S HAND
IT READS: ROUBIER BOOK SHOP
28 RUE DE CHARLOT

SOUND: A MATCH BEING STRUCK
WE SEE THE FLAME IGNITE THE PAPER.
AS IT BEGINS TO BURN WE
DISSOLVE TO:
INTERIOR - BOOK SHOP
LONG SHOT - HELENE
(SHOOTING FROM THE DOOR)
HELENE SITS IN THE REAR OF THE
SHOP ON A SMALL STOOL. SHE IS
HUNCHED OVER A BOOK, COMPLETELY
ABSORBED WITH IT. WE DON'T SEE HER
FACE, HER BACK IS TO THE CAMERA.

THE BIG STORY

AMERICAN CIGARETTE & CIGAR CO.	BIG STORY TELEVISION
PALL MALL FAMOUS CIGARETTES	OPENING COMMERCIAL - FILM #15

SIGHT	SOUND
Little man takes PALL MALL from pack.	CHAPPELL: Smokers ... listen!
Little people march, in rhythm, carrying cigarette on their shoulders.	GROUP: (SINGING) Guard against throat-scratch! Guard against throat-scratch! Guard against throat-scratch!
CU of Man #1.	Enjoy the smooth, smooth smoking of fine tobaccos. Smoke a PELL MELL!
	CHAPPELL: Yes, smoke PELL MELL - the cigarette whose mildness you can measure.
Insert approved Puff Chart.	Puff by puff you are always ahead when you smoke PELL MELL. The further the smoke is filtered through fine tobaccos, the milder it becomes.
At the word "5" cigarettes are cut off. Between the words "5" and "17" cigarettes shrink gradually.	At the first puff PELL MELL smoke is filtered further than that of any other leading cigarette. Moreover, after 5 puffs of each cigarette, or 10, or 17, by actual measure, PELL MELL'S greater length of tradition-ally fine tobaccos still travels the smoke further - filters the smoke and makes it mild.
CU of Man #1.	Thus, PELL MELL'S fine mellow tobaccos give you a smoothness, mildness and satisfaction no other cigarette offers you.
Dissolve to pack in Man's hand.	Smoke PELL MELL FAMOUS CIGARETTES -
Pack zooms through screen.	"Outstanding!" And - they are mild!

Arnold Perl

THE BIG STORY

(Paul Hochuli: Houston (Texas) Press)

1. (F) PELL MELL pack ZOOMS up to CU: the title "BIG STORY" drops over the pack.

        (L) CHAPPELL: PELL MELL FAMOUS CIGARETTES present ... THE BIG STORY!

            FADE IN:

                MUSIC: BIG, FOREBODING, BEHIND .....

2. (F) GENERAL SHOT OF HOUSTON.

Houston, Texas.

            DISSOLVE TO:

3. (F) PRESS BLDG. AND LETTERING.

The Houston Press. And tonight to Paul Hochuli of the Houston Press, for his BIG STORY.

           (MORE)

4. (L) PRESS CITY ROOM. HOC is 43, big, athletic, likable. He is a Texan, proud of it, a man with a good amount of modesty as well as pride. HE is seated at his desk, and his attitude reveals the state of weariness as described in the story. HE has been keyed-up for sometime and that feeling permiates his speech.

> HOC:
> My name is Paul Hochuli. They tell me I'm the number one police beat man on the paper. That means that I'm in from the start and there at the end. I got to the police beat by way of Rice Institute (got All Conference mention), and the sports desk. As you know, we in Texas breed them big: big men, big women -- and sometimes, big crimes. This is a story about the biggest 36 hours I ever spent in my life. This is just how it happened, taken from the pages of my paper.

5. (L) BIG STORY title card.

6. (F) HOC, weary, is walking slowly down the steps, out of a coffee shop and goes across the street, where HE enters the building which is a hospital There is no rush about it, he has got time and he takes it -- needs it.

> DISSOLVE TO:

7. (L) The HOSPITAL ANTEROOM. CAPTAIN DAVE BLAZER, a man about 15 years HOC's junior is peeking in a door of a hospital room. HE closes it because he is not yet allowed to go in. From his actions, we know he is anxious to get in and talk to the patient. He nods as he sees HOC, but pays little attention to him, being preoccupied with his problem.

> HOC:
> How's he doing?

DAVE shakes his head sadly.

> HOC:
> Leave it to the kids. Where a cop wouldn't go near a punk like that with two guns drawn and a squad with him, a 14 year old will go running up and try to stop him.

> DAVE:
> Well, he ain't going to go running up to anybody anymore. He'll be lucky if he can ever walk.

> HOC: (DISTRESSED)
> I didn't know that.

the makers of PELL MELL FAMOUS CIGARETTES are proud to have presented the PELL MELL Award.

MUSIC: BRIDGE

NARR:
There had been three robberies in the last 24 hours. And that meant that you hadn't slept in the last 24 hours. In that time you had seen the manager at the William Penn Eat Shoppe ($200 from the till), a man from a moving and storage warehouse ($475 and a crack on the head), and a little while ago, the front office of a furniture store (no money, because the robber was interrupted). And it was that interruption that

sent you here now, to the Misericordia Hospital. Because the person who had tried the interrupting was a kid, 14 years old, and he had it bad.

During this last speech, DAVE has once again
opened the door and now apparently he can go
in and does so. He is the center of attention.
and he walks into the hospital room where ERNIE,
the kid, is in bed. ERNIE is a young negro,
about 14, who has no real idea of the seriousness of his injury or any real concern for his
own minor heroism. He is enjoying the situation. During the ensuing action HOC walks in
not sure that he will be allowed to stay, but
taking full advantage when DAVE doesn't throw
him out.

> ERNIE:
> Hello, Captain. Hey, I'm getting to
> be a big man! Six doctors come to
> see me, a couple of aunts I hadn't
> seen in five years, and now you. Hey,
> this is all right!

> DAVE:
> How do you feel!

> ERNIE:
> Fine. You know what I had for lunch?
> Half a chicken -- a whole half a chicken
> with coleslaw. But I'm worried.

> DAVE:
> What's the matter, Ernie?

> ERNIE:
> Well, the doc said I had to stay in the
> bed -- he didn't know how long. Prac-
> tising starts this Friday.

> DAVE:
> Practising?

> ERNIE:
> Didn't you know I'm the hottest first
> baseman in the Morton Street League?

> DAVE:
> No, I didn't know -- Oh, sure, sure.
> I remember.

> ERNIE:
> Stole 31 bases last year. Better than
> Jackie -- but that's not saying Jackie
> might not beat me out this year. Hey,
> you don't think it's going to interfere
> with my ball playing, do you?

> DAVE:
> I don't know. No, no -- I don't think so.

> ERNIE:
> That's what I told the doc. You know,
> those guys worry. They worry all the time
> about a scratch. (AFFABLY) And I don't
> feel nothing.

> DAVE:
> How good a look did you get at the guy,
> Ernie?

ERNIE:
Well, not too good on account of he was
running away. You know I ran after him.
Only when he turned around to fire the
shot and then I saw him a little bit.
But I kind of fell down -- you know what
I mean. (HE LAUGHS)

DAVE:
You did all right.

ERNIE:
But I saw the car. That tan coupe.
Even when I was laying on the ground
and my leg was hurting then -- I said
to myself "The cops are going to ask
you what the car looked like." I
couldn't see the license but the right
fender was crumbled, white wall tires
and the car was a '32 Chrysler. The
tires was all new.

DAVE:
But you didn't see the guy at all?

ERNIE:
Well, you know -- a guy running from
the back. Just looked like a guy.
White man. Kind of a runty type of
guy.

DAVE:
What was he wearing?

ERNIE:
Gee, I didn't really look. I didn't
do a very good job, did I?

DAVE:
You did swell, kid.

HOC:
What's your whole name, Ernie?

ERNIE:
Ernie Crighton. C-R-I-G-H-T-O-N.

HOC:
I'm going to put you in the papers,
Ernie.

ERNIE:
Hey, no kidding! Hey you know, I
never had my name in the papers before.
What paper, mister?

HOC:
The Press.

ERNIE:
I'm going to buy about 10 copies.

HOC:
Don't you buy anything, Ernie. I'll
send you about 10 copies.

ERNIE:
Will you?

                    HOC:
                 Sure, Ernie.

This conversation has been the end of
movement headed by DAVE out of the room.
Both DAVE & HOC wave "so long."

                    DAVE: (SOMBER)
                 Take it easy, kid.

The two men move outside the room.

                    DAVE:
                 I didn't want to spoil it for you,
                 but no paper stuff.

                    HOC:
                 What's the matter? I mean, the kid
                 deserves it.

                    DAVE:
                 Sure, sure. I just don't want to go
                 around tipping the guy off that we
                 know what his car looks like. I don't
                 want us printing the fact that we know
                 he's a sharp man with a gun.

                    HOC:
                 I didn't know he was a sharpie.

                    DAVE:
                 Well, between you and me, he could have
                 laid that kid out, but he didn't. He
                 just took one bullet and buried it in
                 that kid's kneecap. Just cut him down
                 like that -- one shot.

                    HOC:
                 That's shooting.

                    DAVE:
                 That's why no Ernie Crighton, no tan
                 coupe, no sharp-shooter mentioned.

                    HOC:
                 I'd like to do something for the kid.

                    DAVE:
                 So would I. Best thing we can do is
                 button it up and get the guy.

                    HOC:
                 You got a point, Dave.

HE offers DAVE a cigarette, and on this WE

                    DISSOLVE TO:

8. (1) CU of a pair of hands holding a
        strong rubber-band and shooting a paper
        clip. WE FOLLOW the flight of the clip
        as it zooms dead center into a small
        target crudely drawn on a piece of a
        cardboard. It hits with a resounding
        smack. As the CAMERA pulls back, it
        reveals BRADFORD, sitting in a shabby
        sitting-room. The light in the room
        reveals that it is night outside.

                    (MORE)

372

There is a pot of coffee standing on a
table with no concern given to whether
the coffee pot burns the table or not.
The room is in general disarray, crumbled
papers on the couch that has obviously
been read. In general, a picture of a
man with insomnia. As he looks at his
watch, the door of the room opens and
EDITH, wearing a nightgown covered by a
shabby robe, enters, rubbing her eyes.

> EDITH:
> I thought you said you were coming
> to bed. (ANGRY) How many times did
> I tell you to put a piece of paper
> down before you put the coffee pot
> down on the table! You got to burn
> everything we got? What're you
> doing? (SEES THE PAPER CLIPS AND
> RUBBER BAND) What're you doing?

> BRAD:
> Go back to sleep.

> EDITH:
> I swear, you ought to have your head
> examined by one of them doctors.
> Every night "Go to sleep, go to
> sleep. I'll come to bed." But you
> don't come to bed. What're you do-
> ing with yourself?

For answer, he fires another paper clip
at the target, hits it, smiles.

> BRAD:
> I got ideas.

> EDITH:
> Sure, sure, you got ideas. You got
> a trade too. Once upon a time you
> were a paper hanger. Once upon a
> time you got up at 9 o'clock and
> went out and earned a day's pay.
> Why don't you get a job and stop
> it?

> BRAD: (FLAT)
> There's no work.

> EDITH: (GESTURES TO PAPER)
> Didn't I mark those three ads in the
> paper for you? And yesterday four of
> them. No work! There's a whole
> government project going up.

> BRAD:
> Look, you starving? Eating regularly?
> Did I give you a new coat? Didn't I
> tell you go to the store and buy a new
> dress, new shoes? Get rid of this
> junky furniture?

> EDITH:
> You ain't starting that again!

BRAD:
What's the matter -- the color of my
money don't please you? The guys in
the stores don't ask questions like
you ask. Now go back to bed will you?
I told you I ain't sleepy and I ain't
going to sleep.

EDITH:
I suppose you're going out again?

BRAD:
What's the matter -- something terrible
going out to get a glass of beer? Is
that the most terrible thing in the
world?

EDITH: (DESPERATE, TRYING TO REACH HIM)
Brad, look -- it ain't the money. I
don't care about the money that much. I
just want it to be regular and decent and
no trouble. I could fix up this place so
it could be nice and -- Don't go out
tonight.

BRAD: (DECIDES TO HUMOR HER)
Okay. Go to sleep. Go ahead. I'll be in
in a little while.

EDITH: (YAWNS)
I don't see how you can stay up. I'm
dead tired.

BRAD:
Well, I told you -- go to sleep. Ten,
fifteen minutes I'll be in.

He goes to her and kisses her. She likes him
very much and grabs him.

TELEVISION: THE NEW CHALLENGE

and, when I made out the guest list, I was surprised to find that more than 120 people worked on the show in one capacity or another. I won't bore you with the entire list, but a few might interest you. Supervisor, producer, director, assistant director, camera director, television director, (sometimes called technical director), audio director, video director, light director, light men and electricians, three camera men (minimum), two dolly men, two boom men, two boom pushers, stage manager, assistant manager, carpenters, property men, make-up director, and so on ad infinitum.

The second question asked by the ambitious television writer is, How can I sell my services? A very high percentage of writers, setting out to try television, begin by trying to originate an entire program idea—a theme for an entire series. This approach, although legitimate and sometimes successful, is fraught with particular difficulty. Even people with long experience and great ability find it difficult to sell a series because they are at the outset in competition with large and well-staffed organizations which make a business of originating television programs and are in a position to know the market. Selling a series is far more than just having an idea. It is a matter of organization, complex budgeting, and cost accounting. Writing for a specific show, the author should know about how many sets and characters an established budget allows.

It is easier for the newcomer to gain entree by attempting to write individual episodes for shows already on the air. Many agencies and program sponsors buy individual episodes and are constantly on the alert for new writers. "When we find a *consistently* good writer, he is welcomed with an enthusiasm only slightly less than that caused by the discovery of a new uranium deposit."

When scripts are bought on the open market rather than on a term contract basis, a definite assignment to write a completed script is made upon the approval of an outline. Outlines are submitted on speculation but are usually extensions of ideas which have been discussed in advance, and the margin of rejection therefore is not very large. An assignment to write a full script is a firm offer to purchase at an agreed price with the agency or network reserving the right to ask for necessary revisions. Writers are not asked for full scripts on speculation. This practice is a protection to recognized writers because it is assumed by the prospective buyer that a story outline, once approved, can be delivered in complete script form. At the same time, the procedure places the newcomer at a disadvantage because buyers uncertain about his ability to deliver will not ask him to write on speculation. It is well for the new writer, therefore, to have in hand a script or scripts of similiar types of shows which he has done to offer as samples of his work. If he has none, he should write something of his own not aimed too specifically at any one particular program, but one which could, with slight revision, be adapted to any one of several. In this way he has what he considers a good sample of his work, and he might sell it in one of several markets.

If his submitted work evidences ability to handle a writing job, he may be asked to proffer a "basic idea" for a story consonant with the format and story design of a "going" series. If this "basic idea" seems to have possibilities, the writer is assigned to do a scene-by-scene outline. When this has been approved, a meeting is arranged with the producer, the director, the writer, and the editor who functions as a coproducer. At this meeting the outline of the potential story is discussed with regard to such details as sets, props, costumes, scene transitions, visual details necessary to support narration, etc. When these details are matters of agreement, the writer starts to work on the completion of the script. If the discussion has been a thorough one and if the writer has the requisite skill, the script when completed will probably need only minor revision. The quotation of a single scene synopsis is here given to illustrate the information the writer sets down in making his presentation of story ideas and details. It is the complete scene sequence which usually is first reviewed and, when approved, the author develops it into a complete acting and directing script.

Opening Scene

(*Office behind door*)

Randolph is giving Carter his assignment. The country has been flooded with counterfeit money in quantities of ten- and twenty-dollar bills. The assumption is that the stuff is being made abroad, presumably for the purpose of undermining the economic stability of the nation. Considerable amounts have been confiscated at ports of entry and by border patrols . . . none lately, but the money still appears. There is no known setup in this country to handle such volume, and no known craftsman to turn out such quality. Carter's assignment is to locate the leader of the ring, and the source of supply, if in this country. He will work alone but is given a code in the event that anyone represents himself as a government agent. . . . Randolph tells Carter he must study up on the basic technique and terminology of photoengraving after which he will be launched with the help of a stool pigeon who is a very small cog in the big wheel, but a helpful one in such matters. Carter's assignment will begin when he is arrested for passing counterfeit money and placed in a cell with the man suspected of being a regional leader of the ring.

In conclusion, it should be emphasized that the writing market is a highly competitive one and is made more so by the shortage of network time. A writer may be able to present an excellent and acceptable idea but be met with the reply, But where can we put it? The best hope for a new series comes from a client who has a good time spot which he wants to keep and who is dissatisfied with his current show. We have been speaking, however, about dramatic writing and particularly about network productions. There are other types of TV continuity and a growing demand for writers by local and independent stations. Although rigid competition and market limitations prevail, writing for television is a challenging and profitable vocational field for those who have the requisite creative talent and ability.

The above explanation of some of the comparative aspects of radio and television may be restated for clarity by arranging the similarities and dissimilarities of the two media in parallel columns.

Radio

1. Microphones: Placed in best acoustical position; cast grouped with no regard for visual relationship. Everything balanced for sound.

2. Radio is a system of audio transmission.

3. Studio: May be a small room, empty or partially empty. Equipped with a single microphone; a microphone, table, and chairs; or with a mobile sound truck and setup arrangements for an orchestra. Several microphones may be used according to the number of performers and various technical requirements.

4. A radio program requires no special sets, properties, or accessories.

Television

1. Microphones: Placement dictated by visual nature of television, stage set, and the fluid nature of the dramatic action. Suspended on cables, hidden behind bits of scenery, or hung on long booms which move over the heads of the actors, they are placed outside the camera pickup frame, and in such position as not to cast shadows in front of the lights. Their positioning must ensure satisfactory audio pickup but, at the same time, exclude background noise and echo.

2. Television embraces two complete transmission systems: audio and video.

3. Studio: A practical working set in which the program is framed for presentation. This set may be either impressionistic or three-dimensional (realistic). The background against which the show is played is particularly important to the dramatic story—its style, locale, period, and atmosphere. The set design is often multiple in character, permitting continuous action as the program progresses from scene to scene and from locale to locale.

4. Set dressings, properties, and accessories are necessary to complement the basic set design. "A set is more than paint and canvas. It's an

Radio

Television

easy chair, too . . . and an office desk . . . a dozen roses and a dice-table . . . a cut-glass decanter and an ivory-handled cane." Properties are selected according to how they will look on the camera under the 10 shades of gray scale used in the black-and-white medium.

5. Costumes: Unnecessary in radio.

5. Costumes: Selected to fit the character's role, period, style, and mood of the show. The television camera is very critical of detail.

6. Lighting: The illumination of a radio studio is purely functional. There must be adequate brilliance for performers to read their scripts.

6. Lighting: Studio lighting is basic to telecasting. The sensitivity and color response of the television camera demand careful selection of background details. Dramatic mood, key, and atmosphere are achieved in large part through careful studio lighting.

7. Sound effects: Mechanical or recorded. Used extensively to create "pictures in the mind."

7. Sound effects. Television combines auditory and visual stimulation and therefore places less reliance on sound effects. The medium, however, uses both recorded and mechanical sound.

8. Video effects: None.

8. Video effects: Uses such tools as film inserts, miniatures, background projections, maps, and cartoons. These are employed to achieve transitions, the reduction of production costs, further animation or eye appeal, and for surprise or novelty effects.

9. Make-up: None required.

9. Make-up: Television performers, like stage and film actors, use make-up, but not for the purpose of creating illusions or compensating for actor-audience distance. The TV camera reproduces what is normally seen by the naked eye. Thus, make-up is used to afford protection, not to give color; to cover natural skin pigments; and to achieve a smooth, monotonous tone for proper light reflection.

Radio

10. Music: Live and recorded. Used at the discretion of the director to identify the program (signature), to introduce, close, and bridge scenes, intensify mood, indicate locale, and implement a montage.

11. Direction: The radio director works with a one-dimensional system —a monaural sound system, directed to one sense only. He can approximate the transmission or projection of vertical and horizontal movements of sound only by varying the distance relationship of microphone and sound source. He must depend on the imagination of the hearer to complete a full delineation of the picture. It is his hope that technical devices common to audio broadcasting will produce a uniform response—that all listeners will "see" the picture in the same way.

Audio pictures as implemented by sound are achieved by

a. Cutting from one sound source to another

b. Fade-in and fade-out of sound

c. Cross-fading

d. Blending of two or more sound sources

e. Use of special electronic effects such as echo chambers and filter microphones

12. Writing: The radio writer tells his story in terms of three elements only: sound, music, and voice.

The radio script writer utilizes the entire page. Sound and music directions, capitalized and underlined, are listed in the dialogue or placed in vertical line with the cast names listed at the left margin of the page.

The number of characters in radio

Television

10. Music: The use which radio makes of music applies in general to television. However, in radio, music is a more functional tool, serving as it does to etch the action which takes place on the stage of the listener's imagination. Somewhat less extensive use of music is required by television continuity.

11. Direction: The television director works with a system which appeals to hearing and sight. While visual elements, too, will be interpreted differently by different viewers, there will be more uniformity of response. The director, knowing what the audience is seeing, has more control over their attention and reactions.

The television director uses these radio tools, but he achieves pictorial effects by employing camera techniques such as

a. Cutting from one camera source to another

b. Fading-in and fading-out his pictures

c. Dissolving one picture into another

d. Superimposing one picture on another

e. Varying camera distance and depth of lighting

f. Creating distortions

g. Changing points of view

12. Writing: Television communication utilizes seen movement: gestures, action, pantomime, facial expression, and stage business. The program is further vivified by the use of costumes, scenery, lighting effects, and properties. This extension of the radio medium expands the scope of the writer's function and responsibility.

Radio

drama is limited by cost factors, of course, but particularly by audience ability to keep each character clearly identified.

13. Acting: The radio actor reads interpretively from a script. His field of movement, or action, is limited by a fixed microphone.

14. Control room: An *engineer* controls the sound output, sound balance, and the blending of microphone levels. Sound effects originate in the studio.

Television

The television script page is divided into two columns: video and audio. The audio (dialogue) column is paralleled with instructions to camera men and film projectionists, and with descriptions of visual action and required sets, etc.

The number of characters in a television drama is restricted by the coverage limitations of the camera.

13. Acting: The television performer, who combines radio and stage acting, must be able to memorize quickly, sustain a performance through many distractions, and control his characterizations according to the intimacy of the medium. In radio, the actor goes to the microphone: in television the microphone and camera come to him.

14. Control room: A *sound engineer* presides over the same type of console as found in the radio control booth. He governs microphone output and provides recorded music and recorded sound effects from turntables adjacent to the audio console.

Video engineer presides over pictures from each camera which are registered on a video control panel. By means of a set of knobs on the front of his monitor panel, he controls the pictures for contrast, brightness, shading, horizontal and vertical adjustments.

Film projectionist provides requisite film sequences, slides, and baloptican pictures. (The projectionist is not situated in the control room, but in an adjacent booth. His work, however, is essentially a part of control room operations.)

Technical director in liaison with the program director, has charge of the crew. In most operations he is the

Radio

Television

"switcher" who, by means of buttons, levers, and switches, cuts from one picture to another and manages dissolves, superimpositions, fades, etc.

Related to the program director and the engineers in the control room, are studio personnel:

Cameramen are stationed on the floor of the studio and assisted by dolly men.

Boom man manipulates a boom microphone to achieve satisfactory pick-up without allowing the mike to enter the picture.

Stage manager, also called the floor manager, is the director's liaison with the program or talent personnel. He receives and transmits instructions concerning stage directions, acting cues, the introduction of title cards, and other production details.

The *radio director* and engineer can converse orally when both are in the control booth. When the director is working from the studio, they communicate by light signals or by sign language.

The *television director* communicates with his associates in the studio by telephone or through head-set receivers. He must be able to maintain contact at all times. The director is also provided with a talk-back system to the studio. This cannot be used, of course, when the program is on the air.

The radio director is concerned only with the transmission of sound patterns. These are monitored by means of earphones or a control-room loud-speaker.

The television director is concerned with sound and picture transmission. On a series of viewing screens in the control room, he scans the product of each camera on a preview monitor, makes necessary corrections requisite to satisfactory transmission, and then rechecks the result on an on-the-air monitor.

QUESTIONS

1. Give a brief, nontechnical explanation of television as a process of transmitting and receiving pictures.

2. To what extent does the technical development of television parallel the development of radio?

3. What was Nikow's contribution to practical television?

4. Why is the name, Zworykin, important in the history of television development?

5. What tests in the United States first demonstrated the potential possibility of transmitting pictures?

6. What is the meaning of "line definition"?

7. Summarize the developments which took place from 1947 to 1949.

8. What prophecies were made in 1950 concerning the future of television's growth and acceptance?

9. What arguments can be made to refute the claim that radio will be "put out of business" by television?

10. What is Phonovision?

11. Summarize in parallel columns the social advantages and disadvantages of television.

12. For what basic reason may television fail to rise above the alleged mediocrity of radio?

13. Discuss TV's educational promise.

14. Should a fixed percentage of TV channels be allocated to the exclusive use of noncommercial organizations?

15. What is color television and how does it work?

16. What is meant by "compatible color television"?

17. Why is television an effective sales medium? Cite examples of TV advertising to illustrate your answer.

18. Contrast television and radio production. In what respects are they similar and dissimilar? Answer from the viewpoints of studios, control rooms, basic equipment, production, and script writing.

19. Writing exercise: (a) Write a straight narrative plot line for a half-hour story using a specific show or type of show as a model. (b) Make a scene-by-scene outline of the story, using four sets and keeping in mind such essential elements as size of cast, properties, and costume. (c) Expand the scene outline into a full-length working script (dialogue and production directions), allowing yourself three cameras.

PART IV

PART IV

PERFORMANCE MANUAL: PRODUCTION
AND ACTING PROBLEMS

The problem and techniques of radio production and acting are covered in the following exercises. They are arranged in the order of increased complexity proceeding from elementary microphone principles to intricate blends of voice, sound, and music.

The first set of exercises establishes an understanding of voice level and microphone distance, and the second set makes clear the application of this understanding. Vocal practice is supplemented by practical drills in the handling of sound and music effects. These three introductory sections then find specific application in short dialogue passages and dramatic scenes illustrating basic acting and production principles. Particular emphasis is given to perspective, balance, suppressed speech, the timing of sound effects, characterization, emotional interpretation, voice differentiation, and the employment of effective music.

LIST OF EXERCISES

A. Voice Level and Microphone Distance
Normal conversational level—Calling—Shouting—Restrained, suppressed emotion—Full release of strong emotion—*Sotto voce*

B. Applications of Voice Level and Microphone Distance
Exit and entrance fades—Balance and perspective

C. Sound and Music Effects
Doors—Steps—General sound—Music

D. Studio Practice
1. Perspective (*Reached a Verdict?*)
2. Balance and proportion (*Order in the Court*)
3. Balance (*Congratulations*)
4. Background, balance, fade (*The Party*)
5. Suppressed dialogue (*Will You Help Me?*)
6. Filtered speech (*So This Is Death*)
7. Timing, sound (*How Much Will They Lend Us?*)
8. Pistol shots (*Outside the Bella Union*)
9. Ad libs, off-mike, fades (*Lady Cornbury*)
10. Crowd voices, sound levels (*Give in, Bryan*)
11. Balance, perspective, footsteps (*Want a Job?*)
12. Voice perspective (*Claim Jumpers*)
13. Crowd chatter, excitement (*I'll Go with You*)
14. Complicated sound (*You've Got to Escape*)
15. Complicated sound (*Rain*)
16. Complicated sound (*Stalled*)
17. Pictured action (*Dig, You Rascal, Dig*)
18. Sustained, complicated sound (*The Wager*)
19. Sound timing, English accent (*Phantom*)
20. Emotion, galloping horse, music to cover (*Don't Leave Me*)
21. Music, sound problem, characterization (*Shoes for Paul*)
22. Sound and acting problem (*Spires*)
23. Narration, background sound, balance (*Clara Barton*)
24. Emotional transitions (*What Do You Want?*)
25. Characterization (*Mrs. Spendover*)
26. Characterization (*Jean Valjean*)
27. Emotional interpretation (*Call from Beyond*)
28. Voice differentiation (*Where's Carol?*)
29. Voice differentiation (*How's the Kid Doing?*)
30. Voice differentiation (*Daily Bugle*)
31. Voice differentiation (*All Right, Hadley*)
32. Picture (*What Did You Lie for?*)

33. Montage (*Unknown Soldier*)
34. Montage (*Dance Band*)
35. Montage (*Lafayette*)
36. Dramatic narration

A. VOICE LEVEL AND MICROPHONE DISTANCE

The radio performer must be familiar with the medium through which he is working. Acting before a microphone is different in several respects from stage acting. The student who has been trained for the stage finds it necessary to make many modifications of established acting habits.

One of the first things a radio actor learns is that he is not concerned with voice projection. There is no balcony, no last row, no dead areas. He will use a voice level requisite to the dramatic scene as it would be played in the actual life situation. In other words, his real audience is the actor or actors associated with him in the scene. A stage, it is said, is a room minus one wall in order that an audience may see and hear what is going on. In the radio play the audience is in the room.

It is difficult for the radio actor at first to appreciate fully the sensitivity of a microphone or the degree to which his voice is amplified—to realize that he can speak very quietly and yet be heard distinctly. The failure to understand and utilize this aspect of his medium leads to a distortion of the dramatic picture he is projecting. In particular he must never give the impression that he is acting. To do so is to lose the immediacy and intimacy of radio drama.

We do not mean that the actor always creeps on tiptoe and shushes his way through his scenes. He will laugh quietly and boisterously, sob softly and shriek hysterically, speak quietly and shout angrily, but always as he would in the precise life situation and without the consciousness that he is addressing an audience.

The actor will learn in a very short time the relationship of voice level and microphone distance. In fact, one develops what may be called a "mike sense" which regulates changes of physical position during the action of the play and the reading of lines. The following exercises are suggested to help you develop this sense. They begin with a series of words and phrases to be spoken in a normal tone but at various distances from the microphone. Then, normal conversational dialogue is stepped up to the more intense voice levels used in scenes requiring *calling* and *shouting*. The interpretation of emotion may call for quietness, restraint, and suppression or, at the other extreme, for unrepressed and vociferous expression. Exercises for this range of tone are also prescribed. There are occasions when the actor will use a very soft speech and others when he may actually whisper. Situations covering these requisites are offered for practice.

Normal Conversational Level

1. Take a position 12 inches from the microphone and speak in a normal voice sufficient for broadcast level, "Good morning."

2. Repeat the words at the same intensity from a distance of 2, 4, and 6 feet. The monitor pot, or rheostat, should not be turned up, but the V.I. (volume indicator) reading should be observed. The effect of moving off-mike to the above stated position will be to reduce sharply the audible tone level. Roughly speaking, the intensity of the tone will diminish according to the formula: *the intensity of sound varies inversely with the square of the distance.*

3. Repeat the experiment, moving off-mike at a 45-degree angle. (You will be partially off-beam.)

4. Repeat the experiment moving off to the side of the microphone facing in the same direction. You will be moving out of the beam into the dead area. What is the effect upon the intensity and intelligibility of the voice? How rapid is the diminution of the sound?

5. Repeat the experiment saying the phrase four times as you gradually turn your back to the microphone. The last speech will be given as you face away from the mike.

6. Repeat these four tests with other phrases, sentences, short speeches, and casual dialogue:

(*a*) Hello there, how are you?
(*b*) I got back yesterday.
(*c*) I couldn't find him.
(*d*) Why do you want to go?
(*e*) He gave me wrong information.
(*f*) Of course I feel sorry for him, but he makes his trouble worse by worrying.
(*g*) Sorry we're late, but we got caught in that crosstown traffic.
(*h*) Take this road down to Five Points and turn right on 22. Benton lives on the left 3 miles out.
(*i*) Gee, Mom, I can't tell him that. He'll know it's just an excuse. I've got to give him a reason.

7. Crosswords

(1) What's the name of a tribal chief of Turkestan?
(2) How many letters?
(1) Eight.
(2) Got any of them?
(1) Blank, blank, H, O, U, blank, I, N.
(2) H-mmm, I don't know. . . . What do you waste your time on that stuff for anyway?
(1) Oh, it's fun.
(2) Silly, if you ask me.
(1) I didn't ask you.

(2) You asked for a tribal chief in Turkestan, eight letters. Who cares?
(1) I do.
(2) Why?
(1) It'll make this puzzle come out.
(2) O.K. I'll help you.

8. Any Mail?

(1) Get any mail today?
(2) Nothing but bills.
(1) We ought to be hearing from Dick.
(2) It takes a long time to get mail from Japan . . . especially this time of the year.
(1) We don't know he's reached there yet.
(2) He left San Francisco on the fourth. That's almost a month.
(1) He might have been held up at Hawaii.
(2) Then we certainly should have heard.
(1) Well, you know Dick. He'll write when he gets ready. No use worrying about him.

9. Overheard at a College Registration Desk

(1) What you got the third period, Jack?
(2) Archeology.
(1) Pete's sake. What you want that stuff for?
(2) Requirement.
(1) Yeah, I know; but what good is it going to be?
(2) Meet the requirement.
(1) Why don't you take chem? Lot more fun.
(2) Not for me, brother. I've got to pass.
(1) Chem ain't tough.
(2) Doc Jackson is.
(1) Oh, he's O.K.
(2) I'll take my chances with old Buzzell. Anybody can get by him. Say, where do I hand in these registration books?
(1) Over there at the east door.
(2) O.K. Be seeing you.
(1) Coming down to the house for lunch?
(2) Yeah, if I get through this line in time.

Calling. The above exercises are prescribed to test the effect of distance on *normal* or *conversational* speech level, but script demands call for voice levels ranging from whispering to shouting. Let us experiment with words and phrases involving emotional excitation and a consequent increase of vocal projection.

How far from the microphone should one stand when calling to someone at a distance? The exact distance cannot be stated. It is obvious, however, that one will not take quite the same position required for normal speech. The actual distance will be determined in part by the speaker's natural vocal intensity. The voice in the present exercise must be on-mike; it should not give an off-mike effect. Speak the following phrases from different distances and from slightly different angles until the best results are obtained:

- (a) Oh, Mary!
- (b) Hello.
- (c) Here we are, up here.
- (d) Look out!
- (e) Stand back, stand back.
- (f) Get those people away from there.
- (g) Don't come any closer. We're warning you.

Shouting. "Shouting" is basically similar to "calling." We differentiate the terms because the former is associated more clearly with emotional motivation and is more impersonal. Various dramatic situations will come to mind wherein characters use top vocal intensity in giving directions or in reactions to dramatic stimuli. Again, the shout may be either on-mike or off-mike, and both situations should be handled in the following practice routine. Often, these shouts are blended with sound (waves, wind, thunder, cannon, crashes), and this combination of sound and voice will be treated under the production problems of balance and perspective.

On-mike
- (a) Help! Help!
- (b) Go on back—back!
- (c) Run—run!
- (d) Bring him out, bring him out.
- (e) You're out too far—come back.
- (f) Where are you? Answer me.

Off-mike
- (a) Look out below!
- (b) Come up and get us.
- (c) Stay where you are.
- (d) We're coming in.
- (e) I can't make it.
- (f) Up here! Hurry!

Restrained, Suppressed Emotion

1. Louise Davis is called from the party she is giving for a group of friends to meet a man whom the maid has shown to the library.

- (1) Yes? Did you—John!
- (2) That's right, keep your voice down and don't call your friends. I'll only be here a minute.

(1) Why, you—you brazen. . . .

(2) Names don't matter, Mrs. Davis. Just listen. You are meeting me tomorrow—at noon—where I said.

(1) Why did you come here? Why didn't you phone?

(2) And have you hang up on me again? It's no run-around you're giving me this time, Louise.

(1) I didn't hang up on you. The operator broke the connection.

(2) But I called back and you didn't answer.

(1) You can't frighten me.

(2) I'm not trying to frighten you.

(1) Please go.

(2) There's a bit of unfinished business. Or, have you forgotten?

(1) All that's done—over. It's no use.

(2) There's something you don't know, Louise.

(1) What do you mean?

(2) The police have found John Edwards.

(1) John Edwards is in Canada.

(2) He came back last Monday night.

(1) Where is he now?

(2) In the city morgue.

2. This scene is played for a quality of simplicity and sincerity. The Senora believes she has found her long lost son. Actually, the young man is an impostor.

SENORA: Hijo mio! Panchito, my little lost one! God has brought you back to me—he has brought you back.

BOY: This is my room, mother?

SENORA: Just as you left it. Even the things you played with before you went away.

BOY: A real room . . . a bed. . . . You must have thought me ungrateful, madre mio, never to write.

SENORA: For 12 years we have searched, written, cabled. Why didn't you let us know?

BOY: I was ashamed, I reckon.

SENORA: It was pride—stubborn pride.

BOY: Why are you wearing black?

SENORA: I have always worn black—since that day.

BOY: Mourning.

SENORA: It was the same as if you were dead, Panchito. You took the sunshine out of my life when you went away.

BOY: You forgive me?

SENORA: There is nothing to forgive—now.

BOY: For the years of suffering?

SENORA: The ways of God are strange, my son, but He is kind. I know not why we have had to suffer. A test perhaps—a test of faith. But now you're home nothing will ever come between us again—nothing. I shall hold you in my arms as I did long ago, here in this room, when I sang you to sleep and prayed that some day you—you would be a good man—that some day. . . .

BOY: You are crying.

SENORA: Because I—I'm so happy.

3. Ligeia.

MAXIM: And then quite suddenly I realized it. Ligeia was dying. . . . She weakened, was forced to bed, and then at high moon on the night she departed she called me to her side.

LIGEIA: Maxim, dearest.

MAXIM: What is it?

LIGEIA: I haven't much longer.

MAXIM: Don't say that, Ligeia. You're going to be all right.

LIGEIA: No, Maxim. The light is fading. Oh, it's so very dim, so very dim.

MAXIM: Fight it. You who have been so strong. You can't give up.

LIGEIA: I shan't give up ever.

MAXIM: Your iron will—your iron will.

LIGEIA: Oh, I had the will to live, Maxim. It's a power in me—I can feel it—strong and certain. But this—this body.

MAXIM: Darling, how could I live without you?

LIGEIA: Oh. Maxim, remember that book we read together—and that passage that interested us so: "Man must not yield himself to the angels, nor unto death, save only through the weakness of his people's will."

MAXIM: Ligeia.

LIGEIA: Watch for me, Maxim. Watch for me.

(*Music*)

Full Release of Strong Emotion

(1)

WOMAN: No! No! I won't believe it.

MAN: It's true. Where are you going?

WOMAN: I won't stay here. You can't keep me. Let me go.

MAN: Out in that storm? I tell you it's too late. Come back, come back.

(2)

Situation. A young woman, overcome by the sudden tragedy of her husband's suicide, calls the police.

Problem. Interpretation of intense emotion without blasting. Music punctuation.

WOMAN: Hello—Hello, police? My husband, Monte Girard, just shot himself. . . . What? . . . Yes, the famous lawyer. Hurry . . . hurry, please.

(*Music: Stab*)

(3)

MAN: Stop it! Do you hear me? I forbid you to touch that picture. I forbid it.
WOMAN: Keep away, Charles.
MAN: Leave it alone. It's been in that place for 20 years. You can't take it down.
WOMAN: I will. It's time we got rid of your old monstrosities.
MAN: How dare you?
WOMAN: I dare anything now. Your abuse—your cruelty—it's got to stop. . . . Charles, you're hurting me. (*Screams*)

Sotto Voce

(a) Don't fall for that blarney. He's trying to sell you a bill of goods.
(b) Do you think he's on the level?
(c) Here comes the fathead. Let him do the talking.
(d) Slip out after the next number. I'll meet you on the balcony.
(e) Crazy as a Madhatter.
(f) Where did you check the box?
(g) Take it easy.
(h) That's the second time she's made a mistake.
(i) Keep your voice down.
(j) Do you think he saw you?
(k) HELEN: Jack, we've got to get out of here.
    JACK: Don't worry, Helen. The old coot is harmless.
    HELEN: But you heard what he said. And he'll be back any minute.
    JACK: Shhh! Here he comes.

B. APPLICATIONS OF VOICE LEVEL AND MICROPHONE DISTANCE

Entrance and Exit Fades. The term, "fade," refers to the increase or decrease of vocal level, also to the increase and diminution of sound and music. Walking into the microphone pickup area may be described as an entrance fade, and stepping out of the pickup area, as an exit fade. The fade may be quick and abrupt, or slow and deliberate. It is controlled either by the actor (live fade) or by the engineer at the monitor panel (board fade). The student should practice the following exercises until he has acquired a consistent skill in making all types of radio fades.

(1)

MAN: What are your plans today, dear? Going over to the flower show?
WOMAN: No, I promised Carol to take her into town.
MAN: Where is the darling daughter? Sleeping in again?
WOMAN: She'll be down. I called her when I got up.
CAROL: (*Fading in*) Good morning, good morning, good morning. Sorry I'm late, Mom. I broke a darn old shoelace. Had an awful time finding a new one. 'Morning, Dad.
MAN: 'Morning, my dear. Mother says she's taking you into town today.

CAROL: She tell you what for?
MAN: No, I'm afraid to ask.
CAROL: It'll cost you money.
MAN: That's why I'm afraid.

(2)

MARIE: Come over to the fire. You're drenched. Sit here, please.
SOLDIER: Thanks. . . . Won't this rain ever stop?
MARIE: Sometime . . . I'll get you something hot to drink.
SOLDIER: Yeah, I need something hot.
MARIE: (*Fading*) We haven't much to offer. . . . I'll be back in a moment.
MARIE: (*Fading in*) Here drink this. It's not very good, but it's all we have.

(3)

WOMAN: (*Fading in*) Mr. De Varville, I'm so glad you could come. We thought you were out of town.

(4)

WOMAN: Marie, dinner will be late tonight. They just phoned from the airport. Flight 903 won't arrive until six. I'm going upstairs to nurse this headache. (*Fading*) If anyone calls tell them to ring back.

(5)

MAN: That's the man. I'm positive.
OFFICER: Take him out, Sergeant.
ACCUSED: 'E's mistaken. I was never in his blinkin' store. I can prove it.
OFFICER: Take him out.
ACCUSED: (*Fading*) And this bloke 'ere I never set eyes on afore. Wot kind of justice you calls this?

(6)

MAN: Yeah, the storm warnings came in an hour ago, Charley. Better close up soon as you take care of this customer. I think the Missus will be needing you. (*Fading*) Take my advice now and lock up. See you later.

(7)

WALTER: It's all set. We know the exact minute Sam will arrive with the truck. We know when the watchman will be on the fourth floor. Jack and I will then have 15 minutes, and when. . . .
(*Sound: Knocks on door, obviously a signal*)
WALTER: Who is it?
CARSON: (*Off*) Carson.
WALTER: Come in.
(*Sound: Door opens . . . closes*)
WALTER: Well?
CARSON: They got one of our boys, Walt.
WALTER: What?
CARSON: (*Coming in*) Outside the restaurant. He was getting in his car when the big fellow flashed a badge and forced him into a patrol car.

(8)

NARRATOR: No argument I could use had any effect. The contract was signed and Joan took a plane the next night for New York. It was her great opportunity for stardom she thought. Six months later I had to go east to a sales conference. I resolved to make no effort to see her, but one night (*Fading*) at a party Henchon was giving at his penthouse . . . .
(*Sound: Dance music and buzz of voices*)

(9)

GEORGE: (*Off*) Carol, where are you?
CAROL: (*On*) In the library.
GEORGE: (*Off*) Did you see my sunglasses?
CAROL: (*On*) They're in here on your desk.
GEORGE: Good. (*Coming in*) I thought I left them at the office. Well, it's time we shoved off if we get to the beach by twelve. Ready?

(10)

WANGEL: Her life with her father at the lighthouse has left a deep impression upon her as you may imagine. In town here people can't understand it at all. They call her the Lady from the Sea.
ELLIDA: (*Off*) Are you there, Wangel?
WANGEL: Here comes the mermaid. In here, Ellida.
ELLIDA: (*Fading in*) Thank Heaven you are safe home again, Wangel. When did you come?
WANGEL: Just now. But have you nothing to say to an old friend?
ELLIDA: Oh, Arnholm. So you really have come. Welcome! And forgive my not being at home.

Balance and Perspective. Proper balance is achieved when voices, sound effects, and musical instruments are so related that no single phase of the over-all tonal picture is distorted or exaggerated beyond the level required for the best dramatic effect. Perspective may be defined as spatial relationship—the presentation of details in such a manner that the auditor's imagination may easily create the dimensional variations inherent in the dramatic picture. Balance and perspective are interrelated. Both involve proportional differences of intensity, and it may be claimed that, since perspective is achieved through balance, they are synonymous. However, for practical purposes, each may be studied with separate emphasis.

It is obvious that recorded wind, waves, airplanes, or an elevated train may so dominate the conversation as to render it confused and even unintelligible. Muisc, played as background, may be too high to effect the desired emotional response. In general, if any part of the sound picture calls attention to itself and subtracts from a unified auditory impression, the balance is wrong. Voices must be balanced. It is seldom true that two people reading lines of the same intellectual or emotional intensity will stand equally distant from the microphone. This is because voices vary in their natural intensity.

It must also be clear that unless the sound levels are skillfully mixed the sense perceptions of depth and physical relationships within the scene portrayed will be lacking. This is why we say that perspective is achieved through balance and that the two terms are differentiated psychologically if not physically.

However, because of the close physical relationship between balance and perspective, the two terms are combined in the following exercises.

(1)

NARRATOR: Mr. Smith has been ready for some time to leave for church services, but there seems to be some delay.

MR. SMITH: We're going to be late again, Mary. What's the alibi today?

MRS. SMITH: Oh, it's Lucy. She has no sense of time. . . . (*Calling*) Hurry, Lucy, we're late.

LUCY: (*Upstairs*) I can't find your gloves, Mom.

MRS. SMITH: I left them on my dresser.

LUCY: They're not here now.

MRS. SMITH: Look in the top drawer.

LUCY: Oh, here they are. Which pair do you want? The tan ones or the black ones?

MR. SMITH: I don't see why we can't get ready on time. Every Sunday it's the same thing—15 minutes late. If it was a picture show instead of church, you'd be on time.

MRS. SMITH: Well, if you'd get down to breakfast on time. I refuse to go off and leave a sink full of dirty dishes.

LUCY: (*Fade in*) Gee, Mom. I'm awful sorry, but I looked all over. Here they are.

MRS. SMITH: Thank you, dear.

MR. SMITH: (*Fading*) Come on, let's get going.

MRS. SMITH: Back door locked?

MR. SMITH: (*Off*) Yeah.

MRS. SMITH: Where's the car?

MR. SMITH: (*Off*) Down in front.

(2)

(*Sound: Ocean surf*)

MAN: I wouldn't go out too far, Miss. Those waves are pretty heavy today.

MARY: Don't worry about Jane. She's got enough swimming medals to fill a trunk. One time in Lake Michigan . . . .

MAN: This is the Pacific Ocean.

JANE: Oh, that's all right. We've got waves in Lake Michigan, too.

MAN: I'm just giving you advice.

MARY: Go on, Jane, I want to see you ride those breakers.

JANE: You coming, too?
MARY: No, I'll sit here and watch.
JANE: Well, here I go. (*Fading*) You'd better come out and join me.
MAN: Pretty confident girl, isn't she?
MARY: Sure. She'll take care of herself. (*Calling*) How is it, Jane?
JANE: (*Off*) Swell. Better come out.
MARY: (*Calling*) There comes a big one. Let's see you go under it. . . . Oh,
    oh—she's not going to time it right. . . . Where are you going?
MAN: (*Fading*) To get your champion before she kills herself.
JANE: (*Off*) (*Scream*)
(*Sound: Surf up. Fade out*)

(3)

(*Sound: Wind. Howling of wolves*)
HARRY: Confounded animals. Wish they'd stop that howling. . . . We've got
    to get out of here, Joe. Snow's 3 feet deep now. By morning . . . .
JOE: Stop worrying and have another drink.
(*Sound: Clink of bottle and glass*)
HARRY: Fine way to spend a furlough. (*Mocking*) Ten days, we got. Sure, let's
    go up to the mountains. . . . Been here 2 days and it's snowed ever
    since. (*Fading*) If we could only get out on this phone.
(*Sound: Phone off cradle . . . jiggles connection*)
HARRY: Still dead.
JOE: Stop worrying, I said. We got plenty of food.
HARRY: Yeah, but we're 20 miles from the base. If this storm doesn't let
    up . . . .
VOICE: (*Distant*) Hello-o-o-o!
HARRY: Hey, what's that?
JOE: What?
HARRY: Someone's calling.
JOE: It's the wolves.
HARRY: No.
VOICE: Hello-o-o-o!
JOE: You're right. Somebody caught in the storm. Get your coat.
(*Sound: Wind up and down*)

(4)

William Legrand comes into possession of a scarabaeus—a gold bug—
which he believes will lead him to buried treasure. Accompanied by a
friend and his Negro servant, Jupiter, he goes to a wild and desolate
spot on Sullivan's Island to carry out a plan of exploration. Arriving at a
particular tulip-tree, he coaxes Jupiter to climb the trunk to a point some
60 feet from the ground.[1]

JUPITER: Which way mus go now, Massa Will?
LEGRAND: Keep up the largest branch—the one on this side. How high up are
    you?

[1] From Edgar Allan Poe, *The Gold Bug*.

JUPITER: Ebber so fur; can see de sky fru de top ob de tree.

LEGRAND: Never mind the sky, but attend to what I say. Look down the trunk and count the limbs below you on this side. How many limbs have you passed?

JUPITER: One, two, tree, four, fibe—I done pass fibe big limb, massa, pon dis side.

LEGRAND: Then go one limb higher. . . . Now, Jup, I want you to work your way out upon that limb as far as you can. If you see anything strange, let me know.

JUPITER: Mos feerd for to venture pon dis limb berry far—'tis dead limb putty much all de way.

LEGRAND: Did you say it was a *dead* limb, Jupiter?

JUPITER: Yes, massa, him dead as de doornail—done up for sartain—done departed dis here life.

LEGRAND: Try the wood well with your knife, and see if you think it *very* rotten.

JUPITER: Mought venture out leetle way pon de limb by myself.

LEGRAND: By yourself!—what do you mean?

JUPITER: Why, I mean de bug. 'Tis *berry* hebby bug. S'pose I drop him down fuss, and den de limb won't break.

LEGRAND: You infernal scoundrel! Drop that beetle and I'll break your neck. Look here, Jupiter, do you hear me?

JUPITER: Yes, massa.

LEGRAND: Well! now listen!—if you will venture out on the limb as far as you think safe, and not let go the beetle, I'll make you a present of a silver dollar as soon as you get down.

JUPITER: I'm gwine, Massa Will—deed I is, mos out to the eend now.

LEGRAND: *Out to the end!* Do you say you are out to the end of that limb?

JUPITER: Soon be to de eend massa—o-o-o-oh! Lor-gol-a-marcy! what is dis here pon de tree?

LEGRAND: Well! What is it?

JUPITER: Why taint noffin but a skull—somebody bin lef him head up de tree, and de crows done gobble ebery bit of de meat off.

LEGRAND: A skull, you say!—very well!—how is it fastened to the limb?—What holds it on?

JUPITER: Dare's a big nail in de skull, what fastens ob it on to de tree.

LEGRAND: Jupiter, do exactly as I tell you—do you hear?

JUPITER: Yes, massa.

LEGRAND: Pay attention, then—find the left eye of the skull.

JUPITER: Why dey ain't no eye left at all.

LEGRAND: Curse your stupidity! Do you know your right hand from your left?

JUPITER: Yes, I knows dat—knows all bout dat—'tis my lef hand what I chops de wood wid.

LEGRAND: To be sure! You are left-handed; and your left eye is on the same side as your left hand. Now, I suppose, you can find the left eye of the skull, or the place where the left eye has been. Have you found it?

JUPITER: Is de lef eye of de skull pon de same side as de lef-hand side of de
skull too?—cause de skull ain't got a bit ob a hand at all—nebber mind! I
got de lef eye now—here de lef eye! What mus do wid it?

LEGRAND: Let the beetle drop through it, as far as the string will reach—but
be careful and not let go your hold of the string.

JUPITER: All dat done, Massa Will; mighty easy ting for to put de bug fru
de hole—look out for him dare below!

C. SOUND AND MUSIC EFFECTS

Many kinds of effects are employed in the following exercises, and
the general principles are comprehensive. We begin with simple effects
and proceed to complicated sequences. The word "simple," however, is
misleading. What appears to be very easy may actually prove difficult.
Indeed, one reason for mistakes is the tendency toward oversimplification.
This leads to carelessness. Give close attention to each problem and
repeat the exercise until satisfactory results are obtained.

Doors. The handling of doors would appear to be the simplest of sound
effects. Are we not opening and closing them every day. The act becomes
an automatic if not autonomic one. But the functional door of everyday
life is quite different from an artificial prop door consciously operated to
simulate the real. The two situations are different.

The radio script will call for several kinds of doors and the sound-
effects man, unless he is working in an elaborately furnished sound-effects
department, will find it difficult to make one or two miniature doors
answer every purpose. Go over in your mind the various kinds of doors
that one might meet in a radio script authored by people especially
concerned with realism. Recall the different doors you have passed
through during the past week. In one sense, of course, doors are doors,
and the point we are making should not be pressed too far. The door of
a jail cell, naturally, is different from a living-room door and one cannot
be substituted for the other. We may admit that, in general, door sounds
have a broad similarity, and it would be bootless to carry our differentiation of door sounds too far. Nevertheless, here is a point which
concerns the sound man and, in so far as practicable within the limits of
available studio materials, he will try to produce the sound that approximates most closely the real door. It will be interesting to you to
pursue the above suggestion and make a catalogue of door effects. Doors
squeak, bang, clang, rattle, thud, slide, roll up, and revolve. They are
fastened or locked with bolts, bolts and chains, snap locks, and keys.
There are screen doors, outside heavy oak doors, inside light pine doors,
cupboard doors, massive castle doors, and sheet-metal doors. Automobile
doors range from the tinny bang of a flivver to the substantial click of a
Cadillac. The list of door effects can be greatly expanded. Again, we

emphasize that minor differentiations are impracticable, but the director will try to achieve as much realism as possible.

The purpose of opening doors on an air show is to interpret or make clear a particular action or incident. It is obvious that the effect must be heard. Now, it is possible, actually, to open a door with very little sound. What is the sound of opening a door? How does this differ from the sound of closing a door? Practice with the door to your room. The two effects are not identical. The opening sound derives from the doorknob that turns the latch; the closing sound is the click of the latch plus the door striking the jam. To make the opening carry it is necessary that the doorknob or handle be turned firmly and that the latch be properly released just after the door opens. To make the closing register effectively, the latch must be allowed to click in place and the door be pushed to with adequate force.

Doors are not always opened and closed in the same way. The action may be slow, quick, easy, or firm to the point of a bang. The action is determined by the line or situation. There is a tendency to close doors with too much force, and this should be carefully governed. Another common fault is to close the door too quickly after it is opened. Give the caller time to get into the room. Too often the listener gets the impression that the visitor is a poltergeist who flashes through a narrow aperture.

The following exercises should be sufficient to give you experience with various door effects. They will be elaborated later in the assigned production problems. You will probably not have the equipment for some of these directions and will have to improvise with whatever you can assemble.

1. Ordinary Door

(a) (Sound: Door opens)
(b) (Sound: Closes)
(c) (Sound: Opens . . . closes)
(d) (Sound: Bursts open)
(e) (Sound: Bangs)

2. Squeaking Door

(a) (Sound: Door opens slowly . . . squeaks)

3. Car Door

(a) (Sound: Car door opens)
(b) (Sound: Closes)
(c) (Sound: Opens . . . closes)
(d) (Sound: Slams shut)

4. Railroad-car Door

(a) (Sound: Door slides open)

5. Jail Door

(a) (*Sound: Door unlocked . . . opens*)
(b) (*Sound: Door closes . . . locked*)

6. Door to Telephone Booth

(a) (*Sound: Door opens . . . closes*)

7. Revolving Door

(a) (*Sound: Revolving office building door*)

8. Screen Door

(a) (*Sound: Door opens . . . slams shut*)

9. Garage Door

(a) (*Sound: Double garage doors open, drag slightly*)

10. Safe Door

(a) (*Sound: Iron safe door opens . . . shuts*)

11. To Differentiate

(a)

MARGE: Mom! Bill is coming up the front walk. I can't talk with him now.
MA: All right, go out the back way. I won't tell him you were here.
MARGE: Thanks. (*Fading*) I'll see you tomorrow if I can get over.
(*Sound: Back door opens and closes off-mike*)
MA: If only my children would grow up.
(*Sound: Front door opens on-mike*)
BILL: Hello, Ma! Got a letter for you.
(*Sound: Door closes*)

(b)

MAN: I'm sure I put it in here.
WOMAN: Look in the filing cabinet.
(*Sound: Steel filing drawer pulled out*)
MAN: Nope.
(*Sound: Drawer closed*)
WOMAN: Did you look in that center desk drawer?
(*Sound: Desk drawer pulled out*)
MAN: Not here.
WOMAN: Well, you may have left it at the office.

Steps. One of the most common sound directions found in radio scripts calls for steps. They may be on-mike (pacing), fading on, fading off, on wood, sand, gravel, stone, or other surface. They may be the action of one person or of two or more persons. Directions may specify that they are slow, fast, excited, halting, labored, weary, dragging. They may take place in a hollow, reverberant hall, room, or chamber or on a city sidewalk against the background or traffic and street noises. Steps on a flat surface are different from those on a staircase. The impression of going upstairs is not the same as going down. The location and conditions pertaining to walking are extremely varied. Therefore, a single stereotyped pattern cannot meet recurring script demands.

In the following exercises the lines are artificial and are intended only to aid the timing of the sound. Each problem may be performed first without lines and then added to the dialogue if desired.

1. Steps on Wood Floor

(*Sound: Doorbell*)
WOMAN: Marie, see who that is, will you?
MARIE: Yes, ma'am.
(*Sound: Steps to door. Door opens*)
MAN: Good morning, I'm Mr. Kennedy. I have an appointment to see Mrs. Brown at eleven.

2. Steps on Linoleum

SECRETARY: Mr. Hughes will see you now.
LIN: Thank you.
(*Sound: Steps across office floor. Tacet*)
LIN: Good morning. I'm James Lin.
HUGHES: How do you do? Will you sit here?

3. Steps on Concrete

(*Sound: Steps on concrete. Off*)
WOMAN: Someone's coming up the drive.
MAN: I hope it's Hank. We're an hour late now.
(*Sound: Steps coming on*)
HANK: Hello, folks. Think I was never coming? Original alibi this time. Guess what?
MAN: Puncture?
HANK: Right.

4. Two People. Hurried Steps on Sidewalk

(*Sound: Two people walking rapidly on sidewalk*)
MARTHA: Come on, Henry. I tell you they'll be closed.
HENRY: Can't you stop in tomorrow?
MARTHA: You know I won't be in town tomorrow. The dressmaker is coming at nine, and if I don't get those buttons today she can't finish the dress.
HENRY: I suppose that would be a disaster. You've got another dress.
MARTHA: Oh, you're impossible. Let's take this bus.
HENRY: It's only two blocks.
MARTHA: But it's 10 minutes to five now. Come on.

5. Hollow Tread Off-mike

WOMAN: There's somebody walking upstairs.
MAN: Couldn't be. You're . . . .

WOMAN: Listen.
(*Sound: Slow heavy tread in room above*)
WOMAN: Do you hear it?
MAN: What do you want me to do? Play hero?
WOMAN: Wait.
MAN: I'm not going anywhere.
WOMAN: Call the police.
MAN: It's stopped now.
WOMAN: But someone is up there.
MAN: Imagination. That old shutter, probably.
(*Sound: Walking resumes*)
WOMAN: There it is again. It is somebody. Go up and see.

6. Slow Weary Steps in Desert Sand

(*Sound: Two men, plodding; weary steps in soft sand*)
   (1) I'm done in, Jack. I'll never make it.
   (2) Hold on, old man. The next hill will be the last.
   (1) We've thought that all morning. We're lost—lost—lost!
   (2) Steady, fellow. Another hour and we'll be in camp. Those flares last night were not more than 5 miles away.

7. Two Men Walking Rapidly through Soft Sand

(*Sound: Two men walking rapidly through soft beach sand*)
   (1) Boy, the Coulters sure got a swell place down here.
   (2) I wish my folks had a place at the beach.
   (1) I wonder if the tide is out.
   (2) Yeah. High tide's at eight.
   (1) Gee, look at that surf. Come on, race you in.
(*Sound: Steps increase to running*)

8. Two People on Firm Beach Sand

(*Sound: Two people walking barefoot on firm beach sand, slightly squashy*)
   (1) When is your vacation up?
   (2) Next Saturday. Wanted another week but I couldn't wangle it. You staying down?
   (1) Till the fourteenth, I guess. Marge and Bob are coming down Tuesday. We're going out after tuna.
   (2) Are they running now?
   (1) Yeah, down off Dana Point.
   (2) Well, I'll be thinking about you when I get back to that stinkpot office.

9. Steps Running On

MAN: Valdemar! Valdemar!
VAL: (*Off*) Yes, master.
MAN: Where are you? Come here.
(*Sound: Steps running on*)
VAL: Here, master.

MAN: You scoundrel. Why didn't you come?

VAL: I didn't hear you, master. I was in the cave where you sent me to fetch the brass box.

10. Two People Running on Concrete

(*Sound: Running steps*)

ONE: Down this way. I know a short cut. . . . Turn right into the alley. (*Fade*)

11. Going Downstairs

MAN: Come on, it'll be faster to walk down. The elevator is up at the fourteenth floor.

(*Sound: Two people walking downstairs*)

WOMAN: I've never seen this store so crowded. Looks like a Christmas rush.

MAN: Yeah, it was a smart deal when they opened for night shoppers.

(*Sound: Steps up. Tacet*)

MAN: Wait for me out in front. I'll bring the car around here.

12. Going Upstairs

MAN: Come on, it'll be faster to walk up. I don't see why they don't have more elevator service in this store.

(*Sound: Steps going upstairs*)

WOMAN: I've never seen such crowds in this place. Looks like a Christmas rush.

MAN: Yeah, it was a smart idea when they opened for night shoppers. Where is the rug department?

WOMAN: On the fourth I think.

(*Sound: Steps up. They reach the floor landing . . . continue*)

WOMAN: Yes, this is the place.

13. Pacing

(*Sound: Deliberate steps back and forth. Man or woman*)

MAN: If I could only solve that one complication . . . the cable breaks and the cage falls to the bottom of the shaft . . . and I have my motivation. But the time schedule doesn't fit. . . . Now if I bring Ranson back from New York on the eve of the wedding. . . . No, that won't do. (*Mumbles in tempo to the steps*)

14. Slow Menacing Steps

MAN: The last chime of that tower clock was the deadline, Thompson. You had your chance and didn't take it. Now I'll take over.

(*Sound: Slow steps*)

And keep away from that desk. . . . You were a fool to think you could double-cross us. . . .

15. Limping

(*Sound: Limping steps*)

BOY: He taunted me—humiliated before all of them. Little lame boy! I'll make him sorry he said those words . . . lame . . . lame . . . lame. (*Fade out*)

16. Steps in Snow

(*Sound: Steps in snow*)
MAN: B-rrrrr! It's cold . . . looks like another blow settin' in. Better get on my
way. (*Steps up and fade*)

General Sound. Particular attention has been given to doors and steps
because they constantly occur in radio scripts and because, as explained, their execution requires more care and judgment than would at
first appear.

Other sound effects will not be particularized here because the list
could not conveniently be terminated and because the general principles
which apply are common to the entire range. The two primary requisites
are realism and prompt timing. This applies to both live and recorded
sound. You can depend on the realism of recorded sound because sound
companies make many of their records under actual conditions. Harbor
noises, cement mixers, construction noises, traffic, clocks, trains, automobiles, theater applause, etc., are transcribed on the scene. The cuing
and timing of the record, however, are technical matters, and the problem becomes difficult when sounds follow each other rapidly, are segued,
or cross-faded.

Music. The problem in each of the following exercises is to select
and execute music suitable to the suggested dramatic transition or background. Although you will be somewhat handicapped by not having
before you the entire continuity, the following lines should be sufficient
to guide you in selecting an adequate musical phrase, stab, or passage.

(1)

MAN 1: I hope you will be very happy with this wonder woman. Shall we
drink to it?
MAN 2: By all means. Let's drink to our happiness.
MAN 1: To your happiness—and to your beautiful lady, Ligeia.
(*Music*)

(2)

MAN: Rowena—what is it?
ROWENA: My medicine.
MAN: I'll get it.
ROWENA: Hurry—hurry!
(*Music*)

(3)

ANNOUNCER: We have prepared for your pleasure tonight a delightful comedy
with a rollicking Irish accent titled, *Kitty Mulvaney Speaks Her Mind*.
(*Music: Introduction to set the mood of the play*)

(4)

WOMAN: How did you come here?
MAN: We bribed your servants, madam.

WOMAN: What is your purpose?
MAN: You will go with us, madam.
WOMAN: Where?
MAN: To a new lodging—to Dumfreyshire.
WOMAN: On whose orders?
MAN: We're not at liberty to tell you that.
WOMAN: I know. I have known from the beginning. So this is the pledged
    word of a sovereign!
MAN: Be quick, madam, the carriage is waiting.
WOMAN: You have come with orders to arrest me.
MAN: Yes, my lady. You are a prisoner.
(*Music: In . . . sock . . . up to end*)

(5)

MAN: There is no sanctuary for you and me together. Another time, perhaps,
    but with the state divided as it is, I can only fight and with their weapons.
    I am leaving at midnight.
WOMAN: But can you win your way through? The castle is surrounded. It will
    be a miracle if you get through their lines now.
MAN: It's a risk I must take. We shall win in the end, believe me; and we will
    be together again, I promise you. Goodbye, my love.
(*Sound: Footsteps fade to door. . . . Door opens . . . closes*)
WOMAN: (*Sobbing*) Oh, my darling—my beloved.
(*Music: Surges with tragic emphasis . . . fades*)

(6)

NARRATOR: The barren summer passed with relentless slowness. The mails
    were slow in this pioneer land, but the Olsens had received three letters
    from St. Louis since Mary had heard from Charles. The pleas of her neigh-
    bors grew more urgent.
ANNA: Mary, in two more months the snows will come again. You cannot face
    the winter alone.
MARY: We've been here too long to give up the land. This is our home, Anna.
ANNA: It's no fit place for humans. Blizzards in winter and grasshoppers that
    destroy the crops in summer.
MARY: You're giving up?
ANNA: It's common sense. Come with us. My man can get his old store back
    and start over again. Your husband will find you if he is alive.
MARY: He is alive. I'm sure of that. . . . No, Anna, this land we have here—
    and this home—such as it is—was a dream. We've worked and suffered too
    much to give it up now. And things will be better—I know it. I can't go
    with you, Anna. I've got to wait—here—for Charles.
(*Music*)

(7)

ROCCO: We know you saw Harper last Friday night. Come on, talk.
MICKY: I was in Philly last Friday night.
ROCCO: Quit stalling, Micky. We got witnesses.
LOU: Let me handle him, Rocco.

Rocco: Wait . . . your neck is out, Micky. You saw Harper and you gave him
the numbers. Now, for the last time, come across. I'm waiting.
Micky: Don't get tired, pal. It's going to be a long wait.
Rocco: O.K., Lou. . . . Let him have it.
(*Music: Stab and under*)

(8)

Narrator: The room was at the end of the ninth floor corridor. I was at the
door almost before the elevator started down. The door was unlocked. I
knew then—almost—what I should find. The furniture was piled in confusion, the upholstery cut to shreds, even the floor covering ripped from
its place. Then I saw her—crumpled in a corner. I was too late. She was
dead!
(*Music*)

D. STUDIO PRACTICE

In the preceding sections we have explained several of the basic techniques applicable to radio acting and production. These included the
adaptation of voice level to the microphone, the execution of fades, the
maintenance of balance, some of the skills requisite to radio acting, and
the utilization of sound and music.

These techniques will now be combined in a series of acting and
production problems. There is necessarily much overlapping although
some effort is made to differentiate and grade the problems in terms of
the problem itself and its production difficulty. No particular effort is
made to segregate acting and production elements in every instance.
The actor will be handicapped more than the director because the lines
in most cases are stereotyped speeches supplied primarily to aid the
technical staff in handling production details. However, some of the following exercises are formulated primarily for the actor, and most of the
skills enumerated and explained in Section B will be encountered.

1. Perspective

Situation. The judge calls on the foreman of the jury to report the
verdict. The foreman replies.

Problem. What is the mental picture? Should the speakers be equally
distant from the mike? Should one be on and the other off? May the
picture be colored somewhat by introducing a slight echo common to a
certain type of courtroom?

(*Sound: Rapping of gavel*)
Judge: Mr. Foreman, has the jury reached a verdict?
Foreman: We have, Your Honor. We find the defendant not guilty.

2. Balance and Proportion

Situation. On the announcement of this decision, the people in the
courtroom, after a brief pause, break into words, cries, and exclamations

of approval. These come like a wave, starting low and rising to a climax of excitement. The judge, or bailiff, bangs his gavel and orders quiet. The voices subside.

Problem. How long a pause should be taken following the foreman's statement? What should be the maximum level of the courtroom voices? How long should it take to bring the voices to complete quiet? Are they faded very gradually or stopped abruptly? Should the voices be recorded or live? Should the words spoken be distinct or blurred and indistinct? The basic element in the problem is to regulate the increase of sound and its gradual diminution.

FOREMAN: We have, Your Honor. We find the defendant not guilty.
(*Effect: Fade in courtroom voices. They rise in enthusiastic approval*)
(*Sound: Gavel*)
BAILIFF: Order! Order in the court! Order!
(*Effect: Voices subside to complete quiet*)

3. Balance

Situation. Following the foreman's decision, the courtroom audience releases its tenseness in words and subdued approval. Against this background of 100 voices the attorney for the defense is congratulated by his associates seated at his table.

Problem. Establish and maintain the correct balance between the voices of the crowd and the speeches of the people at the attorney's table. Play the latter against the general background.

(*Effect: Background of voices*)
ALLAN: Congratulations, Ross. You've done it again.
Ross: Thank you.
ALLAN: It was a great speech. You had them all the way.
Ross: We won. That's enough, I guess. . . . Well, Mr. Young, you're a free man.
YOUNG: And I owe it to you, Mr. Ross. I'll never forget you.
ALLAN: Here're the photographers, Ross. They want some pictures.
(*Effect: Bring up slightly background of voices and take out*)

4. Background, Balance, Fade

Situation. A party is in progress at the home of Monte Girard, the lawyer.

Problem. The problem is threefold: to create a realistic effect of a party, to put dialogue in the foreground, and to picture a fade-in.

GIRARD: I can't remember exactly when they met, but I knew from the first she was attracted to him. That night after the trial I realized how much Catherine was attracted. She insisted on giving a party and Ross was the man of the hour.

(Sound: Music and background chatter)

MAN: Another victory in the legal books for the combination of Ross and Girard, eh, Monte? You know, old boy, you're pretty lucky you got Ross. Does he make those jurors eat out of his hand?

GIRARD: Yes, he's learning fast. I might say too fast.

MAN: Ummmm! I see what you mean, Monte. They do make a nice couple on the dance floor, don't they?

WOMAN: *(Fading in)* Oh, there you are, Monte, dear. Congratulations on the verdict. I hear Allan was superb. Where is the darling, anyway? Oh, I see him—dancing with Catherine. Oh, he's so handsome.

GIRARD: And that's the way it was all the time—handsome—wonderful—impressive in the court room. . . .

5. Suppressed Dialogue

Situation. A man and woman, in a secluded corner of a terrace, are overheard planning a murder.

Problem. To lead from narration to dialogue scene, to create the impression of a suppressed dialogue being overheard by an eavesdropper some feet away.

GIRARD: Later that same evening I was searching for Catherine. I wanted to dance with her myself. I found her—with Allan—on the terrace. They didn't notice me as I slipped behind a box elm.

CATHERINE: Allan, darling, we're taking too many chances. If Monte finds out. . . .

ALLAN: He's got to find out. You're demanding a divorce—now.

CATHERINE: No. It's no use. He'll never give it to me.

ALLAN: You're sure?

CATHERINE: Positive.

ALLAN: Then there's only one way out.

CATHERINE: What?

ALLAN: Will you help me?

CATHERINE: I . . . .

ALLAN: Will you help me?

CATHERINE: Yes, Allan.

(Music)

6. Filtered Speech

Situation. A murder has been committed.

Problem. To make words clear and effective over a filter mike. A filter microphone distorts the normal speech frequencies by suppressing either the high or the low frequencies. For this reason, filtered speech is not so intelligible as when the complete sound spectrum in employed. The speaker should work close to the filter and be careful that the articulative elements in his lines are not blurred.

GIRARD: (*On filter*) So, this is death. Funny. I didn't feel any pain; didn't feel anything at all. But I could see everything as plain as day. The room had been dark and still was to human eyes, but to me it was brightly lighted. And I saw my own lifeless body on the floor. I heard voices—their voices—from the other room. Allan was talking in that steely convincing tone of his.

ALLAN: Get hold of yourself, Kathy. It's done. We've got work to do.

CATHERINE: But why did we have to shoot him? Oh, it was horrible.

ALLAN: You know why it was done that way. It was the only way we could make out a suicide case. Let's move fast. Somebody might have heard the shot and already called the police.

CATHERINE: All right, Allan, we'll do everything we planned.

GIRARD: (*Filter*) Everything they had planned. It was so terribly clear now. The beach cottage, the double insurance, my display of jealousy. What a perfect brief my young protégé had made for a perfect murder.

7. Timing, Sound

Situation. A man and woman are walking along the street looking for the number of a commercial shop. They arrive at the door and enter the building. The situation is complicated as a production exercise by adding other elements of sound and background.

Problem. To time sound and dialogue; to integrate sound and words; to create pictures involving perspective and balance.

(a)

(*Sound: Steps of man and woman on sidewalk*)

MAN: It should be here in this block.

WOMAN: How much do you think they will lend us?

MAN: Fifty bucks, I hope. . . . Here it is. Seacoast Finance.

WOMAN: Are you sure this is the right thing to do?

MAN: Sure. Come on, let's go in.

(*Sound: Door opens . . . closes*)

(*Steps: From door to counter*)

(b)

(*Sound: Traffic . . . street noises. Steps of man and woman on sidewalk*)

MAN: It should be here in this block.

WOMAN: How much do you think they will lend us?

MAN: Fifty bucks, I hope. . . . Here it is. Seacoast Finance.

WOMAN: Are you sure this is the right thing to do?

MAN: Sure. Come on, let's go in.

(*Sound: Door opens . . . closes. Steps from door to counter*)

CLERK: Good morning. Something we can do for you?

MAN: Yes. We want to see about a small loan.

(c)

(*Sound: Traffic . . . street noise. Newsboy in background. Steps of man and woman on sidewalk*)

MAN: It should be here in this block.

WOMAN: How much do you think they will lend us?

MAN: Fifty bucks, I hope. . . . Here it is. Seacoast Finance.

WOMAN: Hm. Looks like a dump.

MAN: It is.

WOMAN: Let's go back to Grove's, Tom. Maybe they will . . . .

MAN: No. Come on.

(*Sound: Door opens . . . tinkle of small bell . . . door closes. Steps to counter*)

CLERK: Good morning. Something we can do for you?

MAN: Yeah. A loan. On this medallion.

(*Sound: Unwraps a small package*)

CLERK: Uh–huh.

MAN: Eighteenth century. Bought it in Italy.

CLERK: I see. I'll call Mr. Samuels. He will give you an appraisal. Will you wait a minute, please?

(*Sound: Steps fade*)

8. Pistol Shots

Situation. Two brothers attempt to carry out a matter of justice which they think has been denied them by the court.

Problem. To produce realistic pistol shots and time them with dialogue.

NARRATOR: Next day at noon, outside the Bella Union, Frank and Houston King. . . .

HOUSTON KING: There he is, Frank, over by that wall in the shade.

FRANK KING: I see him. Come on.

(*Sound: Slow footsteps . . . 8 seconds. Tacet*)

FRANK: We want to talk to you, Carlisle.

CARLISLE: Oh, hello, boys. My what nice, fancy shooting irons. Very pretty.

FRANK: Carlisle, you going to apologize to our brother?

CARLISLE: Can't he take care of himself?

FRANK: He's an officer. He can't tend to a personal grudge.

CARLISLE: Meaning me, maybe?

FRANK: Not maybe.

CARLISLE: Take it slow, boys, I'm kind of quick on the draw myself.

FRANK: Not quick—enough.

(*Sound: Pistol shot*)

HOUSTON: You got him, Frank.

CARLISLE: In the shoulder . . . .

(*Sound: Pistol shot*)

FRANK: (*Groans*)

HOUSTON: Frank.

CARLISLE: Talk louder, he can't hear you.

HOUSTON: Carlisle, you've done for my brother . . . . I—

CARLISLE: Yes, and for you.

(*Sound: Pistol shot*)

9. Ad Libs, Off-mike, Fades

Situation. A group of ladies have gathered by invitation at the "mansion" of the Colonial Governor. They have been invited for tea, but a quarter-hour has passed and Her Ladyship has not appeared.

Problem. The problem is (1) to introduce a quiet buzz of conversation following the announcer's line to establish the scene and ensuing dialogue, (2) to set the proper distance for the off-mike butler's voice, and (3) to effect an entrance fade.

ANNOUNCER: In the drawing room of the governor's mansion, several ladies are waiting for their hostess.
(*Effect: Ad-lib conversation*)
WOMAN 1: I think this is very strange.
WOMAN 2: The invitation said 4 o'clock; I'm sure of it.
WOMAN 3: All of us couldn't be mistaken.
BUTLER: (*Off*) Her Ladyship, Lady Augustus Cornbury.
LADY C: (*Fading in*) Ah, ladies, so nice of you to come to tea. Please forgive me for the delay.

10. Crowd Voices, Sound Levels

Situation. A mob of townspeople is milling about outside the house. The sound of voices creeps in during the first lines of dialogue. Mr. Brian goes to the window to speak with the mob.

Problem. To bring in the crowd, keeping it in proper perspective; raising the level on the opening of the window; and retaining the presence of the crowd after the window is closed.

MAN 1: You're a stubborn fool, Brian. Give in.
BRIAN: And take my chances with the rabble in this town?
MAN 1: That's what it will be if you don't go with us.
MAN 2: Judge Barreson promised you a fair trial.
BRIAN: I'd never get a fair trial in this country.
(*Sound: Sneak in mob voices*)
MAN 1: Listen to us, man. We're your friends, and we know the feeling out there in town against you. . . . Listen.
MAN 2: They're coming' now, Brian. This is the pay-off unless you use your head.
BRIAN: I won't budge.
MAN 1: How long do you think you can keep that mob out of here?
BRIAN: Let me talk to them. I'll make them understand.
MAN 1: Keep away from that window.
BRIAN: No.
(*Sound: Window up . . . crowd level up*)
VOICES: (1) There he is. (2) Bring him down. (3) We're comin' in, Brian.
MAN 1: Shut that window, you fool.

BRIAN: Let me alone.

(*Sound: Window banged down. Crowd level down*)

MAN 1: There's only one chance for you now, Brian. Help me, Morgan. I think the back way is still clear.

(*Sound: Struggle. Board fade the scene*)

11. Balance, Perspective, Footsteps

Situation. A young man is working on his fishing boat moored to a pier. The water laps gently at the pilings. A girl, who has been watching him for some minutes, speaks to him from the pier above.

Problem. To blend the sound of waves with the last line of narration, establish briefly, and project the dialogue with proper perspective and balance. Another sound element, fading footsteps, is introduced at the end of the scene.

NARRATOR: It is midday in the tropics. There is little activity in the streets of San Juan and the fishing boats are tied to the pier. But Rick Farrell has not yet acquired the habits of the natives. A workday is still a workday to him, and he is more concerned with repairs to his boat than with a siesta. The lazy tide beats a gentle tattoo against the pilings as he works on a motor assembly.

(*Sound: Water against the pilings*)

RICK: Now, if I can make this gasket fit. (*Whistles*) There—she's all right.

GIRL: (*From the pier slightly above*) Looks all right to me, too.

RICK: Oh, hello!

GIRL: Hello!

RICK: Didn't see you. Where did you come from?

GIRL: Over there. *Pocahontas II.*

RICK: That's a swell yacht. Saw you come in last night.

GIRL: Are you Mr. Farrell?

RICK: Right.

GIRL: We're looking for a guide—fishing trip tomorrow.

RICK: There are a lot of guides in San Juan.

GIRL: I hear you're the best. Want a job?

RICK: Well, that's my business.

GIRL: What time should we start?

RICK: Four o'clock. The fish get hungry early down here.

GIRL: O.K. We'll be ready. So long.

RICK: So long.

(*Sound: Steps on pier fade out*)

12. Voice Perspective

Situation. Colonel John C. Frémont is on his way from San Francisco to a land grant in the California Mariposa region where he had started mining operation. He is met on the road by one of his men and told that claim jumpers have taken possession of the mine.

Problem. To establish perspective of voices and sound.

TOM: Colonel Frémont, I'm glad you've come, sir.
FREMONT: What's up, Tom?
TOM: We saw you from the point up there and I. . . .
FREMONT: What's happened?
TOM: It's the boys of the Merced Company, sir. They jumped a claim of ours last night and are holding it against us.
FREMONT: Which one?
TOM: The Black Drift.
FREMONT: Haven't you ordered them to clear out?
TOM: Yes, sir, and we tried to force them out, but you know how it is— the trail down to the drift is too narrow for more than one man at a time. Pat Kyler has already been killed.
FREMONT: Claim jumpers, eh? Thieving scoundrels. . . . Drive on Fox, we'll blast them out with dynamite.
(*Music: Transition*)
(*Effect: Confusion of voices*)
VOICES: (1) We can never get near the place. (2) How many are there? (3) They're armed and they mean business. (4) The Colonel says we'll blow them out. (4) They've barricaded the mine road. Etc.
FREMONT: Quiet.
(*Voices: Tacet*)
FREMONT: (*Calling*) Hello, down there. . . . Hello! Answer if anyone is down there.
(*Sound: Two shots from the mine*)
FREMONT: Down on your faces—quick. Anyone hurt?
TOM: They was firin' wild—over our heads.
FREMONT: (*Calling*) Hold your fire. I want to talk to you.
PETE: (*Distant*) Come out alone, then—hands in the air.
TOM: Don't do it, Colonel. Let one of us go.
FREMONT: They won't shoot. Stay here.
PETE: (*Distant*) And don't any of your men follow you.
FREMONT: (*Calling*) They won't follow—and I am not armed.
PETE: (*Calling*) All right. Come ahead.

13. Crowd Chatter, Excitement

Situation. Mr. Walter Colton, one of the first civil authorities in early California, is entertaining two visitors. He is telling them something about the work of an alcalde when a group of townspeople descend on his house with the news that gold has been discovered on the American River and that they are leaving immediately for brighter prospects.

Problem. To fade in small crowd chatter and excitement and to keep it in balance and perspective.

COLTON: Yes, that's our real difficulty. The Mexican code is a complicated set of legal provisions quite different from our own.

(*Sound: Fade in sound of small crowd approaching Colton's house*)

COLTON: Quite often the written laws don't cover the offense and all we can do is apply common sense. My friend, William Blackburn, at Santa Cruz, had a queer case not long ago. A young man was brought before him charged with. . . .

MRS. HART: Listen, Mr. Colton, what are those voices?

(*Sound: Lift voices slightly*)

MRS. HART: I declare, it sounds like a mob.

COLTON: Oh, no. Just some little excitement, I suppose.

MRS. HART: I do believe they're coming here to your house, Mr. Colton.

COLTON: Quite possible. I'm frequently called on to settle little disputes. Let's go outside. I'll meet them on the porch. You'll probably see a new kind of town meeting.

(*Sound: Steps to door . . . door opens . . . voices up*)

COLTON: What's wrong here?

MAN: They've discovered gold, Mr. Colton.

COLTON: How's that?

(*Voices: Excited and blurred, confusion*)

COLTON: Quiet! Quiet! One man at a time.

(*Sound: Voices down to mumble but never completely out*)

MAN: On the American Fork—they were digging for a mill race at Captain Sutter's place and they found gold.

COLTON: Who told you?

MAN 2: We saw it with our own eyes. It's the real thing.

COLTON: I wouldn't get excited if I were you. A report like this is always exaggerated.

MAN 3: We come to tell you we're quittin' the town-hall job.

MAN 2: Yes, and us carpenters at the new schoolhouse are quittin', too.

MAN: We're *all* going to the river.

(*Sound: Voices up*)

COLTON: Now wait a minute—wait a minute.

MAN: We can't work here for $5 a day when we make a hundred at the mine.

COLTON: Be quiet. Quiet, please.

(*Sound: Crowd almost out*)

COLTON: Now listen to me. Of course I don't expect you to stay here *if* there is gold up there. But it's 400 miles a round trip to the American Fork. I'll tell you what I'll do. I'll send a messenger up there right away. He will ride night and day. He will get the exact truth. If he tells us there's a real gold strike up there—you can all go at once—and I'll go with you!

(*Sound: Voices in excited debate. Board fade*)

14. Complicated Sound

Situation. A woman runs from her house, across the porch, and to the garage. She climbs into an automobile, starts the engine, and "guns out" at top speed to the highway. The car accelerates to almost maximum speed and crashes over an embankment.

Problem. To execute a series of sound effects timed with narration. Execute the effects (1) without dialogue and then try (2) to integrate them with words.

(a)

(*Sound: Woman runs across room . . . opens door . . . steps on cement porch . . . steps on gravel driveway . . . car door opens . . . closes . . . car starts . . . guns out . . . picks up speed . . . car crashes*)

(b)

GIRARD: So, you've got to escape, Catherine. Pick up the car keys. Detective Green left them on the table. I'm right with you as you go out the front door. (*Steps*) You'll find the car in the garage (*Door opens*) just 50 feet away. There's not much traffic on the highway this time in the morning. (*Steps across porch*) You can get away before the teletypes tick out the order for your arrest. (*Steps on gravel*) And where we're going, they may never find you. Get in the car, Catherine. (*Car door opens*) You're headed toward the Palisades Road. One step on the starter and you're away. (*Car starts*) I'm glad you're taking this way out, Catherine. You could never defend yourself alone. (*Car guns away*) The police would twist your story around your neck. Come on, step on it; you're going too slow. (*Car gains speed*) . . . faster . . . faster . . . faster. . . . Ah, this is better now, you're up to seventy, but this crate will do a hundred. . . .

CATHERINE: Monte . . . Monte! Don't make me do it!

GIRARD: Don't worry, dear. We'll all be together in that other world.

(*Sound: Car crashes through a guard rail and rolls down an embankment*)

15. Complicated Sound

Situation. A young man and woman on the way to a party are stalled on a country road. Seeing an isolated home, they run for shelter.

Problem. Complicated sound.

(*Sound: Rain*)

WALTER: Well, there's nothing to do but run for it. Come on.

(*Sound: Running steps*)

JANE: I hope somebody's at home.

WALTER: There ought to be a porch anyway. All I want is a roof over my head.

JANE: And I want to get to the dance.

WALTER: Pretty picture we'd be at a dance now.

(*Pause: Steps up*)

JANE: The place is dark.

WALTER: Yeah, but there is a porch.

(*Sound: Steps up and on porch. Stomps*)

WALTER: What we need is a boat. . . . What are you doing?

JANE: Looking for a doorbell. Here it is.

(*Sound: Bell sounds back. Repeat*)

JANE: They must be here.
WALTER: Give them time.
JANE: How far is the garage?
WALTER: I don't know until I get to a telephone.
(*Sound: Door opens*)
VOICE: Yes?
WALTER: Sorry, sir, but our car's stuck. Do you have a phone?
VOICE: Nope, no phone. Never had one. Come in, you look nigh drowned.
WALTER: Thank you.
(*Sound: They walk into room. . . . Door closes. . . . Rain down*)

16. Complicated Sound

Situation. A man asks directions. He drives away through a heavy rain. The car stalls.

Problem. Complicated sound timed with narration.

(*Sound: Heavy rain*)
MAN: Five miles? Take 71? Thanks, Mister.
(*Sound: Car pulls away*)
NARRATOR: The rain was driving hard now. John tensed forward to peer
   through the blurred windshield. A skid on one of these curves would be
   the end. Five miles to Highway 71, and he would be safe on the straight-
   away. Suddenly the motor began to sputter. He couldn't be out of gas.
   Might be a clogged fuel line, or maybe the distributor. He felt the engine
   die. What a place to be stalled! Rolling slowly to a stop he reached for a
   flashlight and climbed out.

17. Pictured Action

Situation. It is the period of the forty-niners. A gentleman from
Tennessee finds his search for gold unproductive. He is so discouraged
that he decides on going home. He is arrested in this intention by his
servant whom he had brought from the East. The servant tells him of
recurring dreams which prove that under a certain cabin there is a
rich deposit of ore. Although incredible and reluctant, the man buys the
cabin in question and begins the exploration guaranteed to bring him
fortune.

Problem. The primary problem is to relate sound to dialogue in creating a picture of movement and activity. The secondary one is to provide
an interpretive musical tag.

(*Sound: Two men digging in hard soil. Carter is very tired*)
CARTER: I was a fool to listen to you, Tom. Of all the crazy ideas.
TOM: Don't give up, Massa Carter. We're going to find it; I know we will.
CARTER: Rabbit's feet, monkey paws, dark of the moon, black magic—and I
   thought I was an intelligent man.
TOM: Didn't you hear what that preacher man say about Daniel and the

golden ladder and the man what dreamed about the cows that stopped giving milk?

CARTER: You're mixed up, Tom.

TOM: I reckon if the epistles had dreams what come true. . . .

CARTER: Wait a minute! Stop!

(*Sound: Sound tacet*)

CARTER: Turn that shovel of dirt over again.

(*Sound: Turn over dirt*)

TOM: (*Pause*) Massa Carter—Massa Carter! There it is—just like the Lord told me. That's a gold nugget sure's I'm born.

CARTER: Dig, you rascal, dig!

(*Music*)

18. Sustained, Complicated Sound

Situation. A party is in progress at the summer home of J. Winfield Van Smythe. Cecily Van Symthe has invited her smart set for a gala week end in honor of her cousin, Sally Ward, newly arrived from the Middle West. Sally becomes the center of attention and the especial object of one Judd Peterson who makes a wager, "I'll bet I'll be kissing you before this party is over and you'll be liking it." One of the competing Romeos invites Sally to go rowing with him on the lake. She accepts. Eluding Judd's vigilance they are on the way to the boathouse.

Problem. This is an extended exercise involving complicated sound.

(*Sound: Night noises . . . footsteps in gravel*)

STEVE: I hope a boat was left out, Sally. We can't waste any time.

SALLY: Are we in a hurry?

STEVE: I won't feel safe until we get away from the pier—not with Judd on the prowl.

SALLY: Judd wouldn't follow us down here—or would he?

STEVE: Don't count on it. Judd has no scruples when he's after something he wants. Let's hurry.

(*Sound: Quicken footsteps . . . slow*)

STEVE: There is a boat still out. Wait here, Sally; I'll get the oars.

SALLY: Don't be long.

(*Sound: Steps fade on board pier*)

SALLY: (*Hums lightly while waiting. After pause*) Steve, someone is coming. Hurry.

STEVE: (*Fading in*) Get in the boat. I've got the oars. Here, let me help you.

SALLY: Careful. I'm not used to boats. I've never been nearer a larger piece of water than a swimming pool.

STEVE: You're all right. Hold these oars while I climb in.

(*Sound: Oars striking as they are shoved into the boat*)

SALLY: Steve, someone is coming.

STEVE: Where?

SALLY: Down the path. He's almost here.

STEVE: We'll be off in a second.

BUTLER: (*Off*) Mr. Mallory! Mr. Mallory!

STEVE: It's Van Smythe's butler. . . . What is it, Fellows?

BUTLER: (*Closer*) Mr. Mallory, there's a long-distance call for you—from New York.

STEVE: Oh, for Pete's sake. You're sure, Fellows?

BUTLER: Yes, sir. It's urgent, the operator said.

STEVE: All right. I'm sorry, Sally. It might be important.

SALLY: Of course, Steve. You must answer it.

STEVE: Wait here. I'll be right back.

(*Sound: Climbs out of boat to pier. Footsteps fade with ad-lib conversation between Steve and Fellows*)

SALLY: Bother! Oh, well, it's a beautiful evening. (*Hums*)

JUDD: It is a beautiful evening, Sally.

SALLY: Judd!

(*Sound: Clatter of Judd getting in rowboat*)

SALLY: What are you doing?

JUDD: Here, let go of those oars.

SALLY: Stop it, Judd. I'm waiting. . . .

JUDD: Thanks for waiting, Sally. I knew I could count on you.

SALLY: Judd, where's Steve?

JUDD: He should be halfway up to the house by now. I can't imagine anyone running off like that . . . from you.

SALLY: Stop untying the boat, Judd. I told Steve. . . .

JUDD: It's all untied. Sit back, Sally. Anchors aweigh!

(*Sound: Oars dipping in and out of the water*)

SALLY: You're impossible, Judd. I told you I was waiting for Steve. He's gone to answer a long-distance call and is coming right back.

JUDD: It might take him a long time. I hate to see you out here all alone. Very rude of Steve, I think.

SALLY: What are you doing down here, anyway?

JUDD: Oh, just out for a breath of fresh air.

SALLY: And what makes you think it might take Steve a long time with that phone call?

JUDD: Just a hunch.

SALLY: Judd Peterson. Did you have something to do with this?

JUDD: Don't ask so many questions, Sally. You sound like a girl detective.

SALLY: You think you can get away with anything, don't you?

JUDD: Now, wait a minute. . . .

SALLY: You're just a spoiled brat. . . .

JUDD: Hold on. . . .

SALLY: You've always had your way, and you think it's smart to pull petty little tricks like this. . . .

JUDD: Sally, please. . . .

SALLY: (*Almost in tears*) You don't care about people, or whose feelings you hurt, just as long as you keep your reputation for getting the upper hand.

JUDD: (*Quietly*) You've got it all wrong this time, Sally. I'll admit I pulled a fast one, but the motive is the important thing, isn't it?

SALLY: What motive?

JUDD: Mine. I've been trying to get you alone all evening to explain.

SALLY: You've been making scenes all evening.

JUDD: Look—you hurt my feet this afternoon, wounded my pride tonight, and now you're stabbing me in the back. Why don't you be nice for a change? The least you could do is go rowing around the lake.

SALLY: Well . . . all right, Judd.

(*Sound: Rowing*)

JUDD: We're right in the middle of your meadow of stars, Sally.

SALLY: It's beautiful, Judd.

JUDD: Can you see the man in the moon, Sally.

SALLY: Yes, he's up there tonight.

JUDD: Is he smiling at you?

SALLY: Why . . . yes, he is.

JUDD: Listen to the breeze.

(*Sound: Rowing out . . . waves gently lapping against the boat*)

JUDD: Does it sound happy?

SALLY: (*Softly*) Yes, it does, Judd.

JUDD: Tell me, is your heart made of ice?

SALLY: No, I don't think so. If it is, it seems to be melting.

(*Sound: Oars being pulled into the locks*)

JUDD: Let me catch my breath after that last remark. You sounded almost human.

SALLY: (*Laughs*) You flatter me. I still say you don't understand me, Judd.

JUDD: No, I don't—but I'm working on it. I may have slung a lot of blarney this afternoon, Sally, but one thing I said was absolutely right.

SALLY: What was that, Judd?

JUDD: You are different from the other girls I've known.

SALLY: And I'll bet you've known a lot.

JUDD: You're so alive—I mean, you're interested in things. . . .

SALLY: Yes?

JUDD: I mean, you're fun to be with—I like to hear you laugh—you laugh when you want to, not just for effect. . . .

SALLY: Why, Judd, that's not at all smooth. It doesn't sound like your old line.

JUDD: It's not a line, Sally. You make me think about what I say to you—and I'm a bit rusty, I guess.

SALLY: Reconversion is always a problem.

JUDD: Well, you're not helping much.

SALLY: Don't get discouraged. You're not doing too badly.

JUDD: I'm not? Why didn't you say so?

(*Sound: Clatter of Judd standing up*)

SALLY: What are you doing?

JUDD: I'm coming to visit you.

SALLY: Don't get so enthusiastic!

JUDD: How can I help it? I want to celebrate your first kind words.

SALLY: Stay there, you're rocking the boat!

JUDD: Here I come!

SALLY: Judd, be careful!

(*Sound: Judd stumbles on oar*)

JUDD: Ouch!

(*Sound: Falls*)

SALLY: Judd, watch out! The boat's tipping over! (*Screams*)

(*Sound: Boat tipping over. Sally and Judd splashing in the water*)

JUDD: Sally, Sally! Where are you?

SALLY: (*Spluttering*) Here, Judd. Here.

JUDD: I'm coming, Sally. Are you all right?

SALLY: Judd, help me!

JUDD: Easy . . . easy. I'm coming.

SALLY: Help me.

JUDD: Hang on to me. It's not far to the shore.

SALLY: Judd, I'm scared.

JUDD: Hang on, Sally, I'll take care of you.

(*Sound: Splashing up*)

JUDD: (*Straining*) Almost there. Should be able to touch bottom now . . . ah, solid ground, Sally.

SALLY: It's slippery, Judd.

JUDD: Grab my hand. I'll pull you up. (*Grunts*) There you are.

SALLY: Whew! That was close!

JUDD: (*Quietly*) I'm sorry, Sally.

SALLY: Sorry! You practically saved my life!

JUDD: I tipped the boat over.

SALLY: Maybe I deserved a ducking.

JUDD: No, it's all my fault. I've been acting like a fool ever since I first met you. I wish this had begun differently, Sally.

SALLY: So do I, Judd.

JUDD: You're beautiful, Sally . . . even when you've half-drowned.

SALLY: You must have water in your eyes.

JUDD: (*Softly*) The most beautiful girl in the world.

SALLY: You're sure of that? You really mean that?

JUDD: Positive. (*Slight pause*)

SALLY: Judd—no, don't. I'm going to win that bet. I'll race you up to the house. It's getting too warm down here . . . when I should be freezing to death.[2]

19. Sound Timing, English Accent

Situation. Two men, Dr. Hetherlegh and young Jack Pansay, are riding back to their quarters. Pansay is suffering from hallucinations. Periodically, he sees a rickshaw and its occupant, Agnes Wessington, although the lady had died and the rickshaw itself had been destroyed.

Problem. (1) Timing sound with lines and (2) English accent.

[2] From Evelyn Bell, *Bets Are Never Safe.*

NARRATOR: When the party at Mannerington's broke up that night, the doctor made a point of riding away with Pansay. (*Fading*) He sensed that something was wrong and decided to see what it was.

(*Sound: Two horses at walk*)

HETHERLEGH: I say, Pansay, what the deuce was the matter with you this evening on the Elysium Road?

JACK: That.

HETHERLEGH: What?

JACK: That! I see it now. So can you.

HETHERLEGH: Man, you're trembling and sweating like a scared pony.

JACK: She follows me everywhere.

HETHERLEGH: There's nothing whatever where you're pointing. You come home with me, young man. You need patching up.

JACK: It keeps moving just ahead of us.

HETHERLEGH: Nonsense. . . . What's the story, though? I'd like to have it.

JACK: Mrs. Agnes Wessington. We were—well, I cut her like a brute. It broke her heart.

HETHERLEGH: Why, I knew that case; but I didn't suppose. . . .

JACK: And she appears to me—day and night—she's there now—the same yellow paneled rickshaw—the same four black-and-white jampanis.

HETHERLEGH: Eyes, Pansay—all eyes, brain, and stomach.

JACK: No, I'm quite well.

HETHERLEGH: I happen to know that every one of those jampanis died with cholera and that the rickshaw itself was broken to splinters.

JACK: It isn't so, Doctor. It isn't true . . . wait a minute!

(*Sound: Horses tacet*)   .

JACK: (*After pause*) It's stopping—under that shale cliff . . . don't go on.

HETHERLEGH: Blast it, man, if you think I'm going to spend a cold night on a hillside for the sake of a stomach-cum-brain-cum-eye illusion. . . . Lord! What's that?

(*Sound: Landslide . . . a muffled report . . . shale, rock, trees fall with a thunderous crash*)

HETHERLEGH: (*After noise subsides*) Man, if we'd gone forward we should be 10 feet in our graves by now. . . . "There are more things in heaven and earth. . . ." Come home, Pansay, and thank God. . . . I want some brandy.

(*Music*)

20. Emotion, Galloping Horse, Music to Cover

Situation. See the situation in Exercise 19.

Problem. (1) Emotional dialogue, (2) galloping horse, (3) music to cover.

NARRATOR: Dr. Hetherlegh went to work on Pansay. He put him through a course of liver pills, cold-water baths, strong exercise, and at the end of a week certified him as mentally cured and sent him off to make love to Miss Kitty who believed her young man had been laid up with a sprained ankle. The doctor had done a good job, and Pansay was in fine fettle as he and Kitty dashed off on a brisk ride to the Sanjowlie Reservoir. But no sooner had they rounded the corner above the convent than Pansay pulled his pony to its haunches. In the center of the level road stood the black-and-white liveries, the yellow-paneled rickshaw, and Mrs. Agnes Wessington. The next moment he was lying in the road, Kitty kneeling above him.

KITTY: (*Crying*) My dear, what is it—what is wrong? You're ill, Jack.

PANSAY: Has it gone—has it gone? Ohhhhh!

KITTY: Has what gone, dear? What?

PANSAY: Right there—in the middle of the road—

KITTY: You must be out of your mind, Jack. There's nothing I tell you—only some ludicrous mistake.

PANSAY: Yes, there is a mistake—a hideous mistake. Come with me—look at it—you've got to look at it. For pity's sake speak to it—tell her we're betrothed—that neither death nor Hell can break the tie between us. . . . Come!

KITTY: Stop dragging me, Jack.

PANSAY: You've got to speak to it. . . . Agnes, you must release me. This torture is driving me insane. Have mercy, Agnes.

KITTY: Stop this babbling, Jack, you're terrifying me.

PANSAY: Speak to her, Kitty.

KITTY: There is nothing here.

PANSAY: I killed her. I broke her heart. She thought I was to marry her—she had reason to believe. It's Mrs. Wessington—tell—her—

KITTY: Thank you, Mr. Pansay—you've said quite enough. Let me go.

PANSAY: No, you must hear me out! You must forgive me.

KITTY: Let go my bridle.

PANSAY: Don't leave me with her.

(*Sound: Two sharp lashes of riding whip across Pansay's face*)

PANSAY: (*Groans*)

(*Sound: Kitty gallops away*)

(*Music: Transition*)

21. Music, Sound Problem, Characterization

Situation. A printer is working at his hand press running off an order of handbills. He is interrupted by his wife who comes in to see how the work is progressing.

Problem. (1) Selection of appropriate opening and closing scene music, (2) creation of the sound of a hand press such as was used by printers in eighteenth century, (3) characterization.

NARRATOR: This is the story of John Peter Zenger and the struggle for free speech in America.

(*Music: Introduce . . . under for narrator and blend with sound*)

NARRATOR: It is a cold afternoon in November. In a small shop adjacent to his living quarter, an immigrant printer is operating a small hand press. . . .

(*Sound: Rhythm of a hand printing press*)

ZENGER: (*Counting to himself in rhythm with the press*) Hundert and forty-one. (*Thump*) Hundert and forty-two. (*Thump*) Hundert and forty-three—

(*Sound: Door opens. Footsteps*)

ANNA: (*Calls off-mike*) John!

ZENGER: Hundert and forty-six. (*Thump*) Hundert and—

ANNA: (*Calls closer*) John!

ZENGER: Hundert and forty-nine. (*Thump*)

ANNA: John Peter Zenger! You—

ZENGER: Hundert and fifty. (*Thump. Stops press*) Yah, Anna?

ANNA: (*Scolding lightly*) When you work dis old press, you hear nutting else.

ZENGER: (*Philosophically*) Yah. I'm just counting and praying she don't quit all togedder.

ANNA: Are you soon finished, John?

ZENGER: (*Sighs*) Yah. Too soon. Three hundert handbills about runaway slaves. (*Shows her a copy*)

ANNA: (*Reads*) "One hundert fifty dollar reward . . . ." (*Encouraging*) It's good and clear, John.

ZENGER: Good enough. All except the capital S; she's printing crooked. Well . . . (*Starts press again*) Hundert and fifty-one. (*Thump*) Hundert—hundert—

ANNA: (*Rather timidly*) John. . . .

ZENGER: —fifty-two. (*Thump. Stops press*) Yah?

ANNA: Is that all you've got to do—just the handbills?

ZENGER: That's all, for sure. Maybe tomorrow comes the boat in from London. Then new goods to advertise.

ANNA: Yah, maybe. (*Sighs*)

ZENGER: You wish I not left the *Gazette,* eh, Anna?

ANNA: No. Is nice to have our own shop. But I wish we have more work. I wish we have a paper of our own to print.

ZENGER: (*Laughs incredulously*) A paper of our own! You think New York iss big enough for two papers?

ANNA: Six thousand people now—in New York!

ZENGER: Yah. And all who can read have a paper, *Gazette.* This new governor —Cosby—he says what to print, what not to print. And the *Gazette* says, "Yah."

ANNA: Two sides there are, John, to every story. If we had a paper. . . .

ZENGER: (*With some impatience*) If we had a paper . . . if we had a paper! It takes money to start a paper. (*Starts the press*) Hundert and fifty-three (*Thump. Stops press*) If we had a paper, Anna, who writes for it? Me? I'm not even talking English so good!

ANNA: Maybe when he grows up—Paul.

ZENGER: (*Softening*) Yah, that could be. . . . He's better today, Anna?

ANNA: Oh—a little. He wants to get up. But he has not shoes. . . .

ZENGER: So—we'll have our own paper to buy shoes for little Paul? Is that it?

ANNA: (*Admits*) Such a good head he has, John! But he coughs all the time. He needs to get out in the sun and play. But. . . .

ZENGER: But he has no shoes. (*Sighs deeply*) Well, first food. The handbills
will buy something for today, eh?

ANNA: Yah.

(*Sound: Sound of press thumping again*)

ZENGER: Go back in where it is warm, Anna.—Hundert and fifty-four. (*Thump*)
Hundert and. . . . (*Fade out*)

(*Music: Bridge*)[3]

22. Sound and Acting Problem

Situation. A fantasy.

Problem. Music, sound, characterization.

VOICE: On a bridge . . . New York City . . . 2 A.M.

(*Sound: Slow footsteps*)

VOICE: A chill mist swirls above the distant rooftops. An occasional foghorn
moans its dreary warning. The slow steps of a solitary walker strike
hollowly through the shrouded gloom.

(*Sound: Steps up 10 seconds. Tacet*)

DIANNE: Max . . . Max, you did a beautiful thing when you built this
bridge . . . but it took you away from me when you fell. . . . Look,
Max. The tired old city . . . asleep . . . no more cares until tomorrow
. . . and then it comes to life again, rumbling, noisy, complaining,
bulging with people . . . some ugly . . . some wonderful . . . all kinds.
Everyone with something on their minds. . . . Max, darling, what's it
like where you are?

(*Sound: Car fades in and stops*)

MADGE: Hey, Honey, whatcha doin' out here all by yourself? Kin we help
you somewhere, maybe?

DIANNE: No . . . No, I'm all right. Thank you. I often walk this bridge.

MADGE: At this time in the morning?

DIANNE: Yes.

MAE: Better make her come with us, Madge.

MADGE: Sure you don't want a lift?

DIANNE: No.

MADGE: O.K. Guess you know what you're doin'.

(*Sound: Car guns away*)

DIANNE: (*After car has faded out*) Did you hear her, Max? She's one of the
people I was telling you about.

MAN: (*Slightly off*) Pardon me, are you Dianne Martin?

DIANNE: Yes, I . . . . Who—where are you?

MAN: I'm here—close by you.

DIANNE: Who are you?

MAN: I have many names.

DIANNE: You don't make sense. What do you want with me?

MAN: I was sent to find you.

DIANNE: What for? Who sent you?

---

[3] From John T. Waterhouse, *Shoes for Paul Zenger.*

MAN: Some one who wants to build and reach the stars and take the whole dead earth with him.

DIANNE: (*Stunned*) Max! That's what Max said.

MAN: He sent me.

DIANNE: Max is dead.

MAN: I can take you to him. Will you come?

DIANNE: Max, will I see you? Will I? Help me, Max. Help me.

(*Sound: Wind up full and gradually fade out*)

DIANNE: Excuse me, can you—Why, you're the girl who spoke to me on the bridge.

MADGE: So ya did it, huh? I thought you was up to something standin' out there all alone.

DIANNE: Am I still alive?

MADGE: Believe me, you're more alive than ever.

DIANNE: But you . . . ?

MADGE: We turned over on the bend just beyond the bridge. You waitin' for someone?

DIANNE: No, he's already here . . . I haven't found him yet. That's what I was doing on the bridge . . . I could talk to him there. I wish I knew where he was. This is such a big place.

MADGE: It is a big place, dearie; (*Fading*) but if he's here, you'll find him. Good luck.

DIANNE: Thank you . . . Max . . . Max . . . I can't find you. You must be here. He said you were here.

(*Sound: Drills and construction sounds*)

DIANNE: Drills! Those are drills. Someone is building . . . that spire! It's touching a star. . . .

(*Sound: Running steps*)

DIANNE: Max! Max!

(*Sound: Up . . . Cross-fade to music*)

23. Narration, Background Sound, Balance

Situation. Clara Barton, addressing a large audience, collapses.

Problem. Dramatic narration, background sound, balance.

ANNOUNCER: Clara Barton—a nurse on the battlefields of the American War between the States. Amidst the leaden hail of Bull Run and Chantilly, at Harper's Ferry and South Mountain; Antietam and Fredericksburg; before the belching walls of Fort Wagner; mired in the muddy swamps of the Wilderness—on through every major engagement up to the climax of the great "Amen" before Richmond, the noble heart of this noble woman beat in tempo to the suffering of her fellow countrymen. (*Pause*) The war was over. Destiny had written a tragic finis to a fratricidal strife. President Lincoln asks her to assume the gigantic task of locating over 80,000 men. Largely at her own expense, Miss Barton set to work and against almost insuperable odds gradually brought order out of chaos. Then early one winter evening in 1868 she stood on a lecture platform in the East. A great throng was listening to the woman whom John B. Gough (Goff) regarded as one of the greatest orators in America.

(*Sound: Mixed chatter and applause on cue, "Lecture platform in the East"*)

CHAIRMAN: Ladies and gentlemen!

(*Sound: Applause up*)

CHAIRMAN: *Ladies and gentlemen!!!!*

(*Sound: Gradually fades and tacets under first words of chairman*)

CHAIRMAN: Your committee has given me the honor of presenting Miss Clara Barton. Language is a poor vehicle to express our appreciation and love for this great woman. Miss Barton is regarded as a sister to the soldiers from Maine to Virginia. As a miracle of mercy, her name is a household word throughout the land. I introduce to you, Miss Clara Barton.

(*Sound: Vigorous applause . . . voices fade. A mike changes to back stage*)

REDDING: Big audience out there tonight, Tom.

TOM: Yes, we turned away hundreds.

REDDING: I tell you she's the grandest woman that ever breathed.

TOM: But she shouldn't be out there lecturing, Mr. Redding. The woman is on the edge of a breakdown.

REDDING: You don't know Clara Barton. I've never seen such stamina in a human being.

(*Sound: Applause out*)

TOM: Yes, but she is a human being. Listen.

CLARA: (*Slight fade-in*) Thank you . . . you are most generous. But if I have been privileged to stand by your loved ones when the trial hour came, and their last look was on my face, not yours, the secret is not mine. It belongs to you. I am by the very circumstances the servant of the people who have sacrificed so much. (*Fading till barely audible*)

TOM: I noticed her when she came in tonight, Mr. Redding. How pale!

REDDING: She has been lecturing every night.

TOM: Against her doctor's orders.

REDDING: No one gives her orders.

CLARA: (*Voice up . . . tired*)

CLARA: (*Voice goes to a whisper*)

TOM: Mr. Redding, something is wrong.

REDDING: She's all right.

TOM: I tell you she is on the point of collapse. She's not talking over the front rows.

I recall an incident which might serve as a type of all those days. Having occasion to pass through a somewhat western city in the winter of '65, my attention was one day suddenly arrested by the figure of a singularly attired, weird, little boy with a basket on his arm standing in front of a bakery. A soldier's cap and pantaloons in which his tiny form seemed nearly lost, and the faded light blue cape of a storm-beaten overcoat reaching to his knees, with the once bright buttons still striving to adorn its tattered edges, comprised the uniform of the little shivering . . . .

(*Sound: Miss Barton falls to the floor*)

REDDING: She has fainted, Tom. Pull the curtain. I'll explain to the audience. Pull the curtain.

(*Transition—Beginning with "I'll explain to the audience"*)

24. Emotional Transitions

Problem. Combined production and acting exercise. The production problem seems very easy, but simple effects essential to sharp mental pictures may require particular care. The element of timing is important. The acting problem involves the clear differentiation of emotions.

SOUND: *Doorbell rings. . . . Steps to door. . . . Door opens)*
MAN: Good morning, Myra.
MYRA: (*Shocked*) Ben!
MAN: (*Sarcastic*) Yes, you recognize me, don't you?
MYRA: (*Fear*) What do you want?
MAN: (*Taunting*) Why don't you invite me in?
MYRA: (*Pleading*) Go away. Leave me alone.
MAN: (*Threateningly*) I've just had a call from your husband. I think you ought to talk with me, Myra.
MYRA: (*Resigned*) All right, come in.
MAN: (*Satisfied*) Thank you.
(*Sound: Door closes*)

25. Characterization

Problem. Acting exercise in characterization. Mrs. Spendover is played as an ultra-ultra. On meeting you for the first time, she is likely to raise her lorgnette, arch her eyebrows, and say "Really?" She is never embarrassed by her ignorance.

Situation. The scene is in the rug and carpet department of a fashionable department store.

MANAGER: Now, this rug, Mrs. Spendover, will never be duplicated. . . . It can't be; hand-woven, native dyes . . . a genuine Sarouk.
MRS. SPENDOVER: I was talking with Mrs. Wentworth yesterday. . . . You know, Mrs. Wentworth of *the* Wentworths . . . and she was saying, "Now, if you can ever find a real Ghordy." Yes, that was it . . . Ghordy . . . the place where Alexander is supposed to have cut the Gordion knot, you know. She said, "Now if you can find a Ghordy be sure to pick it up. It's priceless."
MANAGER: She was quite right . . . "priceless." But the only place you will find one is in a museum. You couldn't buy one for $25,000.
SPENDOVER: Really?
MANAGER: If you want a fine rug, Mrs. Spendover, I would advise either a Sarouk like this or possibly a Kerman.
SPENDOVER: Are orientals really as good today as they were . . . oh . . . 20 years ago?
MANAGER: That depends on the rug.
SPENDOVER: Well, Mrs. Wentworth was saying that most of them were domestic fabrications, stained with . . . what was it . . . an . . . aniline dyes, and that. . . .

MANAGER: I'm sorry to contradict her but that's not quite true. There was a short period when the Persian and Turkish rugmakers tried to use aniline dyes, but their product was so inferior that Turkey now, by law, requires the use of vegetable dyes altogether. Now this Sarouk . . .

SPENDOVER: I don't think I shall buy one today, Mr. Coleman. What I really came in about was that piece I have hanging between my candelabra . . . the one with the funny name . . . the eh—Kish . . . What do you call it?

MANAGER: The Kis Khilim.

SPENDOVER: That's it . . . Kis Khilim. Well, my maid let it fall yesterday and it's damaged . . . one corner of it. Can it be repaired?

MANAGER: Oh, certainly. We'll restore it for you perfectly.

SPENDOVER: Of course, I don't know very much about Armenian handicraft but I don't see how an American weaver. . . .

MANAGER: We send our repair work to an old Armenian who learned his art in the Near East over 50 years ago. . . . He works at home on a special loom. But I wish I could interest you in this Sarouk, Mrs. Spendover. At this price. . . .

SPENDOVER: No, I can't use it . . . really I can't. Will you send for the Kis Khilim this afternoon?

MANAGER: Certainly.

SPENDOVER: And when can I get it?

MANAGER: I'm not sure. The man I spoke of is very particular . . . refuses to be hurried; but his work is absolutely reliable, I promise you.

SPENDOVER: Very well. But have him start right away; we're entertaining next weekend and I must have it.

26. Characterization

Problem. Voice and character differentiation. Five voices are used in this short scene, and each one should be clearly recognized.

Situation. The incident occurs in *Les Miserables*. Hearing that the long-lost Jean Valjean has been apprehended and is on trial in a distant city, the real Jean Valjean, now a prosperous and respected figure, decides to avow his identity. When he reaches the courtroom, the trial is almost over. The last witnesses are being being examined. To convict Brevet, the judge commands.

JUDGE: Brevet, look well on the prisoner. Say on your soul and conscience. You recognize the prisoner as your former friend in the galleys, Jean Valjean?

BREVET: Yes, your Honor. I was the first to recognize him. He is Jean Valjean. I recognize him positively.

VOICES: (*Slight stir in courtroom. Use as transition*)

JUDGE: Antonie, say on your soul and conscience if you recognize this prisoner. Collect your rememberance.

ANTONIE: Gad, do I recognize him? We were 5 years on the same chain.

VOICES: (*Buzz . . . up . . . fade*)

JUDGE: Cochepaille, you are to testify in this case. Swear on your soul and conscience; do you recognize the accused?

COCHEPAILLE: It *is* Jean Valjean. The same they call Jean the Jack, he was so strong.

VOICE: (*Increased buzz*)

JUDGE: Officers. Enforce order. I am about to sum up the case.

(*Sound: Rap on table*)

VALJEAN: Your Honor—gentleman—of the jury—a moment please.

JUDGE: Who—who are—

VALJEAN: Release the accused. Your Honor, order *my* arrest. He is not the man whom you seek. It is I; I am Jean Valjean.

27. Emotional Interpretation

Situation. A plane has crashed in the Rocky Mountains. Contact is made with Salt Lake City, but owing to a heavy snowstorm rescue parties cannot possibly reach the survivors. The plane's radio is intact but can operate only 15 or 20 minutes longer. It is arranged that six of the survivors may each have 2 minutes for a final message. Their words are to be picked up from the short-wave transmitter and rebroadcast over a national radio hookup.

Problem. Emotional interpretation and characterization.

MRS. HANSEN: This is Margaret Hansen. Hello, Jim. They've told us everyone will be listening. I don't really know what I can say. Jimmy is alive and here beside me. He got shaken up a little by the crash but wasn't hurt badly at all. Thank Heaven for that. He's going to speak next. He had a wonderful time at the folks . . . If Mother and Dad are listening in, I . . . well, I just don't know what I can say. Words are so inadequate, but *faith* is adequate. We haven't given up hope. We know that some way, somehow, rescue will come. We wouldn't have been spared this long if it wasn't meant to turn out that way. My faith and trust is in God, and so is Jimmy's whose hand I hold. You'd be proud of him, darling, as I am. Jim . . . in case something should happen . . . if this was meant to turn out some other way . . . I want to thank you for the precious years of happiness our marriage has brought, for our son, Jimmy, and for being the father you have been. No matter what happens, I've had more than my share of happiness. But everything will be all right. When two people love each other as much as we do, everything has to turn out right. Don't worry, dear. Jimmy wants to talk to you. Daddy is listening, Jimmy.

JIMMY: Hello, daddy. How are you? It's awful cold where I am. It's been snowing real hard and it sure is pretty but I don't like it so much. Golly, it was a big crash. I wasn't scared though, daddy, honest. Mommy held on to me and after we crashed we slid for a long ways. The pilot's a swell guy. He lets me help him do things. We're living in part of the airplane.

I'd like to come home and see you, but Mommy says we can't leave until the people come and get us, because everyone is too hurt to go anywhere. I'm not hurt, but I don't want to go anywhere without Mommy. (*Pause*) Well. . . .

MRS. HANSEN: (*Whisper*) Tell daddy you love him, dear.

JIMMY: I love you, daddy. G'by.

TRAVIS: This is Harry Travis from Pennsylvania. If anybody from Oil City is listening in, you can give my best to the home town. I'll bet no one there ever expected to get out of bed at six in the morning to hear me on the radio! (*Laugh*) You can tell old Judge Peterson that I finally found a place that's colder than his jail. (*Chuckle*) Well, it looks like we're in a pretty tight spot up here. If I had my choice, I think I'd take Peterson's jail again; at least the meals are more regular there. But I've been in tough places before, so I know it don't help none to stew about it. Here's the way I figure it . . . if it's in the cards that my number is up, well, it's up, and there's nothing that me or anybody else can do about it. This lady here says she's got faith in God. Well, I guess that's O.K., if that's what she wants. It's probably good for the kid, I don't know. I'm not one to argue about that stuff; religion is one thing I don't monkey with. I say let 'em believe whatever they want. Me, I believe in Harry Travis. If I get out of this, it'll be because I pulled myself through it. Like I say, it's all in the cards. Well, I just wanted to put in my two cents worth. Harry Travis from Oil City, Pennsylvania, signing off.

ALICE: (With difficulty) My name is Alice O'Connor. I really shouldn't be taking up any time like this because I don't have any family or anyone particular to say goodby to. I told them to leave me out when they drew lots to speak so that people with someone listening could be sure to talk before the radio gives out like they think it will. I'll make it short. It hurts a little to talk, anyway. This hasn't been easy, but I'll never forget how wonderful and brave these people have been, considering the predicament we're all in. Up to now I've been a nobody as far as you people listening in are concerned. But now I'm somebody worth listening to, because I'm going to die, and I can tell you what it's like. For one thing, you find out that being important doesn't make much difference, and that maybe being famous isn't so important after all. If we'd only stop long enough to think about it, we would realize that there is more to life than just the individuals who run around living it. It's big, it's very big. We fool ourselves into thinking that we're big until something like this happens. Then the balloon breaks and there we are, just a little wet speck. No, it doesn't matter much who you are, but it does matter what you are. What I mean is, death is no respecter of prominence, but it has to respect courage. Like Mr. Travis, I've always accepted everything as being in the cards, so to speak. I guess I still believe that, only now I'm wondering if there isn't someone or something somewhere who shuffles the cards and deals them out. I'm going to let someone else talk now. Good-by, everyone.

DIECKMANN: This is Charles R. Dieckmann speaking. I want to speak first to my wife and family, then to my colleagues on the faculty at the

American Institute of Technology, and finally to the radio audience which I understand is listening in. For Marta Dieckmann and to my sons Frank and Robert, I have a personal message. First, I must assure you that I have not suffered extensive physical pain. My legs and one shoulder were injured in the accident, but the injuries are not of an especially painful nature. I trust that your knowledge of this will be of some relief to your minds. Truly, the most painful aspect of this experience is knowing how distraught you must be and the mental anguish which you no doubt are suffering. Hence I am deeply grateful for this opportunity to speak to you personally. I need not reaffirm my love for any of you. I am certain you understand it, though you will never realize its depth. To Dr. Barnett, my associate, and to Professor Tassey and the others with whom I have worked for many eventful years, I submit a word of appreciation. Gentlemen, together we have explored life in our laboratory. We have succeeded in unveiling some of its mysteries. It has been satisfying and not a little exciting. But I submit to you the recent observation that there is more to life than that which is explored in the laboratory and tested in the crucible. It is my unusual experience to reflect upon life as it approaches an end, and to be in this unique position to comment upon it. The words which I would now use to explain life and the meaning of life would not be included in the best scientific journals. To the radio audience, to all my friends, and to those whom I do not know, I implore you to accept the observations of one who has devoted his life to seeking scientific truths. Human lives are significant only so far as human happiness makes them so. And the nucleus of happiness is love. Good-by, Martha; good-by, boys.

GLORIA: Hello, everyone, this is Gloria Freeman speaking. I understand this is to be somewhat of a farewell performance. It comes rather early in my career, and because it is so premature, I am not prepared for it. As the hours pass by, it seems that individual identity is lost. Personalities decrease in significance as the outcome of the situation becomes more and more apparent. (*Choking*) It's hopeless! (*Gasp . . . then more collected*) At a time like this, it would be foolish to maintain a theatrical relationship with so interested a public. So with your permission, I will speak not as an actress, but as a temporary survivor of tragedy which has not yet been concluded. It was Miss O'Connor who said that personal importance is of little value at a time such as this. She is right, very right . . . and she was referring to me. I am not ashamed to admit that I would gladly exchange my fame and career for just half the faith of Mrs. Hansen, of Jimmy, or for just a part of the real love which some of these people have known. Personal glory is no substitute for the real meaning of life; I've found that out. I've made a mess of my own life, cluttering it with marriages that glittered but failed. (*Slightly hysterical*) Yes, this is Gloria Freeman speaking, the famous Gloria Freeman whom no one could possibly recognize now. The wealthy Gloria Freeman who can't find a hot dinner to buy. My biggest audience, and I'm afraid, deathly afraid. The curtain . . . is so final. (*Sobbing*)[4]

[4] From George Willey, *Call from Beyond.*

28. Voice Differentiation

Problem. Voice differentiation: three women's voices—daughter, mother, grandmother.

MOTHER: Mother, where's Carol?

GRANDMOTHER: She hasn't come home yet.

MOTHER: It's eleven-thirty—and a school night. It's bad enough for her to stay out on party nights.

GRANDMOTHER: Well, maybe something happened.

MOTHER: That's what I'm afraid of.

GRANDMOTHER: Oh, I don't mean anything serious. Maybe the show was late or Billy had tire trouble. Maybe they stopped in at Mabel's to see the television.

MOTHER: Then she could have phoned. Really, mother, if I had behaved like Carol when I was her age you would have curbed me plenty.

GRANDMOTHER: Well, don't worry anymore. She just came in the front door.

DAUGHTER: Hello, Mom. I'm awfully sorry, but—Why, Grandma, you still up?

GRANDMOTHER: Yes. I have to stay up to keep your mother from having hysterics.

DAUGHTER: I tried to call you, Mom, but the line was busy.

GRANDMOTHER: That must have been when I was chinning with Mrs. Dolly.

MOTHER: You could have tried again.

DAUGHTER: But we were in the show, and on the way home—well, anyway I thought you would understand, Mom. It's only eleven-thirty.

29. Voice Differentiation

Problem. Voice differentiation. Two fighters, a fight trainer, and a fight promoter.

EDDIE: How's the kid doing, Doc?

DOC: He can hit but that's about all.

EDDIE: Do you think he will make it?

DOC: Not in a million years. He takes a terrible beating trying to get his right hand in.

EDDIE: Isn't he coming along at all?

DOC: Some guys can box and some can't. Now, you for instance. With your natural footwork, you could have been a ballet dancer. Jerry just hasn't got it. He can go a little way with his punch, but a real fighter will cut him to ribbons.

EDDIE: I was afraid of that.

DOC: He's getting anxious for a little action. What do you want me to do?

EDDIE: Maybe I can talk him into going back to school. If not, you'll have to put him in the ring.

DOC: Well, we can bring him along a way if we match him right for a while . . . here he comes now. Say, isn't that Maxie Kline with him?

EDDIE: Yeah. What's the kid doing with a guy like Kline? Hey, Jerry, come on over.

JERRY: (*Fading in*) Hello, Eddie. Doc, you know Maxie Kline?

EDDIE: Yeah, we know him.

MAXIE: How are you, champ?

EDDIE: I didn't know you were acquainted with Kline, Jerry.

MAXIE: Oh, we've been batting the breeze off and on, eh kid?

JERRY: Yeah. I came in looking for you, Eddie. Have you got a robe I can borrow for tomorrow night?

MAXIE: My new boy is making his debut at the beach.

EDDIE: Your new boy?

JERRY: Yeah, I'm changing managers. I signed with Maxie this morning.

30. Voice Differentiation

Situation. Two escaping bandits have found their way to an isolated mountain cabin. They are surprised by someone pounding on the door. It is the rural mail carrier. Hiding in an adjoining room, they tell the owner to open the door.

Problem. Voice differentiation. Sound.

(*Sound: Heavy wind heard from inside cabin. Pounding on door of cabin*)

SCOTTY: Hey, in there! Open up before I kick it in! Kennedy! Kennedy, open up!

(*Sound: More pounding*)

HERMAN: All right, let him in, but don't forget, we're in the next room. And don't let him spot us. Open up.

(*Sound: Steps to door. Door opens. Storm up*)

OLD MAN: Hi, Scotty, come on in.

(*Sound: Door closes. Storm down*)

SCOTTY: It's about time, 'bout went to sleep out here.

OLD MAN: What did you bring me, Scotty?

SCOTTY: The *Daily Bugle*.

(*Sound: Folded newspaper thrown on table*)

SCOTTY: (*Good-natured*) Four miles out of my way every day—six days a week. For what? So a white whiskered old sheep farmer can look at the pictures in the *Bugle*—so he can have a newspaper to start his morning fire.

OLD MAN: Now, Scotty, don't blow up.

SCOTTY: Aw . . .

OLD MAN: I got a pot of chile on the stove. And some hot coffee, too. Shuck that sheepskin and pull up at the table.

(*Sound: Heavy coat thrown down. Dishes. Chair pulled out*)

OLD MAN: How long you think this storm'll last, Scotty?

SCOTTY: Don't know, but if it gets any worse you're not going to have any callers for a while.

OLD MAN: Here, this'll warm your insides. Don't mind if I read my paper while you eat?

SCOTTY: What? Uh . . . no. Go ahead.
(*Sound: Tears wrapper off paper and unfolds it. Sound of dishes as Scotty eats*)
OLD MAN: Huh! Must've been quite a robbery you folks had in town.
SCOTTY: What?
OLD MAN: Says here bandits stuck up the First National. . . .
SCOTTY: Yeah, killed the cashier and got away with 12,000 in cash.

31. Voice Differentiation

Situation. A farmer drives a poacher off his land.
Problem. Voice differentiation.

LUD: All right, Hadley. I can't prove it was you that left the gate open and
  let all my pigs loose to run their fool heads off through the woods, but
  you'd better do your fishing somewhere else from now on. I'm giving you
  fair warning. Stay off my land.
HADLEY: Who you trying to scare, Rucker? . . . Come on, Vinton, let's go.
  This is beginning to bore me.
VINTON: Yes, sir.
HADLEY: Take me back to the house. I think I'll take it easy before dinner.
(*Sound: Car starts*)
VINTON: You know, sir, I have the feeling Rucker hopes you'll come back.
  He's the kind that would take a shot at you if you riled him any more.
HADLEY: Young punk! You ought to know by now, Vinton, that no one—
  no one—tells J. B. Hadley what he can and can't do.
(*Sound: Car fades out*)

32. Picture

Situation. A father is trying to force his boy to make a confession.
Problem. To time sound and dialogue.

MAN: What did you lie for, Tommy? Why did you? Tell me . . . all right,
  if you want it this way. Stand up! Stand up!! Stubborn, eh? O.K., this
  will take it out of you. (*Sound: Belt striking flesh*) You want to be a
  hoodlum, huh? (*Sound*) Stay out all night. (*Sound*) Run around with
  a bunch of pack rats. (*Sound*) Little big shot. (*Sound*) Talk, won't you?
  Tell me the truth. Where did you get that money? Do you think I like
  beating it out of you? All right, so you want to be a hard, (*Sound*),
  tough (*Sound*), rough (*Sound*) guy. Cry—cry! Say something. (*Sound-
  sound-sound*) O.K., O.K., I can't strap any more. Go to the dogs. I'm
  through. There's nothing I can do for you now.

33. Montage

(*Music: Fades*)
NARRATOR: Always on guard! Day or night, fair weather or foul! They guard
  a memory!
(*Music: Up, then down and out*)
NARRATOR: Just opposite the teeming capital of the United States, and across
  the winding, historic Potomac River in the shadow of the weird Pentagon

Building stand two men on guard. They are sometimes soldiers, sometimes marines, and sometimes bluejackets. Theirs is a proud duty for they are watching over one of their own. Inscribed on the tomb past which beats their measured tread:

(*Music: In softly*)

NARRATOR: "Here lies in everlasting glory an American soldier known but to God."

(*Music: Up and out*)

NARRATOR: He could be a private in the Army. A Marine major. A pharmacist's mate. He could be any of thousands of men. He might even be George Bennett of Columbus, Ohio, who one sunny April morning in 1942 (*Fade*) . . .

(*Sound: Hubbub of crowd. Band music in background*)

GEORGE: I'll say good-by here, honey. It's quieter. I'm gonna miss you, sweet, more than you'll ever know.

GEORGIA: Oh, George, George, why, why do you have to go? You've got a wife and a baby. They wouldn't draft you, darling. Why did you do it?

GEORGE: Hey, baby, take it easy. We decided this a long time ago, remember. There're lots of reasons, honey, and I thought I had you convinced.

GEORGIA: I was lying, George. Just agreeing with you so you'd think I was the brave little wife. I don't want you to go, George.

GEORGE: It's too late, darling. But don't worry your pretty little head. I'll be back before you miss me.

(*Sound: Crowd noise builds. Sounds of train steaming. Whistle toots*)

GEORGE: Good-by, darling. (*Fades*) I'll be back before you realize I've gone.

(*Music: Up and out*)

NARRATOR: But George didn't come back. All that came was a telegram. Among the blur of words were three that hit his wife right between the eyes—"missing in action."

(*Music: Up and out*)

NARRATOR: Lots of good-bys were said during those dark days of struggle.

(*Music: Up and out*)

MAN 1: Take it easy, son, and God bless you.

GIRL: Good-by, Johnny, and hurry back.

WOMAN: (*Tearfully*) Good-by for now, Tommy. Take care of yourself.

MAN 2: So long, Joe.

BOY: 'By, Daddy.

MAN 1: Good-by.

GIRL: Good-by.

WOMAN: Good-by.

MAN 2: Good-by.

BOY: Good-by.

(*Music: Up and out*)

NARRATOR: And for many, it was truly good-by.

(*Music: Up and out*)

MAN 1: (*Softly and huskily*) Missing in action.

GIRL: (*With disbelief*) Missing in action.

WOMAN: (On verge of hysterics) Missing in action.
MAN 2: Missing in action.
BOY: Where's daddy, Mommy?
MAN 1: Missing in action.
GIRL: Missing in action.
WOMAN: Missing in action.
MAN 2: Missing in action.
BOY: Where's daddy, Mommy?
(*Music: Up and out*)
NARRATOR: (*Slowly*) "Missing in action." An odd phrase. At first a flame
of hope surged in the hearts of the recipients, dying daily as no further
word came. Ofttimes, good news followed. Often, too, came nothing.
But America remembers. And day and night, year after year, in foul
weather and in fair, the soldier, the American soldier, whose name is
known but to God, rests peacefully while his comrades watch above.[5]

34. Montage

Purpose. To show the scope of a popular dance-band tour. Use of filter
mike.

(*Music: Fade in popular dance-band tune. Establish. Same tune used through-*
out sequence, growing louder and with more pronounced rhythm toward end
of sequence. Music down, blend with)
(*Sound: Telephone bell. Click of receiver lifted*)
BARBARA: Hello!
OPERATOR: (*Filter*) Is this Barbara Simmons at Los Angeles 1700?
BARBARA: Yes.
OPERATOR: (*Filter*) One moment, please. Las Vegas is calling. Go ahead,
please.
JACK: (*Filter*) Hello, honey, this is Jack. How does it feel to be engaged to a
famous band leader?
BARBARA: They liked you?
JACK: (*Filter*) Liked us? They loved us. Want us back next season.
BARBARA: What's the next stop?
JACK: (*Filter*) Dallas. I'll call you.
BARBARA: Don't forget, and take care of yourself.
(*Music: Up, down into telephone bell*)
OPERATOR: (*Filter*) Just a moment, please. Dallas is calling.
JACK: (*Filter*) Hello, baby.
BARBARA: Hello, band leader. How's everything down South?
JACK: (*Filter*) We fractured 'em. Cotton jumped 10 points. Miss me?
BARBARA: You bet I do.
JACK: (*Filter*) I'll blow you a kiss from St. Louis.
(*Music: Up . . . down*)
OPERATOR: (*Filter*) St. Louis calling Los Angeles. For Barbara Simmons.
JACK: (*Filter*) Hello, darling, did I wake you up? I forgot about the time
change.

[5] Jack Geyer.

BARBARA: (*Sleepily*) 'S all right. You have to pay the phone bill.

JACK: (*Filter*) Baby, the way we're going, we'll have a phone in every room.

(*Music: Up . . . down*)

JACK: (*Filter*) A 2-week holdover and more invitations for next year. Throw away your old coat, baby. It's open season on mink.

(*Music: Up . . . down*)

OPERATOR: (*Filter*) Go ahead, Cleveland.

OPERATOR: (*Filter*) Go ahead, Pittsburgh.

OPERATOR: (*Filter*) Go ahead, Boston.

(*Music: Up to climax . . . end*)

JACK: (*Filter*) And we took the big city without losing a man.

BARBARA: Darling, that's wonderful. What about the critics?

JACK: (*Filter*) They surrendered completely. We're using them to carry the band instruments.

BARBARA: The home folks are proud of you, darling. When are you coming back?

JACK: (*Filter*) On the first plane.[6]

35. Montage

NARRATOR: The young Marquis de Lafayette was set to work anew in order that he could soon qualify for the social demands of his grandfather's salon.

(*Sound: Clash of fencing foils, 10 seconds*)

INSTRUCTOR: Arrete!

(*Sound: Tacet*)

INSTRUCTOR: Parry, quart!

(*Sound: Blades strike*)

INSTRUCTOR: Non, non! Turn the nails upward, thumb slightly to the right; and this time move the hand and foil across the body to the left. Again. Parry, quart.

(*Sound: Clash of blades*)

INSTRUCTOR: Better. . . . Again, parry!

(*Sound: Clash of blades*)

INSTRUCTOR: Parry, tierce!

(*Sound: Blades touch*)

INSTRUCTOR: Marquis, you must concentrate. Three time I have corrected you. Now, nails down, hand to the right. Parry, tierce!

(*Sound: Blades meet*)

INSTRUCTOR: Again, parry.

(*Sound: Repeat*)

INSTRUCTOR: Better, now, on guard. This time we practice the vault, a side movement necessary when facing several opponents.

LAFAYETTE: I am tired.

INSTRUCTOR: Why, we have only begun, Marquis.

LAFAYETTE: I am not interested. Why must I spend an hour a day doing such monkey tricks? Tell me that. Put the foils away.

INSTRUCTOR: But Marquis de la Rivière—he has instructed me—

[6] Paul Brett.

LAFAYETTE: And so do I. Put the foils away.

INSTRUCTOR: Every gentleman, Monsieur, should learn the art of self-defense. It is a point of honor and skill to learn—

LAFAYETTE: There are other marks of a gentleman that please me more. Monsieur, the lesson is finished. (*Fade*) You are excused. (*Pause*)

(*Music: Sneak in minuet played on spinet*)

MASTER: One, two, three . . . one, two, three. (*Talks at intervals through music*) Relax your shoulders . . . Nod with the gesture . . . One, two, three . . . more on your toes . . . (*Music stops*) Marquis, you will pardon me—but—but—

LAFAYETTE: Say it, if you wish. I am awkward, I lack grace, I am stupid. Suppose I don't want to learn to dance?

MASTER: Let's try again. Remember, now, the minuet is a slow and graceful dance. It consists of a couple, a high step, a balance—three-four time. Ready. (*Music begins*) One, two, three; one, two, three. . . . Don't shuffle . . . don't sway . . . keep yourself erect. (*Exasperated*) No, no, no!! (*Music stops discord*) You do not have your mind on what you are doing, Marquis; you do not concentrate. Now watch me. You must make the picture of lightness, ease, courtliness, rhythm. You will never grace the salons of the great Marquis unless you learn to dance. Begin again, like this. One, two, three; (*Fading*) one, two, three; . . .

(*Pause*)

PERE: (*Fading in*) Marquis de Lafayette, I must insist upon your giving close attention to your Latin composition. Now give me the conjugation again—subjunctive, audio.

LAFAYETTE: Active voice?

PERE: Yes.

LAFAYETTE: Audiam, audias, audiat, audiamus, audiatis, audiant.

PERE: Now passive voice.

LAFAYETTE: Audi—Audi—

PERE: Audior.

LAFAYETTE: Audior . . . auditis . . . au—dimur—

PERE: (*Sharply*) No.

LAFAYETTE: I don't know the passive. . . . And why should I know? It's a dead language. No one speaks it and I don't want to waste my time. There are other marks of a gentleman that please me more. Monsieur, the lesson is finished. You are excused. (*Fade*)

36. Dramatic Narration[7]

(1)

(*Orchestra*)

NARRATOR: It is one o'clock in the morning of October 1, 1910. While the city sleeps, a band of men who toil by night and rest by day is working at top speed. From the far corners of the world another page of history's

[7] The first nine practice exercises in this section are quoted from the radio series, *Calling All Cars* and are supplied by the courtesy of Hixson-Jorgensen, Inc., Advertising, Los Angeles, Calif.

book has been assembled—the morning paper is going to press. In the composing room on the second floor of the *Times* building, a line of men, green eyeshades clamped to their heads, clatter at the Linotype machines. In the engraving room on the sixth floor, mercury lamps throw their ghoulish glare. The dogwatch in the city room sleepily eyes the clock, hoping that no big story will break to disturb their somnolent ease until thirty comes for them at half past four. Seated by their silent telegraph keys, two men stand by in the wire room for last-minute news flashes. In the basement, the huge presses hungrily await the plates for the final edition. Horses and wagons stand ready in the alley to dash away with the ink-wet edition to carriers all over the city, that Los Angeles may have her news with her morning coffee. The hands of the clock slowly move on. Activity increases as press time approaches. It is now one-five —one-six—in ink alley, by the pressroom. Another clock ticks ominously, unnoticed by any of the busy workmen in the building. The seconds pass, the clock says one-seven. And then—

(*Sound: Terrific explosion. Suitcase of 80 per cent dynamite*)

(*Orchestra: Up—after explosion*)

NARRATOR: With a roar that is heard 10 miles, the center of the *Times* building blows up. The force of the explosion snaps the girders supporting the second and third floors as so many toothpicks. Down into the gaping hole hurtle the heavy Linotype and stereotyping machinery, carrying their operators to a crushing death. The gas main which feeds the building is ripped open and instantly ignited. A seering fountain of flame leaps through the building. Within a moment the entire structure is a blaze. Workmen clutched in the freezing maw of horror rush to the fire escapes to be met by a fiery wall through which escape is an impossibility. The two telegraph editors, trapped in their room, slowly burn to death. Compositors and Linotype operators, horribly maimed, arms torn off and legs broken, lie helpless on the floor as the vicious fire creeps toward them. Their pitiful cries reach the street below where all the downtown fire apparatus has already arrived, but rescue is an impossibility. No man can enter that seething funeral pyre and live. The reporters and the editors on the dogwatch in the city room on the third floor are forced to jump to the street. Those who survive the jump are crippled for life. Within a few minutes after the explosion, the last cry of the helpless victims trapped in the building has been smothered in the fevered embrace of the flames. In an astonishingly short time, the entire building is gutted and then a new danger threatens as, one after another, the walls, lacking any support, sway,

(*Sound: Crashing walls*)

totter, and crash to the street where a huge crowd of citizens, hurled from their beds by the explosion, are straining at the hastily rigged guard rope. (*Pause*) All night long the fire rages, completely ruining the plant of the *Times*, yet just a little later than usual the next morning, the *Times* is delivered to its subscribers, printed at an emergency plant by the battered, bruised, and bandaged survivors of the catastrophe. (*Pause*)

(*Orchestra: Up*)

Before the last smoldering ember has died away, the law swings into action.

(2)

NARRATOR: The sleek, little, mechanical red bird skims across the green of the airdrome, shears the top of the grass, and vaults toward the heavens. Circling effortlessly, it is soon 1,000 feet in the air. Below lies the panorama of Southern California, a glimmering jewel in the noonday sun—the mountains to the east—the desert beyond shimmering in the heat—below the matchless blue of Santa Monica Bay, half circled by the frothing half scallop of the beach, and toward the west the mysterious peaks of the channel islands—a day to dream—a day to soar. . . . A shout goes up from the field—the monocoupe falters in its flight, turns over, flops into a spin—hurtles earthward—

(*Sound: Trombone dive*)

down . . . down . . . down. . . .

(3)

NARRATOR: On a lonely hill on the east side of Los Angeles stands an old house surrounded by a weed-grown garden, screened by scabby eucalyptus trees. It is a mystery house, a silent house, to the children of the neighborhood, a haunted house!

(*Sound: Wind*)

One night, a year ago, the wind blew around its bleak corners out of a dark cloud which glowed dully from the reflected lights of the city. The wind moaned and whined, it rustled the dry branches of the trees, it plucked up the scaling bark of the eucalyptus and whirled it away; it nipped at the noses of two small boys taking a short cut home past the old, dark house. . . .

(*Sound: Wind moaning. Footsteps on gravel*)

BOBBY: I kinda wish we hadn't taken the short cut, Dick.

DICK: Why?

BOBBY: Well, of course, I ain't afraid, but well—I might scuff up my new shoes on this gravel walk—

DICK: Aw, that's what shoes are for—to scuff.

(4)

NARRATOR: The Tortolitas Mountains outside Tuscon, Arizona, are crowned with gray clouds. Lightning flashes about the crest of Mount Lemmon. The dying sun sends one somber streak of red across the desolate, overcast desert and then chokes to extinction the soft tentacles of a thunderhead around its throat.

(*Sound: Thunder*)

The drums of heaven beat a dirge, and far below a rickety Model T Ford chugs up a sandy hill, the first drops of

(*Sound: Distant Model T fading in*)

rain splattering its dust-caked windshield—and as it reaches the top of the rise—

(*Sound: Clap of thunder. Model T in full. Slows down—two shots . . . clatter of windshield glass*)

MAN: (*Screams*)

(*Sound: Colossal clap of thunder . . . furious downpour of rain*)

(*Orchestra*)

NARRATOR: The reborn sun next morning rises in a clear, blue rain-washed sky, sends the last storm clouds scudding west toward the Pacific, sets about drying up the drenched desert. Up the same lonely road near Tucson, chugs another automobile containing two men. . . .

(*Sound: Motor . . . low gear*)

BUFFER: That rain last night sure did the country a lot of good, George.

GEORGE: Sure did.

(5)

NARRATOR: Slowly the Los Angeles officers follow the gunrunners. At 15 miles an hour they creep along Telegraph Road, through Santa Fe Springs. The sun splashes flat, dying yellow against the brown, burned hills of La Habra as the caravan tediously rolls onward. Early in the evening they arrive in Santa Ana. O'Buff and his men watch the trucks put up in a garage for the night. Keeping the drivers and their assistants, or "swampers," under constant watch, O'Buff and his men follow them about town. Toward 10 o'clock, the Captain takes a room in a hotel facing the main street. He is joined there by Captain Hook, the Federal man.

(6)

NARRATOR: September 13, 1928. The *Lark,* Los Angeles bound, is standing in a small watering station only a few miles from its destination. In the club car a group of San Francisco and Los Angeles businessmen are discussing plans for the coming year: golf, business, and the usual small talk of the smoking cars. Suddenly the door at the end of the coach opens, letting in a blast of cold, September air. Two men and a woman step in, and the travelers find themselves looking into the business end of two guns held by the men.

SIMPSON: If you'll be so kind, gentlemen, as to just line up over there against the bar and put your hands above your heads, I assure you there will be no violence.

(7)

NARRATOR: As Sergeant Bunner turns his back to unlock the door, he hears the scuffle of feet and whirls around to find that his prisoner has dived headfirst through the window. Rushing to the window, Bunner faces Sander for a brief instant across the fire escape and then the daredevil bandit hurls himself into space. Horror-stricken, Bunner watches Sander's body turn over and over as he falls three stories on to a vacant lot beside the rooming house. Sounding the alarm to McLachlin, Bunner runs down the fire escape. When he reaches the second-floor landing, to his amazement he sees Sander jump to his feet and run toward Pine Street. Bunner jumps from the second-floor landing. . . . His ankle crumples under him as he hits the ground. McLachlin, rounding the side of the building, cannot shoot at Sander because his brother officer is in the line of fire. This momentary break enables Sander to escape in the crowds on Pine Street, and discouraged, the two officers, Bunner limping badly, climb the stairs to the room where the frightened Percy waits for them.

(8)

NARRATOR: The secretary of the Prison Board immediately phones the prison of his whereabouts. With orders to hold fire as long as possible, the army of the law goes into action. From San Francisco, from Oakland, from Berkeley come officers. Quickly the peace forces are organized, and with police radio blaring last-minute flashes . . . a posse composed of hundreds of men, in scores of police cars, block every highway and byway in Petaluma and Marin counties. The posse closes in, combing the hilly north coast country. As the convict's car swoops into the Hick's Valley Road, the posse sights them. The chase is on. Deputy sheriffs pull down their shotguns from the roofs of their high-powered police cars. State patrolmen crouch over their white motorcycles, unlimber their guns. Sirens scream. Ten miles—12—14 miles, they roar west of Petaluma. The law holds its guns in readiness. The convicts, still out of range, apprehensively look backward. Then, when they are 18 miles away from Petaluma, the convicts' car takes a turn too sharply . . . the car skids . . . the law is within range. . . .

(*Sound: Fusillade of shots continues through scene. Motor roar*)

(9)

NARRATOR: Fog settles silently through the streets of San Francisco . . . cold—dank fog that swirled and eddied about the close-packed streets of Chinatown. Amoebalike blobs of humanity drifted through the murky gloom.

(*Orchestra out. . . . Sound back of narration . . . faint footsteps, etc.*)

In the doorway a hag of a woman waited . . . sniffling . . . shifting uneasily . . . peering, perplexed, into the gloom. The faint tread of footsteps came cautiously toward her . . . paused. The shabby figure of a man loomed out of the fog.

MAN: Got the stuff?

HAG: Yeah.

MAN: Gimme.

HAG: How much?

MAN: Two bindles.

HAG: Here . . . two bucks.

MAN: For this junk? Buck and a half is my limit.

HAG: Aw, how's a lady goin' to make a livin'?

MAN: That ain't nothing to me. That's all I'll pay.

HAG: Okay! Okay! Gimme it!

MAN: Here. Dollar bill and two quarters.

NARRATOR: He pressed a crumpled bill and two coins into her hand and received two small envelopes. He slipped out of the doorway and was swallowed up in the fog. The hag waited a second or two, then emerged from the black hole of the building and headed along the pavement in the opposite direction. Suddenly, out of the murk, two figures swung into step beside the woman. Steel fingers tightened on her arm.

HAG: Say—what's comin' off here?

AUGEN: Take it easy, sister.

ALLEN: You're under arrest.

(10)

ANNOUNCER: Today we bring you a concluding series of incident's in the life of the great actor, Robert Bruce Mantell. Many years have passed since the night young Mantell, then playing under an alias, Robert Hudson, fell asleep on a railway station platform and dreamed that the great Henry Irving had summoned him to London; years of casual employment and dire poverty. But ambition burned with increased intensity. Again he comes to the United States, but this time on contract. New York discovers a new idol. Mantell scores a tremendous hit playing opposite Fanny Davenport in Sardou's new play, *Fedora*. Then followed a series of triumphs that raised the Belfast actor to fame and fortune; but a few years later circumstances conspired to exile Mantell from New York and his tide of success began to ebb from the affluence of Broadway to the poverty of the barnstormer. On the night of July 2, 1898, in Rockford, Illinois. . . .

(11)

(*Signature*)

ANNOUNCER: Presenting *Drama in Literature*.

(*Music: Up . . . fade*)

ANNOUNCER: The conversation of the villagers gathered in the big kitchen of the Rainbow Inn concerning the supernatural is given a touch of unexpected realism as the figure of Silas Marner drenched with rain, hatless, wild-eyed, breaks into the room and babbles incoherently that he has been robbed. The room is in an uproar. Some believe the gaunt old miser; and others deem him out of his head. However, the landlord and Mr. Macey go back with Silas to investigate his story.

(12)

(*Signature*)

ANNOUNCER: Presenting *Drama in Literature*, brought to you by the Division of Adult and Continuation Education, State Department of Education. Today it is our pleasure to bring you the first in a series of dramatizations based on George Eliot's famous novel, *Silas Marner*.

(*Music: Up*)

ANNOUNCER: In the days when the spinning wheels hummed busily in the farmhouses—and even great ladies, clothed in silk and threadlace, had their toy spinning-wheels of polished oak! Silas Marner, a pallid young man, with prominent shortsighted brown eyes, was highly thought of in the little hidden world of Lantern Yard; but a peculiar interest had been centered in him ever since he had fallen, at a prayer meeting, into a mysterious rigidity and suspension of consciousness, which, lasting for an hour or more, had been mistaken for death. It was William Dane, alone, Silas' closest friend, who interpreted the occurrence as a possible manifestation of evil.

(13)

(*Signature: Up . . . fade under*)

ANNOUNCER: The _____ brings you a radio dramatization based on, *The Making of an American,* the story of Jacob Riis. It is a story of a Viking of our own time which proves that the North Sea country can still send forth as stanch and fearless men as those who sailed in their dragon ships the whole roads of the uncharted seas, found a new world, and forgot about it long before Columbus dreamed his dream. The setting for the prologue of our drama is the little town of Ribe, Denmark, with its wide view to the sea, its green meadows, the lonesome flight of shore birds and the melancholy curlew's call. The clatter of the mill wheel comes up with drowsy hum. The sweet smells of meadow and field are in the air. Upon a wooden bridge spanning the Nibs River with twin arches like the humps of a dromedary—

(*Music: Tacet*)

A boy and a girl.

(14)

(*Signature*)

ANNOUNCER: Presenting *Sands of Time,* the record of men and women whose daring, sacrifice, and achievement constitute a challenge to heroic living.

(*Organ: Up . . . fade*)

ANNOUNCER: Today we conclude our account of the tragic Donner party— that ill-starred expedition of emigrants to California in 1846. The situation, briefly, is as follows: advised to take a cutoff, the pioneers were delayed in reaching the Sierras where an early snowfall blocked their advance. On October 23, at Prosser Creek, 3 miles below Truckee, they find 6 inches of snow and realize they must make camp and wait until some of their party can cross the Sierras on foot and bring back relief. Although this saga of adventure is historically labeled with the name of George Donner, the central figures of the drama as we recount it from this point are Mrs. Jim Reed and her children. Reed himself had been banished from the expedition, charged with unjustifiable homicide. He had gone ahead alone without food or equipment. Our story opens in a snow-locked camp in the Sierras.

(15)

(*Signature*)

ANNOUNCER: Presenting *Sands of Time,* brought to you by _____.

(*Organ: Up . . . fade*)

ANNOUNCER: Tonight we tell the story of Florence Nightingale—liberator of womanhood—who devoted her life to the alleviation of human suffering. . . . Florence Nightingale—a portrait. "Attractive . . . remarkable for

grace of figure and movement . . . a sweet voice, and the air of a woman
of unaffected high breeding . . . great reserve and self-control . . . "
It is our purpose to draw the picture of a sensitive, thoughtful, ambitious
young woman, restricted by convention, who succeeded eventually in
mounting the barriers which blocked her pathway to a great ideal. Our
scene opens at the family estate at Embley. It is after breakfast. Mr.
Nightingale, according to his custom, is reading aloud from a London
journal. . . .

APPENDIX I

TELEVISION 1950—IS IT GOOD OR BAD?[1]

Announcer:

Welcome, friends, to historic Town Hall in New York City to the 593d broadcast of America's Town Meeting. After nearly 15 years on the air as an hour-long program, we're changing tonight to a new streamlined format of 30 minutes. As you know, nearly all full hour programs on the air have been condensed to half an hour with great success. To keep in step with the times and in consideration of your own valuable time, we're presenting this half-hour program for your enjoyment and profit.

On future Town Meetings, you'll hear the Nation's leaders of thought and opinion in lively but orderly discussion of subjects of greatest interest to you, the American people. You've helped us select these subjects and you've helped us make Town Meeting the Nation's most popular radio forum. For your past and continuing interest, we are most grateful.

Now to preside over our discussion, here is your moderator, the president of Town Hall and founder of America's Town Meeting, George V. Denny, Jr. Mr. Denny. (*Applause*)

Moderator Denny:

Good evening, neighbors. We're beginning the New Year and the second half of the 20th century with a discussion of television for a very important reason. In our opinion, television—good or bad—will be the most powerful single medium of communication and, therefore, the greatest influence among the peoples of this earth that we shall know during the next 50 years.

Now we have not asked our speakers to prophesy, but, in the highest interest of the human race, we've asked them to examine television in the light of what we've done with it to date and where we seem to be headed.

Both Mr. Cousins and Mr. Capp have watched television's development with eager and friendly interest. While Mr. Cousins views much that he has seen with alarm, Mr. Capp has seen much to applaud and that's what makes a good Town Meeting.

[1] This was the question discussed on the Town Meeting (*America's Town Meeting of the Air*) program, Jan. 3, 1950, and broadcast by the stations of the ABC. Reprinted with the permission of The Town Hall, Inc., 123 West 43d St., New York 18, N.Y,

In the last analysis, we, the people, will decide the future of television by the way we exercise our freedom of choice.

I'm sure that at this stage of the game those who are preparing the things we choose—both those who manufacture sets and those who build television programs—will be glad to know your opinions after you've heard both sides on this Town Meeting. So listen carefully and let us know what you think.

We'll hear first from the editor of one of the great cultural forces of this country, *The Saturday Review of Literature*, which reaches one of the most influential audiences in America. Mr. Cousins, we invite you to tell us freely and frankly the things you think that are bad about television today. Norman Cousins. (*Applause*)

Mr. Cousins:

Mr. Denny, I hope that Al Capp will make radio history here tonight— Town Hall Meeting history—by agreeing with me. You see, we both like television, both have faith in its future; we both see it, as Mr. Denny says, somewhat differently. My feelings about television right now is that it's being murdered.

Now I'm not talking about television as a gadget. I'm talking about the promise of television.

Let's think of television in terms of what it could do and what it can be and ask ourselves whether television is living up to its early promise. Now is the time, while TV is young, for the American people to speak up about television. When we do speak up, I hope the first thing we hit and hit hard, Mr. Capp, is the notion, now apparently governing television as it has governed the movies, that the American people must be talked down to.

You know the theory—it's the idea that the average American has the mentality of a 12-year-old child and you've got to spoon-feed him with entertainment that makes no demands on his supposedly limited intellectual resources.

I contend that this theory, this Idiot's Fable, is one of the biggest myths of our time. I contend that it is a blunder and a billion dollar blunder.

It is a blunder that has already come close to putting the skids under Hollywood, has devitalized and disfigured much of radio, and has already wrecked some of the largest pulp magazines in America. Despite all the evidence, television today is apparently repeating that blunder, and I'm afraid with the same results.

Out of the wizardry of the television tube these days, there is coming such an assault against the human mind, such a mobilized attack on the intelligence, such a mass invasion against good taste, as no communication medium has known.

There are millions of dollars for perfecting television mechanically, but only pennies, comparatively, for programs. Expensive research and equipment will make color on television possible within a year or two, but a Grade C program in technicolor is still a Grade C program.

What television needs right now—even more than technicolor and mechanical improvement—is better programing, more respect for the intelligence of the average American, more imagination, more originality, more of the pioneering spirit that was behind much of TV only two years ago.

Television needs to get over the notion and get over it fast that all you have to do to have a successful television programing schedule is to take mediocre radio shows and put them before a TV camera.

Increasingly, the fabulous possibilities within television are being brushed aside in favor of radio stereotypes—dramatizations that stick to the usual patter and pattern: get-rick-quick, get-kissed-quick, get-killed-quick. (*Laughter*)

It isn't as though TV lacks the people who realize this, people who believe that television is an art of its own and not the visual extension of radio or another outlet for Hollywood. But these people need front office backing. Even more than that, they need the support of the American people.

Incidentally, if you enjoy Kukla, Fran, and Ollie, to my mind the best program on TV for children—and I confess it's one of my own favorite programs—write to them and tell them so. I'm sorry that more people haven't written to the Jon Gnagys and the Ivan Sandersons and Roy K. Marshalls, just to mention a few whose programs gave some idea of the promise of television but who haven't had the support from the television industry itself.

Am I arguing here for television without starch or dramatic appeal? Certainly not.

Am I arguing for highbrowism in television, or for converting it into an extension of the classroom? Certainly not.

I expect my television set to bring me entertainment, bring magnificent entertainment to my home, but I said *entertainment*, not an endless procession of murders, gang wars, terror and horror specials, substandard variety shows, and wrestling matches.

I expect TV, too, Mr. Denny, to live up to its billing as the supreme triumph of invention, a magic eye that can bring into the home the wonders of entertainment, information, and education; something that can be a tool for the making of an enlightened democracy, such as the world has never known.

But, Mr. Denny and Mr. Capp, I'm afraid there is no point right now in painting any rosy pictures about the future of television, the promise of television, until we face up to the hard fact that right now it is being murdered in the cradle. (*Applause*)

Moderator Denny:

Thank you, Norman Cousins. Well, like all pictures on Town Meeting, there's another side of the ball, so let's take a look at the other side with one of the most successful creative artists in one of the greatest mass media of communications—the comic strip.

Mr. Capp, the creator of Li'l Abner, the Shmoo, the Kigmy, and now a contributor to the *Atlantic Monthly Magazine*. Al Capp. (*Applause*)

Al Capp:

Thank you, Dick Tracy fans. I agree with Mr. Cousins—isn't that a lovable way to begin an argument—to agree with the other guy? I agree that the

American people should not be talked down to. Well, all of us are Americans and quite a few of us here are people.

I'm afraid that Mr. Cousins has been talking down to us, so I'm going to raise the level of this discussion. I'm going to bring it up from the murky depths of Mr. Cousins' vague generalities, his over-all damning, up to the revealing sunlight of fact.

I'm going to compare Mr. Cousins' beef that television programing is substandard and mediocre with the facts of television life.

Oh, yes, I've done research. I've gone into this thing fully. There is no sacrifice too great for me to make for you. I spent three seconds clipping out tonight's television program. (*Laughter*)

And it proves that anyone who takes the trouble to get off his canvas-backed chair (*Laughter*) and turn a knob can get from television tonight and any night the most fabulous, the most imaginative, the most varied entertainment, delight, and culture ever offered by man to man.

You've heard Mr. Cousins' picture of television. Well, here's television's record. From 6 to 7 tonight, American kids—that is, good little kids who've finished reading Li'l Abner (*laughter*)—have a choice of the most charming juvenile entertainment—Kukla, Fran, and Ollie; the Lucky Pup; the Small Fry Club.

Now as one whose profession is whomping up wholesome fantasy—well, pretty wholesome fantasy—I'm amazed and I'm a little frightened at the consistent goodness, the endless invention of the artists who created these things for our children.

At seven, the little kids should be put to bed, and the adults and the older kids ought to dine. That is, if they can tear themselves away from the monster called television. But if they can't, there is a solid scientific film. There's Doug Edwards' News Show. There is sweet music by Sonny Kendis and Vincent Lopez. There is honest and wholesome humor by a wonderful guy named Herb Shriner.

Then at eight o'clock, television tonight brings you the most beloved funny man of our time—Milton Berle—and with him the opera star, Patrice Munsel.

Or, if you want ideas and free and authoritative debate from 8 to 9, there is the Court of Current Issues. This is television's record. This is what's true. This is what's true tonight.

There is the Court of Current Issues with two college professors—two, count 'em, two—and Robert Nathan, one of America's great economists.

Or, if you want the finest in music at eight o'clock tonight, there is the Sylvan Levin Opera Concert with a soprano, Ann Ayres.

At nine o'clock, the Actors' Studio gives you, as it always does, excellent drama, with Broadway's best actors. Or, if you want sports, there are the fights from Westchester.

At 9:30, there is a film with a couple of substandard, mediocre hams, named Lawrence Olivier and Gertrude Lawrence. (*Laughter*) Later, there are more sports. There is a charming light comedy show. There is news.

What do you want, Mr. Cousins, an egg in your beer? (*Laughter*)

The record shows that television will give you whatever you want. If you want the light entertainment and information, television will give it to you. If you just want to gripe about it, you can. But by carefully manipulating your dials so that you bypass all the wonderful things of television, you can find murder and horror and ugliness.

Now, to me, that seems like being confronted by Rita Hayworth in a bathing suit—Mr. Denny made me put a bathing suit on her here, to protect your morals or your sanity (*laughter*)—to see a picture of Rita Hayworth in a bathing suit, but refuse to look at anything except a wart on her thumb and insist that that's what all of Rita Hayworth looks like.

Television isn't being murdered in its cradle, Mr. Cousins. Take a good look at it. It's a lusty brat; it's bright and intelligent. Sure, sometimes it yowls, and its bed-wetting annoys sensitive souls like you, but watch it grow into the greatest blessing and the greatest delight of American family life.

Take off those mud-covered glasses and take a good look at the kid. See its wonderful promise and give it a chance. After all, Norman, we—editors, cartoonists, and television producers—are all cousins under the skin. (*Laughter*) Television isn't a Kigmy—it's a Shmoo. (*Applause*)

Moderator Denny:

Thank you, Al Capp. I don't know whether I can appreciate your making Tuesday night sound so attractive on television and robbing us of our listeners, but now while we get ready for our Question Period, here's a special message for our Town Meeting listeners.

Announcer:

Well, friends, what's your opinion now? In today's world we can't be like the judge who said he could never listen to more than one side of a case because it confused him.

. . . .

Our Town Hall audience is ready with questions, and so for our question period, we return you to Mr. Denny.

QUESTIONS, PLEASE!

Mr. Denny: Are we ready for our questions here in Town Hall? We'll start with this gentleman right over here.

Man: Mr. Denny, I'd like to observe offhand first that if Mr. Capp finally gets tired of drawing comics he probably has a great future as a politician. (*Laughter*) He made a rather magnificent defense of an untenable position, I think, there for a while, if I might sympathize with Mr. Cousins. But instead of getting in the middle on this thing, I'd like to ask him a question which maybe he can't answer so offhandedly, that is to get it down to an economic level.

He cited some very nice programs that are on the air tonight on television— and I think some of them are very good programs, too—but the question is, are any of them profitable?

I read the other day that television has lost sixteen million dollars this year and had lost fifteen million dollars last year, and some months ago I got rather curious about how long that can happen. I'm an economist, and I get to asking these questions that nobody else wants. So I just added up how much it would cost if we had national television of the same kind on a thousand stations, and I come up with the rather gruesome figure of $1,740,000,000.

That's how much it would cost to give the whole United States these wonderful programs that he's been itemizing. I just want to know how we are going to make that pay. When we answer that question, maybe we can talk about how we're going to make the programs better.

Mr. Denny: Mr. Capp, that's Mr. Faught, who has just made an extensive survey of television that's just out this last month. Perhaps you'd like to handle his question.

Mr. Capp: Yes, I read his book and it's an excellent book. (*Laughter*) As a matter of fact, you've all just heard his book. (*Laughter*) Mr. Faught, don't expect me to worry about the fact that television is losing fifteen million dollars a year. I'm a cartoonist, and what's a week's pay!

What do we expect? I think that we'll pay for television. We'll pay for television by buying the soap, the automobiles, the oil, the gasoline, and all the things that television sponsors want us to buy to pay for the programs that we like. We've always paid for everything we've gotten. We'll pay for it and it'll be worth it. (*Applause*)

Mr. Denny: All right. Mr. Cousins has a comment on that. Mr. Cousins.

Mr. Cousins: Mr. Capp says that a cartoonist makes fifteen million dollars a week. I don't think he was kidding. Mr. Capp, why don't you just take over the television and support it? (*Laughter*) I think that you could probably help it a lot.

Mr. Capp: No, I want to say this fast: To every kid that's throwing his school books away and beginning to draw pictures—cartoonists don't make fifteen million dollars a week. Some of them don't make that in a year, kids! (*Laughter*)

Mr. Denny: We're first going to call on Mr. Capp to make up our Town Hall deficit. All right.

Lady: Mr. Cousins, would you approve a government-run station for non-profit cultural and intellectual programing to satisfy the so-called malcontents, and, possibly, become a standard or measuring rod for the TV audience, and, accordingly, for the advertisers?

Mr. Cousins: No, I notice that you were very careful not to say "government-sponsored television or government-sponsored radio" because they're two different things. You said, "a television station," somewhat comparable to the radio station New York City has. I think it'd be an excellent idea, yes.

Mr. Denny: All right, thank you. Now the gentleman back there right under the balcony with a question for Mr. Capp.

Man: What is the general effect of TV on the high school pupil?

Mr. Capp: What is the general effect of TV on the high school pupil? Well, it may seem unbelievable to you who see me, but it's been, oh, five years since I've been in high school. (*Laughter*) I think the general effect on the high school pupil is fine; for instance, it's got to be dark where you look at television. (*Laughter and applause*)

Mr. Denny: All right, Mr. Cousins, do you have a comment there?

Mr. Cousins: That's one way to get educated, Mr. Capp. (*Laughter*)

Mr. Denny: I think the high school students know more about that than Mr. Capp does, don't you? (*Laughter*)

Mr. Cousins: Well, Mr. Capp can draw pictures. He has an advantage.

I have before me a copy of the *Congressional Record* of early last year which publishes a speech by the Chairman of the Criminal Law Section of the American Bar Association in which he says that no one medium—television, radio, or comic books—damages the child by itself.

But he makes this very good point: "No one of the media alone at any one time or over any extended period can be said to be more harmful than another, but the insistent and continued repetition of these influences, each complementing the other, must produce a deteriorating effect upon the minds of the impressionable. Immature and undeveloped minds are molded to the concept that crime and criminal conduct is the norm of human behavior. Ethical concepts are twisted from reality, weakened, and all too frequently destroyed." This was based on a very careful study.

Mr. Denny: All right, Mr. Cousins. Now that you've raised that question let me bring up this one here. This is the same kind of thing, Mr. Capp. It's a question from Mrs. Clara S. Logan, president of the Southern California Association for Better Radio and Television. She sends in this question: "In one week's time over six stations, there were 91 murders and numerous other crimes shown on the television screen during children's listening hours. Should we excuse this breach of its pledge 'to operate in the public interest' because of present financial difficulties?" That's for you, Mr. Capp. Would you comment on that?

Mr. Capp: Yes, let's go ahead on Clara's reasoning—on Mrs. Logan's reasoning—that anything with murders in it isn't any good, so we chuck out all the radio shows that excite us. Then we get on to Shakespeare, Romeo and Juliet goes out—poisoning, starving; Macbeth—lots of innocent Scottish soldiers are killed—let's cross that out; Huckleberry Finn—there's a grave robbing, there's truancy—let's chuck that out. Let's chuck out the dictionary because it explains very carefully "communism" and "free love." (*Laughter*)

This sort of reasoning is idiotic. It's as idiotic as the reasoning in the *Congressional Record*. I'd like to know what would happen to those kids' minds if they didn't listen to television shows, if they didn't read comic strips, but if they just read the *Congressional Record*. (*Laughter and applause*)

Mr. Cousins: That sounds pretty good, doesn't it, Mr. Capp? Let's think what you have said. You have said, in effect, to throw out all education—education is not important. That no influence on a child is important. I think, Mr. Capp, that we can't burlesque what is happening today. Let's read the rest of that total. You gave a very good summary before of what goes on on television.

The organization that Mr. Denny quoted before, the Southern California Association for Better Radio and Television, lists the following: the week's total—91 murders, 7 staged holdups, 3 kidnapings, 10 thefts, 4 burglaries, 2 cases of arson, 2 jail breaks, 1 murder by explosion of 15 to 20 people, 2 suicides, 1 case of blackmail, cases of assault and battery too numerous to tabulate, also cases of attempted murder. Much of the action takes place in saloons, brawls all too numerous to mention, crooked judges, crooked sheriffs, crooked juries.

Now, Mr. Capp, I think it's very easy to brush this all aside and say, "Sure it doesn't make any difference, the children aren't influenced by all this." But you know it as well as I do, Mr. Capp, this is serious. So serious is it that, in radio, the National Broadcasting Company has agreed to suspend all programs of this nature until after nine o'clock at night. If radio does it, apparently there must be something to it. (*Applause*)

Mr. Capp: One thing I will say is that the Southern Association of the Ladies Upward and Onward League—I think I have that name right—must have a wonderful time listening to all that stuff. (*Laughter*) I'll bet they had to belt their kids out from in front of the television machine.

But, here, American kids have been reading comic strips. They've been listening to radio shows. Now, they look at television. As a whole, American kids are pretty decent kids. They're pretty decent. There is a whole nation of kids who never saw comic strips, who never saw television, who never heard horror radio shows—a nation of kids under Adolf Hitler. They grew up to destroy all civilization, to murder, to burn, to destroy, and to kill. That's my answer. (*Applause*)

Mr. Cousins: It's a question of fact, Mr. Capp. Let's get this down. The medium most used by Joseph Goebbels in propagandizing the German youth was the technique of a comic strip. Now, I'm not opposed to comic strips as such. I think Mr. Capp does the best comic strip in America and I'm all for it. My only regret is that there aren't more Capps who have good taste and real imagination, and do not have to rely on the stereotypes of bloodlust in order to get an audience. (*Applause*)

Mr. Denny: Thank you. A question from the gentleman up in the balcony.

Man: Mr. Cousins, is it necessary to pose an artificial dilemma of control of programing by Government versus control of programing by advertisers when instead we might have television programing as magazine content is produced? For example, each magazine determines its own editorial content. Advertisers buy only advertising space. Couldn't we have television on the same basis?

Mr. Denny: Take it, Mr. Cousins.

Mr. Cousins: I don't know about that. One thing I am certain of is that the worst solution for this would be to have the Government take over. What I am anxious to see happen is to have the television industry itself raise its own sights, recognizing that there are certain limitations at present, and that it is actually endangering the future of television by not putting it on a high level. By high level I am not talking about a highbrow level.

I don't think you can use any other technique—the magazine technique, the radio technique, or the movie technique. Television is an art of its own and must be so recognized.

Mr. Denny: Thank you. Now, Mr. Capp, we've got time for this question:

"With the high cost of entertainment and the high cost of baby sitters, don't you think television will be a big factor in eliminating boredom and monotony for parents with babies and young children?" (*Laughter*)

Mr. Capp: Well, one thing I say is that I think all parents should have children. (*Laughter*) I haven't much time left, and so I want to end this with a summation of everything I have said. "Television, you are misshapen, you are small. You have warts, but, gee, I love you." (*Laughter and applause*)

Mr. Denny: Thank you, Al Capp, and thank you, Norman Cousins.

APPENDIX II

WHO SHOULD BE RESPONSIBLE FOR EDUCATION ON TELEVISION? [1]

Moderator Denny:

Good evening, neighbors. When the late H. G. Wells was being chided by a friend of his for being pessimistic in his book, *The Shape of Things to Come,* Wells replied, "Pessimistic, old chap? Not at all, I was exceedingly optimistic. I let the human race survive. What reason have you to assume that mankind will continue to inhabit this earth? Other animals have become extinct because they didn't learn how to use their brains for survival."

In the face of today's news, we may well ponder this statement. We spend billions developing our machine age each year and a pathetic few millions teaching ourselves how to live with these machines without destroying civilization itself.

Now comes a great new medium of communication many times more powerful than any we've yet developed—television. It has the power to influence and control the activities of vast populations. But who should be responsible for its use in the field of education? We're not limiting our definition of education to literacy, only, for we'll embrace in our discussion tonight the question of who should be responsible for the use of television to help the American people find the right answer to the problems of living today, in the last half of the twentieth century.

We are fortunate in having the advice of a member of the Federal Communications Commission, the Honorable Frieda B. Hennock, who was previously a successful practicing attorney here in New York City, and Dr. Ernest Dichter, business and psychological research consultant for some of the largest sponsors of radio and television programs in the country. Also in our audience are representative American educators, who will probably challenge both of our speakers tonight during our discussion. We'll hear first from the Honorable Frieda B. Hennock. (*Applause*)

Miss Hennock:

Mr. Denny, I want to alert the millions of friends and listeners of America's Town Meeting of the Air to the hearings currently being held by the Federal

[1] A discussion heard on *America's Town Meeting of the Air* radio program, Nov. 28, 1950, and broadcast by the stations of the ABC. Reprinted with the permission of The Town Hall, Inc., 123 West 43d St., New York 18, N.Y.

Communications Commission in Washington, D.C., on the question of reserving television channels for educators.

Two years ago, the FCC established a freeze, halting the grant of any new television licenses. Because of this freeze, there are only 107 television stations in operation. Now, Dr. Dichter, these television channels represent one of America's most valuable natural resources. Unlike other mass communications media, such as newspapers, magazines, or motion pictures, the radio and television air waves belong to the people.

Television is at the crossroads. There are about 2,000 television frequencies remaining to be handed out, and once these are gone, there will be no more to be had. Shall the FCC hand out television licenses to commercial broadcasters on a first-come-first-serve basis, as was done in radio, until all the channels are exhausted, or will the Commission take a far-sighted view of the great potential value of television as a medium for education and set aside these channels exclusively for the use of noncommercial educational stations? I hope the Commission will do the latter. I hope they will invite the educators into the banquet when they assign these valuable frequencies, rather than leave them to scramble after crumbs, once the best channels are gone.

Dr. Dichter, television is the cheapest and most effective means of mass education ever developed. If one picture is worth a thousand words, then one television should be worth an entire library shelf. That is why I firmly believe that 25 per cent of all television channels should be assigned to educators. I do not think our commercial broadcasters ever have accepted or ever will accept the full responsibility for educating our listening and viewing public.

Of course, a distinguished broadcaster once said that a famous comedy program was educational, because it taught people to brush their teeth twice a day and see their dentist twice a year, but that is not my idea of the potential educational value of television in this world of ours.

At the turn of the century in America, there was great opposition to the enactment of compulsory school attendance laws. Industrial expansion called for sources of cheap, unskilled labor, and many people agreed to the principle of having children work, saying it kept them out of idle mischief. I think today we realize the wisdom of these school laws. I hope that we do not have to wait another half century to realize the fallacy of considering television exclusively as a medium of advertising. We will be too late.

Television can be put to better use as an electronic blackboard than as an electronic billboard, bringing roadside advertising messages into the home. Seventy-five per cent of all television channels are more than adequate for the needs of advertising and soap operas. Education cannot safely be left to commercial interests. Commercial interests are too concerned with their own problems of sales, and profits and loss.

Education cannot do a decent job when it is subject to the vicissitudes of commercial broadcasting. Education should be handled by educators, skilled and trained in that field. Commercial broadcasters, granting their merits as entertainers and advertisers, are not qualified in the field of education and never have made such a pretense.

The FCC, by licensing 2,200 commercial radio stations, has not created

2,200 additional educational institutions. But there is no compromise necessary here. Building more schools does not interfere with building more theaters, but I think few parents would want to send their children to the movies for six hours every day.

Our educators hold the key to the future of America. They are qualified to undertake making America a better-informed, better-educated society in an expanding democracy, rather than a nation of household gadgets, $50,000 jackpots, and home libraries stacked with comic books.

Making television channels available for colleges, universities, municipalities, and public-school systems is putting the responsibility for education on television in the hands where it belongs—the hands that have guided America into its position as the best-informed and most progressive nation on earth. (*Applause*)

Moderator Denny:

Thank you, Commissioner Hennock.

Our next speaker is a psychological research consultant to many of the outstanding business concerns that sponsor radio and television programs today. He has also served in a similar capacity to one of the large radio networks, and he is particularly interested in television. His views differ sharply from those of Commissioner Hennock. Now it's your turn, Dr. Ernest Dichter. (*Applause*)

Dr. Dichter:

Commissioner Hennock, I want to challenge the right of educators to usurp this title exclusively. Education in its realistic analysis is education for life, and, as Mr. Denny has indicated, today it is education for survival.

I accuse the educators who bestow this title upon themselves and who look arrogantly down on anyone who does not use starch in his language and his collar of being responsible for the failure of education in this country. It is the educators themselves who have refused to give people their badly needed education.

Educators, who have held much more sales territory for a much longer time than television, have failed to build up a sizable audience because of four major kinks in their professional armor.

First, arrogance. Education is surrounded by puritanical duty concepts. Education has been presented as something on the same level with cold showers, spinach, getting-up exercises, and self-improvement programs. It is good for us, but its taste is bitter and boring. Education that does not pinch or hurt is not dignified.

Two, autocracy. Most educators insist that their messages be accepted on their terms. A magazine editor who would explain his low circulation by the fact that his readers are too dumb to like his articles would be fired instantly. Most educators righteously regret the ignorance of their pupils and get away with it.

Three, superficiality. Many educational attempts are focused more on burdening the pupils with interesting but useless information and indexed knowledge than with the realistic techniques of living and insight into the complexities of modern everyday life.

Four, isolationism. Most educators make sure to let the pupil know when he is being educated. Times of the day are set aside for it. Sharp dividing lines are drawn between education and fun. That division is carried on later in life. A book, to many people—as a study I did for the Book-of-the-Month Club showed—remains an assignment, a job for which time has to be set aside.

To approach intelligently the controversial issue put before the Town Hall Meeting today is to clarify our thinking about education along these four lines. To devote 25 per cent of television frequencies to education—label it one thing or another—would perpetuate the very pitfalls and dangers of education I have outlined.

We cannot say, Commissioner Hennock, that now we are going to educate and now we are going to entertain. Anything that happens around us, any television program, labeled as such or not, educates in its basic sense. That is, it exerts influence, changes attitudes and opinions, affects our adjustments to life.

Miss Hennock, do you think for an instant that by giving 25 per cent of the frequencies to educational institutions you automatically ensure their getting 25 per cent of the audience? Entertainment and education can, and often must, go together in mass media. The Goldbergs, in one half-hour, can get across a lesson in living which equals in value a discussion of the wisdom of the Greek philosophers. Education through mass media has to be brought to people in a format which is psychologically accessible and understandable.

Rather than fight a losing battle against Tommy's and Susie's hunger for Hopalong Cassidy, let us realize that they must have a reason, a psychological need for this kind of literary diet. I wonder whether Hoppy's good-deed philosophy may not have a more lasting effect and therefore be more educational, in this true sense, for Tommy's and Susie's later life than extended lectures on proper behavior.

Social scientists, teachers, educators, and those advertisers who have shown that they can reach people through the mass communications channels are not enemies. They all want the same thing. It is time they learned from one another.

It is time for the educator to shed his dignity and arrogance and for the TV practitioner to recognize that he, too, must concern himself with the kind of education which insures survival. If both learn to work together to give people help in adjusting to the cares of modern life, which all of us so sorely need, they will have made TV a commercially profitable and culturally beneficial medium. (*Applause*)

Moderator Denny:

Thank you, Dr. Dichter. Well, them's fighting words, in the language of the educators, but we're going to hear first from Miss Hennock, who may have a comment or two on what you've just said.

Miss Hennock:

Dr. Dichter, you know you've completely avoided the crucial issue here, and that is education's last chance to get into television. There is only one alternative. Either we reserve part of the remaining television channels for educational use, or we allow all of them to go to commercial interests as an advertising medium and forever bar education from playing a substantial role in television.

I think it a good thing that you've pointed out the faults that educators may fall into, and I hope that educators profit from your criticism, but there's no reason to deny educators access to this great electronic innovation of television. And believe me, as a Commissioner, I know how great an innovation it is and I grant you that this great industry has created it. But don't forget that to deny television to educators is the same as to deny our generals modern weapons, such as tanks, planes, and rockets, because they made some errors in the past while using the spear and musket.

Education is a powerful part of our armament. It must also be able to use modern techniques to properly prepare all of us for life in today's modern serious world. Television has given broadcasting the gift of sight. We must have the vision, Dr. Dichter, to make proper use of it. (*Applause*)

Mr. Denny:

Thank you, Commissioner Hennock. Well, Dr. Dichter, what do you say to that?

Dr. Dichter:

Well, I don't disagree with Commissioner Hennock that a certain number of channels should be reserved for educational purposes. But I try to be a realist, and I have to be one in my kind of business, being sort of in between, being an educator and also serving the advertising industry at the same time.

Miss Hennock:

Well, thank you for giving the educators some channels! You never admitted that before. (*Laughter*)

Dr. Dichter:

I wanted to stress that we have to be realistic. What I'm asking for is not only that 25 per cent of the channels be turned over to education. What I tried to point out in my previous speech is that actually 100 per cent of the television channels should be turned over to education—the right kind of education.

Miss Hennock:

You mean such as entertainment, which, according to your definition, is always informing—especially, according to the survey made in California, children's programs? In one week, there were 91 murders on these television stations in California, seven stage holdups, three kidnapings, 10 thefts, four burglaries, two cases of arson, two jailbreaks, the murder of 15 to 20 people by explosion, two suicides, one case of blackmail, cases of assaults and battery too numerous to tabulate, also cases of attempted murder. Much of the action takes place in saloons. Brawls are too numerous to mention. Also drunkenness, crooked judges, crooked sheriffs, and crooked juries. If you think that's good education for your children, all right, then make that 100 per cent of the channels for education. (*Applause*)

Dr. Dichter:

I certainly don't think that this is good education, but in the meantime, while we're waiting for these educational channels to be used by educators, television is going on, and more and more people—hundreds of thousands of people, probably millions of people—are being attracted to these television shows and are actually being influenced by them. So what I'm asking for is that something be done in the meantime to control them, and to use the educators to exert their influence on the existing programs.

Miss Hennock:

You mean that educators should hurry up and get in here? You're absolutely right, Doctor. (*Applause*)

Dr. Dichter:

Well, I'd like to ask Miss Hennock a question myself now. It takes approximately a quarter of a million dollars to start a station and about as much to run a station. Who is going to pay for the 200 stations which will be involved in that 25 per cent of the channels?

Miss Hennock:

Who pays for education today? Who pays for the gymnasiums? Who pays for these beautiful campuses? And who pays for new school buildings? These things take many, many millions. And you know the cheapest form of mass education is television. (*Applause*)

Mr. Denny:

All right, thank you very much, Miss Hennock and Dr. Dichter.

. . . .

Announcer:

And now for our question period, here is your moderator, Mr. Denny.

QUESTIONS, PLEASE!

Lady: Miss Hennock, I'd like to ask you whether you think all the television programs on the air now are bad?

Miss Hennock: Oh, no. I think there are both good and bad programs. I think it is true, though, that it is very difficult to get good programs because of a tendency on the part of broadcasters to underestimate the taste and standards of the listening public.

Man: Dr. Dichter, how much Class A time do you believe will be devoted consistently by the commercial TV networks to honestly educational programs?

Dr. Dichter: Well, I have to come back to what I tried to say before, to define what educational programs are. I think we simply have to meet the public on their own level. We cannot set our own standards and call one particular type of program an educational program and another type of program an entertainment program. It has been my experience that the intelligent advertiser can be convinced and quite readily convinced that it is in his interest to put on programs that have a social responsibility.

Lady: Miss Hennock, according to ratings, it seems that the public wants comedians like Berle and Caesar. Should we insist on giving the public educational programs when no one seems to want them?

Miss Hennock: Up until now, the public has had no choice in the matter. They have had to choose between Milton Berle and mysteries or wrestling matches, or turn their sets off. However, 70 million people go to the movies at least once a week. Other millions attend the theater or go dancing, but this does not mean that there should not be any more schools, or that the children should spend eight hours a day looking at their television sets.

Now, I'd like to read a quote here from a very great critic in this town known as John Crosby. I'd like to read quotes from Jack Gould, also, but I just don't have the time. But let me read you this one. "There will be plenty of room on the other 75 per cent of the frequencies for the Milton Berles and the Captain Videos," says John Crosby. "Along with Mr. Berle, we badly need some learning, some wisdom to reinstill in us something that is slipping away— a philosophy of life, a set of guiding principles somewhat higher than a two-line joke about Rita Hayworth. If we lose our philosophy, we lose our power to think. And if we lose our power to think, we lose our ability to govern ourselves. And if we lose that, well, the stakes in this game are pretty high, with the world as it is today." (*Applause*)

Lady: Dr. Dichter, why should either educational or commercial interests be exclusively responsible for education on television? Why not share the responsibility?

Dr. Dichter: I think that is an excellent question and an excellent statement. Actually, what I want to suggest, in order that this broadcast will be constructive, is that educators and advertisers get together and form some sort of council. If Commissioner Hennock is willing to talk to the educators, I'm perfectly willing to talk to the advertisers and arrange a mutual meeting where some sort of over-all organization might be created, which would not necessarily have censorship rights, but a moral control over the type of programs that are put on the air.

And I'm coming back again to my viewpoint. It is not sufficient to turn over two or three per cent of the audience to purely educational attempts, and that's the only percentage of audience that you are really going to reach. It is much more important, in the meantime, to try to improve all those programs which are actually reaching the public. The advertisers have shown at least one thing, that they can interest people and can exert influence on them, and I think what is necessary, in order to be constructive, is that both parties and both sides really get together. (*Applause*)

Miss Hennock: Just a moment. Get together where? Where is this television time that is available for educators? I understand that every bit in New York is sold out to commercial interests and with the few interesting shows that they do on current events and discussion—well, I'm giving these commercial interests credit for the good programs they put on, as well as saying that education must get on the air.

Now, I don't have to talk to educators, Dr. Dichter. I know what they want, and they don't want the crumbs and they don't want a 15-minute period for education at the wrong time in the afternoon, and they don't want to be kicked around 17 times with that one fine Dr. Marshall program in Philadelphia. They want their own stations. In 1934 they were promised 25 per cent, or 20 per cent of Standard Broadcasting. What happened? They got nothing. They got a good swift kicking around from the commercial interests.

Let's get together and use these fine commercial techniques. Yes, I'm all for it. Let's get these fine developments in the arts, and in programming, and let's give some of the air to the educators. Seventy-five per cent for commercial interests is enough. These air waves belong to the people. (*Applause*)

Dr. Dichter: Well, I'm very much afraid that many of the advertisers, particularly those that deserve the criticism, will be quite glad to have 25 per cent of the frequencies turned over to education, because then they could have the permanent excuse that, "You got what you wanted; now let us do on our programs what we want." And that's exactly the thing I'm trying to avoid. I have found, in my experience as a research psychologist for the advertising industry and radio industry, that that is exactly where the danger lies.

Mr. Denny: Thank you, Dr. Dichter. Well, Town Meeting would welcome a sponsor that either one of you could get—a commercial sponsor on television. (*Laughter*)

All right, Mr. Boutwell, of Scholastic Press.

Mr. Boutwell: Miss Hennock, could the FCC require commercial television stations to devote a certain number of hours each week to educational programs?

Miss Hennock: Well, I think so. I don't know. We haven't gotten into that. We've always left it up to their bounty, but I must say, look what happened to the Philharmonic, and look what happened to the Symphony Orchestra in New York. We used to get fine, live programs. Now the hours have been changed, and they are recorded, and pretty soon they will be decreasing in number. Now, you know those are very fine cultural and entertaining programs, too. You know that's not strictly just dull education.

Now, what do you want us to do? To rely on this very expensive medium and on the charity and the bounty of the commercial interests again? I don't know whether they can afford to give the time that is necessary for education.

Mr. Rosen: Dr. Dichter, are you aware that this beautiful idea of getting radio educators and commercial people together was tried twenty years ago? The Federal Radio Education Committee announced last week that the pittance of $5,000 which the National Association of Broadcasters used to give for their service bulletin has been discontinued because the rich radio industry cannot afford to help educational radio.

Dr. Dichter: I would say that because it has been tried twenty years ago is no reason not to try it again. I definitely want to stress that the advertising industry, together with all the other sections of the population, has definitely made important progress and there would be a good chance to take the problem up again.

Miss Hennock: How can you try it again, when all the time is sold commercially in the New York network? What are you going to use for air waves?

Dr. Dichter: But we're still talking about separation of time, and what I have in mind and what I'm trying to say. . . .

Miss Hennock: What are you going to separate, when it no longer is available?

Dr. Dichter: Well, where are you going to get the 25 per cent of the frequencies from?

Miss Hennock: We're going to build the stations. Twenty-five per cent of these channels will be set aside for building these stations. Ownership—diversity of ownership—is what we're seeking, and these stations will be built and owned by educators. (*Applause*)

Dr. Dichter: But you still haven't solved the problem that you are only going to reach 2 or 3 per cent of the people. What's going to happen to the 98 per cent of the people?

Miss Hennock: Well, I don't know why you talk about 2 or 3 per cent of the people when there are more than 30 million adults in the country today who are touched by education in one form or another. There are 31 million school children in this country. Now please get up on your percentages. (*Applause*)

Dr. Dichter: There are also millions of people listening to television and radio, and they are being influenced day after day. There are 20 million women listening to soap operas day after day.

Miss Hennock: That's exactly what I'm afraid of. I want them to get the right influence. (*Laughter, applause*)

Dr. Dichter: Yes, but you still have not found a solution, and in the meantime these 20 million women keep on listening to soap operas, and the educators just simply sneer at any kind of an attempt to improve those soap operas. Why is that council not created, and why are improvements not brought into the soap operas? (*Applause*)

Miss Hennock: Show me the channels. That's what I'm looking for and that's what I want set aside for the educators.

Mr. Denny: Thank you, Frieda Hennock and Dr. Dichter, and our friends from the field of education who have contributed so much to our discussion.

.   .   .   .

GLOSSARY

RADIO TERMS

AAAA (*a*) American Association of Advertising Agencies; (*b*) Association of Actors and Artists of America.

ACCOUNT A program sponsor or buyer of radio time.

ACCOUNT EXECUTIVE An advertising agency's representative who serves the sponsor's account.

ACROSS THE BOARD The board in this case refers to the weekly time chart. "Across the board" means that a program is scheduled at the same time on at least five consecutive days.

ACROSS THE MIKE Applied to the direction of sound across the face of the microphone.

AFFILIATE An independent station associated by contractural arrangements with a radio network.

AGENCY An advertising firm which represents and assists the radio advertiser.

AGENCY COMMISSION The standard commission charged the advertiser by the agency; 15 per cent of net billing.

AM Amplitude modulation.

ANNOUNCEMENT The advertising message: (*a*) straight, (*b*) spot, (*c*) station break, (*d*) cutin, (*e*) participating, (*f*) hitchhike, (*g*) cowcatcher, (*h*) dialogue leadin, (*i*) dialogue. The conventional straight announcement runs about 1 minute; the spot announcement is slightly less; and the station break, inserted in the 30-second interval between programs, is still less. The cutin is usually a local "plug" introduced in the network program. The participating announcement is so named because it is the statement of one of several cooperating sponsors. The hitchhike refers to the sales presentation of another product offered by the sponsor not advertised on the program proper; it comes within the time period purchased by the advertiser but is "hitched on" at the close of the main program. The cowcatcher is a similar announcement introduced at the beginning of the program. The dialogue leadin is a commercial which begins with a short dialogue and flows into conventional announcing copy. The entire commercial may be given as a dialogue.

ASCAP The American Society of Composers, Authors, and Publishers.

AUDIMETER A device attached to home radio receivers which records the listening data on which is based the Neilsen Radio Index.

Balance   The relationships of voice, sound, and music in the audio picture; the blending of different kinds of sounds to achieve proper volume relationships.

BBC   British Broadcasting Corporation.

BBM   Bureau of Broadcast Measurement.

Beam   The pickup angle of the microphone.

Blank groove   The groove or grooves on a recording disk on which nothing is inscribed or recorded.

BMB   Broadcast Measurement Bureau.

BMI   Broadcast Music, Inc.

Board   The control panel in the monitor booth or control room, through which the program elements (voice, sound, and music) are controlled as to balance and intensity. The board is also referred to as a mixing panel.

Board fade   A diminution of program sound elements at the technician's panel; contrasted with live fade which is achieved by the performers.

Bridge   A device for linking parts of a dramatic program. Usually achieved through music, sound, and pause.

Bring it up   A direction to increase volume.

CAB   (a) Cooperative Analysis of Broadcasting, (b) Canadian Association of Broadcasters.

Canned music   Transcribed or recorded music.

Cans   Headphones or earphones.

CBC   Canadian Broadcasting Corporation.

Channel   The particular frequency band in the electromagnetic spectrum assigned to particular stations. Channels are classified as clear, regional, or local according to the power allocated them by the FCC.

Clear a number   To obtain permission from copyright owners to use a desired musical number.

Clear time   To arrange with a station or stations for a free time period, or the freeing of time already contracted for a particular broadcast.

Coincidental   The name applied to one method of measuring radio listening response. Radio users are called by telephone and asked to report the program to which they are listening.

Commercial   A program paid for by an advertiser.

Continuity   Applied to all script material prepared for broadcasting.

Control room   A small, soundproofed, windowed room adjacent to the broadcasting studio which contains the monitor panel.

Coverage   The geographical area over which the station's signal is received.

Cowcatcher   See *Announcement*.

Creeper   A performer who persists in inching-in closer and closer to the microphone instead of maintaining the required distance.

Crossfade   An overlapping of sound and sound, sound and music, or voices. As one sound element is faded out, another is faded in over it.

Cue   A signal to speaker, actor, sound men, music director, engineer, or other personnel to start or otherwise perform a given operation.

Cushion   Program material which may be inserted or added to the continuity to guarantee that the broadcast will fill the required time.

CUT   Stop operations.

DEAD AIR   A period of silence when nothing is being broadcast.

DEAD SIDE   The side of a microphone from which there is no effective pickup of sound waves.

DELAYED BROADCAST   A broadcast presented by means of electrical transcription subsequent to its original transmission.

DISK JOCKEY   One who conducts a record (transcribed music) program.

DRESS   A program rehearsed for the last time exactly as it is to be broadcast.

DUBBING   A re-recording.

ECHO CHAMBER   A reverberant space so employed as to give voices a hollow, distant, and echolike effect; a small room with resounding walls may be used. If the studio output is run into the echo chamber on a loud-speaker and picked up again on another microphone, an echo effect will be the result. In modern studios, however, the effect is produced by running the studio output through a mechanism which delays part of the sound and then feeds it back into the main line.

EIGHT-BALL   A type of nondirectional dynamic microphone, so named because of its resemblance to a black billiard ball.

ET   Electrical transcription.

FACSIMILE BROADCASTING   Radio transmission and reception of printed matter.

FADER   The rheostat or potentiometer by which the volume of sound can be controlled.

FCC   Federal Communications Commission.

FILL   Material employed to supply the unused portion of program time.

FILTER MIKE   A microphone which changes the normal sound frequencies, producing varying degrees of intelligibility.

FM   Frequency modulation. A major advantage of FM over AM is the elimination of interference.

GAIN   The amount of amplification or increased volume. Less gain or more gain, respectively, is secured by manipulating the gain controls (pots) on the monitor panel or sound table.

INDEPENDENT STATION   A station which is not owned by one of the networks. Independents may or may not be affiliates.

IN THE BEAM   Within the effective pickup range of the microphone.

KEY STATION   The station where a network program is produced.

LIVE END   The part of the radio studio which has the greater degree of sound-reflecting qualities.

LIVE MIKE   A connected microphone which transmits sound.

LOG   A complete record of broadcasting operations.

MASTER CONTROL   The central control room through which programs are relayed for transmission.

MBS   Mutual Broadcasting System.

MC   Master of ceremonies, sometimes spelled "emcee."

MIKE HOG   One who does not share a microphone with other performers.

MIXER   The panel of switches and dials by which program sound elements are blended and controlled as to balance and broadcast level.

MUSICAL CURTAIN   Music employed to end a dramatic scene.

NBC   National Broadcasting System.

NETWORK   A series of stations linked by telephone lines. Networks vary in size from coast-to-coast chains to regional and local hookups.

OFF-BEAM   A position outside the angle of pickup.

OFF-MIKE   A position, on-beam, but too far removed from the microphone itself for the most effective pickup of the voice.

ON THE HEAD   Signifying that the program starts on the precise scheduled time.

ON THE NOSE   Signifying that the program ends on precise scheduled time. Also used to designate that the program is running on scheduled time.

OUTLET   A radio program which carries the program.

PA   Public address system.

PACKAGE   A fully designed program together with talent (writing, production, acting) ready for broadcast. Usually bought by the advertiser or his agent for a specified lump sum.

PEAKS   High points in the variation of sound which are the natural result of changes of pitch, accent, and explosions of certain consonants and vowel sounds causing the volume indicator to fluctuate in accordance with the volume of these respective sounds. To say that the performer is "peaking" means that he is speaking with such disproportionate stress that it is difficult for the engineer to maintain a smooth outflow of energy.

PERSPECTIVE   Spatial relationship of program sound elements; that is, from the standpoint of the imaginative pictures created by the production, balances and distances must be carefully governed.

PIPE   To transmit or send a program from one point to another—from one studio to another or from one station to another station.

PLATTER   A record.

PROGRAM RATING   The estimated number of radio families or individual listeners tuned to a program.

REMOTE   A broadcast originating at a point outside of the station. Fights, football games, dance bands, and street-corner broadcasts are examples.

RIBBON   A velocity microphone.

RWG   Radio Writers Guild.

SCHMALZ   Sentimental rendition.

SEGUE   A smooth and direct transition from one musical effect to another. Also applies to dramatic scene transitions and sound effects. Pronounced, "seg-way."

SIGNATURE   The identifying music, sound, or combining device employed by a program.

SNEAK IN   Bring in softly. "Sneak in the theme. Sneak in the traffic sounds."

SOAP OPERAS   Daytime dramatic serial programs.

SOUND TABLE   A mobile table or truck equipped with turntables and some built-in sound effects.

SPLIT CHANNEL   A network may be divided into two or more sections, different programs being transmitted simultaneously to the respective sections.

SPONSOR   An advertiser who uses radio to sell his products and services.

STAND BY   Get ready; wait for cue to begin.

STRETCH   Slow the tempo of your reading or music.

STRIP SHOW   A serial program.

SUSTAINING SHOW   Nonsponsored program paid for by station or network.

TACET   Bring to stop or silence.

TIE-IN ANNOUNCEMENT   A commercial announcement given by the local station immediately after a prearranged cue given on the network. The sales promotion involved in this announcement is designed for local consumers.

TIGHT   There is barely sufficient time to complete the program in the scheduled time.

TRANSCRIPTION   A recording made particularly for broadcasting.

TRANSITION   Movement from one scene to another. Accomplished in several ways such as by the use of music, fades, or silence.

TURNTABLE   A rotating disk or plate from which records may be played.

VELOCITY MIKE   A ribbon type of mike.

V.I.   A volume indicator which is placed on the monitor panel and by which the engineer regulates the output of sound to the transmitter.

WALLAWALLA   Confused mumbling, crowd chatter, ad-lib talking.

WARMUP   A prebroadcast period during which the announcer or MC talks with the studio audience to arouse receptive attitudes and general rapport.

WE ARE UNDER   Our program is "short"; we are coming out (finishing) ahead of our allotted time.

WOW   An unpleasant sound resulting when a recording is tuned in before it reaches the proper speed or revolutions per minute.

TELEVISION TERMS[1]

AMPLIFIERS   Electrical circuits through which a sound or picture signal passes and is strengthened.

ANGLE SHOT   A camera technique in which a subject or scene is shot from an abnormal, unusual, or extreme angle, such as side view, or looking down from a high boom level, or looking up from a low boom level. Angle shots are generally used for dramatic effect.

ANTENNA   A structure for sending or receiving radio waves.

ASPECT RATIO   The ratio of width to height in a frame.

BACKDROP   An upstage curtain used as a setting for a television act; a cyclorama.

BACKGROUND   The rear space of the stage area, or the drapes or painted scenery forming the walls of a stage set; anything that can be seen behind the actors on the set or outdoors.

BACKGROUND PROJECTION   The use of moving pictures, slides, or silhouettes projected on a translucent screen to be used as a background.

BACKGROUND SOUND   Any sounds used behind dialogue, narration, or the main sound, such as background music, sound effects, or mixed voices.

[1] For the glossary of television terms, the author gratefully acknowledges the assistance of Edgar C. Pierce.

BALOPTICON   An optical projector which can project either opaque or transparent slides, of a size larger than 35 mm., into a film camera in the projection room.

BAND WIDTH   The number of cycles per second in the band of frequency required to transmit the visual or aural signal. Present television is transmitted in channels 6 megacycles wide which accommodate both picture and sound signals.

BASE   The panchromatic toning color used in television makeup.

BIG SCREEN   Theater size television pictures.

BLACK SCREEN   Elimination of all traces of a picture being televised; *i.e.*, switching or fading all cameras off the on-the-air line. Nothing visible to a viewer on his receiving set.

BLANKING   Elimination from a television picture of the visible results of the action of the scanning beam as it returns from right to left.

BLOOM   Glare caused by an object reflecting light into the lens of the cameras.

BLOWUP   The photographic enlargement of printed material in order that it be legible when transmitted through television.

BOOM   A mechanical gadget designed for suspending a microphone.

BOOMUP or DOWN   The raised or lowered position of the camera dolly boom and consequently of the camera.

BOTTOM FLARE   The washing out of the detail in the lower part of a television picture.

BOUNCE   The reflected radiation of a h-f signal.

BREAK   A stop in rehearsal or timing.

BREAK CAMERA   An order or direction to move the camera from one shooting position to the next as soon as it goes off the air. Specific directions to break camera are given when rapid moves are necessary.

BRIGHTNESS   The brilliance of the television image.

BUSINESS   Incidental action, devices, or props used to create additional interest or atmosphere to the general idea of the show.

BUSY   A stage with too many props, details, tonalities, or gadgets that detract from the main object or characters.

CAMERA CABLE   The wire that carries the picture from the camera to the control room.

CAMERA CHAIN   A television camera and the necessary electronic equipment to deliver a picture for broadcasting.

CAMERA LIGHT   A little red light which designates when the camera is on or off and is located on the front side of the camera to be seen by the actors.

CAMERA SCRIPT   A cue sheet indicating sequential camera positions for a telecast.

CAMERA SHOTS   Various views or pictures obtained by moving cameras about during a performance. The major camera shots and their abbreviations or script notations are:

Close-up   CU

Medium close-up   MCU or Med. CU

Tight or big close-up   TCU or BCU (BCU used by movie industry)

Long shot LS

Medium shot MS or Med. S

Pan Pan right or pan left

Tilt Tilt up or Tilt down

Two-shot 2-shot or 2-S

Boom up BU, or Boom down—BD

Follow shot Follow

CAMERA SWITCHING The control-room operation by the technical director (TD) or video operator, by which he switches camera channels on the air or mixes camera channels on the air by depressing the controlling keys associated with the camera channels.

CAMERA TUBE The tube that converts light energy into corresponding electrical energy.

CANS Earphones worn by cameramen, stage manager, and rest of crew.

CARRIER WAVES Radio waves on which television impulses are sent. Two separate waves are needed for television: one for sound and one for sight.

CATHODE-RAY TUBE An electronic tube in which streams of electrons are shot from a cathode and are formed into a narrow beam directed by means of electrostatic or magnetic fields over a target, usually a photosensitive plate or a fluorescent screen which glows wherever the beam strikes it.

CATWALKS Elevated walkways alongside a stage set, normally used for mounting equipment.

CENTERING CONTROL A control on the receiver for centering the picture either vertically or horizontally.

CENTER UP To center the composition of a picture and bring it into proper frame.

CHANGE POLARITY Technique used to change polarity of film projector with opaque slides or negative film used. Reverses blacks and whites.

CHANNEL A certain wavelength or set of frequencies on which the television program is transmitted.

CHANNEL ALLOCATION The channel or band in the radio spectrum to which a television station is assigned, or the channel space in the radio spectrum to which a communication service is assigned.

CHEAT An acting technique, peculiar to all camera work, by which the performer "cheats" on perspective or normal position relation to other performers or objects. A performer, for instance, would cheat in body position when talking to a seated companion. (He would stand close against the chair, facing forward, inclining the head slightly toward the other person without actually looking at him.) Thus the television audience could see both persons and they would appear in "normal" perspective to each other on the receiving screen.

CHINESE The feature of a camera dolly which allows the boom to be rotated, thus moving the camera in a horizontal circle without moving the dolly.

CLOSED CIRCUIT The picture is not broadcast but fed to viewing screens at certain locations by wire; a private showing.

CLOSE-UP   CU; a shot taken at close range in which the object or person practically fills the screen.

COAXIAL CABLE   A special type of cable composed of a copper tube with a single wire in its center, capable of conveying television signals. A pair can provide 480 telephone circuits, or both the visual images and accompanying sound for television programs.

CONSOLE   A control desk.

CONTRAST   The ratio of the dark to the light portions of a television picture. Pictures having high contrast have very deep blacks and brilliant whites while a picture with low contrast has an over-all gray appearance.

CUT   A control technique by which a scene on a camera is instantaneously switched on or off the air.

CYCLE   A unit of electrical measurement; one complete alternation of an electric wave.

DEPTH OF FOCUS   Limits of distances between which everything appears in sharp focus.

DIPOLE   A type of antenna used for reception of h-f broadcasts.

DISSECTOR   A nonstorage type of pickup tube developed by Farnsworth.

DISSOLVE   A control technique by which a picture on a second camera is made to merge with a picture on the air and is gradually brought into full view while the other picture is gradually faded out.

DISTORTION   Any change in the original frequency, amplitude, or phase of a radio signal, consequently distorting the picture at the receiver.

DOLLY   A wheeled trucklike platform used to move the camera into different positions on the set.

DOLLY MAN   The operator who pushes or moves the camera dolly about during a telecast.

DOLLY SHOT   A shot taken when the camera is moving upon a dolly.

DOUBLE BANK   To erect on stage a setting in front of a second, later setting.

DOWNSTAGE   Toward the camera.

DRESS   To arrange the minor properties of a stage setting preparatory to telecasting.

EDGE FLARE   A rim of illumination around the edge of the picture on the receiver tube.

EFFECT SHOT   A special camera shot that produces a desired effect.

ELECTRON GUN   That part of a cathode-ray tube from which the electrons are emitted and formed into a beam.

FADE-IN or FADE-OUT   A control technique by which a scene is gradually brought into view from black level or is gradually dimmed from view to black level.

FIELD PICKUP   The use of mobile-unit cameras to transmit out-of-studio events.

FILM LOOP   A short piece of motion-picture film spliced end to end to form a loop, which can be threaded on a projector and run continuously during a show so that it can be brought into the picture sequence as desired.

FILM PICKUP   The electronic transmission of motion pictures from film by means of television.

FILM SEQUENCE A portion of a telecast made up of various motion-picture scenes; or in a motion picture, the relation of various views of a scene into which can be built an incident climax.

FLAT LIGHT Lighting a scene or stage set with over-all brightness without modeling or high lights.

FLATS The canvas sections used for room walls, or backgrounds in stage sets. Usually 9 feet high and from 1 to 6 feet wide.

FLOOR LIGHT Light at studio floor level used for modeling; light so placed and of such intensity as to bring out the contours and volume of a subject. The antithesis of a flat light.

FLOOR PLAN A scale diagram indicating the position of stage sets in the studio for a program or series of programs.

FLY To lift a stage setting above the stage.

FOCUS A control for bringing the picture into the sharpest definition possible.

FOOT-CANDLE A unit of illumination. The foot-candle is the unit of illumination when the foot is taken as the unit of length. It is the illumination on a surface 1 square foot in area on which there is uniformly distributed flux of 1 lumen, or the illumination produced at a surface all points of which are at a distance of 1 foot from a uniform point source of 1 candle.

FRAMES One complete picture. In present standards, transmitted at the rate of 30 frames per second.

FREQUENCY Number of cycles per second. Radio waves fall into low frequencies, high frequencies, and UHFs and microwaves.

GELATIN A gelatinous screen used to diffuse the beam of a light source.

GHOST A secondary image or picture formed on a television receiver screen by a signal from the transmitter which reaches the antenna by more than one path. Ghosts are usually caused by the reflection of the signal by large buildings, hills, etc., near the receiving antenna.

GRAY SCALE The achromatic color scale or table from white through grays to black, the intermediate grays differing from each other only through a proportional admixture of white and black. For practical printing and photographic purposes, it is a 10-step transition from white through the grays to black.

HALF-LAP A control technique by which two pictures in a dissolve or overlap are both held at maximum simultaneous definition (50 per cent each) so that both are visible to viewers.

HAND PROPS Movable small items used to dress up a set, including those carried by the actors.

HEADROOM The space between the actor's head and the actual top of the setting. Refers to the amount of upward camera movement possible without overshooting a set.

HIGH LIGHT Emphasizing a subject or scene by special lighting or painting effects to make the subject stand out from the rest of the picture. May be rim lighting, halo effects, etc.

HOT CAMERA; HOT MIKE Meaning that the apparatus is energized.

HOT LIGHT A concentrated light used in the studio for emphasizing features and bringing out contours.

HORIZONTAL CENTERING   The position of a picture with respect to the axis of the cathode-ray tube. This is accomplished by a control on the receiver.

ICONOSCOPE   "Ike." A type of television camera tube converting light and shadow of a scene into electrical impulses. Developed by RCA.

IMAGE   The picture or scene focused on the mosaic of the camera tube, or the picture reproduced electronically on the face of the picture tube.

IMAGE DISSECTOR   A television pickup tube developed by Farnsworth.

IMAGE ORTHICON   Ultrasensitive pickup tube developed by RCA.

INTERFERENCE   Spurious electrical signals which cause noise in the sound reproduced by a receiver and which disrupt or tear the received picture.

INTERLACING   A technique of dividing each picture into two sets of lines, one set transmitted after the other, to eliminate flicker.

IRIS   An adjustable opaque shutter having a circular opening that is used to regulate the light admittance of a lens.

KILOCYCLE   A thousand cycles.

KILL   To order the elimination of anything in the studio; e.g., "kill the light" or "kill the chair."

KINESCOPE   A cathode-ray tube having a fluorescent screen used to reproduce the television picture in the receiver or monitor.

KINESCOPE RECORDING   A sound motion picture, usually on 16-mm. film, photographed off the end of a kinescope tube during a television show.

LAP DISSOLVE   A control technique by which a picture held by a camera is made to merge with another camera picture on the air. The term, derived from overlap dissolve, has come to mean to hold both pictures at half-lap so that the montage can be seen by viewers before one or the other is gradually taken out.

LENS TURRET   A movable disk on the front of the television camera permitting four lenses to be mounted for rapid interchanging.

LEVEL   Measurement of an electrical circuit.

LIGHT LEVEL   The general intensity of illumination on a subject or scene measured in foot-candles.

LIGHT PLOT   A cue sheet for lighting arrangement.

LINE   A single scanning line across the picture containing high lights, shadows, and half tones; 525-line definition is the standard for television.

LINEARITY   The uniformity of distribution of a regular pattern on a picture tube. Technically, the term refers to the straightness of a characteristic curve or a portion of that curve that shows the relation between two quantities or circuit factors.

LINE OF SIGHT   A straight, unobstructed path between two points.

LIVE TALENT   Studio or on-the-spot televising of events and people in contrast to the transmission of film material.

LIVE TITLES   Title cards or effects that are photographed directly by television cameras in the studio rather than supplied from slides or film.

LOCK IN   When the televised image is properly synchronized.

LONG SHOT   LS; an establishing shot taken from a distance sufficient to include a complete view of the scene.

MEDIUM SHOT   MS; a camera position from a middle distance. It might include an actor from about the knee level to his head.

MEGACYCLE   A measure of frequency; 1 million cycles per second.

MICROWAVE   This term generally refers to radio waves having a wavelength of less than 1 meter; *e.g.*, one having a frequency greater than 300 megacycles. Signal sent from television station to the transmitter by microwave.

MIKE BOOM   The arm which carries the microphone above the playing area being televised.

MILLIMETER   35 mm. is standard motion-picture size film, and 16 mm. is small size, generally home movie film. Both are used in video.

MOBILE UNIT   A truck or van equipped with camera, control and monitoring equipment, and transmitter, which can be driven to the scene to be televised. In effect, a mobile unit is a television station on wheels. It relays pictures and sound back to the main transmitter so they can be broadcast to the home audience.

MONAURAL   Of one sound perspective.

MONITOR   To control the picture shading and other factors involved in the transmission of both a scene and the accompanying sound. Monitoring usually occurs in the control room and at the transmitter.

MONOCHROMATIC   Of one color.

MONOSCOPE   A television camera tube which contains a simple picture or pattern used for test purposes.

MONTAGE   A series of three or more pictures achieved by superimposing one camera picture over another by means of dissolves.

MOSAIC   The photosensitive plate used in an iconoscope or camera tube. The term is also applied to the test pattern placard on which cameras are focused for testing purposes.

MULTIPATH TRANSMISSION   The condition in which the radio signal from the transmitter travels by more than one route to a receiver antenna usually because of reflections from obstacles. This condition usually results in ghost pictures.

NEGATIVE GHOSTS   Ghost pictures in which the black-and-white areas are reversed.

NOODLE   To play a few bars of background music or improvisation, usually behind titles.

OFF THE CUFF   Phrase used in connection with program productions, indicating that such programs are televised without preliminary camera preparation or rehearsal. Most on-the-scene events are produced off the cuff. Many studio productions receive off-the-cuff production, the producer calling for camera switches and takes as action occurs.

ORTHICON   An RCA development of a more sensitive "pickup" tube. It requires less light than the iconoscope.

PAN   To follow action to the right or left or up and down with the camera.

PARABOLA   A special directional microphone mounting used to pick up crowd noise, band music, etc.

PEDESTAL   The solid base on which a camera may be mounted. Such a base is equipped with small casters so that the pedestal and camera can be moved rapidly from position to position.

PICTURE NOISE   Interference signals causing spots of light and other irregular patterns on the receiver picture.

PIPE   To telephone. Sound is carried by this means.

PLAYING AREA   The physical space in a studio occupied by a stage set in which a scene is played.

PROJECTION RECEIVER   A large-screen receiver where the picture is reproduced on a projection screen, rather than the face of a cathode-ray tube.

PROPS   All the physical items of a show or program—except the costumes and scenery—required for performer business or to furnish the stage set.

RELAY STATION   A station used to receive picture and sound signals from a master station and to transmit them to a second relay station or to a television station transmitter.

REMOTE PICKUPS   Events televised away from the studio by a mobile unit or by permanently installed equipment at the remote location.

ROLL IT   A cue to start the film projector.

SCANNING   The process of deflecting the electron beam in a camera or picture tube so that it moves at high speed from left to right in a sequence of rows or lines from top to bottom, thus changing light and shadows of a scene into electrical impulses to form the image on the receiver tube.

SET   This term may refer to (*a*) a stage set or (*b*) a television receiver.

SHADING   Eliminating electrically the undesired signals in a picture caused by scanning.

SIGNAL   Any transmission of electronic waves; two signals involved in television transmission: the picture or video signal and the sound or audio signal. Each signal contains electrical impulses representing elements transmitted.

SLIDE   A card, a piece of glass, or film of specific size on which is a drawing or picture which is to be televised through a film or slide projector. Slides may be made on 35-mm. film, or on 3¼ by 4-inch glass, film, or opaque cards, to be used in the balopticon.

SPECIAL EFFECTS   Miniature special devices, and gadgets used when full-scale operations are impossible in the studio.

SPECIAL EVENTS   Programs of news interest, sporting events, parades, and other events not regularly scheduled.

SPLIT FOCUS   Adjusting the focus of a television camera midway between two subjects when one is in the foreground and the other in the rear. This is usually done in two shots to give both subjects equal dramatic value.

STAGING PLAN   A scaled plan of the stage floor showing location of walls, settings, doorways, furniture, sound effects, orchestra, and other working areas.

STOCK SHOTS   Film shots taken of people, objects, or places as they made news, or special portions of motion pictures, which have been filed for possible reuse. These shots are usually available at film libraries or from the files of newsreel or motion-picture organizations. Stock shots can be used for pictorial value or story emphasis in televising studio programs.

STRETCH   To stall for time or to slow up action or dialogue.

STRIKE SET   To dismantle a stage set.

SUPERIMPOSE   To impose the picture from one camera on to the picture from another; to put the output of two cameras on the line at the same time.

SWEEP   A term used to describe the motion of the electron beams in a picture or camera tube.

SWITCH   To change from one camera to another; a change of camera angles.

SYNCHRONIZATION   The process of keeping the moving beam of electrons in a picture tube in a receiver in step with the beam in the studio camera tube so that both beams move in synchronism.

TAKE   As a noun: (*a*) a picture or scene held by a television camera, (*b*) such a scene so televised or filmed. As a verb: to switch a camera on the air.

TALK BACK   Phone circuits from director to studio and announcer.

TD   The TD is the technical director, in charge of the technical portion of the program.

TEAR   The horizontal disturbance in a television picture caused by noise which makes the picture appear to tear apart.

TELECAST   A television program, or a television broadcast.

TELEVISION GRAY SCALE   This scale, which indicates the resolution of colors in scenery, costumes, and performers' faces into corresponding gray values in black-and-white television, has a contrast range from white through grays to black, depending upon light sources and equipment factors.

TELEGENIC   Having good pictorial qualities when seen over television.

TELEPHOTO   A long lens used to get large-size images at extreme distances.

TEST PATTERNS   A drawing or design broadcast before a telecast to aid in receiver alignment and adjustment, and transmitter test purposes; a standard used to check camera and system resolution.

TILT   A camera technique by which additional portions of a scene are shown by aiming the camera up or down (tilting it) in a vertical plane.

TITLES   Any titles used on a program; show credits.

TOP LIGHT   Light from above the set.

TRUCK SHOT   A camera technique by which a line of performers (*e.g.,* a chorus) or a scene is covered by dollying the camera along the line of subjects or along the scene while the camera is on the air.

TWO-SHOT (or 2-SHOT)   A camera shot of two people or objects.

UHF   Ultra-high frequency, normally above 300 megacycles.

VHF   Very high frequency, normally between 30 and 300 megacycles.

VERTICAL CENTERING   The control which regulates the position of the picture vertically on the screen of the receiver tube.

VIDEO   "I see"; that portion of the television signal which contains the picture information. Video is also loosely used as a synonym for television.

VIEW FINDER   The optical or electronic equipment connected with the focusing lens system in a camera enabling the cameraman to compose and focus a scene on the mosaic of the camera tube.

WALK-THROUGH   A rehearsal in which all stage business is observed without cameras.

WIDE-ANGLE LENS   Lens having a wide angle of view that picks up a broad area of the set at a short distance.

WINGS   The sides of a television set normally off stage.

WIPE   A control technique whereby a picture is replaced by any other by apparently pushing the first picture off the screen by the edge of another. The bottom edge of the top picture pushes the top of the bottom picture down off the screen. In a horizontal wipe, the action is from the side of the picture; in a fan wipe, it is semicircular.

WOMP   A sudden surge in signal strength resulting in a flare-up of light in the picture.

X   A stage direction meaning to cross or move.

BIBLIOGRAPHY

Comprehensive bibliographies are easily available to anyone who wishes to pursue an extensive study of any phase of wireless communication. *Radio Broadcasting and Television*, edited by Oscar Rose and published by the H. W. Wilson Company, New York, 1947, is an annotated bibliography which covers substantially "the entire field of radio broadcasting and television except the technological." Another general coverage of radio literature, *Radio Reference Books and Other Publications*, was prepared by the Reference Department of CBS for the 1946 *Broadcasting Yearbook*. These references cover the following subjects: general, advertising, statistical services, drama, script anthologies, education, children's programs, frequency modulation, listener and market data, news and special events, other countries, regulation and legal aspects, shortwave, technical aspects, techniques and careers, and television. Attention is also directed to "Selected Bibliography on Radio and Television," compiled by S. S. Gilburt, *English Journal*, 38, 295–297, May, 1949, and to "Radio and Television," compiled by G. G. Broderick and H. Moskowitz, *U.S. Office of Education Bulletin*, 17, 1–30, 1948. For an excellent review of radio development year by year, the reader will profit much from the radio section in the *Britannica Yearbook*. For specific material of especial interest to education and speech majors, we suggest the many articles which have appeared in the *Quarterly Journal of Speech*.

The author is aware that, in the compilation of references to support the study of radio and television many excellent books, articles, and reports are necessarily omitted. The following listings, however, are made in connection with the various aspects of communication discussed in this book. They should provide a fully adequate schedule of collateral reading and a basis for expanded discussion.

BOOKS

GENERAL:

Abbot, Waldo: *Handbook of Broadcasting*, McGraw-Hill Book Company, Inc., New York, 1950.

Broadcasting-Telecasting Yearbooks, Broadcasting Magazine, Washington, D.C.

Chester, Giraud, and Garnett R. Garrison: *Radio and Television*, Appleton-Century-Crofts, Inc., New York, 1950.

Federal Communications Commission: *Annual Reports*, Washington, D.C.

A Free and Responsible Press, Commission on Freedom of the Press, University of Chicago Press, Chicago, 1947. A general report on mass communication: newspapers, radio, motion pictures, magazines, and books.

Hayes, John S., and Horace J. Gardner: *Both Sides of the Microphone*, J. B. Lippincott Company, Philadelphia, 1938.

Siepmann, Charles A.: *Radio, Television and Society*, Oxford University Press, New York, 1950.

Waller, Judith C.: *Radio: The Fifth Estate*, Houghton Mifflin Company, Boston, 1946.

White, Llewellyn: *The American Radio*, University of Chicago Press, Chicago, 1947.

Willis, Edgar E.: *Foundations in Broadcasting*, Oxford University Press, New York, 1951.

CHAPTER 1:

Electronics at Work: A Practical Introduction to a Practical Science, Westinghouse Electric and Manufacturing Co., 1943.

Goldsmith, Alfred N., and Austin C. Lescarbouro: *This Thing Called Broadcasting: A Simple Tale of an Idea, an Experiment, a Mighty Industry, a Daily Habit, and a Basic Influence in Our Modern Civilization*, Henry Holt and Company, Inc., New York, 1930.

Landry, Robert J.: *This Fascinating Radio Business*, Bobbs-Merrill Company, Indianapolis, 1946.

————: *Who, What, Why Is Radio?*, 2d ed., George W. Stewart, Publisher, Inc., New York, 1942.

National Association of Broadcasters (FM Department): *Broadcasting's Better Mousetrap*, Washington, D.C., 1940.

————: *History of Frequency Modulation*, Washington, D.C., 1944.

Rowe, George: *F.M. for You*, U.S. Department of Agriculture, Washington, D.C., 1945.

The Sound of Your Life, Columbia Broadcasting System, New York, 1950. A record of radio's first generation.

Thomas, Lowell: *Magic Dials: The Story of Radio and Television*, Lee Furman, Inc., Publisher, New York, 1939.

CHAPTER 2:

Archer, Gleason L.: *History of Radio to 1926*, American Historical Society, New York, 1938.

Chappell, Matthew N., and C. E. Hooper: *Radio Audience Measurement*, Stephen Daye Press, New York, 1944.

Chase, Francis, Jr.: *Sound and Fury: An Informal History of Broadcasting*, Harper & Brothers, New York, 1942.

Coe, Douglas: *Marconi, Pioneer of Radio*, Julian Messner, Inc., Publishers, New York, 1943.

Cooperating Analysis of Broadcasting,. *Program Popularity*, Annual summaries since 1938 of radio audience high lights.

————: *Ten Years of Network Program Analysis*, a compilation of listening and program data developed by the CAB, 1930–1939.

————: *This Is Your New and Expanded CAB*, a handbook describing the purpose, history, workings, and aims of CAB, 1945.

Dunlap, Orrin E., Jr.: *Marconi, The Man and His Wireless*, The Macmillan Company, New York, 1937.

————: *Radio's One Hundred Men of Science*, Harper & Brothers, New York, 1944.

————: *The Story of Radio*, Dial Press, Inc., New York, 1935.

Dygert, Warren B.: *Radio As an Advertising Medium*, McGraw-Hill Book Company, Inc., New York, 1939.

Federal Communications Commission: *An Economic Study of Standard Broadcasting*, Washington, D.C., Oct. 31, 1947.

Grumbine, Evalyns: *Reaching Juvenile Markets* (How to advertise, sell, and merchandise through boys and girls), McGraw-Hill Book Company, Inc., New York, 1938.

Hettinger, Herman S.: *A Decade of Radio Advertising*, University of Chicago Press, Chicago, 1933.

National Association of Broadcasters: *Results from Radio*, 1939 to date.

Palmer, B. J.: *Radio Salesmanship*, Station WHO, Des Moines, Iowa, 1943.

CHAPTER 3:

Chappelle, Matthew N., and C. E. Hooper: *Radio Audience Measurement*, Stephen Daye Press, New York, 1944.

Midgley, Ned: *The Advertising and Business Side of Radio*, Prentice-Hall, Inc., New York, 1948.

Radio Industry: *The Story of Its Development*, McGraw-Hill Book Company, Inc., New York, 1928. A series of lectures delivered at the Harvard Graduate School of Business Administration during the academic year, 1927–1928.

Shurick, E. P. J.: *The First Quarter-Century of American Broadcasting*, Midland Publishing Company, Kansas City, 1946.

Sill, Jerome: *The Radio Station*, George W. Stewart, Publisher, Inc., New York, 1946.

CHAPTER 4:

Archer, Gleason L.: *Big Business and Radio* (History of Radio from 1927), American Historical Society, New York, 1939.

Robinson, Thomas P.: *Radio Networks and the Federal Government*, Columbia University Press, New York, 1943.

Sandage, C. H.: *Radio Advertising for Retailers*, Harvard University Press, Cambridge, Mass., 1945.

Sarnoff, David: *Principles and Practices of Network Broadcasting*, RCA Institute Technical Press, New York, 1939.

Wolfe, Charles Hull: *Modern Radio Advertising*, Funk & Wagnalls Company, New York, 1949.

CHAPTER 5:

Broadcasting and the Bill of Rights, National Association of Broadcasters. Statements presented by representatives of the broadcasting industry during hearings on the White bill—S. 1333—to amend the Communications Act of 1934, before a subcommittee of the Senate Committee on Interstate and Foreign Commerce, Washington, D.C.

Canadian Broadcasting Corporation: *Political and Controversial Broadcasting*. Policies and rulings of the CBC issued Feb. 31, 1944.

Communications Act of 1934: With Amendment and Index Thereto, U.S. Federal Communications Commission, Washington, D.C.

Federal Communications Commission: *A Short History of Radio Regulation*, Washington, D.C., 1941.

————: *Report on Chain Broadcasting*, U.S. Government Printing Office, Washington, D.C., 1941.

Fly, James Lawrence: "Regulation of Radio Broadcasting in the Public Interest," *Annals of the American Academy of Political and Social Science*, January, 1941.

Friedrich, Karl, and Evelyn Sternberg: *Congress and the Control of Radio Broadcasting*, Harvard Radio Broadcasting Research Project, Cambridge, Mass., 1944.

Kerwin, Jerome G.: *The Control of Radio*, University of Chicago Press, Chicago, 1934.

Public Service Responsibility of Broadcast Licensees (The Blue Book), FCC Report, Washington, D.C., Mar. 7, 1946.

Maine, Basil: The BBC and Its Audience, Thomas Nelson & Sons, New York, 1939.

Rose, C. B., Jr.: National Policy for Radio Broadcasting, Harper & Brothers, New York, 1940.

Schmeckebier, Lawrence F.: Federal Radio Commission, Brookings Institution, Washington, D.C., 1932. History, activities, and organization of the predecessor of the FCC.

Socolow, A. Walter: The Law of Radio Broadcasting, Baker, Voorhis and Company, New York, 1939.

CHAPTER 6:

American Broadcasting Company: Children's Radio Program Preferences, 1943.

Beville, Hugh M., Jr.: Social Stratification of the Radio Audience, Princeton Research Project, 1939. (Now, Office of Radio Research, Columbia University.)

Cantril, Hadley, and G. W. Allport: The Psychology of Radio, Harper & Brothers, New York, 1935.

Eisenberg, Azriel L.: Children and Radio Programs, Columbia University Press, New York, 1936. A study of more than 3,000 children in the New York metropolitan area.

Federal Council of the Churches of Christ in America: Broadcasting and the Public: A Case Study in Social Ethics, Abingdon Press, New York, 1938.

Friedrich, Karl J., and Jeanette Sayre Smith: Radio Broadcasting and Higher Education, Harvard Radio Broadcasting Research Project, Harvard University, Cambridge, Mass., 1942.

Gruenberg, Sidonie M.: Radio and Children, Radio Institute of the Audible Arts, New York, 1935.

Herzog, Herta: Survey of Research on Children's Radio Listening, Office of Radio Research, Columbia University, New York, 1941.

Lazarsfeld, Paul F., and Harry Field: The People Look at Radio, University of North Carolina Press, Chapel Hill, 1946.

——— and Patricia L. Kendall: Radio Listening in America, Prentice-Hall, Inc., New York, 1948.

Lewis, Dorothy: Broadcasting to the Youth of America, National Association of Radio Broadcasters, Washington, D.C., 1941. A report on present-day activities in the field of children's radio programs.

———: Radio Patterns for Children's Programs, National Association of Broadcasters, Washington, D.C., 1943.

———: Program Patterns for Young Radio Listeners, National Association of Broadcasters, Washington, D.C., 1945.

Peatman, John Gray, and Tore Hallonquist: The Patterning of Listening Attitudes toward Radio Broadcasts, Stanford University Press, Stanford University, Calif. 1945.

Rowland, Howard I., Keith Tyler, and Norman Woelfel: Criteria for Children's Radio Programs, Federal Radio Education Committee, Washington, D.C., 1942.

Siepmann, Charles A.: Radio's Second Chance, Little, Brown & Company, Boston, 1946.

CHAPTER 7:

Arnold, Frank A.: Do You Want to Get into Radio?, J. B. Lippincott Company, Philadelphia, 1940.

Bartlett, Kenneth G., and Douglas W. Miller: *Occupations in Radio*, Science Research Associates, 1940.

Carlisle, Norman V., and Conrad C. Rice: *Your Career in Radio*, E. P. Dutton & Co.. Inc., New York, 1941.

De Haven, Robert, and Harold S. Kahm: *How to Break into Radio*, Harper & Brothers, New York, 1941.

Hornung, J. L.: *Radio As a Career*, Funk & Wagnalls Company, New York, 1940.

Ranson, Jo, and Richard Pack: *Opportunities in Radio*, Vocational Guidance Manuals, Inc., 1946.

Working for Radio, 2d ed., National Association of Broadcasters, 1944.

CHAPTER 9:

Consult the references to Abbot, Chester and Garrison, and Willis under General.

CHAPTER 10:

Barnouw, Erik: *Handbook of Radio Writing*, Little, Brown & Company, Boston, 1947.

Bender, James F.: *NBC Handbook of Pronunciation*, The Thomas Y. Crowell Company, New York, 1946.

Crews, Albert: *Professional Radio Writing*, Houghton Mifflin Company, Boston, 1946.

Dunlap, Orrin E., Jr.: *Talking on the Radio*, Greenberg; Publisher, Inc., New York, 1936.

Hoffman, William G., and Ralph L. Rogers: *Effective Radio Speaking*, McGraw-Hill Book Company, Inc., New York, 1944.

Pear, T. H.: *Voice and Personality*, Chapman & Hall, Ltd., London, 1931.

Pillsbury and Meader: *The Psychology of Language*, Appleton-Century-Crofts, Inc., New York, 1928.

Weaver, Luther: *The Technique of Radio Writing*, Prentice-Hall, Inc., New York, 1948.

Zimmerman, Jane Dorsey: *Radio Pronunciations*, Columbia University Press, New York, 1946.

CHAPTER 11:

Gilmore, Art, and Glenn Middleton: *Radio Announcing*, Hollywood Radio Publishers, Hollywood, Calif., 1947.

Gould, S. B., and S. A. Dimond: *Training the Local Announcer*, Longmans, Green & Co., Inc., New York, 1950.

CHAPTER 14:

Duerr, Edwin: *Radio and Television Acting*, Rinehart & Company, Inc., New York, 1950.

Herman, Lewis, and Marguerite S. Herman: *Manual of Foreign Dialects for Radio, Stage and Screen*, Ziff-Davis Publishing Company, Chicago, 1943.

CHAPTER 15:

Barnouw, Erik: *Handbook of Radio Production*, D. C. Heath and Company, Boston, 1949.

Carlile, John S.: *Production and Direction of Radio Programs*, Prentice-Hall, Inc., New York, 1939.

Chase, Gilbert, ed.: *Music in Radio Broadcasting*, McGraw-Hill Book Company, Inc., New York, 1946.

Crews, Albert: *Radio Production-Directing*, Houghton Mifflin Company, Boston, 1944.
McGill, Earle: *Radio Direction*, McGraw-Hill Book Company, Inc., New York, 1940.
Turnbull, Robert B.: *Sound Effects*, Rinehart & Company, Inc., New York, 1951.

CHAPTER 17:

Allan, Douglas: *How to Write for Television*, E. P. Dutton & Co., Inc., New York, 1946.
Dunlap, Orrin E., Jr.: *Understanding Television*, Greenberg: Publisher, Inc., New York, 1948.
Eddy, William C.: *Television: The Eyes of Tomorrow*, Prentice-Hall, Inc., New York, 1945.
Hubbell, Richard W.: 4000 *Years of Television: The Story of Seeing at a Distance*, G. P. Putnam's Sons, New York, 1942.
————: *Television Programming and Production*, Murray Hill Books, Inc., New York, 1945.
Royal, John F.: *Television Production Problems*, McGraw-Hill Book Company, Inc., New York, 1948.

PERIODICALS

ADVERTISING:

"Plugs Limited; C.B.S. Rescues Its Listeners from Commercial Patter," *Business Week*, Sept. 30, 1943, p. 99.
"Old Nostrum Rides Again," *American Journal of Public Health*, **34**, 182–183, February, 1944.
"Media Slug It Out," *Business Week*, June 3, 1944, p. 84.
Cunningham, R. M., Jr.: "Medicine Men of the Air," *New Republic*, **111**, 515–517, Oct. 23, 1944.
"Radio Record; Networks 26% Gain Carries Industry to Another High," *Business Week*, Jan. 30, 1945, p. 88.
"Radio Revisited," *New Republic*, **112**, 296–298, Jan. 30, 1945.
"Plug-ugly Time: *St. Louis Post-Dispatch* Crusades against Sandwiching of Palliative Advertising into News Broadcasts," *Business Week*, Feb. 24, 1945, p. 82.
General Mills of Minneapolis: "Some of the Lustiest Advertising of the Day," ill., *Fortune*, **31**, 116–121, April, 1945.
"Capsulating or Crooning," *Newsweek*, **25**, 89–90, Apr. 23, 1945.
Gannett, L.: "Feeling Tired?" *Atlantic Monthly*, **176**, 115, August, 1945.
Porter, P. A.: "Radio Must Grow Up," *American Magazine*, **140**, 24–25, October, 1945.
Hollister, P.: "Yes, I'm Tired; Reply to L. Gannett," ill., *Atlantic Monthly*, **177**, 133–135, January, 1946.
Riley, F.: "While Soap Sells; Why So Many Radio Commercials a Day?" *Commonweal*, **43**, 401–403, Feb. 1, 1946.
"Sponsor Trouble," *Newsweek*, **27**, 62, Mar. 25, 1946.
"Radio Advertising Snaps Back," *Business Week*, June 15, 1946, p. 66.
Doyle, L. F.: "There's Never a Shortage of Ham," *Catholic World*, **163**, 251–256, June, 1946.
"Recent Experiments in Radio Advertising," *Publishers' Weekly*, **150**, 47, July 6, 1946.
Tree, L.: "What Can Be Done to Improve Radio? Fight Begun on Excessive Commercialism," ill., *New York Times Magazine*, Aug. 25, 1946, p. 9.

Williams, A. N.: "Slings and Arrows," *Saturday Review of Literature,* 29, 42–44, Nov. 30, 1946.
Williams, A. N.: "Original Sin," *Saturday Review of Literature,* 30, 24–25, Jan 18, 1947.
"Radio at the Crossroads," *Business Week,* Mar. 22, 1947, pp. 62–64.
"How Commercial Should Radio Be? New Code," *Scholastic,* 51, 5, Oct. 6, 1947.
Knepper, K.: "Why Broadcasting Has Failed," *Forum,* 109, 7–10, 79–82 January-February, 1948.
"Free Gifts, Cheap Ads: Radio Giveaway Programs," ill., *Business Week,* Feb. 7, 1948, p. 42.
Klein, A.: "Challenge of Mass Media," *Yale Review,* 39, No. 4, 675–691, June, 1950.

CENSORSHIP:

Howe, Q.: "Policing the Commentator: A New Analysis. What Do the Network, the Sponsor, and the F.C.C. Do to the Opinions?" *Atlantic Monthly,* 172, 46–49, November, 1943.
"Take the Chains off Radio," *Collier's,* 113, 66, Feb. 5, 1944.
"You Can't Say That," *Newsweek,* 29, 67, May 26, 1947.
Lear, J.: "You Can't Say That on the Air," ill., *Saturday Evening Post,* 220, 22–23, July 12, 1947.
"Diaper Cleanup on NBC," *Newsweek,* 30, 57, Dec. 15, 1947.
"People's Air Lanes Need Scrubbing," *Christian Century,* 67, 52, Apr. 12, 1950.
"Who Is Competent to Decide Which News Is Slanted?" *Saturday Evening Post,* 222, 10, May 27, 1950.

CRITICISM:

Hutchins, J. K.: "Same Time, Same Station," *Saturday Review of Literature,* 29, 16–17, May 4, 1946.
"Revolt against Radio," *Fortune,* 35, 100–103, March, 1947.
"Social Problems on the Air; An Audience Study," *Public Opinion Quarterly,* 11, No. 3, 402–411, 1947.
White, L.: "Shortcomings of Radio," *Atlantic Monthly,* 179, 64–70, April, 1947.
Larrabee, C. H.: "Radio, a Public Servant," *English Journal,* 38, 92–94, February, 1949.

POLITICAL USES:

Kaltenborn, R.: "Is Radio Politically Impartial?" *American Mercury,* 62, 665–669, June, 1946.
Arndt, J. A.: "Know Your Legislature: Connecticut's State Radio Programs," ill., *Christian Science Monitor Magazine,* Jan. 18, 1947, p. 3.
"Rally by Air," *Newsweek,* 30, 58, Sept. 15, 1947.
"Jockeying for Votes," ill., *Newsweek,* 32, 66, Oct. 25, 1948.
"Voices and Voters; Election by Radio," *Newsweek,* 32, 52, Nov. 1, 1948.

PROPAGANDA:

"Beamed to Europe: O.W.I.'s Propaganda Paves the Way for Military Advances," ill., *Newsweek,* 22, 73, Sept. 27, 1943.
Rennie, J. O.: "Dr. Goebbel's Awkward Squad," *Atlantic Monthly,* 172, 107, September, 1943.
Shirer, W. L.: "America's Radio Traitors," *Harper's,* 187, 397–404, October, 1943.

Bayles, W. D.: "England's Radio Blitz," *Reader's Digest*, **44**, 61–63, April, 1944.

Witkin, R.: "World Radio," *United Nations World*, **1**, 62–63, March, 1947.

Carson, S.: "Mayflower: 1948," *New Republic*, **117**, 33–34, Oct. 27, 1947.

Smith, W. C.: "Broadcasting in Peace and War," *Contemporary Review*, **173**, 47–50, January, 1948.

Heffron, E. J.: "Should Radio Be as Free as the Press? Freedom to Editorialize," *Commonweal*, **47**, 466–469, Feb. 20, 1948.

Siepmann, C. A.: "Shall Radio Take Sides?" *Nation*, **166**, 210–211, Feb. 21, 1948.

SOCIAL ASPECTS:

White, L.: "Radio Could Be So Much Better," *Reader's Digest*, **51**, 33–35, January, 1947.

Bartlett, K. G.: "Social Impacts of the Radio," Bibliography F, *Annals of the American Academy of Political and Social Science*, **250**, 89–97, March, 1947.

"Is Radio Operating in the Public Interest?" Broadcast of the American Town Meeting of the Air, *Education*, **67**, 534–548, May, 1947.

Crosby, J.: "Radio and Who Makes It," *Atlantic Monthly*, **181**, 23–29, January, 1948.

Godman, S.: "Menace of Radio," *Catholic World*, **169**, 312, January, 1949.

INDEX